THE RENAISSANCE AND REFORMATION IN NORTHERN EUROPE

THE RENAISSANCE AND REFORMATION IN NORTHERN EUROPE

EDITED BY KENNETH R. BARTLETT AND MARGARET McGLYNN

UNIVERSITY OF TORONTO PRESS

Copyright © University of Toronto Press 2014

Higher Education Division

www.utppublishing.com

All rights reserved. The use of any part of this publication reproduced, transmitted in any form or by any means, electronic, mechanical, photocopying, recording, or otherwise, or stored in a retrieval system, without prior written consent of the publisher—or in the case of photocopying, a licence from Access Copyright (Canadian Copyright Licensing Agency), One Yonge Street, Suite 1900, Toronto, Ontario M5E 1E5—is an infringement of the copyright law.

LIBRARY AND ARCHIVES CANADA CATALOGUING IN PUBLICATION

The Renaissance and Reformation in northern Europe /
    edited by Kenneth R. Bartlett and Margaret McGlynn.

Includes bibliographical references.
Issued in print and electronic formats.
ISBN 978-1-4426-0825-2 (bound).—ISBN 978-1-4426-0714-9 (pbk.)—
ISBN 978-1-4426-0715-6 (pdf).—ISBN 978-1-4426-0716-3 (epub)

    1. Renaissance—Europe, Northern—Sources. 2. Reformation—Europe, Northern—Sources.
3. Humanism—Europe, Northern—Sources. 4. Europe, Northern—Civilization—Sources.
5. Europe, Northern—History—Sources. I. Bartlett, Kenneth R., 1948–, editor II. McGlynn, Margaret, 1968–, editor

CB361.R33 2014   940.2'1   C2014–902026–0
                                           C2014–902027–9

We welcome comments and suggestions regarding any aspect of our publications—please feel free to contact us at news@utphighereducation.com or visit our Internet site at www.utppublishing.com.

North America
5201 Dufferin Street
North York, Ontario, Canada, M3H 5T8

2250 Military Road
Tonawanda, New York, USA, 14150

ORDERS PHONE: 1-800-565-9523
ORDERS FAX: 1-800-221-9985
ORDERS E-MAIL: utpbooks@utpress.utoronto.ca

UK, Ireland, and continental Europe
NBN International
Estover Road, Plymouth, PL6 7PY, UK
ORDERS PHONE: 44 (0) 1752 202301
ORDERS FAX: 44 (0) 1752 202333
ORDERS E-MAIL: enquiries@nbninternational.com

Every effort has been made to contact copyright holders; in the event of an error or omission, please notify the publisher.

This book is printed on paper containing 100% post-consumer fibre.

The University of Toronto Press acknowledges the financial support for its publishing activities of the Government of Canada through the Canada Book Fund.

To the memory of our mutual friend and colleague, Tom Mayer, 1951–2014

Contents

Acknowledgements xiii
Introduction xv
How to Read a Historical Document xxiii

1   THE BACKGROUND TO REFORM   3

1. Cardinal Guillaume Filastre (1348–1428)
Diary of the Council of Constance   3

2. Peter of Mladonovice (1390s–1451)
The End of the Saintly and Reverend Master John Hus   10

3. Aeneas Silvius Piccolomini (Pius II) (1405–64)
First Book of the *Commentaries*   15

4. John Wyclif (c. 1330–84)
Of Wedded Men and Wives and of Their Children Also   18

5. Thomas à Kempis (1379/80–1471)
The Imitation of Christ   24

2   EARLY NORTHERN HUMANISM   28

6. Conrad Celtis (1459–1508)
Oration Delivered Publicly in the University of Ingolstadt   28

7. Sir Thomas More (1478–1535)
Letter to the Professors and Masters of the University of Oxford   35

8. Desiderius Erasmus of Rotterdam (1466?–1536)
Letter to Jodocus Jonus on Vitrier and Colet   39

9. William Roper (c. 1495–1578)
The Life of Sir Thomas More   44

10. **Desiderius Erasmus of Rotterdam (1466?–1536)**
    The Paraclesis 49

11. **Cardinal Francisco Ximenes (1436–1517)**
    Prologue to the *Polyglot* 54

12. **Desiderius Erasmus of Rotterdam (1466?–1536)**
    A Pilgrimage for Religion's Sake 56

3 THE PROTESTANT REFORMATION 62

LUTHER 62

13. **Martin Luther (1483–1546)**
    To the Christian Nobility 63

THE RADICAL REFORMATION 70

14. **Anonymous (1525)**
    The Twelve Articles 70

15. **Martin Luther (1483–1546)**
    An Admonition to Peace 73

16. **Martin Luther (1483–1546)**
    Against the Robbing and Murdering Hordes 77

17. **Thomas Müntzer (1489–1525)**
    A Highly Provoked Defense 80

MOTHERS OF THE CHURCH 83

18. **Katharina Schütz Zell (1498–1562)**
    Letter to . . . Strasbourg 84

19. **Argula von Grumbach (c. 1492–1554)**
    To Adam von Thering 88

CALVIN 90

20. **Michael Servetus (1511–53)**
    On the Errors of the Trinity 91

21. **John Calvin (1509–64)**
    Reply to Sadoleto 93

ENGLAND 97

22. **Simon Fish (d. 1531)**
    A Supplication for the Beggars 98

23. **Prohibition of Appeals to Rome** 99

24. **Anne Askew (c. 1520–46)**
    The Two Examinations 104

CONTENTS

LUTHER'S IMPACT   109

 25. Philip Melanchthon (1497–1560)
   Funeral Oration over Luther   110

4 THE CATHOLIC REFORMATION   114

 26. *Consilium de Emendanda Ecclesia,* 1537   114

 27. The Capuchin Constitutions of 1536   120

 28. Ignatius Loyola (1491–1556)
   Letter on Obedience   126

 29. Teresa of Avila (1515–82)
   Spiritual Testimonies   131

5 SOCIAL RELATIONS   137

 30. *The Trial of Mary and Joseph*   137

 31. *Malleus Maleficarum*   142

 32. Sir Thomas More (1478–1535)
   Utopia, Book I   147

 33. Martin Luther (1483–1546)
   On the Family   155

 34. Marguerite de Navarre (1492–1549)
   The Heptameron   160

 35. Hans Sachs (1494–1576)
   The Old Game   166

 36. Michel de Montaigne (1533–92)
   On Experience   170

 37. Thomas Deloney
   Jack of Newbury   174

 38. Juan Luis Vives (1492–1540)
   On Assistance to the Poor   180

 39. William Shakespeare (1564–1616)
   Ulysses on Degree, from *Troilus and Cressida*   185

6 DISCOVERING NEW WORLDS ABROAD   187

GOING WEST   187

 40. Christopher Columbus (1451–1506)
   The Privileges Accorded to Columbus by Ferdinand and Isabella   188

41. **Gonzalo Fernandez de Oviedo (1478–1557)**
    General and Natural History of the Indies   191

42. **Bernal Díaz (1492–1581)**
    The Expedition of Francisco Hernández de Córdoba   195

43. **Stephen Parmenius of Buda (c. 1541–83)**
    Letter to … Richard Hakluyt … From St. John's Harbor, Newfoundland, 1583   202

   GOING EAST   203

44. **Richard Hakluyt (c. 1552–1616)**
    The book made by … Mr. Robert Thorne in the year 1527 in Seville, to Dr. Ley   204

45. **Sir Martin Frobisher (c. 1535–94)**
    The second voyage of Captain Frobisher, made to the West and Northwest regions, in the yere 1577   206

46. **Richard Hakluyt (c. 1552–1616)**
    Notes given in 1580 to Mr. Arthur Pet, and to Mr. Charles Jackman, sent by the merchants of the Muscovy Company for the discovery of the Northeast Strait   210

7   IMAGINING NEW WORLDS AT HOME   214

47. **William Caxton (b. 1415–24, d. 1492)**
    Prologue to the Translation of the Eneydos   214

48. **Miguel de Cervantes (1547–1616)**
    Don Quixote: Dedication to the Duke of Béjar and the Prologue   216

49. **Miguel de Cervantes (1547–1616)**
    Don Quixote   219

50. **Nostradamus (Michel de Nostradame) (1503–66)**
    Letter to King Henri II of France   227

51. **The Fugger Newsletters (1568–1604)**   232

52. **Galileo Galilei (1564–1642)**
    Letter to the Grand Duchess Christina   236

53. **John Shute (d. 1563)**
    The First and Chief Groundes of Architecture   241

54. **Jean Bodin (1530–96)**
    Method for the Easy Comprehension of History   244

55. **François Rabelais (c. 1483–1533)**
    Gargantua and *Pantagruel*   247

56. **William Shakespeare (1564–1616)**
    The Merchant of Venice   252

8   RENAISSANCE AND REFORMATION POLITICS   255

57. **Sir Thomas Elyot (c. 1490–1546)**
    The Boke Named the Governour   256

58. **Desiderius Erasmus of Rotterdam (c. 1466–1536)**
    The Education of a Christian Prince   260

59. **Juan Luis Vives (1492–1540)**
    On the Writing of Letters   267

60. **Emperor Charles V (1500–58)**
    Advice to His Son   270

61. **John Knox (c. 1514–72)**
    The First Blast of the Trumpet against the Monstrous Regiment of Women   273

62. **Queen Elizabeth I of England (1533–1603)**
    Queen Elizabeth's First Speech, Hatfield, November 20, 1558   278
    and Richard Mulcaster's Account of Queen Elizabeth's Speech   279

63. **Theodore Beza (1519–1605)**
    On the Right of Magistrates   281

Sources   286

Acknowledgements

A book such as this is the work of many hands. We would like to thank our many colleagues and their publishers who generously granted permission to include their translations and editions of the primary source material contained in this text. In addition, we want to offer our sincere thanks to Canadian Scholars' Press for releasing their portion of the copyright to us so that this revised and enlarged reader might appear with the University of Toronto Press.

This new version of our reader resulted from the enthusiasm for the text on the part of our editor with the University of Toronto Press, Natalie Fingerhut. Without her encouragement, this new text would not have appeared. We are greatly in her debt for this and for her championing of our book. Ashley Rayner was a creative and imaginative presence in the production of the book, as was Beate Schwirtlich. Our copy editor, Martin Boyne, caught a great many errors and inconsistencies on our part and worked cooperatively and professionally with us as the book proceeded through the press.

This collection began in a Renaissance Europe course at the University of Toronto and has developed through the responses of many students there and at York University, Wellesley College, and the University of Western Ontario, who have not hesitated to let us know what they found interesting, inspirational, bemusing, amusing, and sometimes just plain odd. Their feedback and insight have helped us as we worked to make this an accessible and coherent entry point to a complex and tumultuous period.

Finally, we must recognize the constant help, support, and good humor of our families: Gillian Bartlett, whose skill and dedication as a teacher has always been an inspiration; Richard Moll, without whose linguistic and practical support this could not have happened; and Niamh and Ardith Moll, who were patient most of the time.

Kenneth Bartlett
Toronto

Margaret McGlynn
London, Ontario

Introduction

Humanism is often defined as the central cultural and intellectual expression of the European Renaissance. Its widest elaboration was seen as the application of classical knowledge—the wisdom of ancient Greece and Rome—to the dominant issues of contemporary life. The style of ancient authors became the model for both spoken and written Latin, and the principles that animated these ancient texts were believed to be broadly appropriate to the needs of Europeans. The essential elements of humanism were established in Italy during the later fourteenth and fifteenth centuries. Beginning with Petrarch (1304–74) Italians began to reevaluate their relationship with the past, both the immediate past of the Middle Ages and the more distant past of classical antiquity. In the midst of dramatic social, economic, and political change, Italians began to search for models of thought, behavior, and society that spoke more directly to their own experience. The great expansion of long-distance trade that followed the Crusades, the resurgence in secular education that resulted, and the creation of a large class of wealthy, learned, sophisticated, and politically ambitious laymen in the Italian city states all contributed to a growing belief that the individual, acting singly or through the community, could improve life in this world. Add to this the dynamic social and political world of the republic of Florence, a world in which social mobility, republican politics, secular values, and practical learning were privileged, and the fundamental character of the Italian Renaissance emerges.

In searching for guides for life, these wealthy, lay, urban patricians of cities like Florence found a model particularly well suited to their circumstances: the ancient world of Greece and Rome. These civilizations were not unlike their own, and their literature and thought provided ideal models for Italians looking for principles relevant to their own lives. Clearly, the civilization of the feudal, rural, agrarian, scholastic Middle Ages held little attraction. Scholastic theology offered no support to men whose lives were dedicated to things of this world, whose riches came from lending at interest or trade and whose professions were practical. However, ancient Roman writers, such as Cicero (Marcus Tullius Cicero, 106–43 BCE) seemed to have shared their experience, giving useful advice for ethical behavior. Moreover, Cicero did so in a rhetorical style so powerful that it seemed necessarily true. For urban patrician merchants who were exercising guild authority or were ambitious for selection as magistrates in their city state, the appeal of

Cicero and other ancient authors like him was compelling. Cicero was, after all, a man like them: a lawyer who worked his way to the top of Roman republican political life, a married man with children, but still concerned with ethical behavior, reflected in his stoic philosophical works.

The problem was, however, that Cicero and his fellow Romans of the golden age were pagans, and their thought consequently made no allowance for the Christian dispensation. The contribution of Petrarch and his followers was the recognition that ancient pagans could still be good men, ethical, learned, and useful for advice on secular matters. This was in no way to diminish Christianity, but rather to admit that the ancients had much to teach modern men in a great many areas. Furthermore, the eloquence and beauty of their Latin style reflected the quality and clarity of their thoughts and minds. The classical belief that good letters mirror good thoughts on the part of good men was widely held. Cicero had to be right and good because his style was so effective and majestic.

Consequently, there was an attempt to recover as much of the ancient world as possible. If individual experience and life in this world are to be recognized and valued, anything that contributed to human experience and understanding would be valuable, especially if written by the ancients, whose knowledge of human nature was celebrated. Italian humanists of the Renaissance sought surviving ancient works throughout Europe, discovering long-lost classical texts. These texts then had to be studied and reviewed to ensure that they accurately reflected the ancient author's actual words. Philology was invented, as were textual editing and comparative stylistics; archaeology was first employed to uncover the ruins of the ancient world so visible throughout Italy. Numismatics told Italians what their ancient ancestors looked like; and new styles of painting, sculpture, and architecture paid tribute to the inspiration of the past. With the new validity of human experience and ancient models, art was made to describe nature accurately: it was to reflect what the eye saw. Correct human anatomy and linear perspective arose, predicated on the belief that man was the measure of all things.

By the late fifteenth century some of these ideas were moving north of the Alps to influence northern Europeans. However, the circumstances in the north were very different from those in Italy. Feudalism was still the dominant political structure, with the landholding knightly class in the position of greatest influence. The economies of the dynastic monarchies remained largely agrarian, and trade mostly local. Education and learning were almost solely clerical, with the universities and schools extensions of church authority and directed mostly toward the training of clergy. The wealthy urban patrician class—the vanguard of humanism in Italy—was small.

Still, there were vehicles for the introduction of Italian humanist learning in the north. The end of the Hundred Years' War and the fall of Constantinople in the middle years of the fifteenth century stimulated trade by making more capital available for peaceful economic activity and breaking the Italian monopoly on the eastern luxury trade. Explorers were beginning to work their way down the coast of Africa, until eventually Vasco da Gama sailed around the continent, opening a direct route from the Atlantic seaboard to India and the East. The consolidation of dynastic monarchies added a measure of security through the enforcement of law and the establishment of standardized procedure. Northern scholars had also enjoyed opportunities to experience Italian humanism through direct contact at Church Councils such as Constance, residence at the papal court, or study at the great universities of the peninsula such as Padua or Bologna; and many Italians—merchants, diplomats, papal collectors or ecclesiastics—spent time in the north, spreading interest in the new learning. Finally, with the invasion of Italy by Charles VIII of France in 1494, there began a period of foreign intervention in the peninsula that would lead to the humiliation of Italy and centuries of foreign domination. However, these events equally resulted in large numbers of northerners spending considerable periods in Italy, bringing home with them the fruits of the Italian Renaissance in all of its manifestations.

By the early sixteenth century the conditions were right for the development of an indigenous humanist culture in the north, dependent upon its different social, political, cultural, and religious traditions. The dominant social class remained the landowning nobility, and the models of behavior were heavily dependent upon the ideals of chivalry and court life.

It is, however, in the area of religion and the Church that the character of northern humanism emerges clearly. Because of the clerical control of education and because of distance from the ruins and traditions of antiquity, the classical past in the north had been transmitted by the Church to a much greater degree than in Italy. Consequently, the place of Christianity in the Northern Renaissance is central. Christianity is a religion of the book and consequently requires at least a learned clergy. Add to this a powerful tradition of lay piety and a significant degree of control over local churches on the part of kings and princes, and the imperative of confessional renewal and ecclesiastical reform and the defining role of religion north of the Alps become clear. Learned humanists applied the techniques developed by Italians for the study of pagan texts to patristic and biblical scholarship. The model of ethical behavior shifted from the justified pagan exemplified by Cicero and Seneca to early doctors of the Church such as Jerome or Augustine, and, ultimately, the example of Christ himself.

Reform of the Church had, of course, deep roots. The late Middle Ages had bequeathed to northern Europeans the heretical movements led by John Wyclif (c. 1330–84) in England and Jan Hus (c. 1370–1415) in Bohemia. Wyclif was to call for a simpler faith modelled on the apostolic church, in which a vernacular Bible, clerical poverty, and upright behavior would be celebrated. Hus shared these ideas and used them as the basis for a program of religious and social reform, a program that soon encountered serious opposition from the established orders and resulted in his trial and burning at the Council of Constance (1414–18). Thomas à Kempis's *Imitation of Christ*, on the other hand, provided an unimpeachably orthodox route to a deeper lay spirituality.

By the early sixteenth century, new ideas, often derived from humanist thought, were animating a powerful new imperative toward church reform and religious enthusiasm. The northern strain of lay piety was finding powerful support among those Christian humanists who united a sincere and personal piety with superb humanist training. This tradition of northern Christian humanism is ideally represented in Thomas More (1478–1535) and Erasmus of Rotterdam (1466?–1536), two friends who, with others such as John Colet (1457–1519) and Juan Luis Vives (1492–1540), sought a regeneration of religion, education, and moral behavior based upon a sound knowledge of scripture and the tools of classical learning.

This element of uniting profound learning with deep, sincere Christian spirituality was a central element of Christian humanism. The ancient dichotomy between

Athens and Jerusalem could be solved by recognizing that for a Christian scholar the purpose of education was to elucidate, propagate, and contemplate Christian revelation and teaching. Hence, Erasmus came to accept and profess that secular knowledge was imperfect without the Christian dispensation. Although it might gratify the intellect, it could not redeem the spirit. Here, then, was the primary difference between northern Christian humanism, exemplified by Erasmus, and Italian humanism. In Italy, man was sufficient and secular knowledge was a goal in itself; but for Erasmus, man was insufficient without God and Christian revelation, to which all human knowledge must defer. This was the *Philosophia Christi*, the Philosophy of Christ, which is the application of human knowledge to divine revelation and the application of the teachings of Christ to each individual's life, to be achieved through a return to the basic elements of the New Testament. The greatest text to be explicated becomes the Bible, and Erasmus noted that it should be approached "with a mind sharpened by culture and a heart purified by reverence."

The biblical scholarship of the Northern humanists enjoyed one advantage over the secular scholarship of the earlier Italian humanists in their ready access to the printing press. Developed in the mid-fifteenth century by Johann Gutenberg, the printing press stabilized and spread texts in a way previously impossible, and it was to play a crucial role in the upheavals of the sixteenth century. Northern humanists were astute users of the press, developing complex new projects such as the complutensian polyglot bible, and using the printed word to engage a new public on issues ranging from William Caxton's pragmatic concern with the standardization of language, to Erasmus's call for deeper scriptural knowledge and spiritual renewal in the *Paraclesis*, the powerful preface to his *Novum Instrumentum*.

The master of the printing press, however, was Martin Luther (1483–1546). In 1517 this German monk began to question the efficacy of church teachings on salvation. His 95 theses, with their emphasis on salvation through faith alone, spread like wildfire though Europe and garnered an astonishing response. Over the next few years, as Luther responded to both supporters and critics, his first insight developed into a broad attack on the structure and teachings of the Roman Church, including the supremacy of the pope. The Reformation he began led to the division of the universal church of the Middle Ages. The authority of lay magistrates and princes was greatly increased in Luther's church, and much church property was secularized, resulting in a social and political as well as a religious revolution.

Luther's emphasis on "scripture alone" as the source of authority in the Church opened the door to a further division of Christendom, and a wide variety of reformers emerged, many claiming that Luther's ideas did not go far enough and arguing for the extension of religious reform into the social, economic, and political spheres. Though Luther had not intended a permanent division of the Church, increasing fragmentation of the reform movement and the hardening of divisions meant that by the 1530s it was becoming increasingly clear that the division in Christianity would prove permanent. By this point second-generation leaders of the Reformation were elaborating new reformed theologies and new models of church government. The most influential of these second-generation leaders was the Frenchman John Calvin (1509–64), whose Genevan church became the "Protestant Rome" and a beacon for aspiring reformers across Europe. Calvin drew on Luther's model of "scripture alone" to begin to frame a new role for the Protestant pastor and preacher, and developed new structures through which church and lay society could be governed together as a model Christian state.

Other models of reform lacked both the passion of Luther's revelation and the clarity of Calvin's governance. The Reformation in England, for example, was undertaken by royal authority and statute when Henry VIII (r. 1509–47) attempted to secure a divorce from his wife, Catherine of Aragon (1485–1536). The "King's Great Matter" started a process that would lead to the definition of a peculiarly English strain of reformed belief and practice. Though the English Reformation did not stem from any fervent religious belief on the part of the king, it aroused such belief in others, as the urbane and thoughtful Thomas More followed his conscience all the way to his death on Tower Hill.

The Protestant Reformations emerged from obvious and undeniable problems in the Church, but even though popular, often local, reform movements had arisen in the late fifteenth and early sixteenth centuries, Rome had a good deal of difficulty responding constructively to its critics. The *Consilium De Emendanda Ecclesia,* produced by the foremost reformers within the Catholic Church, reflects the beginning of a pragmatic recognition of both its critics and their criticism. In the 1530s and 1540s this Catholic reform program accelerated and gained new authority with the formation of new religious orders such as the Jesuits, the reformation of existing religious orders, and the calling of the Council of Trent in 1545. This council was to sit, with some interruptions, for almost 20 years, and it reaffirmed the core beliefs and values of the Catholic Church while reforming a wide variety of abuses. By the late sixteenth century the cumulative effect of the reforms was to produce a Church drawing on medieval traditions of spirituality and education, reinforced by the advances of humanism, and governed by a disciplined hierarchy increasingly focused on unity and obedience.

The conjunction of intellectual renewal, religious reform, and the economic pressures developing from changing landholding patterns propelled a wave of unrest across Europe in the early years of the sixteenth century. The most powerful and widespread example of violent revolt remains the peasant revolt in Germany in 1524–25, where the rebels, incited by radical preachers like the Anabaptist Thomas Müntzer (1489–1525), attempted to transfer ideals of religious reform into the social and economic sphere, much to the disgust of Martin Luther. Müntzer's role and the response of more traditional reformers like Luther to such radical positions injected an element of social revolution and a concomitant backlash that resulted in much suffering and death and generated great anxiety. But though the vast majority of people rejected radical social change, questions about growing levels of poverty and social dislocation and the role of Christian morals and Christian theology in solving those problems circulated widely among both Protestants and Catholics, discussed by men such as Thomas More, Simon Fish (d. 1531), and Juan Luis Vives.

The stimulation of this age of upheaval and renewal also brought forth a new world of the imagination. Literature and culture in general were engaged to celebrate or attempt to explain the complexities of the period and the manifold ambiguities of the human condition. Interior voyages mapped the infinite channels of human experience, and satirical commentary introduced an element of irony into debates that too often proved uncompromising. Literary works such as Erasmus's *Colloquies,* More's *Utopia* (1516), Miguel de Cervantes's *Don Quixote* (1605), Thomas Deloney's *Jack of Newbury,* François Rabelais's *Gargantua* and *Pantagruel,* Marguerite de Navarre's *Heptameron*

(1558), and especially the genius of William Shakespeare (1564–1616) all introduced a humane element of occasionally playful but also sensitive and astute observation to the age.

The printing press that allowed the Reformation to explode across Europe thus created a forum for a broad discussion of its consequences and implications, but it also allowed women to play a much more active role in that discussion than had been possible before. Female leaders emerged in the early years of the Reformation, women such as Argula von Grumbach (c. 1492–1554) and Katharina Zell (1498–1562), with strong views on their rights and duties in the new Church. For the most part, reformers who agreed on little else agreed that female equality within the Church was even less desirable than social equality, but the role of women in the churches, in the family, and in political life was discussed broadly across the sixteenth century, and women were increasingly able to contribute to those discussions.

The voyages of discovery similarly drew upon a number of the new streams feeding change. Seeking the riches of the spice islands and the alliance of a mythical Christian king, the Portuguese found their way around the coast of Africa by the end of the fifteenth century and spent much of the sixteenth gathering the riches of the East and trying to create Christians where none had been before. The Spanish attempted to circumvent the Portuguese by venturing west to China and in the process stumbled upon a new continent to be exploited and converted. Both nations brought with them the zealous evangelizing of the Jesuits who were determined that native inhabitants of the Spanish and Portuguese empires would be Catholic, indicating the renewed vigor of the Church after Trent and replacing European souls lost to the Reformation. But the Portuguese and Spanish voyages of discovery did not just open markets and draw missionaries; they also forced Europeans to reconsider their place in the world and to reassess the human condition. Were the native inhabitants of the new-world empires people whom Christ forgot, since they were not part of the Christian dispensation? Equally, if the ancients had not known of the existence of entire continents inhabited by other humans and possessed of vast riches, what else might they not have known, where else might they have erred? These questions are implied in texts like More's *Utopia*, which used the new world as a corrective or at least a comparison with the old. Writers such as Bernal Díaz (1492–1581) and Gonzalo Fernandez de Oviedo (1478–1557) were sophisticated observers of the events of their times. The contacts they record between the old world and the new reflect the complexity of the experience for Europeans and the new need to integrate learning gathered by experience with the learning of the ancients valorized in humanist thought.

Tensions between medieval models of knowledge, humanist rediscoveries of classical learning, and the growing value of practical experience played an important role in the voyages of exploration, but they also rippled through the broader worlds of science and society. The beginnings of modern science coexisted with the still powerful forces of the occult. Charlatans such as those exposed by the *Fugger Newsletters* shared a continent with Nostradamus (1503–66), a physician whose opaque predictions were widely read and continue to be quoted; but, by the turn of the century Galileo Galilei (1564–1642) was practicing and defining modern scientific method by posing a hypothesis, testing it through experimentation, and publishing his results so that the hypothesis could be independently replicated or disproved by others.

INTRODUCTION

European rulers presided over this growing mass of contradictions, forced for the first time to confront the challenges of divided religious allegiance, along with the growth of market economies, rapid rises in prices and in poverty, a new reading public increasingly willing to share their views on all aspects of society, and an expanding planet replete with economic, political, and religious opportunities and catastrophes. The nature of authority was questioned in religious, intellectual, and scientific circles, and such questioning naturally extended to political authority. Great rulers such as Charles V of Habsburg (r. 1519–56), who ruled a vast dynastic accumulation of territory in the old world and the new, saw their power as gifts from God to settle accounts in Church and state. In Charles's case, though, the effort was not fully rewarded: he could not stop Martin Luther, nor could he halt the advance of the Turks into Europe and the Mediterranean. He recognized at the end of his life the impossibility of ruling effectively the greatest empire since Charlemagne; he abdicated and spent the last years of his life in monastic seclusion, having divided his territories. His brother, Ferdinand of Habsburg (1503–64), was given the territories in Germany and in central and eastern Europe; his son, Philip (1527–98), received Spain, the Low Countries, and parts of Italy, as well as the new world. Other rulers, such as Elizabeth I of England (r. 1558–1603), handled their new circumstances well. Turning the perceived weaknesses of her gender into a strength, Elizabeth managed the competing claims and concerns of subjects of different religious allegiances and worked with their political and mercantile impulses to turn England into a seafaring, Protestant, and fiercely nationalistic nation by the end of her reign.

Other responses to the new challenges sought refuge in education, rational dialogue, and broader understanding. Writers such as Sir Thomas Elyot (c. 1490–1546) advocated a new style of education for the ruling elite that would incorporate a formal humanist curriculum and reflect the social skills necessary to navigate changing social and political waters. Erasmus continued the discussion in his treatise written for the future Charles V in which he identified the essential virtues needed to properly execute royal duties. And that most civilized and astute of authors, Michel de Montaigne (1533–92), would attempt to bring a skeptical wisdom to an age deeply divided and steeped in violence. His *Essays* are among the most insightful responses to the crisis around him and his skeptical question of "Que sais-je?" (What do I know?) brings an element of uncertainty and openness to a time too often characterized by lethal dogmatism. His humanist education in the classics and his political experience merged with a profound insight into human nature that reflects well on his intentions.

A corollary to this questioning and creative response to the problems engendered by religious, social, economic, and cultural challenges were new perspectives on the nature of the state and society itself. How is it best to structure a community or government in the face of such dynamic change? What are the limits on royal—or papal—power, and how much authority do the citizens of a state, or the faithful in a church, exercise on their and their fellows' behalf? What constitutes law and justice? How does the temporal authority of princes or civic government operate in matters of religion or government? Authors such as Calvin, Jean Bodin (1530–96), and Theodore Beza (1519–1605) addressed these issues, as did John Knox (c. 1514–72).

Humanism and Renaissance ideals continued to develop in the north, aided by the zeal of religion and the wealth of the new world. The desire for fame and glory, so brilliantly

INTRODUCTION

satirized by Cervantes, remained, as did the search for individual autonomy and insight into the secrets of man and nature. The selections excerpted in this collection of readings illustrate the richness of that experience and the magnificence of its achievement in so many areas of human endeavor. They also illustrate some of the failures, inconsistencies, and mistakes that helped shape one of the most chaotic, brilliant, and formative centuries of the modern era.

Kenneth Bartlett
Victoria College
University of Toronto

Margaret McGlynn
Department of History
University of Western Ontario

How to Read a Historical Document

When studying the past it is necessary to access the society, culture, and minds of those men and women who lived at that time, rather than simply rehearse the analysis of historians who lived long after. To do this we need to look at the documents a society produced for itself. These can come from a great many sources and in many forms: some are legal or official documents; some are personal letters or journals; others are creative works, such as poetry or fiction; some are biographical or autobiographical; still others are rhetorical, such as speeches and sermons; finally some are historiographical, that is, historians writing about their own time or the past.

The collection of materials in this book are all primary source documents, sources written in the past which historians of all kinds use to enter the civilization of the Northern Renaissance and Reformation. What follows are suggestions for reading primary source documents that should help in the use of this text.

1. Read the document carefully and closely, looking up any words or terms you do not know: often these unusual words or technical terms are keys to the significance of the document.
2. What is the genre of the passage: is it an official document, a creative work or a personal statement, for example? Why did the author choose this form to communicate his perspective?
3. Ask yourself who wrote the document and when. The introductions to the chapters and entries will help. Does what we know about the author add authority to the ideas contained within it? Did the author enjoy some special knowledge or privileged access to the information? Was the document written during the time of the events described in the document or after? Finally, did the author have any particular prejudice, personal advantage or animus (a political or national allegiance, for example) that might affect the content of the document?
4. What was the intended audience of the document? Was it a personal reflection sent to an individual friend or relation? Was it a formal, official analysis of a situation or

person? Was it intended for a whole community (such as a law) or for a privileged elite in that community (for example, a Latin oration)? Was it to be read only in the context in which it was written, or was it intended to be used over a long period of time (such as a work of history)? Was the author addressing people like him or herself or people unlike him or herself: for example, a patrician writing to other nobles, a scholar addressing other scholars, or a powerful individual addressing poor or politically disadvantaged groups, or a man speaking to women or women to men?

5. How "factual" or correct is the information in the document? Is the author intentionally spreading erroneous or misinterpreted evidence for a particular purpose or because he or she is unaware of the real situation? Even if the content of the document contains incorrect information, is the source still useful in our understanding of the context in which it was written?

6. Finally, what is NOT in the document? Negative evidence is often an important tool in understanding a historical source. Is more than one point of view offered? Are positive elements surrounding an event privileged or suppressed to drive the reader to embrace negative impressions or vice versa; for example, are the biographical or autobiographical selections designed to leave a favorable or unfavorable impression of a person in the reader's mind?

Not every document will yield answers to all of the questions above. The important element that does operate in every case, however, is that historical documents are complex materials that greatly assist modern readers in understanding the past by providing access to what contemporaries thought was happening and also in developing an historical critical awareness, conditioning us to recognize that documents are extremely important sources of information but are sometimes not what they seem to be and need to be used cautiously and critically.

THE RENAISSANCE AND REFORMATION IN NORTHERN EUROPE

1

The Background to Reform

1. CARDINAL GUILLAUME FILASTRE (1348–1428)

Filastre was born in La Suze, France, educated in law at Paris, and taught jurisprudence at Rheims. Although an early defender of French ecclesiastical rights and a proponent of the Avignon pope during the Great Schism, he came eventually to recognize the need for unity in the church at the Council of Constance. Named a cardinal in 1411 and archbishop of Aix in 1413, he joined with other powerful clerics to try to contain the reform movement supported by the Emperor Sigismund (r. 1433–37) and others. With the end of the Great Schism and the election of Martin V (r. 1417–31) as the singular head of the Church, Filastre was sent as papal legate to France to work for church unity. Filastre was an important scholar as well. He translated several works of Plato and wrote an influential treatise on usury. It is his Diary of the Council of Constance *(the general council of the Church called to end the Great Schism) that is best known today, as it provides a detailed commentary on those complex proceedings. Filastre died in Rome in 1428.*

Diary of the Council of Constance

The General Council of Constance had its origin in the Council of Pisa. The great and terrible Schism had lasted thirty years, from its commencement at Rome after the death of Gregory XI, in the year of our Lord 1378, when, first, Bartholomew, Archbishop of Bari, was elected Pope, because of the tumults and pressure of the Romans and took the name of Urban VI, and, later, the same cardinals abandoned him, declaring they had been frightened into the election, and chose Cardinal Robert of Geneva, who took the name of Clement VII. Under these two men the famous Great Schism began, unlike any other that has preceded it, in the length of its duration—for it is now in its thirty-seventh year—the perplexing nature of its cause and continuance, and the divisions created by it in kingdoms and provinces.

Those who submitted to Clement were all the Gauls from the Alps inclusive as far as the British Ocean, except Flanders, Hainault, Brabant, and Liège, also all the Spains but Portugal, also Scotland, Cyprus, Rhodes, Majorca, the islands subject to Spain, and finally Genoa. Those who obeyed Urban were the other kingdoms and provinces, such as Italy with her islands, all the Germanies, Bohemia, Hungary, Poland, and England. Urban fixed his seat at Rome, Clement at Avignon....

When the Schism had lasted thirty years, the said Benedict and Gregory promised and made arrangements to abdicate in order to restore unity to the Church, and agreed upon Savona as the place to meet for their abdication. But when the time of meeting drew near, they both, acting, it is supposed, in collusion, discovered so many insuperable obstacles in the way of obtaining safeguards that they never came together at all. Whereupon the cardinals of both obediences took the situation into consideration and withdrew from them. Pedro de Luna, called Benedict, fled from Portovenere to Perpignan in Aragon, in dread of the King of France, who had now retracted his obedience. Angelo, called Gregory, retired to Siena.

Then cardinals from both obediences assembled and acting in concert summoned a council to meet at Pisa. There the said Benedict and Gregory were deposed from the papacy and the Cardinal of Milan, Peter of Candia, a Franciscan, was elected Pope. He was a native of Crete, also known as Candia, whence he took his title, and a distinguished doctor of theology at Paris. He called himself Alexander V. But all the Spains, except Portugal, still obeyed Pedro de Luna, while the Neapolitan kingdom of Sicily, Charles Malatesta and his lands and all the dukes of Bavaria and the Archbishop of Trier, with the lands subject to them, obeyed Angelo, the deposition at Pisa notwithstanding....

After the election of Alexander at Pisa, the Council was ordered by him with its own approval to meet again in three years. The place and day of meeting were to be selected and announced by whoever was pope at the time. But Alexander died at Bologna less than a year after his election and the present John XXIII, cardinal of St. Eustachius, legate at Bologna, known as Baldasarre Cossa of Naples, was elected in his stead. It is said that the election was corrupt, and certainly it was so as regards the merits of the man elected. However, at the end of the three years, he carried out the order to resume the Council of Pisa and convoked a general council at Rome, on the first of April, in the year 1412. But because of the remoteness of the place and the perils of travel no one came but members of the Curia, for everywhere around Rome wars were being fought and there was no safe route of approach. Many people said and believed that these obstructions had been created or aggravated by Pope John so that the council might not be held.

At length, Rome was captured by Ladislas, king of Sicily, and the Curia abruptly forced to take flight, not without some deep connivance on the part of Pope John. He and the Curia then established themselves at Florence. Thither the serene prince Sigismund, king of the Romans and Hungary, sent envoys to ask the Pope for authorization to summon a general council and choose the place and the time. The cardinals then, perceiving that the Pope was trying to escape a general council, put such pressure on him that he sent the Cardinals of Florence and Challant to Sigismund at Como in Italy with power to fix the place and time of holding the council with the advice and consent of the King. So they chose Constance and the day of November first in the year 1414, the fifth of Lord John's pontificate. They also agreed with the King on a day in November in the year 1413, when the Pope and the King would meet in the city of Lodi. There in due time they met with all the cardinals in the presence of the King, and the Pope in a general consistory ordained that the General Council of Constance be convened on the said date and convened it by apostolic decree....

After the Pope had thus ordained the calling of the Council, he returned with his Curia to Bologna at the beginning of Lent and in the month of August following, Ladislas, ruler of the kingdom of Sicily, died. He had taken Rome, as I said before, and was occupying it and all the patrimony and lands of the Church, especially those in Tuscany, the March [of Ancona] and Campania. So our lord Pope John XXIII was bent on going back to Rome to recover it and the lands of the Church. But the cardinals were well aware that if they went back they would not return to the Council and the Council would not be held and the union and reformation of the Church would not be accomplished, and they dreaded the dire consequences to the Church that would probably ensue. They therefore opposed him stubbornly and all in concert urged him by word of mouth and in writing to carry on himself in person his spiritual and ecclesiastical duty, namely, the Council, and to delegate his temporal duty to vicars and legates. He yielded to them but with reluctance.

On the first day of October, he set out from Bologna for Constance. On his way through Merano, a city belonging to Frederick, duke of Austria, he made a compact with him. For a financial consideration the Duke promised to guarantee the Pope's security, even in Constance, to keep him safe and free there, conduct him out of Constance whenever he wished and preserve him safe and free against all comers. Later, in Constance, our lord Pope disclosed this compact, as will appear further on. Hence it may be inferred that the lord Pope did not approach the Council with any sincere intent.

On Sunday, October 28, the feast of Simon and Jude, our lord Pope entered Constance in state, the cardinals having already arrived. He was lodged in the bishop's palace. Later, the order was given to hold a procession and Solemn Mass on Saturday, the third of November, for the opening of the Council. And on that day the Pope, the cardinals and all the prelates and clergy of Constance gathered in the palace, robed in their sacred vestments, and the whole procession was drawn up. But just as it was starting and the Pope had come out from his chamber in pontifical array, he was seized with an illness and obliged to retire again and take off his vestments and lie down on his bed. So the entire performance was at an end for that day. On the following Monday, November 5, the Pope was well again and the procession was held, followed by a Solemn Mass with sermon in the cathedral of Constance. Master John of Vincelles of the Order of Cluny and proctor for that order, doctor of theology at Paris, preached the sermon in the Pope's presence. Thus the Council was opened.

[*Session 1.*] Then on Friday, the 16th of the month, the first session was held. The Council sat in the place appointed for holding meetings, that is, the nave of the cathedral of Constance. The Pope presided and said Mass and preached a sermon, the text of which was "Love truth."... Then lord Francis, cardinal of Florence, read from the high pulpit the Pope's memorandum providing for the successful conduct and termination of the Council, as follows: ...

In accordance with the laudable custom of the ancient councils our chief concern is with matters of faith. We exhort all with knowledge of sacred letters to reflect deeply and discuss with themselves and others the things which seem to them helpful and opportune.... In particular, let them consider the errors which for some time past, they say, have been springing up in certain regions, those especially that originated with a certain John, called Wyclif....

[All who come to the Council are asked to share their wisdom with us.] For it is our will and intention that all who gather here for this reason shall be free to speak, consult, and act in perfect liberty on all and every subject they think pertains to the above.

... Note that even before the first of November the Pope and the cardinals had assembled in the city of Constance as related above, and also many prelates from Italy, and until after the feast of Our Lord's Nativity few from other nations arrived. So in this general Council of Constance, in which measures were to be taken for the peace and perfect union of the Church and then for its reformation, nothing whatever was achieved from the beginning of November, 1414, when the Pope and the college met there, until the end of January, and the subject of union was not touched upon. For some of the members had the disease *Noli me tangere,* and others who were eager for action did not dare to broach that subject because the French and the English, from whom everyone expected most, were still absent. Meanwhile a few preparations were made but nothing for the reform of the Church was effected. Some cardinals, appointed for the purpose, made certain suggestions but they were always hindered from reaching a conclusion.

However at the first assembly in the palace [December 7], the Pope being absent, a memorandum was presented in the name of the Italian nation on the subject of the Council, to the effect that first of all action should be taken in the Council to confirm the Council of Pisa and put its sentences into execution by an increase of penalties and other methods. But when this memorandum had been read aloud, the lord Cardinal of Cambrai [Pierre d'Ailly] at once offered another and opposing memorandum which he had shown beforehand to the Cardinal of St. Mark [Filastre] and some other French prelates and doctors. It argued, in effect, that they should at least wait until they had heard the ambassadors who were coming from Pedro de Luna and Angelo Corario. So the matter was dropped. Meanwhile some action was taken against the Bohemian heretic, named John Hus, and against the errors of the Englishman, John Wyclif.

The tenor of the memorandum of the lord Cardinal of Cambrai was as follows: "Some conclusions, for the proof and defence of which certain prelates and doctors offer themselves to the general Council and beg the Council, now sufficiently assembled, to deliberate on them.

"The sacred Council of Pisa has bound the lord Pope and the lords cardinals to strive in the present Council by every reasonable way and method for the perfect and complete union and peace of the Church and its due reformation in head and members. To this they are bound not only by the said Council of Pisa but also by the laws of nature and of God. To this the prelates of the Church also are bound, both those already gathered in the present Council and those yet to come. Such persons as obstinately insist that the Council of Constance should be dissolved or prorogued for continuation at another council, when the said union and reformation—in case they cannot now be brought about—may at last be accomplished, are promoters of schism and subject to grave suspicion of heresy.

"Within the present Council no doubt should be raised as to the Council of Pisa. We should maintain as our fundamental hypothesis that that Council was lawfully and canonically held and was therefore valid and authoritative. The Council of Pisa and the present Council are one by continuation and ought to be called one Council. With respect to the Council of Pisa, this

Council has properly no power to confirm or sanction it but merely, since it derives from it, the power to continue its work. The request to have the Council of Pisa confirmed by the present Council, before action is taken in full congregation on the ways and means to bring about the union and reformation of the Church, should not at present be either granted or discussed.

"These conclusions will promote the unity of the Church and true faith. Contrary conclusions would promote schism and imply support of heresy."

In time the King of the Romans arrived, during the night of the Lord's Nativity. After his arrival the envoys of Angelo and Pedro de Luna came, some of whom were anti-cardinals. There was then a violent dispute as to whether they should be permitted to enter the city wearing their red hats. For the sake of peace they were permitted to do so and in that garb made their entry. Louis, duke of Bavaria, of the obedience of Angelo Corario, also came.

[As discussions stalled, the Cardinal of St. Mark (Filastre) composed and circulated the following memorandum]: "In the general Council of Constance two objects chiefly are to be accomplished and for that purpose the Council was called together, namely, first, the perfect pacification and union of the Church, second, the reformation of the ecclesiastical state.

"For the pacification and true union of the Church and the ending of the Schism various methods were proposed long before the Council of Pisa. The first was to reduce the disobedient by force. The second was to argue the case and decide by law between the contestants. The third was to bring about the abdication of both contestants.... [Both before and since the Council of Pisa the first two methods have been proved impracticable.]

"Hence it is plain that neither of these two methods should be tried again so long as one other remains, easy and practicable, namely, the last, the abdication of all contestants. This is obviously easy and practicable and advantageous for many reasons.

"Let us ask then whether, circumstances being as they are, the method of abdication should now be tried in the hope of achieving a perfect union; second, whether Lord John should be asked to take that method. (As for the other two, we say we do them a grace if we allow them to take it.) Third, whether, circumstances being as they are, our lord may lawfully be compelled to take it.

"In reply to the first question, I maintain the following propositions.... [Circumstances being as they are, the method of abdication should be tried and preferred above all others to bring about the peace and union of the Church. Obviously it is the quickest and easiest way to reach the goal of peace and perfect union. The other ways look desperate because of their difficulty and numerous other drawbacks.]

"Finally, in the situation in which the Supreme Pontiff now palpably stands, the more truly he is the shepherd of the Church, the more eagerly, ardently, and promptly will he propose and embrace the way of abdication for the peace and union of the Church. This conclusion is plainly supported by the words of the Chief Shepherd, who said: 'The good shepherd lays down his life for his sheep.' It is a mark of a good shepherd that he lays down his life for his sheep, whenever needed. If he does not lay it down, he is not a good shepherd. And if he is bound to lay down his life, how much more should he lay down the accidents of life, honor, power, dominion! ... Nor do I understand Christ's teaching of the good shepherd, if, in view of the present condition of the Church, a true shepherd may not be required to renounce his office for the peace of the Church, seeing that Christ may require him to lay down his life....

"A soldier in an armed troop is bound to face death for the state; so also is a soldier of Christ. The Vicar of Christ is bound even more than an inferior to follow Christ because of his close relationship to Christ and his obligation to furnish an example to his inferiors, whom he is bound to teach by word and example, even as Jesus began first to do and then to teach....

"In view of the condition of the Church ... the Supreme Pontiff and shepherd of the Church may be compelled for the peace and unity of the Church to offer to abdicate, on condition that the others agree to cease their usurpation of office and carry out their abdications honestly and freely. This conclusion follows plainly from the above. For since he is bound to abdicate, he may be compelled to do so, if he refuses; that is, he may be commanded to do so and compelled, if he does not obey, in order to save God's Church from being rent asunder. For when a man is commanded to make restitution and fails to obey the command, his property may be taken from him by armed force, or other means may be used to oblige him to perform his duty. If the Pope does not obey, he may be deposed as bringing scandal on the Church of God, which he is bound to protect and cherish....

"Nor should we doubt that a general council is competent to judge in such a case. Otherwise the Council of Pisa would not have possessed its power or passed judgment by the same authority and on the same fundamental grounds....

"Many other reasons might be adduced from the laws of God, of nature and of man to prove that a general Council is superior to a Pope in matters which concern the universal state of the Church, such as the present case and numerous others. Nevertheless, although these conclusions are correct, we recognize the propriety of proceeding mildly at the outset.

"In closing, let us humbly and devoutly entreat our most holy lord John, the true Supreme Pontiff and shepherd of the Lord's flock, that His Holiness deign to open the eyes of a true and good shepherd to the condition of his flock.... Unquestionably the Lord's flock stands in danger of lasting destruction, for already it has experienced grave divisions and suffered for many years the schism of the Greeks. In addition, at the present moment, we are threatened with the loss not only of Spain, as large a part of Christendom as Christian Greece, but of many nations in Germany and Italy besides. It is a fearful spectacle—so many heads for the one body of the Church.

"Let him deign—I will not call him bound—to lay down his life, his soul and his members or, less than that, the office of his members and his body.... to end this spectacle by the sure, easy, and honorable way of abdication. Let him offer to do it on condition that the other members of the flock agree truthfully to renounce the rights they claim and pursue the same way to the goal by sincere and honest paths. Undoubtedly, if he does this, peace will return to the Universal Church of God and the hearts of all Christians will rejoice in secure tranquility. No nobler act has ever been recorded nor will any Roman pontiff ever possess fame, glory, and renown wider or more lasting than his.

"He must be assured that the Church will provide more richly for his future position than he would ask. No fear of poverty should deter him a moment from so great a benefaction, so bright a glory, and so splendid a reward. But if he refuses to heed, let him consider the two wolves in God's flock, in what scandals they have involved themselves for their causes, and what weapons he may take to resist and eventually overcome them."

In response to this memorandum some sycophants—to describe them correctly—wrote memoranda made up of invectives. Not daring to risk any assertions, they composed them in the form of questions.... "[Does not the course proposed by Filastre involve a repudiation of the work of the Council of Pisa and the reduction of the true Pope to the level of schismatics and heretics?]"

In reply to these memoranda the lord Cardinal of Cambrai composed a memorandum, the tenor of which was.... "[It is no derogation to Pope John or to the Council of Pisa to ask him at this juncture to take the lead on the road to peace by voluntarily abdicating. In fact the method of abdication was the one chosen at Pisa as most likely to end the Schism. The Universal Church may depose anyone, even the chief minister of the Church, if its state is disturbed by his continuance in office, and even without guilt on his part.]" The Cardinal of St. Mark also drew up answers to those who were attacking his previous conclusions and advocating compulsory deposition.... Still other memoranda were put forward in the name of the nations, to the effect that the chief business on hand was the union of the Church, and these memoranda were made public.

While all this was going on, the question arose as to who should be admitted to vote on measures in the Council. Some wanted only the bishops and greater prelates and abbots admitted. In opposition to their opinion the cardinal of Cambrai prepared a memorandum, the tenor of which was:

"The following considerations are presented to oppose the pride and ignorance of those who maintain that in this holy Council of Constance, through all its sessions, only the greater prelates, bishops, and abbots should vote in the final verdict on the problems before us.

"To begin with, a distinction should be drawn between the subjects to be treated in the Council. They may either be such as relate solely to the Catholic faith, the sacraments and purely spiritual aspects of the Church, with which the holy fathers of old dealt in their general councils. In such a case the canon law has much to say and what I am now writing nothing at all. Or else they may relate to the ending of the present Schism and the establishment of unbroken unity and peace. In which case the following remarks are pertinent.

"First, we should understand that, just as from the time of the primitive Church different methods were employed in the election of the supreme pontiff, as the laws and ancient histories tell us, so there were differences in the method of convening and conducting general councils. For, as one may read in the Acts of the Apostles and the *History* of Eusebius, which joins directly on to the Acts of the Apostles, at times the whole community of Christians was convened for a council, at other times the bishops, priests, and deacons, at times the bishops alone without the abbots, at other times both bishops and abbots, at times the Emperor summoned and assembled the council and was present in person, while the Pope whose case was under discussion was absent. So a variation in method finds support in the law of nature and of God and in the histories aforesaid....

"Further, we ought to realize that when bishops alone had the final vote in general councils, it was because they had the administration of the people and were themselves holy and learned men, chosen above the rest in the Christian Church. Later, abbots were added for the same reason and because they had administration over persons subject to them. On the same score priors should now be added and heads of every congregation, in place of the useless bishops or abbots who have merely a titular office and lack the qualifications just mentioned and are possibly under suspicion in this present situation. It seems strange that one such archbishop or bishop or abbot, with few or no suffragans and few or none subject to him, should have as large a vote in the Council as the Archbishop of Mainz or the other great prelates and princes of the Empire or as all the separate archbishops and bishops of France and England and other kingdoms, who govern many parochial churches in which there is a greater congregation than in many of the archbishoprics and bishoprics aforesaid.

"On the same grounds as above the doctors of sacred theology and canon and civil law should not be excluded from the vote. For they, particularly the theologians, have been granted authority to preach and teach everywhere in the world, which is no small authority among Christian people and far greater than that of an ignorant bishop or abbot with merely a titular office. In ancient times, the authority of doctors had not been introduced through the institution of universities, though today it is sanctioned by the church's authority. So there is no mention of them in the ancient common laws, but in the Councils of Pisa and Rome their authority was quoted, and they signed their names to the final decrees. Hence it would be not only absurd but a kind of repudiation of the Council of Pisa if the present Council, which is a continuation of that council, should exclude theologians from similar participation.

"Further, by the same or similar reasoning an equal claim may be made out for kings and princes and their ambassadors and for the proctors of absent prelates and chapters. This is proved by the bull of our lord Pope in which he instructs the members of the present Council that if, through some canonical impediment, they are unable to attend the Council in person at this time and place, those who are thus prevented shall send in their stead, without delay, God-fearing men, equipped with learning and practical experience and furnished with warrant sufficient to fill in the Council the posts of those who sent them.

"With regard to the question of putting an end to the present Schism and restoring peace to the Church, it would seem neither just, right, nor rational to attempt to exclude kings, princes, or their ambassadors from a vote or share in the final decision, since they make up a large and honorable part of the Council and the establishment of peace intimately concerns them and the people under them, and without their advice, assistance and favor the decisions of the Council cannot be put into execution."

The Cardinal of St. Mark composed another memorandum on the same topic, as follows....

"Whoever you are.... I venture to tell you that in the Gauls, the Germanies, England, and Spain there are a thousand priests of parish churches, each one of whom has a larger district to administer than many prelates, and the care of more souls. Justice would admit these men and no one should exclude them. Would you shut out those whose interest is the keenest because of their great administrative responsibilities?

"For my part, I say we should admit every man in orders or ecclesiastical office, because he is interested, and every doctor, because he may be of use, and should shut none of them out. I do not find they were debarred from the ancient councils. On the contrary, look at the Council of Pisa, of which this is supposed to be a part! You will find in it almost a hundred persons of this sort, especially doctors and licentiates, officially admitted and subscribers to the verdict against Pedro de Luna and Angelo. Why you should make another, contrary rule for this Council, that derives its power from Pisa, I fail to see. Indeed you will find many councils that admitted priests and deacons. Sometimes, when you do not read they were admitted, we know they were but the names of only the principal men were recorded, so that the numbers might not be too cumbersome.

"It may be that their poverty and distance from this place will keep them from coming. But if they come, I know of no reason, nor do you, why they should be shut out. You admit abbots without discrimination. I do not know why you exclude priests of parish churches, who have definite jurisdiction and an established office in the ecclesiastical hierarchy. They have a more extended cure of souls and administration than abbots. Many of them have a thousand— no, two, three, four, ten thousand—souls under their charge, while some abbots have ten monks or twenty or a handful more. Very few have a hundred. The place of these priests must be within the ecclesiastical order and hierarchy. The abbots minister outside the order and the hierarchy.

"Admit then, of necessity and for our own interest, men of this rank within the body whose ordained and indispensable members they are. Admit also the doctors both for their sakes and for yours, that they may direct and teach you what you do not know. Do not shut out the wise, lest you shut out wisdom and God shut you out.

Let Him instruct you by their learning and guide you in the way of eternal salvation.

"As for the proctors of archbishops, bishops, and others above-mentioned, who have the right to admittance but whom you would indiscriminately exclude, I say now that they should neither be altogether excluded nor everyone admitted. I say that proctors for persons who have legitimate excuses for absence should be admitted but others not. That is the rule I find applied in elections.... As for ambassadors of kings and princes, clearly they should be given a voice in matters that concern the Universal Church, such as church union and faith. But in questions of faith they ought to abide by the decision of the scholars and doctors. Other matters too affecting ecclesiastical conduct and orders are not their affair...."

While this problem was still under debate, another arose as to how decisions should be reached and votes counted on measures before the Council, whether by nations voting as a body—there being four of them, namely, Italy, France, Germany, and England—or by heads! Now the law was clear, that votes should be counted by heads, but there were more poverty-stricken prelates from Italy than from well-nigh all the other nations put together. Besides, our lord Pope had created an excessive number of prelates *in camera*, over fifty. There was also a rumor that he had tried to attach many more to himself by means of promises, bribes, and threats. So if votes were counted by heads, nothing would be done except what our lord wanted. Unquestionably the majority inclined towards the way of abdication. Over these questions the Council halted in suspense a long while.

In the interim, action was taken on the errors of Wyclif and a sentence was written out. But that whole matter was postponed by further developments in the proceedings for abdication. Our lord Pope at last said he was entirely willing to give peace to the Church. Meanwhile the nations, that is, France, Germany, and England, and, later, Italy, were assembling by themselves and so deciding *de facto* the question whether procedure should be by nations or by individuals, for they assembled separately. Finally they all inclined to the method of abdication in accordance with the idea of the first memorandum presented on the subject by the Cardinal of St. Mark, which began: "In the general Councils etc."

ONE: THE BACKGROUND TO REFORM

2. PETER OF MLADONOVICE (1390S–1451)

Peter was born in the village of Mladonovice in Moravia near the end of the fourteenth century. He received his B.A. from Prague University in 1409 and was closely associated with John Hus there. While at the Council of Constance he shared the same lodging as Hus and was thus an eyewitness to the proceedings he narrates. He kept in close touch with Hus even after the latter's imprisonment. Peter also played a role in keeping Czech supporters aware of political machinations against Hus at the Council. After Hus's martyrdom, Peter returned to Bohemia to complete his account, part of which had been written while he was in Constance. His account of Hus's death was regularly read along with the Gospel lesson on July 6, a day that became a national holiday.

John (Jan) Hus (c. 1370–1415)

Prague was a center for reform-minded thinkers from the 1360s, and early in his career Hus took a leading position among Czech reform leaders. At first he used the typical reform ideas, calling for a reform in morality, true repentance, and the pursuit of holiness in sermons addressed almost entirely to the laity. By 1405, however, he was preaching sermons to the clergy calling for clerical reform and arguing that priests who live in concubinage or commit adultery cannot enter heaven and so should be suspended from their office. He also lashed out against the financial exactions of the clergy and began to turn against the papacy itself; this may represent the beginning of Wycliffite views, which were well known in Prague.

As a parish priest Hus was under pressure to resist the Lollard heresy, but as rector of the university he led the fight against clerical abuses and against German domination of Bohemia. In 1409 the Germans were expelled from the university and the reform movement in Prague intensified. The Czech clergy split over their loyalty to the various popes, and Hus was a victim of the rift. In 1409 he was charged with Wycliffite heresies.

Hus's real troubles began, however, when he objected to King Wenceslas's involvement in the selling of indulgences. When the pope turned against Hus, the king was no longer willing to protect him. John XXIII ordered Hus to come to Rome for trial, but Hus refused and was excommunicated. Riots broke out in Prague, and Hus appealed to the patriotism of the people against the popes (there were three at the time) and the German clergy that dominated the church in Bohemia. Finally, under a safe-conduct guaranteed by Emperor Sigismund, Hus agreed to attend the Council of Constance to defend his views.

The End of the Saintly and Reverend Master John Hus

In like manner in that year of the Lord 1415, on July 5, the Friday after St. Procopius, the noble lords Wenceslas of Dubá and John of Chlum were sent by Sigismund, king of the Romans and of Hungary, along with four bishops, to the prison of the Brothers Minor in Constance to hear the final decision of Master John Hus: if he would hold the above-mentioned articles which had been, as has already been said, abstracted from his books, as well as those that had been produced against him during the course of the trial, and the depositions of the witnesses; or if he would, according to the exhortation of the Council, abjure and recant them, as has been said. When he was brought out of the prison, Lord John of Chlum said to him: "Look, Master John! we are laymen and know not how to advise you; therefore see if you feel yourself guilty in anything of that which is charged against you. Do not fear to be instructed therein and to recant. But if, indeed, you do not feel guilty of those things that are charged against you, follow the dictates of your conscience. Under no circumstances do anything against your conscience or lie in the sight of God: but rather be steadfast until death in what you know to be the truth." And he, Master John Hus, weeping, replied with humility: "Lord John, be sure that if I knew that I had written or preached anything erroneous against the law and against the holy mother Church, I would desire humbly to recant it—God is my witness! I have ever desired to be shown better and more relevant Scripture than those that I have written and taught. And if they were shown me, I am ready most willingly to recant." To those words one of the bishops present replied to Master John: "Do you wish to be wiser than the whole Council?" The Master said to him: "I do not wish to be wiser than the whole Council, but I pray, give me the least one of the Council who would instruct me by better and more relevant Scripture, and I am ready instantly to recant!" To these words the bishops responded: "See, how obstinate he is in his heresy!" And with these words they ordered him to be taken back to the prison and went away.

Then the next day, which was July 6, or the Saturday after St. Procopius, in the octave of the blessed apostles Peter and Paul, the said Master John Hus was led by the archbishop of Riga to the cathedral of the city of Constance, where the general session of the prelates was held, presided over by the king of the Romans and of Hungary wearing his crown. In the midst of that session and church a bench like a table was elevated and on it a kind of pedestal was placed, on which the vestments and the chasuble for the mass and the sacerdotal garments were arranged for the purpose of unfrocking him, Master Hus. When, therefore, he was brought into the church and approached the said elevated bench, he fell on his knees and prayed for a long time. In the meantime the bishop of Lodi, ascending the pulpit, delivered a sermon concerning heresies, declaring among other things how much harm heresies cause in the Church of God and how they tear it asunder, and how it is the duty of the king to extirpate such heresies, particularly the heresy of simony, from the Church of God.

In the meantime Henry of Piro, procurator of the Council, rising, made a motion requesting that the Council continue the trial of Master John Hus until a definite decision [could be reached]. Then one of the bishops, deputed by the Council, stood up in the pulpit and read the proceedings of the trial that had been carried on between Master John and the Prague archbishop and the prelates in the Roman curia and elsewhere; and after other matters, read the articles against Master Hus himself, drawn from his books and from the trial proceedings, a copy of which, containing the comments and qualifications from the hand of Master John Hus himself, and signed by him in the prison, were delivered to us, as will be further clearly described. Some of them I shall put in here, as to set down the words which he actually used at the time.

The first of these articles was this: the holy universal Church is one, which is the totality of the predestinate, etc. To that, when it was read and finished, as well as to others subsequently, Master John replied in a loud voice with the same qualifications that he had appended to them and signed with his own hand, as has been mentioned previously. When, however, he answered, the cardinal of Cambrai (Pierre d'Ailly) told him: "Be silent now; it were better that you reply later to all of them together." Master John replied: "And how should I reply to all of them together when I cannot reflect upon them all together?" When, therefore, he again attempted to reply to other charges that were being brought up against him, the cardinal of Florence rose and told him: "Be silent now. For we have already heard you enough!" And again rising, he said to the guard: "Order him to be silent!" Master Hus, clasping his hands, implored in a loud voice, saying: "I beseech you for God's sake, hear me, so that those standing about would not believe that I have ever held such errors; then afterward do with me as you please!" When, on the contrary, he was forbidden to say anything whatever or to respond to the charges against him, he fell upon his knees, and clasping his hands and lifting his eyes to heaven, he prayed most devoutly, committing his cause to God, the most just Judge. He did this repeatedly.

After the conclusion of the articles drawn from his books, the articles from the proceedings of the trial were read, which the depositions of the witnesses were said to have proved against him and objected to him. And to each individual accusation they adduced as witnesses pastors, canons, doctors, and other prelates without naming them personally, but mentioning them merely by their official titles and places. Among those articles was the one that after the consecration of the host there remains on the altar the material bread or the substance of the bread. Also another, that a priest in mortal sin does not transubstantiate, nor consecrate, nor baptize; and so forth about others. Then when Master John again arose, wishing to respond, the cardinal of Florence, again shouting at him, forbade him. And he [Hus], responding nonetheless, said: "I pray, for God's sake, hear my meaning at least on account of those standing here, lest they believe that I have held those errors. I declare that I have never held, nor taught, nor preached that in the sacrament of the altar the material bread remains after the consecration." And subsequently he responded to other [charges] in accordance with what he had signed with his own hand.

Among other things they also accused him of the article that he wished to be and is the fourth person of the Godhead, as they stated. They attempted to prove that article by [citing] a certain doctor. And the Master cried: "Name that doctor who testified that against me!" But the bishop who was reading it said: "There is no need here now that he be named." And the Master, responding, said among other things: "Be it far from me, a miserable wretch, that I should want to name myself the fourth person of the Godhead, for that has never entered my heart; but I unswervingly assert that the Father, the Son, and the Holy Spirit are one God, one essence, and a trinity of persons."

Thereupon the said lectors read that Master John Hus had appealed to God, and condemned such an appeal as an error. To that Master John responded in a loud voice: "O Lord God, see how this Council already condemns Thy acts and law as an error; and Thou, when Thou wast gravely oppressed by Thine enemies, Thou didst commend Thy cause to God, Thy Father, the most just Judge. Thus Thou hast given us wretches an example, that in all grave cases we should resort to Thee, the most just Judge, most humbly asking Thy help in rendering a righteous decision." And to that he added: "I continue to declare that there is no safer appeal than to the Lord Jesus Christ, Who will not be suborned by a perverse bribe, nor deceived by a false testimony, but will render to each one what he deserves."

Among other things they stated that Master John Hus, although excommunicated, bore it contumaciously, etc. He responded: "I did not bear it contumaciously, but having appealed, I preached and celebrated the mass. But although I have twice sent procurators to the Roman curia, advancing reasons for not appearing personally, I was never able to obtain a hearing: instead, some of my procurators were incarcerated and others were ill-treated. In all these matters I refer you to the acts of the trial in which all these things are more fully contained. Above all, I even came to this Council freely, having the safe-conduct of the lord king here present, desiring to show my innocence and to give account of my faith."

When therefore all the articles offered against him were completed and read, a certain old and bald auditor, a prelate of the Italian nation commissioned thereto, read the definitive sentence upon Master John Hus. And he, Master John, responded, replying to certain points in the sentence, although they forbade it. And particularly when he was declared to be obstinate in his error and heresy, he replied in a loud voice: "I have never been obstinate, and am not now. But I have ever desired, and to this day I desire, more relevant instruction from the Scriptures. And today I declare that if even with one word I could destroy and uproot all errors, I would most gladly do so!" And when all his books, either in Latin written by himself or translated into whatever other language, likewise in that sentence condemned as suspect of heresy, were for that reason condemned to be burned—of which some were burned later, particularly the book *De ecclesia* and *Contra Paletz and Contra Stanislaum,* as they were called—he, Master John, responded: "Why do you condemn my books, when I have ever desired and demanded better Scriptural proofs against what I said and set forth in them, and even today I so desire? But you have so far neither adduced any more relevant Scripture in opposition, nor have shown one erroneous word in them. Indeed, how can you condemn the books in the vernacular Czech or those translated into another language when you have never even seen them?" While the rest of the sentence was being read, he heard it kneeling and praying, looking up to heaven. When the sentence was concluded, as has already been mentioned concerning particular points, Master John Hus again knelt and in a loud voice prayed for all his enemies and said: "Lord Jesus Christ, I implore Thee, forgive all my enemies for Thy great mercy's sake; and Thou knowest that they have falsely accused me and have produced false witnesses and have concocted false articles against me! Forgive them for Thy boundless mercy's sake!" And when he said this, many, especially the principal clergy, looked indignantly and jeered at him.

Then at the command of the seven bishops who assisted at his unfrocking, he put on the altar vestments as if he were about to celebrate the mass. When he put on the alb, he said: "My Lord Jesus Christ, when He was led from Herod to Pilate, was mocked in a white garment." And when he was already so dressed and was exhorted by those bishops to recant and abjure, he rose, and ascending the table before which he was being dressed, and turning toward the multitude, weeping sorrowfully, he exclaimed: "Behold, these bishops exhort me to recant and abjure. But I fear to do so, lest I be a liar in the sight of the Lord, and also lest I offend my own conscience and the truth of God. For I have never held those articles that are falsely witnessed against me, but rather have written, taught, and preached their opposite; and also lest I offend the multitude to whom I have preached and others who faithfully preach the Word of God." When he said this, the prelates sitting nearby and others of the said Council remarked: "We see now how obdurate he is in his wickedness and obstinate in heresy."

After he descended from the table, the said bishops at once began to unfrock him. First they took the cup from his hands, pronouncing this curse: "O cursed Judas, because you have abandoned the counsel of peace and have counseled with the Jews, we take away from you this cup of redemption." He replied in a loud voice: "I trust in the Lord God Almighty, for whose name I patiently bear this vilification, that He will not take away from me the cup of His redemption; but I firmly hope to drink from it today in His kingdom." And subsequently taking away from him the other vestments—that is, the stole, the chasuble, and others, etc.—they pronounced in each instance an appropriate curse. And he responded that he humbly and gladly embraced the vilifications for the name of our Lord Jesus Christ. When he was divested of all vestments, as already mentioned, the said bishops proceeded to obliterate his tonsure. Thereupon they began an altercation among themselves, for some wished to shave him with a razor while others asserted that it suffices to obliterate the tonsure merely with scissors; he, turning toward the king presiding on the throne, said: "Look, these bishops so far do not know how to agree in this vilification!" And when they cut his tonsure with scissors into four parts—namely, right, left, front, and back—they spoke during it these words: "The Church has already deprived him of all ecclesiastical rights, and has nothing more to do with him. Therefore, we turn him over to the secular court." But prior to that they placed on his head a paper crown for vilification, saying to him among other things: "We commit your soul to the devil!" And he, joining his hands and lifting his eyes to heaven, said: "And I commit it to the most merciful Lord Jesus Christ." Seeing that crown he said: "My Lord Jesus Christ on account of me, a miserable wretch, bore a much heavier and harsher crown of thorns. Being innocent, he was deemed deserving of the most shameful death. Therefore I, a miserable wretch and sinner, will humbly bear this much lighter, even though vilifying crown for His name and truth." The paper crown was round, almost eighteen inches high, and on it were shown three horrible devils about to seize a soul and to tear it among themselves with claws. The inscription on that crown describing his guilt read: "This is a heresiarch." Then the king said to Duke Ludwig, the son of the late Clem of Bavaria, who then stood before him in his robes, holding the golden orb with the cross in his hands: "Go, receive him!" And the said Clem's son then received the Master, giving him into the hands of the executioners to be led to death.

When so crowned he was then led from the said church; they were burning his books at that hour in the church cemetery. When in passing by he saw it, he smiled at this their act. On his way indeed he exhorted those standing around or following him not to believe that he was to die on account of the errors falsely ascribed to him and deposed by the false testimony of his chief enemies. Indeed, almost all the inhabitants of that city, bearing arms, accompanied him to death.

And having come to the place of execution, he, bending his knees and stretching his hands and turning his eyes toward heaven, most devoutly sang psalms, and particularly, "Have mercy on me, God," and "In Thee, Lord, have I trusted," repeating the verse "In Thy hand, Lord" [Psalms 51:3 and 31:2, 6]. His own [friends] who stood about then heard him praying joyfully and with a glad countenance. The place of execution was among gardens in a certain meadow as one goes from Constance toward the fortress of Gottlieben, between the gates and the moats of the suburbs of the said city. Some of the lay people standing about said: "We do not know what or how he acted and spoke formerly, but now in truth we see and hear that he prays and speaks with holy words." And others said: "It would certainly be well that he have a confessor that he might be heard." But a certain priest in a green suit with a red silk lining, sitting on a horse, said: "He should not be heard, nor a confessor be given him, for he is a heretic." But Master John, while he was still in prison, had confessed to a certain doctor, a monk, and had been kindly heard and absolved by him, as he himself stated in one of his letters to his [friends] from prison.

When he was praying, the offensive crown already mentioned, painted with three devils, fell from his head. When he perceived it, he smiled. Some of the hired soldiers standing by said: "Put it on him again so that he might be burned along with the devils, his masters, whom he served here on earth." And rising at the order of the executioner from the place where he was praying, he said in a loud and clear voice, so that his [friends] could plainly hear him: "Lord Jesus Christ, I am willing to bear most patiently and humbly this dreadful, ignominious, and cruel death for Thy gospel and for the preaching of Thy Word." Then they decided to take him among the bystanders. He urged and begged them not to believe that he in any way held, preached, or taught the articles with which he had been charged by false witnesses. Then having been divested of his clothing he was tied to a stake with ropes, his hands tied behind his back. And when he was turned facing east, some of the bystanders said: "Let him not be turned toward the east, because he is a heretic; but turn him toward the west." So that was done. When he was bound by the neck with a sooty chain, he looked at it and, smiling, said to the executioners: "The Lord Jesus Christ, my Redeemer and Savior, was bound by a harder and heavier chain. And I, a miserable wretch, am not ashamed to bear being bound for His name by this one." The stake was like a thick post half a foot thick; they sharpened one end of it and fixed it in the ground of that meadow. They placed two bound bundles of wood under the Master's feet. When tied to that stake, he still had his shoes on and one shackle on his feet. Indeed, the said bundles of wood, interspersed with straw, were piled around his body so that they reached up to his chin. For the wood amounted to two wagon- or cartloads.

Before it was kindled, the imperial marshal, Hoppe of Poppenheim, approached him along with the son of the late Clem, as it was said, exhorting him to save his life by abjuring and recanting his former preaching and teaching. But he, looking up to heaven, replied in a loud voice: "God is my witness," he exclaimed, "that those things that are falsely ascribed to me and of which the false witnesses accuse me, I have never taught or preached. But that the principal intention of my preaching and of all my other acts or writings was solely that I might turn men from sin. And in that truth of the Gospel that I wrote, taught, and preached in accordance with the sayings and expositions of the holy doctors, I am willing gladly to die today." And hearing that, the said marshal with the son of Clem immediately clapped their hands and retreated.

When the executioners at once lit [the fire], the Master immediately began to sing in a loud voice, at first "Christ, Thou son of the living God, have mercy upon us," and secondly, "Christ, Thou son of the living God, have mercy upon me," and in the third place, "Thou Who art born of Mary the Virgin." And when he began to sing the third time, the wind blew the flame into his face. And thus praying within himself and moving his lips and the head, he expired in the Lord. While he was silent, he seemed to move before he actually died for about the time one can quickly recite "Our Father" two or at most three times.

When the wood of those bundles and the ropes were consumed, but the remains of the body still stood in those chains, hanging by the neck, the executioners pulled the charred body along with the stake down to the ground and burned them further by adding wood from the third wagon to the fire. And walking around, they broke the bones with clubs so that they would be incinerated more quickly. And finding the head, they broke it to pieces with the clubs and again threw it into the fire. And when they found his heart among the intestines, they sharpened a club like a spit, and, impaling it on its end, they took particular [care] to roast and consume it, piercing it with spears until finally the whole mass was turned into ashes. And at the order of the said Clem and the marshal, the executioners threw the clothing into the fire along with the shoes, saying: "So that the Czechs would not regard it as relics; we will pay you money for it." Which they did. So they loaded all the ashes in a cart and threw it into the river Rhine flowing nearby.

Thus I have therefore described clearly and in detail the sequence of the death and agony of the celebrated Master John Hus, the eminent preacher of the evangelical truth, so that in the course of time his memory might be vividly recollected. My principle has been not to dress up the account in a mass of highly embellished diction lacking the kernel of fact and deed, wherewith to tickle the itching ears desirous to feast thereon; but rather to speak of the marrow of the substance of the trial proceedings mentioned above, of what I have clearly learned from what I myself have seen and heard. He who knows all things is my witness that I lie not. I would rather suffer the blame of having used inept and awkward words so that it may be recognized that I have brought forth testimony to the truth, that the memory of the Master, its most steadfast champion, may thus live in the future!

3. AENEAS SILVIUS PICCOLOMINI (PIUS II) (1405–64)

Aeneas Silvius was born in 1405 into the noble Sienese family of Piccolomini. He studied law, but he was more interested in classical letters and humanist learning. In 1431 Aeneas attended the Council of Basle (Basel), where his abilities as a scholar and diplomat were widely used; and in 1436 his eloquence and his ambition resulted in his becoming the spokesman for the conciliarist faction.

Aeneas was sent by the Council to the Imperial Diet of Frankfurt. He so impressed the Emperor Frederick III that he was crowned poet laureate in 1442 and appointed an imperial secretary. He had also decided to enter the Church, taking holy orders in 1446, and soon after he was given the see of Trieste. In 1450 he was translated to the see of his native city, Siena, and in December 1456 he was raised to the sacred college as a cardinal. Then, in the conclave of 1458, a moment Aeneas himself so powerfully describes in his Commentaries, *he emerged as pope, taking the name Pius II.*

Although guilty of the usual papal nepotism, Pius patronized humanists, and he himself continued to write, despite the demands upon his time. In particular, he completed his Commentaries, *which represents one of the great contributions to Renaissance autobiography and the unique example of the genre by a Renaissance pope.*

The great issue of his papacy was his calling for a new crusade to liberate Constantinople from the Turks who had conquered the city in 1453. Unfortunately Pius died in 1464 before his plans could be realized.

First Book of the Commentaries

While this was happening at Mainz no little uncertainty arose among the theologians who had stayed behind at Basle as to whether [Pope] Eugenius [IV; r. 1431–47] could be called a heretic, seeing that he was showing such rebellious contempt of the instructions of the Church. Meeting together for that reason, they held a long discussion, some maintaining the negative, some the positive view, knowing that this was the old Socratic method of arguing against another's opinion. For Socrates thought that in this way what was closest to the truth could most easily be discovered. In the course of the discussion three views emerged; some maintained that Eugenius was a heretic, some that he was not only a heretic but relapsed, and the third group was unwilling to admit that he was either relapsed or a heretic. Prominent among the theologians both in authority and knowledge was the bishop of Hebron, ambassador of the serene and puissant king of Castile. Prominent too was a certain Scottish abbot. These, like active boxers putting on an exhibition fight, floored some of their opponents; others either accepted their pleas or gave way to them, and by their efforts the weightier view in the end prevailed: that Eugenius be called both a heretic and relapsed. Eight short resolutions were approved among these theologians, which they asserted to be truths; they published a copy of them. This affair began towards the middle of April, through the industry and shrewdness of a certain Nicolas, a Dominican friar from Burgundy, an acute man with a mind far larger than his body, who did not stop dinning it in the ears of members of deputations and congregations until the matter was accepted and brought to a conclusion. I should not hesitate to assert that the matter would have remained unattempted had not this little man's diligence roused the Fathers, although to look at him you would not have considered him capable of so much. But men are not to be judged by their appearance.

Now when the ambassadors had returned from Mainz, and certainty was felt about the acceptance of the decrees, the Fathers resolved to discuss with greater care and at greater length the short resolutions of the masters, and there were summoned at the order of the deputations all masters and doctors of civil and canon law to the chapter-house of the cathedral to discuss in public with the prelates the heresy of Eugenius. This was a matter very troublesome to the archbishop of Milan, who feared that this discussion might involve the deprivation of Eugenius, which he, as he said, had always opposed through fear of a schism. On that account he admonished some, stirred the sluggish, frightened the bold, and used all his energy to cause confusion in the matter, and though of the duke's ambassadors he alone remained at Basle, yet with notable success he acted for the others as well. For if one works with a will nothing seems hard, and three together would not have done more than he accomplished alone. For as far as he was able he inspired the absent members of his party by letters and those present by words to defend Eugenius. They came to the chapter-house and there was a crowded meeting, for all had been enticed by their eagerness to speak or listen. Discussion lasted for six days altogether, both morning and afternoon. In the midst of them all and occupying first place as judge of faith and director and controller of the whole discussion was Cardinal Louis, archbishop of Arles, a prelate notable for many virtues and in particular for courage and steadfastness. Nicolas Amici, who too is a procurator of faith and very well known among the theologians of Paris, asked each man for his opinion. The votes were recorded by the notary Jean Dieulifist, and there was an excellent discussion and wise examination of several topics. If I were willing to make mention of these, I am afraid some would consider that my judgment was at fault when I entered upon so great a task, as this is very far removed from my promise and my aim. Yet I shall suit myself, and shall not consider that by trespassing within the bounds of holy writings I have "peered into the temple of that goddess from whom males are scared away." Now in beginning to make mention of the actual subject I will state at the outset the resolutions of the theologians as being the foundation of the discussion. I shall not, however, use the same words as they did. It will be sufficient to report the sense. The resolutions were of this nature:

1. It is a truth of the catholic faith that the holy general Council holds power over the pope and anyone else.
2. The Roman pontiff of his own authority can neither dissolve nor transfer nor prorogue the general Council when lawfully assembled without its own consent, and that is part of the same truth.
3. Whoever obdurately opposes those truths must be deemed a heretic.
4. Pope Eugenius IV attacked these truths when first from the plenitude of his apostolic power he attempted to dissolve or transfer the Council of Basle.
5. Eugenius at the warning of the holy Council eventually renounced the errors at variance with these truths.
6. Eugenius's second attempt at dissolution or transference is inimical to the aforesaid truths and contains unpardonable error as regards the faith.
7. Eugenius in attempting a second time to dissolve or transfer the Council is relapsing into the errors he renounced.
8. Eugenius, when warned by the Council to renounce his second attempt at dissolution or transference, by persisting in rebellion after his evident contumacy and by upholding the Assembly of Ferrara, shows himself to be obdurate.

Of this nature, I think, were the resolutions, and when these had been read again and again in the chapter-house in the presence of the Fathers, all were asked individually to give their opinion, and almost all voted for the resolutions. The archbishop of Palermo, however, a man eminent among all for learning, argued at length to the contrary. So too did that ornament of the prelates, the bishop of Burgos, and the almoner of the king of Aragon, distinguished not less for eloquence than learning. These, however, did not oppose the earlier resolutions, but only those affecting Eugenius, and with the subtlety of a most astute mind Panormitanus [i.e., Nicolò de' Tudeschi, 1386–1445] held forth against the later resolutions, and worked energetically to show that Eugenius was not relapsed; and he had a great dispute with three theologians, the bishop of Ardjisch, John of Segovia, and François de Fuxe. He made a threefold division of the articles of the faith, precise as in the Creed, broad as in declarations made by the Church, very broad as in the consequences of the first two, holding that Eugenius had under none of these headings harmed the faith in the first dissolution that he made, because neither in the Creed nor in the canons of the Church was it maintained that the pope could not dissolve councils; nor did it appear to him that this was a consequence of the canons previously made, but rather of the decrees of the Council of Constance. Such an occasion had been, as it were, left out of account, and was reserved for the pope's ordering, since in the decree *Frequens* the place for a future council was chosen by the pope with the Council's approval, and nothing at all was said about this. But if perhaps Eugenius had done wrong in the first dissolution he ought to be considered excused, as he had acted in accordance with the advice of cardinals representing the Roman Church, the authority of which (he said) was so great that its judgment would be preferred to the whole world's, and which was affirmed by a singular gloss; nor was it found that the holy Council had ever proceeded against Eugenius as a heretic, a sign that it did not think that he had turned aside from the faith. He himself attached no weight to what was said about adherence [to the Council] and about renounced errors. He had read the whole text of [Eugenius's] adherence, and the pope had not renounced the dissolution as contrary to the faith, but as an occasion of scandal. Moreover, in the last dissolution there was nothing of this kind, since in a similar way he had ordered the dissolution on the advice of the cardinals, and to facilitate union with the Greeks, and he should not be compelled to give answer in a criminal case through an agent when he could not put in a personal appearance owing to bad health. So, since from the first dissolution he had not fallen into an error of faith, he was persuaded that Eugenius could not now be called relapsed, seeing that he had not harmed the faith either by the first or the second dissolution.

The speech of Panormitanus met with more general praise than approval. It was, however, so far effective that later the word "relapsed" was taken out of the resolutions, and in its place was put "lapsed." Panormitanus did not venture to clear Eugenius completely of heresy, and placed more weight on the first than the second dissolution, nor did he withdraw without a reply. For John of Segovia, who was very distinguished in theology, rose, and replied with reverence and modesty as befitted so great a prelate. He said he agreed with the remarks of Panormitanus about the threefold division of the articles of the faith, and that supported his own case, because if those things were to be held as articles of faith which were consequences of the canons of the Church, it would be obvious that the resolutions under discussion proceeded from the canons of the Church, that is, the Council of Constance; because if there the pope was in subjection to the general Council, who might say that the Pope had any command over the Council which was his superior? Eugenius should have halted, because he could not dissolve against its will a Council that was superior to himself; and this article he certainly violated. If anyone wished it to be expressly stated that in the first dissolution this article was not infringed because the declaration had not yet been made, the holder of this view should realize that the Roman pontiff must know not only the explicit matters of the faith but the implicit ones too. For being the vicar of Christ and head of all, he had to teach and instruct all men. But if he should dodge this completely, he would be convicted under the head that he persisted in his dissolution for a long time after the declaration of the Council, and did not accept a canon of the Church, and therefore if he did not perhaps commit an error in faith in making the dissolution, he most certainly did in his obduracy. That conclusion was very neatly drawn from a saying of Clement often quoted by Panormitanus to the effect that he who lived in rebellion and neglected to do what was right was shown to be a member of the devil rather than of Christ, and was revealed as being an unbeliever rather than a believer. So it was not absurd to call Eugenius an unbeliever as not obedient to the Church. Nor was it true that the pope was not attacked on a matter of faith. For both in the reply beginning "Considering," and in the other, "They hope, when the pope's ambassadors are given up," these words were openly found: "This article concerns the faith, and we prefer death to a cowardly surrender"; from which remark it was clear enough that the Synod had warned the pope that he was going against the faith. So when afterwards by his adherence Eugenius had renounced the dissolution, he clearly renounced the error of faith contained in it as well; and the scandal moreover, of which mention was made, arose because of the error of faith, since some said the pope was beneath the Council, others denied this, and the very discrepancy of doctrine brought scandal with it. In the pope's act of adherence those assertions were also expressly renounced which had been made in the name of the pope against the authority of the Council. Though in retractions like these the style and order of legal documents were not observed, still what was done in such matters was enough since the Council was acting against the pope; in which case only the truth was to be respected; nor was the Council subject to positive law that it should keep [legal] terms and follow judicial procedure. Further that "singular gloss" which "preferred the Roman Church to the world," he held in utter contempt; it was a good thing it was "singular," since it made such a fatuous statement, and it did not deserve to have anyone following it. He was surprised at Panormitanus and other doctors of our times who, while thinking they praised the authority of glosses, actually lessened it by adding the "singularity." For a "singular gloss" was one that stood alone; but who would not value more a gloss possessing the same meaning in all places, and always consistently expressed, than one making an assertion in only a single place, which could without doubt seem to have been made in error? As far as the truth was concerned he took Jerome, the most learned of doctors, to be in opposition to that gloss, for he had no doubt that as regards authority the world was greater than the city, that is than Rome.

John of Segovia was not able to finish without interruption. For often Panormitanus broke in upon his words, and actively tried to confute now one remark now another. There rose also the bishop of Ardjisch, a man not only of eloquence but full of courage, who sharply demolished the remarks and arguments of Panormitanus, and matters between them went beyond the requirements of moderate discussion, for they did not refrain from abuse. Yet afterwards (though perhaps he was less at fault), the bishop of Ardjisch asked pardon, as usually happens because subordinates should always submit. The bishop of Ardjisch had happened to say that the Roman pontiff was the servant of the Church, which Panormitanus could not tolerate; and that day so far forgot himself and his learning, which is very great, as not to shrink from claiming that the pope was ruler of the Church. John of Segovia replied, "Watch what you are saying, Panormitanus. It is a very honorable title of the Roman pontiff when he calls himself 'servant of the servants of God.' For that is taken from what Christ said to his disciples when they were asking which of them would be the greatest. For you know he replied that 'the princes of the Gentiles exercise lordship over them, but ye shall not be so' [Luke 22:25], and so on, when he completely forbade lordship, and Peter, who himself was the first vicar of Christ, says: 'Feed the flock of God which is among you, taking the oversight thereof, not by constraint but willingly'; and a little later: 'neither as being lords over [God's] heritage' [1 Peter 5:2–3]. But if Christ, the son of God, 'came not to be ministered unto, but to minister' [Matt. 20:28], how will his vicar exercise lordship or be able to be called lord, as you wish, Panormitanus? For 'the disciple is not above his master, nor the servant above his lord,' 'neither be ye called masters,' saith the Lord [Matt. 10:24], 'for one is your master [even] Christ,' and 'he that is greatest among you shall be your servant'" [Matt. 20:26].

Panormitanus was rather perturbed by this reply, and the meeting broke up.

4. JOHN WYCLIF (C. 1330–84)

Wyclif was a trained Oxford theologian who sought to publicize his views outside the university. He objected to pluralism, simony, and the accumulation of church property, which were common targets for church reformers. Wyclif, however, moved into dangerous territory by advocating both the return of ecclesiastical property to secular hands and an important role for the secular authority in the reform of the Church. He also believed that the Bible should be available in the vernacular for everyone to read; he made a start on the first English bible, completed after his death.

Up to about 1378 he cannot be considered a heretic, because although his opinions did not follow those of the Church, they had not been condemned. In 1377, however, Pope Gregory XI (r. 1370–78) condemned Wyclif's teachings and ordered him to be arrested and examined. He was protected by John of Gaunt (1340–99), the uncle of the king, and the examination did not take place, but after this point Wyclif was in defiance of the Church.

The Peasants' Revolt of 1381 discredited Wyclif, though there is no evidence that he either was involved with it or agreed with its aims. He was placed under house arrest in 1382, when he seems to have suffered a stroke. It was followed by a second one that killed him two years later. Wyclif's followers became known as Lollards, and the movement passed largely into lay hands. The authorities took measures to suppress it, and persecution by Henry IV (r. 1399–1413) forced the Lollards to go underground in 1401. Because Wyclif had never been formally excommunicated, he was buried in hallowed ground. His condemnation came at the council of Constance, in 1415. In 1421 Wyclif's body was dug up and burnt and the ashes thrown into a nearby stream.

Of Wedded Men and Wives and of Their Children Also

Chapter I

Our Lord God Almighty speaks in his law of two matrimonies or wedlocks. The first is spiritual matrimony, between Christ and holy Church, that is, Christian souls ordained to bliss. The second matrimony is bodily or spiritual, between man and woman, by just consent, after God's law.

God speaks of the first matrimony by the prophet Hosea to holy Church; and to each person of holy Church God himself says, I shall espouse you or wed you to me, in righteousness, in judgment, in mercy and in faith; and I shall wed you without end. This is the first matrimony and the best, as God and the soul of true men are better than men's bodies. And this best matrimony is broken for a time by the breaking of the said faith, and default of righteous living. And therefore God says often by his prophets, that his people fornicated and committed adultery, for they worshipped false gods; and St. James (iv.4) says that men that love the world are spiritual adulterers. For he writes thus: you adulterers, do you not know that friendship of this world is enmity of God? And thus all men that love worldly worship or goods of the world more than God and his law and true life are spiritual adulterers, if they were Christian before; and this is worse adultery than breaking fleshly matrimony.

God speaks of the second matrimony, that is bodily, in the first book of Holy Scriptures, when he made matrimony between Adam and Eve in Paradise in the state of innocence, before they sinned. And because God himself made this order of matrimony and he did not make these new religious orders, it is better and more to praise than these new orders. And also Jesus Christ would not be born of the Virgin Mary, nor conceived, but in true matrimony, as the gospel of Luke, and St. Ambrose, and other saints witness. Also Jesus Christ was present in his own person with his mother in bodily matrimony, to approve it, as the gospel of John teaches, when he turned water into wine. Also the Holy Spirit warns Christian men, how in the last days some heretics shall depart from the faith of God's law, paying heed to spirits of error, and to teaching of devils, telling lies in hypocrisy, forbidding men and women to be married and teaching men to abstain from meat, which God has made to be eaten by faithful men, thanking God and listening to Him. Also, this bodily matrimony is a sacrament and figure of the spiritual wedlock between Christ and holy Church, as St. Paul says. Also, this wedlock is necessary to save mankind by generation until the day of judgment, and to restore and fulfill the number of angels, damned for pride, and the number of saints in heaven, and to save men and women from fornication. And therefore he that forbids or hinders true matrimony is an enemy of God and the saints in heaven and all mankind. And therefore man punished fornication and adultery in the old law by stoning to death, and in the law of grace by damning in hell, unless men are truly sorry for it.

And therefore, since fornication is so perilous, and men and women so frail, God ordained priests in the old law to have wives, and never forbade it in the new law, neither by Christ nor by his apostles, but rather approved it. But now, by hypocrisy of fiends and false men, many bind themselves to priesthood and chastity, and forsake wives by God's law, and ruin maidens and wives and fall foul of all. For there are many priests and religious, carrying-on, who have a pleasure-loving easy life, being young and strong of complexion, faring well in meat and drink, and they will not toil, neither in penance, nor study of God's law, nor teaching, nor labor with their hands; and therefore they fall into lechery in diverse degrees and in sin against nature. For many gentlemen's sons and daughters have been made religious against their will, when they were children without discretion, in order to give the inheritance wholly to one child that is most loved. And when they come to age, either for fear of their friends or for fear of poverty if they should leave, and for hypocrisy and flattering and fair promises of the religious or for fear of taking their body to prison, they dare not show their heart or leave this state, though they know that they are incapable of it. And from this comes lechery and sometimes murdering of many men.

Nevertheless, though matrimony is good and greatly commended by God, yet pure virginity is much better—and wedlock also, as St. Paul says publicly; for Jesus Christ, who lived most perfectly, was always a pure virgin and not married bodily, and so was his mother ever virgin, and John the Evangelist. St. Augustine and Jerome specially witness this well in many books. Nevertheless, virginity is so high and so noble that Christ did not command it generally, but said, who may take, take it. And therefore Paul gave no commandment of virginity, but gave counsel to them that were able to do it. And thus priests who keep pure chastity in body and soul do best; but many take this burden unwisely and scandalize themselves foully before God and his saints, for new bonds made needlessly by sinful men. And this is a great deceit of the devil under color of perfection and chastity. For he stirs men to high points of perfection, when he knows or supposes them unable, not for their good, but so that they will fall fouler and deeper in more sin, as St. Augustine teaches. And thus the fiend Satan transfigures or turns himself falsely into an angel of light, to deceive men by color of holiness.

Chapter II

See now how this wedlock ought to be kept in both sides. First this wedlock should be made with full consent of both parties, principally to the worship of God, to live cleanly in the order that he made, and bring forth children to fulfill the chosen number of saints in bliss, and not to have fleshly lusts without reason and fear of God, as mules and horses and swine that have no understanding. For the angel Raphael warned Tobit, that the fiend has mastery upon such men as are wedded, to have thus lusts of flesh as beasts without reason and fear of God. Also this contract should not be made between a young man and an old barren widow, past child-bearing, for love of worldly muck, as men full of covetousness do sometimes—for then comes soon wrangling and adultery and enmity and waste of goods, and sorrow and care enough. And it is a great despite to God to color thus their wicked covetousness, lechery and adultery by the holy order of matrimony. And many men sin much, for they befoul many women, and hinder them from matrimony and undo them in this world and are sometimes the cause of their damnation; for they are made common women, when they have lost their friends and know no craft to live by. Many hot and courageous men will not take a poor gentlewoman as his wife in God's law, and make her a gentlewoman, and save her own soul, but live in the devil's service all their life, or the more part; and befoul many temples of God to the great peril of their soul, and abide to have a rich woman for muck, and then waste their goods in harlotry and foolish pride, in adultery on gay strumpets, and ever live in wrath and chiding, and in bondage of sin to the fiends of hell. Also some mighty men marry their children where their heart does not consent willingly, but pretends for fear. For commonly they look for riches and worthiness to the world and not after goodness of virtuous life. And so God and his side is put behind, and the devil and the world and the flesh now have mastery here.

A man may know his rightful wife fleshly for three reasons, the first to beget children, to fulfill the number of men and women that will be saved; the second to keep his wife from lechery with other men; the third is to keep himself from lechery with other women. And no party may keep himself chaste from the acts of wedlock without the assent of the other commonly, for the man has power over the wife's body, and the wife has power over the man's body, as St. Paul says. And if the party desires to be chaste, he should endure without his own lust the acts of matrimony for the other party and he will have God's favor, both for allowing his mate and for the will he has to be chaste; for God gives reward for the good will and not only the deed. Also men say, if both parties assent willingly to perfect chastity, both of will and deed, that it is better than to use forth the acts of matrimony; and if they assent both parties at the beginning to live ever chaste, without bodily knowing, that it is the best kept matrimony of all other, as did our Lady and Joseph, when they were married. Look that each party live well before God and the world, and stir each other to charity, righteousness, and meekness and patience, and all goodness. And each man should beware lest he procure any false divorce, for money or friendship or enmity; for Christ bids that no man divide those that God has joined; but only for adultery the one that keeps himself clean may leave the other's bed, and for no other reason, as Christ himself says. And yet then the clean party may live chaste forever while the other lives, or else be reconciled again to the other. Nevertheless the clean one may dwell forth with the other that forfeits, by way of charity. And men suppose that that way is great charity, if there is evidence that the other party will do well afterwards.

Chapter III

See now how the wife ought to be subject to the husband and he ought to rule his wife, and how they both ought to rule their children in God's law. First St. Peter bids that wives be subject to their husbands, insomuch that those who do not believe by word of preaching may be gained without word of preaching through the holy living of women, when men behold the chaste living of women. And these women should not have crimped hair, or garlands of gold or over precious or curious clothing on the outside, but they should have a clean soul, peaceable and meek and humble, which is rich in the sight of God. And once upon a time holy women, hoping in God, honored Him in this manner and were subject to their own husbands, as Sara, Abraham's wife, obeyed Abraham, calling him lord; and women doing well are spiritual daughters of Sara. St. Peter says all this. Also St. Paul speaks thus of husbands and wives; I wish that men would pray in each place, lifting up clean hands, that is, clean works, without wrath and strife. Also I wish that women were in suitable dress, with modesty and soberness adorning them or making fair, not in twisted hair nor in gold, nor in margery stones, or pearls, nor in precious cloth, but in that that becomes women, inspiring pity by good works. A woman ought to learn in silence, with all obedience and subjection. But Paul says, I will not allow a woman to teach, that is, openly in church, as Paul says in a letter to Corinth, and I will not allow a woman to have lordship over her husband but to be in silence and stillness. For, as Paul says in many places, the husband is the head of the wife; and Paul gives this reason, that Adam was first formed and Eve afterwards, and Adam was not deceived in faith, but the woman was deceived in faith, in trespassing against God's commandment. Paul says all this in divers places of holy writ. Also Paul bids that bishops and priests teach wives to love their husbands, to be prudent and chaste and sober, and to have care of the house, and to be benign and submissive or subject to their husbands—so that the word of God is not blasphemed. And that old women should be in holy dress, not putting false crime or sin to another, nor suing too much wine and to teach well, so that they teach prudence. Also Paul teaches thus—that women are submissive or subject, to their husbands as to the Lord. For the husband is head of the woman as Christ is head of the church, he is savior of the body thereof, that is, the great multitude of all worthy to be saved. But as holy church is subject to Christ, so women are subject to their husbands in all things. Husbands, love your wives, just as Christ loved holy church and took himself willingly to suffer and die for holy church, to make it clean and holy; and made it clean by washing with water in the word of life, to give the church glorious to himself, not having blemish nor reveling nor any such filth, but that it should be holy and without spot or blemish. And husbands ought to love their wives as their own bodies, for he that loves his wife loves himself. For no man has ever hated his body, but nourishes and furthers it, as Christ does holy church. For we are members of his body, of his flesh and of his bones. For this thing a man shall forsake, or leave, his father and his mother and shall cleave to his wife and they shall be two in one flesh. This sacrament is great, but I say, says Paul, in Christ and holy church. But forsooth, you husbands, each by himself, love your wife as yourself and wives, fear your husbands. Children, honor your elders, father and mother, in the Lord, for this is the right thing to do. Worship your father and mother—that is the first commandment in behest; that Christ will look after you and you will live long upon earth. And, fathers, don't stir your children to wrath, but nourish them and bring them forth in discipline or learning and chastising of God. St. Paul says all this together. Also Paul commands thus in another letter; women be submissive to your husbands, as it behooves in the Lord. Men, love your wives and be not bitter to them. Children, honor your elders in all things, for this is pleasing to the Lord. Fathers, stir not your children to indignation, lest they of little understanding offend or trespass against God or man.

Here obstinate husbands and cruel fighters with their wives, without reasonable cause, are blamed by God. But many, when they are drunk, come home to their wives and sometimes from their cursed strumpets and throwers of dice, and chide and fight with their wife and household, as if they were Satan's brats and they allow neither rest, peace nor charity among them. But they shall pay dearly for this bitterness, for if they will have mercy from God they must have mercy on other men, though they had deserved beating—amend them in fair manner.

Chapter IV

Of this may wedded men and wives know, how they ought to live together and teach their children God's law. For at the beginning a child may easily be taught, and good morals and manners, according to God's law, are easily printed in his heart; and then he may easily hold them forth and increase in goodness. And therefore Paul bids that the father nourish his children in the lore and chastising of God; and God commands in the old law that the fathers should tell God's commandments to their children and the wonders and miracles that he did in the land of Egypt, and in the Red Sea, and in the water of the Jordan and in the promised land. And much more are fathers and mothers bound to teach their children to the belief of the Trinity, and of Jesus Christ, how he is true God without beginning, and was made man through most fervent charity, to save mankind by strong penance, hard torment, and bitter death. And so all come in points of Christian belief, but they are most beholden to teach them God's commandments, and the works of mercy, and points of charity, and to govern their five wits well, and to fear God before all other things, and to love him most of all things, for his endless might, endless wisdom, endless goodness, mercy and charity. And if they trespass against God's deeds, they ought to blame them for it sharply, and chastise them a thousand-fold more than for spite or unkindness done against their own person. And this teaching and chastising will in a few years make good Christian men and women, and namely the good example of holy life of old men and women, for that is the best teaching to their children.

And Christian men, above all many priests, charge godfathers and godmothers to teach the children the Our Father and the Creed; and this is well done; but it is most needful to teach them the commandments of God, and give them good example by their own life. For though they have been christened and know the common points of belief, yet they will not be saved without keeping God's commandments, but will be full hard and deep damned in hell, more than heathen men. And it would have been better for them never to have received Christendom, unless they continue truly in God's commandments, as St. Peter teaches plainly.

But some teach their children stories of battles and false chronicles not needful to their souls. Some teach new songs to stir men to jollity and harlotry. Some set them to needless crafts, for pride and greed; and some allow them in idleness and lying flattery to breed forth strumpets and thieves; and some with great cost set them to law, for gain and worldly honor, and for this spend hugely in many ways. But in all this God's law is left behind, and thereof hardly any man speaks a good word, to magnify God and that, and to save men's souls. Some teach their children to swear and stare and fight, and curse all men about, and have great joy in their hearts from this. But certainly they are Satan's teachers, and procurators to lead them to hell, by their cursed example and teaching and nourishing and maintaining in sin; and they are cruel slayers of their own children, indeed more cruel than if they hacked their children as small as morsels to their pot or mouth. For by this cursed teaching, and ending therein, their children's bodies and souls are damned without end in hell. And though their bodies were thus hacked so small, both body and soul will be in bliss of heaven, if they truly keep God's commandments. And St. Paul says a dreadful thing about such negligent fathers and mothers, that do not teach their children God's laws and do not chastise them when they trespass against God's commandments. He that has not care of his own and especially of his household has denied the faith and he is worse than a man outside Christendom. And such fathers and mothers, who maintain their children knowingly in sin, and teach them wickedness are worse than the cursed fathers that kill their children, and offer them up to sticks, worshipping false idols. For those children in their youth were dead and destroyed and did no more sin; but these children of cursed fathers and mothers, that teach them pride, theft, lechery, anger, covetousness and gluttony and keep them in them, have a long life and increase in sin to the greater damnation of both [parent and child]. And thus little wonder though he take vengeance on our people both old and young, for all commonly despise God and have joy and mirth at his anger and reproving. And God must punish this sin for his rightful majesty.

Chapter V

But though husbands thus have power over their wives' bodies, nevertheless they ought to use this in measure and reason, and somewhat refrain their foul lusts and not take a superfluity of hot wines and spiced ale and delicate meats to delight them in this occupation, but consider that they are guests and pilgrims in the world and do not have a dwelling place here forever. And therefore they must give themselves to holiness, without which no man shall see God; and they must abstain from fleshly desires that fight against the soul, as Peter and Paul teach by the authority of God himself; and think on this word of Saint Paul; the time is short; the other part is that they that have wives are as if they have none; that is to say, that they use them for and in dread of God, and measure, not to fulfill their lusts, as beasts without understanding; and that they keep in mind the dreadful coming of Christ to the last judgment, how they shall then answer for each deed, each word, and each thought—and each evil sufferance of their children and household, and principally of evil example to their subjects. And no quibbling or procurator shall be there, but their own good life to save them, or cursed life to damn them. And fleshly lusts, and gluttony, drunkenness, and over much liking in fleshly deeds, make men most to forget this dreadful judgment. And therefore the gospel says, that the third servant that had married a wife, said that he could not come to the supper of Christ; and that servant is understood to be he that gives himself to over much liking in fleshly lusts. And therefore Christ bids in the Gospel, that we take heed that our hearts are not charged with gluttony and drunkenness and business of this life, for the day of judgment will come as a snare, or trap, upon all those that sit upon the face of all the earth.

But wives beware that they stir not their husbands to wrath, nor envy against their neighbors, nor to falseness and over-much business of the world, to find too costly estate. For the wife was made to be as a helper to the husband, each to help the other in cleanness and holy life, and true before God and man. But if the husband is stirred to vengeance and pride and envy, the wife ought to stir him to penance and patience, meekness and charity, and all good manner of Christian life. And when God's law bids the husband and wife to love each other, they should beware that they do not turn this love all to fleshly love, and not to love of the soul, for they are encouraged to love the soul much more than the body, for God loves that more than the body, and for the soul Christ died. And indeed love of the body is truly hate unless it is in help to save the soul and keep it in holy life.

But yet three great faults fall many times among married men and women. The first fault is, as Saint John with the gilded mouth says, that they make sorrow if their children are naked or poor, but though their children are naked of virtues in their soul, they think nothing of it. And with much labor and cost they get great riches and high status and benefices for their children, often to their greater damnation, but they will not get their children goods of grace and virtuous life, nor allow them to receive such goods, freely offered by God, but hinder it as much as they can; and say, if their child is inclined to meekness and poverty, and flees covetousness and pride, for dread of sin and to please God, that he will never be a man, and they never spend a penny on him, and curse him if he lives well and teaches other men God's law, to save men's souls. For by this deed the child gains many enemies for his elders and they say that he slanders all their noble kin, that were always considered true and honorable men.

The second fault is, that wives give their husband's goods to strong and rich beggars and other churls, to get them sweet morsels and sometimes spend their husband's goods about fornicators and lechers, while their husbands travel in far countries or grievous travels. And to remain holy and excuse this wickedness, wives many times give a little alms openly, and find hypocrites to say mass and make the silly husbands maintain such hypocrites in their falseness, to rob the poor and hinder true men from teaching God's law, and to favor false slanders of their brethren. And if wives favor and maintain such hypocrites and stir their husbands to it, for private lechery between themselves, and for false security that the hypocrites give them, though they dwell still as swine in sin, it is so much the worse.

The third fault is this; if Almighty God, of his righteousness and mercy, takes their children out of this world by fair death, these rich wives weep, grumble and cry against God, as though God should not act against their will; and ask God why he takes their children from them rather than taking a poor man's, since they may better care for their children than poor men. See now the insanity of this grumbling! It is a great mercy of God to take a child out of this world; for if it shall be safe, it is delivered out of woe into bliss, lest malice turned the understanding of children to sin, and that is a great mercy of God, and therefore all men should be glad. If he shall be damned, yet it is a mercy of God to take him soon to death, lest he live longer and do more sin and therefore be in more pain. And since they grumble thus against God's rightful judgment, they tell God that he is unjust, unaware, that he does not know when is the best time for the child and, without mercy and charity he punishes so sorely the child and its elders. But indeed they are cursed Lucifer's children, wayward anti-Christs, and unnatural heretics and blasphemers. Therefore they should be glad and thank God for all his mercies and benefices and rightful judgments. Amen.

Also each party should look to keep the order made by God, and do not break it for any temptation or liking of the flesh. And many reasons help this. First, because God, who is the author of this order, loves it to be kept in cleanness, and present in every place, and for his righteousness must punish him that breaks it. And no defouling of it may escape unpained, for he knows all things, no matter how secret; and nothing, no matter how mighty, may stand against his punishing. Also, think how soon this stinking flesh, that now delights in lechery, shall turn to ashes and powder, and earth and worm's meat; and for such short liking to lose everlasting bliss and get everlasting pain in hell, in body and soul, were a cursed exchange; and no man knows how soon he will die and in what state. Also good angels, keepers of men and women, present to God a grievous complaint when this holy order is thus broken, and Christian souls, temples of the Holy Ghost, are thus wickedly blackened with filth of sin and made like the fiends of hell. And for this reason, men and women should be well occupied in good works and not idle, for idleness is the devil's snare, to tempt men to sin; and they should live in devout prayers and reasonable abstinence of meat, and namely of hot and strong drinks, and visit their poor neighbors that are bedridden, and clothe them, and lodge them, to get remission of over-much liking of fleshly deeds; and ever cry to God, with great desire and good life, that he grant them grace to keep cleanly his holy order, and do true penance for their old sins, to end in perfect charity, and so ever have their true spouse, Jesus Christ, in bliss of heaven without end. Amen.

5. THOMAS À KEMPIS (1379/80–1471)

Thomas's surname comes from his birthplace of Kempen in the Rhineland. The younger of two sons of a blacksmith and a schoolteacher, in 1393 he began his studies at Deventer. The school at Deventer was run by the Brethren of the Common Life, and during his time there Thomas was greatly influenced by Florens Radewijns (1350–1400), successor to the founder of the Brethren, Gerhard Groote (1340–84). In 1399 Thomas left the house at Deventer to join a house of regular canons at Mount St. Agnes (near Zwolle), where his older brother John was prior. After some delay Thomas was professed in 1407 and ordained in 1413 or 1414.

Thomas remained at Mount St. Agnes for the rest of his long life and was a prolific writer of devotional works, homilies, and saints' lives. He also wrote a chronicle of his monastery, which provides much of our knowledge of his life. His most famous work, The Imitation of Christ *is one of the most-published and best-known works of Christian devotion. It is a prime example of the message and methods of the* Devotio Moderna *inspired by the Brethren of the Common Life.*

The Imitation of Christ

Admonitions Profitable for the Spiritual Life

CHAPTER I

OF THE IMITATION OF CHRIST, AND
OF CONTEMPT OF THE WORLD AND ALL
ITS VANITIES

He that follows me shall not walk in darkness, says the Lord. These are the words of Christ; and they teach us how far we must imitate His life and character, if we seek true illumination, and deliverance from all blindness of heart. Let it be our most earnest study, therefore, to dwell upon the life of Jesus Christ.

His teaching surpasses all teaching of holy men; and such as have His Spirit find therein the hidden manna. But there are many who, though they frequently hear the Gospel, yet feel but little longing after it, because they have not the mind of Christ. He, therefore, that will fully and with true wisdom understand the words of Christ, let him strive to conform his whole life to that mind of Christ.

What doth it profit you to enter into deep discussion concerning the Holy Trinity, if you lack humility, and be thus displeasing to the Trinity? For truly it is not deep words that make a man holy and upright; it is a good life which makes a man dear to God. I had rather feel contrition than be skillful in the definition thereof. If you knew the whole Bible, and the sayings of all the philosophers, what should all this profit you without the love and grace of God? Vanity of vanities, all is vanity, save to love God, and Him only to serve. That is the highest wisdom, to cast the world behind us, and to reach forward to the heavenly kingdom.

It is vanity then to seek after, and to trust in, the riches that shall perish. It is vanity, too, to covet honors, and to lift up ourselves on high. It is vanity to follow the desires of the flesh and be led by them, for this shall bring misery at the last. It is vanity to desire a long life, and to have little care for a good life. It is vanity to take thought only for the life which now is, and not to look forward to the things which shall be hereafter. It is vanity to love that which quickly passes away, and not to have seen where eternal joy abides.

Be often times mindful of the saying, The eye is not satisfied with seeing, nor the ear with hearing. Strive, therefore, to turn away your heart from the love of the things that are seen, and to set it upon the things that are not seen. For they who follow after their own fleshly lusts defile the conscience and destroy the grace of God.

CHAPTER II

OF THINKING HUMBLY OF ONESELF

There is naturally in every man a desire to know, but what profit is knowledge without the fear of God? Better of a surety is a lowly peasant who serves God, than a proud philosopher who watches the stars and neglects the knowledge of himself. He who knows himself well is vile in his own sight; neither does he regard the praises of men. If I knew all the things that are in the world, and were not in charity, what should it help me before God, who is to judge me according to my deeds?

Rest from inordinate desire of knowledge, for therein is found much distraction and deceit. Those who have knowledge desire to appear learned, and to be called wise. Many things there are to know which profits little or nothing to the soul. And foolish out of measure is he who attends upon other things rather than those which serve to his soul's health. Many words satisfy not the soul, but a good life refreshes the mind, and a pure conscience gives great confidence towards God.

The greater and more complete your knowledge, the more severely shall you be judged, unless you have lived holily. Therefore be not lifted up by any skill or knowledge that you have; but rather fear concerning the knowledge which is given to you. If it seems to you that you know many things, and understand them well, know also that there are many more things which you know not. Be not high-minded, but rather confess your ignorance. Why do you desire to lift yourself above another, when there are found many more learned and more skilled in the Scripture than you? If you will know and learn anything with profit, love to be yourself unknown and to be counted for nothing.

That is the highest and most profitable lesson, when a man truly knows and judges lowly of himself. To account nothing of one's self, and to think always kindly and highly of others, this is great and perfect wisdom. Even should you see your neighbor sin openly or grievously, yet you ought not to reckon yourself better than he, for you know not how long you shall keep your integrity. All of us are weak and frail; hold you no man frailer than yourself.

CHAPTER III

OF THE KNOWLEDGE OF TRUTH

Happy is the man whom Truth by itself doth teach, not by figures and transient words, but as it is in itself.

Our own judgment and feelings often deceive us, and we discern but little of the truth. What doth it profit to argue about hidden and dark things, concerning which we shall not be even reproved in the judgment, because we knew them not? Oh, grievous folly, to neglect the things which are profitable and necessary, and to give our minds to things which are curious and hurtful! Having eyes, we see not.

And what have we to do with talk about genus and species! He to whom the Eternal Word speaks is free from multiplied questionings. From this One Word are all things, and all things speak of Him; and this is the Beginning which also speaks unto us. No man without Him understands or rightly judges. The man to whom all things are one, who brings all things to one, who sees all things in one, he is able to remain steadfast of spirit, and at rest in God. O God, who art the Truth, make me one with You in everlasting love. It wearies me oftentimes to read and listen to many things; in You is all that I wish for and desire. Let all the doctors hold their peace; let all creation keep silence before You: speak You alone to me.

The more a man hath unity and simplicity in himself, the more things and the deeper things he understands; and that without labor, because he receives the light of understanding from above. The spirit which is pure, sincere, and steadfast, is not distracted though it hath many works to do, because it doth all things to the honor of God, and strives to be free from all thoughts of self-seeking. Who is so full of hindrance and annoyance to you as your own undisciplined heart? A man who is good and devout arranges beforehand within his own heart the works which he hath to do abroad; and so is not drawn away by the desires of his evil will, but subjects everything to the judgment of right reason. Who hath a harder battle to fight than he who strives for self-mastery? And this should be our endeavor, even to master self and thus daily to grow stronger than self, and go on unto perfection.

All perfection hath some imperfection joined to it in this life, and all our power of sight is not without some darkness. A lowly knowledge of yourself is a surer way to God than the deep searching of man's learning. Not that learning is to be blamed, nor the taking account of anything that is good; but a good conscience and a holy life is better than all. And because many seek knowledge rather than good living, therefore they go astray, and bear little or no fruit.

O if they would give that diligence to the rooting out of vice and the planting of virtue which they give unto vain questionings: there had not been so many evil doings and stumbling-blocks among the laity, nor such ill living among houses of religion. Of a surety, at the Day of Judgment it will be demanded of us, not what we have read, but what we have done; not how well we have spoken, but how holily we have lived. Tell me, where now are all those masters and teachers, whom you knew well, whilst they were yet with you, and flourished in learning? Their stalls are now filled by others, who perhaps never have one thought concerning them. Whilst they lived they seemed to be somewhat, but now no one speaks of them.

Oh how quickly passes the glory of the world away! Would that their life and knowledge had agreed together! For then would they have read and inquired unto good purpose. How many perish through empty learning in this world, those who care little for serving God. And because they love to be great more than to be humble, therefore they "have become vain in their imaginations." He only is truly great, who hath great charity. He is truly great who deems himself small, and counts all height of honor as nothing. He is the truly wise man, who counts all earthly things as dung that he may win Christ. And he is the truly learned man, who doeth the will of God, and forsakes his own will.

CHAPTER IV

OF PRUDENCE IN ACTION
We must not trust every word of others or feeling within ourselves, but cautiously and patiently try the matter, whether it be of God. Unhappily we are so weak that we find it easier to believe and speak evil of others, rather than good. But they that are perfect do not give ready heed to every news-bearer, for they know man's weakness that it is prone to evil and unstable in words.

This is great wisdom, not to be hasty in action, or stubborn in our own opinions. A part of this wisdom also is not to believe every word we hear, nor to tell others all that we hear, even though we believe it. Take counsel with a man who is wise and of a good conscience; and seek to be instructed by one better than yourself, rather than to follow your own inventions. A good life makes a man wise toward God, and gives him experience in many things. The more humble a man is in himself, and the more obedient towards God, the wiser will he be in all things, and the more shall his soul be at peace.

CHAPTER V

OF THE READING OF HOLY SCRIPTURES

It is Truth which we must look for in Holy Writ, not cunning of words. All Scripture ought to be read in the spirit in which it was written. We must rather seek for what is profitable in Scripture, than for what ministers to subtlety in discourse. Therefore we ought to read books which are devotional and simple, as well as those which are deep and difficult. And let not the weight of the writer be a stumbling-block to you, whether he be of little or much learning, but let the love of the pure Truth draw you to read. Ask not, who hath said this or that, but look to what he says.

Men pass away, but the truth of the Lord endures for ever. Without respect of persons God speaks to us in divers manners. Our own curiosity often hinders us in the reading of holy writings, when we seek to understand and discuss, where we should pass simply on. If you would profit by your reading, read humbly, simply, honestly, and not desire to win a reputation for learning. Ask freely, and hear in silence the words of holy men; nor be displeased at the hard sayings of older men than you, for they are not uttered without cause.

CHAPTER VI

OF INORDINATE AFFECTIONS

Whenever a man desires anything above measure, immediately he becomes restless. The proud and the avaricious man are never at rest; while the poor and lowly of heart abide in the multitude of peace. The man who is not yet wholly dead to self is soon tempted, and is overcome in small and trifling matters. It is hard for him who is weak in spirit, and still in part carnal and inclined to the pleasures of sense, to withdraw himself altogether from earthly desires. And therefore, when he withdraws himself from these, he is often sad, and easily angered too if any oppose his will.

But if, on the other hand, he yields to his inclination, immediately he is weighed down by the condemnation of his conscience; for that he hath followed his own desire, and yet in no way attained the peace which he hoped for. For true peace of heart is to be found in resisting passion, not in yielding to it. And therefore there is no peace in the heart of a man who is carnal, nor in him who is given up to the things that are without him, but only in him who is fervent towards God and living the life of the Spirit.

CHAPTER VII

OF FLEEING FROM VAIN HOPE AND PRIDE

Vain is the life of that man who puts his trust in men or in any created Thing. Be not ashamed to be the servant of others for the love of Jesus Christ, and to be reckoned poor in this life. Rest not upon yourself, but build your hope in God. Do what lies in your power, and God will help your good intent. Trust not in your learning, nor in the cleverness of any that lives, but rather trust in the favor of God, who resists the proud and gives grace to the humble.

Boast not yourself in your riches if you have them, nor in your friends if they be powerful, but in God, who gives all things, and in addition to all things desires to give even Himself. Be not lifted up because of your strength or beauty of body, for with only a slight sickness it will fail and wither away. Be not vain of your skillfulness or ability, lest you displease God, from whom comes every good gift which we have.

Count not yourself better than others, lest perchance you appear worse in the sight of God, who knows what is in man. Be not proud of your good works, for God's judgments are of another sort than the judgments of man, and what pleases man is often times displeasing to Him. If you have any good, believe that others have more, and so you may preserve your humility. It is no harm to you if you place yourself below all others; but it is great harm if you place yourself above even one. Peace is ever with the humble man, but in the heart of the proud there is envy and continual wrath.

CHAPTER VIII

OF THE DANGER OF TOO MUCH FAMILIARITY

Open not your heart to every man, but deal with one who is wise and fears God. Be seldom with the young and with strangers. Be not a flatterer of the rich; nor willingly seek the society of the great. Let your company be the humble and the simple, the devout and the gentle, and let your discourse be concerning things which edify. Be not familiar with any woman, but commend all good women alike unto God. Choose for your companions God and His Angels only, and flee from the notice of men.

We must love all men, but not make close companions of all. It sometimes falls out that one who is unknown to us is highly regarded through good report of him, whose actual person is nevertheless unpleasing to those who behold it. We sometimes think to please others by our intimacy, and forthwith displease them the more by the faultiness of character which they perceive in us.

CHAPTER IX

OF OBEDIENCE AND SUBJECTION

It is verily a great thing to live in obedience, to be under authority, and not to be at our own disposal. Far safer is it to live in subjection than in a place of authority. Many are in obedience from necessity rather than from love; these take it amiss, and repine for small cause. Nor will they gain freedom of spirit, unless with all their heart they submit themselves for the love of God. Though you run here and there, you will not find peace, save in humble subjection to the authority of him who is set over you. Fancies about places and change of them have deceived many.

True it is that every man willingly follows his own bent, and is the more inclined to those who agree with him. But if Christ is amongst us, then it is necessary that we sometimes yield up our own opinion for the sake of peace. Who is so wise as to have perfect knowledge of all things? Therefore trust not too much to your own opinion, but be ready also to hear the opinions of others. Though your own opinion be good, yet if for the love of God you forego it, and follow that of another, you shall have the more profit thereby.

Often times I have heard that it is safer to hearken and to receive counsel than to give it. It may also come to pass that each opinion may be good; but to refuse to listen to others when reason or occasion requires it, is a mark of pride or willfulness.

CHAPTER X

OF THE DANGER OF SUPERFLUITY OF WORDS

Avoid as far as you can the tumult of men; for talk concerning worldly things, though it be innocently undertaken, is a hindrance, so quickly are we led captive and defiled by vanity. Many a time I wish I had held my tongue, and had not gone among men. But why do we talk and gossip so continually, seeing that we so rarely resume our silence without some hurt done to our conscience? We like talking so much because we hope by our conversations to gain some mutual comfort, and because we seek to refresh our wearied spirits by variety of thoughts. And we very willingly talk and think of those things which we love or desire, or else of those which we most dislike.

But alas! It is often to no purpose and in vain. For this outward consolation is no small hindrance to the inner comfort which cometh from God. Therefore must we watch and pray that time pass not idly away. If it be right and desirable for you to speak, speak things which are to edification. Evil custom and neglect of our real profit tend much to make us heedless of watching over our lips. Nevertheless, devout conversation on spiritual things helps not a little to spiritual progress, most of all where those of kindred mind and spirit find their ground of fellowship in God.

2

Early Northern Humanism

6. CONRAD CELTIS (1459–1508)

Celtis rose through learning from the peasantry to appointments at the universities of Ingolstadt and Vienna. After studies in Germany he visited Italy (1487) but returned to the north where the Emperor Maximilian granted him a professorship in Vienna. He was also a major neo-Latin poet, crowned poet laureate by the Emperor Frederick III. Concerned that German humanist scholars should enjoy mutual support against both the Italians and the medieval scholastics, Celtis established academies or sodalities in Cracow, Budapest, and Heidelberg and encouraged particularist German scholarship and style. His own research discovered the plays of the medieval German nun Hrotswitha (fl. tenth century), and, in his Oration Delivered Publicly in the University of Ingolstadt *(August 1492) on the occasion of his acceptance of his professorship in that university, he encouraged German students to apply themselves to humanist disciplines.*

Oration Delivered Publicly in the University of Ingolstadt

I would not have considered it something special, most excellent fathers and distinguished youths, that I, a German and your fellow countryman, can speak to you in Latin, if those ancient talents of our Germany still flourished, and if that age had returned in which our ambassadors are said to have spoken Greek rather than Latin. But, since through the adverseness of the ages and the change of the times, not only amongst us but even in Italy, the mother and ancient parent of letters, all the past splendor of literature has perished or been extinguished, and all the noble disciplines have been driven away and ruined by barbaric tumults, I am not at all confident that, given the slowness of my mind and the poverty of my powers, I can speak to you adequately in Latin. This is especially true since I have not lacked industry or good teaching, which many of you have up till now experienced and deplored in yourselves. However, lest I be accused of coming in total silence to this place, so richly adorned by your presence, I would rather offend by stammering than lightly pass over by silence your love for me and for the commonwealth of letters. I shall hope for your indulgence if you consider that a little man born in the midst of barbarity and drunkenness, as they say, cannot speak so sensibly as is required by your most sagacious ears and by this auditorium, assigned to me for oratory and poetry by the most illustrious prince, our [Duke] George [the Rich of Bavaria-Landshut], and by you most distinguished gentlemen who are privy to all his counsels.

I have decided, moreover, that I can say nothing to you more worthy and pleasant, or more appropriate for me and fitting for you to hear, than to exhort your minds to virtue and the study of the liberal arts. For through them true glory, immortal fame, and happiness can be attained even in this brief life of ours. None of you should be found so sluggish and lazy that you do not regard it as a beautiful, excellent, and magnificent thing to strive toward these lofty goals which can make one truly happy. I have not thought it necessary to discuss with any particular acumen the favors of fortune and the delights of the body, or those sensual pleasures, worthy of slaves, that extinguish the light of the spirit. For these are all perishable, transitory, and destined to die with their body in a brief moment of time or will soon have other masters. Wherefore no wise man is remembered to have striven for these things. Rather, if we examine their lives, we find that these wise men of ancient times so loved learning and wisdom, with which the human spirit is nourished as with nectar and ambrosia, that in order to attain them they left their fatherland, wives, and beloved children, dispersed the richest patrimonies, endured injustices, insults, and infamy at the hands of the common crowd, and suffered exile with the greatest patience and peace of mind. Moreover, it is related that they willingly accepted labors, suffered cold and heat, and undertook arduous journeys because they wished to perceive and to see with their sense what they had learned, tired out by their deepest reflection and constant reading—so great was their incredible zeal to acquire wisdom and their love for searching into celestial things and nature. For these accomplishments they finally attained divine honors and are destined to have an immortal name. Greatly venerated and reverenced by all posterity, they come to be solemnly named "philosophers."

The Scythian race is so brutish, uncultivated, and horrid, like wild beasts, that they wander about in vast and inaccessible solitudes like herds of cattle, protecting themselves from the inclemency of the atmosphere and the harshness of the climate only with the skins of wild animals and their hides, from which they take their name. Nevertheless, glory and the desire for praise have so inspired them that three times they ruled over vanquished Asia. Nor did they carry away any gold or silver, things which we most desire, but considered it more glorious for it to be said of them that by their bravery they added such great splendor and amplitude to their dominion. We thus have great examples of a barbarous people for the pursuit of virtue and glory. While they were not able by genius and learning or by gentle customs, contrary to their nature, to contend with other mortals, they at least seem to have provided for their glory and immortality by their unbridled barbarity and the impetuosity of their spirits, which they regarded as a virtue. But if I were to turn my address to the histories of other tribes and what they did in peace and war, I would have a very broad field for recounting, and this present day would not be long enough to tell them all. So I purposely pass over what you are easily able to apply to this subject from your reading of illustrious authors.

I shall regard it as enough, and more than enough, men of Germany and illustrious youths, if by my presentation today, such as it is, I shall have added, impressed, and as it were, branded upon your spirits some stimulus to glory and virtue, so that you keep ever before your eyes that immortality which you must seek only from the fountain of philosophy and the study of eloquence. I cannot easily declare with what great labors and vigils you must linger and sweat over these two things—that is to say, over the writings of the ancient philosophers, poets, and orators. For they alone have prescribed for us the way to live well and happily and have set before us Nature, which is both the parent of the human race and the cause of all things (as it were), as an example and mirror of life to be imitated. From them you will learn to praise good deeds and to detest evil deeds, and from them you will learn to console yourselves, to exhort, to impel, and to hold back. You will strive to contemplate the Ruler of all things and Nature itself, which is the summit of human happiness. Although all these things can be done by others, nevertheless, and I still do not understand just how, the power to arouse compassion, to reawaken, and to repress the whole spirit lies in the hand of the orator and the poet. Indeed, those ornaments of words and thoughts, which like stars illumine the oration, are the proper instruments of the orator and poet. You must borrow them and use them as the occasion demands for your own use in your daily conversations. For what, by the immortal gods, does it profit us to know many things, to understand the beautiful and the sublime, if we are prevented from speaking of them with dignity, elegance, and gravity, and if we are not able to transmit our thoughts to posterity, which is the unique ornament of human happiness? So it is, by the faith of men: nothing shows a man to be learned and erudite unless it be the pen and the tongue—the two things which eloquence governs.

But to you, excellent gentlemen and noble youths, I now direct my address, to whom, thanks to ancestral virtue and invincible German strength, the empire of Italy has passed and who frequent this university rather than all the other centers of study in our Germany, make it fruitful, and serve as a great adornment and elegance. I exhort you to turn first to those studies that can render your minds gentle and cultured and call you away from the habits of the common crowd, so that you dedicate yourselves to higher studies. Keep before your eyes true nobility of mind, and consider that you are bringing not refinement but dishonor to our empire if you merely feed horses and dogs and pursue ecclesiastical prebends rather than the study of letters. As you seek splendor for your dignities with virtue, knowledge, and erudition, reflect on how to add honor to your holy morals so that men may esteem you worthy of those honors, so that they pursue you, and not you them, like fowlers a flock of birds. Noble men, emulate the ancient Roman nobility who, after they had taken over the empire of the Greeks, combined all their wisdom and eloquence so that it is a question as to whether they equalled or actually surpassed all the Greek faculty of invention and apparatus of learning. So you, too, having taken over the rule of the Italians and having cast off your vile barbarity, must strive after the Roman arts. Take away that infamy of the Germans among the Greek, Latin, and Hebrew writers, who ascribe to us drunkenness, barbarism, cruelty, and whatever is bestial and foolish. Regard it as a great shame for yourselves not to know the histories of the Greeks and the Latins, and beyond all shamelessness not to know the situation, the stars, rivers, mountains, antiquities, peoples of our region and land—briefly, all that foreigners have shrewdly gathered together concerning us. It seems a great miracle to me how the Greeks and Romans with such precise diligence and exquisite learning surveyed our land—"the greatest part of Europe," to use their own words, but rough and crude, I think, compared with the South; and they expressed our morals, affections, and spirits with words like paintings and the lineaments of bodies. Cast out, noble men, cast out and eliminate those villainies which they relate were bestowed among us as proofs of manly excellence. It is a wonder that this native sickness has endured for nearly fifteen hundred years in some parts of Germany. For even now we still do not compel the chiefs of that robber band to surrender, in a happier climate when we have eliminated bogs, cut down vast forests, and peopled our land with famous cities—so difficult is it to correct what has become a custom, spread about for ages, because it is generally approved. Thus it has happened that neighboring peoples make us smart and persecute our name with such awful eternal envy and calumny, proclaiming that with the Empire we have taken on many vices of the foreign nations. They always distrust and fear our talents. We should feel ashamed, noble gentlemen, that certain contemporary historians [Sabellicus, 1436–1506], by publishing an edition of new *Decades*, so glory in having equalled the ancient Roman Empire, that they insult and bitterly jeer the German name, and that they call our most glorious princes barbarians, suppressing their natal names. So great has been the old and inexpiable hatred between us and the ancient hatred of our gods, that because of the hostility on both sides we would never have been restrained from mutual slaughter if provident nature had not separated us by the Alps and by cliffs raised up to the stars. Let us feel ashamed, I pray, that although we have successfully waged many memorable wars in Pannonia [Hungary], Gaul, and Italy, and against the most monstrous tyrant of Asia [the Turk], brandishing his sword wet with Christian blood, there is no one found among you today who records for eternity the deeds performed by German courage. But there will be many foreigners who will in their histories, without regard for the law of history, hiss like vipers against our bravery with a great verbal show and enticement of speech, not to say with fictions and mendacious invention, with which that kind of men are most effusive in singing their own praises and belittling the most glorious deeds which we perform. I do not really know whether it is due to our wisdom or to our thoughtlessness that in recent times we returned the insignia of writers and the accompanying imperial laurel beyond to the Tarpeian Hill [Rome]. It is an unhappy omen for our Empire, since having conceded to others the license for bestowing the laurel wreath, that finally no honor of the Empire remains ours.

O men of Germany, assume those ancient passions by which you were so often a dread and terror to the Romans, and turn your eyes to the wants of Germany and consider her lacerated and divided borders. What a shame to have a yoke of servitude imposed on our nation and to pay tributes and taxes to foreign and barbaric kings. O free and strong people, O noble and brave nation, clearly worthy of the Roman Empire, your renowned seaport [Danzig] is held by the Pole and your ocean gateway is occupied by the Dane! In the east the most vigorous tribes are held as slaves; the Marcomanni [Bohemians], Quadi [Moravians], and Bastarnae [Slovaks] live, as it were, separate from the body of our Germany. I do not even speak of the Transylvania Saxons, who also use our national culture and native language. In the west, however, upper Gaul [France] is so friendly and munificent toward us, thanks to the immortal virtue and incredible wisdom of Philipp of the Rhenish Palatinate, who rules the shore on either side of its renowned river and ever will rule with an auspicious reign, "As long as the pole rotates the stars, as long as the breezes strike the shores." But to the south we are burdened with a kind of distinguished servitude, for new colonies are continually being established, thanks to that ancient and detestable avarice for fostering luxuries by which our land is being emptied of its wonderful natural resources, while we pay from the public treasury to others what we need for ourselves [papal exploitation]. So determined is fortune or fate to pursue and destroy the Germans, the remnants of the Roman Empire. But I fear I have progressed more freely than I desire, so disgusted am I with my Germany when I consider the things in the store of books taken from the Greeks and the Latins and preserved by the power of our Emperors, books which we have till now abandoned like the detested spoils of the enemies, as if locked in a prison, covered with dust, untouched, and not well protected from the rain.

I come back to you, O noble youths, and admonish above all things that you recall to mind before you proceed to the science of law that the knowledge of many things is necessary for you, because that discipline can teach you nothing beyond opinion. For if one is to believe antiquity, the philosophers and poets, the first theologians, called out the people, who were roaming and wandering about, from the haunts and caves of animals to the cities and social abodes, after their crude spirits had been tamed by speech. They taught them religion and the fear of the gods with many and varied arguments and then ruled with laws and ordinances. Who of you will doubt, O most distinguished fathers, that before the study of law it is necessary to pay close attention to true philosophy and especially to those things by which eloquence can be acquired, which you agree are very necessary for the lawyer. Therefore you will also consider those people quite mistaken and responsible for many abuses who, passing by all philosophy (except the low variety), make themselves leaders in law and religion without reflecting on what kind of legislators there were in ancient times—men who spent their day on laws and arms but spent every night on the study of philosophy. Inasmuch as philosophy, like a kind of seminary, teaches fully the knowledge of things human and divine and their jurisdiction, who without drinking of the fountain of philosophy shall judge himself able to manage these two things? I shall not at this point offer as evidence for you the Greeks: Solon, Plato, Alcibiades, Themistocles, or Philip, the father of Alexander the Great. With what great care he commended his son to Aristotle, the greatest philosopher of that age, and with what great joy he eagerly desired a son born to him at a time when philosophers enjoyed such very great prestige! For that master of arms, so experienced in ruling the state, knew that if his own son were initiated into the precepts and ordinances of philosophy, he would be worthy to be entrusted with the administration of the whole universe. Nor shall I remind you of Anacharsi who, when he introduced his laws to Scythia, first wanted to learn philosophy from the Attic philosophers. I remain silent about the Roman kings, Numa, Cato, the Scipios, the Caesars, and the later ones, the Antonians, the Valerians, the Aurelians, Theodosius, finally also Charlemagne, born of the noble stem of the Franks, by whose learning and by whose concern and zeal for the liberal arts a most glorious empire was procured and preserved, which flourished as long as it maintained philosophy as its partner and assistant. I now pass over Moses the legislator of our ancient religion, most wise in all philosophy, who was a most prudent governor in impelling, curbing, and overcoming the minds of the masses. In writing the sacred laws he began with the creation of the world and with the remembrance of the majesty of Nature and its Maker. He thereby clearly demonstrated that any legislator or student of the legal discipline must first be initiated into the precepts of philosophy as though into sacred rites.

But such great men do not move us, for by the narrow boundary of destiny now among us, by fortune, circumstances, and the dregs of these last times, the Empire grows old; and we, neglecting all philosophy, prostitute our servile spirits to base complaint alone and hire them out for mercenary wages. Hence, when we come from such pursuits to the princes, we suggest to them only those which we have learned. And these are the reasons—I say with great bitterness—why our princes despise learning and always remain unlearned, why they are regarded with derision by others and are ridiculed as "barbarous," because, even in these otherwise prosperous times, they neglect the liberal arts and their proponents. There is nothing more vile and abject at their courts than those who profess with a word or gesture a knowledge of letters—so greatly our barbarity pleases us and the sickness of an intractable mind. Even among our high churchmen and, to use an ancient term, the "sacred flames," to whom the care and protection of letters rightly belongs, they have been so contemptuous of the trifling value of letters and of those devoted to them that they prefer the wild animals of the forests, the long-eared dogs, the snorting and spirited horses, and other pleasures and amusements like Rhea, the wife of Mars [mother of Romulus and Remus], [Emperor] Claudius, and Sardanapalus [effeminate king of Assyria]. We know some bishops, come up from obscure origins, who, when they receive studious men from abroad at their courts, refuse to speak to them to show their knowledge, to such an extent does the silence of Pythagoras please them, lest they seem to be dishonored in their barbarous majesty by the parsimony of the Roman language. Meanwhile they pant with greed like rapacious hawks for money or for the approbations of kings, which they dare exhibit before their doors like common eager whores. So much has Italian luxury and savage cruelty in extorting pernicious silver corrupted us that it would clearly have been more godly and holy had we lived that rude and silvan life of olden times, when we lived within the limits of moderation, rather than bringing in so many instruments of gluttony and luxury, and adopting foreign manners. So it happens that our rulers take those men into their familiar circle who are similarly inclined and exclude those who cherish learning and wisdom. The founders of the Greek and Roman Empire, in contrast, so honored wise men that they bestowed upon them imperial honors and called their secretaries friends. They ordered that those who died should be interred in their own sepulchers, because they believed that power and immortality were preserved for them by those wise men through the benefit and use of letters by which alone immortality is attained. That way they could aid mankind not only while alive but even after they had died. Therefore they live until today and will continue to live as long as Roman and Greek letters exist. I will give no other reason for Italy's flourishing than that they excel us in no other felicity than the love and study of letters. With these they intimidate other nations as though with weapons and lead others to admire them by their talent and industry. But with us there are frequent changes, and among us there is an improper desire for new things, so that a very wise poet says of us:

Brothers eager to know new things and mad with hate
Of peace and with genius and quick desire.

So that our horses do not contract the gout and our weapons rust, we raise a tumult among ourselves by dissension like Sulla and Marius of Caesar and Pompey. I cannot be temperate as long as we are involved in our vices and domestic strifes and neglect our very rich territories, whose titles we brandish as though for our own consolation, while we tie bootstraps and stretch out the deliberations in our councils up to the fifth new moon, as a certain historian has written of us, by nature given to worthless goods and eager for small advantages. Meanwhile in the heart of our Germany we tolerate the reign of a pertinacious religion most sumptuous in its use of a foreign tongue [Hussites in Bohemia]. Although their university [Charles University in Prague] weeps and sighs over the ruin of its ancient felicity, they must nevertheless render thanks to the gods because an Italian is their leader [Augustinus Lucianus of Vicenza]. Because the university had no cultivators of true philosophy, it left behind a strong proof by its fall that the foundations of religion can be strengthened and preserved by no one better than by a true philosopher, rather than by those who regard the highest wisdom as ignorance and who merely accommodate themselves by habit to ostentation for the common crowd and set forth only a small shadow of learning and virtue. They are very much like little scarecrows that peasants put up in their orchards and fields to frighten away small birds, but if you come closer you see that they have neither movement nor sense.

I now return to you, then, youths of Germany. Act no longer in a childish manner, but learn to know the secrets of literature, for those writers relate that you flee from them and sing to our shame:

The Castalian liquids [wines] and the prescient rivers
  of fate
No barbarian shall ever drink with his polluted mouth.

It should shame us that such things should be read and applied to you, the possessors of the Roman Empire, and persist down to the present day. Someone might want to argue against me on the basis of the large number of our universities, of which we have fourteen, and might say that because of them barbarity has been eliminated and care has been taken for good morals and honorable arts, and the way has been opened while the crowd flatters and exults us with the titles of masters and doctors! With tears I say it—you will find few who acquire a true knowledge of things and search into the nature and purity of the Roman language or retain it. This is because in our studies of (not to say triflings with) such subjects those who interpret the poets and the writers of the Roman language are repressed and those who uncover the work of nature and the wisdom of its governor with mathematical truthfulness and who think a bit more deeply than the common crowd are regarded as infamous. To such an extent is philosophy trampled underfoot and boiled down by some who have deformed the most beautiful majesty of Nature into incorporeal thoughts and monstrous abstractions and empty chimeras, like poets. For poets with their imagery and apt fables have transposed natural things figuratively so that sacred things should be hidden from the common crowd, for they know that open and naked exposure is inimical to Nature and that Nature must therefore be revealed under respectable coverings and a sacramental veil. For should the common crowd understand certain mysteries as the philosophers do, it might be difficult to restrain their impulses.

Nor shall I now interpret the fables of the Greek and the Latin poets in the manner of the naturalists, who reveal the foundations of all divine inventions under the cloud of poetic fiction to the truly wise. But we accuse such poets of lies and execrate them as imposters and vile men. So much do our baseness and our foul barbarity please us, the gods being hostile, I believe, that we do not, together with the Roman imperium, also assume the splendor of Italian letters and seek to rival them in this most beautiful kind of writing, even though we admire them. We may to be sure find among us those who labor with my vice, usurping for themselves the name "poet" and "orator." But they, ignoring every precept of philosophy and rhetoric, strain every nerve of their genius to produce futile banter and to allure the minds of the adolescents with strange fantasies. They devise smoothness with watery words, spewing forth shamelessly whatever comes into their mouths, making chaste ears drunk with obscene and shameful fables, as if vices should be opened up to us for our understanding, although they always sprout up more densely of their own accord without encouragement, like useless weeds. If someone would give more careful attention to our erudition such as it is, he would come upon an arena without a goal and a voice without blood, although we are quite prepared to fault others for their vocabulary, like schoolboys. But our own stench we do not smell, and I think that the immortal gods have decreed well toward us, for they have conceded to us at least a certain plebeian and vulgar learning. Otherwise by our bleating and vile medley of words we would not permit others who are more learned than we to murmur a sound. Although it pleases us to hear such men, it is not because they nourish our minds with true teaching, while we persecute with hatred those who cry out against and carp at our obsolete manner of teaching, offer new approaches from the true Roman instruction, and compel the aged, trifling grammarians to learn the elements of the Greek language and to cry once again in learning the art of grammar, like infants in the cradle. As if Cato were not at hand as an example, a most serious man and most learned in all erudition and doctrine, who when already an octogenarian began to learn Greek in order to be able to speak Latin correctly. We, boys and old men alike, neglect both languages and, in defense of our slothfulness and inertia, ascribe divine power and miracle to St. James and St. Augustine because they learned so many languages and wrote so many books, which we do not attain in our whole age, rather than crediting their long vigils, the greatest labors, and longest journeys. For by these efforts learning, sanctity, and an eternal name are handed on to all posterity, not by sleep and gluttony, spending on feasting, with dice and Venus, evils with which we are inflamed, thanks to our stupidity; we gormandize our whole life as though we had been born for this alone. But we who wish to appear more cultivated in learning tarry in childish contention about our terms and quiddities on which we grow old and die, as on the rocks of the Sirens. Nor do we want others to know anything except what is stained with our dregs. Therefore we are chosen as leaders and princes of our most beautiful religion. We look longingly with the zeal of avarice and burn with an insatiable thirst for all powers, while we bury away money with ourselves like the corpses of the dead beneath the earth. This is what our vulgar philosophy has taught us with its worthless harvest of empty words, for which we neglect the most restrained and the most fluent writers of our religion. We are able to attain nothing magnificent, high and excellent, while we seek only inferior things, as though certain basic teachings of our religion were not to be found in Plato and Pythagoras, in whom the most beautiful association of the light of nature and of grace may be perceived. But concerning this another time.

For that reason turn, O Germans, turn about to the more gentle studies, which philosophy and eloquence alone can teach you. Consider well that it is not without reason that the Greek and Roman founders of the Empire devoted such great efforts and watchful attentions to those matters and decorated the teachers of those subjects with the highest honors, for they understood that by the power of language and the lessons of wisdom the assemblies of men, cities, religions, the worship of the gods, the most holy morals, and the broadest empires could be preserved and governed. That divine poet [Virgil], the ornament and delight of Roman eloquence, splendidly expressed this truth thus when he sang:

And, as in times of revolt, which often afflict a great nation,
When the ignoble throng are roused to a frenzy of
*   passion,*
Fire brands and stones are beginning to fly, for fury
*   finds weapons,—*
Then, if they chance to behold some man, for his faith
*   and his virtue*
Highly revered, they are awed, and attentively listen
*   in silence,*
While he controls their minds by his words, and quiets
*   their passion.*

[Virgil, *Aeneid*, I, X 48–53]

Great indeed was that nearly divine element in administering their state that they aimed to join wisdom with eloquence; and, in order to master these, they instituted public performances in which by sublime persuasion and remarkable inventive faculties, they exhorted the spirits of the viewers to virtue, piety, modesty, fortitude, and endurance of all things. They deterred the idle youth from vices and inflamed them to glory, so that whatever they owed to the fatherland, friends, strangers, and their dear parents, they learned as from living portraits. Therefore that allegory of the poets is not unseemly, according to which Orpheus is said to have tamed wild animals, moved stones, and led them where he wished; for it shows by metaphor the power of eloquence and the duty of the poet, who is able to move ferocious, monstrous, and intractable spirits to gentleness, a right spirit, and love for the fatherland. These things being so, the states of Greece and now of Italy wisely educated their boys from the very beginning with the hymns of poets. In those hymns they learned to perceive musical tunes and the sweetest modulations of harmony, on which that age is very keen; and they provided for those tender spirits, inclined to inertia and laziness, a stimulant to industry so that they were excited to learning with a cheerful zeal, a lively spirit, and eagerness. The gravity of words and meanings imbibed by tender minds will thus endure to a more advanced age and until death, and will continually sprout forth again through an entire lifetime. Aristotle prescribes this plan when he stipulates that adolescents should be educated in musical hymns. Because it—that is, harmony—stirs up the talents of boys and impels them to the acumen of oratory and the production of song. That discipline is very well adapted for relaxing the spirit and for consoling and uplifting minds; it sounds forth in sacred hymns their praises of the gods and carries them off in divine meditations. For this reason Pythagoras and Plato, the loftiest philosophers, named poetry the first philosophy and theology, which uses hymns for its demonstrations and arouses with melodious speech. But the other discipline—that is, oratory—spreads out with humble, loose, and free speech. Poetry is more concise in rhythm and a bit more free with words, but similar and almost equal in many kinds of embellishment. Neither the one nor the other must be neglected; but from the very beginning, O men of Germany, the minds of the boys must be instructed in and, if I may say so, allured with songs. And when the sublime admiration of things resides in these, the beauty and polish of words, the spirits of the youths easily gain strength from them. In an intellectually stronger age, when the youthful spirit has already been hardened by those beginnings, and thought has been invigorated, they are better instructed and better prepared to lead themselves to the reading of more serious philosophers and orators. From these they can finally rise to their own inventions and to the sublimity of the poetic discipline and its figures, attaining to the praises of illustrious authors in writing histories and poems. They will then procure immortality for themselves and glory and praise for the fatherland. I have spoken.

7. SIR THOMAS MORE (1478–1535)

Thomas More was born in London and educated in the law. He considered taking monastic vows but decided instead to marry and devote himself to the service of the Crown, holding among others the offices of Speaker of the House of Commons (1523) and Lord Chancellor of England (1529–32). The issue of Henry VIII's divorce from Catherine of Aragon resulted in More's resignation; and after his refusal to acknowledge the king as head of the English Church (the Act of Supremacy), he was charged with treason. After an unfair trial, he was executed in July 1535.

More is remembered not only as King Henry's most principled opponent but also as the author of Utopia *(1516), one of the great books of the Northern Renaissance (see selection 32). Sharing with his close friends Erasmus (c. 1466–1536) and John Colet (1457–1519) a strong belief in the need for church reform, he wrote of a previously unknown island where charity, reason, cooperation, and virtue operated. This mythical island of Utopia (No Place) he contrasted to the England he knew. The book is also an evocative expression of the values of northern humanism, a movement More strongly supported both privately and officially.*

> *In 1518 he learned that the opposition to Erasmus's Greek New Testament included his own university of Oxford and that gangs of students calling themselves Trojans were interfering in their fellow students' attempts to learn Greek. More responded with a letter to Oxford University supporting the new learning, especially Greek studies, a discipline, he notes, also favored by the King and by the Lord Chancellor, Thomas Wolsey (1473–1530).*

Letter to the Professors and Masters of the University of Oxford

Abingdon

29 March [1518]

Thomas More to the Reverend Fathers, the commissary [i.e., the Vice-Chancellor], proctors, and others of the guild of masters of the University of Oxford, greeting.

I have been wondering, gentlemen, whether I might be permitted to communicate to scholars of your distinction certain conclusions to which I have recently come. Yet I have hesitated in approaching so brilliant a group, not so much on the ground of my style as on that of seeming to give an exhibition of pride and arrogance. Who am I, the possessor of little prudence and less practice, a scholar of mediocre proportions, to arrogate to myself the right to advise you in anything? And how can I dare to offer advice in the field of letters especially, when any one of you is fitted by his wisdom and erudition to give advice in that field to thousands?

At first sight, Venerable Fathers, I was therefore deterred by your unique wisdom. But, on second thought, I was encouraged; for it occurred to me that only ignorant and arrogant fools would disdain to give a man a hearing, and that the wiser and more learned you were, the less likely you would be to think highly of yourselves or to scorn the advice of others. I was further emboldened by the thought that no one was ever harmed by just judges, such as you are above all, simply on the ground that he offered advice without thinking of the consequences. On the contrary, loyal and affectionate advice, even if imprudent, has always deserved praise and thanks.

Finally, when I consider that, with God's help, I ought to offer you whatever slight learning I have acquired, since it was at your University that my education began, it seems the duty of a loyal friend not to pass over in silence what I deem it serviceable to bring to your attention. Since, then, the only danger in putting my pen to paper seemed to lie in the fact that a few might deem me too audacious; while I know that my silence would be condemned by many as ingratitude, I have preferred that the whole world should condemn my audacity rather than that anyone should have the chance to say that I showed myself ungrateful to your University, the honor of which I feel myself bound to defend to the uttermost. Moreover, no situation has, I believe, arisen in recent years, which, if you desire to maintain the honor of that institution, more urgently requires your serious attention.

The matter is as follows: when I was in London recently, I rather frequently heard that some members of your teaching body, either because they despised Greek or were simply devoted to other disciplines, or most likely because they possessed a perverse sense of humor, had proceeded to form a society named after the Trojans. The senior sage christened himself Priam; others called themselves Hector, Paris, and so forth; the idea, whether as a joke or a piece of anti-Greek academic politics, being to pour ridicule on those devoted to the study of Greek. And I hear that things have come to such a pass that no one can admit in public or private that he enjoys Greek, without being subjected to the jeers of these ludicrous "Trojans," who think Greek is a joke for the simple reason that they don't know what good literature is. To these modern "Trojans" applies the old saw, "Trojans always learn too late."

The affair aroused much comment, all very critical; and I myself felt somewhat bitter that even a few academics among you had nothing better to do in their spare time than to cast slurs on their colleagues' subjects. But I kept in mind that one could not expect the whole crowd of academics to possess wisdom, temperance, and humility; and so I began to dismiss the matter as a triviality. However, since I have been here in Abingdon in attendance at the court of His Victorious Majesty [Henry VIII], I have found that the silliness is developing into a form of insanity. For one of the "Trojans," a scholar in his own estimation, a wit of the first water in that of his friends, though slightly deranged in that of anyone observing his actions, has chosen during Lent to babble in a sermon against not only Greek but Roman literature, and finally against all polite learning, liberally berating all the liberal arts.

His whole performance was of a piece. Perhaps such a body of nonsense could not be preached on the basis of any sensible text; in any case, he followed neither the old custom of elucidating a whole passage of Scripture, nor the recent one of expounding some few words of Scripture; instead he elaborated on some stupid British proverbs. So I have no doubt that his frivolous sermon very deeply disturbed those who heard it; since I see that all who have heard fragmentary reports of it are unfavorably impressed.

What man in the audience, in whose breast burned even a spark of Christianity, would not groan at the degradation of the royal office of sacred preaching, which gained the world for Christ—above all at the hands of those whose supreme duty it was to protect it with the authority of their office? Who could possibly have devised a more outrageous insult than for an avowed preacher, during the most solemn season of the Church's year, in the presence of a large Christian congregation, in the sanctuary itself, from the elevation of the pulpit (as it were from the throne of Christ), and in view of the Sacred Body of Christ, to turn a Lenten sermon into Bacchanalian ravings? What a look must have been on the faces of the audience, who had come to hear spiritual wisdom, and saw the laughable pantomime he put on in the pulpit! They had expected to listen in reverence to the Word of Life; when they departed, all they could record they had heard was an attack on humane letters and a defamation of the preaching office by a fatuous preacher.

It would have been no reproach to secular learning if some good man, who had retired from the world to monastic life, suddenly returned and used this speaker's phrases: "much in watchings, much in prayer" or "the path to be trod by those who seek for heaven" or "other matters like humanistic education, trivial if not a positive hindrance to the spiritual life," or "simple country folk, and the unlettered, flying quicker to heaven," etc., etc. All this could have been borne from such a man. His simplicity would have been pardoned by his audience. They would have generously admitted his saintliness, and given serious consideration to his piety, devotion, and righteousness. But when they saw a man with the academic ermine over his shoulders, step on to the platform in the midst of a gathering composed solely of academics, and calmly proceed to rant against all humane learning, one would have had to be stone blind not to notice a signal pride and wickedness, a positive hatred of the higher arts. Many must have wondered indeed how such a man could get the idea that he had to preach either about Latin, of which he did not know much, or about the liberal arts, of which he knew less, or about Greek—in which he could not even grunt that it was "all Greek" to him!

If such an abundance of material had been supplied by the seven deadly sins, an altogether suitable theme for sermons, who would have believed him totally inexperienced therein! Though, as a matter of fact, what is it but sloth, when one is in the habit of denouncing rather than of learning that of which one is ignorant? And what is it but hatred, when one defames those who know what one deprecates but does not comprehend? And what is it but supreme pride, when he wishes no kind of knowledge to be prized save what he has falsely persuaded himself that he knows, and when he even—not from modesty, as might be the case with other people—arrogates more praise to himself for his ignorance than for his knowledge?

Now as to the question of humanistic education being secular. No one has ever claimed that a man needed Greek and Latin, or indeed any education in order to be saved. Still, this education which he calls secular does train the soul in virtue. In any event, few will question that humanistic education is the chief, almost the sole reason why men come to Oxford; children can receive a good education at home from their mothers, all except cultivation and book learning. Moreover, even if men come to Oxford to study theology, they do not start with that discipline. They must first study the laws of human nature and conduct, a thing not useless to theologians; without such study they might possibly preach a sermon acceptable to an academic group, without it they would certainly fail to reach the common man. And from whom could they acquire such skill better than from the poets, orators, and historians?

Moreover, there are some who through knowledge of things natural (i.e., rational) construct a ladder by which to rise to the contemplation of things supernatural; they build a path to theology through philosophy and the liberal arts, which this man condemns as secular; they adorn the queen of heaven with the spoils of the Egyptians! This fellow declares that only theology should be studied; but if he admits even that, I don't see how he can accomplish his aim without some knowledge of languages, whether Hebrew or Greek or Latin; unless, of course, the elegant gentleman has convinced himself that there is enough theology written in English or that all theology can be squeezed into the limits of those [late scholastic] "questions" which he likes to pose and answer, for which a modicum of Latin would, I admit, suffice.

But really, I cannot admit that theology, that august queen of heaven, can be thus confined. Does she not dwell and abide in Holy Scripture? Does she not pursue her pilgrim way through the cells of the holy Fathers: Augustine and Jerome; Ambrose and Cyprian; Chrysostom, Gregory, Basil, and their like? The study of theology has been solidly based on these now despised expositors of fundamental truth during all the Christian centuries until the invention of these petty and meretricious "questions" which alone are today glibly tossed back and forth. Anyone who boasts that he can understand the works of the Fathers without an uncommon acquaintance with the languages of each and all of them will in his ignorance boast for a long time before the learned trust his judgment.

But if this foolish preacher pretends that he was not condemning humanistic education in general but only an immoderate thirst for it, I can't see that this desire was such a sin that he had to deal with it in a public assembly, as if it were causing society to rush headlong to ruin. I haven't heard that many have gone so far in such studies that they will soon be overstepping the golden mean. Further, this fellow, just to show how immoderate *he* could be in a sermon, specifically called students of Greek "heretics," teachers of Greek "chief devils," and pupils in Greek "lesser devils" or, more modestly and facetiously as he thought, "little devils"; and the zeal of this holy man drove him to call by the name of devil one whom everybody knows the Devil himself could hardly bear to see occupy a pulpit. He did everything but name that one [Erasmus], as everybody realized just as clearly as they realized the folly of the speaker.

Joking aside, I have no desire to pose as the sole defender of Greek learning; for I know how obvious it must be to scholars of your eminence that the study of Greek is tried and true. To whom is it *not* obvious that to the Greeks we owe all our precision in the liberal arts generally and in theology particularly; for the Greeks either made the great discoveries themselves or passed them on as part of their heritage. Take philosophy, for example. If you leave out Cicero and Seneca, the Romans wrote their philosophy in Greek or translated it from Greek.

I need hardly mention that the New Testament is in Greek, or that the best New Testament scholars were Greeks and wrote in Greek. I am but repeating the consensus of scholarship when I say: however much was translated of old from Greek, and however much more has been recently and better translated, not half of Greek learning has yet been made available to the West; and, however good the translations have been, the text of the original still remains a surer and more convincing presentation. For that very reason all the Doctors of the Latin Church—Jerome, Augustine, Bede, and a host of others—assiduously gave themselves to learning Greek; and even though many works had already been translated, they were much more accustomed to reading them in the original than are many of our contemporaries who claim to be erudite; nor did they merely learn it themselves, but counseled those among their successors who wanted to be theologians above all to do the same.

So it is not as if I were just giving your Worships good advice about preserving the study of Greek. I am rather exhorting you to do your duty. You should not allow anyone in your university to be frightened away from the study of Greek, either by public assemblies or private inanities, since Greek is a subject required in every place of learning by the Church Universal. Common sense is surely enough to convince you that not all of your number who give themselves to the study of Greek can be blockheads; in fact, it is in part from these studies that your university had acquired its pedagogical prestige both at home and abroad.

There seems to be an increasing number of cases where Oxford has benefitted from the presence of men nominally studying Greek only, but really taking the whole liberal arts course. It will be a wonder if their enthusiasm for you does not evaporate when they realize that so serious an enterprise is held in such contempt. Just think, too, what they are doing at Cambridge, which you have always outshone; those who are *not* studying Greek are so moved by common interest in their university that they are actually making large individual contributions to the salary of the Greek professor!

You see what I mean; and much more could be said to the point by men with better minds than mine. All I am doing is warning you of what others are saying and thinking, not telling you what it behooves you to do. You see much better than I that, if wicked factions are not suppressed at birth, a contagious disease will spread, and the better half be slowly absorbed by the worse, and that outsiders will be forced to take a hand in helping the good and wise among you. Any former student of the university takes its welfare as much to heart as you who are its living members. And I am sure that the Reverend Father in Christ who occupies the See of Canterbury [William Warham], who is the Primate of all our Clergy, and who is also the Chancellor of your university will not fail to do his part. Whether for the clergy's sake or yours, he rightly feels interested in preventing the decay of learning; and learning will perish if the university continues to suffer from the contentions of lazy idiots, and the liberal arts are allowed to be made sport of with impunity. And what about the Reverend Father in Christ, the Cardinal of York [Thomas Wolsey], who is both a patron of learning and himself the most learned of the episcopate? Would he endure patiently if aspersions were cast in your university on the liberal arts and the study of languages? Will he not rather aim the shafts of his learning, virtue, and authority at these witless detractors from the arts?

Last but not least: what of our Most Christian King? His Sacred Majesty has cultivated all the liberal arts as much as ever a king did; indeed, he possesses greater erudition and judgment than any previous monarch. Will his wisdom and piety suffer him to allow the liberal arts to fail—through the interests of evil and lazy men—in a place where his most illustrious ancestors wished that there be an illustrious seat of letters, a place which is an ancient nursery of learning, whose products have been an ornament not only to England but to the whole Church, a place which possesses so many colleges that have perpetual endowments specially designated for the support of students (in which respect there is no university outside the kingdom that can compare with Oxford), a place in which the aim of all its colleges and the purpose of all its endowments is none other than that a great body of academics, delivered from the necessity of earning their daily bread, might there pursue the liberal arts?

I have no doubt that you yourselves will easily in your wisdom find a way to end this dispute and quiet these stupid factions; that you will see to it not only that all the liberal arts may be free from derision and contempt but that they shall be held in dignity and honor. By such diligence in intellectual pursuits you will reap benefit for yourselves; and it can hardly be said how much you will gain favor with our Illustrious Prince and with the above-mentioned Reverend Fathers in Christ. You will forge an almost miraculous bond between yourselves and myself, who have thought that all this had to be written now in my own hand out of my deep personal affection for you. You know that my services are at the disposal of each and all of you. May God preserve your glorious seat of learning unharmed; and may He grant that it flourish continually in virtue and in all the liberal arts.

Thomas More

8. DESIDERIUS ERASMUS OF ROTTERDAM (1466?–1536)

Erasmus was the greatest figure of the Northern, or Christian, Renaissance. He used his encyclopedic scholarship in ancient Greek and Latin literature and patristic texts to define a new ideal of Christian learning. His biblical scholarship was equally profound, producing in 1516 his Novum Instrumentum, *a new translation of the New Testament with the original Greek on facing pages.*

Erasmus's influence during his lifetime and after was immense. His wide circle of friends and acquaintances throughout Europe resulted in a voluminous correspondence. Producing both learned and popular books, he was the best-read author of his age. Works such as The Praise of Folly *(1509), the* Adagia *and the* Colloquies *contributed to northern Europe's appreciation of the heritage of the classical world and publicized Erasmus's concerns for religious reform. This central element of Erasmus's work and thought—indeed of northern Christian humanism more broadly—was defined as learned piety (*docta pietas*) and the philosophy of Christ (*philosophia Christi*), an attitude toward religion and scholarship that helped shape the culture of the Northern Renaissance and Reformation. Although initially sympathetic to some of Martin Luther's program of reform, Erasmus refused to join with the Lutherans, preferring a single, united Church but reformed to reflect more clearly what he saw as the simple message of Scripture.*

Letter to Jodocus Jonus on Vitrier and Colet

[June 13, 1521]

…It may indeed be that [John] Colet [1457–1519] deserves the greater praise of the two on this account, namely, that neither the smiles of fortune nor the impulse of a far different natural bent could divert him from the pursuit of a Gospel life. For he was the son of wealthy and distinguished parents; born, too, in London, where his father had twice filled the highest municipal office in his city, called by them the mayoralty. His mother, who still survives, is a most worthy woman. She bore her husband eleven sons and as many daughters; of whom John, as the eldest, would have been heir to the entire estate, according to the English law, even had the others been alive. But at the time when my acquaintance with him began, he was the sole survivor of the band. To these advantages of fortune was added that of a tall and graceful figure.

During his younger days in England he diligently mastered all the philosophy of the schools and gained the title expressive of a knowledge of the seven liberal arts. Of these arts there was not one in which he had not been industriously and successfully trained. For he had both eagerly devoured the works of Cicero and diligently searched into those of Plato and Plotinus, while there was no branch of mathematics that he left untouched.

After this, like a merchant seeking goodly wares, he visited France and then Italy. While there, he devoted himself entirely to the study of the sacred writers. He had previously, however, roamed with great zest through literature of every kind, finding most pleasure in the early writers, Dionysius, Origen, Cyprian, Ambrose, and Jerome. I should add that among the old authors there was none to whom he was more unfavorable than Augustine. At the same time he did not omit to read Scotus and Thomas [Aquinas] and others of that stamp, if the occasion ever required it. He was also carefully versed in treatises of civil and canon law. In a word, there was no work containing either the chronicles or enactments of our forefathers which he had not perused. The English nation has poets who have done among their own countrymen what Dante and Petrarch have done in Italy. And by the study of their writings he perfected his style, preparing himself even at this date for preaching the Gospel.

Soon after his return from Italy he left his father's house, as he preferred to reside at Oxford, and there he publicly and gratuitously expounded all St. Paul's Epistles. It was at Oxford that my acquaintance with him began, some kind providence having brought me at that time to the same spot. He was then about thirty years old, some two or three months younger than myself. Though he had neither obtained nor sought for any degree in divinity, yet there was no doctor there, either of divinity or law, no abbot or other dignitary but came to hear him and brought his textbooks with him as well. The credit of this may have been due to Colet's personal influence, or it may have been due to their own good will in not being ashamed to learn, the old from the young, doctors from one who was no doctor. However, the title of doctor was spontaneously offered him some time later and accepted by him, though rather to oblige the offerers than because he sought it.

From these sacred occupations he was called back to London by the favor of Henry VII and made dean of St. Paul's, so as to preside over the cathedral of that Apostle whose epistles he loved so much. This takes precedence over all the deaneries in England, though there are others with richer incomes. Hereupon our good Colet, feeling his call to be for the work and not for the empty honor, restored the decayed discipline of the cathedral body and—what was a novelty there—commenced preaching at every festival in his cathedral, over and above the special sermons he had to deliver now at Court, now in various other places. In his own cathedral, moreover, he would not take isolated texts from the Gospels or Apostolic Epistles but would start with some connected subject and pursue it right to the end in a course of sermons: for example, St. Matthew's Gospel, the Creed, or the Lord's Prayer. He used to have a crowded congregation, including most of the leading men both of the city and the court.

The dean's table, which in former days had ministered to luxury under the guise of hospitality, he brought within the bounds of moderation. For having done without suppers entirely for some years before, he was thus free from company in the evening. Moreover, as he dined rather late, he had fewer guests on those occasions as well, and all the fewer because the repast, though neat, was frugal, and the sitting at table short, and lastly, the conversation such as to have no charms but for the good and learned. When grace had been said, a servant would read aloud in a clear, distinct voice a chapter from St. Paul's Epistles or the Proverbs of Solomon. He would then usually repeat some passage selected from the part read and draw a topic of conversation from it, inquiring of any scholars present, or even of intelligent laymen, what this or that expression meant. And he would so season the discourse that, though both serious and religious, it had nothing tedious or affected about it. Again, towards the end of the meal, when the requirements of nature, at any rate, if not of pleasure had been satisfied, he started some other topic; and thus bade farewell to his guests, refreshed in mind as well as in body and better men at leaving than they came, though with no overloaded stomachs. The pleasure he took in conversing with friends was extreme, and he would often prolong the talk till late at night. But still it was all either about literature or about Christ. If there was no agreeable person at hand to chat with—and it was not every sort that suited him—a servant would read aloud some passage from Holy Scripture. Occasionally he took me with him for company on a journey, and then nothing could be more pleasant than he was. But a book was ever his companion on the road, and his talk was always of Christ.

He could not endure any slovenliness, so much so as not to tolerate even an ungrammatical or illiterate mode of expression. All his household furniture, his service at table, his dress, his books he would have neat; as for splendor, he did not trouble himself. He used to wear only dark-colored robes, though priests and divines in England are usually robed in scarlet. His outer garment was always of woolen cloth, not lined; but if the cold required it, he would protect himself with an inner lining of fur.

All the revenue that came in from his preferments he left in his steward's hands, to be laid out in household expenses. His private fortune, a very large one, he would himself dispose of for charitable purposes. At his father's death he had inherited a large sum of money; and fearing lest, if he hoarded it up, it might breed some distemper of mind in him, he built with it in St. Paul's Churchyard a new school of splendid structure, dedicated to the Child Jesus. He attached to it also a handsome residence for the two masters to dwell in and assigned them a liberal stipend to teach free of charge, but on condition that the school should only admit a fixed number. The school was divided by him into four partitions. The one first entered contains those whom we may call the catechumens, none being admitted but such as can already both read and write. The second contains those under the surmaster's teaching, and the third those who are instructed by the high master. Each of these partitions is separated from the others by a curtain, drawn to or drawn aside at pleasure. Over the high master's chair is a beautifully wrought figure of the Child Jesus seated in the attitude of one teaching, and all the young flock as they enter and leave school salute it with a hymn. Over it is the countenance of God the Father, saying: HEAR YE HIM (an inscription added at my suggestion). At the far end is a chapel in which divine service may be held. The whole school has no bays or recesses, so much so that there is neither any dining room nor dormitory. Every boy has his own proper seat on regularly ascending tiers with gangways left between. Each class contains sixteen, and the head boy in each class has a stall somewhat higher than the rest. Boys of all kinds are not admitted promiscuously, but a selection is made according to natural capacity and ability.

A most farsighted man, Colet saw that a nation's chief hope lay in having the rising generation trained in good principles. But though the undertaking cost him a very large sum of money, he allowed no one to share it. Some person had left a legacy of a hundred pounds sterling toward the building. But when Colet perceived that on the strength of this outsiders were claiming some rights or other, he obtained his bishop's sanction to apply the sum toward providing sacred vestments for the cathedral. Over the revenues and the entire management of his school he placed neither priests, nor the bishop, nor the chapter (as they call it), nor noblemen, but some married citizens of established reputation. And when asked the reason, he said that, while there was nothing certain in human affairs, he yet found the least corruption in these.

This was a work that no one failed to approve. But many were surprised at his building a magnificent dwelling within the precincts of the Carthusian monastery, not far from what is called Richmond Palace. He said that he was preparing an abode for his old age, when he should be no longer equal to his work or be enfeebled by sickness and so compelled to retire from society. There he was minded to philosophize with two or three chosen old friends, among whom he was accustomed to reckon myself. But death forestalled him. For having been seized a few years before with the sweating sickness (a disease that is the special scourge of England), he was now for the third time attacked by it; and though he recovered from it to some degree, an internal disorder ensued from what the disease left behind it, of which he died. One physician pronounced him dropsical. Nothing fresh was discovered by the postmortem examination except that the liver was found to have the extremities of the lobes rough with tuftlike excrescences. He was buried at the south side of the choir in his cathedral, in a modest grave chosen by himself some years before for the purpose, with the inscription placed over it: IOAN. COL. [John Colet]

Before I conclude, my friend Jonas, I will mention a few particulars, first of his natural disposition, then of his peculiar opinions, and lastly of the stormy scenes in which his sincere religion was put to the test. It was but a very small portion of this religious spirit that he owed to nature. For he was gifted with a temper singularly high and impatient of affront; he was, as he himself confessed to me, naturally prone to incontinence, luxuriousness, and indulgence in sleep; overmuch disposed to jests and raillery; and he was besides not wholly exempt from the taint of covetousness. But these tendencies he combatted so successfully by philosophy and sacred studies, by watching, fasting, and prayer that he led the whole course of his life free from the pollutions of the world. As far as I could gather from my intimate acquaintance and conversations with him, he kept the flower of chastity even unto death. His fortune he spent on charitable uses. Against his high temper he contended with the help of reason, so as to brook admonition even from a servant. Incontinence, love of sleep, and luxuriousness he vanquished by a uniform abstinence from supper, by constant sobriety, by unwearied exertions in study, and by religious conversation. Yet if an occasion had ever presented itself either of conversing with ladies or being a guest at sumptuous repasts, you might have seen some traces of the old nature in him. And on that account he kept away, as a rule, from laymen's society, and especially from banquets. If forced at times to attend them, he would take me or some similar companion with him in order, by talking Latin, to avoid worldly conversation. Meanwhile he would partake sparingly of one dish only and be satisfied with a single draught or two of ale. He was abstemious in respect of wine, appreciating it if choice, but most temperate in the use of it. Thus keeping a constant watch upon himself, he carefully avoided everything by which he might cause anyone to stumble, not forgetting that the eyes of all were upon him.

I never saw a more highly gifted intellect. But though he felt a peculiar pleasure on this account in kindred intellects, he liked better to bend his mind to such things as fitted it for the immortality of the life to come. If at times he sought relaxation in sprightlier talk, he would still philosophize on every topic. He took a delight in the purity and simplicity of nature that is in children, a nature that Christ bids His disciples imitate, and he was wont to compare them to angels.

To complete, now, the second part of my promised account, his opinions differed widely from those commonly received. But in this matter he showed a remarkable discretion in adapting himself to others, so as to avoid giving offence to any persons or bringing any slur on his good name. For he knew well how unfair men's judgments are, how ready they are to believe evil, and how much easier a thing it is for slanderous tongues to tarnish a man's good name than for kind-spoken ones to repair it. Among friends and scholars, however, he would express his sentiments with the utmost freedom. As to the Scotists, for example, to whom the common run of men ascribe a subtlety peculiarly their own, he said that he considered them dull and stupid and anything but intellectual. For it was the sign of a poor and barren intellect, he would say, to be quibbling about the words and opinions of others, carping first at one thing and then at another, and analyzing everything so minutely. Yet for some reason he was even harder on Aquinas than on Scotus. For when I once praised Aquinas to him as a writer not to be despised among the moderns, since he appeared to me to have studied both the scriptures and the early Fathers—such being the impression I had formed from his *Catena aurea*—and had also a certain unction in his writings, he checked himself more than once from replying and did not betray his dislike. But when in another conversation I was reiterating the same opinions more strongly, he looked hard at me, as if watching whether I were saying this in seriousness or in irony. And on perceiving that I was serious in what I said, he broke out like one possessed: "Why do you preach up that writer to me? For without a full share of presumption, he never would have defined everything in that rash and overweening manner; and without something of a worldly spirit, he would not have so tainted the whole doctrine of Christ with his profane philosophy." Struck with his impetuous manner, I began a more careful study of this author's writings, and, to be brief, my estimate of him was undoubtedly diminished.

Though no one approved of Christian devotion more warmly than he, he had yet but very little liking for monasteries—undeserving of the name as many of them now are. The gifts he bestowed upon them were either none or the smallest possible, and he left them no share of his property even at his death. The reason was not that he disliked religious orders but that those who took them did not come up to their profession. It was in fact his own wish to disconnect himself entirely from the world, if he could only have found a fraternity anywhere really bound together for a Gospel life. And he had even commissioned me to seek for such a one when I was about to visit Italy, telling me that among the Italians he had discovered some monks of true wisdom and piety. Moreover, he did not consider what is popularly deemed religion to be really such, being as it often is mere poverty of intellect. He was accustomed also to praise certain Germans, among whom there even yet lingered, as he said, some traces of primitive religion. He was in the habit of declaring that he nowhere found more unblemished characters than among married people, on whom such restraints were laid by natural affection and family and household cares that they were withheld, as by so many barriers, from rushing into all kinds of wickedness. Though himself living in perfect chastity, yet of all in the list of offenders he was less hard on those—were they priests or even monks—whose only offence was incontinence. It was not that he failed to abhor the vice of unchastity but that he found such persons not nearly so bad, in comparison, as some others who thought no small things of themselves—though overweening, envious, slanderous, backbiters, hypocrites, empty-headed, ignorant, given up heart and soul to money-making and ambition—while their acknowledged infirmity rendered the former more humble and unassuming. Covetousness and pride, he would say, were more detestable in a priest than keeping a hundred concubines.

I would not have anyone strain these opinions to such a degree as to suppose incontinence in a priest or monk to be a slight offence, but only to infer from them that those of the other kind are still further removed from true religion.

There was no class of persons to whom he was more opposed or for whom he had a greater abhorrence than those bishops who acted the part of wolves instead of shepherds, showing themselves off before the people with their guise of sanctity, their ceremonies, benedictions, and paltry indulgences, while at heart they were slaves to the world, that is, to ostentation and gain. He had a leaning to some opinions derived from Dionysius and the other early divines, though not to such a degree as to make him contravene in any points the decisions of the Church. Still, they made him less hard on such as disapproved of the universal adoration of images in churches, whether painted or of wood, or stone, or bronze, or silver; or again, on those who doubted whether a priest, openly and notoriously wicked, had any efficacy in the administration of the sacraments. Not that he in any way leaned to this error of theirs, but he was indignant against such as, by a life of open and unmixed depravity, gave occasion to surmises of this kind.

The colleges established in England at a great and imposing cost he used to say were a hindrance to profitable studies and merely centers of attraction for the lazy. And in like manner he did not attach much value to the public schools, on the ground that the race for professorships and fees spoilt everything and adulterated the purity of all branches of learning.

While strongly approving of auricular confession, saying that there was nothing from which he derived so much comfort and spiritual advantage, he yet as strongly condemned its too solicitous and frequent repetition. It is the custom in England for priests to celebrate the Holy Eucharist every day. But Colet was content to do so on Sundays and festivals, or at the most on some few days in addition, either because it kept him away from the sacred studies by which he used to prepare for preaching and from the necessary business of the cathedral, or because he found that he sacrificed with devouter feelings if he let an interval elapse. At the same time he was far from disapproving of the principles of those who liked to come every day to the Table of the Lord.

Himself a most learned man, he did not approve of that painful and laborious erudition which is made complete at all points, so to speak, by an acquaintance with all branches of learning and the perusal of every author. It was his constant remark that the natural soundness and simplicity of men's intellects were impaired by it, and they were rendered less healthy-minded and less fitted for Christian innocence and for pure and simple charity. He set a very high value on the Apostolic Epistles; but he had such a reverence for the wonderful majesty of Christ that the writings of the Apostles seemed to grow poor by the side of it. He had with great ability reduced almost all the sayings of Christ to triplets, intending to make a book of them. The rule that priests, even though busily occupied, must say long prayers right through every day, no matter whether at home or on a journey, was a thing that he greatly wondered at. As to the public service of the Church, he was quite of the opinion that that should be performed with proper dignity.

From numbers of the tenets most generally received in the public schools at the present day he widely dissented and would at times discuss them among his private friends. When with others, he would keep his opinions to himself for fear of coming to harm in two ways; that is to say, only making matters worse by his efforts, and sacrificing his own reputation. There was no book so heretical but he read it with attention. For from such, he said, he many a time received more benefit than from the books of those who so define everything as often to flatter their party leaders, and not seldom their own selves as well.

He could not endure that the faculty of speaking correctly should be sought from the trivial rules of grammarians. For he insisted that these were a hindrance to expressing oneself well and that result was obtained only by the study of the best authors. But he paid the penalty for this notion himself. For though eloquent both by nature and training, and though he had at his command a singularly copious flow of words while speaking, yet when writing, he would now and then trip on such points as critics are given to mark. And it was on this account, if I mistake not, that he refrained from writing books, though I wish he had not so refrained, for I should have been glad of the thoughts of such a man, no matter in what language expressed.

And now, that nothing may be thought wanting to the finished religious character of Colet, listen to the storms by which he was harassed. He had never been on good terms with his bishop, who was, to say nothing about his principles, a superstitious and impracticable Scotist, and thinking himself on that account something more than mortal. I may say that, whilst I have known many of this school whom I should not like to call bad men, I have yet never to this day seen one who, in my opinion at least, could be termed a real and sincere Christian. Colet was no great favorite either with many of his own college, being too strict about canonical discipline; and these were every now and then complaining of being treated as monks, though in fact this college was formerly what in ancient deeds it is styled, the Eastern Monastery. However, when the animosity of the old bishop (who was, I should have said, full eighty years of age) was too virulent to be suppressed, he took as his coadjutors two other bishops, as wise and as acrimonious as himself, and began to give Colet trouble. His weapons were just what such persons resort to when plotting anyone's destruction, that is to say, he laid an information against him before the archbishop of Canterbury, specifying certain articles taken from his sermons. One was that he had taught that images ought not to be worshiped. Another, that he had done away with the hospitality commended by St. Paul, seeing that in expounding the passage from the Gospel with its thrice repeated "feed my sheep," while he was in accordance with other expositors on the first two heads (feed by example of life; feed by the word of doctrine), he had disagreed with them on the third, saying that it was not meet that the Apostles, poor as they then were, should be bidden to feed their sheep in the way of any temporal support; and he had substituted some other interpretation in lieu of it. A third article was that having said in the pulpit that there were some who preached written sermons—the stiff and formal way of many in England—he had indirectly reflected on his bishop, who, from his old age, was in the habit of so doing. The archbishop, to whom Colet's high qualities were perfectly well known, undertook the protection of the innocent, and as Colet himself disdained any reply to these and still more frivolous charges, he became a protector instead of a judge. Still the old bishop's animosity was not allayed. He tried to excite the court, with the king at its head, against Colet, having now got hold of another weapon against him. This was that he had openly declared in a sermon "an unjust peace was to be preferred to the justest war," a war being at that very time in preparation against the French. A leading part in this play was being taken by two Franciscan friars, of whom one, a very firebrand of war, earned a miter while the other used to declaim like a Stentor in his sermons against poets—meaning Colet, who had not the least taste for poetry, though in other respects not unskilled in music. At this juncture the noble young king gave a conspicuous token of his kingly disposition, for he privately encouraged Colet to go on without restraint, and improve by his teaching the corrupt morals of the age, and not to withdraw his light from those dark times. He was not unaware, he said, of the motive that incited those bishops against him, nor unconscious of the benefits he had conferred on the English nation by his life and doctrine. He added, that he would put such a check on their attempts that others should clearly see that whoever assailed Colet would not go unpunished. On this, Colet expressed his gratitude for such kind feeling on the king's part but prayed leave to decline the offer. He would have no one, he said, worse off on his account: sooner than that, he would resign the office which he bore.

Some time afterwards, however, the faction had an occasion given them for hoping that now at last Colet might be crushed. An expedition was being got ready against the French, to start after Easter. On Good Friday, Colet preached a noble sermon before the king and his court on the victory of Christ, exhorting all Christians to war and conquer under the banner of Him their proper King. For they, he said, who through hatred or ambition were fighting, the bad with the bad, and slaughtering one another by turns, were warring under the banner not of Christ but of the Devil. At the same time, he pointed out to them how hard a thing it is to die a Christian death, how few entered on a war unsullied by hatred or love of gain, how incompatible a thing it was that a man should have that brotherly love without which no one would see God and yet bury his sword in his brother's heart. Let them follow, he added, the example of Christ as their Prince, not that of Julius Caesar or an Alexander. Much more to the same effect he gave utterance to on that occasion, so that the king was in some apprehension lest the soldiers whom he was on the point of leading abroad should feel their courage gone through this discourse. On this, all the mischief-makers flocked together like birds setting upon an owl, in the hope that now at last the mind of the king might be exasperated against him. By the king's order Colet was sent for. He came and had luncheon in the Franciscan convent adjoining Greenwich Palace. When the king was apprised of his arrival, he went down into the convent garden, dismissing his attendants as Colet came out to meet him. As soon as they were alone, the courteous young prince bade him be covered and converse with him without ceremony, himself beginning in these terms: "To spare you any groundless alarm, Mr. Dean, we have not sent for you hither to disturb your sacred labors, which have our entire approval, but that we may unburden our conscience of some scruples, and with the help of your counsel may better discharge the duties of our office." (I will not, however, repeat the whole conversation, which lasted nearly an hour.) Meanwhile Bricot, who from a Franciscan friar had now become a bishop, was in high spirits in the palace, supposing Colet to be in danger; whereas the king and he were at one upon all points, save only that the king wished him to say at some other time, with clearer explanation, what he had already said with perfect truth, namely, that for Christians no war was a just one. And this was for the sake of the rough soldiers, who might put a different construction on his words from that which he had intended. Colet, as became his good sense and remarkable moderation of temper, not only set the king's mind at rest but even increased the favor in which he stood before. On returning to the palace, the king had a wine cup brought to him and pledged Colet in it before he would let him depart. Then embracing him most courteously and promising all that could be expected from the most gracious of sovereigns, he let him go. And as the throng of courtiers was now standing round, eager to hear the result of this conference, the king, in the hearing of all, said, "Let every man have his own doctor, and every one follow his liking; but this is the doctor for me." Thus they departed, like the baffled wolves in the adage, Bricot more than all; nor did anyone from that day forward venture to molest Colet....

9. WILLIAM ROPER (C. 1495–1578)

Roper was Thomas More's son-in-law, having married his daughter, Margaret (d. 1544), in 1521. The son of a lawyer, Roper entered More's household in 1518, the same year the young man was admitted to Lincoln's Inn to study law, and continued to live with More even after the marriage. Originally a follower of the Reformation, Roper was brought back to the Catholic faith by More and remained loyal for the rest of his life. He served as chief clerk of the court of King's Bench (1524) and as Member of Parliament for Bramber in 1529. After his resignation as Lord Chancellor in 1532, More assigned some of his Chelsea property to Roper.

Unlike his father-in-law, Roper swore the oath attached to the Act of Supremacy but continued to live as a Catholic. He refused to flee England for the continent, although he sent aid to those of his family who did. Under Mary he received much honor, being elected M.P. in 1554, 1555 and 1558, and serving as Sheriff of Kent. With the religious settlement of Elizabeth, Roper was harassed as a Catholic but remained steadfast in his faith. He died in 1578.

The Life of Sir Thomas More

In the fourteenth year of his grace's reign [April 1523] was there a Parliament held, whereof Sir Thomas More was chosen Speaker. Who, being very loath to take that room upon him, made an oration (not now extant) to the King's highness for his discharge thereof. Whereunto when the King would not consent, he spoke unto his grace in the form following:

> Since I perceive, most redoubted Sovereign, that it stands not with your high pleasure

to revoke this election and cause it to be changed, but have by the mouth of the most reverend father in God, the legate, your highness's Chancellor, thereunto given your most royal assent, and have of your benignity determined—far above that I may bear—to enable me, and for this office to declare me qualified, rather than you should seem to impute unto your Commons that they had inappropriately chosen, I am therefore, and always shall be, ready obediently to conform myself to the accomplishment of your high commandment—in my most humble wise beseeching your most noble majesty that I may with your grace's favor, before I farther enter thereunto, make mine humble intercession unto your highness for two lowly petitions; the one privately concerning myself, the other the whole assembly of your Common House.

For myself, gracious Sovereign, that if it is my bad luck in anything hereafter that is on the behalf of your Commons in your high presence to be declared, to mistake my message, and in the lack of good utterance, by my misrepresentation to pervert or impair their prudent instructions, it may then like your most noble majesty, of your abundant grace, with the eye of your accustomed pity, to pardon my simplicity—giving me leave to repair again to the Common House and there to confer with them, and to take their substantial advice what thing and in what wise I shall on their behalf utter and speak before your noble grace, to the intent their prudent devices and affairs be not by my simplicity and folly hindered or impaired. Which thing, if it should so mishap, as it were well likely to mishap in me, if your gracious benignity relieved not my oversight, it could not fail to be during my life a perpetual grudge and heaviness to my heart. The help and remedy whereof, in manner aforesaid remembered, is, most gracious Sovereign, my first lowly suit and humble petition unto your most noble grace.

Mine other humble request, most excellent prince, is this: forasmuch as there be of your Commons, here by your high commandment assembled for your Parliament, a great number which are after the accustomed manner appointed in the Common House to treat and advise of the common affairs among themselves apart; and albeit, most dear liege-lord, that according to your prudent advice, by your honorable writs everywhere declared, there hath been as due diligence used in sending up to your highness's Court of Parliament the most discreet persons out of every quarter that men could esteem meet thereunto—whereby it is not to be doubted but that there is a very substantial assembly of right wise and politick persons; yet, most victorious prince, since among so many wise men neither is every man wise alike, nor among so many men, like well-witted, every man like well-spoken. And it often happens that, likewise, as much folly is uttered with painted, polished speech; so many boisterous and rude in language see deep indeed, and give right substantial counsel.

And since also in matters of great importance, the mind is often so occupied in the matter that a man rather studies what to say than how, by reason whereof the wisest man and the best spoken in a whole country now and then among, while his mind is fervent in the matter, somewhat to speak in such wise as he would afterward wish to have been uttered otherwise, and yet no worse will had when he spoke it than he hath when he would so gladly change it; therefore, most gracious Sovereign, considering that in your high Court of Parliament is nothing treated but matter of weight and importance concerning your realm and your own royal estate, it could not fail to hinder and put to silence from the giving of their advice and counsel many of your discreet commons, to the great hindrance of the common affairs, except that every of your Commons were utterly relieved of all doubt and fear how anything that it should happen them to speak should happen of your highness to be interpreted. And in this point, though your well known and proved benignity puts every man in right good hope, yet such is the weight of the matter, such is the reverenced fear that the timorous hearts of your natural subjects conceive toward your high majesty, our most redoubted King and undoubted Sovereign, that they cannot in this point find themselves satisfied, except your gracious bounty therein declared put away the scruple of their timorous minds, and animate and encourage them, and put them out of doubt.

It may therefore like your most abundant grace, our most benign and godly King, to give all your Commons here assembled your most gracious license and pardon, freely, without doubt of your dreadful displeasure, every man to discharge his conscience, and boldly in everything incident among us to declare his advice. And whatsoever happen any man to say that it may like your noble majesty, of your inestimable goodness, to take all in good part, interpreting every man's words, however unskilfully they be couched, to proceed yet of good zeal towards the profit of your realm and honor of your royal person, the prosperous estate and preservation whereof, most excellent Sovereign, is the thing which we all, your most humble loving subjects, according to the most bounden duty of our natural allegiance, most highly desire and pray for.

At this Parliament Cardinal Wolsey found himself much grieved with the burgesses thereof, for that nothing was so soon done or spoken therein but that it was immediately blown abroad in every alehouse. It fortuned at that Parliament a very great tax to be demanded, which the Cardinal fearing would not pass the Common House, determined for the furtherance thereof to be personally present there. Before whose coming, after long debating there, whether it were better but with a few of his lords (as the most opinion of the house was) or with his whole train royally to receive him there amongst them—"Masters," said Sir Thomas More, "forasmuch as my Lord Cardinal lately, ye know well, laid to our charge the looseness of our tongues for things uttered out of this house, it shall not in my mind be amiss with all his pomp to receive him, with his maces, his pillars, his pole-axes, his crosses, his hat, and Great Seal, too—to the intent, if he find the like fault with us hereafter, we may be the bolder from ourselves to lay the blame on those that his grace bringeth hither with him." Whereunto the house wholly agreeing, he was received accordingly.

Where, after that he had in a solemn oration by many reasons proved how necessary it was the demand there moved to be granted, and further showed that less would not serve to maintain the prince's purpose, he—seeing the company sitting still silent, and thereunto nothing answering and contrary to his expectation showing in themselves towards his requests no readiness to accede said unto them:

Masters, you have many wise and learned men among you, and since I am from the King's own person sent hither unto you for the preservation of yourselves and all the realm, I think it meet you give me some reasonable answer.

Whereat every man holding his peace, then began he to speak to one Master Marney, after Lord Marney: "How say you," said he, "Master Marney?" Who making him no answer neither, he severally asked the same question of divers others accounted the wisest of the company.

To whom, when none of them all would give so much as one word, being before agreed, as the custom was, by their speaker to make answer—"Masters," said the Cardinal, "unless it be the manner of your house, as of likelihood it is, by the mouth of your speaker, whom you have chosen for trusty and wise, as indeed he is, in such cases to utter your minds, here is without doubt a marvellous obstinate silence."

And thereupon he required answer of Master Speaker. Who first reverently upon his knees excusing the silence of the house, abashed at the presence of so noble a personage, able to amaze the wisest and best learned in a realm, and after by many probable arguments proving that for them to make answer was it neither expedient nor agreeable with the ancient liberty of the house, in conclusion for himself showed that though they had all with their voices trusted him, yet except every one of them could put into his one head all their several minds, he alone in so weighty a matter was inappropriate to make his grace answer.

Whereupon the Cardinal, displeased with Sir Thomas More, that had not in this Parliament in all things satisfied his desire, suddenly arose and departed.

And after the Parliament ended, in his gallery at Whitehall in Westminster, uttered unto him his complaints, saying: "Would to God you had been at Rome, Master More, when I made you Speaker!"

"Your grace not offended, so would I too, my lord," said he. And to wind such quarrels out of the Cardinal's head, he began to talk of that gallery and said: "I like this gallery of yours, my lord, much better than your gallery at Hampton Court." Wherewith so wisely brake he off the Cardinal's unpleasant talk that the Cardinal at that present (as it seemed) knew not what more to say to him. But to revenge of his displeasure counselled the King to send him ambassador into Spain, commending to his highness his wisdom, learning, and appropriateness for that voyage; and, the difficulty of the cause considered, none was there, he said, so well able to serve his grace therein.

Which, when the King had broken to Sir Thomas More, and that he had declared unto his grace how unfit a journey it was for him, the nature of the country and disposition of his constitution, so disagreeing together, that he should never be likely to do his grace acceptable service there, knowing right well that if his grace sent him thither, he should send him to his grave. But showing himself nevertheless ready, according to his duty (all were it with the loss of his life), to fulfill his grace's pleasure in that behalf.

The King, accepting his answer, said unto him: "It is not our meaning, Master More, to do you hurt, but to do you good would we be glad. We will therefore for this purpose devise upon some other, and employ your service otherwise." And such entire favor did the King bear him that he made him Chancellor of the Duchy of Lancaster upon the death of Sir Richard Wingfield, who had that office before.

And for the pleasure he took in his company would his grace suddenly sometimes come home to his house at Chelsea to be merry with him. Whither on a time, unlooked for, he came to dinner to him; and after dinner, in a fair garden of his, walked with him by the space of an hour, holding his arm about his neck.

As soon as his grace was gone, I, rejoicing thereat, told Sir Thomas More how happy he was, whom the King had so familiarly entertained, as I never had seen him to do to any other except Cardinal Wolsey, whom I saw his grace once walk with, arm in arm. "I thank our Lord, son," said he, "I find his grace my very good lord indeed; and I believe he doth as singularly favor me as any subject within this realm. Howbeit, son Roper, I may tell thee I have no cause to be proud thereof, for if my head could win him a castle in France (for then was there war between us) it should not fail to go."

This Sir Thomas More, among all other his virtues, was of such meekness that, if it had fortuned him with any learned men resorting to him from Oxford, Cambridge, or elsewhere, as there did sundry occasions, some for desire of his acquaintance, some for the famous report of his wisdom and learning, and some for petitions from the universities, to have entered into argument (wherein few were comparable unto him) and so far to have discoursed with them therein that he might perceive they could not, without some inconvenience, hold out much further disputation with him, then lest he should discomfort them—as he that sought not his own glory but rather would seem conquered than to discourage students in their studies, ever showing himself more desirous to learn than to teach—would he by some witty device courteously break off into some other matter and give over.

Of whom for his wisdom and learning had the King such an opinion that at such time as he attended upon his highness, taking his royal visit either to Oxford or Cambridge, where he was received with very eloquent orations, his grace would always assign him, as one that was prompt and ready therein, *ex tempore* to make answer thereunto. Whose manner was, whensoever he had occasion either here or beyond the sea to be in any university, not only to be present at the readings and disputations there commonly used, but also learnedly to dispute among them himself. Who being Chancellor of the Duchy was made ambassador twice, joined in commission with Cardinal Wolsey—once to the Emperor Charles into Flanders, the other time to the French King into France.

Not long after this, the Water-bailly of London [an important official, one of four attendants upon the Lord Mayor of London] sometime his servant, hearing (where he had been at dinner) certain merchants liberally to rail against his old master, waxed so discontented therewith that he hastily came to him and told him what he had heard. "And were I, sir," said he, "in such favor and authority with my prince as you are, such men surely should not be suffered so villainously and falsely to misreport and slander me. Wherefore I would wish you to call them before you, and to their shame for their evil malice to punish them."

Who, smiling upon him, said: "Why, Master Water-bailly, would you have me punish those by whom I receive more benefit than by you all that be my friends? Let them, [in] God's name, speak as lewdly as they list of me and shoot never so many arrows at me. As long as they do not hit me, what am I the worse? But if they should once hit me, then would it indeed not a little trouble me. Howbeit I trust, by God's help, there shall none of them all at once be able to touch me. I have more cause, I assure thee, Master Water-bailly, to pity them than to be angry with them." Such fruitful communication had he oft-times with his familiar friends.

So on a time, walking with me along the Thames-side at Chelsea [the site of More's house, up the Thames from London] in talking of other things he said unto me: "Now would to our Lord, son Roper, upon condition that three things were well established in Christendom, I were put in a sack and here presently cast into the Thames."

"What great things be those, sir," said I, "that should move you so to wish?"

"Wouldst thou know what they be, son Roper?" said he.

"Yea, marry, with goodwill, sir, if it please you," said I.

"In faith, son, they be these," said he. "The first is that where the most part of Christian princes be at mortal war, they were all at an universal peace. The second, that where the Church of Christ is at this present sore afflicted with many errors and heresies, it were settled in a perfect uniformity of religion. The third, that where the King's matter of his marriage is now come in question, it were to the glory of God and quietness of all parts brought to a good conclusion." Whereby, as I could gather, he judged that otherwise it would be a disturbance to a great part of Christendom.

Thus did it by his doings throughout the whole course of his life appear that all his travail and pains, without respect of earthly profits either to himself or any of his, were only upon the service of God, the prince, and the realm, wholly bestowed and employed. Whom I heard in his later time to say that he never asked the King for himself the value of one penny.

As Sir Thomas More's custom was daily, if he were at home, besides his private prayers, with his children to say the Seven Psalms, Litany and Suffrages following, so was his custom nightly before he went to bed, with his wife, children, and household, to go to his chapel and there upon his knees ordinarily to say certain psalms and prayers with them. And because he was desirous for godly purposes sometime to be solitary, and sequester himself from worldly company, a good distance from his mansion house built he a place called the New Building, wherein there was a chapel, a library, and a gallery. In which, as his use was upon other days to occupy himself in prayer and study together, so in the Friday there usually continued he from morning to evening, spending his time only in devout prayers and spiritual exercises.

And to stimulate his wife and children to the desire of heavenly things, he would sometimes use these words unto them:

> It is now no achievement for you children to go to heaven, for everybody gives you good counsel, everybody gives you good example—you see virtue rewarded and vice punished. So that you are carried up to heaven even by the chins. But if you live the time that no man will give you good counsel, nor no man will give you good example, when you shall see virtue punished and vice rewarded, if you will then stand fast and firmly stick to God, upon pain of my life, though you be but half good, God will allow you for whole good.

If his wife or any of his children had been diseased or troubled, he would say unto them: "We may not look at our pleasure to go to heaven in featherbeds. It is not the way, for our Lord himself went thither with great pain and by many tribulations, which was the path wherein he walked thither. For the servant may not look to be in better case than his master."

And as he would in this sort persuade them to take their troubles patiently, so would he in like sort teach them to withstand the devil and his temptations valiantly, saying:

> Whosoever will mark the devil and his temptations shall find him therein much like to an ape. For, like as an ape, not well looked unto, will be busy and bold to do shrewd turns and contrariwise, being spied, will suddenly leap backward and adventure no farther, so the devil finding a man idle, slothful, and without resistance ready to receive his temptations, waxes so hardy that he will not fail still to continue with him until to his purpose he have thoroughly brought him. But, on the other side, if he see a man with diligence persevere to prevent and withstand his temptations, he waxes so weary that in conclusion he utterly forsakes him. For as the devil of disposition is a spirit of so high a pride that he cannot abide to be mocked, so is he of nature so envious that he fears any more to assault him, lest he should thereby not only catch a foul fall himself but also minister to the man more matter of merit.

Thus delighted he evermore not only in virtuous exercises to be occupied himself, but also to exhort his wife, children, and household to embrace and follow the same.

10. DESIDERIUS ERASMUS OF ROTTERDAM (1466?–1536)

The Paraclesis *is Erasmus's preface to his new translation of the New Testament (*Novum Instrumentum*) of 1516. Although only a few pages in length, it contains many of his fundamental beliefs about learning and religion. It argues for a vernacular bible, for placing Christ's teachings above all else, and for the essential harmony between scholarship and revelation, but observes that Christ's teaching is the ultimate wisdom.*

The Paraclesis

The illustrious Lactantius Firmianus, good reader, whose eloquence Jerome especially admires, as he begins to defend the Christian religion against the pagans desires especially an eloquence second only to Cicero's be given him, thinking it wrong, I believe, to want an equal eloquence. But I indeed might heartily wish, if anything is to be gained by wishes of this kind, so long as I exhort all men to the most holy and wholesome study of Christian philosophy and summon them as if with the blast of a trumpet, that an eloquence far different than Cicero's be given me: an eloquence certainly much more efficacious, if less ornate than his. Or rather [I might wish for that kind of eloquence], if such power of speech was ever granted anyone, as the tales of the ancient poets not entirely without cause attributed to Mercury, who as if with a magic wand and a divine lyre induces sleep when he wishes and likewise snatches sleep away, plunging whom he wished into hell and again calling them forth from hell; or as the ancient tales assigned to Amphion and Orpheus, one of whom is supposed to have moved hard rocks, the other to have attracted oaks and ashes with a lyre; or as the Gauls ascribed to their Ogmius, leading about whither he wished all men by little chains fastened to their ears from his tongue; or as fabled antiquity attributed to Marsyas; or really, lest we linger too long on fables, as Alcibiades imputed to Socrates and old comedy to Pericles, an eloquence which not only captivates the ear with its fleeting delight but which leaves a lasting sting in the minds of its hearers, which grips, which transforms, which sends away a far different listener than it had received. One reads that the noble musician Timotheus, singing Doric melodies, was wont to rouse Alexander the Great to a desire for war. Nor were they lacking in former times who considered nothing more effective than the entreaties which the Greeks call *epodes*. But if there were any such kind of incantation anywhere, if there were any power of song which truly could inspire, if any Pytho truly swayed the heart, I would desire that it be at hand for me so that I might convince all of the most wholesome truth of all. However, it is more desirable that Christ Himself, whose business we are about, so guide the strings of our lyre that this song might deeply affect and move the minds of all, and, in fact, to accomplish this there is no need for the syllogisms and exclamations of the orators. What we desire is that nothing may stand forth with greater certainty than the truth itself, whose expression is the more powerful, the simpler it is.

And in the first place it is not pleasing to renew at the present time this complaint, not entirely new but, alas, only too just—and perhaps never more just than in these days—that when men are devoting themselves with such ardent spirit to all their studies, this philosophy of Christ alone is derided by some, even Christians, is neglected by many, and is discussed by a few, but in a cold manner (I shall not say insincerely). Moreover, in all other branches of learning which human industry has brought forth, nothing is so hidden and obscure which the keenness of genius has not explored, nothing is so difficult which tremendous exertion has not overcome. Yet how is it that even those of us who profess to be Christian fail to embrace with the proper spirit this philosophy alone? Platonists, Pythagoreans, Academics, Stoics, Cynics, Peripatetics, Epicureans not only have a deep understanding of the doctrines of their respective sects, but they commit them to memory, and they fight fiercely in their behalf, willing even to die rather than abandon the defense of their author. Then why do not we evince far greater spirit for Christ, our Author and Prince? Who does not judge it very shameful for one professing Aristotle's philosophy not to know that man's opinion about the causes of lightning, about prime matter, about the infinite? And neither does this knowledge render a man happy, nor does the lack of it render him unhappy. And do not we, initiated in so many ways, drawn by so many sacraments to Christ, think it shameful and base to know nothing of His doctrines, which offer the most certain happiness to all? But what purpose is served to exaggerate the matter by controversy, since it is what I might call a kind of wicked madness to wish to compare Christ with Zeno or Aristotle and His teaching with, to put it mildly, the paltry precepts of those men? Let them magnify the leaders of their sect as much as they can or wish. Certainly He alone was a teacher who came forth from heaven, He alone could teach certain doctrine, since it is eternal wisdom, He alone, the sole author of human salvation, taught what pertains to salvation, He alone fully vouches for whatsoever He taught, He alone is able to grant whatsoever He has promised. If anything is brought to us from the Chaldeans or Egyptians, we desire more eagerly to examine it because of the fact that it comes from a strange world, and part of its value is to have come from far off; and oftentimes we are anxiously tormented by the fancies of an insignificant man, not to say an impostor, not only to no avail but with great loss of time (I am not adding a more serious note, for the matter as it stands is most serious). But why does not such a desire also excite Christian minds who are convinced—and it is a fact—that this teaching has come not from Egypt or Syria but from heaven itself? Why do not all of us ponder within ourselves that this must be a new and wonderful kind of philosophy since, in order to transmit it to mortals, He who was God became man, He who was immortal became mortal, He who was in the heart of the Father descended to earth? It must be a great matter, and in no sense a commonplace one, whatever it is, because that wondrous Author came to teach after so many families of distinguished philosophers, after so many remarkable prophets. Why, then, out of pious curiosity do we not investigate, examine, explore each tenet? Especially since this kind of wisdom, so extraordinary that once for all it renders foolish the entire wisdom of this world, may be drawn from its few books as from the most limpid springs with far less labor than Aristotle's doctrine is extracted from so many obscure volumes, from those huge commentaries of the interpreters at odds with one another—and I shall not add with how much greater reward. Indeed, here there is no requirement that you approach equipped with so many troublesome sciences. The journey is simple, and it is ready for anyone. Only bring a pious and open mind, possessed above all with a pure and simple faith. Only be docile, and you have advanced far in this philosophy. It itself supplies inspiration as a teacher which communicates itself to no one more gladly than to minds that are without guile. The teachings of the others, besides the fact that they give hope of a false happiness, drive off the natural talents of many by the very difficulty, it is clear, of their precepts. This doctrine in an equal degree accommodates itself to all, lowers itself to the little ones, adjusts itself to their measure, nourishing them with milk, bearing, fostering, sustaining them, doing everything until we grow in Christ. Again, not only does it serve the lowliest, but it is also an object of wonder to those at the top. And the more you shall have progressed in its riches, the more you shall have withdrawn it from the shadow of the power of any other. It is a small affair to the little ones and more than the highest affair to the great. It casts aside no age, no sex, no fortune or position in life. The sun itself is not as common and accessible to all as is Christ's teaching. It keeps no one at a distance, unless a person, begrudging himself, keeps himself away.

Indeed, I disagree very much with those who are unwilling that Holy Scripture, translated into the vulgar tongue, be read by the uneducated, as if Christ taught such intricate doctrines that they could scarcely be understood by very few theologians, or as if the strength of the Christian religion consisted in men's ignorance of it. The mysteries of kings, perhaps, are better concealed, but Christ wishes his mysteries published as openly as possible. I would that even the lowliest women read the Gospels and the Pauline Epistles. And I would that they were translated into all languages so that they could be read and understood not only by Scots and Irish but also by Turks and Saracens. Surely the first step is to understand in one way or another. It may be that many will ridicule, but some may be taken captive. Would that, as a result, the farmer sing some portion of them at the plow, the weaver hum some parts of them to the movement of his shuttle, the traveler lighten the weariness of the journey with stories of this kind! Let all the conversations of every Christian be drawn from this source. For in general our daily conversations reveal what we are. Let each one comprehend what he can, let him express what he can. Whoever lags behind, let him not envy him who is ahead; whoever is in the front rank, let him encourage him who follows, not despair of him. Why do we restrict a profession common to all to a few? For it is not fitting, since Baptism is common in an equal degree to all Christians, wherein there is the first profession of Christian philosophy, and since the other sacraments and at length the reward of immortality belong equally to all, that doctrines alone should be reserved for those very few whom today the crowd call theologians or monks, the very persons whom, although they comprise one of the smallest parts of the Christian populace, yet I might wish to be in greater measure what they are styled. For I fear that one may find among the theologians men who are far removed from the title they bear, that is, men who discuss earthly matters, not divine, and that among the monks who profess the poverty of Christ and the contempt of the world you may find something more than worldliness. To me he is truly a theologian who teaches not by skill with intricate syllogisms but by a disposition of mind, by the very expression and the eyes, by the very life that riches should be disdained, that the Christian should not put his trust in the supports of this world but must rely entirely on heaven, that a wrong should not be avenged, that a good should be wished for those wishing it, that we should deserve well of those deserving ill, that all good men should be loved and cherished equally as members of the same body, that the evil should be tolerated if they cannot be corrected, that those who are stripped of their goods, those who are turned away from possessions, those who mourn are blessed and should not be deplored, and that death should even be desired by the devout, since it is nothing other than a passage to immortality. And if anyone under the inspiration of the spirit of Christ preaches this kind of doctrine, inculcates it, exhorts, incites, and encourages men to it, he indeed is truly a theologian, even if he should be a common laborer or weaver. And if anyone exemplifies this doctrine in his life itself, he is in fact a great doctor. Another, perhaps, even a non-Christian, may discuss more subtly how the angels understand, but to persuade us to lead here an angelic life, free from every stain, this indeed is the duty of the Christian theologian.

But if anyone objects that these notions are somewhat stupid and vulgar, I should respond to him only that Christ particularly taught these rude doctrines, that the Apostles inculcated them, that however vulgar they are, they have brought forth for us so many sincerely Christian and so great a throng of illustrious martyrs. This philosophy, unlettered as it appears to these very objectors, has drawn the highest princes of the world and so many kingdoms and peoples to its laws, an achievement which the power of tyrants and the erudition of philosophers cannot claim. Indeed I do not object to having that latter wisdom, if it seems worthwhile, discussed among the educated. But let the lowly mass of Christians console themselves certainly with this title because, whether the Apostles knew or other Fathers understood these subtleties or not, they surely didn't teach them. If princes in the execution of their duties would manifest what I have referred to as a vulgar doctrine, if priests would inculcate it in sermons, if schoolmasters would instill it in students rather than that erudition which they draw from the fonts of Aristotle and Averroës, Christendom would not be so disturbed on all sides by almost continuous war, everything would not be boiling over with such a mad desire to heap up riches by fair means or foul, every subject, sacred as well as profane, would not be made to resound everywhere with so much noisy disputation, and, finally, we would not differ from those who do not profess the philosophy of Christ merely in name and ceremonial. For upon these three ranks of men principally the task of either renewing or advancing the Christian religion has been placed: on the princes and the magistrates who serve in their place, on the bishops and their delegated priests, and on those who instruct the young eager for all knowledge. If it happen that they, having laid aside their own affairs, should sincerely cooperate in Christ, we would certainly see in not so many years a true and, as Paul says, a genuine race of Christians everywhere emerge, a people who would restore the philosophy of Christ not in ceremonies alone and in syllogistic propositions but in the heart itself and in the whole life. The enemies of the Christian name will far more quickly be drawn to the faith of Christ by these weapons than by threats or arms. In the conquest of every citadel nothing is more powerful than the truth itself. He is not a Platonist who has not read the works of Plato; and is he a theologian, let alone a Christian, who has not read the literature of Christ? Who loves me, Christ says, keeps my word, a distinguishing mark which He himself prescribed. Therefore, if we are truly and sincerely Christian, if we truly believe in Him who has been sent from Heaven to teach us that which the wisdom of the philosophers could not do, if we truly expect from Him what no prince, however powerful, can give, why is anything more important to us than His literature? Why indeed does anything seem learned that is not in harmony with His decrees? Why in the case of this literature that should be revered do we also allow ourselves, and I shall say almost to a greater extent than do the secular interpreters in the case of the imperial laws or the books of the physicians, to speak what ever comes to mind, to distort, to obscure? We drag heavenly doctrines down to the level of our own life as if it were a Lydian rule, and while we seek to avoid by every means appearing to be ignorant and for this reason gather in whatever is of account in secular literature, that which is of special value in Christian philosophy I shall not say we corrupt, but—and no one can deny it—we restrict to a few, although Christ wished nothing to be more public. In this kind of philosophy, located as it is more truly in the disposition of the mind than in syllogisms, life means more than debate, inspiration is preferable to erudition, transformation is a more important matter than intellectual comprehension. Only a very few can be learned, but all can be Christian, all can be devout, and—I shall boldly add—all can be theologians.

Indeed, this philosophy easily penetrates into the minds of all, an action in especial accord with human nature. Moreover, what else is the philosophy of Christ, which He himself calls a rebirth, than the restoration of human nature originally well formed? By the same token, although no one has taught this more perfectly and more effectively than Christ, nevertheless one may find in the books of the pagans very much which does agree with His teaching. There was never so coarse a school of philosophy that taught that money rendered a man happy. Nor has there ever been one so shameless that fixed the chief good in those vulgar honors and pleasures. The Stoics understood that no one was wise unless he was good; they understood that nothing was truly good or noble save real virtue and nothing fearful or evil save baseness alone. According to Plato, Socrates teaches in many different ways that a wrong must not be repaid with a wrong, and also that since the soul is immortal, those should not be lamented who depart this life for a happier one with the assurance of having led an upright life. In addition, he teaches that the soul must be drawn away from the inclinations of the body and led to those which are its real objectives although they are not seen. Aristotle has written in the *Politics* that nothing can be a delight to us, even though it is not in any way despised, except virtue alone. Epicurus also acknowledges that nothing in man's life can bring delight unless the mind is conscious of no evil, from which awareness true pleasure gushes forth as from a spring. What shall we say of this, that many—notably Socrates, Diogenes, and Epictetus—have presented a good portion of His teaching? But since Christ both taught and presented the same doctrine so much more fully, is it not a monstrous thing that Christians either disregard or neglect or even ridicule it? If there are things that belong particularly to Christianity in these ancient writers, let us follow them. But if these alone can truly make a Christian, why do we consider them as almost more obsolete and replaced than the Mosaic books? The first step, however, is to know what He taught; the next is to carry it into effect. Therefore, I believe, anyone should not think himself to be Christian if he disputes about instances, relations, quiddities, and formalities with an obscure and irksome confusion of words, but rather if he holds and exhibits what Christ taught and showed forth. Not that I condemn the industry of those who not without merit employ their native intellectual powers in such subtle discourse, for I do not wish anyone to be offended, but that I think, and rightly so, unless I am mistaken, that that pure and genuine philosophy of Christ is not to be drawn from any source more abundantly than from the evangelical books and from the Apostolic Letters, about which, if anyone should devoutly philosophize, praying more than arguing, and seeking to be transformed rather than armed for battle, he would without a doubt find that there is nothing pertaining to the happiness of man and the living of his life which is not taught, examined, and unraveled in these works. If we desire to learn, why is another author more pleasing than Christ himself? If we seek a model for life, why does another example take precedence for us over that of Christ himself? If we wish some medicine against the troublesome desires of the soul, why do we think the remedy to be more at hand somewhere else? If we want to arouse a soul that is idle and growing listless by reading, where, I ask, will you find sparks equally alive and efficacious? If the soul seems distracted by the vexations of this life, why are other delights more pleasing? Why have we steadfastly preferred to learn the wisdom of Christ from the writings of men than from Christ himself? And He, since He promised to be with us all days, even unto the consummation of the world, stands forth especially in this literature, in which He lives for us even at this time, breathes and speaks, I should say almost more effectively than when He dwelt among men. The Jews saw and heard less than you see and hear in the books of the Gospels, to the extent that you make use of your eyes and ears, whereby this can be perceived and heard.

And what kind of a situation is this, I ask? We preserve the letters written by a dear friend, we kiss them fondly, we carry them about, we read them again and again, yet there are many thousands of Christians who, although they are learned in other respects, never read, however, the evangelical and apostolic books in an entire lifetime. The Mohammedans hold fast to their doctrines, the Jews also today from the very cradle study the books of Moses. Why do not we in the same way distinguish ourselves in Christ? Those who profess the way of life of Benedict hold, study, absorb a rule written by man, and by one nearly uneducated for the uneducated. Those who are in the Augustinian order are well versed in the rule of their founder. The Franciscans reverence and love the little traditions of their Francis, and to whatever corner of the earth they go, they carry them with them; they do not feel safe unless the little book is on their person. Why do these men attribute more to a rule written by man than does the Christian world to its rule, which Christ delivered to all and which all have equally professed in baptism? Finally, although you may even cite a thousand rules, can anything be holier than this? And I wish that this may come to pass: just as

Paul wrote that the law of Moses was not full of glory compared with the glory of the Gospel succeeding it, so may all Christians hold the Gospels and Letters of the Apostles as so holy that in comparison with them these other writings do not seem holy. What others may wish to concede to Albert the Great, to Alexander, to Thomas, to Egidio [Giles], to Richard, to Occam [all medieval thinkers], they will certainly be free, as far as I am concerned, to do, for I do not want to diminish the fame of anyone or contend with the studies of men that are now of long standing. However learned these may be, however subtle, however seraphic, if they like, yet they must admit that the former are the most tried and true. Paul wishes that the spirits of those prophesying be judged whether they are of God. Augustine, reading every kind of book with discretion, asks nothing more than a just hearing also for his own works. But in this literature alone [i.e., Holy Scripture] what I do not comprehend, I nevertheless revere. It is no school of theologians who has attested to this Author for us but the Heavenly Father Himself through the testimony of the divine voice, and He has done this on two occasions: first at the Jordan at the time of the Baptism, then on Mount Tabor at the Transfiguration. "This is my beloved Son," He says, "in whom I am well pleased; hear Him" [Matthew 3:17, 17:5]. O solid and truly irrefragable authority, as the theologians say! What is this phrase, "Hear Him"? Certainly He is the one and only teacher, let us be the disciples of Him alone. Let each one extol in his studies his own author as much as he will wish, this utterance has been said without exception of Christ alone. A dove first descended on Him, the confirmation of the Father's testimony. Peter next bears His spirit, to whom the highest Pastor three times entrusted the feeding of His sheep, feeding them without a doubt, however, on the food of Christian doctrine. This spirit was born again, as it were, in Paul, whom He himself called a "chosen vessel" and an extraordinary herald of His name [Acts 9:15]. What John had drawn from that sacred font of His heart, he expressed in his own writings. What, I pray, is like this in Scotus (I do not wish that this remark be taken as a pretext for abuse), what is like this in Thomas? Nevertheless, I admire the talents of the one, and I also revere the sanctity of the other. But why do not all of us apply ourselves to philosophy in these authors of such great value? Why do we not carry them about on our persons, have them ever in our hands? Why do we not hunt through these authors, thoroughly examine them, assiduously investigate them? Why devote the greater part of life to Averroës rather than to the Gospels? Why spend nearly all of life on the ordinances of men and on opinions in contradiction with themselves? The latter, in fact, may now be the views of the more eminent theologians, if you please; but certainly the first steps of the great theologian in the days to come will be in these authors [of Holy Scripture].

Let all those of us who have pledged in baptism in the words prescribed by Christ, if we have pledged sincerely, be directly imbued with the teachings of Christ in the midst of the very embraces of parents and the caresses of nurses. For that which the new earthen pot of the soul first imbibes settles most deeply and clings most tenaciously. Let the first lispings utter Christ, let earliest childhood be formed by the Gospels of Him whom I would wish particularly presented in such a way that children also might love Him. For as the severity of some teachers causes children to hate literature before they come to know it, so there are those who make the philosophy of Christ sad and morose, although nothing is more sweet than it. In these studies, then, let them engage themselves until at length in silent growth they mature into strong manhood in Christ. The literature of others is such that many have greatly repented the effort expended upon it, and it happens again and again that those who have fought through all their life up to death to defend the principles of that literature, free themselves from the faction of their author at the very hour of death. But happy is that man whom death takes as he meditates upon this literature [of Christ]. Let us all, therefore, with our whole heart covet this literature, let us embrace it, let us continually occupy ourselves with it, let us fondly kiss it, at length let us die in its embrace, let us be transformed in it, since indeed studies are transmuted into morals. As for him who cannot pursue this course (but who cannot do it, if only he wishes?), let him at least reverence this literature enveloping, as it were, His divine heart. If anyone shows us the footprints of Christ, in what manner, as Christians, do we prostrate ourselves, how we adore them! But why do we not venerate instead the living and breathing likeness of Him in these books? If anyone displays the tunic of Christ, to what corner of the earth shall we not hasten so that we may kiss it? Yet were you to bring forth His entire wardrobe, it would not manifest Christ more clearly and truly than the Gospel writings. We embellish a wooden or stone statue with gems and gold for the love of Christ. Why not, rather, mark with gold and gems and with ornaments of greater value than these, if such there be, these writings which bring Christ to us so much more effectively than any paltry image? The latter represents only the form of the body—if indeed it represents anything of Him—but these writings bring you the living image of His holy mind and the speaking, healing, dying, rising Christ himself, and thus they render Him so fully present that you would see less if you gazed upon Him with your very eyes.

11. CARDINAL FRANCISCO XIMENES (1436–1517)

Francisco Ximenes de Cisneros was born in 1436 in Castile, the son of a minor official. He studied both civil and canon law in Spain and worked in Rome, but he returned to Spain in 1459. He earned a reputation as an episcopal administrator but in 1484 abandoned his benefices to become an Observant Franciscan monk, adopting a rigorously ascetic life. Despite his humility he was obliged to accept the influential position of confessor to Queen Isabella of Castile in 1492. His wisdom and prudence resulted in Isabella having him appointed archbishop of Toledo and chancellor of Castile, honors he tried conscientiously to avoid. He was a man of unbending character and rigor: he forced Franciscan monks to live according to their vows, driving many to leave the order; he forced the conversion of Moors in newly conquered Granada, destroyed Arabic manuscripts, and turned all mosques into churches, acts that resulted in widespread opposition, even revolt. He personally funded a crusade against North Africa, from which King Ferdinand of Aragon received most of the benefit. But he was loyal to the Crown, so Ferdinand arranged his elevation to Grand Inquisitor and Cardinal. On the death of Ferdinand, Ximenes became regent of Spain for the young Charles of Habsburg, the future emperor Charles V; however, his high-handed and autocratic actions alienated both the Spanish nobility and the young Charles V who, on his arrival in Spain, dismissed Ximenes, who died en route to meet the new king in 1517.

Ximenes was a great patron of learning, especially theology. He was responsible for the foundation of the Complutensian University of Alcala and for the complutensian (polyglot) bible begun in 1502. This massive work of scholarship arranged the original biblical languages of Aramaic, Hebrew, Greek, and Latin beside the translation so that the meaning could be compared. The massive five-volume bible finally appeared in 1517, but Ximenes died before he could see a printed copy.

Prologue to the Polyglot

Prologue to the Books of the Old and New Testaments Printed in Their Various Languages

There are many reasons, Holy Father, that impel us to print the languages of the original text of Holy Scripture. These are the principal ones. Words have their own unique character, and no translation of them, however complete, can entirely express their full meaning. This is especially the case in that language through which the Lord Himself spoke. The letter here of itself may be dead and like flesh which profits nought ("for it is the spirit that gives life" [2 Cor. 3:6]) because Christ concealed by the form of the words remains enclosed within its womb. But there is no doubt that there is a rich fecundity so astonishing and an abundance of sacred mysteries so teeming that since it is ever full to overflowing "streams of living water shall flow out from His breast" [John 7:38]. And from this source those to whom it has been given "to behold the glory of the Lord with an unveiled face and thus be transformed into that very image" [2 Cor. 3:18] can continually draw the marvelous secrets of His divinity. Indeed there can be no language or combination of letters from which the most hidden meanings of heavenly wisdom do not emerge and burgeon forth, as it were. Since, however, the most learned translator can present only a part of this, the full Scripture in translation inevitably remains up to the present time laden with a variety of sublime truths which cannot be understood from any source other than the original language.

Moreover, wherever there is diversity in the Latin manuscripts or the suspicion of a corrupted reading (we know how frequently this occurs because of the ignorance and negligence of copyists), it is necessary to go back to the original source of Scripture, as St. Jerome and St. Augustine and other ecclesiastical writers advise us to do, to examine the authenticity of the books of the Old Testament in the light of the correctness of the Hebrew text and of the New Testament in the light of the Greek copies. And so that every student of Holy Scripture might have at hand the original texts themselves and be able to quench his thirst at the very fountainhead of the water that flows unto life everlasting and not have to content himself with rivulets alone, we ordered the original languages of Holy Scripture with their translations adjoined to be printed and dedicated to your Holiness. And we first took care to print the New Testament in Greek and Latin together with a lexicon of all the Greek expressions that can help those reading that language. Thus we spared no effort on behalf of those who have not acquired a full knowledge of the Greek tongue. Then before we began the Old Testament we prepared a dictionary of the Hebrew and Chaldean words of the entire Old Instrument [Testament]. There not only the various meanings of each expression are given, but (we believe this will be most useful to students) the place in Scripture where each meaning occurs is cited.

Also, since not only the shell of the letter that kills but above all the kernel of the life-giving spirit that lies hidden within must be sought by the student of Holy Scripture, and since an important part of this derives from the translation of proper names, we ordered that their translation be worked out with the greatest care by men who excelled in the knowledge of languages and that they be arranged alphabetically and the list appended to the dictionary. The ascribing of these names, foreseen from eternity, is of incredible help in revealing spiritual and concealed meanings and uncovering hidden mysteries that the Holy Spirit has veiled under the shadow of the literal text. After this list come instruction in reading the Hebrew characters and a grammar of that language compiled from many Hebrew authors of accepted reliability and arranged according to the Latin method.

After we completed all this as a prelude, so to speak, we printed the different languages of the Old Testament and added the Latin translation for each of them. We can frankly state, Most Holy Father, that the greatest part of our labor was expended here. We employed men the most outstanding for their knowledge of languages, and we had the most accurate and the oldest manuscripts for our base texts. We made the greatest effort to gather from various places a large number of Hebrew as well as Greek and Latin codices. Indeed we are indebted to your Holiness for the Greek texts. With the greatest kindness you sent us the most ancient codices of both the Old and the New Testaments from your Apostolic Library, and these were of the greatest help to us in this undertaking.

And so, having completed the printing of the New Testament in Greek and Latin together with its lexicon and also the Hebrew and Chaldean dictionary, to which we appended a grammar as well as the translation of proper names, and in addition having finished annotating variant readings in the Old Testament, annotations which our scholars added in many places since Nicholas of Lyra had not fully completed the task, at last with divine assistance we printed the Old Testament in its various languages. We now send this entire work to your Holiness, for to whom should all our vigilant efforts be dedicated than to that Apostolic See to whom we owe everything? Or who with greater joy ought to accept and embrace the sacred books of the Christian religion than the sacred Vicar of Christ? May your Holiness receive, therefore, with a joyful heart this humble gift which we offer unto the Lord so that the hitherto dormant study of Holy Scripture may now at last begin to revive.

We beseech your Blessedness most earnestly, however, that you examine these books that now prostrate themselves before you and pass the most severe judgment on them so that, if it seems they will be of use to the Christian commonwealth, they may receive permission from your Holiness to be published. We have held them back until now, waiting to consult that sacred oracle of the Apostolic Office.

12. DESIDERIUS ERASMUS OF ROTTERDAM (1466?–1536)

The Colloquies, *or* Dialogues, *of Erasmus were first printed in 1518 and saw twelve editions before 1533. Colloquies were often used in teaching Latin because of the rich vocabulary, brilliant style, and engaging dialogue. These dialogues are amusing, insightful, but often biting in their irony, as they illustrate the problems Erasmus identified in contemporary religious practice, especially when superstition supplanted faith and outward practice replaced personal belief in or understanding of the Christian message.*

Pilgrimage, the subject of Erasmus's concern here, developed as a penitential exercise in the early Middle Ages, when a journey to Jerusalem, Rome, or Santiago de Compostela (Spain), was both expensive and dangerous. Though these pilgrimages remained popular and could still be gruelling, by the later Middle Ages local pilgrimage sites had sprouted up all over Europe, allowing pilgrims to take trips that might be as much a break from the everyday as a religious experience, a view most famously expressed in Chaucer's Canterbury Tales. *The most famous pilgrimage sites also benefited from the generosity of their visitors, amassing vast wealth that seemed incongruous in a penitential environment to reformers like Erasmus.*

A Pilgrimage for Religion's Sake

MENEDEMUS.
Did you pass by Thomas Archbishop of Canterbury?
OGYGIUS.
No, I think I did not. It is one of the most religious pilgrimages in the world.
MEN.
I'd love to hear it, if it won't be too much trouble to you.
OGY.
Far from it; I want you to hear of it. That part of England that looks towards Flanders and France is called Kent: The major city is Canterbury. There are two monasteries in it that are almost contiguous; and they are both of Benedictines. St Augustine's is the older of the two; the one now called by the name of St. Thomas, seems to have been the seat of St. Thomas the Archbishop, where he led his life with a few monks whom he chose for his companions, as now deans have their palaces near the church, though separated from the houses of other canons. For, previously, both bishops and canons were monks, as surviving evidence shows clearly. But the church dedicated to St. Thomas rises up towards heaven with such majesty that it strikes those who see from a great distance with an awe of religion, and now, with its splendor, makes the neighboring palaces look dim, and even obscures the place that was in ancient times the most celebrated for religion. There are two lofty turrets which stand, as it were, bidding visitors welcome from afar; and a peal of bells that make the adjacent countryside echo far and wide with their rolling sound. In the south porch of the church stand three stone statues of men in armor, who wickedly murdered the holy man, with their names added, *Tusci, Fusci,* and *Berti*.

MEN.
Why are such wicked men so honored?
OGY.
They have the same honor done to them that is done to Judas, Pilate, Caiaphas, and the band of wicked soldiers whose images you may see carved upon stately altars. And their names are added so nobody afterwards might ever think anything of them but evil. They are set there in open sight, to be a warning to other wicked courtiers that no one may hereafter lay a hand on either bishops or the possessions of the church. These three scoundrels went mad from recognizing the horror of the murder they had committed; and they would not come to their senses again, had not holy Thomas been implored to heal of them.
MEN.
O the perpetual mercy of martyrs!
OGY.
When you entered, a certain spacious grandeur appears to you, which is free for everyone.
MEN.
Is there nothing to be seen there?
OGY.
Nothing but the size of the building, and some books chained to the pillars, containing the Gospel of Nicodemus, and the tomb of someone I don't know.
MEN.
And what else?
OGY.
Iron gates enclose the place called the choir, so that there's no entrance; but the sightline is still open

from one end of the church to the other. You ascend by a great many steps under which there is a vault that opens a passage to the north side. There they show a wooden altar, consecrated to the holy Virgin; it is a very small one, and remarkable for nothing, except as a monument of antiquity, reproaching the luxury of the present time. In that place the holy man is said to have taken his last leave of the Virgin, when he was at the point of death. Upon the altar is the point of the sword with which the top of the head of that good archbishop was wounded, and some of his brains that were beaten out to make sure he died. We most religiously kissed the sacred rust on this weapon out of love for the martyr. Leaving this place, we went down into a vault underground where there are two keepers of relics. The first thing they show you is the skull of the martyr where it was cut through; the upper part is left open to be kissed, all the rest is covered with silver. There also is shown you a lead plate with this inscription, *Thomas Acrensis* [Thomas of Acre]. And hung up to see are his hair shirt, the belts, and breeches which this prelate used to mortify his flesh. The very sight of these was enough to strike us with horror, and to reproach the softness and delicacy of our age.

MEN.
And perhaps of the monks themselves, too.
OGY.
That I can neither prove nor deny, nor does it matter much to me.
MEN.
You're right.
OGY.
From there we return to the choir. On the north side they opened a private place. It is incredible what a world of bones they brought out of it: skulls, chins, teeth, hands, fingers, whole arms, all of which we first adored, then kissed. This would never have ended, had it not been for one of my fellow travelers, who indiscreetly interrupted the official who was showing them to us.
MEN.
Who was he?
OGY.
He was an Englishman, named Gratian Pullus [John Colet, Dean of St. Paul's], a man of learning and piety, but not as devoted to this aspect of religion as I wish he were.
MEN.
I expect he was a follower of John Wickliffe [i.e., Wyclif, or a Lollard].
OGY.
No, I don't think so, although he had read his books; but I don't know where he got them.
MEN.
Did he make the official angry?
OGY.
He took out an arm having yet some bloody flesh on it; he showed a reluctance to kiss it, and a sort of uneasiness in his expression. So, the official put away all his relics. After this we viewed the table of the altar, and the ornaments; and after that the things under the altar. All was very rich; you would have said Midas and Crœsus were beggars compared to them, if you saw the great quantities of gold and silver.
MEN.
And was there kissing here?
OGY.
No, but I was inspired to imagine something quite different.
MEN.
What was it?
OGY.
It made me sad to think I had no relics in my own house.
MEN.
A sacrilegious wish!
OGY.
I confess it, and I humbly begged the pardon of the saint, before I set foot out of the church. After this we were carried into the vestry. Good God! What a display of silk vestments we saw there: Golden candlesticks! There we saw also St. Thomas's pastoral staff. It looked like a reed covered with silver; it had little weight, and not much workmanship, and was no longer than up to my belt.
MEN.
Was there a cross?
OGY.
I didn't see one. There was a gown shown: it was silk indeed, but coarse, and without embroidery or jewels; and a handkerchief, still having plain marks of sweat and blood from the saint's neck. We readily kissed these reminders of former simple living.

MEN.
Are these shown to everybody?
OGY.
No certainly not, my good friend.
MEN.
How did you come to have such a reputation with them that none of their secrets were kept from you?
OGY.
I had used to know the reverend prelate William Warham the Archbishop, and he recommended me.
MEN.
I have heard he was a man of great humanity.
OGY.
Really, if you knew the man, you would take him for humanity itself. He was a man of such learning, candor of manners, and piety of life that there was nothing missing in him to make him a most accomplished prelate. From hence we were conducted up higher; because behind the high Altar, there is another staircase, as into another church. In a certain chapel there was shown the whole face of the holy man set in gold, and adorned with jewels; and here a certain unexpected incident almost interrupted all our joy.
MEN.
I want to hear what nasty thing this was.
OGY.
My friend Gratian really lost himself here. After a short prayer, he says to the assistant who showed us the relics: Good father, is it true, as I have heard, that Thomas, when alive, was very charitable to the poor? Very true, he replied, and began to relate a great many examples of his charity. Then, answers Gratian, I don't believe that good tendency in him is changed, unless it is for the better. The official agreed. Then, says he again, if this holy man was so generous to the poor when he was a poor man himself, and stood in need of charity for his own support don't you think he would be pleased now that he is grown so rich and wants for nothing, if some poor woman with many children at home about to starve, or daughters in danger of having to prostitute themselves for not having a dowry, or a husband sick in bed, and destitute of all comfort should ask him leave to make a gift of these vast riches for the relief of her family? The assistant did not answer this question. Gratian, being an impulsive man, says, "I am fully persuaded that the holy man would be certainly glad in his heart that when he is dead he could be able to relieve the needs of the poor with his wealth." Upon this the keeper of the relics began to frown and pout and look at us as with Gorgon eyes; and I don't doubt but he would have spit in our faces and thrown us out of the church by the neck and shoulders, except that we had the archbishop's recommendation. Indeed I did pacify him a little with kind words, telling him that Gratian did not really mean what he said but had a droll way with him. And I also put down a little money.

MEN.
Indeed I greatly approve of your piety. But I sometimes seriously think about how they can possibly excuse themselves from being guilty of an error by using such vast sums in building, beautifying, and enriching churches, setting no limits to their expenses. I allow that there ought to be a dignity to sacred vestments; the vessels of a church should be agreeable to the solemn service; and I would have the structure of it to have a certain air of majesty. But to what purpose are so many golden fonts, so many candlesticks, and so many images? To what purpose is such a profusion of expense upon organs, as they call them? Nor are we indeed content with one pair. What signify those concerts of music, hired at so great an expense, when in the meantime our brothers and sisters, Christ's living temples, are about to perish for hunger and thirst?

OGY.
There is no man of piety or wisdom, who would not wish for moderation in these matters; but since this error results from a certain extreme of piety, it deserves some praise, especially when we see on the other hand, the error of others, those who rob churches rather than build them up. Such buildings are commonly endowed by great men and monarchs who would waste the money in gambling or war. And moreover, if you take anything away from the church, it is called sacrilege; and it discourages others from donating; and besides, it is a temptation to despoil the Church. The churchmen are rather guardians of these things than owners of them. And lastly, I had rather see a church luxurious with sacred furniture than appear as some of them do: naked and sordid, more like stables than churches.

Men.

But we read that the bishops of old were commended for selling sacred vessels and relieving the poor with the money.

Ogy.

And so they are commended today; but they are only commended. I believe they neither have the power nor the will to follow that example.

Men.

But I am interrupting you. I now want to hear the conclusion of your story.

Ogy.

Well, you shall have it, and I'll be very brief. At this point, out comes the head of the college.

Men.

Who was he? The abbot of the place?

Ogy.

He wears a mitre and has the revenue of an abbot; so he lacks nothing but the name. He is called the Prior, because the archbishop serves as abbot. For a long time ago, every archbishop of the diocese was a monk.

Men.

I wouldn't care if I was called a camel, if I had but the income of an abbot.

Ogy.

He seemed to me to be a godly and prudent man, and not unacquainted with the theology of the Scotists. For us, he opened the box in which the remains of the holy man's body is said to rest.

Men.

Did you see the bones?

Ogy.

That is not permitted; nor can it be done without a ladder. But a wooden box covers a golden one, and that when hauled up with ropes reveals an inestimable treasure.

Men.

What are you saying?

Ogy.

Gold was the basest part. Everything sparkled and shone with very large and rare jewels, some of them bigger than a goose egg. Some monks stood about with the greatest veneration. The cover was taken off, and we all worshipped. The prior, with a white wand, touched every stone one by one, telling us the name in French, the value of it, and who was the donor. The largest of them were presents from Kings.

Men.

He must have had a good memory.

Ogy.

You guessed right; and yet practice goes a long way, for he does this frequently. From there, he took us back into a vault, where the Virgin Mary has her residence. It's rather dark, with a double rail in and surrounded by iron bars.

Men.

What is she afraid of?

Ogy.

Nothing, I suppose, but thieves. And I never in my life saw anything more laden with riches.

Men.

You tell me of riches in the dark?

Ogy.

Candles being brought in, we saw more than a royal sight.

Men.

What, does it go beyond the *Parathalassian* Virgin [Our Lady of Walsingham, literally "the Virgin by the Sea"] in wealth?

Ogy.

It goes far beyond that! What is hidden she knows best. These things are shown to none but great persons, or particular friends. In the end, we were led back into the vestry where a chest was pulled out covered with black leather. It was put on the table and opened. Everyone fell down on their knees, and worshipped what they saw.

Men.

What was it?

Ogy.

Pieces of linen rags, a great many of them which still had the marks of the saint's snot. The rags were those, they say, that the holy man used to wipe off the sweat from his face and neck, the snot out of his nose, or any other such sort of dirt which human bodies produce. Here again my friend Gratian behaved not in the most obliging manner. For the gentle prior offered him, as an Englishman, an acquaintance and a man of considerable authority, one of the rags as a present, thinking he had presented him with a very appropriate gift. But Gratian ungraciously took it squeamishly in his fingers, and laid it down with an air of contempt, making a face at it, as if he would have tossed it. This was what he did, if anything caused him to feel disgust. I was both ashamed and afraid. Nevertheless the good prior, although not unaware of the affront, seemed to take no notice of it; and after he had civilly entertained us with a glass of wine, dismissed us, and we went back to London.

...

MEN.
... But, I have led you way from your story. Go on.
OGY.
On our journey to London, not far from Canterbury, there's a narrow, hollow, steep road, and a cragged, steep bank on either side, so that you can't escape it. There is no other way to go. Upon the left hand of that route, there is a little cottage of old beggars. As soon as they spy a man on horseback coming, one of them runs out and sprinkles him with holy water, and then offers him the upper leather of a shoe, with a brass ring attached to it in which is a glass, as if it were some gem. Having kissed it, you then give the beggar a small bit of money.
MEN.
On a road like this, I had rather meet with a cottage of old beggars than a gang of tough robbers.
OGY.
Gratian rode on my left, next to the cottage. He was sprinkled with holy water, and took it pretty well; but upon presented with the shoe, he asked what was meant by it? This, says the poor man, was St. Thomas's shoe. Gratian fell into a fit of anger, and turning to me, said, "What would these brutes have? Will they make us kiss the shoes of all good men? Why don't they give us their spit as well, and the other excrement from their bodies to kiss?" I pitied the sad, poor old man, and comforted him by giving him a little money.
MEN.
In my opinion, Gratian was not angry without cause. If these shoes and slippers were preserved as an argument of moderation in living, I shouldn't mind it. But I think it impudent to thrust slippers, and shoes, and stockings, upon any one to be kissed. If anyone does it of their own free choice, from a great affection to piety, I think they deserve to be left free to do so.
OGY.
I'm not going to pretend: I think those things had better be let alone. But in such instances where you can't do a quick fix, my view is to make the best of them. In the meantime my mind was delighted with this prospect that a good man was like a sheep and a wicked man like a predatory beast. A viper cannot bite when it is dead, yet it is infectious because of its stink and corruption. A sheep, while it lives, nourishes us with its milk, clothes us with its wool, and enriches us by its lambs; when it is dead, it supplies us with leather, and every part of it is good to eat. Similarly, men that are vexatious and devoted to this world are troublesome to all persons while they live, and when they are dead, they are a disturbance to those that are alive, with the noise of the bells and a pompous funeral—and sometimes a problem to their successors on inheriting their possessions by causing new exactions. But good men make themselves useful in every way to the whole world. So was this saint, who while he was alive, by the example of his teaching and encouragement, invited others to piety, comforted the lonely, and helped the needy. Now that he is dead, he is in some ways more useful. He built this magnificent church, and advanced the authority of the priesthood all over England; and now, after all, this fragment of his shoe maintains a conventicle of poor men.
MEN.
That indeed is a very pious thought. But I wonder, given your predilections, that you never went to see St. Patrick's Den, which people say so many prodigious things about. I can scarcely think this likely to be true.
OGY.
No, there is no report of it can be so remarkable, but the reality itself exceeds it.
MEN.
Then you did go into it?
OGY.
Yes, I have ferried over a truly *stygian* lake, and descended into the very jaws of *Avernus*, and seen all that is done in Hell.
MEN.
You'll honor me if you tell me about it.
OGY.
I think this preface of our conversation has been wordy enough. I am going home to give orders to get supper ready; for I have not dined yet.
MEN.
Why haven't you had dinner? Is it for a religious reason?
OGY.
No, rather out of spite.
MEN.

What, do you spite your own belly?

Ogy.

No, but dishonest publicans, who, although they serve you with what is not fit to eat, make no scruple of demanding an unreasonable price for their slop. This is how I revenge myself on them: If I anticipate a good supper, either at an acquaintance's, or at a tavern—anything tolerable—my stomach fails me at dinner. If Fortune delivers up a dinner I like, then my stomach fails me at supper-time.

Men.

And are you not ashamed to be so stingy and sneaky?

Ogy.

Believe me, Menedemus, in such cases modesty is the wrong response. I have learned to keep my bashfulness for other purposes.

Men.

I really want to hear the rest of your story, so expect me for supper, where you may tell it more at leisure.

Ogy.

Truly, thanks for taking the liberty of inviting yourself, when many who are invited with sincerity won't accept. But I will thank you over and over, if you dine at home tonight. My time will be taken up in congratulating my family. But I have advice to give you that will be more comfortable for us both. If you provide a dinner at your house for me and my wife tomorrow, I'll proceed with my story till supper-time. When you say you have had your bellyful and if you are in agreement, we won't leave you before supper either. Why are you scratching your head? Just get everything ready and I give you my word we will come without fail.

Men.

I like free stories best. However, come, I'll provide a dinner for you, but it'll be an unsavory one, if you don't make it spicy with your stories.

Ogy.

But listen, aren't you getting excited to go on pilgrimages?

Men.

Perhaps I might be by the time you have finished your story; but I find at present that I have enough to do to travel my Roman stations.

Ogy.

Roman? You who've never been to Rome?

Men.

I'll tell you about it. I walk about my house, I go to my study, and check on my daughter's chastity; then I go into my shop to see what my servants are doing; then into the kitchen to see if anything is amiss there; and so from one place to another, to observe what my wife and children are doing, taking care that everyone is at their proper business. These are my Roman stations.

Ogy.

But St. James would take care of these things for you.

Men.

The holy scriptures require me to look after them myself, because I can't find any text instructing me to leave them to the saints.

3

The Protestant Reformation

LUTHER

13. MARTIN LUTHER (1483–1546)

Luther was born in Saxony in 1483 and educated by the Brethren of the Common Life. In 1501 he went to university at Erfurt and by 1505 he had become a Master of Arts. In 1508 he was sent to the Augustinian house at Wittenberg to teach in the university that had recently been founded there. As he lectured on St. Paul's letters to the Romans in Wittenberg, Luther came to the realization that salvation was possible only through faith. Luther was only starting to work out the implications of this new revelation when he was prompted into the publication of his views in 1517 by his outrage at the sale of indulgences.

Luther's 95 theses were quickly printed and flew through Germany. The enthusiasm his ideas generated in Germany was not shared in Rome, and between 1518 and 1520 Luther worked to avoid an open breach with the Church. At the same time he developed and publicized his ideas in a number of pamphlets, including the Appeal to the Christian Nobility of the German Nation *(published in the summer of 1520), which became best sellers.*

In July 1521, Luther was formally excommunicated by Pope Leo X, and the pope called on the emperor to enforce the bull. Charles V would have been glad to enforce the proclamation, but the political situation in Germany simply did not allow it. Luther was receiving a great deal of support from the German princes, and the emperor could not afford to antagonize them.

Luther wanted to return the Church to a purer form of what it had been, not to create something entirely new, and so he stood against extreme reform. Luther was always concerned to play down any kind of social revolution or any kind of reorganization of the temporal world. His concern was with the spiritual world, and he had no desire to put forward ideas on the reorganization of the temporal world that would raise difficulties in having his entirely spiritual ideas accepted.

To the Christian Nobility

To His Most Illustrious, Most Mighty, and Imperial Majesty [the Holy Roman Emperor Charles V], and to the Christian Nobility of the German Nation, from Doctor Martin Luther

Grace and power from God, Most Illustrious Majesty, and most gracious and dear lords.

It is not from sheer impertinence or rashness that I, one poor man, have taken it upon myself to address your worships. All the estates of Christendom, particularly in Germany, are now oppressed by distress and affliction, and this has stirred not only me but everybody else to cry out time and time again and to pray for help. It has even compelled me now at this time to cry aloud that God may inspire someone with his Spirit to lend a helping hand to this distressed and wretched nation. Often the councils have made some pretense at reformation, but their attempts have been cleverly frustrated by the guile of certain men, and things have gone from bad to worse. With God's help I intend to expose the wiles and wickedness of these men, so that they are shown up for what they are and may never again be so obstructive and destructive. God has given us a young man of noble birth as head of state, and in him has awakened great hopes of good in many hearts. Presented with such an opportunity we ought to apply ourselves and use this time of grace profitably.

The first and most important thing to do in this matter is to prepare ourselves in all seriousness. We must not start something by trusting in great power or human reason, even if all the power in the world were ours. For God cannot and will not suffer that a good work begin by relying upon one's own power and reason. He dashes such works to the ground, they do no good at all. As it says in Psalm 33[:16], "No king is saved by his great might and no lord is saved by the greatness of his strength." I fear that this is why the good emperors Frederick I and Frederick II and many other German emperors were in former times shamefully oppressed and trodden underfoot by the popes, although all the world feared the emperors. It may be that they relied on their own might more than on God, and therefore had to fall. What was it in our own times that raised the bloodthirsty Julius II to such heights? Nothing else, I fear, except that France, the Germans, and Venice relied upon themselves. The children of Benjamin slew forty-two thousand Israelites because the latter relied on their own strength, Judges 30[:21].

That it may not so fare with us and our noble Charles, we must realize that in this matter we are not dealing with men, but with the princes of hell. These princes could fill the world with war and bloodshed, but war and bloodshed do not overcome them. We must tackle this job by renouncing trust in physical force and trusting humbly in God. We must seek God's help through earnest prayer and fix our minds on nothing else than the misery and distress of suffering Christendom without regard to what evil men deserve. Otherwise, we may start the game with great prospects of success, but when we get into it the evil spirits will stir up such confusion that the whole world will swim in blood, and then nothing will come of it all. Let us act wisely, therefore, and in the fear of God. The more force we use, the greater our disaster if we do not act humbly and in the fear of God. If the popes and Romanists have hitherto been able to set kings against each other by the devil's help, they may well be able to do it again if we were to go ahead without the help of God on our own strength and by our own cunning.

The Romanists have very cleverly built three walls around themselves. Hitherto they have protected themselves by these walls in such a way that no one has been able to reform them. As a result, the whole of Christendom has fallen abominably.

In the first place, when pressed by the temporal power they have made decrees and declared that the temporal power had no jurisdiction over them, but that, on the contrary, the spiritual power is above the temporal. In the second place, when the attempt is made to reprove them with the Scriptures, they raise the objection that only the pope may interpret the Scriptures. In the third place, if threatened with a council, their story is that no one may summon a council but the pope.

...

May God help us, and give us just one of those trumpets with which the walls of Jericho were overthrown to blast down these walls of straw and paper in the same way and set free the Christian rods for the punishment of sin, [and] bring to light the craft and deceit of the devil, to the end that through punishment we may reform ourselves and once more attain God's favor.

Let us begin by attacking the first wall. It is pure invention that pope, bishop, priests, and monks are called the spiritual estate while princes, lords, artisans, and farmers are called the temporal estate. This is indeed a piece of deceit and hypocrisy. Yet no one need be intimidated by it, and for this reason: all Christians are truly of the spiritual estate, and there is no difference among them except that of office. Paul says in 1 Corinthians 12[:12–13] that we are all one body, yet every member has its own work by which it serves the others. This is because we all have one baptism, one gospel, one faith, and are all Christians alike; for baptism, gospel, and faith alone make us spiritual and a Christian people.

The pope or bishop anoints, shaves heads, ordains, consecrates, and prescribes garb different from that of the laity, but he can never make a man into a Christian or into a spiritual man by so doing. He might well make a man into a hypocrite or a humbug and blockhead, but never a Christian or a spiritual man. As far as that goes, we are all consecrated priests through baptism, as St. Peter says in 1 Peter 2[:9], "You are a royal priesthood and a priestly realm." The Apocalypse says, "Thou hast made us to be priests and kings by thy blood" [Rev. 5:9–10]. The consecration by pope or bishop would never make a priest, and if we had no higher consecration than that which pope or bishop gives, no one could say mass or preach a sermon or give absolution.

Therefore, when a bishop consecrates it is nothing else than that in the place and stead of the whole community, all of whom have like power, he takes a person and charges him to exercise this power on behalf of the others. It is like ten brothers, all king's sons and equal heirs, choosing one of themselves to rule the inheritance in the interests of all. In one sense they are all kings and of equal power, and yet one of them is charged with the responsibility of ruling. To put it still more clearly: suppose a group of earnest Christian laymen were taken prisoner and set down in a desert without an episcopally ordained priest among them. And suppose they were to come to a common mind there and then in the desert and elect one of their number, whether he were married or not, and charge him to baptize, say mass, pronounce absolution, and preach the gospel. Such a man would be as truly a priest as though he had been ordained by all the bishops and popes in the world. That is why in cases of necessity anyone can baptize and give absolution. This would be impossible if we were not all priests. Through canon law the Romanists have almost destroyed and made unknown the wondrous grace and authority of baptism and justification. In times gone by Christians used to choose their bishops and priests in this way from among their own number, and they were confirmed in their office by the other bishops without all the fuss that goes on nowadays. St. Augustine, Ambrose, and Cyprian each became [a bishop in this way].

Since those who exercise secular authority have been baptized with the same baptism, and have the same faith and the same gospel as the rest of us, we must admit that they are priests and bishops and we must regard their office as one which has a proper and useful place in the Christian community. For whoever comes out of the water of baptism can boast that he is already a consecrated priest, bishop, and pope, although of course it is not seemly that just anybody should exercise such office. Because we are all priests of equal standing, no one must push himself forward and take it upon himself, without our consent and election, to do that for which we all have equal authority. For no one dare take upon himself what is common to all without the authority and consent of the community. And should it happen that a person chosen for such office were deposed for abuse of trust, he would then be exactly what he was before. Therefore, a priest in Christendom is nothing else but an officeholder. As long as he holds office he takes precedence; where he is deposed, he is a peasant or a townsman like anybody else. Indeed, a priest is never a priest when he is deposed. But now the Romanists have invented *characteres indelebiles* and say that a deposed priest is nevertheless something different from a mere layman. They hold the illusion that a priest can never be anything other than a priest, or ever become a layman. All this is just contrived talk, and human regulation.

It follows from this argument that there is no true, basic difference between laymen and priests, princes and bishops, between religious and secular, except for the sake of office and work, but not for the sake of status. They are all of the spiritual estate, all are truly priests, bishops, and popes. But they do not all have the same work to do. Just as all priests and monks do not have the same work. This is the teaching of St. Paul in Romans 12[:4–5] and 1 Corinthians 12[:12] and in 1 Peter 2[:9], as I have said above, namely, that we are all one body of Christ the Head, and all members one of another. Christ does not have two different bodies, one temporal, the other spiritual. There is but one Head and one body.

Therefore, just as those who are now called "spiritual," that is, priests, bishops, or popes, are neither different from other Christians nor superior to them, except that they are charged with the administration of the word of God and the sacraments, which is their work and office, so it is with the temporal authorities. They bear the sword and rod in their hand to punish the wicked and protect the good. A cobbler, a smith, a peasant—each has the work and office of his trade, and yet they are all alike consecrated priests and bishops. Further, everyone must benefit and serve every other by means of his own work or office so that in this way many kinds of work may be done for the bodily and spiritual welfare of the community, just as all the members of the body serve one another [1 Cor. 12:14–26].

Consider for a moment how Christian is the decree which says that the temporal power is not above the "spiritual estate" and has no right to punish it. That is as much as to say that the hand shall not help the eye when it suffers pain. Is it not unnatural, not to mention un-Christian, that one member does not help another and prevent its destruction? In fact, the more honorable the member, the more the others ought to help. I say therefore that since the temporal power is ordained of God to punish the wicked and protect the good, it should be left free to perform its office in the whole body of Christendom without restriction and without respect to persons, whether it affects pope, bishops, priests, monks, nuns, or anyone else. If it were right to say that the temporal power is inferior to all the spiritual estates (preacher, confessor, or any spiritual office), and so prevent the temporal power from doing its proper work, then the tailors, cobblers, stonemasons, carpenters, cooks, innkeepers, farmers, and all the temporal craftsmen should be prevented from providing pope, bishops, priests, and monks with shoes, clothes, house, meat and drink, as well as from paying them any tribute. But if these laymen are allowed to do their proper work without restriction, what then are the Romanist scribes doing with their own laws, which exempt them from the jurisdiction of the temporal Christian authority? It is just so that they can be free to do evil and fulfill what St. Peter said, "False teachers will rise up among you who will deceive you, and with their false and fanciful talk, they will take advantage of you" [2 Pet. 2:1–3].

For these reasons the temporal Christian authority ought to exercise its office without hindrance, regardless of whether it is pope, bishop, or priest whom it affects. Whoever is guilty, let him suffer. All that canon law has said to the contrary is the invention of Romanist presumption. For thus St. Paul says to all Christians, "Let every soul (I take that to mean the pope's soul also) be subject to the temporal authority; for it does not bear the sword in vain, but serves God by punishing the wicked and benefiting the good" [Rom. 13:1, 4]. St. Peter, too, says, "Be subject to all human ordinances for the sake of the Lord, who so wills it" [1 Pet. 2:13, 15]. He has also prophesied in 2 Peter 2[:1] that such men would arise and despise the temporal authority. This is exactly what has happened through the canon law.

So, then, I think this first paper wall is overthrown. Inasmuch as the temporal power has become a member of the Christian body it is a spiritual estate, even though its work is physical. Therefore, its work should extend without hindrance to all the members of the whole body to punish and use force whenever guilt deserves or necessity demands, without regard to whether the culprit is pope, bishop, or priest. Let the Romanists hurl threats and bans about as they like. That is why guilty priests, when they are handed over to secular law, are first deprived of their priestly dignities. This would not be right unless the secular sword previously had had authority over these priests by divine right. Moreover, it is intolerable that in canon law so much importance is attached to the freedom, life, and property of the clergy, as though the laity were not also as spiritual and as good Christians as they, or did not also belong to the church. Why are your life and limb, your property and honor, so cheap and mine not, inasmuch as we are all Christians and have the same baptism, the same faith, the same Spirit, and all the rest? If a priest is murdered, the whole country is placed under interdict. Why not when a peasant is murdered? How does this great difference come about between two men who are both Christians? It comes from the laws and fabrications of men.

The second wall is still more loosely built and less substantial. The Romanists want to be the only masters of Holy Scripture, although they never learn a thing from the Bible all their life long. They assume the sole authority for themselves, and, quite unashamed, they play about with words before our very eyes, trying to persuade us that the pope cannot err in matters of faith, regardless of whether he is righteous or wicked. Yet they cannot point to a single letter. This is why so many heretical and un-Christian, even unnatural, ordinances stand in the canon law. But there is no need to talk about these ordinances at present. Since these Romanists think the Holy Spirit never leaves them, no matter how ignorant and wicked they are, they become bold and decree only what they want. And if what they claim were true, why have Holy Scripture at all? Of what use is Scripture? Let us burn the Scripture and be satisfied with the unlearned gentlemen at Rome who possess the Holy Spirit! And yet the Holy Spirit can be possessed only by pious hearts. If I had not read the words with my own eyes, I would not have believed it possible for the devil to have made such stupid claims at Rome, and to have won supporters for them.

Therefore, their claim that only the pope may interpret Scripture is an outrageous fancied fable. They cannot produce a single letter [of Scripture] to maintain that the interpretation of Scripture or the confirmation of its interpretation belongs to the pope alone. They themselves have usurped this power. And although they allege that this power was given to St. Peter when the keys were given him, it is clear enough that the keys were not given to Peter alone but to the whole community. Further, the keys were not ordained for doctrine or government, but only for the binding or loosing of sin. Whatever else or whatever more they arrogate to themselves on the basis of the keys is a mere fabrication. But Christ's words to Peter, "I have prayed for you that your faith fail not" [Luke 22:32], cannot be applied to the pope, since the majority of the popes have been without faith, as they must themselves confess. Besides, it is not only for Peter that Christ prayed, but also for all apostles and Christians, as he says in John 17[:9, 20], "Father, I pray for those whom thou hast given me, and not for these only, but for all who believe in me through their word." Is that not clear enough?

Just think of it! The Romanists must admit that there are among us good Christians who have the true faith, spirit, understanding, word, and mind of Christ. Why, then, should we reject the word and understanding of good Christians and follow the pope, who has neither faith nor the Spirit? To follow the pope would be to deny the whole faith as well as the Christian church. Again, if the article, "I believe in one holy Christian church," is correct, then the pope cannot be the only one who is right. Otherwise, we would have to confess, "I believe in the pope at Rome": This would reduce the Christian church to one man, and be nothing else than a devilish and hellish error. [...]

The third wall falls of itself when the first two are down. When the pope acts contrary to the Scriptures, it is our duty to stand by the Scriptures, to reprove him and to constrain him, according to the word of Christ, Matthew 18[:15–17], "If your brother sins against you, go and tell it to him, between you and him alone; if he does not listen to you, then take one or two others with you; if he does not listen to them, tell it to the church; if he does not listen to the church, consider him a heathen." Here every member is commanded to care for every other. How much more should we do this when the member that does evil is responsible for the government of the church, and by his evil-doing is the cause of much harm and offense to the rest! But if I am to accuse him before the church, I must naturally call the church together.

The Romanists have no basis in Scripture for their claim that the pope alone has the right to call or confirm a council. This is just their own ruling, and it is only valid as long as it is not harmful to Christendom or contrary to the laws of God. Now when the pope deserves punishment, this ruling no longer obtains, for not to punish him by authority of a council is harmful to Christendom.

Thus we read in Acts 15 that it was not St. Peter who called the Apostolic Council but the apostles and elders. If then that right had belonged to St. Peter alone, the council would not have been a Christian council, but a heretical *conciliabulum*. Even the Council of Nicaea, the most famous of all councils, was neither called nor confirmed by the bishop of Rome, but by the emperor Constantine. Many other emperors after him have done the same, and yet these councils were the most Christian of all. But if the pope alone has the right to convene councils, then these councils would all have been heretical. Further, when I examine the councils the pope did summon, I find that they did nothing of special importance.

Therefore, when necessity demands it, and the pope is an offense to Christendom, the first man who is able should, as a true member of the whole body, do what he can to bring about a truly free council. No one can do this so well as the temporal authorities, especially since they are also fellow-Christians, fellow-priests, fellow-members of the spiritual estate, fellow-lords over all things. Whenever it is necessary or profitable they ought to exercise the office and work which they have received from God over everyone. Would it not be unnatural if a fire broke out in a city and everybody were to stand by and let it burn on and on and consume everything that could burn because nobody had the authority of the mayor, or because, perhaps, the fire broke out in the mayor's house? In such a situation is it not the duty of every citizen to arouse and summon the rest? How much more should this be done in the spiritual city of Christ if a fire of offense breaks out, whether in the papal government, or anywhere else! The same argument holds if an enemy were to attack the city. The man who first aroused the others deserves honor and gratitude. Why, then, should he not deserve honor who makes known the presence of the enemy from hell and rouses Christian people and calls them together?

But all their boasting about an authority which dare not be opposed amounts to nothing at all. Nobody in Christendom has authority to do injury or to forbid the resisting of injury. There is no authority in the church except to promote good. Therefore, if the pope were to use his authority to prevent the calling of a free council, thereby preventing the improvement of the church, we should have regard neither for him nor for his authority. And if he were to hurl his bans and thunderbolts, we should despise his conduct as that of a madman. On the contrary, we should excommunicate him and drive him out as best we could, relying completely upon God. This presumptuous authority of his is nothing. He does not even have such authority. He is quickly defeated by a single text of Scripture, where Paul says to the Corinthians, "God has given us authority not to ruin Christendom, but to build it up" [2 Cor. 10:8]. Who wants to leap over the hurdle of this text? It is the power of the devil and of Antichrist which resists the things that serve to build up Christendom. Such power is not to be obeyed, but rather resisted with life, property, and with all our might and main. [...]

Now, although I am too insignificant a man to make propositions for the improvement of this dreadful state of affairs, nevertheless I shall sing my fool's song through to the end and say, so far as I am able, what could and should be done, either by the temporal authority or by a general council.

1. Every prince, every noble, every city should henceforth forbid their subjects to pay annates to Rome and should abolish them entirely. The pope has broken the agreement and made the annates a robbery to the injury and shame of the whole German nation. He gives them to his friends, sells them for huge sums of money, and uses them to endow offices. In so doing he has lost his right to them and deserves punishment. Consequently the temporal authority is under obligation to protect the innocent and prevent injustice, as Paul teaches in Romans 13, and St. Peter in 1 Peter 2[:14], and even the canon law in Case 16, Question 7, in the *de filiis* clause. Thus it has come about that they say to the pope and his crowd, "*Tu ora*, thou shalt pray"; to the emperor and his servants, "*Tu protege*, thou shalt protect"; to the common man, "*Tu labora*, thou shalt work," not however as though everyone were not to pray, protect, and work. For the man who is diligent in his work prays, protects, and works in all that he does. But everyone should have his own special work assigned him.

2. Since the pope with his Romanist practices—his commends, coadjutors, reservations, *gratiae expectativae*, papal months, incorporations, unions, pensions, pallia, chancery rules, and such knavery—usurps for himself all the German foundations without authority and right, and gives and sells them to foreigners at Rome who do nothing for Germany in return, and since he robs the local bishops of their rights and makes mere ciphers and dummies of them, and thereby acts contrary to his own canon law, common sense, and reason, it has finally reached the point where the livings and benefices are sold to coarse, unlettered asses and ignorant knaves at Rome out of sheer greed. Pious and learned people do not benefit from the service or skill of these fellows. Consequently the poor German people must go without competent and learned prelates and go from bad to worse.

For this reason the Christian nobility should set itself against the pope as against a common enemy and destroyer of Christendom for the salvation of the poor souls who perish because of this tyranny. The Christian nobility should ordain, order, and decree that henceforth no further benefice shall be drawn into the hands of Rome, and that hereafter no appointment shall be obtained there in any manner whatsoever, but that the benefices should be dragged from this tyrannical authority and kept out of his reach. The nobility should restore to the local bishops their right and responsibility to administer the benefices in the German nation to the best of their ability. And when a lackey comes along from Rome he should be given a strict order to keep out, to jump into the Rhine or the nearest river, and give the Romish ban with all its seals and letters a nice, cool dip. If this happened they would sit up and take notice in Rome. They would not think that the Germans are always dull and drunk, but have really become Christian again. They would realize that the Germans do not intend to permit the holy name of Christ, in whose name all this knavery and destruction of souls goes on, to be scoffed and scorned any longer, and that they have more regard for God's honor than for the authority of men.

3. An imperial law should be issued that no bishop's cloak and no confirmation of any dignity whatsoever shall henceforth be secured from Rome, but that the ordinance of the most holy and famous Council of Nicaea be restored. This ordinance decreed that a bishop shall be confirmed by the two nearest-bishops or by the archbishop. If the pope breaks the statutes of this and of all other councils, what is the use of holding councils? Who has given him the authority to despise the decisions of councils and tear them to shreds like this?

This is all the more reason for us to depose all bishops, archbishops, and primates and make ordinary parsons of them, with only the pope as their superior, as he now is. The pope allows no proper authority or responsibility to the bishops, archbishops, and primates. He usurps everything for himself and lets them keep only the name and the empty title. It has even gone so far that by papal exemption the monasteries, abbots, and prelates as well are excepted from the regular authority of the bishops. Consequently there is no longer any order in Christendom. The inevitable result of all this is what has happened already: relaxation of punishment, and license to do evil all over the world. I certainly fear that the pope may properly be called "the man of sin" [2 Thess. 2:3]. Who but the pope can be blamed for there being no discipline, no punishment, no rule, no order in Christendom? By his usurpation of power he ties the prelates' hands and takes away their rod of discipline. He opens his hands to all those set under him, and gives away or sells their release.

Lest the pope complain that he is being robbed of his authority, it should be decreed that in those cases where the primates or the archbishops are unable to settle a case, or when a dispute arises between them, then the matter should be laid before the pope, but not every little thing. It was done this way in former times, and this was the way the famous Council of Nicaea decreed. Whatever can be settled without the pope, then, should be so settled so that his holiness is not burdened with such minor matters, but gives himself to prayer, study, and the care of all Christendom. This is what he claims to do. This is what the apostles did. They said in Acts 6[:2–4], "It is not right that we should leave the Word of God and serve tables, but we will hold to preaching and prayer, and set others over that work." But now Rome stands for nothing else than the despising of the gospel and prayer, and for the serving of tables, that is, temporal things. The rule of the apostles and of the pope have as much in common as Christ has with Lucifer, heaven with hell, night with day. Yet the pope is called "Vicar of Christ" and "Successor to the Apostles."

...

9. The pope should have no authority over the emperor, except the right to anoint and crown him at the altar just as a bishop crowns a king. We should never again yield to that devilish pride which requires the emperor to kiss the pope's feet, or sit at his feet, or, as they say, hold his stirrup or the bridle of his mule when he mounts to go riding. Still less should he do homage and swear faithful allegiance to the pope as the popes brazenly demand as though they had a right to it....

The pope is not a vicar of Christ in heaven, but only of Christ as he walked the earth. Christ in heaven, in the form of a ruler, needs no vicar, but sits on his throne and sees everything, does everything, knows everything, and has all power. But Christ needs a vicar in the form of a servant, the form in which he went about on earth, working, preaching, suffering, and dying. Now the Romanists turn all that upside down. They take the heavenly and kingly form from Christ and give it to the pope, and leave the form of a servant to perish completely. He might almost be the Counter-Christ, whom the Scriptures call Antichrist, for all his nature, work, and pretensions run counter to Christ and only blot out Christ's nature and destroy his work.

...

14. We also see how the priesthood has fallen, and how many a poor priest is overburdened with wife and child, his conscience troubled. Yet no one does anything to help him, though he could easily be helped. Though pope and bishops may let things go on as they are, and allow what is heading for ruin to go to ruin, yet I will redeem my conscience and open my mouth freely, whether it vexes pope, bishop, or anybody else. And this is what I say: according to the institution of Christ and the apostles, every city should have a priest or bishop, as St. Paul clearly says in Titus 1[:5]. And this priest should not be compelled to live without a wedded wife, but should be permitted to have one, as St. Paul writes in 1 Timothy 3[:2, 4] and Titus 1[:8–7] saying, "A bishop shall be a man who is blameless, and the husband of but one wife, whose children are obedient and well behaved," etc. According to St. Paul, and also St. Jerome, a bishop and a priest are one and the same thing. But of bishops as they now are the Scriptures know nothing. Bishops have been appointed by ordinance of the Christian church, so that one of them may have authority over several priests.

So then, we clearly learn from the Apostle that it should be the custom for every town to choose from among the congregation a learned and pious citizen, entrust to him the office of the ministry, and support him at the expense of the congregation. He should be free to marry or not. He should have several priests or deacons, also free to marry or not as they choose, to help him minister to the congregation and the community with word and sacrament, as is still the practice in the Greek church. Because there was sometimes so much persecution and controversy with heretics after the apostolic age, there were many holy fathers who voluntarily abstained from matrimony that they might better devote themselves to study and be prepared at any moment for death or battle.

But the Roman See has interfered and out of its own wanton wickedness made a universal commandment forbidding priests to marry. This was done at the bidding of the devil, as St. Paul declares in 1 Timothy 4[:1, 3], "There shall come teachers who bring the devil's teaching and forbid marriage." Unfortunately so much misery has arisen from this that tongue could never tell it. Moreover, this caused the Greek church to separate, and discord, sin, shame, and scandal were increased no end. But this always happens when the devil starts and carries on. What, then, shall we do about it?

My advice is, restore freedom to everybody and leave every man free to marry or not to marry. But then there would have to be a very different kind of government and administration of church property; the whole canon law would have to be demolished; and few benefices would be allowed to get into Roman hands. I fear that greed is a cause of this wretched, unchaste celibacy. As a result, everyone has wanted to become a priest and everyone wants his son to study for the priesthood, not with the idea of living in chastity, for that could be done outside the priesthood. [Their idea is to] be supported in temporal things without work or worry, contrary to God's command in Genesis 3[:19] that "in the sweat of your face you shall eat your bread." The Romanists have colored this to mean that their labor is to pray and say mass.

I am not referring here to popes, bishops, canons, and monks. God has not instituted these offices. They have taken these burdens upon themselves, so they will have to bear them themselves. I want to speak only of the ministry which God has instituted, the responsibility of which is to minister word and sacrament to a congregation, among whom they reside. Such ministers should be given liberty by a Christian council to marry to avoid temptation and sin. For since God has not bound them, no one else ought to bind them or can bind them, even if he were an angel from heaven, let alone a pope. Everything that canon law decrees to the contrary is mere fable and idle talk.

Furthermore, I advise anyone henceforth being ordained a priest or anything else that he in no wise vow to the bishop that he will remain celibate. On the contrary, he should tell the bishop that he has no right whatsoever to require such a vow, and that it is a devilish tyranny to make such a demand. But if anyone is compelled to say, or even wants to say, "so far as human frailty permits," as indeed many do, let him frankly interpret these same words in a negative manner to mean "I do not promise chastity." For human frailty does not permit a man to live chastely, but only the strength of angels and the power of heaven. In this way he should keep his conscience free of all vows.

I will advise neither for nor against marrying or remaining single. I leave that to common Christian order and to everyone's better judgment. I will not conceal my real opinion or withhold comfort from that pitiful band who with wives and children have fallen into disgrace and whose consciences are burdened because people call them priests' whores and their children priests' children. As the court-jester I say this openly.

You will find many a pious priest against whom nobody has anything to say except that he is weak and has come to shame with a woman. From the bottom of their hearts both are of a mind to live together in lawful wedded love, if only they could do it with a clear conscience. But even though they both have to bear public shame, the two are certainly married in the sight of God. And I say that where they are so minded and live together, they should appeal anew to their conscience. Let the priest take and keep her as his lawful wedded wife, and live honestly with her as her husband, whether the pope likes it or not, whether it be against canon or human law. The salvation of your soul is more important than the observance of tyrannical, arbitrary, and wanton laws which are not necessary to salvation or commanded by God....

First, not every priest can do without a woman, not only on account of human frailty, but much more on account of keeping house. If he then may keep a woman, and the pope allows that, and yet may not have her in marriage, what is that but leaving a man and a woman alone together and yet forbidding them to fall? It is just like putting straw and fire together and forbidding them to smoke or burn!

Second, the pope has as little power to command this as he has to forbid eating, drinking, the natural movement of the bowels, or growing fat. Therefore, no one is bound to keep it, but the pope is responsible for all the sins which are committed against this ordinance, for all the souls which are lost, and for all the consciences which are confused and tortured because of this ordinance. He has strangled so many wretched souls with this devilish rope that he has long deserved to be driven out of this world. Yet it is my firm belief that God has been more gracious to many souls at their last hour than the pope was to them in their whole lifetime. No good has ever come nor will come out of the papacy and its laws.

Third, although the law of the pope is against it, nevertheless, when the estate of matrimony has been entered against the pope's law, then his law is already at an end and is no longer valid. For God's commandment, which enjoins that no man shall put husband and wife asunder [Matt. 19:6], is above the pope's law. And the commandments of God must not be broken or neglected because of the pope's commandment. Nevertheless, many foolish jurists, along with the pope, have devised impediments and thereby prevented, broken, and brought confusion to the estate of matrimony so that God's commandment concerning it has altogether disappeared. Need I say more? In the entire canon law of the pope there are not even two lines which could instruct a devout Christian, and, unfortunately, there are so many mistaken and dangerous laws that nothing would be better than to make a bonfire of it.

But if you say that marriage of the clergy would give offense, and that the pope must first grant dispensation,

I reply that whatever offense there is in it is the fault of the Roman See which has established such laws with no right and against God. Before God and the Holy Scriptures marriage of the clergy is no offense. Moreover, if the pope can grant dispensations from his greedy and tyrannical laws for money, then every Christian can grant dispensations from these very same laws for God's sake and for the salvation of souls. For Christ has set us free from all man-made laws, especially when they are opposed to God and the salvation of souls, as St. Paul teaches in Galatians 5[:1] and 1 Corinthians 10[:23].

THE RADICAL REFORMATION

14. ANONYMOUS: *THE TWELVE ARTICLES* (1525)

The language of religious reform quickly melded with the language of social and political reform in Germany, for in contemporary thought it was difficult, if not impossible, to separate the two. This blending of religious and social life reached from the top of society to the bottom, where reformers argued that communal life should be guided by Christian values of morality, charity, and obedience to the will of God. Nothing in this was inherently novel, but the suggestion that those currently in positions of authority, whether secular or religious, had failed in their duty to observe those precepts and that the obligation should be taken up by local communities as a reflection of their commitment to the equality of the gospel was quite radical. The Twelve Articles does not advocate violence, but the calm assertion of control over such matters as the appointment of pastors, tithes, labor services, and economic resources such as woodlands is revolutionary.

The Twelve Articles of the Upper Swabian Peasants: 27 February–1 March 1525

The fundamental and correct chief articles of all the peasants and of those subject to ecclesiastical lords, relating to these matters in which they feel themselves aggrieved.

Peace to the Christian Reader and the Grace of God through Christ

There are many evil writings put forth of late which take occasion, on account of the assembling of the peasants, to cast scorn upon the gospel, saying: "Is this the fruit of the new teaching, that no one should obey but all should everywhere rise in revolt and rush together to reform or perhaps destroy altogether the authorities, both ecclesiastic and lay?" The articles below shall answer these godless and criminal fault-finders, and serve in the first place to remove the reproach from the word of God, and in the second place to give a Christian excuse for the disobedience or even the revolt of the entire peasantry.

In the first place the gospel is not the cause of revolt and disorder, since it is the message of Christ, the promised Messiah, the Word of Life, teaching only love, peace, patience and concord. Thus, all who believe in Christ should learn to be loving, peaceful, long-suffering and harmonious. This is the foundation of all the articles of the peasants (as will be seen) who accept the gospel and live according to it. How then can the evil reports declare the gospel to be a cause of revolt and disobedience? That the authors of the evil reports and the enemies of the gospel oppose themselves to these demands is due, not to the gospel, but to the devil, the worst enemy of the gospel, who causes this opposition by raising doubts in the minds of his followers, and thus the word of God, which teaches love, peace and concord, is overcome.

In the second place, it is clear that the peasants demand that this Gospel be taught them as a guide in life and they ought not to be called disobedient or disorderly. Whether God grant the peasants (earnestly wishing to live according to His word) their requests or no, who shall find fault with the will of the Most High? Who shall meddle in His judgments or oppose his majesty? Did he not hear the children of Israel when they called upon Him and saved them out of the hands of Pharaoh? Can He not save His own today? Yes, He will save them and that speedily. Therefore, Christian reader, read the following articles with care and then judge. Here follow the articles:

The First Article. First, it is our humble petition and desire, as also our will and resolution, that in the future we should have power and authority so that each community should choose and appoint a pastor, and that we should have the right to depose him should he conduct himself improperly. The pastor thus chosen should teach us the gospel pure and simple, without any addition, doctrine or ordinance of man. For to teach us continually the true faith will lead us to pray God that through His grace this faith may increase within us and become part of us. For if His grace work not within us we remain flesh and blood, which avails nothing; since the Scripture clearly teaches that only through true faith can we come to God. Only through His mercy can we become holy. Hence such a guide and pastor is necessary and in this fashion grounded upon the Scriptures.

The Second Article. According as the just tithe is established by the Old Testament and fulfilled in the New, we are ready and willing to pay the fair tithe of grain. The word of God plainly provided that in giving according to right to God and distributing to His people the services of a pastor are required. We will that, for the future, our church provost, whomsoever the community may appoint, shall gather and receive this tithe. From this he shall give to the pastor, elected by the whole community, a decent and sufficient maintenance for him and his, as shall seem right to the whole community (or, with the knowledge of the community). What remains over shall be given to the poor of the place, as the circumstances and the general opinion demand. Should anything farther remain, let it be kept, lest anyone should have to leave the country from poverty. Provision should also be made from this surplus to avoid laying any land tax on the poor.

In case one or more villages themselves have sold their tithes on account of want, and each village has taken action as a whole, the buyer should not suffer loss, but we will that some proper agreement be reached with him for the repayment of the sum by the village with due interest. But those who have tithes which they have not purchased from a village, but which were appropriated by their ancestors, should not, and ought not, to be paid anything farther by the village which shall apply its tithes to the support of the pastors elected as above indicated, or to solace the poor as is taught by the Scriptures. The small tithes, whether ecclesiastical or lay, we will not pay at all, for the Lord God created cattle for the free use of man. We will not, therefore, pay farther an unseemly tithe which is of man's invention.

The Third Article. It has been the custom hitherto for men to hold us as their own property, which is pitiable enough, considering that Christ has delivered and redeemed us all, without exception, by the shedding of His precious blood, the lowly as well as the great. Accordingly, it is consistent with Scripture that we should be free and wish to be so. Not that we would wish to be absolutely free and under no authority. God does not teach us that we should lead a disorderly life in the lusts of the flesh, but that we should love the Lord our God and our neighbor. We would gladly observe all this as God has commanded us in the celebration of the communion. He has not commanded us not to obey the authorities, but rather that we should be humble, not only towards those in authority, but towards every one. We are thus ready to yield obedience according to God's law to our elected and regular authorities in all proper things becoming to a Christian. We, therefore, take it for granted that you will release us from serfdom as true Christians, unless it should be shown us from the Gospel that we are serfs.

The Fourth Article. In the fourth place it has been the custom heretofore, that no poor man should be allowed to catch venison or wild fowl or fish in flowing water, which seems to us quite unseemly and unbrotherly as well as selfish and not agreeable to the word of God. In some places the authorities preserve the game to our great annoyance and loss, recklessly permitting the unreasoning animals to destroy to no purpose our crops which God suffers to grow for the use of man, and yet we must remain quiet. This is neither godly or neighborly. For when God created man he gave him dominion over all the animals, over the birds of the air and over the fish in the water. Accordingly it is our desire if a man holds possession of waters that he should prove from satisfactory documents that his right has been unwittingly acquired by purchase. We do not wish to take it from him by force, but his rights should be exercised in a Christian and brotherly fashion. But whosoever cannot produce such evidence should surrender his claim with good grace.

The Fifth Article. In the fifth place we are aggrieved in the matter of wood-cutting, for the noble folk have appropriated all the woods to themselves alone. If a poor man requires wood he must pay double for it. It is our opinion in regard to wood which has fallen into the hands of a lord whether spiritual or temporal, that unless it was duly purchased it should revert again to the community. It should, moreover, be free to every member of the community to help himself to such fire-wood as he needs in his home. Also, if a man requires wood for carpenter's purposes he should have it free, but with the knowledge of a person appointed by the community for that purpose. Should, however, no such forest be at the disposal of the community let that which has been duly bought be administered in a brotherly and Christian manner. If the forest, although unfairly appropriated in the first instance, was later duly sold let the matter be adjusted in a friendly spirit and according to the Scriptures.

The Sixth Article. Our sixth complaint is in regard to the excessive services demanded of us which are increasing from day to day. We ask that this matter be properly looked into so that we shall not continue to be oppressed in this way, but that some gracious consideration be given us, since our forefathers were required only to serve according to the word of God.

The Seventh Article. Seventh, we will not hereafter allow ourselves to be farther oppressed by our lords, but will let them demand only what is just and proper according to the word of the agreement between the lord and the peasant. The lord should no longer try to force more services or other dues from the peasant without payment, but permit the peasant to enjoy his holding in peace and quiet. The peasant should, however, help the lord when it is necessary, and at proper times when it will not be disadvantageous to the peasant and for a suitable payment.

The Eighth Article. In the eighth place, we are greatly burdened by holdings which cannot support the rent exacted from them. The peasants suffer loss in this way and are ruined, and we ask that the lords may appoint persons of honor to inspect these holdings, and fix a rent in accordance with justice, so that the peasants shall not work for nothing, since the laborer is worthy of his hire.

The Ninth Article. In the ninth place, we are burdened with a great evil in the constant making of new laws. We are not judged according to the offense, but sometimes with great ill will, and sometimes much too leniently. In our opinion we should be judged according to the old written law so that the case shall be decided according to its merits, and not with partiality.

The Tenth Article. In the tenth place, we are aggrieved by the appropriation by individuals of meadows and fields which at one time belonged to a community. These we will take again into our own hands. It may, however, happen that the land was rightfully purchased. When, however, the land has unfortunately been purchased in this way, some brotherly arrangement should be made according to circumstances.

The Eleventh Article. In the eleventh place we will entirely abolish the due called heriot and will no longer endure it, nor allow widows and orphans to be thus shamefully robbed against God's will, and in violation of justice and right, as has been done in many places, and by those who should shield and protect them. These have disgraced and despoiled us, and although they had little authority they assumed it. God will suffer this no more, but it shall be wholly done away with, and for the future no man shall be bound to give little or much.

Conclusion. In the twelfth place it is our conclusion and final resolution, that if any one or more of the articles here set forth should not be in agreement with the word of God, as we think they are, such article we will willingly recede from when it is proved really to be against the word of God by a clear explanation of the Scripture. Or if articles should now be conceded to us that are hereafter discovered to be unjust, from that hour they shall be dead and null and without force. Likewise, if more complaints should be discovered which are based upon truth and the Scriptures and relate to offenses against God and our neighbor, we have determined to reserve the right to present these also, and to exercise ourselves in all Christian teaching. For this we shall pray God, since He can grant these, and He alone. The peace of Christ abide with us all.

15. MARTIN LUTHER (1483–1546)

Luther (see selection 13) wrote this tract in response to the growing demand among the German peasantry for the kinds of changes enunciated in The Twelve Articles *(see selection 14). Afraid that his religious insights would be tainted by an association with social and economic upheaval and that the religious reforms underway would be halted by secular rulers anxious to avoid insurrection, he called on the peasants to offer due obedience to the authorities established by God, while exhorting the authorities, both secular and religious, to mend their behavior and look after both the spiritual and the physical needs of their subordinates. Though Luther hoped to avoid the outbreak of violence with this tract, by the time it was published the peasants' revolt was already underway in Germany.*

An Admonition to Peace

The peasants who have now banded together in Swabia have formulated their intolerable grievances against the rulers in twelve articles, and have undertaken to support them with certain passages of Scripture. Now they have published them in printed form. The thing about them that pleases me most is that, in the twelfth article, they offer to accept instruction gladly and willingly, if there is need or necessity for it, and are willing to be corrected, to the extent that it can be done by clear, plain, undeniable passages of Scripture. And it is indeed right and proper that no one's conscience should be instructed or corrected except by Holy Scripture.

Now if that is their serious and sincere meaning—and it would not be right for me to interpret it otherwise, because in these articles they come out into the open and do not shy away from the light—then there is good reason to hope that things will be well. Since I have a reputation for being one of those who deal with the Holy Scriptures here on earth, and especially as one whom they mention and call upon by name in the second document, I have all the more courage and confidence in openly publishing my instruction, I do this in a friendly and Christian spirit, as a duty of brotherly love, so that if any misfortune or disaster comes out of this matter, it may not be attributed to me, nor will I be blamed before God and men because of my silence. But if this offer of theirs is only pretense and show (without a doubt there are some people like that among them for it is impossible for so big a crowd all to be true Christians and have good intentions; a large part of them must be using the good intentions of the rest for their own selfish purposes and seeking their own advantage) then without doubt it will accomplish very little, or, in fact, it will contribute to their great injury and eternal ruin.

This, then, is a great and dangerous matter. It concerns both the kingdom of God and the kingdom of the world. If this rebellion were to continue and get the upper hand, both kingdoms would be destroyed and there would be neither worldly government nor word of God, which would ultimately result in the permanent destruction of all Germany. Therefore it is necessary for us to speak boldly and to give advice without regard to anyone. It is also necessary that we be willing to listen and allow things to be said to us, so that we do not now—as we have done before—harden our hearts and stop our ears, and so that God's wrath not run its full course. For the many terrible signs that are seen both in heaven and earth point to a great disaster and a mighty change in Germany. Sad to say, however, we care little about it. Nevertheless, God goes on his way, and someday he will soften our hardheadedness.

To the Princes and Lords

We have no one on earth to thank for this disastrous rebellion, except you princes and lords, and especially you blind bishops and mad priests and monks, whose hearts are hardened, even to the present day. You do not cease to rant and rave against the holy gospel, even though you know that it is true and that you cannot refute it. In addition, as temporal rulers you do nothing but cheat and rob the people so that you may lead a life of luxury and extravagance. The poor common people cannot bear it any longer. The sword is already at your throats, but you think that you sit so firm in the saddle that no one can unhorse you. This false security and stubborn perversity will break your necks, as you will discover. I have often told you before to beware of the saying, in Psalm 107[:40], "*Effundit contemptum super principes*" "He pours contempt upon princes." You, however, keep on asking for trouble and want to be hit over the head. And no warning or exhortation will keep you from getting what you want.

Well, then, since you are the cause of this wrath of God, it will undoubtedly come upon you, unless you mend your ways in time. The signs in heaven and the wonders on earth are meant for you, dear lords; they bode no good for you, and no good will come to you. A great part of God's wrath has already come, for God is sending many false teachers and prophets among us, so that through our error and blasphemy we may richly deserve hell and everlasting damnation. The rest of it is now here, for the peasants are banding together, and, unless our repentance moves God to prevent it, this must result in the ruin, destruction, and desolation of Germany by cruel murder and bloodshed.

For you ought to know, dear lords, that God is doing this because this raging of yours cannot, will not, and ought not be endured for long. You must become different men and yield to God's word. If you do not do this amicably and willingly, then you will be compelled to do it by force and destruction. If these peasants do not compel you, others will. Even though you were to defeat them all, they would still not be defeated, for God will raise up others. It is his will to defeat you, and you will be defeated. It is not the peasants, dear lords, who are resisting you; it is God himself, to visit your raging upon you. Some of you have said that you will stake land and people on exterminating the Lutheran teaching. What would you think if you were to turn out to be your own prophets, and your land and people were already at stake? Do not joke with God, dear lords! The Jews, too, said, "We have no king" [John 19:15], and they meant it so seriously that they must be without a king forever.

To make your sin still greater, and guarantee your merciless destruction, some of you are beginning to blame this affair on the gospel and say that it is the fruit of my teaching. Well, well, slander away, dear lords! You did not want to know what I taught or what the gospel is; now the one who will soon teach you is at the door, unless you change your ways. You, and everyone else, must bear witness that I have taught with all quietness, have striven earnestly against rebellion, and have energetically encouraged and exhorted people to obey and respect even you wild and dictatorial tyrants. This rebellion cannot be coming from me. Rather the murder-prophets, who hate me as they hate you, have come among these people and have gone about among them for more than three years, and no one has resisted and fought against them except me.

Therefore, if God intends to punish you and allows the devil through his false prophets to stir up the people against you, and if it is, perhaps, God's will that I shall not be able to prevent it any longer, what can I or my gospel do? Not only have we suffered your persecution and murdering and raging; we have also prayed for you and helped to protect and maintain your rule over the common people. If I desired revenge, I could laugh up my sleeve and simply watch what the peasants are doing or even join in with them and help make matters worse;

may God keep me from this in the future as he has in the past.

…

To the Peasants

So far, dear friends, you have learned only that I agree that it is unfortunately all too true that the princes and lords who forbid the preaching of the gospel and oppress the people unbearably deserve to have God put them down from their thrones [Luke 1:52] because they have sinned so greatly against both God and man. And they have no excuse. Nevertheless, you, too, must be careful that you take up your cause justly and with a good conscience. If you have a good conscience, you have the comforting advantage that God will be with you, and will help you. Even though you did not succeed for a while, or even suffered death, you would win in the end, and you would preserve your souls eternally with all the saints. But if you act unjustly and have a bad conscience, you will be defeated. And even though you might win for a while and even kill all the princes, you would suffer the eternal loss of your body and soul in the end. For you, therefore, this is no laughing matter. The eternal fate of your body and soul is involved. And you must most seriously consider not merely how strong you are and how wrong the princes are, but whether you act justly and with a good conscience.

Therefore, dear brethren, I beg you in a kindly and brotherly way to look carefully at what you are doing and not to believe all kinds of spirits and preachers [1 John 4:1]. For Satan has now raised up many evil spirits of disorder and of murder, and filled the world with them. Just listen attentively, as you offer many times to do. I will not spare you the earnest warning that I owe you, even though some of you have been so poisoned by the murderous spirits that you will hate me for it and call me a hypocrite. That does not worry me; it is enough for me if I save some of the goodhearted and upright men among you from the danger of God's wrath. The rest I fear as little as they despise me much; and they shall not harm me. I know One who is greater and mightier than they are, and he teaches me in Psalm 3[:6], "I am not afraid of ten thousands of people who have set themselves against me round about." My confidence shall outlast their confidence; that I know for sure.

In the first place, dear brethren, you bear the name of God and call yourselves a "Christian association" or union, and you allege that you want to live and act according to divine law. Now you know that the name, word, and titles of God are not to be assumed idly or in vain, as he says in the second commandment, "Thou shalt not take the name of the Lord your God in vain," and adds, "for the Lord will not hold him guiltless who takes his name in vain" [Deut. 5:11]. Here is a clear, plain text, which applies to you, as to all men. It threatens you, as well as us and all others, with God's wrath without regard to your great numbers, rights, and terror. God is mighty enough and strong enough to punish you as he here threatens if his name is taken in vain, and you know it. So if you take his name in vain, you may expect no good fortune but only trouble. Learn from this how to judge yourselves and accept this friendly warning. It would be a simple thing for God, who once drowned the whole world with a flood [Gen. 7:17–24] and destroyed Sodom with fire [Gen. 19:24–28], to kill or defeat so many thousands of peasants. He is an almighty and terrible God.

Second, it is easy to prove that you are taking God's name in vain and putting it to shame; nor is there any doubt that you will, in the end, encounter all misfortune, unless God is not true. For here is God's word, spoken through the mouth of Christ, "All who take the sword will perish by the sword" [Matt. 26:52]. That means nothing else than that no one, by his own violence, shall arrogate authority to himself; but as Paul says, "Let every person be subject to the governing authorities with fear and reverence" [Rom. 13:1].

How can you get around these passages and laws of God when you boast that you are acting according to divine law, and yet take the sword in your own hands, and revolt against "the governing authorities that are instituted by God?" Do you think that Paul's judgment in Romans 13[:2] will not strike you, "He who resists the authorities will incur judgment"? You take God's name in vain when you pretend to be seeking divine right, and under the pretense of his name work contrary to divine right. Be careful, dear sirs. It will not turn out that way in the end.

Third, you say that the rulers are wicked and intolerable, for they will not allow us to have the gospel; they oppress us too hard with the burdens they lay on our property, and they are ruining us in body and soul. I answer: The fact that the rulers are wicked and unjust does not excuse disorder and rebellion, for the punishing of wickedness is not the responsibility of everyone, but of the worldly rulers who bear the sword. Thus Paul says in Romans 13[:4] and Peter, in 1 Peter 3 [2:14], that the rulers are instituted by God for the punishment of the wicked. Then, too, there is the natural law of all the world, which says that no one may sit as judge in his own case or take his own revenge. The proverb is true, "Whoever hits back is in the wrong." Or as it is said, it takes two to start a fight. The divine law agrees with this, and says, in Deuteronomy 32[:35], "Vengeance is mine; I will repay, says the Lord." Now you cannot deny that your rebellion actually involves you in such a way that you make yourselves your own judges and avenge yourselves. You are quite unwilling to suffer any wrong. That is contrary not only to Christian law and the gospel, but also to natural law and all equity.

If your cause is to prosper when the divine and Christian law of the Old and New Testaments and even the natural law are all against you, you must produce a new and special command of God, confirmed by signs and wonders, which commands you to do these things. Otherwise God will not allow his word and ordinance to be broken by your violence. On the contrary, because you boast of the divine law and yet act against it, he will let you fall and be punished terribly, as men who dishonor his name. Then he will condemn you eternally, as was said above. For the word of Christ in Matthew 7[:3] applies to you; you see the speck in the eye of the rulers, but do not see the log in your own eye. The word of Paul in Romans 3[:8] also applies, "Why not do evil that good may come? Their condemnation is just." It is true that the rulers do wrong when they suppress the gospel and oppress you in temporal matters. But you do far greater wrong when you not only suppress God's word, but tread it underfoot, invade his authority and law, and put yourselves above God. Besides, you take from the rulers their authority and right, indeed, everything they have. What do they have left when they have lost their authority?

I make you the judges and leave it to you to decide who is the worse robber, the man who takes a large part of another's goods, but leaves him something, or the man who takes everything that he has, and takes his life besides. The rulers unjustly take your property; that is the one side. On the other hand, you take from them their authority, in which their whole property and life and being consist. Therefore you are far greater robbers than they, and you intend to do worse things than they have done. "Indeed not," you say, "We are going to leave them enough to live on." If anyone wants to believe that, let him! I do not believe it. Anyone who dares go so far as to use force to take away authority, which is the main thing, will not stop at that, but will take the other, smaller thing that depends upon it. The wolf that eats a whole sheep will also eat its ear. And even if you permitted them to keep their life and some property, nevertheless, you would take the best thing they have, namely, their authority, and make yourselves lords over them. That would be too great a robbery and wrong. God will declare you to be the greatest robbers.

Can you not think it through, dear friends? If your enterprise were right, then any man might become judge over another. Then authority, government, law, and order would disappear from the world and there would be nothing but murder and bloodshed. As soon as anyone saw that someone was wronging him, he would begin to judge and punish him. Now if that is unjust and intolerable when done by an individual, we cannot allow a mob or a crowd to do it. However, if we do permit a mob or a crowd to do it, then we cannot rightly and fairly forbid an individual to do it. For in both cases the cause is the same, that is, an injustice. What would you yourselves do if disorder broke out in your ranks and one man set himself against another and took vengeance on him? Would you put up with that? Would you not say that he must let others, whom you appointed, do the judging and avenging? What do you expect God and the world to think when you pass judgment and avenge yourselves on those who have injured you and even upon your rulers, whom God has appointed.

...

Admonition to Both Rulers and Peasants

Now, dear sirs, there is nothing Christian on either side and nothing Christian is at issue between you; both lords and peasants are discussing questions of justice and injustice in heathen, or worldly, terms. Furthermore, both parties are acting against God and are under his wrath, as you have heard. For God's sake, then, take my advice! Take a hold of these matters properly, with justice and not with force or violence and do not start endless bloodshed in Germany. For because both of you are wrong, and both of you want to avenge and defend yourselves, both of you will destroy yourselves and God will use one rascal to flog another.

Both Scripture and history are against you lords, for both tell how tyrants are punished. Even the heathen poets say that tyrants seldom die a dry death, but are usually slain and perish in their own blood. Because, then, it is an established fact that you rule tyrannically and with rage, prohibit preaching of the gospel, and cheat and oppress the poor, you have no reason to be confident or to hope that you will perish in any other way than your kind have always perished.

Look at all the kingdoms that have come to their end by the sword—Assyria, Persia, Israel, Judah, and Rome. In the end they were all destroyed in the same way they destroyed others. Thus God shows that he is Judge upon earth and that he leaves no wrong unpunished. Therefore nothing is more certain than that this same judgment is breathing down your necks, whether it comes now or later, unless you reform.

Scripture and experience are also against you peasants. They teach that rebellion has never had a good end and that God always keeps his word exactly, "He that takes the sword will perish by the sword" [Matt. 26:52]. You are certainly under the wrath of God, because you are doing wrong by judging your own case and avenging yourselves and are bearing the name Christian unworthily. Even though you win and destroy all the lords, you will finally start tearing the flesh from one another's bones, like wild beasts. For because flesh and blood, not spirit, prevails among you, God will soon send an evil spirit among you, as he did to the men of Shechem and to Abimelech [Judg. 9:22–57]. See the end that finally comes to rebellion in the story of Korah, Numbers 16[:31–35], and of Absalom [2 Sam. 18:14–15], of Sheba [2 Sam. 20:22], Zimri [1 Kings 16:18], and others like them. In short, God hates both tyrants and rebels; therefore he sets them against each other, so that both parties perish shamefully, and his wrath and judgment upon the godless are fulfilled.

As I see it, the worst thing about this completely miserable affair is that both sides will sustain irreparable damage; and I would gladly risk my life and even die if I could prevent that from happening. Since neither side fights with a good conscience, but both fight to uphold injustice, it must follow, in the first place, that those who are slain are lost eternally, body and soul, as men who die in their sins, without penitence and without grace, under the wrath of God. Nothing can be done for them. The lords would be fighting to strengthen and maintain their tyranny, their persecution of the gospel, and their unjust oppression of the poor, or else to help that kind of ruler. That is a terrible injustice and is against God. He who commits such a sin must be lost eternally. The peasants, on the other hand, would fight to defend their rebellion and their abuse of the name Christian. Both these things are great sins against God, and he who dies in them or for them must also be lost eternally, and nothing can prevent it.

The second injury is that Germany will be laid waste, and if this bloodshed once starts, it will not stop until everything is destroyed. It is easy to start a fight, but we cannot stop the fighting whenever we want to. What have all these innocent women, children, and old people, whom you fools are drawing with you into such danger, ever done to you? Why do you insist on filling the land with blood and robbery, widows and orphans? Oh, the devil has wicked plans! And God is angry; he threatens to let the devil loose upon us and cool his rage in our blood and souls. Beware, dear sirs, and be wise! Both of you are equally involved! What good will it do you intentionally to damn yourselves for all eternity and, in addition, to bequeath a desolate, devastated, and bloody land to your descendants, when you still have time to find a better solution by repenting before God, by concluding a friendly agreement, or even by voluntarily suffering for the sake of humanity?

You will accomplish nothing through strife and violence.

I, therefore, sincerely advise you to choose certain counts and lords from among the nobility and certain councilmen from the cities and ask them to arbitrate and settle this dispute amicably. You lords, stop being so stubborn! You will finally have to stop being such oppressive tyrants—whether you want to or not. Give these poor people room in which to live and air to breathe. You peasants, let yourselves be instructed and give up the excessive demands of some of your articles. In this way it may be possible to reach a solution of this dispute through human laws and agreements, if not through Christian means.

If you do not follow this advice—God forbid!—I must let you come to blows. But I am innocent of your souls, your blood, or your property. The guilt is yours alone. I have told you that you are both wrong and that what you are fighting for is wrong. You lords are not fighting against Christians—Christians do nothing against you; they prefer to suffer all things—but against outright robbers and defamers of the Christian name. Those of them who die are already condemned eternally. On the other hand, you peasants are not fighting against Christians, but against tyrants, and persecutors of God and man, and murderers of the saints of Christ. Those of them who die are also condemned eternally. There you have God's sure verdict upon both parties. This I know. Do what you please to preserve your bodies and souls, if you will not accept my advice.

I, however, will pray to my God that he will either reconcile you both and bring about an agreement between you, or else graciously prevent things from turning out as you intend. Nonetheless, the terrible signs and wonders that have come to pass in these times give me a heavy heart and make me fear that God's wrath has grown too great; as he says in Jeremiah [15:1; and Ezek. 14:14], "Though Noah, Job, and Daniel stood before me, I would have no pleasure in the people." Would to God that you might fear his wrath and amend your ways that this disaster might be delayed and postponed a while! In any case, my conscience assures me that I have faithfully given you my Christian and fraternal advice. God grant that it helps! Amen.

16. MARTIN LUTHER (1483–1546)

Probably the most infamous of Luther's treatises, Against the Robbing and Murdering Hordes *was published in May 1525 as a reaction to the peasants' revolt. Here Luther (see selection 13) moves away from his moderate sympathy for peasant grievances to wholly and heartily condemn their choice to act violently against the authorities erected by God. He urges the authorities to take whatever means are necessary to suppress the revolt, characterizing any death in that cause as a martyrdom. He does not waste the opportunity to remind both peasants and rulers that the religious reform he is calling for is a purely spiritual one, and that both groups should look to the state of their souls and then behave as appropriate for Christians: while he notes that the rulers may have brought the violence upon themselves by their bad behavior, he makes no concessions to the rebels as a result. This treatise was condemned by many reformers after the revolt was brutally suppressed, but Luther stood by his arguments.*

Against the Robbing and Murdering Hordes

In my earlier book on this matter, I did not venture to judge the peasants, since they had offered to be corrected and to be instructed; and Christ in Matthew 7[:1] commands us not to judge. But before I could even inspect the situation, they forgot their promise and violently took matters into their own hands and are robbing and raging like mad dogs. All this now makes it clear that they were trying to deceive us and that the assertions they made in their *Twelve Articles* were nothing but lies presented under the name of the gospel. To put it briefly, they are doing the devil's work. This is particularly the work of that archdevil who rules at Muhlhausen [Thomas Müntzer, 1489–1525], and does nothing except stir up robbery, murder, and bloodshed; as Christ describes him in John 8[:44], "He was a murderer from the beginning." Since these peasants and wretched people have now let themselves be misled and are acting differently than they promised, I, too, must write differently of them than I have written, and begin by setting their sin before them, as God commands Isaiah [58:1] and Ezekiel [2:7], on the chance that some of them may see themselves for what they are. Then I must instruct the rulers how they are to conduct themselves in these circumstances.

The peasants have taken upon themselves the burden of three terrible sins against God and man; by this they have abundantly merited death in body and soul. In the first place, they have sworn to be true and faithful, submissive and obedient, to their rulers, as Christ commands when he says, "Render to Caesar the things that are Caesars" [Luke 20:25]. And Romans 13[:1] says, "Let every person be subject to the governing authorities." Since they are now deliberately and violently breaking this oath of obedience and setting themselves in opposition to their masters, they have forfeited body and soul, as faithless, perjured, lying, disobedient rascals and scoundrels usually do. St. Paul passed this judgment on them in Romans 13[:2] when he said that those who resist the authorities will bring a judgment upon themselves. This saying will smite the peasants sooner or later, for God wants people to be loyal and to do their duty.

In the second place, they are starting a rebellion, and are violently robbing and plundering monasteries and castles which are not theirs; by this they have doubly deserved death in body and soul as highwaymen and murderers. Furthermore, anyone who can be proved to be a seditious person is an outlaw before God and the emperor; and whoever is the first to put him to death does right and well. For if a man is in open rebellion, everyone is both his judge and his executioner; just as when a fire starts, the first man who can put it out is the best man to do the job. For rebellion is not just simple murder; it is like a great fire, which attacks and devastates a whole land. Thus rebellion brings with it a land filled with murder and bloodshed; it makes widows and orphans, and turns everything upside down, like the worst disaster. Therefore let everyone who can, smite, slay, and stab, secretly or openly, remembering that nothing can be more poisonous, hurtful, or devilish than a rebel. It is just as when one must kill a mad dog; if you do not strike him, he will strike you, and a whole land with you.

In the third place, they cloak this terrible and horrible sin with the gospel, call themselves "Christian brethren," take oaths and submit to them, and compel people to go along with them in these abominations. Thus they become the worst blasphemers of God and slanderers of his holy name. Under the outward appearance of the gospel, they honor and serve the devil, thus deserving death in body and soul ten times over. I have never heard of a more hideous sin. I suspect that the devil feels that the Last Day is coming and therefore he undertakes such an unheard-of act, as though saying to himself, "This is the end, therefore it shall be the worst; I will stir up the dregs and knock out the bottom." God will guard us against him! See what a mighty prince the devil is, how he has the world in his hands and can throw everything into confusion, when he can so quickly catch so many thousands of peasants, deceive them, blind them, harden them, and throw them into revolt, and do with them whatever his raging fury undertakes.

It does not help the peasants when they pretend that according to Genesis 1 and 2 all things were created free and common, and that all of us alike have been baptized. For under the New Testament, Moses does not count; for there stands our Master, Christ, and subjects us, along with our bodies and our property, to the emperor and the law of this world, when he says, "Render to Caesar the things that are Caesars" [Luke 20:25]. Paul, too, speaking in Romans 12 [13:1] [sic] to all baptized Christians, says, "Let every person be subject to the governing authorities." And Peter says, "Be subject to every ordinance of man" [1 Pet. 2:13]. We are bound to live according to this teaching of Christ, as the Father commands from heaven, saying, "This is my beloved Son, listen to him" [Matt 17:5].

For baptism does not make men free in body and property, but in soul; and the gospel does not make goods common, except in the case of those who, of their own free will, do what the apostles and disciples did in Acts 4[:32–37]. They did not demand, as do our insane peasants in their raging, that the goods of others—of Pilate and Herod—should be common, but only their own goods. Our peasants, however, want to make the goods of other men common, and keep their own for themselves. Fine Christians they are! I think there is not a devil left in hell; they have all gone into the peasants. Their raving has gone beyond all measure. Now since the peasants have brought [the wrath of] both God and man down upon themselves and are already many times guilty of death in body and soul, and since they submit to no court and wait for no verdict, but only rage on, I must instruct the temporal authorities on how they may act with a clear conscience in this matter.

First, I will not oppose a ruler who, even though he does not tolerate the gospel, will smite and punish these peasants without first offering to submit the case to judgment. He is within his rights, since the peasants are not contending any longer for the gospel, but have become faithless, perjured, disobedient, rebellious murderers, robbers, and blasphemers, whom even a heathen ruler has the right and authority to punish. Indeed, it is his duty to punish such scoundrels, for this is why he bears the sword and is "the servant of God to execute his wrath on the wrongdoer," Romans 13[:4].

But if the ruler is a Christian and tolerates the gospel, so that the peasants have no appearance of a case against him, he should proceed with fear. First he must take the matter to God, confessing that we have deserved these things, and remembering that God may, perhaps, have thus aroused the devil as a punishment upon all Germany. Then he should humbly pray for help against the devil, for we are contending not only "against flesh and blood," but "against the spiritual hosts of wickedness in the air" [Eph. 6:12; 2:2], which must be attacked with prayer. Then, when our hearts are so turned to God that we are ready to let his divine will be done, whether he will or will not have us to be princes and lords, we must go beyond our duty, and offer the mad peasants an opportunity to come to terms, even though they are not worthy of it. Finally, if that does not help, then swiftly take to the sword.

For in this case a prince and lord must remember that according to Romans 13[:4] he is God's minister and the servant of his wrath and that the sword has been given him to use against such people. If he does not fulfill the duties of his office by punishing some and protecting others, he commits as great a sin before God as when someone who has not been given the sword commits murder. If he is able to punish and does not do it—even though he would have had to kill someone or shed blood—he becomes guilty of all the murder and evil that these people commit. For by deliberately disregarding God's command he permits such rascals to go about their wicked business, even though he was able to prevent it and it was his duty to do so. This is not a time to sleep. And there is no place for patience or mercy. This is the time of the sword, not the day of grace.

The rulers, then, should press on and take action in this matter with a good conscience as long as their hearts still beat. It is to the rulers' advantage that the peasants have a bad conscience and an unjust cause, and that any peasant who is killed is lost in body and soul and is eternally the devil's. But the rulers have a good conscience and a just cause; they can, therefore, say to God with all confidence of heart, "Behold, my God, you have appointed me prince or lord, of this I can have no doubt; and you have given me the sword to use against evildoers, Romans 13[:4]. It is your word, and it cannot lie, so I must fulfill the duties of my office, or forfeit your grace. It is also plain that these peasants have deserved death many times over, in your eyes and in the eyes of the world, and have been committed to me for punishment. If you will me to be slain by them, and let my authority be taken from me and destroyed, so be it: let your will be done. I shall be defeated and die because of your divine command and word and shall die while obeying your command and fulfilling the duties of my office. Therefore I will punish and smite as long as my heart beats. You will be the judge and make things right."

Thus, anyone who is killed fighting on the side of the rulers may be a true martyr in the eyes of God, if he fights with the kind of conscience I have just described, for he acts in obedience to God's word. On the other hand, anyone who perishes on the peasants' side is an eternal firebrand of hell, for he bears the sword against God's word and is disobedient to him, and is a member of the devil. And even if the peasants happen to gain the upper hand (God forbid!)—for to God all things are possible, and we do not know whether it may be his will, through the devil, to destroy all rule and order and cast the world upon a desolate heap, as a prelude to the Last Day, which cannot be far off—nevertheless, those who are found exercising the duties of their office can die without worry and go to the scaffold with a good conscience, and leave the kingdom of this world to the devil and take in exchange the everlasting kingdom. These are strange times, when a prince can win heaven with bloodshed better than other men with prayer!

Finally, there is another thing that ought to motivate the rulers. The peasants are not content with belonging to the devil themselves; they force and compel many good people to join their devilish league against their wills, and so make them partakers of all of their own wickedness and damnation. Anyone who consorts with them goes to the devil with them and is guilty of all the evil deeds that they commit, even though he has to do this because he is so weak in faith that he could not resist them. A pious Christian ought to suffer a hundred deaths rather than give a hairsbreadth of consent to the peasants' cause. O how many martyrs could now be made by the bloodthirsty peasants and the prophets of murder! Now the rulers ought to have mercy on these prisoners of the peasants, and if they had no other reason to use the sword with a good conscience against the peasants, and to risk their own lives and property in fighting them, this would be reason enough, and more than enough: they would be rescuing and helping these souls whom the peasants have forced into their devilish league and who, without willing it, are sinning so horribly and must be damned. For truly these souls are in purgatory; indeed, they are in the bonds of hell and the devil.

Therefore, dear lords, here is a place where you can release, rescue, help. Have mercy on these poor people!

Let whoever can stab, smite, slay. If you die in doing it, good for you! A more blessed death can never be yours, for you die while obeying the divine word and commandment in Romans 13[:1, 2], and in loving service of your neighbor, whom you are rescuing from the bonds of hell and of the devil. And so I beg everyone who can to flee from the peasants as from the devil himself; those who do not flee, I pray that God will enlighten and convert. As for those who are not to be converted, God grant that they may have neither fortune nor success. To this let every pious Christian say, "Amen!" For this prayer is right and good, and pleases God; this I know. If anyone thinks this too harsh, let him remember that rebellion is intolerable and that the destruction of the world is to be expected every hour.

17. THOMAS MÜNTZER (1489–1525)

Müntzer was born in 1489 and was educated at Leipzig and Frankfurt, becoming skilled in Hebrew, Greek, and Latin. He entered a monastery but was convinced to leave by Luther's revolt and traveled to Wittenberg. Luther fell out with Müntzer, however, and Müntzer left, arriving eventually in Prague in 1521, where he wrote his Prague Manifesto, *a provocative and anticlerical tract that indicated how closely he had moved toward the radical reformation. He was also becoming more apocalyptic in his preaching, sympathetic to Anabaptism and convinced of his access to divine prophecy. His beliefs were also becoming more politically radical, leading to his formation in the town of Mulhausen of a communist experiment, led by a radical committee of the Eternal League of God. In May 1525 he led a peasant army during the Peasants' War in the Battle of Frankenhausen. He was defeated, captured, and beheaded at Mulhausen.*

A Highly Provoked Defense

Vindication and Refutation

A highly provoked vindication and a refutation of the unspiritual soft-living flesh in Wittenberg, whose robbery and distortion of scripture has so grievously polluted our wretched Christian church.

[From] Thomas Müntzer of Allstedt: From the cave of Elijah, whose zeal spares no one. [1] Kings 18; Matthew 17[:10]; Luke 1[:17]; Revelation 11[:3– 6]; Anno 1524. O Lord, deliver me from the calumnies of men that I may keep your commandments, and I will proclaim the truth hidden in your son, lest the wiles of the evil-doers continue to flourish.

To his Eminence, the first-born prince and almighty lord, Jesus Christ, the kindly king of kings, the valiant leader of all believers, to my most gracious lord and true protector, and to his grieving and only bride, the poor Christian Church.

All glory, fame and honor, all dignity and splendor and acclamation be given to you alone, eternal son of God, Philippians 2[:9]. Your holy spirit has always suffered the fate of being treated by these merciless lions, the biblical scholars, as the worst of devils, John 8[:48]; although the holy spirit was yours in inexhaustible measure from the very beginning, John 3[:34], and all the elect have received it from your fullness, John 1[:16], and it has dwelt in them. 1 Cor. 3[:16], 6[:19]; 2 Cor. 1[:21]; Eph. 1[:13]; Psalm 5[:8]. You give it to all who hasten towards you, according to the measure of their faith, Eph.

4[:7]; Psalm 68[:18]. Anyone, on the other hand, who does not have it to give infallible testimony to his own spirit has nothing to do with you, O Christ; Romans 8[:9] gives you the irrefutable testimony to that, Psalm 92[:5].

Hence there is nothing so very surprising about Doctor Liar [i.e., Luther], that most ambitious of all the biblical scholars, becoming a more arrogant fool every day, covering himself up with your Holy Scripture and most deceitfully arming himself with it, but in no way renouncing fame and easy living. For the last thing he intends is to make you his first concern, Isaiah 58[:6]. As if he had access (through you, the very portal of truth) to your judgments, he is insolent to your very face, utterly despising your true spirit for, driven by his raging envy and his most bitter hate, he has betrayed his true colors by denouncing me. Without true or just cause he has made me a laughing-stock among his scornful, jeering, ruthless companions and has jeeringly traduced my name in the eyes of the simple, making me out to be a satan or a devil, although I am a ransomed member of your body. Such scandalous conduct can never be made good.

In you, however, my joy is full, and your gentle consolation satisfies me completely, for as you have proclaimed so graciously to your real friends in Matthew 10[:24]: "The pupil will not have it any better than the master." Now if they were blasphemous enough to call you Beelzebub, my innocent leader and comforting savior, how much more will they do this to me, your tireless warrior, once I have shaken off that flattering rascal at Wittenberg and followed your voice, John 10[:4]. Yes, this is how things are bound to be, if one is not prepared to let soft-living and self-willed men get away with their counterfeit faith and their pharisaical dodges, but sees to it that their fame and pomp declines. Even you [Christ] were not able to get them to recognize your superiority. They preferred to think that they were more learned than you and your disciples. Indeed they probably were more learned, with their stubborn literalism, than our Doctor Lampooner [i.e., Luther] can ever be. Even though their fame and reputation were so widespread throughout the world they had no right to devise clever plans against you, trying to refute you from the clear word of Scripture, as in their reproof of Nicodemus, John 7[:50] and in their arguments about the Sabbath, John 5[:9], and in [John] chapter 9[:14]. They mobilized the whole of Scripture against you with all the energy at their command, saying that you would and should die for daring to confess boldly that you were a son of God, born of the eternal father, as we confess of your spirit. Hence they said: We have a law, and according to it he must die. For they twisted the text of Deuteronomy 13[:1–5] and 18[:10] to refer to you, and refused to look at it in a broader context. I am now being treated in exactly the same way by that sly robber of Scripture, who pours out his scorn at just those points where Scripture is clearest, in his fiery jealousy calling the spirit of God a devil.

…

All I have done to that wily black crow released by Noah from the Ark as a sign is this: like an innocent dove I have flapped my wings, covered them with silver, which has been purified seven times and gilded my back, Psalm 68, and flown over the carrion on which he likes to perch. How I loathed it! I will let the whole world know his hypocrisy towards these godless rascals, as seen in his book against me. He is, in brief, their advocate. It is quite clear then, that Doctor Liar does not dwell in the house of God, Psalm 15[:4] since he does not despise the godless, but denounces many God-fearing men as devils or rebellious spirits in order to serve the interests of the godless. The black crow knows this very well. He pecks out the eyes of the pigs to turn them into carrion, he blinds these pleasure-loving people. For he is indulgent about their faults in order to eat his fill of their wealth and honors and especially of the fine-sounding titles at their disposal.

The Jews wanted to see Christ insulted and humiliated on every occasion, just as Luther now tries to treat me. He denounces me fiercely and reproaches me with the mercifulness of the son of God and of his dear friends. This is his retort to my preaching about the earnestness of the law, and the punishment of unspiritual sinners. For (even if they happen to be rulers) this is not abolished but is to be executed with the very greatest severity. Paul instructed Timothy (and through him all pastors) to preach this to the people, 1 Tim. 1[:9]. He says clearly that (punishment) will visit all who combat and try to subvert sound teaching. No one can deny this. It is stated clearly and unambiguously in Deuteronomy, chapter 13[:6], and Paul pronounces the same judgment against the unchaste sinner. 1 Cor. 5[:1–5]. Although I have had my sermon printed in which, arguing from Scripture, I told the princes of Saxony quite frankly that if they were to avert an uprising they must use the sword: that, in short, disobedience must be punished, and neither great or small would be exempt, Numbers 25[:4].

Despite all this that indulgent fellow, Father Pussyfoot [i.e., Luther], comes along and says I want to stir up an insurrection. This is how he understands my letter to the mine-workers. He says one thing, but suppresses the most vital point for, as I expounded quite clearly to the princes, the power of the sword as well as the key to release sins is in the hands of the whole community. From the passages in Daniel 7[:27], Revelation 6[:15], Romans 13[:1], and 1 Samuel 8, I pointed out that the princes are not lords over the sword but servants of it. They should not act as they please, but execute justice, Deut. 17[:18]. Hence it is a good old custom that the people must be present if someone is to be judged properly by the law of God, Num. 15[:35]. Why? So that if the authorities try to give a corrupt judgment, Isaiah 10[:1] the Christians present can object and prevent this happening, since anyone spilling innocent blood will be accountable to God, Psalm 79. There is no greater abomination on earth than the fact that no one is prepared to take up the cause of the needy. The great do whatever they please, as Job describes in chapter 41.

The poor flatterer tries to use Christ to cover himself, adducing a counterfeit type of clemency which is contrary to Paul's text in 1 Timothy 1[:7–11]. In his book about trade, however, he says that the princes should not hesitate to join the thieves and robbers in their raids. He suppresses here, however, the basic reason for all theft. He is a herald, who hopes to earn gratitude by approving the spilling of people's blood for the sake of their earthly goods; something which God has never commanded or approved. Open your eyes! What is the evil brew from which all usury, theft and robbery springs but the assumption of our lords and princes that all creatures are their property? The fish in the water, the birds in the air, the plants on the face of the earth—it all has to belong to them! Isaiah 5[:8]. To add insult to injury, they have God's commandment proclaimed to the poor: God has commanded that you should not steal. But it avails them nothing. For while they do violence to everyone, flay and fleece the poor farm worker, tradesman and everything that breathes, Micah 3[:2], yet should any of the latter commit the pettiest crime, he must hang. And Doctor Liar responds, Amen. It is the lords themselves who make the poor man their enemy. If they refuse to do away with the causes of insurrection how can trouble be avoided in the long run? If saying that makes me an inciter to insurrection, so be it!

...

He claims that he will deal with everything by discussion, but refuses to start discussing my case, so it can be justified or condemned. All he does is urge the mighty that no one should follow my teaching since it leads to insurrection. Anyone who wants to judge this matter fairly should neither love insurrection nor, on the other hand, should he be averse to a justified uprising. His outlook must be a balanced one; otherwise he will either hate my teaching too much or have ulterior reasons for loving it too much. This is the last thing I want.

It would certainly be more profitable for me to spend my time instructing the poor people with good teaching rather than getting myself entangled with this blasphemous monk, who now makes himself out to be a new Christ, one who has purchased so many good things for the Christian people by his blood and striven as well for this noble cause: that priests may take wives. What should I answer to that? Perhaps I will find nothing to say, for (or so you think) you have an answer to everything. Look how nobly you sacrificed the poor priests to the chopping block, saying in your comment on the Emperor's first edict: It had to be endured, in order to safeguard the teaching you had initiated. For in your hypocritical way you would be happy enough to have them taken away. In this way you would steadily accumulate new martyrs and could have sung a song or two about them, and would then have been confirmed as a genuine savior. Then indeed you would sing—as only you can—*Nunc dimittis* etc. [Luke 2:2], for all to sing after you. All you need to do, monk, is dance and the whole world falls at your feet.

But if you are a savior, then a mighty strange one! Christ renders all glory to his father, John 8[:54] and says: "If I pursue my own honor then it is nothing." But what you want from the people in Orlamünde is a great title. You go and steal (like the black crow you are) the name "son of God" and expect the gratitude of your prince. Have you not read, you most learned wretch, what God says through Isaiah in chapter 42[:8]: "I will give my glory to no one?" Why not call the good people what Festus is called by Paul in the histories of the apostles, chapter 25[:1]? Why do you call the princes "Your Eminences"? For the title does not belong to them but to Christ, Hebrews 1[:3], John 1, 8[:12]. Why do you call them "High-born"? I thought you were a Christian, but in fact you are an arch-heathen, making them your Joves, your Muses; perhaps not born from the shame of women, as the Wisdom of Solomon puts it, chapter 7[:2], but out of the forehead. It is all too much, too much!

You should be ashamed of yourself, you arch-wretch! Are you trying to patch up a hypocritical accommodation with this erring world? Luke 9[:25]. You who wanted to judge all men! You choose well, though, the objects of your insults. The poor monks and priests and merchants cannot defend themselves. So it is easy for you to insult them! But the godless rulers are to be immune from criticism, even if they tread Christ underfoot. But to satisfy the peasants you write that the princes will meet their end through the word of God, and in your gloss on the latest imperial edict you say: The princes will be cast down from their seats. You prefer them, though, to the merchants. You should give your princes a tug at the nose too! Is it not conceivable that they have merited it more than the others? What concessions do they make? On the interest they charge, on their extortions? But though you have scolded the princes you can give them fresh courage again, you new pope, by presenting them with monasteries and churches. Then they will be happy with you. That's what I would advise you, lest the peasants take matters into their own hands. You are always talking about faith and alleging that I want to do battle with you while shielded and sheltered by you, but that just illustrates my uprightness and your folly. I have been as much shielded and sheltered by you as a sheep by a wolf, Matthew 10[:16]. Is it not a fact that you had more power over me there than anywhere else? Couldn't you take that into consideration? What other consequences could that have had? The reason I was in your princedom was to give you no excuse. Under your shield and shelter you say. Oho! how you give yourself away! I take it you're a prince too? What right have you to puff yourself up about your shield and shelter? ... Do you imagine that the whole province doesn't know how you shield and shelter them? God have mercy on the Christian people. Is not he who has created it its protector? Psalm 111.

MOTHERS OF THE CHURCH
18. KATHARINA SCHÜTZ ZELL (1498–1562)

Katharina Schütz was born in 1498 to artisan parents in Strasbourg, then part of the Holy Roman Empire, where she received a good vernacular education. Her family was devout, and at a young age Katharina dedicated herself to a life of virginity. She seems to have suffered from great anxiety about her salvation and was attracted to Luther's teachings at an early date. Matthew Zell was one of the most popular preachers of Luther's ideas in Strasbourg, and Katharina seems to have accepted his preaching some time in 1522 and married him in December 1523. The Reformation in Strasbourg was still insecure, and the decision to marry was a risky one for them both. This led to her first writing, a defense of clerical marriage originally sent to the local bishop and published in September 1524. Since Catholic priests were forbidden to marry, not only was this marriage a clear statement of faith for both Katharina and Matthew, but it also meant that she had to develop a new role for herself as one of the first-ever pastor's wives under the critical eyes of both Catholic and Protestant critics. The task was made easier by the fact that her marriage was a happy one and her husband seems to have accepted her as an equal partner both in the household and, increasingly, in his ministry. Their two children died young, in 1528 and c. 1532, so Katharina had more time for the ministry than most pastor's wives.

Strasbourg was torn by the Reformation, as were many German cities, but by 1525 the city government had accepted the new religious teaching and by 1529 had abolished the Mass completely. Growing divisions between the reformers and conflict with the Catholic emperor meant that the next two decades were challenging, and in 1547 the Protestant Schmalkaldic League was defeated by the emperor's forces. Matthew Zell died in January 1548, just as the city was working out the implications of the Augsburg Interim and seeing the return of Catholic worship. By the 1550s the Protestants had split among themselves and there was a good deal of tension in Strasbourg between the various groups. Katharina had difficulty accepting the tensions of the second-generation reformers, valuing the teaching of all who broke with Rome and held to the central tenets of the Gospel and refusing to be classified as belonging to any faction. This letter is one of her last writings, in which she clashes with Ludwig Rabus (1523–92), Matthew Zell's successor, over the legacy of the early Strasbourg reform and her role in it, and makes clear just how radical her husband's assumption of equality was for a second-generation reformer. A response from Rabus follows. Katharina died in September 1562.

Letter to . . . Strasbourg

I, Katharina Zell, the respectable widow of Matthew Zell, the blessed departed preacher of Strasbourg, wish you, dear Church and Citizenship of Strasbourg (in which I was born, brought up, and still live), peace and increase of the grace of God, through true faith in the resurrected Son of God, our Lord Jesus Christ, who is preached to you with such great faithfulness and diligence [Rom. 1:7].

Through His special grace and undeserved love, this Christ called me, a poor woman, to the holy and true knowledge of Him. Yes, from my youth on He drew me to Him, and so it is fitting that I extol and praise His holy name and always speak of His love and goodness. I hope I have done that till now, and I ought and wish to do so to the end, in this weak struggling church on earth. And then, in the victorious triumphant church of the communion of all the angels and saints, I will eternally honor and confess the Lamb of God who is the lion of the race of Judah and branch of the root of David [Gal. 1:15; Psalm 103:1; Rev. 5:5]. With the holy old Anna in the temple of God, I praise the Lord and speak of His Son Christ to all who wait with me for redemption and the coming of His glorious appearing [Luke 2:36–38].

Since then the Lord drew me from my mother's womb and taught me from my youth, I have diligently busied myself with His church and its household affairs, working gladly and constantly. I have dealt faithfully according to the measure of my understanding and the graces given to me, without deception, and I have earnestly sought what is of the Lord Jesus [Rom. 12:6; Eph. 4:7]. So when I was still young all the parish priests and those related to the church loved and feared me. Therefore also my devout husband Matthew Zell, at the beginning of his preaching of the Gospel, sought me for his wedded companion. I was also a faithful help to him in his [ecclesiastical] office and household management, to the honor of Christ, who will also bear witness to this before all believers and unbelievers on the great day of His judgment, when all will be revealed. It will be seen that I have not acted according to the measure of a woman but have done faithfully and simply according to the measure of the gift that God through His Spirit has given to me, with great joy and effort, day and night. So, constantly, joyously, and strongly, with all good will have I given my body, strength, honor, and goods for you, dear Strasbourg; I have made them a footstool for you [Matt. 25:31ff; Rev. 20:12; Eph. 4:7; Psalm 110:1]. My devout husband too was very heartily glad to allow this, and he also loved me very much for it; he often allowed there to be something lacking in his own physical and household needs because of my absence and gladly sent me as a gift to the community; also, at his death he commended me to continue such activity—not with a command, but with a friendly request.

Also I hope that I have faithfully followed that. For I remained in the pastor's house still two years and eleven weeks after his death. I received refugees and the poor, helped to maintain the church, and did good to them all at my own expense without anyone's financial support; I harbored faithful and upright preachers as guests. Among others, namely, there was the dear man Marx Heilandt from Kalb in Württemberg when he was put out of his pulpit; I maintained and recommended him and, against the will of some of the clergy (who were beginning to be overly irritable), he came again to the pulpit of a church and also served there until the end of his life. So up till now, besides bearing my own great crosses and severe illnesses, I have gladly served many with counsel and deed, according to my ability (as much as God has bestowed on me)—as I was also obligated before God to do, and as my husband commended to me at the end. I have gladly followed his behest since I know that it is godly and came out of God's behest [Matt. 25:31ff].

Meanwhile, then, O Strasbourg, my good husband, who served you for thirty years in the office of preacher, who loved you so much and cared for you so faithfully (you know that, don't you?), also at his end, when he was in great difficulty and misery, he did not forget you; he faithfully prayed to God for you and with great earnestness commended you to the chief shepherd Christ Himself [1 Peter 5:4]. And I also have loved and served you, Strasbourg, from my youth, as I still also do in my old age and almost sixty years. And I seek to serve you until the end, while I am able, and also to defend you with mind and body. So I must also tell you what has now happened to me—not for the sake of getting your help, and also not so that you should be provoked to anger with anyone, but only that you may pray to God for me, that He may give me patience, joy, and a sure conscience in this matter.

Since I was ten years old I have been a church mother, a nurturer of the pulpit and school. I have loved all the clergy, visited many, and had conversations with them—not about dances, worldly pleasures, riches, or carnival, but about the kingdom of God. Therefore also my father, mother, friends, and fellow citizens, and also many clergy (whom I have much questioned in order to learn) have held me in great love, honor, and fear. Since, however, my distress about the kingdom of heaven grew great and in all my hard works, worship, and great pain of body I could not find or obtain from all the clergy any comfort or certainty of the love and grace of God, I became weak and sick to death in soul and body [Luke 7:2; Phil. 2:27]. I was like the poor little woman in the Gospel who spent all her property and strength with doctors but lost yet more. However, when she heard of Christ and came to Him, then she was helped and healed by Him [Mark 5:25–34].

So it was for me also and for many afflicted hearts who were then in great distress along with me: many honorable old women and virgins who sought out my company and were glad to be my companions. We were in such anxiety and worry about the grace of God, but we could never find any peace in all our many works, practices, and sacraments of that [Roman] church. Then God had mercy on us and many people. He awakened and sent out by tongue and writings the dear and now blessed Dr. Martin Luther, who described the Lord Jesus Christ for me and others in such a lovely way that I thought I had been drawn up out of the depths of the earth, yes, out of grim bitter hell, into the sweet lovely kingdom of heaven. So I thought of the word that the Lord Christ said to Peter, "I will make you a fisher of people and henceforth you shall catch people" [Luke 5:10]. And I have striven day and night that I might grasp the way of the truth of God, which is Christ the Son of God [John 14:6]. What distress I have drawn upon myself because I have here learned to know and helped to confess the Gospel that I commit to God. Then when I married my good husband, that was counted as a disgrace, outrage, calumny, and falsehood. God knows it all! And the work that fell on me, in the house and out, those who now rest in God and those who still live can well testify to it, and to how I have helped build up the Gospel, received refugees, comforted the sorrowing, and loved and furthered the church, pulpit, and school. All those things will console my good conscience before God [1 Peter 3:16] (even if the world has forgotten or disregarded them): how I have honored, loved, sheltered so many fine learned men with my dear husband and with him—and with much work and expense—I have visited many dear men in cities and lands far and near. I did not cease to persevere: I heard their sayings and sermons, read their books, received their letters with joy, and they received mine with joy. All this will be known after my death, what I left behind.

In summary, I am writing all this because I must show how in my younger days I was so dear to the fine old learned men and architects of the church of Christ—those who now rest in the Lord from their work and some who are still alive. They never withheld from me their conversation about holy matters and they gladly (from the heart) heard mine [Heb. 4:10]. I devoted myself to that conversation about holy matters and gave no place to any worldly foolishness. Since I was waiting for the kingdom of God, my desire, longing, and joy was always only to speak of and be busy with these same (holy) things. Therefore also the dear saintly men sought my company and took pleasure in it—to God be all the glory.

Now, however, in my old age, this is all forgotten and disregarded by these [new] clergy, as well as all the honor, faithfulness, love, and motherly heart that I have shown to them themselves. Yes, it is not only forgotten, but reckoned as disgrace and outrage, although not by all, but only by some, and namely one, whom you, dear church in Strasbourg, received in his youth, loved and honored. But he has ungratefully turned his back on you, on account of which unworthy act I could not keep silence. I wrote to him in an admonishing and rebuking way—for I have seen that all the world practices hypocrisy with each other, including brothers in the faith with each other; no one calls another to account (to his face) as Saint Paul did with dear Peter over a lesser matter [Gal. 2:11–14]. I was also grieved for and motivated by many dear people who have been so greatly scandalized by him, who have come to me, weeping and afflicted, as one to whom they can still come for refuge, as still a little piece of the rib of the blessed Matthew Zell [Gen. 2:21–22].

This one is namely Mr. Ludwig Rabus, now preacher in the city of Ulm. Dear Strasbourg, I must let you read what disrespect this man has shown me and what he has written in answer to my faithful writing, which I sent to him on account of his injudicious departure. Since, however, I cannot carry it from house to house, to each one individually, I have permitted it to be published so that all may read and judge for themselves. For I think he may well suffer this, and perhaps think that it is ostensibly an honor (to have his name in print, since he was so eager to publish his martyrology). So I also am not ashamed of letting what he said to me be known, because of the words of Christ: "They will malign you for the sake of the truth and my name; rejoice when they speak evil of you and lie about you, your reward is great in heaven" [Matt. 5:11–12]. Therefore I do not seek to have him injured by a sharp word said to him on my account; I am not at all distressed by a letter like his and quite at peace with it because my heart and conscience are right before God. Yes, his letter gives me more reason to thank God that I am not as Rabus describes me and to ask God also to continue to protect me from such. Furthermore, if I could do Mr. Ludwig good in soul or body, I would, despite this wicked letter and other brutality that he has done to me verbally, and also despite the wicked and false reputation about me that he has spread in city and country: that I have fallen away from the Gospel and am no longer of the faith and teaching of my dear husband and of other Christians.

All of that (abuse and lies) would not hinder me from doing good to him and his, according to the saying and teaching of the Lord Christ [Matt. 5:44]. He encountered greater insults than I, but as Saint Peter said, "He did not strike back when He was struck" [1 Peter 2:23]. If God wills, that is also what I want to do toward Rabus: he should not make me upset or angry with his wicked letter; as the wise man teaches me and says, "When someone stronger than you goes against your will, do not let yourself be provoked" [Eccl. 6:10]. That is what I want to do, as much as I am able. What I wrote to him, which motivated him and gave him reason to write me such an injudicious wicked letter, I have also permitted to be put here so that you can read both letters, mine and his, and can recognize with Christian judgment who has behaved in a less heated, more friendly, more Christian fashion toward the other. I also wrote to him alone in private, so that he might consider his injustice in private and pray to God for it, and I wanted to let what I wrote remain between him and me. Since, however, he has sent me such an insulting letter as answer, I cannot leave the matter as if he were in the right and keep silence as if I were the way he describes me. For that I take an example from our Lord Christ, when He spoke to the bishop's servant: "If I have spoken evil, give witness to that; but if I have spoken rightly, why then do you strike me?" [John 18:(22–)23]. So I say also to Mr. Ludwig, if what I have spoken and written is evil, then he should give truthful witness to it and tell me what is wrong with it; but if it is not wrong, why then does he insult and condemn me this way? Otherwise, according to the teaching of Christ our Lord, I will gladly do good to my enemy, and according to the saying of Saint Paul, put burning coals on his head [Matt. 5:44; Rom. 12:20].

So that you, dear Strasbourg, may know why I have first introduced this long speech about how I was loved in my youth and marriage (a speech that should be unnecessary!), so read now also what disrespect and judgment I have received in my old age. Therefore I have put here the letter that Mr. Ludwig sent to me. See how he ascribes to me insult, dishonor, and godlessness together with all errors and heresies before God and human beings. He hands me over to the devil, with whom (God be praised) I have nothing to do forever; but I belong to my Lord Jesus Christ, who with His own blood redeemed me from the devil. So besides showing Rabus's letter, I also seek to give a full accounting of my faith to anyone who wants it. [1 Cor. 5:5; Rev. 1:5; 1 Peter 3:15]. In this account you may see whether my good husband's faith and mine are alike or unlike or whether my confidence and faith in the Lord Jesus have changed or not. However, I will clearly show Rabus that he and others have not kept to the pure knowledge of Jesus Christ as the old architects of our church taught us, in the sacraments and other matters. But I know what the Holy Spirit and the old ones through Him have taught me, when at the beginning of the Gospel we were still in fear, great zeal, and under the cross. If God wills, I shall remain with that to the end, when I wish to say with joy the prayer of the dear Simeon: "Now, O Lord, let me, a poor woman, go hence in peace and rest, for the eye of my faith has seen Your savior in my heart and held Him in the arms of my desire" [Luke 2:28–30].

Well then, this is now enough. However, if Mr. Ludwig is not satisfied with his injudicious condemnation of me, a poor solitary woman, then I want to take God as my helper and further recount my dear husband's and my faith, teaching, and life, and let anyone who wants to do so judge who has fallen away or climbed out of the right way! Now, dear Strasbourg, read this letter that Mr. Ludwig Rabus sent to me and judge without any favor and ill humor toward him or me. If I am owed this and have behaved as he describes, then I will gladly bear my punishment. But I believe that no Jew would give me such a testimony and bring such a judgment on me! I am also assured in my heart that I stand before my Lord Christ and His heavenly Father in a fitting way through the power of His Spirit; I stand before Him through the great and high merit of Christ in whom I believe, who also will bring to light this wicked letter or witness by Mr. Ludwig (which lies about me) on the great day of His glorious appearance, when all the books of the conscience will stand open [Tit. 2:13; Rev. 20:12]. Yes, here I stand also before many people who know me, who know my life story and have seen me from youth: as a young woman in my father's house, in my marriage, and now in my grieving widowhood—let them also judge this matter between Mr. Ludwig and me.

To God alone be all honor and glory in His Son Jesus Christ who, with His Father and the Holy Spirit, lives and reigns in the same honor and divine majesty, in the indivisible being of God, true God and true Man, our God and Lord, now and forever. Amen.

Letter of Ludwig Rabus to Katharina Schütz Zell (April 1557)

My glory, honor, and comfort are in the crucified Christ.

Your heathen, unchristian, stinking, lying letter reached me on April 16, Good Friday, when I was busy and much laden with preaching. I find in the same poisonous, envious, stinking, and lying writing that, although God has wonderfully visited you, yet there is no improvement left to hope for you—you are more and more hardened in your frightful error of false witness and devilish gossip about devout people. So I commit you to the just judgment of God and have no doubt that He will someday give you the well-deserved reward for your pharisaic arrogance.

Your letter was produced not from the Spirit of God, who is a Spirit of truth, but from the devil's spirit, who was a liar from the beginning, this I will diligently hold up as witness of your shameless mouth, since you dare boldly to slander and revile a servant of Christ, unheard, without inquiry, accusing him of all devilishness, so that one well may see the beautiful little fruit of the stinking Schwenckfelder weed and other such heretical hearts and spirits. And you say (as your shameless mouth spews forth and as you previously accused me) that I wanted to quarrel with and provoke the magistrates [of Strasbourg] with a three-day limit. That is a stinking, lying saying from the devil without any truth. Also you shamelessly and dishonorably lie about me in your other writing.

Are you to be prayed for that God may forgive you? You made such trouble in the church in Strasbourg from the beginning, and also for your devout husband himself, that I believe God's judgment will someday catch up with you. From now on leave me alone with your lying and slanderous writing.

If you think this letter is too harsh, remember that one must answer the fool as he deserves. April 19, 1557.

Ludwig Rabus, Doctor in the Holy Scriptures and Superintendent of the Church at Ulm, against all Zwinglian, Stenckfelder, Anabaptist spirits. But besides that a poor weak servant of the crucified Christ and of His poor church.

....

19. ARGULA VON GRUMBACH (C. 1492–1554)

Argula von Stauff was born around 1492 to a cultured and deeply religious noble family. Around the age of 15 she joined the Bavarian court as lady-in-waiting to Queen Kunigunde, daughter of Emperor Frederick III, and a few years later married Friedrich von Grumbach, who seems to have been less intellectual than his wife, and who certainly tried to undermine her fervent Protestantism. They had at least four children, though only one was alive at the time of her death in 1554. Argula seems to have engaged deeply with Luther's ideas from the beginning, though her connections and interests moved beyond Wittenberg to Nuremberg and other centers of reform. She emerged into public view with her first letter on the Arascius Seehofer affair in 1523. Seehofer was an eighteen-year-old student at the University of Ingolstadt who persisted in spreading the ideas to which he had been exposed during a recent visit to Wittenberg. He was arrested and found in possession of banned material, agreed to recant, and was banished to a distant monastery. Argula was appalled at what she saw as a show trial and wrote a letter of protest to the University and another to Duke Wilhelm of Bavaria calling for reform, both of which were coldly received. Despite the response of the Bavarian authorities, Argula's letter to Ingolstadt appeared in fourteen editions, making her the first Protestant woman to use the printing press to express her views. In all she published eight pamphlets, though none of the others had the same success as her first, and her career was short, with her last piece appearing in 1524, though she remained active in reforming circles throughout the rest of her life. Argula's writing reflects a brief window of opportunity for women to engage publicly on religious and political issues in the early years of the Reformation, but that window was firmly shut by the middle of the decade, and women like Argula quickly found that some elements of the old church would be carried into the new. The letter here was probably written in December 1523 to her mother's cousin, Adam Von Thering. Von Thering was a prominent and successful man who had publicly criticized her behavior. In the letter she argues for her obligation to express her religious views and expresses her profound desire for greater moral and religious leadership in Bavaria.

To the noble and honorable Adam von Thering, the Count Palatine's Administrator in Neuburg: an open letter from Argula von Grumbach, née von Stauff

To the noble and honorable lord Adam von Thering, my gracious lord the Count Palatine's administrator in Neuburg…, my dear lord and cousin.

The grace and peace of God and the presence of his Holy Spirit be with you, my beloved lord and cousin. I have been told that you were informed of my letter to the University of Ingolstadt, and that this made you more than a little angry with me. Perhaps you thought it unbecoming of me as a foolish woman. Which is, of course, exactly how I see myself. However, the wisdom needed to confess God does not derive from human reason, but is to be seen as a gift of God. From this has come—and more may yet come—much malicious gossip on the part of the worldly wise, tending to my disgrace, shame or ridicule.

As my family friend, you also paid careful attention to this. I conclude from this that you love me as your family friend, and for this I express to you my deep and sincere thanks. For it is obvious to me that if you did not mean me well, you would have paid little heed to any gossip about me, be it good or evil. In recognition of what is clearly your friendship to me, I have been moved to write to you to advise you of the truth of the matter. I am therefore sending you a copy of what I have written, which I beseech you to read faithfully and to judge me according to the Spirit of God.

For the wisdom of the world cannot comprehend God's Spirit, as Hosea chapter 4[:1b, 7b] shows. There is nothing good in human nature, but what is in us is sin: "I will change their glory into shame." And as Paul says in 1 Corinthians 3[:19]: Human wisdom is foolishness to God. If I have acted wrongly I will, of course, gladly endure the punishment. But do not think you should be criticizing me, for no one should criticize us for doing what God has commanded us to do. And indeed in this case, too, I am not under constraint to obey any one at all, for I vowed at baptism to believe in God, to confess him, and to renounce the Devil and all his illusions. I can never hope to fulfill such a lofty vow, until I am born anew through death. For while we live in the flesh we are sinners. As it says in the Book of Proverbs, chapter 20[:9]: Who can say "my heart is pure and I am without sin?" And in Jeremiah chapter 17[:5, 7]: "Cursed is the one who trusts in mortals, but blessed is the one who trusts in God."

Now you well know that we all make the same vow: I believe/I renounce etc. Which doctor has made a greater vow in baptism than I have? Which pope, or emperor, or prince? And so every day I pray God for grace to be able to fulfill the vow that was made on my behalf by my godfather. Now that I have come to understand this, having been instructed in the Christian faith, I have accepted and affirmed it, and so it is confirmed by faith.

Therefore do not be astonished, my dear lord and cousin, that I confess God; for whoever does not confess God is no Christian, though he be baptized a thousand times. Each individual must give an account of himself at the Last Judgment. Neither pope, king, prince nor doctor will settle my account. That is what I keep in mind. Nor will wealth be any help, as Ezekiel 7[:19, 25] says: Their silver and their gold will not redeem them in the day of the Lord; when they are aghast they will seek peace but will not find it. And Hosea chapter 8[:7]: "They sow wind and reap wind." Such is the fate of those who trust in riches and all its works.

So my beloved lord and cousin, I beg you not to be vexed if you hear that I am being abused or ridiculed because I confess Christ. Be alarmed only if you hear that I have denied God (which may God forfend). I count it a great honor to be abused for the sake of God's honor; and it is a trifle to be cursed by those whom God has shamed and blinded for trusting in their human wisdom. For, as it says in Isaiah 40[:6–8]: "All flesh is grass, its fame like a wilted flower. But the word of God remains forever." I speak as Paul did in his first chapter to the Galatians [1:10]: "If I continued to please people, I would not be a servant of the Lord." For God says in Hosea chapter 13[:4]: "You shall know no God or savior apart from me." And John 12[:48]: "He who holds me in contempt and rejects my word will find he has one who judges him."

And it is our preachers who prevent us from recognizing God, for the Lord says in Jeremiah 50[:6]: "My people have lost their way like a flock of sheep; their shepherds have led them astray." And Jeremiah 6[:10, 19]: "The word of God has become an object of scorn to them and they will not receive it." And Jeremiah 10[:21]: "The shepherds did foolishly. They did not seek the Lord, so they understood nothing, and all their flock is scattered." And Jeremiah 23[:36, 40]: "You have perverted the word of the living God and have imposed burdens, therefore I will give you an eternal disgrace and shame which will never be taken away." And Paul says in 2 Timothy 4[:3–4]: "They claim to be teachers, and yet do not know what they are talking about, and they will pay attention to lies...." How often did our faithful shepherd, Christ, warn us to beware of the false prophets and their teaching. He calls it a sour dough, a little of which can leaven a large amount of dough, as in Matthew chapters 7[:15] and 13[:33].

In Matthew 17[:5], when [Christ] is transfigured, it says: "This is my dear son in whom I am well pleased; it is to him that you are to listen." In Isaiah 42[:8]: "My glory I give to another," and in John, chapter 1[:12]: "To as many as received him he gave power to become children of God." I am called a follower of Luther, but I am not. I was baptized in the name of Christ; it is him I confess and not Luther. But I confess that Martin, too, as a faithful Christian, confesses him. God help us never to deny this, whether faced by disgrace, abuse, imprisonment, breaking on the wheel and even death—God helping and enabling all Christians in this. Amen.

I have heard that you are reported as saying that if my own husband would not do it, some relative should act, and wall me up. But don't believe him. Alas, he is doing far too much to persecute Christ in me. In 2 Corinthians 4[:8–11] Paul says: "We endure all things without complaint for the name of the Lord." So it is no difficulty for me, and I am not liable to obey him in this matter, for God says in Matthew 10[:21, 37] and Mark 8[:36–37]: "We must forsake father, mother, brother, sister, children, life and limb," and then says: "What good does it do someone to gain the whole world but ruin one's soul? With what would one repurchase one's soul?"

That's the way it is; otherwise, God says, he will not confess us. But forsaking friendship, honor, property, and life does not appeal to the flesh. Of ourselves we are as feeble as Saint Peter was, who promised to die with the Lord, then denied him three times [Matthew 26:35, 75]. God allowed him to see what it means to be human, but finally God gave him the Spirit which enabled him to die joyfully for the sake of the Lord. God must give this Spirit, not flesh and blood. What does the Lord say in Matthew 7[:7–13]: "Whoever asks God for a good spirit will be given it from the Father."

I cannot pity our authorities enough, who are not taking this to heart at all. I have yet to meet one, either in the clerical or the secular realm, who was prepared to undertake the reading of the Bible, so they could discover with certainty God's command. Instead they curse, kill and rage away, devoid of all knowledge and grounding in Scripture. And still no one denounces such behavior as unchristian.

What Christian could keep silence in this situation? To say that God has spoken means no more to them than if some fool or some deformed person had spoken. All this is because they are as well informed about the Bible as a cow is about chess. While it certainly isn't my task to deal with their stock retort: "I believe what my parents believed"—that is not the end of the matter. For all Christians do have a responsibility to know the word of God. Paul says that faith comes from hearing [Romans 10:17]. The princes and much of the nobility are the same. I have heard many say: "If my mother and father were in hell I don't want to go to heaven." Not me!

Even if all my friends were there (God forbid) I fear they could not do much to entertain me! It's the fault of the parents for failing to have their children taught. If by chance they have been to school it's Terence and Ovid they are taught; for the reason given above. But what is in these books? How to make love, be lover-boys and whores and so on. That's an option, for sure, and every level of society is full of people like that, whether married or not, who boast about it rather than being ashamed of it. Sadly it has come to the stage where whores and their partners often show more fidelity to each other than occurs in marriage.

This surely fulfills the words of St. Paul in 1 Corinthians 5[:1]: "Immorality is said to have arisen among you, which is even more notorious than that among the heathen." From this arises whining, quarreling, fighting and violence. No peace, day or night. Prosperity and morale plummet. There is no way out, whatever a woman does; and so often it leads her to disaster. May God preserve all who fight against it, and help those who have fallen to rise again. Everyone turns a blind eye to this; if one complains to friends about it, one meets with laughter. It doesn't do to criticize. The authorities have cut their cloth from the same bolt.

I have scant enthusiasm or expectation about this meeting of the Reichstag that has been summoned. May God send his Spirit to teach them to recognize the truth when they see it, so that this Reichstag meeting deserves the name, and we may become rich in soul and body; all be governed in true Christian faith, and the wealth of land and people no longer be dissipated, making us poorer still. If as much attention were given to God's word as to eating, drinking, banqueting, gambling, masques and the like, things would soon improve. What hundreds of thousands of florins I can remember being wasted in such Reichstag meetings. And to what purpose? You know better than I! What deliberation is possible when they are so busy gorging themselves day and night that they can hardly sit upright?

I have seen it all at Nuremberg myself: that childish behavior on the part of the Princes will be before my eyes as long as I live. But oh, how difficult it will be when the Lord says: "Give an account of your stewardship. Henceforth you will no longer be a steward" [Luke 16:1–2]. And what does God say in Hosea chapter 8[:4]? "They governed, but not at my behest; they were princes, but I do not recognize them as such." May God remedy matters, so that they do not perish like Pharaoh for all their splendor. May the Princes in their deliberations comprehend the word of God—not that the word of God should be subject to them, but rather that they may be subject to the same sure and steadfast word of God.

Therefore, my beloved lord and cousin, I plead with you as a friend to devote yourself to the holy Scriptures. You have long been a counselor of the Princes; it is now time for you to take counsel for your own immortal soul—so that at least you could read through the four gospels before you die. May God grant, though, that you may read the whole Bible, the book which contains all the commands of God. It was never Luther's intent, after all, that one should have faith in his books; they should serve simply as guidebooks to the word of God. You could do a great deal of good in your territory, especially if you were to see to it that the posts of pastor and preacher were occupied by learned men.

For all salvation is wrought by the word of God, as it says in Isaiah 55[:10f]: "As the rain gives food and seed to the sower, and makes the earth green, so does the word, which goes out from my mouth; it does not return to me without fruit." Jeremiah 22 [23:29]: "My words are like a fire, like a hammer which smashes rock."

I have been told that they wish to deprive my husband of his office. I cannot help that; I weighed everything up carefully beforehand. It will not stand in the way of my salvation, as was the case with Pilate. I am prepared to lose everything—even life and limb. May God stand by me! Of myself I can do nothing but sin; pray to God earnestly for me, that he may increase my faith. Even if that should mean the end of me, do not regard that as a disgrace but rather praise God. Had I the grace, my soul would be like a precious jewel to the Lord God.

The property they can take from me is almost nothing. You know that my father was ruined under the princes of Bavaria, and his children became beggars—although they have treated me and my children well by giving employment to my husband. May God be their reward. Although the priests of Würzburg have devoured my husband's property, God will surely care for my four children, and send the birds of the air to feed them and clothe them with the flowers of the field [Matthew 6:26–30; 1 Kings 17:6]. He has said it; he cannot lie.

I had intended to keep my writing private; now I see that God wishes to have it made public. That I am now abused for this is a good indication that it is of God, for if the world were to praise it, it would not be of God. Therefore, my beloved lord and cousin, I commend you now and forever to the grace of God; may it be with you now and forever. Grunbach [sic].

Argula von Grunbach, nee von Stauffen [sic].

CALVIN

20. MICHAEL SERVETUS (1511–53)

During his law studies at Toulouse the young Spaniard Michael Servetus had a moving religious experience in discovering in the Scriptures the historical person of Jesus of Nazareth, the Christ, who became the object and center of his faith. He turned against the traditional formulations of the nature of Christ and the relation of the persons of the Trinity. He believed that such terms as hypostases or persons, substance, essence, and the like were imposed upon biblical conceptions from Greek metaphysics and as such were abstract, speculative, artificial, and unrelated to the living God. Having failed to convince the reformers in Basel and Strasbourg of the propriety of his views, in 1531 Servetus published his treatise On the Errors of the Trinity. *In so doing he left the impression that he was reviving the ancient Arian heresy that Jesus was not the pre-existent Word who was with God the Father from eternity. His subsequent apology and his larger work on* The Restoration of Christianity *(1553) did not improve his reputation for orthodoxy. He was condemned on all sides and was recognized, tried, and burned at the stake in Geneva in 1553, a victim of a misguided zeal for truth on the part of Calvin and his followers, who acted even out of a concern for the man himself. The first paragraphs of the treatise* On the Errors of the Trinity *suggest the tone and general argument of the work.*

On the Errors of the Trinity

In investigating the holy mysteries of the divine Triad, I have thought that one ought to start from the man; for I see most men approaching their lofty speculation about the Word without having any fundamental understanding of Christ, and they attach little or no importance to the man, and give the true Christ quite over to oblivion. But I shall endeavor to recall to their memories who the Christ is. However, what and how much importance is to be attached to Christ, the Church shall decide.

Seeing that the pronoun [the Christ] indicates a man, whom they call the human nature, I shall admit these three things: first, this man is Jesus Christ; second, he is the Son of God; third, he is God.

That he was called Jesus at the beginning, who would deny? That is, in accordance with the angel's command, the boy was on the day of his circumcision given a name, even as you were called John, and this man, Peter. Jesus, as Tertullian says, is a man's proper name, and Christ is a surname. The Jews all admitted that he was Jesus, but denied that he was Christ, asking about Jesus who is called Christ, and they put out of the synagogue those who confessed that he was Christ; and the Apostles had frequent disputes with them about him, as to whether Jesus were the Christ. But as to Jesus, there was never any doubt or question, nor did anyone ever deny this name. See what the discourse is aiming at, and with what purpose Paul testifies to the Jews that Jesus is the Christ; with what fervor of spirit Apollos of Alexandria publicly confuted the Jews, showing by the Scriptures that Jesus was the Messiah. Of what Jesus do you suppose those things were said? Do you think they disputed there about a hypostasis [person]? I am bound therefore to admit that he was Christ as well as Jesus, since I admit that he was anointed of God; for this is thy Holy Servant, whom thou didst anoint. This is the most holy, who, [the Hebrew prophet] Daniel foretold, should be anointed. And [the Apostle] Peter spoke of it as an accomplished fact: Ye yourselves know, for the saying about Jesus is known to all men, namely, that God anointed Jesus of Nazareth with the Holy Spirit and with power, for God was with Him; and, This is He who is ordained of God to be the Judge of the living and the dead; and, Let all the house of Israel know assuredly, that this Jesus whom ye crucified God hath made both Lord and Christ, that is, anointed. Some, however, try to show that these pronouns mean another being. But John calls him a liar that denies that this Jesus is anointed of God; and, He that admits that Jesus is the Christ is begotten of God.

Tertullian also says that the term Christ is a word belonging to a human nature. And although he makes careful inquiry concerning the word Christ, he makes no mention of that being which some make Christ out to be. Who, he also says, is the Son of man, if not himself a man, born of a man, a body born of a body? For the Hebrew expression son of man, son of Adam, means nothing else than man. Again, the way the word is used implies this, for to be anointed can refer only to a human nature. If, then, being anointed, as he says, is an affair of the body, who can deny that the one anointed is a man? Moreover, in the *Clementine Recognitions* Peter brings out the meaning of the word: because kings used to be called Christs, therefore He, being distinguished above others by His anointing, is called Christ the king;

because just as God made an angel chief over the angels, and a beast over the beasts, and a heavenly body over the heavenly bodies, so he made the man Christ chief over men.

Again, on the authority of Holy Scripture we are taught very plainly that Christ is called a man, since even an earthly king is called Christ. Again, Of whom was born Jesus, the one who is called [the] Christ. Note the article, and note the surname; for these words and the pronouns are to be understood in the simplest sense: they denote something perceived by the senses. Again, "Thou shalt call his name Jesus" [Luke 1:31]; and he is very evidently writing of Jesus as a man, when he says, "And Jesus himself began to be thirty years of age, and was supposed to be the son of Joseph" [Luke 3:23]. And, "Of David's seed hath God according to promise brought Jesus" [Acts 13:23]. And John [the Baptist] said, "Think not that I am Christ." How absurd John's disclaimer would be, if the word Christ cannot refer to a man. Moreover, to what end does Christ warn us to shun those men that called themselves Christs? Christ's question and Peter's answer would be silly, when Christ said, "Who do men say that I, the Son of man, am?" And Peter answered, "Thou art the Christ, thou art the Son of the living God." Nor would it mean the living Word of God, for in speaking to a man he ought to have said, "Christ is in thee, the Son of God is in thee, and not, Thou art." And when he charged them there that they should tell no man that he was Christ, tell me, what did he mean by that pronoun? For it is clearer than day that he meant himself, and was speaking of himself. Do you not blush to say that he was without a name, and that the Apostles had preached about him so long [a] time without having called him by his own name; and do you on your own authority impose upon him a new and unfitting name, and one unheard of by the Apostles, calling him only the human nature?

Again, let not the Greek title [*Christos*] deceive you; but take the word [Messiah] or the Latin word *unctus*, and see whether you, who admit that we have been anointed, will venture to admit that he was anointed. Nor should I so strongly insist upon proving this point, which is clear enough at the very outset, were it not that I see that the minds of some are misled. Again, Christ's testimony is very clear, when he calls himself a man: "Ye seek to kill me, a man that hath told you the truth" [John 8:40]. And, "A mediator between God and men, the man Christ Jesus" [1 Tim. 2:5]. Again, pay no regard to the word *homo* [man], which, if you hold to the *communicatio idiomatum*, has been corrupted in meaning; but take the word *vir* [man], and hear Peter when he says that Christ was a man approved. And, "Concerning Jesus the Nazarene, who was a man, a mighty prophet" [Luke 24:19]. And, "After me cometh a man; and, Rejected of men, a man of sorrows; and, Behold, the man, whose name is the Branch; and, God will judge by that man, namely, Christ" [from Isaiah 53:3; Zech. 62; Romans 2:16].

Again, do not misrepresent the law of God by circumlocutions. Consider rather the nature of the demonstrative pronoun, and you will see that this is the original meaning of the word; for when he is pointed out to the eye it is very often admitted, "This is the Christ, Thou art Jesus; and that he speaks, asks, answers, eats, and that they saw him walking upon the water. Likewise, I am he whom ye seek, Jesus of Nazareth; and Whomsoever I shall kiss, that is he: take him." And in another place, "It is I myself: handle me, and see; and, This Jesus, whom ye slew, did God raise up, whereof we all are witnesses." Just what will you mean by such pronouns? As for an eyewitness, are we not in worse case than the Samaritan woman who said, "Come and see a man, who told me all things that ever I did: can this be the Christ?" No wonder that a woman founded on Christ spoke thus, for when she was herself looking for a Messiah to come, who is called Christ, he replied, "I that speak unto thee am he"—I, I, not the being, but he who speaks.

Again, to what man do you understand that that word of the Apostle refers, "As by the trespass of one man, ... so by the grace of one man Jesus Christ"; and, "As by a man came death, so by a man came the resurrection of the dead" [1 Corinthians 15:21]? For the Scripture does not take man connotatively; it calls him not only man, but Adam. Yet for our basis we would have a connotative man, and a speculative substance. Away, I pray, with these sophistical tricks, and you shall see a great light. The foundation of the Church is the words of Christ, which are most simple and plain. Let us imitate the Apostles, who preached Christ not with words composed by art of man. The words of the Lord are pure words; they are to be received with simplicity. And witness the Apostle: Not with excellence of speech is the testimony of Christ to be proclaimed, but plainly, and as if we had become babes, and as if we knew nothing else save Jesus Christ, and him crucified.

21. JOHN CALVIN (1509–64)

Calvin was born in Noyon, north-east of Paris, in 1509. He began his education in theology but turned to the law at the direction of his father. Following his father's death he dabbled in the classics, but in the early 1530s he underwent a conversion to Protestantism that changed his life.

In the early 1530s, Francis I of France (r. 1515–47) seemed open to the possibilities of reform, until the affair of the Placards (1534) led him to clamp down on religious innovation. This is probably one of the reasons for Calvin's move to Switzerland, where he published the first edition of his major work, the Institutes of the Christian Religion, *in 1536, with a preface addressed to the French king. Expanded and republished several times between 1536 and 1559, the* Institutes *were not only an explication of Calvin's theology but also a plan for constructing the kingdom of God on earth. Calvin had the opportunity to put his plan into action as he worked as a pastor and teacher in both Strasbourg and Geneva. Calvin lived in Geneva from 1536–38 and again from 1541–64, when he succeeded in establishing a "godly city." Geneva became a center of Protestant thought; during Calvin's residence it was filled with Protestant refugees from France, England, and northern Italy.*

Calvin held the traditional view that government exists for maintaining order and protecting religion, but he raised the possibility that if the ruler failed in his duties and acted as a barrier to true religion, lesser magistrates might be justified in opposing such tyranny. This idea was developed by many of the Protestant exiles in Geneva and elsewhere into various theories of resistance to constituted authority.

The passage below is Calvin's reply to the Italian Cardinal Jacopo Sadoleto (1477–1547), bishop of Carpentras in France, who wrote to the city of Geneva in 1539 proposing that the community return to its former confessional allegiance to the Catholic Church. Calvin at the time was in exile in Strasbourg because of a conflict with the civic authorities of Geneva. Calvin's position below is a statement of reformed belief that differs fundamentally from Sadoleto's orthodox Catholic position on matters central to the Reformation, such as the nature of the Church, the primacy of biblical texts, the efficacy of good works in salvation, and the authority of the papacy.

Reply to Sadoleto

John Calvin to Jacopo Sadoleto, cardinal, greetings.

In the great abundance of learned men whom our ages has produced, your excellent learning and distinguished eloquence having deservedly procured you a place among the few whom all, who would be thought studious of liberal arts, look up to and revere, it is with great reluctance I bring forward your name before the learned world, and address to you the following expostulation. Nor, indeed, would I have done it if I had not been dragged into this arena by a strong necessity. For I am not unaware how reprehensible it would be to show any eagerness in attacking a man who has deserved so well of literature, nor how odious I should become to all the learned were they to see me stimulated by passion merely, and not impelled by any just cause, turning my pen against one whom, for his admirable endowments, they, not without good reason, deem worthy of love and honor. I trust, however, that after explaining the nature of my undertaking, I shall not only be exempted from all blame, but there will not be an individual who will not admit that the cause which I have undertaken I could not on any account have abandoned without basely deserting my duty.

You lately addressed a letter to the Senate and people of Geneva, in which you sounded their inclination as to whether, after having once shaken off the yoke of the Roman Pontiff, they would submit to have it again imposed upon them. In that letter, as it was not expedient to wound the feelings of those whose favor you required to gain your cause, you acted the part of a good pleader;

for you endeavored to soothe them by abundance of flattery, in order that you might gain them over to your views. Anything of obloquy and bitterness you directed against those whose exertions had produced the revolt from that tyranny. And here (so help you) you bear down full sail upon those who, under pretense of the gospel, have by wicked arts urged on the city to what you deplore as the subversion of religion and of the Church. I, however, Sadoleto, profess to be one of those whom with so much enmity you assail and stigmatize. For though religion was already established, and the form of the Church corrected, before I was invited to Geneva, yet having not only approved by my suffrage, but studied as much as in me lay to preserve and confirm what had been done by [Pierre] Viret [1511–71] and [Guillaume] Farel [1489–1565], I cannot separate my case from theirs. Still, if you had attacked me in my private character, I could easily have forgiven the attack in consideration of your learning, and in honor of letters. But when I see that my ministry, which I feel assured is supported and sanctioned by a call from God, is wounded through my side, it would be perfidy, not patience, were I here to be silent and connive.

In that Church I have held the office first of Doctor, and then of Pastor. In my own right, I maintain that in undertaking these offices I had a legitimate vocation. How faithfully and religiously I have performed them, there is no occasion for now showing at length. Perspicuity, erudition, prudence, ability, not even industry, will I now claim for myself, but that I certainly labored with the sincerity which became me in the work of the Lord, I can in conscience appeal to Christ, my Judge, and all His angels, while all good men bear clear testimony in my favor. This ministry, therefore, when it shall appear to have been of God (as it certainly shall appear, after the cause has been heard), were I in silence to allow you to tear and defame, who would not condemn such silence as treachery? Every person, therefore, now sees that the strongest obligations of duty—obligations which I cannot evade—constrain me to meet your accusations, if I would not with manifest perfidy desert and betray a cause with which the Lord has entrusted me.

...

Although your letter has many windings, its whole purport substantially is to recover the Genevans to the power of the Roman Pontiff, or to what you call the faith and obedience of the Church. But as, from the nature of the case, their feelings required to be softened, you preface with a long oration concerning the incomparable value of eternal life. You afterward come nearer to the point, when you show that there is nothing more pestiferous to souls than a perverse worship of God; and again, that the best rule for the due worship of God is that which is prescribed by the Church, and that, therefore, there is no salvation for those who have violated the unity of the Church unless they repent. But you next contend that separation from your fellowship is manifest revolt from the Church, and then that the gospel which the Genevans received from us is nothing but a large farrago of impious dogmas. From this you infer what kind of divine judgment awaits them if they attend not to your admonitions. But as it was of the greatest importance to your cause to throw complete discredit on our words, you labor to the utmost to fill them with sinister suspicions of the zeal which they saw us manifest for their salvation. Accordingly, you captiously allege that we had no other end in view than to gratify our avarice and ambition. Since, then, your device has been to cast some stain upon us, in order that the minds of your readers, being preoccupied with hatred might give us no credit, I will, before proceeding to other matters, briefly reply to that objection.

I am unwilling to speak of myself, but since you do not permit me to be altogether silent, I will say what I can consistent with modesty. Had I wished to consult my own interest, I would never have left your party. I will not, indeed, boast that there the road to preferment had been easy to me. I never desired it, and I could never bring my mind to catch at it; although I certainly know not a few of my own age who have crept up to some eminence—among them some whom I might have equalled, and others outstripped. This only I will be contented to say, it would not have been difficult for me to reach the summit of my wishes, viz., the enjoyment of literary ease with something of a free and honorable station. Therefore, I have no fear that anyone not possessed of shameless effrontery will object to me that out of the kingdom of the Pope I sought for any personal advantage which was not there ready to my hand.

And who dare object this to Farel? Had it been necessary for him to live by his own industry, he had already made attainments in literature, which would not have allowed him to suffer want, and he was of a more distinguished family than to require external aid. As to those of us to whom you pointed as with the finger, it seemed proper for us to reply in our town name. But since you seem to throw out indirect insinuations against all who in the present day are united with us in sustaining the same cause, I would have you understand that not one can be mentioned for whom I cannot give you a better answer than for Farel and myself. Some of our [reformers] are known to you by fame. As to them, I appeal to your own conscience. Think you it was hunger which drove them away from you, and made them in despair flee to that change as a means of bettering their fortunes? But not to go over a long catalogue, this I say, that of those who first engaged in this cause, there was none who with you might not have been in better place and fortune than require on such grounds to look out for some new plan of life.

...

But here you bring a charge against us. For you teach that all which has been approved for fifteen hundred years or more, by the uniform consent of the faithful, is, by our headstrong rashness, torn up and destroyed. Here I will not require you to deal truly and candidly by us (though this should be spontaneously offered by a philosopher, not to say a Christian). I will only ask you not to stoop to an illiberal indulgence in calumny, which, even though we be silent, must be extremely injurious to your reputation with grave and honest men. You know, Sadoleto, and if you venture to deny, I will make it palpable to all that you knew, yet cunningly and craftily disguised the fact, not only that our agreement with antiquity is far closer than yours, but that all we have attempted has been to renew that ancient form of the Church, which, at first sullied and distorted by illiterate men of indifferent character, was afterward flagitiously mangled and almost destroyed by the Roman Pontiff and his faction.

I will not press you so closely as to call you back to that form which the Apostles instituted (though in it we have the only model of a true Church, and whosoever deviates from it in the smallest degree is in error), but to indulge you so far, place, I pray, before your eyes, that ancient form of the Church, such as their writings prove it to have been in the age of Chrysostom and Basil, among the Greeks, and of Cyprian, Ambrose, and Augustine, among the Latins; after so doing, contemplate the ruins of that Church, as now surviving among yourselves. Assuredly, the difference will appear as great as that which the Prophets describe between the famous Church which flourished under David and Solomon, and that which under Zedekiah and Jehoiakim had lapsed into every kind of superstition, and utterly vitiated the purity of divine worship. Will you here give the name of an enemy of antiquity to him who, zealous for ancient piety and holiness, and dissatisfied with the state of matters as existing in a dissolute and depraved Church, attempts to ameliorate its condition, and restore it to pristine splendor?

Since there are three things on which the safety of the Church is founded, viz., doctrine, discipline, and the sacraments, and to these a fourth is added, viz., ceremonies, by which to exercise the people in offices of piety, in order that we may be most sparing of the honor of your Church, by which of these things would you have us to judge her? The truth of prophetical and evangelical doctrine, on which the Church ought to be founded, has not only in a great measure perished in your Church, but is violently driven away by fire and sword. Will you obtrude upon me, for the Church, a body which furiously persecutes everything sanctioned by our religion, both as delivered by the oracles of God, and embodied in the writings of holy Fathers, and approved by ancient Councils? Where, pray, exist among you any vestiges of that true and holy discipline which the ancient bishops exercised in the Church? Have you not scorned all their institutions? Have you not trampled all the canons under foot? Then, your nefarious profanation of the sacraments I cannot think of without the utmost horror.

Of ceremonies, indeed, you have more than enough, but all or the most part so childish in their import, and vitiated by innumerable forms of superstition, as to be utterly unavailing for the preservation of the Church. None of these things, you must be aware, is exaggerated by me in a captious spirit. They all appear so openly that they may be pointed out with the finger wherever there are eyes to behold them. Now, if you please, test us in the same way. You will, assuredly, fall far short of making good the charges which you have brought against us.

In the sacraments, all we have attempted is to restore the native purity from which they had degenerated, and so enable them to resume their dignity. Ceremonies we have in a great measure abolished, but we were compelled to do so; partly because by their multitude they had degenerated into a kind of Judaism, partly because they had filled the minds of the people with superstition, and could not possibly remain without doing the greatest injury to the piety which it was their office to promote. Still we have retained those which seemed sufficient for the circumstances of the times.

That our discipline is not such as the ancient Church professed we do not deny. But with what fairness is a charge of subverting discipline brought against us by those who themselves have utterly abolished it, and in our attempts to reinstate it in its rights have hitherto opposed us? As to our doctrine, we hesitate not to appeal to the ancient Church. And since, for the sake of example, you have touched on certain heads, as to which you thought had some ground for accusing us, I will briefly show how unfairly and falsely you allege that these are things which have been devised by us against the opinion of the Church.

Before descending to particulars, however, I have already cautioned you, and would have you again and again consider with what reason you can charge it upon our people, as a fault, that they have studied to explain the Scriptures. For you are aware that by this study they have thrown such light on the Word of God, that, in this respect, even Envy herself is ashamed to defraud them of all praise. You are just as un-candid when you aver that we have seduced the people by thorny and subtle questions, and so enticed them by that philosophy of which Paul bids Christians beware. What? Do you remember what kind of time it was when our [reformers] appeared, and what kind of doctrine candidates for the ministry learned in the schools? You yourself know that it was mere sophistry, and sophistry so twisted, involved, tortuous, and puzzling, that scholastic theology might well be described as a species of secret magic. The denser the darkness in which any one shrouded a subject, the more he puzzled himself and others with preposterous riddles, the greater his fame for acumen and learning. And when those who had been formed in that forge wished to carry the fruit of their learning to the people, with what skill, I ask, did they edify the Church?

Not to go over every point, what sermons in Europe then exhibited that simplicity with which Paul wishes a Christian people to be always occupied? Nay, what one sermon was there from which old wives might not carry off more whimsies than they could devise at their own fireside in a month? For as sermons were then usually divided, the first half was devoted to those misty questions of the schools which might astonish the rude populace, while the second contained sweet stories, or not unamusing speculations, by which the hearers might be kept on the alert. Only a few expressions were thrown in from the Word of God, that by their majesty they might procure credit for these frivolities. But as soon as our [reformers] raised the standard, all these absurdities, in one moment, disappeared from amongst us. Your preachers, again, partly profited by our books, and partly compelled by shame and the general murmur, conformed to our example, though they still, with open throat, exhale the old absurdity. Hence, anyone who compares our method of procedure with the old method, or with that which is still in repute among you, will perceive that you have done us no small injustice. But had you continued your quotation from Paul a little farther, any boy would easily have perceived that the charge which you bring against us is undoubtedly applicable to yourselves. For Paul there interprets "vain philosophy" to mean that which preys upon pious souls by means of the constitutions of men and the elements of this world: and by these you have ruined the Church.

Even you yourself afterwards acquit us by your own testimony; for among those of our doctrines which you have thought proper to assail, you do not adduce one, the knowledge of which is not essentially necessary for the edification of the Church.

You, in the first place, touch upon justification by faith, the first and keenest subject of controversy between us. Is this a knotty and useless question? Wherever the knowledge of it is taken away, the glory of Christ is extinguished, religion abolished, the Church destroyed, and the hope of salvation utterly overthrown. That doctrine, then, though of the highest moment, we maintain that you have nefariously effaced from the memory of men. Our books are filled with convincing proofs of this fact, and the gross ignorance of this doctrine, which even still continues in all your churches, declares that our complaint is by no means ill-founded. But you very maliciously stir up prejudice against us, alleging that by attributing everything to faith, we leave no room for works.

I will not now enter upon a full discussion, which would require a large volume; but if you would look into the Catechism which I myself drew up for the Genevans, when I held the office of Pastor among them, three words would silence you. Here, however, I will briefly explain to you how we speak on this subject.

First, we bid a man begin by examining himself, and this not in a superficial and perfunctory manner, but to cite his conscience before the tribunal of God, and when sufficiently convinced of his iniquity, to reflect on the strictness of the sentence pronounced upon all sinners. Thus confounded and amazed at his misery, he is prostrated and humbled before God; and, casting away all self-confidence, groans as if given up to final perdition. Then we show that the only haven of safety is in the mercy of God, as manifested in Christ, in whom every part of our salvation is complete. As all mankind are, in the sight of God, lost sinners, we hold that Christ is their only righteousness, since, by His obedience, He has wiped out our transgressions; by His sacrifice, appeased the divine anger; by His blood, washed away our sins; by His cross, borne our curse; and by His death, made satisfaction for us. We maintain that in this way man is reconciled in Christ to God the Father, by no merit of his own, by no value of works, but by gratuitous mercy. When we embrace Christ by faith, and come, as it were, into communion with Him, this we term, after the manner of Scripture, the righteousness of faith.

What have you here, Sadoleto, to bite or carp at? Is it that we leave no room for works? Assuredly we do deny that in justifying a man they are worth one single straw. For Scripture everywhere cries aloud, that all are lost; and every man's own conscience bitterly accuses him. The same Scripture teaches that no hope is left but in the mere goodness of God, by which sin is pardoned, and righteousness imputed to us. It declares both to be gratuitous, and finally concludes that a man is justified without works (Rom. iv. 7). But what notion, you ask, does the very term righteousness suggest to us if respect is not paid to good works? I answer, if you would attend to the true meaning of the term justifying in Scripture, you would have no difficulty. For it does not refer to a man's own righteousness, but to the mercy of God, which contrary to the sinner's deserts, accepts of a righteousness for him, and that by not imputing his unrighteousness. Our righteousness, I say, is that which is described by Paul (2 Cor. v. 19) that God hath reconciled us to Himself in Jesus Christ. The mode is afterwards subjoined—by not imputing sin. He demonstrates that it is by faith only we become partakers of that blessing, when he says that the ministry of reconciliation is contained in the gospel. But faith, you say, is a general term, and has a larger signification. I answer that Paul, whenever he attributes to it the power of justifying, at the same time restricts it to a gratuitous promise of the divine favor, and keeps it far removed from all respect to works. Hence his familiar inference—if by faith, then not by works. On the other hand—if by works, then not by faith.

But, it seems, injury is done to Christ, if, under the pretense of His grace, good works are repudiated; He having come to prepare a people acceptable to God, zealous of good works, while to the same effect are many similar passages which prove that Christ came in order that we, doing good works, might, through Him, be accepted by God. This calumny, which our opponents have ever in their mouths, viz., that we take away the desire of well-doing from the Christian life by recommending gratuitous righteousness, is too frivolous to give us much concern. We deny that good works have any share in justification, but we claim full authority for them in the lives of the righteous. For if he who has obtained justification possesses Christ, and at the same time, Christ never is where His Spirit is not, it is obvious that gratuitous righteousness is necessarily connected with regeneration. Therefore, if you would duly understand how inseparable faith and works are, look to Christ, who, as the Apostle teaches (1 Cor. i. 30) has been given to us for justification and for sanctification. Wherever, therefore, that righteousness of faith, which we maintain to be gratuitous, is, there too Christ is, and where Christ is, there too is the Spirit of holiness, who regenerates the soul to newness of life. On the contrary, where zeal for integrity and holiness is not in vigor, there neither is the Spirit of Christ nor Christ Himself; and wherever Christ is not, there is no righteousness, nay, there is no faith; for faith cannot apprehend Christ for righteousness without the Spirit of sanctification.

ENGLAND

22. SIMON FISH (D. 1531)

Simon Fish was an influential pamphleteer who in many ways linked the earlier Lollard tradition of opposition to clerical wealth and power with the Reformation. He himself was of good birth and had studied at Oxford before entering Gray's Inn about 1525. He was very much involved as a student in the popular hostility to Cardinal Wolsey and felt the wrath of the powerful cardinal as a result of taking part in a play that attacked him. He was driven abroad to Antwerp, where he wrote A Supplication for the Beggars, *a 16-page invective asking the king's intervention on behalf of his poor subjects against the abuses of the clergy. The pamphlet was circulating in London by early 1529, and in May of 1530 it was declared heretical. And so it was: it recommended nationalization of the Church's wealth, attacked many Catholic practices, such as the doctrine of Purgatory and the sale of indulgences, and claimed that clerics were guilty of every kind of crime, including murder and treason. Fish dedicated it to Henry VIII.*

John Fox, the author of Acts and Monuments, *proposes that it was Anne Boleyn who gave a copy to Henry, who so appreciated it that he took Fish hunting with him and granted him his protection. Nevertheless, Fish was seen as a heretic by the ecclesiastical authorities and Lord Chancellor Sir Thomas More, but he escaped any punishment by dying of the plague in 1531.*

A Supplication for the Beggars

Most lamentably complaineth their woeful misery unto Your Highness, your poor daily [bedesmen] [one who prays for another's soul], the wretched hideous monsters (on whom scarcely for horror any of you dare look), the foul unhappy sort of lepers and other sore people, needy, impotent, blind, lame and sick, that live only by alms; how that their number is daily so sore increased that all the alms of all well-disposed people of this your realm is not half enough for to sustain them, but that for very constraint they die for hunger. And this most pestilent mischief is come upon your said poor bedesmen, by the reason that there is in the time of your noble predecessors passed craftily crept into this your realm another sort (not of impotent but) of strong, puissant and counterfeit holy and idle beggars and vagabonds, which since the time of their first entry by all the craft and wiliness of Satan are now increased under your sight not only into a great number, but also into a kingdom. These are (not the herds, but the ravenous wolves going in herds' clothing devouring the flock) the bishops, abbots, priors, deacons, archdeacons, suffragans, priests, monks, canons, friars, pardoners and summoners. And who is able to number this idle ravenous sort, which (setting all labor aside) have begged so importunately that they have gotten into their hands more than the third part of all your realm? The goodliest lordships, manors, lands and territories are theirs. Besides this they have the tenth part of all the corn, meadow, pasture, grass, wool, colts, calves, lambs, pigs, geese and chickens. Over and besides, the tenth part of every servant's wages [and] the tenth part of the wool, milk, honey, wax, cheese and butter. Yes, and they look so narrowly upon their profits that the poor wives must be accountable to them of every tenth egg or else she gets not her rights at Easter [and] shall be taken as a heretic. Hereto have they their four offering days. What money pull they in by probates of testaments, privy tithes, and by men's offerings to their pilgrimages, and at their first masses? Every man and child that is buried must pay somewhat for masses and dirges to be sung for him or else they will accuse the dead's friends and executors of heresy. What money get they by mortuaries, by hearing of confessions (and yet they will keep thereof no counsel), by hallowing of churches, altars, super-altars, chapels and bells, by cursing of men and absolving them again for money? What a multitude of money gather the pardoners in a year? How much money get the summoners by extortion in a year, by citing the people to the commissary's court and afterward releasing their appearance for money? Finally, the infinite number of begging friars, what get they in a year? Here, if it please your grace to mark, you shall see a thing far out of joint.... Oh grievous and painful exactions thus yearly to be paid, from the [sic] which the people of your noble predecessors, the kings of the ancient Britons, ever stood free! And this will they have or else they will procure him that will not give it them to be taken as a heretic. What tyrant ever oppressed the people like this cruel and vengeful generation? What subjects shall be able to help their prince that be after this fashion yearly polled? What good Christian people can be able to succor us poor lepers, blind, sore and lame, that be thus yearly oppressed? Is it any marvel that your people so complain of poverty? Is it any marvel that the taxes, fifteen[th]s and subsidies that your grace most tenderly of great compassion hath taken in among your people to defend them from the threatened ruin of their commonwealth, have been so slothfully, yes, painfully levied? Seeing that almost the utmost penny that might have been levied hath been gathered before yearly by this ravenous, cruel and insatiable generation....

Yes, and what do they more? Truly nothing but apply themselves by all the slights they may have to do with every man's wife, every man's daughter, and every man's maid, that cuckoldry and bawdry should reign over all among your subjects, that no man should know his own child, that their bastards might inherit the possessions of every man to put the right begotten children clear beside their inheritance in subversion of all estates and godly order. These be they that by their abstaining from marriage do [prevent] the generation of the people, whereby all the realm at length, if it should be continued, shall be made desert and unhabitable.... Oh, the grievous shipwreck of the commonwealth, which in ancient time before the coming in of these ravenous wolves was so prosperous....

Set these sturdy loobies [awkward or stupid persons] abroad in the world to get them wives of their own, to get their living with their labor in the sweat of their brows, according to the commandment of God, to give other idle people by their example occasion to go to labor. Tie these holy idle thieves to the carts, to be whipped naked about every market town until they will fall to labor; that they, by their importunate begging take not away the alms that the good Christian people would give unto us sore, impotent, miserable people, your bedesmen. Then shall as well the number of our aforesaid monstrous sort, as of the bawds, whores, thieves and idle people decrease. Then shall these great exactions cease. Then shall not your sword, power, crown, dignity and obedience of your people be translated from you. Then shall you have full obedience of your people. Then shall the idle people be set to work. Then shall matrimony be much better kept. Then shall your commons increase in riches. Then shall the gospel be preached. Then shall none beg our alms from us. Then shall we have enough and more than shall suffice us, which shall be the best hospital that ever was founded for us. Then shall we daily pray to God for your most noble estate long to endure.

23. PROHIBITION OF APPEALS TO ROME

The Act of Appeals *was a necessary part of Henry VIII's divorce and became an important element of both the English Reformation and English identity. Having failed to procure a divorce from Pope Clement VII, Henry moved his case against Catherine of Aragon to the English ecclesiastical courts. In January 1533 he secretly married Anne Boleyn, anticipating a favorable response from the court. Even with a divorce from the English court, however, Catherine could appeal her case back to Rome, and the* Act in Restraint of Appeals *was designed to forestall such a possibility. Its famous opening line declared resoundingly that "this realm of England is an empire," and the act went on to proclaim England's independence from any outside power, whether temporal or, more to the point, spiritual. The* Act *therefore recognized the independence of the English church from Rome and laid out the way in which ecclesiastical causes would be dealt with within the kingdom. Apart from its content, the* Act of Appeals *marks the growth of the importance of parliament as a vehicle for change and the beginning of England's reformation through statute.*

While the Act *was making its way through parliament, Convocation found that the pope could not sanction marriage with a brother's widow (the basis of Henry's case) and on May 23, 1533, Henry's marriage to Catherine was declared null and void. A few days later his marriage to Anne Boleyn was declared valid, and on June 1, 1533, she was crowned queen. The following year the* Act of Supremacy *complemented the* Act of Appeals *by confirming the king's position as head of the church in England.*

24 Hen. VIII, c. 12: An Act that the Appeals in such cases as have been used to be pursued to the See of Rome shall not be from henceforth had nor used but within this Realm

Where by divers sundry old authentic histories and chronicles it is manifestly declared and expressed that this realm of England is an empire, and so has been accepted in the world, governed by one supreme head and king having the dignity and royal estate of the imperial crown of the same, unto whom a body politic, made up of all sorts and degrees of people divided in terms and by names of spirituality and temporality, are bound and ought to bear next to God a natural and humble obedience; he being also instituted and furnished by the goodness and sufferance of Almighty God with plenary, whole, and entire power, preeminence, authority, prerogative, and jurisdiction to render and yield justice and final determination to all manner of folk resident or subject within this his realm, in all causes, matters, debates, and contentions happening to occur, insurge, or begin within the limits thereof, without restraint or provocation to any foreign princes or potentates of the world: the body spiritual having power when any cause of divine law or of spiritual learning happened to come in question, then it was declared, interpreted, and showed by that part of the said body politic called the spirituality, now usually called the English Church, which always has been reputed and also found of that kind that both for knowledge, integrity, and sufficiency of number, it has been always thought and is also at this hour sufficient and meet of itself, without the meddling of any exterior person or persons, to declare and determine all such doubts and to administer all such offices and duties as pertains to their spiritual roles. For the due administration of this and to keep them from corruption and sinister affection, the king's most noble progenitors and the antecessors of the nobles of this realm have sufficiently endowed the said Church both with honor and possessions.

And the laws temporal for trial of propriety of lands and goods, and for the conservation of the people of this realm in unity and peace without plunder or spoil, was and yet is administered, adjudged, and executed by sundry judges and administrators of the other part of the said body politic called the temporality, and both their authorities and jurisdictions do conjoin together in the due administration of justice the one to help the other: And whereas the king his most noble progenitors, and the nobility and commons of this said realm, at divers and sundry parliaments as well in the time of King Edward the first, Edward the third, Richard the second, Henry the fourth, and other noble kings of this realm, made sundry ordinances, laws, statutes, and provisions for the entire and sure conservation of the prerogatives, liberties, and preeminences of the said imperial Crown of this realm, and of the jurisdictions spiritual and temporal of the same, to keep it from the annoyance as well of the see of Rome as from the authority of other foreign potentates attempting the diminution or violation thereof as often and from time to time as any such annoyance or attempt might be known or espied: And notwithstanding the said good statutes and ordinances made in the time of the king's most noble progenitors in preservation of the authority and prerogative of the said imperial Crown as is aforesaid, yet nevertheless since the making of the said good statutes and ordinances divers and sundry inconveniences and dangers not provided for plainly by the said former acts, statutes, and ordinances have risen and sprung by reason of appeals sued out of this realm to the see of Rome, in causes testamentary, causes of matrimony and divorces, right of tithes, oblations, and obventions, not only to the great inquietation, vexation, trouble, costs, and charges of the king's highness and many of his subjects and residents in this his realm, but also to the great delay and let to the true and speedy determination of the said causes, for so much as the parties appealing to the said court of Rome most commonly do the same for the delay of justice:

And forasmuch as the great distance of way is so far out of this realm, so that the necessary witnesses nor the true knowledge of the cause can neither there be so well known nor the witnesses there so well examined as within this realm, so that the parties grieved by means of the said appeals be most times without remedy: in consideration whereof the king's highness, his nobles and commons, considering the great enormities, dangers, long delays, and hurts that as well to his highness as to his said nobles, subjects, commons, and residents of this his realm in the said causes testamentary, causes of matrimony and divorces, tithes, oblations, and obventions do daily ensue, does therefore by his royal assent and by the assent of the Lords spiritual and temporal and the commons in this present parliament assembled and by authority of the same, enact, establish, and ordain that all causes testamentary, causes of matrimony and divorces, rights of tithes, oblations, and obventions, the knowledge whereof by the goodness of princes of this realm and by the laws and customs of the same pertains to the spiritual jurisdiction of this realm already commenced, moved, depending, being, happening, or hereafter coming in contention, debate, or question within this realm or within any the king's dominions or marches of the same or elsewhere, whether they concern the king our sovereign lord, his heirs or successors, or any other subjects or residents within the same of what degree soever they be, shall be from henceforth heard, examined, discussed, clearly finally and definitively adjudged and determined, within the king's jurisdiction and authority and not elsewhere, in such courts spiritual and temporal of the same as the natures, conditions, and qualities of the causes and matters aforesaid in contention or hereafter happening in contention shall require, without having any respect to any custom, use, or sufferance in hindrance, let, or prejudice of the same or to any other thing used or suffered to the contrary thereof by any other manner person or persons in any manner of wise ...

And that it shall be lawful to the king our sovereign lord and to his heirs and successors, and to all other subjects or residents within this realm or within any the king's dominions or marches of the same, notwithstanding that hereafter it should happen any excommengement, excommunication, interdiction, citation, or any other censures or foreign process out of any outward parties to be fulminate, proclaimed, declared, or put in execution within this said realm or in any other place or places for any of the causes before rehearsed, in prejudice, derogation, or contempt of this said Act and the very true meaning and execution thereof, may and shall nevertheless as well pursue, execute, have, and enjoy the effects, profits, benefits, and commodities of all such processes, sentences, judgments, and determinations, done or hereafter to be done in any of the said courts spiritual or temporal as the cases shall require, within the limits, power, and authority of this the King's said realm and dominions and marches of the same, and those only and none other to take place and to be firmly observed and obeyed within the same:

As also that all spiritual prelates, pastors, ministers, and curates within this realm and the dominions of the same shall and may use, minister, execute, and do, or cause to be used, ministered, executed, and done, all sacraments, sacramentals, divine services, and all other things within the said realm and dominions unto all the subjects of the same as Catholic and Christian men owe to do; any foreign citations, processes, inhibitions, suspensions, interdictions, excommunications, or appeals for or touching any of the causes aforesaid from or to the see of Rome or any other foreign prince or foreign courts to the let or contrary thereof in any wise notwithstanding. And if any of the said spiritual persons, by the occasion of the said fulminations of any of the same interdictions, censures, inhibitions, excommunications, appeals, suspensions, summons, or other foreign citations for the causes beforesaid or for any of them, do at any time hereafter refuse to minister or to cause to be ministered the said sacraments and sacramentals and other divine services in form as is aforesaid, shall for every such time or times that they or any of them do refuse so to do or to cause to be done, have one year's imprisonment and to make fine and ransom at the King's pleasure.

II. And it is further enacted ... that if any person or persons ... do attempt, move, purchase, or procure, from or to the see of Rome or from or to any other foreign court or courts out of this realm, any manner foreign process, inhibitions, appeals, sentences, summons, citations, suspensions, interdictions, excommunications, restraints, or judgments, of what nature, kind, or quality soever they be, or execute any of the same process, or do any act or acts to the let, impediment, hindrance, or derogation of any process, sentence, judgment, or determination had, made, done, or hereafter to be had, done, or made in any courts of this realm or the king's said dominions or marches of the same for any of the causes aforesaid ... that then every person or persons so doing, and their supporters, comforters, abettors, procurers, executors, and counsellors, and every of them being convict of the same, for every such default shall incur and run in the same pains, penalties, and forfeitures ordained and provided by the statute of provision and praemunire made in the sixteenth year of the reign of ... King Richard the second....

III. And furthermore in eschewing the said great enormities, inquietations, delays, charges, and expenses hereafter to be sustained in pursuing of such appeals and foreign process ... do therefore ... ordain and enact that in such cases where heretofore any of the King's subjects or residents have used to pursue, provoke, or procure any appeal to the see of Rome ... they ... shall from henceforth take, have, and use their appeals within this realm and not elsewhere, in manner and form as hereafter follows and not otherwise; that is to say, First from the archdeacon or his official, if the matter or cause be there begun, to the bishop diocesan of the said see ... ; And likewise, if it is commenced before the bishop diocesan or his commissary, from the bishop diocesan or his commissary, within fifteen days next following the judgment or sentence thereof there given, to the archbishop of the province of Canterbury, if it is within his province, and if it is within the province of York then to the archbishop of York; and so likewise to all other archbishops in other the King's dominions as the case by the order of justice shall require; and there to be definitively and finally ordered, decreed, and adjudged according to justice, without any other appellation or provocation to any other person or persons, court or courts: And if the matter or contention for any of the causes aforesaid be or shall be commenced ... before the archdeacon of any archbishop or his commissary, then the party grieved shall or may take his appeal, within fifteen days next after judgment or sentence there given, to the Court of the Arches or Audience of the same archbishop or archbishops, and from the said Court of the Arches or Audience, within fifteen days then next following after judgment or sentence there given, to the archbishop of the same province, there to be definitively and finally determined without any other or further process or appeal thereupon to be had or sued.

IV. ... And in case any cause, matter, or contention ... which has, does, shall, or may touch the king, his heirs or successors kings of this realm, that in all and every such case or cases the party grieved ... shall or may appeal ... to the spiritual prelates and other abbots and priors of the Upper House assembled and gathered by the king's writ in the convocation being or next ensuing within the province or provinces where the same matter of contention is or shall be begun; so that every such appeal be taken by the party grieved within fifteen days next after the judgment or sentence thereupon given or to be given. And that whatsoever be done or shall be done and affirmed, determined, decreed, and adjudged by the foresaid prelates, abbots, and priors of the upper house of the said convocation as is aforesaid, pertaining, concerning, or belonging to the king, his heirs or successors, in any of these foresaid causes of appeals, shall stand and be taken for a final decree, sentence, judgment, definition, and determination, and the same matter so determined never after to come in question and debate to be examined in any other court or courts: And if it shall happen any person or persons hereafter to pursue or provoke any appeal contrary to the effect of this Act, or refuse to obey, execute, and observe all things comprised within the same ... that then every person and persons so doing, refusing, or offending, ... their procurers, supporters, advocates, counsellors, and abettors, and every of them, shall incur the pains, forfeitures, and penalties ordained and provided in the said statute made in the said sixteenth year of King Richard the Second....

26 Hen. VIII, c. 1: An Act concerning the King's Highness to be Supreme Head of the Church of England and to have authority to reform and redress all errors, heresies, and abuses in the same

Albeit the king's majesty justly and rightfully is and ought to be the supreme head of the Church of England, and so is recognized by the clergy of this realm in their convocations; yet nevertheless for corroboration and confirmation thereof, and for increase of virtue in Christ's religion within this realm of England, and to repress and extirp all errors, heresies, and other enormities and abuses heretofore used in the same,

Be it enacted by authority of this present parliament that the king our sovereign lord, his heirs and successors kings of this realm, shall be taken, accepted, and reputed the only Supreme Head in earth of the Church of England called *Anglicana Ecclesia*, and shall have and enjoy annexed and united to the imperial crown of this realm as well the title and style thereof, as all honours, dignities, preeminences, jurisdictions, privileges, authorities, immunities, profits, and commodities, to the said dignity of supreme head of the same Church belonging and pertaining: And that our said sovereign lord, his heirs and successors kings of this realm, shall have full power and authority from time to time to visit, repress, redress, reform, order, correct, restrain, and amend all such errors, heresies, abuses, offences, contempts, and enormities, whatsoever they be, which by any manner of spiritual authority or jurisdiction ought or may lawfully be reformed, repressed, ordered, redressed, corrected, restrained, or amended, to the pleasure of Almighty God, the increase of virtue in Christ's religion, and for the conservation of the peace, unity, and tranquility of this realm: any usage, custom, foreign laws, foreign authority, prescription, or any other thing or things to the contrary hereof notwithstanding.

28 Hen. VIII, c. 10: An Act extinguishing the authority of the Bishop of Rome

Forasmuch as notwithstanding the good and wholesome laws, ordinances, and statutes heretofore enacted, made, and established ... for the extirpation, abolition, and extinguishment out of this realm and other his grace's dominions, lordships, and countries of the pretended power and usurped authority of the bishop of Rome, by some called the pope, used within the same or elsewhere concerning the same realm, dominions, lordships, or countries, which obfuscated and wrested God's holy word and testament a long season from the spiritual and true meaning thereof, to his worldly and carnal affections, as pomp, glory, avarice, ambition, and tyranny, covering and shadowing the same with his human and politic devices, traditions, and inventions, set forth to promote and establish his only dominion, both upon the souls and also the bodies and goods of all Christian people, excluding Christ out of his kingdom and the rule of man's soul as much as he may, and all other temporal kings and princes out of their dominions which they ought to have by God's law upon the bodies and goods of their subjects; whereby he did not only rob the king's majesty, being only the supreme head of this his realm of England immediately under God, of his honor, right, and preeminence due unto him by the law of God, but spoiled this his realm yearly of innumerable treasure, and with the loss of the same deceived the king's loving and obedient subjects, persuading them by his laws, bulls, and other deceivable means, of such dreams, vanities, and phantasies as by the same many of them were seduced and conveyed to superstitious and erroneous opinions; so that the king's majesty, the lords spiritual and temporal, and the commons in this realm, being wearied and fatigued with the experience of the infinite abominations and mischiefs proceeding of his impostures and craftily coloring of his deceits, to the great damages of souls, bodies, and goods, were forced of necessity for the public weal of this realm to exclude that foreign pretended power, jurisdiction, and authority, used and usurped within this realm, and to devise such remedies for their relief in the same as does not only redound to the honor of God, the high praise and advancement of the king's majesty and of his realm, but also to the great and inestimable utility of the same; and notwithstanding the said wholesome laws so made and heretofore established, yet it is come to the knowledge of the king's highness and also to divers and many his loving, faithful, and obedient subjects, how that divers seditious and contentious persons, being imps of the said bishop of Rome and his see, and in heart members of his pretended monarchy, do in corners and elsewhere, as they dare, whisper, inculcate, preach, and persuade, and from time to time instill into the ears and heads of the poor, simple, and unlettered people the advancement and continuance of the said bishop's feigned and pretended authority, pretending the same to have his ground and original of God's law, whereby the opinions of many are suspended, their judgments corrupted and deceived, and diversity in opinions is augmented and increased, to the great displeasure of Almighty God, the high discontent of our said most dread sovereign lord, and the interruption of the unity, love, charity, concord, and agreement that ought to be in a Christian region and congregation:

For avoiding whereof, and repression of the follies of such seditious persons as are the means and authors of such inconveniences, Be it enacted, ordained, and established ... That if any person or persons, dwelling, demurring, inhabiting, or resident within this realm or within any other of the king's dominions, lordships, or countries, or the marches of the same, or elsewhere within or under his obeisance and power, of what estate, dignity, preeminence, order, degree, or condition soever he or they be, after the last day of July in the year of our Lord God 1536 shall, by writing, ciphering, printing, preaching, or teaching, deed, or act, obstinately or maliciously hold or stand with to extol, set forth, maintain, or defend the authority, jurisdiction, or power of the bishop of Rome or of his see, heretofore used, claimed, or usurped within this realm or in any dominion or country of, within, or under the King's power or obeisance, or by any pretense obstinately or maliciously invents anything for the extolling, advancement, setting forth, maintenance, or defence of the same or any part thereof, or by any pretense obstinately or maliciously attributes any manner of jurisdiction, authority, or preeminence to the said see of Rome, or to any bishop of the same see for the time being, within this realm or in any of the king's dominions or countries, that then every such person or persons so doing or offending, their aiders, assistants, comforters, abettors, procurers, maintainers, supporters, counsellors, concealors, and every of them, being thereof lawfully convicted according to the laws of this realm, for every such default and offence shall incur and run into the dangers, penalties, pains, and forfeitures ordained and provided by the Statute of Provision and Praemunire made in the sixteenth year of the reign of the noble and valiant prince King Richard the second against such as attempt, procure, or make provision to the see of Rome or elsewhere for any thing or things to the derogation, or contrary to the prerogative royal or jurisdiction, of the Crown and dignity of this realm.

24. ANNE ASKEW (C. 1520–46)

Anne Askew was arrested for heresy in London in March 1545 and interrogated on doctrines central to the Henrician Reformation: the nature of the Mass and the Eucharist and the role of the priest. She then signed a confession of faith written by Edmund Bonner, bishop of London, and was released. Her first examination shows her in a battle of wits with both clerical and lay leaders of London's government, but it also shows that although her views were quite distinctly heretical, Bishop Bonner, though often represented as a bloodthirsty advocate of repression, chose to let her go. The reasons for this are not entirely clear. Askew was young, about 24 years old at the time, and well connected. One of her brothers was a gentleman of the king's privy chamber, and another was in the service of Archbishop Cranmer. It is likely that the archbishop knew her, and that she had some connections with the ladies of Queen Catherine Parr's household. A rigorous persecution of Anne might well have been something of a political or at least public-relations disaster, and Bonner seems to have chosen to frighten, to warn, but not to punish her.

Though Henrician policy had varied substantially through the 1530s, in the early 1540s evangelicals generally felt cautiously optimistic about the development of a genuinely reformed church in England, but that optimism was severely threatened in April 1546 when Edward Crome (d. 1562), a London preacher and friend of Anne Askew, preached a sermon denying the sacrificial nature of the Mass. This provocative sermon fuelled a new round of persecutions driven by conservative members of Henry's Privy Council, and it was in this context that Askew was arrested again by the Privy Council in June 1546 under the Act of Six Articles (1539) for denying transubstantiation. Her new examiners were less flexible than Bishop Bonner and hoped to use her to root out evangelical belief at court, particularly in the household of Catherine Parr. Askew resisted their questions under torture but was condemned for heresy nonetheless. She seems to have wished to re-frame her first examination and submission in the context of her impending martyrdom, and John Bale (1495–1563) and John Foxe (1517–87), two prominent promoters of English reform, publicized both the event and the text of her examinations widely, making her the most prominent female martyr of the English Reformation.

The two examinations of the worthy servant of God, Mistress Anne Askew, daughter of Sir William Askew, knight, of Lincolnshire, martyred in Smithfield for the constant and faithful testimony of the truth

The first examination before the inquisitors,
A.D. 1545

To satisfy your expectation, good people, [said she,] this was my first examination, in the year of our Lord 1545, and in the month of March. First, Christopher Dare examined me at Sadler's Hall, being one of the inquest, and asked if I did not believe that the sacrament hanging over the altar was the true body of Christ. Then I asked this question of him, "Wherefore was St. Stephen stoned to death?" and he said he could not tell. Then I answered that no more would I pardon his vain question.

Secondly, he said that there was a woman who testified that I would read, how God was not in temples made with hands. Then I showed him chapters VII and XVII. of the Acts of the Apostles; what Stephen and Paul had said therein. Whereupon he asked me how I took those sentences? I answered, I would not throw pearls amongst swine, for acorns were good enough.

Thirdly, he asked me, whether I said that I would rather read five lines in the Bible, than hear five masses in the temple. I confessed that I said no less; not for the dispraise of either of the Epistle or the Gospel, but because the one greatly edified me, and the other nothing at all. As St. Paul witnesses in 1 Cor. XIV., where he says, "If the trumpet gives an uncertain sound, who will prepare himself to the battle?"

Fourthly, he charged me, that I would say that if an ill priest ministered, it was the devil, and not God. My answer was that I never said any such thing. But this was my saying: that whosoever he were that ministered to me, his ill conditions could not hurt my faith, but in spirit I received, nevertheless, the body and blood of Christ.

Fifthly, he asked me what I said concerning confession. I answered him my meaning, which was, as St. James says, that every man ought to acknowledge his faults to other, and the one to pray for the other....

Seventhly, he asked me if I had the Spirit of God in me. I answered, that if I had not, I was but a reprobate or castaway. Then he said he had sent for a priest to examine me, who was there at hand. The priest asked me what I said to the sacrament of the altar, and required much to know my meaning therein. But I desired him again to hold me excused concerning that matter: no other answer would I make him, because I perceived him to be a papist.

Eighthly, he asked me if I did not think that private masses helped the souls departed. I said it was great idolatry to believe more in them, than in the death which Christ died for us.

Then they had me from there to the lord mayor, and he examined me, as they had before, and I answered him directly in all things, as I answered the inquest before. Besides this, my lord mayor laid one thing to my charge, which was never spoken of me, but by them; and that was, whether a mouse, eating the host, received God or no? This question did I never ask, but indeed they asked it of me, whereunto I made them no answer, but smiled.

Then the bishop's chancellor rebuked me, and said that I was much to blame for uttering the Scriptures. For St. Paul, he said, forbade women to speak or to talk of the word of God. I answered him that I knew Paul's meaning as well as he, which is, in 1 Cor. XIV., that a woman ought not to speak in the congregation by the way of teaching: and then I asked him how many women he had seen go into the pulpit and preach? He said he never saw any. Then I said, he ought to find no fault in poor women, unless they had offended the law.

Then the lord mayor commanded me to ward. I asked him if sureties would not serve me; and he made me short answer, that he would take none; then was I taken to the Compter, and there remained eleven days, no friend admitted to speak with me.

On the next day [March 24], the bishop of London sent for me at one o'clock, his hour being appointed at three, and as I came before him, he said he was very sorry for my trouble, and wished to know my opinions in such matters as were laid against me. He required me also, in any way, boldly to utter the secrets of my heart, bidding me not to fear in any point, for whatever I said in his house, no man should hurt me for it. I answered, "Forasmuch as your Lordship appointed three o' clock, and my friends will not come till that hour, I desire you to pardon me of giving answer till they come."...

Anon afterwards he went into his gallery with Master Spilman, and willed him in any way that he should exhort me to utter all that I thought. In the meantime he commanded his archdeacon to talk with me, who said to me, "Mistress, wherefore are you accused and thus troubled here before the bishop?" To whom I answered again and said, "Sir, ask, I pray you, my accusers; for I know not as yet." Then he took my book out of my hand, and said, "Such books as this have brought you to the trouble that you are in. Beware," said he, "beware, for he that made this book, and was the author thereof, was a heretic, I warrant you, and burned in Smithfield."...

Immediately afterwards my cousin Brittayne came in with divers others, as Master Hall of Gray's Inn, and such other like. Then my Lord of London persuaded my cousin Brittayne, as he had done often before, which was, that I should utter the bottom of my heart in any wise. My Lord said after that to me that he would I should credit the counsel of such as were my friends and well-willers in this behalf, which was, that I should utter all things that burdened my conscience; for he assured me that I should not need to stand in doubt to say any thing. For, like as he promised them, (he said,) he promised me, and would perform it; which was, that neither he, nor any man for him, should take me at advantage for any word that I should speak; and therefore he bade me say my mind without fear. I answered him, that I had nought to say, for my conscience (I thanked God) was burdened with nothing....

"Then you drive me," he said, "to lay to your charge your own report, which is this: you said, 'He that receives the sacrament by the hands of an ill priest, or a sinner, receives the devil, and not God.'" To that I answered, "I never spoke such words: but, as I said before, both to the inquest and to my lord mayor, so say I now again, that the wickedness of the priest should not hurt me, but in spirit and faith I received no less than the body and blood of Christ." Then the bishop said to me, "What saying is this, in spirit? I will not take you at that advantage." Then I answered, "My Lord, without faith and spirit I cannot receive him worthily."...

Then said my Lord unto me, that I had alleged a certain text of the Scripture. I answered that I alleged none other but St. Paul's own saying to the Athenians, in the seventeenth chapter of the Acts of the Apostles, that "God dwelleth not in temples made with hands." Then asked he me, what my faith and belief was in that matter? I answered him, "I believe as the Scripture doth teach me."

Then he inquired of me, "What if the Scripture says that it is in the body of Christ?" "I believe," said I, "as the Scripture teaches me." Then asked he again, "What if the Scripture says that it is not the body of Christ?" My answer was still, "I believe as the Scripture informs me." And upon this argument he lingered a great while, to have driven me to make him an answer to his mind: but I would not, but concluded this with him, that I believed in this and in all other things as Christ and his holy apostles did leave them.

Then he asked me why I had so few words? And I answered, "God has given me the gift of knowledge, but not of utterance: and Solomon says That a woman of few words is the gift of God," Prov. IX. 13.

Thirdly, my Lord laid unto my charge, that I should say that the mass was superstitious, wicked, and no better than idolatry. I answered him, "No, I said not so. But I say the inquest asked me whether private mass relieved departed souls or not? Unto whom then I answered, 'O Lord! what idolatry is this, that we should rather believe in private masses, than in the healthsome death of the dear Son of God?'" Then my Lord said again, "What an answer is that!" "Though it is but mean," said I, "yet it is good enough for the question."

[Anne eventually signed a confession, though she disputed its terms, and after some manoeuvering on the part of her sureties was allowed to go free.]

The latter apprehension and examination of the worthy martyr of God, Mistress Anne Askew, A.D. 1546

[…]

The sum of my examination before the king's council at Greenwich

Your request as concerning my prison-fellows I am not able to satisfy, because I did not hear their examinations. But the effect of mine was this: I, being before the council, was asked of Master Kyme. I answered, that my lord chancellor knew already my mind in that matter. They were not contented with that answer, but said it was the king's pleasure that I should open the matter to them. I answered them plainly, I would not so do; but if it were the king's pleasure to hear me, I would show him the truth. Then they said, it was not appropriate for the king to be troubled with me. I answered, that Solomon was reckoned the wisest king that ever lived, yet he did not mind listening to two poor common women, much more his Grace a simple woman and his faithful subject. So, in conclusion, I made them no other answer in that matter. Then my lord chancellor asked me my opinion in the sacrament. My answer was this, "I believe that so often as I, in a Christian congregation, receive the bread in remembrance of Christ's death, and with thanksgiving, according to his holy institution, I receive therewith the fruits, also, of his most glorious passion." The bishop of Winchester told me to make a direct answer: I said I would not sing a new song of the Lord in a strange land. Then the bishop said I spoke in parables. I answered, it was best for him, "for if I show the open truth," quoth I, "you will not accept it." Then he said I was a parrot. I told him again, I was ready to suffer all things at his hands, not only his rebukes, but all that should follow besides, yes, and all that gladly....

The next day I was brought again before the council.... Then came my Lord Lisle, my Lord of Essex, and the bishop of Winchester, requiring me earnestly that I should confess the sacrament to be flesh, blood, and bone. Then said I to my Lord Parre and my Lord Lisle, that it was a great shame for them to counsel contrary to their knowledge. Whereunto, in few words, they did say, that they would gladly all things were well.

Then the bishop said he would speak with me familiarly. I said, "So did Judas, when he unfriendly betrayed Christ." Then the bishop desired to speak with me alone. But that I refused. He asked me why. I said that in the mouth of two or three witnesses every matter should stand, after Christ's and Paul's doctrine.

Then my lord chancellor began to examine me again of the sacrament. Then I asked him how long he would halt on both sides. Then would he needs know where I found that. I said, in the Scripture. Then he went his way. Then the bishop said I should be burned. I answered, that I had searched all the Scriptures, yet could I never find that either Christ or his apostles put any creature to death. "Well, well," said I, "God will laugh your threatenings to scorn."...

The sum of the condemnation of me, Anne Askew, at the Guildhall

They said to me there that I was a heretic, and condemned by the law, if I would stand in my opinion. I answered that I was no heretic, neither yet deserved I any death by the law of God. But, as concerning the faith which I uttered and wrote to the council, I would not, I said, deny it, because I knew it true. Then they wanted to know if I would deny the sacrament to be Christ's body and blood. I said, "Yes: for the same Son of God that was born of the Virgin Mary, is now glorious in heaven, and will come again from thence at the latter day like as he went up. And as for that ye call your God, it is a piece of bread. For a more proof thereof … let it but lie in the box three months, and it will be moldy, and so turn to nothing that is good. Whereupon I am persuaded that it cannot be God."

After that, they willed me to have a priest and then I smiled. Then they asked me if it were not good; I said, I would confess my faults unto God, for I was sure that he would hear with favor. And so we were condemned by an inquest.

My belief which I wrote to the council was this: "That the sacramental bread was left us to be received with thanksgiving, in remembrance of Christ's death, the only remedy of our soul's recovery; and that thereby we also receive the whole benefits and fruits of his most glorious passion." Then would they needs know, whether the bread in the box were God or no: I said, "God is a Spirit, and will be worshipped in spirit and truth." Then they demanded, "Will you plainly deny Christ to be in the sacrament?" I answered, that I believe faithfully the eternal Son of God not to dwell there; in witness whereof I recited again the history of Bel, Dan. XIX., Acts VII. and XVII., and Matt. XXIV., concluding thus: "I neither wish death, nor yet fear his might; God have the praise thereof with thanks."

[…]

My faith briefly written to the king's Grace

I, Anne Askew, of good memory, although God hath given me the bread of adversity, and the water of trouble, yet not so much as my sins have deserved, desire this to be known unto your Grace, that, forasmuch as I am by the law condemned for an evil doer, here I take heaven and earth to record, that I shall die in my innocency: and, according to that I have said first, and will say last, I utterly abhor and detest all heresies. And as concerning the supper of the Lord, I believe so much as Christ hath said therein, which he confirmed with his most blessed blood. I believe also so much as he willed me to follow and believe, and so much as the catholic church of him teaches: for I will not forsake the commandment of his holy lips. But look, what God has charged me with his mouth, that have I shut up in my heart. And thus briefly I end, for lack of learning.

The effect of my examination and handling since my departure from Newgate

On Tuesday I was sent from Newgate to the sign of the Crown, where Master Rich and the bishop of London, with all their power and flattering words, went about to persuade me from God: but I did not esteem their coaxing pretences. Then came there to me Nicholas Shaxton, and counselled me to recant as he had done. I said to him, that it had been good for him never to have been born; with many other like words. Then Master Rich sent me to the Tower, where I remained till three o'clock.

Then came Rich and one of the council, charging me upon my obedience, to show unto them if I knew any man or woman of my sect. My answer was, that I knew none. Then they asked me of my Lady of Suffolk, my Lady of Sussex, my Lady of Hertford, my Lady Denny, and my Lady Fitzwilliam. To whom I answered, if I should pronounce any thing against them, that I were not able to prove it. Then said they unto me that the king was informed that I could name, if I would, a great number of my sect. I answered, that the king was as well deceived in that behalf, as dissembled with in other matters. Then they commanded me to show how I was maintained in the Compter, and who willed me to stick to my opinion. I said, that there was no creature that therein did strengthen me: and as for the help that I had in the Compter, it was by means of my maid. For as she went abroad in the streets, she made moan to the prentices, and they, by her, did send me money; but who they were I never knew. Then they said that there were divers gentlewomen that gave me money: but I knew not their names. Then they said that there were divers ladies that had sent me money. I answered, that there was a man in a blue coat who delivered me ten shillings, and said that my Lady of Hertford sent it me; and another in a violet coat gave me eight shillings, and said my Lady Denny sent it me: whether it were true or no, I cannot tell; for I am not sure who sent it me, but as the maid did say. Then they said, there were of the council that did maintain me: and I said, No.

Then they put me on the rack, because I confessed no ladies or gentlewomen to be of my opinion, and thereon they kept me a long time; and because I lay still, and did not cry, my lord chancellor and Master Rich took pains to rack me with their own hands, till I was nigh dead. Then the lieutenant caused me to be loosed from the rack. Incontinently I swooned, and then they recovered me again. After that I sat two long hours reasoning with my lord chancellor upon the bare floor; where he, with many flattering words, persuaded me to leave my opinion. But my Lord God (I thank his everlasting goodness) gave me grace to persevere, and will do, I hope, to the very end. Then was I brought to a house, and laid in a bed, with as weary and painful bones as ever had patient Job; I thank my Lord God there-for. Then my lord chancellor sent me word, if I would leave my opinion, I should want nothing: if I would not, I should forthwith to Newgate, and so be burned. I sent him again word, that I would rather die, than break my faith. Thus the Lord open the eyes of their blind hearts, that the truth may take place. Farewell, dear friend, and pray, pray, pray! …

The confession of faith which Anne Askew made in Newgate, before she suffered

I, Anne Askew, of good memory, although my merciful Father has given me the bread of adversity, and the water of trouble, yet not so much as my sins have deserved, confess myself here a sinner before the throne of his heavenly Majesty, desiring his forgiveness and mercy. And forasmuch as I am by the law unrighteously condemned for an evil doer concerning opinions, I take the same most merciful God of mine, who has made both heaven and earth, to record, that I hold no opinions contrary to his most holy word. And I trust in my merciful Lord, who is the giver of all grace, that he will graciously assist me against all evil opinions which are contrary to his blessed verity. For I take him to witness, that I have done, and will, unto my life's end, utterly abhor them to the uttermost of my power.

But this is the heresy which they report me to hold: that after the priest has spoken the words of consecration, there remains bread still. They both say, and also teach it for a necessary article of faith, that after those words be once spoken, there remains no bread, but even the self-same body that hung upon the cross on Good Friday, both flesh, blood, and bone. To this belief of theirs say I, nay. For then were our common creed false, which says, that he sits on the right hand of God the Father Almighty, and from thence shall come to judge the quick and the dead. Lo, this is the heresy that I hold, and for it must suffer the death. But as touching the holy and blessed supper of the Lord, I believe it to be a most necessary remembrance of his glorious sufferings and death. Moreover, I believe as much therein as my eternal and only Redeemer Jesus Christ would I should believe.

Finally, I believe all those Scriptures to be true which he has confirmed with his most precious blood. Yes, and as St. Paul says, those Scriptures that Christ has left here with us are sufficient for our learning and salvation so that I believe we need no unwritten truths to rule his church with. Therefore look, what he has said to me with his own mouth in his holy gospel, that I have, with God's grace, closed up in my heart, and my full trust is, as David says, that it shall be a lantern to my footsteps.

There are some who say that I deny the Eucharist or sacrament of thanksgiving, but those people untruly report of me. For I both say and believe it, that if it were ordered as Christ instituted it and left it, it would be a most singular comfort to us all. But as concerning your mass, as it is now used in our days, I do say and believe it to be the most abominable idol that is in the world: for my God will not be eaten with teeth, neither does he die again. And upon these words that I have now spoken, will I suffer death.

[John Foxe:] Hitherto we have treated of this good woman: now it remains that we touch somewhat as concerning her end and martyrdom. After she (being born of such stock and kindred that she might have lived in great wealth and prosperity, if she would rather have followed the world than Christ) now had been so tormented, that she could neither live long in so great distress, neither yet by her adversaries be suffered to die in secret, the day of her execution being appointed, she was brought into Smithfield in a chair, because she could not go on her feet, because of her great torments. When she was brought to the stake, she was tied by the middle with a chain, that held up her body. When all things were thus prepared for the fire, Dr. Shaxton, who was then appointed to preach, began his sermon. Anne Askew, hearing and answering again unto him, where he said well, confirmed the same; where he said amiss, "There," said she, "he misses, and speaks without the book."

Once the sermon was finished, the martyrs, standing there tied at three stakes ready to their martyrdom, began their prayers. The multitude and concourse of the people was exceeding; the place where they stood being railed about to keep out the press. Upon the bench under St. Bartholomew's church sat Wriothesley, chancellor of England; the old duke of Norfolk, the old earl of Bedford, the lord mayor, with various others. Before the fire was set to them, one of the bench, hearing that they had gunpowder about them, and being alarmed lest the faggots, by strength of the gunpowder, would come flying about their ears, began to be afraid: but the earl of Bedford, declaring unto him how the gunpowder was not laid under the faggots, but only about their bodies, to rid them out of their pain, which having vent, there was no danger to them of the faggots, so diminished that fear.

Then Wriothesley, lord chancellor, sent to Anne Askew letters, offering to her the king's pardon if she would recant; who, refusing once to look upon them, made this answer again, that she came not thither to deny her Lord and Master. Then were the letters likewise offered unto the others, who, in like manner, following the constancy of the woman, refused not only to receive them, but also to look upon them. Whereupon the lord mayor, commanding fire to be put unto them, cried with a loud voice, *Fiat justitia*.

And thus the good Anne Askew, with these blessed martyrs, being troubled so many manner of ways, and having passed through so many torments, having now ended the long course of her agonies, being compassed in with flames of fire, as a blessed sacrifice unto God, she slept in the Lord A.D. 1546, leaving behind her a singular example of Christian constancy for all men to follow.

LUTHER'S IMPACT
25. PHILIP MELANCHTHON (1497–1560)

Melanchthon was born Philip Schwartzerd in Bretten in the Palatinate, where his father was armorer to the Count Palatine. He received an excellent classical education in Latin and Greek and consequently translated his German name (literally meaning "Black Earth") into the Greek equivalent: Melanchthon. He attended the universities of both Heidelberg and Tübingen, where he studied classical languages, literature, and philosophy. In 1516 he was awarded an M.A. and began the serious study of theology, influenced by his humanist studies and his great uncle, Johannes Reuchlin (1455–1522), who secured for him the professorship of Greek at Wittenberg, Luther's university, in 1518.

At Wittenberg Melanchthon increasingly studied biblical texts and was subsequently moved to the theology faculty. He began a spirited defense of Luther's position and sustained hope that the cause of the Reformation might be accepted by the emperor and that the divisions emerging in the Protestant movement could be healed through negotiation. The consequence of this was the 1530 Augsburg Confession, which was largely written by Melanchthon. His moderate position and openness to other theological perspectives led to his being attacked from all sides; even Luther occasionally doubted his commitment to the Lutheran position. Nevertheless, on Luther's death Melanchthon became the leading theologian and spokesman for the Lutheran cause. He also served as the most effective and inspired of the Protestant educational reformers, largely responsible for Lutheran manuals and texts. His humanist training and deep knowledge of the classics ensured that humanist methods and content would in future form an important element of Protestant educational practices and textbooks.

It was Melanchthon who was given the responsibility of delivering Luther's funeral oration, and it was he who made the official announcement of the reformer's death to the University of Wittenberg. Although they did not always agree, Luther and Melanchthon had great respect for one another, as is evident from the almost classical oration below. In it, Melanchthon the historian recognizes Luther's role in the Reformation and his place in history; Melanchthon the theologian witnesses for the Protestant return to biblical authority; and Melanchthon the teacher makes clear the contribution Luther made to the institution of confessional learning.

After a life of scholarship, teaching, and writing, Melanchthon died in 1560.

Funeral Oration over Luther

Though amid the public sorrow my voice is obstructed by grief and tears, yet in this vast assembly something ought to be said, not, as among the heathen, only in praise of the deceased. Much rather is this assembly to be reminded of the wonderful government of the Church, and of her perils, that in our distress we may consider what we are, most of all, to desire, and by what examples we are to regulate our lives. There are ungodly men, who, in the confused condition of human affairs, think that everything is the result of accident. But we who are illumined by the many explicit declarations of God, distinguish the Church from the profane multitude; and we know that it is in reality governed and preserved by God. We fix our eye on this Church. We acknowledge lawful rulers and consider their manner of life. We also select suitable leaders and teachers, whom we may piously follow and reverence.

It is necessary to think on and to speak of these things so often as we name the name of the reverend doctor Martin Luther, our most dear Father and Preceptor, whom many wicked men have most bitterly hated; but whom we, who know that he was a minister of the gospel raised up by God, love and applaud. We also have the evidence to show that his doctrine did not consist of seditious opinions scattered by blind impulse, as men of epicurean tastes suppose; but that it is an exhibition of the will of God and of true worship, an exposition of the Holy Scriptures, a preaching of the Word of God, that is, of the gospel of Jesus Christ.

In orations delivered on occasions like the present, it is the custom to say many things about the personal endowments of those who are panegyrized. But I will omit this and will speak only on the main subject, viz., his relation to the Church; for good men will always judge that if he promoted sound and necessary doctrine in the Church, we should give thanks to God because He raised him up; and all good men should praise his labors, fidelity, constancy and other virtues, and should most affectionately cherish his memory.

So much for the exordium of my oration. The Son of God, as Paul observes, sits at the right hand of the Eternal Father and gives gifts unto men, viz., the gospel and the Holy Spirit. That He might bestow these He raises up prophets, apostles, teachers and pastors, and selects from our midst those who study, hear and delight in the writings of the prophets and apostles. Nor does He call into this service only those who occupy the ordinary stations; but He often makes war upon those very ones by teachers chosen from other stations. It is both pleasant and profitable to contemplate the Church of all ages and to consider the goodness of God in sending useful teachers, one after another, that as some fall in the ranks, others may at once press into their places.

Behold the patriarchs: Adam, Seth, Enoch, Methuselah, Noah, Shem. When in the time of the last named, who lived in the neighborhood of the Sodomites, the nations forgot the teaching of Noah and Shem, and worshipped idols, Abraham was raised up to be Shem's companion and to assist him in his great work and in propagating sound doctrine. He was succeeded by Isaac, Jacob and Joseph, which last lighted the torch of truth in all the land of Egypt, which at that time was the most flourishing kingdom in all the world. Then came Moses, Joshua, Samuel, David, Elijah, Elisha, Isaiah, Jeremiah, Daniel, Zechariah. Then Ezra, Onias, and the Maccabees. Then Simeon, Zacharias, the Baptist, Christ and the apostles. It is a delight to contemplate this unbroken succession, inasmuch as it is a manifest proof of the presence of God in the Church.

After the apostles comes a long line, inferior, indeed, but distinguished by the divine attestations: Polycarp, Irenaeus, Gregory of Neocaesarea, Basil, Augustine, Prosper, Maximus, Hugo, Bernard, Tauler and others. And though these later times have been less fruitful, yet God has always preserved a remnant; and that a more splendid light of the gospel has been kindled by the voice of Luther cannot be denied.

To that splendid list of most illustrious men raised up by God to gather and establish the Church, and recognized as the chief glory of the human race, must be added the name of Martin Luther. Solon, Themistocles, Scipio, Augustus and others who established or ruled over vast empires were great men indeed: but far inferior were they to our leaders, Isaiah, John the Baptist, Paul, Augustine and Luther. It is proper that we of the Church should understand this manifest difference.

What, then, are the great and splendid things disclosed by Luther which render his life illustrious? Many are crying out that confusion has come upon the Church, and that inexplicable controversies have arisen. I reply that this belongs to the regulation of the Church. When the Holy Spirit reproves the world, disorders arise on account of the obstinacy of the wicked. The fault is with those who will not hear the Son of God, of Whom the Heavenly Father says: "Hear ye him." Luther brought to light the true and necessary doctrine. That the densest darkness existed touching the doctrine of repentance is evident. In his discussions he showed what true repentance is, and what is the refuge and the sure comfort of the soul which quails under the sense of the wrath of God. He expounded Paul's doctrine, which says that man is justified by faith. He showed the difference between the law and the gospel, between the righteousness of faith and civil righteousness. He also showed what the true worship of God is: and [he] recalled the church from [the] heathenish superstition which imagined that God is worshipped, even though the mind, agitated by some academic doubt, turns away from God. He bade us worship in faith and with a good conscience, and led us to the one Mediator, the Son of God, who sits at the right hand of the Eternal Father and makes intercession for us—not to images or to dead men, that by a shocking superstition impious men might worship images and dead men.

He also pointed out other services acceptable to God, and so adorned and guarded civil life as it had never been adorned and guarded by any other man's writings. Then from necessary services he separated the puerilities of human ceremonies, the rites and institutions which hinder the true worship of God. And that the heavenly truth might be handed down to posterity he translated the prophetical and apostolic Scriptures into the German language with so much accuracy that his version is more easily understood by the reader than most commentaries.

He also published many expositions, which Erasmus was wont to say excelled all others. And as it is recorded respecting the rebuilding of Jerusalem that with one hand they built and with the other they held the sword, so he fought with the enemies of the true doctrine, and at the same time composed annotations replete with heavenly truth, and by his pious counsel brought assistance to the consciences of many.

Inasmuch as a large part of the doctrine cannot be understood by human reason, as the doctrine of the remission of sins and of faith, it must be acknowledged that he was taught of God; and many of us witnessed the struggles through which he passed in establishing the principle that by faith are we received and heard of God.

Hence throughout eternity pious souls will magnify the benefits which God has bestowed on the Church through Luther. First they will give thanks to God. Then they will own that they owe much to the labors of this man, even though atheists who mock the Church declare that these splendid achievements are empty and superstitious nothings.

It is not true, as some falsely affirm, that intricate disputes have arisen, that the apple of discord has been thrown into the Church, that the riddles of the Sphinx have been proposed. It is an easy matter for discreet and pious persons, and for those who do not judge maliciously, to see, by a comparison of views, which [agree] with the heavenly doctrine and which do not. Yea, without doubt these controversies have already been settled in the minds of all pious persons. For since God wills to reveal himself and his purposes in the language of prophets and apostles, it is not to be imagined that that language is as ambiguous as the leaves of the Sibyl, which, when disturbed, fly away, the sport of the winds.

Some by no means evil-minded persons have complained that Luther displayed too much severity. I will not deny this. But I answer in the language of Erasmus: "Because of the magnitude of the disorders God gave this age a violent physician." When God raised up this instrument against the proud and impudent enemies of the truth, he spoke as he did to Jeremiah: "Behold I place my words in thy mouth; destroy and build." Over against these enemies God set this mighty destroyer. In vain do they find fault with God. Moreover, God does not govern the Church by human counsels; nor does He choose instruments very like those of men. It is natural for mediocre and inferior minds to dislike those of more ardent character, whether good or bad. When Aristides saw Themistocles by the mighty impulse of genius undertake and successfully accomplish great achievements, though he congratulated the State, he sought to turn the zealous mind of Themistocles from its course.

I do not deny that the more ardent characters sometimes make mistakes, for amid the weakness of human nature no one is without fault. But we may say of such a one what the ancients said of Hercules, Cimon and others: "rough indeed, but worthy of all praise." And in the Church, if, as Paul says, he fights a good fight, holding faith and a good conscience, he is to be held in the highest esteem by us.

That Luther was such we do know, for he constantly defended purity of doctrine and kept a good conscience. There is no one who knew him who does not know that he was possessed of the greatest kindness and of the greatest affability in the society of his friends, and that he was in no sense contentious or quarrelsome. He also exhibited, as such a man ought, the greatest dignity of demeanor. He possessed "an upright character, a gracious speech."

Rather may we apply to him the words of Paul: "Whatsoever things are true, whatsoever things are honest, whatsoever things are just, whatsoever things are pure, whatsoever things are lovely, whatsoever things are of good report." If he was severe, it was the severity of zeal for the truth, not the love of strife or of harshness. Of these things we and many others are witnesses. To his sixty-third year he spent his life in the most ardent study of religion and of all the liberal arts. No speech of mine can worthily set forth the praises of such a man. No lewd passions were ever detected in him, no seditious counsels. He was emphatically the advocate of peace. He never mingled the arts of politics with the affairs of the Church for the purpose of augmenting his own authority or that of his friends. Such wisdom and virtue, I am persuaded, do not arise from mere human diligence. Brave, lofty, ardent souls, such as Luther had, must be divinely guided.

What shall I say of his other virtues? Often have I found him weeping and praying for the whole Church. He spent a part of almost every day reading the Psalms, with which he mingled his own supplications amid tears and groans. Often did he express his indignation at those who through indifference or pretence of other occupations are indifferent in the matter of prayer. On this account, he said, Divine Wisdom has prescribed forms of prayer, that by reading them our minds may be quickened, and the voice ever may proclaim the God we worship.

In the many grave deliberations incident to the public perils, we observed the transcendent vigor of his mind, his valor, his unshaken courage where terror reigned. God was his anchor, and faith never failed him.

As regards the penetration of his mind, in the midst of uncertainties he alone saw what was to be done. Nor was he indifferent, as many suppose, to the public weal. On the contrary he knew the wants of the state, and clearly understood the feelings and wishes of his fellow-citizens. And though his genius was so extraordinary, yet he read with the greatest eagerness both ancient and modern ecclesiastical writings and all histories, that he might find in them examples applicable to present conditions.

The immortal monuments of his eloquence remain, nor has the power of his oratory ever been surpassed.

The removal of such a man from our midst, a man of the most transcendent genius, skilled in learning, trained by long experience, adorned with many superb and heroic virtues, chosen of God for the reformation of the Church, loving us all with a paternal affection—the removal of such a man from our midst calls for tears and lamentations. We are like orphans bereft of a distinguished and faithful father. But though we must bow to God, yet let us not permit the memory of his virtues and of his good offices to perish from among us. And let us rejoice that he now holds that familiar and delightful intercourse with God and His Son, our Lord Jesus Christ, which by faith in the Son of God he always sought and expected. Where, by the manifestations of God and by the testimony of the whole Church in heaven, he not only hears the applause of his toils in the service of the gospel, but is also delivered from the mortal body as from a prison, and has entered that vastly higher school, where he can contemplate the essence of God, the two natures joined in Christ, and the whole purpose set forth in founding and redeeming the Church—which great things, contained and set forth in the sacred oracles, he contemplated by faith; but seeing them now face to face, he rejoices with unspeakable joy; and with his whole soul he ardently pours forth thanks to God for His great goodness.

There he knows why the Son of God is called the Word and the Image of the Eternal Father, and in what way the Holy Spirit is the bond of mutual affection, not only between the Father and Son, but also between them and the Church. The first principles of these truths he had learned in this mortal life, and often did he most earnestly and wisely discourse on these lofty themes, on the distinction between true and false worship, on the true knowledge of God and of divine revelation, on the true God as distinguished from false deities.

Many persons in this assembly have heard him discourse on these words: "Ye shall see the heaven open, and the angels of God ascending and descending upon the Son of man." He bade his hearers fix their minds on that large word of comfort which declares that heaven is open, that God is revealed to us; that the bolts of the divine wrath are turned away from those who flee to the Son; that God is now with us, and that those who call upon Him are received, guided and kept by him.

This purpose of God, pronounced by atheists to be a fable, admonishes us to banish doubt and to cast out those fears which restrain our timid souls from calling on God and from resting in Him.

He was wont to say that the angels, ascending and descending in the body of Christ, are ministers of the gospel, who first under the direction of Christ ascend to God and receive from Him the light of the gospel and the Holy Spirit. Then they descend, that is, discharge the office of teaching among men. He was also accustomed to add that these heavenly spirits, these angels who behold the Son, study and rejoice over the mysterious union of the two natures; and that since they are the armed servants of the Lord in defending the Church, they are directed by His hand.

Of these glorious things he is now a spectator, and as once under the direction of Christ he ascended and descended among the ministers of the gospel, so now he beholds the angels sent by Christ, and enjoys with them the contemplation of the divine wisdom and the divine works.

We remember the great delight with which he recounted the course, the counsels, the perils and escapes of the prophets, and the learning with which he discoursed on all the ages of the Church, thereby showing that he was inflamed by no ordinary passion for those wonderful men. Now he embraces them and rejoices to hear them speak, and to speak to them in turn. Now they hail him gladly as a companion, and thank God with him for having gathered and preserved the Church.

Hence we do not doubt that Luther is eternally happy. We mourn over our bereavement; and though it is necessary to bow to the will of God who has called him hence, let us know that it is the will of God that we should cherish the memory of this man's virtues and services. That duty let us now discharge. Let us acknowledge that this man was a blessed instrument of God, and let us studiously learn his doctrine. Let us in our humble station imitate his virtues, so necessary for us: his fear of God, his faith, his devoutness in prayer, his uprightness in the ministry, his chastity, his diligence in avoiding seditious counsels, his eagerness for learning. And as we ought frequently to reflect on those other pious leaders of the Church, Jeremiah, John the Baptist and Paul, so let us consider the doctrine and the course of this man. Let us also join in thanksgiving and prayer, as is meet in this assembly. Follow me then with devout hearts:—We give thanks to thee, Almighty God, the Eternal Father of our Lord Jesus Christ, the Founder of Thy Church, together with Thy Coeternal Son, and the Holy Spirit, wise, good, merciful, just, true, powerful Sovereign, because Thou dost gather a heritage for Thy Son from among the human race, and dost maintain the ministry of the gospel, and hast now reformed Thy Church by means of Luther. We present our ardent supplications that Thou wouldst henceforth preserve, fix and impress upon our hearts the doctrines of truth, as Isaiah prayed for his disciples; and that by Thy Holy Spirit Thou wouldst inflame our minds with a pure devotion and direct our feet into the paths of holy obedience.

As the death of illustrious rulers often portends dire punishment to the survivors, we beseech you, we, especially, to whom is committed the office of teaching, beseech you to reflect on the perils that now threaten the whole world. Yonder, the Turks are advancing; here, civil discord is threatened; there, other adversaries, released at last from the fear of Luther's censure, will corrupt the truth more boldly than ever.

That God may avert these calamities, let us be more diligent in regulating our lives and in directing our studies, always holding fast this sentiment: that so long as we retain, hear, learn and love the pure teaching of the gospel, we shall be the House and Church of God, as the Son of God says: "If a man love me, he will keep my words; and my Father will love him, and we will come unto him, and make our abode with him." Encouraged by this ample promise, let us be quickened in teaching the truth of heaven, and let us not forget that the human race and governments are preserved for the sake of the Church; and let us fix our eyes on that eternity to which God has called our attention, Who has not revealed Himself by such splendid witnesses and sent His Son in vain, but truly loves and cares for those who magnify His benefits. Amen.

4

The Catholic Reformation

26. *CONSILIUM DE EMENDANDA ECCLESIA*, 1537

The Consilium *is one of the earliest documents of the Catholic reform movement. The pontificate of Paul III (1534–49) marked the beginning of the Church's recognition of the serious need for reform. With a general council of the Church scheduled to meet in May 1537, in July 1536 the pope called together a reform commission to consider the major issues that needed to be addressed. The commission was headed by Cardinal Gasparo Contarini (1483–1542), and was composed of nine of the most prominent Catholic reformers of the period, including Gian Pietro Carafa (1476–1559), the leader of the Theatines and the future Pope Paul IV, Jacopo Sadoleto (1477–1547), bishop of Carpentras, and Reginald Pole (1500–58). The commission deliberated for three months, and presented its report to the pope in March 1537. It was harshly critical of abuses within the papal curia and urged the Church to respond to the need for more emphasis on pastoral care. Paul III's response to the report can be gauged by his elevation of three of the commissioners—Carafa, Sadoleto, and Pole—to the cardinalate.*

Despite the insight of the report, the credentials of the commissioners and the approval of the pope, the Consilium *had a limited impact on the conduct of church business in the short term. Indeed, it proved to be something of a liability. Copies of it were soon leaked to the Protestant reformers, who used it as further evidence of the degeneracy of the Catholic Church and the rightness of their reforms. Nevertheless it marked the opening of the reform campaign within the Church and identified the directions in which that reform should progress.*

Consilium de Emendanda Ecclesia, *1537*

Most Holy Father, we are so far from being able to express in words the great thanks the Christian Commonwealth should render to Almighty God because He has appointed you Pope in these times and pastor of His flock and has given you that resolve which you have that we scarcely hope we can do justice in thought to the gratitude we owe God. For that Spirit of God by whom the power of the heavens has been established, as the prophet says, has determined to rebuild through you the Church of Christ, tottering, nay, in fact collapsed, and, as we see, to apply your hand to this ruin, and to raise it up to its original height and restore it to its pristine beauty. We shall hope to make the surest interpretation of this divine purpose—we whom your Holiness has called to Rome and ordered to make known to you, without regard for your advantage or for anyone else's, those abuses, indeed those most serious diseases, which now for a long time afflict God's Church and especially this Roman Curia and which have now led, with these diseases gradually becoming more troublesome and destructive, to this great ruin which we see.

And your Holiness, taught by the Spirit of God who (as Augustine says) speaks in hearts without the din of words, had rightly acknowledged that the origin of these evils was due to the fact that some popes, your predecessors, in the words of the Apostle Paul, "having itching ears heaped up to themselves teachers according to their own lusts" [2 Timothy 4:3], not that they might learn from them what they should do, but that they might find through the application and cleverness of these teachers a justification for what it pleased them to do. Thence it came about, besides the fact that flattery follows all dominion as the shadow does the body and that truth's access to the ears of princes has always been most difficult, that teachers at once appeared who taught that the pope is the lord of all benefices and that therefore, since a lord may sell by right what is his own, it necessarily follows that the pope cannot be guilty of simony. Thus the will of the pope, of whatever kind it may be, is the rule governing his activities and deeds: whence it may be shown without doubt that whatever is pleasing is also permitted.

From this source as from a Trojan horse so many abuses and such grave diseases have rushed in upon the Church of God that we now see her afflicted almost to the despair of salvation and the news of these things spread even to the infidels (let your Holiness believe those who know), who for this reason especially deride the Christian religion, so that through us—through us, we say—the name of Christ is blasphemed among the heathens.

But you, Most Holy Father, and truly Most Holy, instructed by the Spirit of God, and with more than that former prudence of yours, since you have devoted yourself fully to the task of curing the ills and restoring good health to the Church of Christ committed to your care, you have seen, and you have rightly seen, that the cure must begin where the disease had its origin, and having followed the teaching of the Apostle Paul you wish to be a steward, not a master, and to be found trustworthy by the Lord, having indeed imitated that servant in the Gospel whom the master set over his household to give them their ration of grain in due time; and on that account you have resolved to turn from what is unlawful, nor do you wish to be able to do what you should not. You have therefore summoned us to you, inexperienced indeed and unequal to so great a task, yet not a little disposed both to the honor and glory of your Holiness and especially to the renewal of the Church of Christ; and you have charged us in the gravest language to compile all the abuses and to make them known to you, having solemnly declared that we shall give an account of this task entrusted to us to Almighty God, if we carelessly or unfaithfully execute it. And you have bound us by oath so that we can discuss all these matters more freely and explain them to you, the penalty of excommunication even having been added lest we disclose anything of our office to anyone.

We have therefore made, in obedience to your command and insofar as it can be briefly done, a compilation of those diseases and their remedies—remedies, we stress, which we were able to devise given the limitations of our talents. But you indeed according to your goodness and wisdom will restore and bring to completion all matters where we have been remiss in view of our limitations. And in order to set ourselves some fixed boundaries, since your Holiness is both the prince of those provinces which are under ecclesiastical authority and the pope of the universal Church as well as bishop of Rome, we have not ventured to say anything about matters which pertain to this principality of the Church, excellently ruled, we see, by your prudence. We shall touch however on those matters which pertain to the office of universal pontiff and to some extent on those which have to do with the bishop of Rome.

This point, we believed, most Holy Father, must be established before everything else, as Aristotle says in the *Politics*, that in this ecclesiastical government of the Church of Christ just as in every body politic this rule must be held supreme, that as far as possible the laws be observed, nor do we think that it is licit for us to dispense from these laws save for a pressing and necessary reason. For no more dangerous custom can be introduced in any commonwealth than this failure to observe the laws, which our ancestors wished to be sacred and whose authority they called venerable and divine. You know all this, excellent pontiff; you have long ago read this in the philosophers and theologians. Indeed we think that the following precept is not only most germane to this, but a greater and higher ordinance by far, that it cannot be permitted even for the Vicar of Christ to obtain any profit in the use of the power of the keys conferred on him by Christ. For truly this is the command of Christ: "Freely you have received, freely give" [Matthew 10:8].

These points having been established at the outset, then [it should be remembered] your Holiness takes care of the Church of Christ with the help of a great many servants through whom he exercises this responsibility. These moreover are all clerics to whom divine worship has been entrusted, priests especially and particularly parish priests and above all bishops. Therefore, if this government is to proceed properly, care must be taken that these servants are qualified for the office which they must discharge.

The first abuse in this respect is the ordination of clerics and especially of priests, in which no care is taken, no diligence employed, so that indiscriminately the most unskilled, men of the vilest stock and of evil morals, adolescents, are admitted to Holy Orders and to the priesthood, to the [indelible] mark, we stress, which above all denotes Christ. From this have come innumerable scandals and a contempt for the ecclesiastical order, and reverence for divine worship has not only been diminished but has almost by now been destroyed. Therefore, we think that it would be an excellent thing if your Holiness first in this city of Rome appointed two or three prelates, learned and upright men, to preside over the ordination of clerics. He should also instruct all bishops, even under pain of censure, to give careful attention to this in their own dioceses. Nor should your Holiness allow anyone to be ordained except by his own bishop or with the permission of deputies in Rome or of his own bishop. Moreover, we think that each bishop should have a teacher in his diocese to instruct clerics in minor orders both in letters and in morals, as the laws prescribe.

Another abuse of the greatest consequence is in the bestowing of ecclesiastical benefices, especially parishes and above all bishoprics, in the matter of which the practice has become entrenched that provision is made for the persons on whom the benefices are bestowed, but not for the flock and Church of Christ. Therefore, in bestowing parish benefices, but above all bishoprics, care must be taken that they be given to good and learned men so that they themselves can perform those duties to which they are bound, and, in addition, that they be conferred on those who will in all likelihood reside. A benefice in Spain or in Britain then must not be conferred on an Italian, or vice versa. This must be observed both in appointments to benefices vacated through death and in the case of resignations, where now only the intention of the person resigning is considered and nothing else. In the case of these resignations we think that it would have good effect if one or several upright men were put in charge of the matter.

Another abuse, when benefices are bestowed or turned over to others, has crept in in connection with the arrangement of payments from the income of these benefices. Indeed, the person resigning the benefice often reserves all the income for himself. In such cases care must be taken that payments can be reserved for no other reason and with no other justification than for alms which ought to be given for pious uses and for the needy. For income is joined to the benefice as the body to the soul. By its very nature then it belongs to him who holds the benefice so that he can live from it respectably according to his station and can at the same time support the expenses for divine worship and for the upkeep of the church and other religious buildings, and so that he may expend what remains for pious uses. For this is the nature of the income of these benefices. But just as in the course of natural events some things occur in particular cases which are contrary to the tendency of nature as a whole, so in the instance of the pope, because he is the universal steward of the goods of the Church, if he sees that that portion of the revenues which should be spent for pious uses or a part of it may more usefully be spent for some other pious purpose, he can without a doubt arrange it. He is able therefore in all justice to set aside payment to aid a person in need, especially a cleric, so that he can live respectably according to his station. For that reason it is a great abuse when all revenues are reserved and everything is taken away which should be allotted to divine service and to the support of him who holds the benefice. And likewise it is certainly a great abuse to make payments to rich clerics who can live satisfactorily and respectably on the income they have. Both abuses must be abolished.

Still another abuse is in the exchanging of benefices which occur under agreements that are all simoniacal and with no consideration except for the profit.

Another abuse must be entirely removed which has now become prevalent in this Curia due to a certain cunning on the part of some experienced persons. For, although the law provides that benefices cannot be bequeathed in a will, since they do not belong to the testator but to the Church, and this so that these ecclesiastical properties may be kept in common for the benefit of all and not become the private possession of anyone, human diligence—but not Christian diligence—has discovered a great many ways whereby this law may be mocked. For first the surrender of bishoprics and other benefices are made with the right of regaining them [*cum regressu*]; the reservation of the income is added, then the reservation of conferring benefices; the reservation of the administration is piled on top of this, and by this stipulation they make him bishop who does not have the rights of a bishop, whereas all the episcopal rights are given to him who is not made bishop. May your Holiness see how far this flattering teaching has advanced, where at length it has led, so that what is pleasing is permitted. What, I pray, is this except appointing an heir for oneself to a benefice? Besides this another trick has been devised, when coadjutors are given to bishops requesting them, men less qualified than they are themselves, so that, unless one wishes to close his eyes, he may clearly see that by this means an heir is appointed.

Also, an ancient law was renewed by Clement [VII] that sons of priests may not have the benefices of their fathers, lest in this way the common property [of the Church] become private property. Nevertheless, dispensations are made (so we hear) in the case of this law which ought to be revered. We have not been willing to be silent in the face of that which any prudent man may judge for himself to be absolutely true, namely, that nothing has stirred up more this ill-will toward the clergy, whence so many quarrels have arisen and others threaten, than this diversion of ecclesiastical revenues and income from the general to private advantage. Formerly everyone was hopeful [that such abuses would be corrected]; now led to despair they sharpen their tongues against this See.

Another abuse is in the matter of expectatives and reservations of benefices, and the occasion is given to desire another's death and to hear of it with pleasure. Indeed the more worthy are excluded when there are vacancies, and cause is given for litigations. All these abuses, we think, must be abolished.

Another abuse has been devised with the same cunning. For certain benefices are by right "incompatible," and they are so designated. By virtue of that term our forefathers have wished to remind us that they should not be conferred on one single person. Now dispensations are granted in these cases, not only for two [such benefices] but for more, and, what is worse, for bishoprics. We feel that this custom which has become so prevalent because of greed must be abolished, especially in the case of bishoprics. What about the lifelong unions of benefices in one man, so that such a plurality of benefices is no obstacle to holding benefices that are "incompatible"? Is that not a pure betrayal of the law?

Another abuse has also become prevalent, that bishoprics are conferred on the most reverend cardinals or that not one but several are put in their charge, an abuse, most Holy Father, which we think is of great importance in God's Church. In the first place, because the offices of cardinal and bishop are "incompatible." For the cardinals are to assist your Holiness in governing the universal Church; the bishop's duty however is to tend his own flock, which he cannot do as well as he should unless he lives with his sheep as a shepherd with his flock.

Furthermore, Holy Father, this practice is especially injurious in the example it sets. For how can this Holy See set straight and correct the abuses of others, if abuses are tolerated in its own principal members? Nor do we think that because they are cardinals they have a greater license to transgress the law; on the contrary, they have far less. For the life of these men ought to be a law for others, nor should they imitate the Pharisees who speak and do not act, but Christ our Savior who began to act and afterwards to teach. This practice is more harmful in the deliberations of the Church, for this license nurtures greed. Besides, the cardinals solicit bishoprics from kings and princes, on whom they are afterwards dependent and about whom they cannot freely pass judgment. Indeed, even if they are able and willing, they are nevertheless led astray, confused in their judgment by their partisanship. Would that this custom be abolished therefore and provision be made that the cardinals can live respectably in accordance with their dignity, each receiving an equal income. We believe that this can easily be done, if we wish to abandon the servitude to Mammon and serve only Christ.

With these abuses corrected which pertain to the appointment of your ministers, through whom as through instruments both the worship of God can be properly directed and the Christian people well instructed and governed in the Christian life, we must now approach those matters which refer to the government of the Christian people. In this regard, most blessed Father, the abuse that first and before all others must be reformed is that bishops above all and then parish priests must not be absent from their churches and parishes except for some grave reason, but must reside, especially bishops, as we have said, because they are the bridegrooms of the church entrusted to their care. For, by the Eternal God, what sight can be more lamentable for the Christian man traveling through the Christian world than this desertion of the churches? Nearly all the shepherds have departed from their flocks, nearly all have been entrusted to hirelings. A heavy penalty, therefore, must be imposed on bishops before the others, and then on parish priests, who are absent from their flocks, not only censures, but also the withholding of the income of absentees, unless the bishops have obtained permission from your Holiness and the parish priests from their bishops to be away for a short period of time. Some laws and the decrees of some Councils may be read in this regard, which provide that the bishop shall not be permitted to be away from his church for more than three Sundays.

It is also an abuse that so many of the most reverend cardinals are absent from this Curia and perform none of the duties incumbent on them as cardinals. Although perhaps not all should reside here, for we think it advantageous that some should live in their provinces—for through them as through some roots spread out into the whole Christian world the peoples are bound together under this Roman See—yet your Holiness therefore should call most to the Curia that they might reside here. For in this way, aside from the fact that the cardinals would be performing their office, provision would also be made for the dignity of the Curia and the gap repaired, if any should occur by the withdrawal of many bishops returning to their own churches.

Another great abuse and one that must by no means be tolerated, whereby the whole Christian people is scandalized, arises from the obstacles the bishops face in the government of their flocks, especially in punishing and correcting evildoers. For in the first place wicked men, chiefly clerics, free themselves in many ways from the jurisdiction of their ordinary. Then, if they have not arranged this exemption, they at once have recourse to the Penitentiary or to the Datary, where they immediately find a way to escape punishment, and, what is worse, they find this in consideration of the payment of money. This scandal, most blessed Father, so greatly disturbs the Christian people that words cannot express it. Let these abuses be abolished, we implore your Holiness by the Blood of Christ, by which He has redeemed for Himself His Church and in which He has bathed her. Let these stains be removed, by which, if any access were given to them in any commonwealth of men or any kingdom, it would at once or very soon fall headlong into ruin, nor could it in any way longer survive. Yet we think that we are at liberty to introduce these monstrosities into the Christian Commonwealth.

Another abuse must be corrected with regard to the religious orders, for many have become so deformed that they are a great scandal to the laity and do grave harm by their example. We think that all conventual orders ought to be done away with, not however that injury be done to anyone, but by prohibiting the admission of novices. Thus they might be quickly abolished without wronging anyone, and good religious could be substituted for them. In fact we now think that it would be best if all boys who have not been professed were removed from their monasteries.

We believe that the appointment of preachers and confessors from among the friars must also be given attention and corrected, first that their superiors take great care that they are qualified and then that they are presented to the bishops, to whom above all others the care of the Church has been entrusted, by whom they may be examined either directly or through capable men. Nor should they be permitted to carry out these tasks without the consent of the bishops.

We have said, most blessed Father, that it is not lawful in any way in the matter of the use of the keys for him exercising this power to obtain any profit. Concerning this there is the firm word of Christ: "Freely you have received, freely give." This pertains not only to your Holiness, but to all who share your power. Therefore we would wish that this same injunction be observed by the legates and nuncios. For just as custom which has now become prevalent dishonors this See and disturbs the people, so, if the contrary were done, this See would win the highest honor and the people would be wonderfully edified.

Another abuse troubles the Christian people with regard to nuns under the care of conventual friars, where in very many convents public sacrilege occurs with the greatest scandal to all. Therefore, let your Holiness take this entire responsibility away from the conventuals and give it either to the ordinaries or to others, whatever will be deemed better.

There is a great and dangerous abuse in the public schools, especially in Italy, where many professors of philosophy teach ungodly things. Indeed, the most ungodly disputations take place in the churches, and, if they are of a religious nature, what pertains to the divine in them is treated before the people with great irreverence. We believe, therefore, that the bishops must be instructed, where there are public schools, to admonish those who lecture that they not teach the young ungodly things, but that they show the weakness of the natural light [of reason] in questions relating to God, to the newness or the eternity of the world, and the like, and guide these youths to what is godly. Likewise, that public disputations on questions of this kind should not be permitted, nor on theological matters either, which disputation certainly destroy much respect among the common people, but that disputations on these matters be held privately and on other questions in the realm of natural science publicly. And the same charge must be imposed on all other bishops, especially of important cities, where disputations of this kind are wont to be held.

The same care must also be employed in the printing of books, and all princes should be instructed by letter to be on their guard lest any books be printed indiscriminately under their authority. Responsibility in this matter should be given to the ordinaries. And because boys in elementary school are now accustomed to read the *Colloquies* of Erasmus, in which there is much to educate unformed minds to ungodly things, the reading of this book and others of this type then must be prohibited in grammar school.

Following these matters which pertain to the instruction of your ministers in the care of the universal Church and in its administration, it must be noted that with regard to privileges granted by your Holiness besides the former abuses other abuses have also been introduced.

The first concerns renegade friars or religious who after a solemn vow withdraw from their order and obtain permission not to wear the habit of their order or even the trace of a habit, but only dignified clerical dress. Let us omit for the moment any reference to gain. For we have already said in the beginning that it is not lawful to make a profit for oneself from the use of the keys and of the power given by Christ, but that one must abstain from this indulgence. For the habit is the sign of profession, whence a dispensation cannot be given even by the bishop to whom these renegades are subject. Therefore this privilege ought not to be granted them, nor should those, when they depart from a vow which binds them to God, be allowed to hold benefices or administrative posts.

Another abuse concerns the pardoners [of the hospital] of the Holy Spirit, [of the hospital] of St. Anthony, and others of this type, who deceive the peasants and simple people and ensnare them with innumerable superstitions. It is our opinion that these pardoners should be abolished.

Another abuse is in connection with dispensing a person established in Holy Orders so that he can take a wife. This dispensation should not be given anyone except for the preservation of a people or a nation, where there is a most serious public reason, especially in these times when the Lutherans lay such great stress on this matter.

There is an abuse in dispensing in the case of marriages between those related by blood or by marriage. Indeed we do not think that this should be done within the second degree [of consanguinity] except for a serious public reason and in other degrees except for a good reason and without any payment of money, as we have already said, unless the parties previously have been united in marriage. In that case it may be permitted in view of the absolution of a sin already committed to impose a money fine after absolution and to allot it to the pious causes to which your Holiness contributes. For just as no money can be demanded when the use of the keys is without sin, so a money fine can be imposed and allotted to pious usage when absolution from sin is sought.

Another abuse concerns the absolution of those guilty of simony. Alas, how this destructive vice holds sway in the Church of God, so that some have no fear of committing simony and then immediately seek absolution from punishment. Indeed they purchase that absolution, and thus they retain the benefice which they have purchased. We do not say that your Holiness is not able to absolve them of that punishment which has been ordained by positive law, but that he ought by no means to do so, so that opposition might be offered to a crime so great that there is none more dangerous or more scandalous.

Also permission should not be given to clerics to bequeath ecclesiastical property except for an urgent reason, lest the possessions of the poor be converted to private pleasure and the enlarging of a person's own estate.

Moreover confessional letters as well as the use of portable altars should not be readily allowed, for this cheapens the devotions of the Church and the most important sacrament of all. Nor should indulgences be granted except once a year in each of the principal cities. And the commutation of vows ought not to be so easily made, except in view of an equivalent good.

It has also been the custom to alter the last wills of testators who bequeath a sum of money for pious causes, which amount is transferred by the authority of your Holiness to an heir or legatee because of alleged poverty, etc., but actually because of greed. Indeed, unless there has been a great change in the household affairs of an heir because of the death of the testator, so that it is likely that the testator would have altered his will in view of that situation, it is wicked to alter the wills of testators. We have already spoken often about greed, wherefore we think that this practice should be entirely avoided.

Having set forth in brief all those matters which pertain to the pontiff of the universal Church as far as we could comprehend them, we shall in conclusion say something about that which pertains to the bishop of Rome. This city and church of Rome is the mother and teacher of the other churches. Therefore in her especially divine worship and integrity of morals ought to flourish. Accordingly, most blessed Father, all strangers are scandalized when they enter the basilica of St. Peter where priests, some of whom are vile, ignorant, and clothed in robes and vestments which they cannot decently wear in poor churches, celebrate mass. This is a great scandal to everyone. Therefore the most reverend archpriest or the most reverend penitentiary must be ordered to attend to this matter and remove this scandal. And the same must be done in other churches.

Also in this city harlots walk about like matrons or ride on mules, attended in broad daylight by noble members of the cardinals' households and by clerics. In no city do we see this corruption except in this model for all cities. Indeed they even dwell in fine houses. This foul abuse must also be corrected.

There are also in this city the hatreds and animosities of private citizens which it is especially the concern of the bishop to compose and conciliate. Therefore, all these animosities must be resolved and the passions of the citizens composed by some cardinals, Romans especially, who are more qualified.

There are in this city hospitals, orphans, widows. Their care especially is the concern of the bishop and the prince. Therefore your Holiness could properly take care of all of these through cardinals who are upright men.

These are the abuses, most blessed Father, which for the present, according to the limitations of our talents, we thought should be compiled, and which seemed to us ought to be corrected. You indeed, in accord with your goodness and wisdom, will direct all these matters. We certainly, if we have not done justice to the magnitude of the task which is far beyond our powers, have nevertheless satisfied our consciences, and we are not without the greatest hope that under your leadership we may see the Church of God cleansed, beautiful as a dove, at peace with herself, agreeing in one body, to the eternal memory of your name. You have taken the name of Paul; you will imitate, we hope, the charity of Paul. He was chosen as the vessel to carry the name of Christ among the nations. Indeed we hope that you have been chosen to restore in our hearts and in our works the name of Christ now forgotten by the nations and by us clerics, to heal the ills, to lead back the sheep of Christ into one fold, to turn away from us the wrath of God and that vengeance which we deserve, already prepared and looming over our heads.

Gasparo, Cardinal Contarini
Gian Pietro [Carafa], Cardinal of Chieti
Jacopo, Cardinal Sadoleto
Reginald [Pole], Cardinal of England
Federigo [Fregoso], Archbishop of Salerno
Jerome [Alexander], Archbishop of Brindisi
Gian Matteo [Giberti], Bishop of Verona
Gregorio [Cortese], Abbot of San Giorgio, Venice
Friar Tommaso [Badia], Master of the Sacred Palace

27. THE CAPUCHIN CONSTITUTIONS OF 1536

The Capuchin order originated with the desire of an Observant Franciscan friar, Matteo da Bascio (1495–1552), to live more strictly according to the rule of St. Francis. The Observant branch had developed as the result of an earlier, similar impulse, but had once again drifted from strict observance of the Rule, and in 1528, driven by the general atmosphere of reform and joined by three other friars, da Bascio gained the pope's approval for a new order. The order's first general chapter was held the following year, with twelve members present, and drew up new constitutions. The Capuchin order grew quickly, reaching 700 by 1536, and in the chapter of that year the constitutions were rewritten to reflect the needs and experience of the growing order. They maintain the desire to return to the simplicity and spirituality of the Franciscan model but are keenly aware of the challenge this represents and the need to choose their members carefully, and to train, support, and monitor them constantly, so that their new order might attain and represent the best of Christian spirituality within, and of Catholic preaching without.

The Capuchin Constitutions

IN THE NAME OF OUR LORD Jesus Christ begin the Constitutions of the Friars Minor Capuchins.

To the end that our Order, as the Vineyard of the Most High Son of God, may the better stand fast in the spiritual observance of the Evangelical and Seraphic Rule, the General Chapter held at Rome in our monastery of

St. Euphemia, the year of the Lord 1536, deemed it advisable to draw up certain statutes which might serve as a fence for our Holy Rule, in order that, like the unconquerable tower of David, it might have a means of protection from whatever might injure the spirit of our Lord Jesus Christ, and keep out all relaxations opposed to the fervent and seraphic zeal bequeathed to us by our Father St. Francis.

Chapter One

1. The doctrine of the Gospel, wholly pure, heavenly, supremely perfect and divine, brought down to us from heaven by the most sweet Son of God, and promulgated and preached by Him in word and deed, approved and authenticated by His Heavenly Father in the river Jordan and on Mt. Tabor, when he declared that "This is My Beloved Son in Whom I am well pleased; hear ye Him," alone teaches and points out the straight path of going to God. Hence, all men, especially all Christians who have professed the Gospel in baptism, and much more we friars, are obliged to observe this holy Gospel. St. Francis, therefore, in the beginning and end of his Rule, expressly mentions the observance of the Holy Gospel; nay, his Rule is simply the incarnation of the Gospel. In his Testament he also declares it was revealed to him that he should live according to the manner of the holy Gospel. In order that the friars may always keep the doctrine and life of our Lord Jesus Christ before the eyes of their mind, and that like the saintly Virgin Cecilia always bear the holy Gospel in the interior of their hearts, it is ordained that in honor of the Most Blessed Trinity the four evangelists be read three times a year, namely, one every month.

2. And since the Rule of St. Francis is like a little mirror in which evangelical perfection is reflected, it is ordained that every Friday in all our friaries, it be read distinctly, with due reverence and devotion, so that being impressed upon our minds, it may be the better observed. Some other pious book shall also be read to the friars, exhorting them to follow Christ crucified.

3. In order that the love of God be enkindled in our hearts, the friars shall always strive to speak of God. Desiring that the evangelical doctrine should bear fruit in our hearts and that all chaff which might suffocate it be extirpated, it is ordained that in no wise shall books that are useless, or frivolous and dangerous to the spirit of Christ, our Lord and God, be kept in our friaries.

4. And since the flames of divine love proceed from the light of divine things, it is ordained that some lesson from the Holy Scripture be read, expounding it by means of saintly and devout doctors. And though the infinite and divine Wisdom be incomprehensible and elevated, still it has humbled itself in Christ, our Savior, to such an extent, that by means of the pure, simple and unaffected eye of faith, even the simple can understand it. It is forbidden, however, that the friars read or study anything irrelevant or frivolous. Let them read and study the Holy Scriptures, nay, Christ Jesus, in Whom, according to St. Paul, are all treasures of wisdom and knowledge.

5. And because it was the desire, not only of our Seraphic Father, but of Christ, our Redeemer, that the Rule should be observed to the letter, with simplicity and without gloss, as it was observed by our first fathers, we renounce all privileges and explanations that relax it, detract from its pure observance and wrest it from the pious, just and holy intentions of Christ, our Lord, Who spoke in St. Francis. We accept only as a living and authentic commentary thereon, the declarations of the supreme pontiffs, and the most holy life, doctrine and example of our Seraphic Father himself.

…

7. Our Father, being wholly divine, contemplated God in every creature, especially in man, and more so in the Christian, but above all in the priest, and in a very singular manner in the supreme pontiff, who is the vicar of Christ our Lord on earth and head of the whole Church militant. He, therefore, wished his friars, in accordance with the apostolic teaching, to be subject to the divine Majesty in every creature, out of love for Him Who humbled Himself so much for us. Wherefore, he called them Friars Minor in order that they should, not only in their hearts deem themselves inferior to all, but that, being called in the Church militant to the marriage-feast of the Most Holy Spouse, Jesus Christ, they should always take the lowest place, in accordance with His counsel and example.

8. Considering that to be free from subjection to the ordinaries by privileges and exemptions is not only proximate to pride, but the enemy of the humble subjection of a Friar Minor, and because such liberty very often disturbs peace and begets scandal in the Church

of God, and in order to conform ourselves to our humble crucified Savior, Who came to serve us, becoming obedient, even unto the bitter death of the cross, and not being subject to the law yet wished to subject Himself to it by paying the temple-tax, and finally, to avoid scandal, the general chapter renounces the privilege of being exempt from ordinaries. By the highest privilege we accept, with our Seraphic Father, to be subject to all. Furthermore, it is ordained, that all vicars, each in their own province, go to their respective ordinary and prelates who are members humbly subject to the supreme pontiff, the head and superior of all. In their name and in the name of all the Friars let them renounce all contrary privileges and humbly offer obedience and reverence in all divine and canonical matters.

...

11. And since to avoid similar privileges our Father St. Francis in his Testament commands his Friars that they shall not dare to ask letters from the Roman court on account of bodily persecution, the general chapter renounces all privileges which relax the Rule and, enervating the way of the spirit, lay the foundation of a sensual life.

Chapter Two

12. As to the second chapter: desiring that our Order grow more in virtue, perfection and spirit, than in numbers; knowing also as the Infallible Truth teaches that "many are called, but few chosen," and that, as our Seraphic Father foretold when near death: nothing is a greater hindrance to the pure observance of the Rule than a multitude of useless, worldly and self-indulgent friars, we ordain that, when any persons apply for admission the vicars shall make careful enquiries as to their condition and character, and they shall not receive them if they do not manifest a very good intention and fervent will. To avoid all wonder and scandal, and that the candidate may know by experience what he must promise, no one shall be received until he is sixteen years of age, or if he should be sixteen but have a youthful face.

13. It is further ordained, that no one be received as a cleric who has not sufficient literary education so that in chanting the divine office he may not offend but understand what he says.

14. We further ordain that those who are admitted in this mode of life shall for some days previous to their clothing, exercise themselves in one of our friaries in all those things which are observed by the friars, so that their good will may be known, and that they may enter on so great an undertaking with greater light, maturity and deliberation. The same is to be understood of those religious who desire to be admitted to our life. In order that this be well observed, it is ordained that the vicars shall not receive any one without the counsel and consent of the majority of the friars dwelling in that place.

15. And since Christ, the wisest of Masters, charged that young man who desired to gain eternal life, that if he wished to become His disciple, he should first sell all that he had, give it to the poor and then follow Him; His imitator, Francis, not only observed that counsel and taught it by example in his own person and in those whom he received, but commanded it in his Rule. In order, therefore, to conform ourselves to Christ, our Lord, and to the will of the Seraphic Father, we ordain that no one shall be clothed, unless first, if able, he has distributed all to the poor as is becoming for one who freely chooses a mendicant life. In this way the friars will be able to determine at least in part, the fervent or tepid spirit; and the candidates will be able to serve God with greater peace of mind and constancy of will. And the friars, avoiding all interference in these matters, shall remain undisturbed in their holy peace.

16. We further ordain that the clothes of the novices who come from the world be kept until the day of profession; those of religious, for some days. If they persevere, the seculars shall give their clothes to the poor; those of religious shall be distributed by the vicars themselves or by the medium of some spiritual person.

17. Lest that should be said of us which our most holy Savior said to the Scribes and Pharisees: "Woe to you, because you go about the sea and the land to make one proselyte, and when he is made, you make him the child of hell twofold more than yourselves," we determine that in every province the novices shall be placed in one or two houses suited to the spiritual life, chosen for this purpose by the chapter. And they shall be given masters who are most mature, refined, and enlightened in the way of God. The masters shall take diligent care to teach the novices not only the ceremonies, but those spiritual matters necessary for the perfect imitation of Christ, our Light, our Way, our Truth, and our Life. By

word and example they shall show them in what the life of a Christian and a Friar Minor consists. No one shall be received to profession unless he know beforehand what he must promise and observe. The masters shall take diligent care that the cleric novices learn the Rule by heart during the time of the novitiate.

18. In order that the novices may in quiet, peace and silence be better strengthened in the spirit we ordain that no one speak much with them except the Father Guardian and their master. Nor shall anyone enter their cells, nor they the cells of others, without special permission.

19. And in order that they may better learn to bear the yoke of the Lord, we determine, that after their profession, they shall remain under the discipline of a master for at least three years, so that they may not easily lose the newly acquired spirit, but growing in strength, may become more fixed and rooted in the love of Jesus Christ, our Lord and God.

20. And since the doctors of the Church hold that those novices who make their profession with proper dispositions are restored to their baptismal innocence, we ordain that they prepare themselves before their profession with great care, by confession, communion and much prayer, their general confession having been made when they entered religion to put on the new man. And before receiving the said novices into religion, as well as admitting them to profession, the prescriptions and ceremonies customary and approved of in the Order shall be observed.

21. And since it was not without reason that Christ commended St. John the Baptist's austerity in clothing when He said: "They that are clothed in soft garments are in the houses of kings," it is ordained that the friars who have chosen to be menials in the house of God, clothe themselves with the more common, abject, austere, coarse and despised cloth that can conveniently be had in the province where they shall be. And let the friars remember that the sack-cloth with which St. Francis would have us mend our habits, and the cord with which he would have us girt, are not suited to the rich ones of this world.

22. The general chapter also exhorts all the friars to be content with the habit alone, as expressed by St. Francis in his Testament, when he said: "And we were content with one tunic, patched inside and out." But should any of the Friars be weak in body or in spirit, then, according to the Rule, a second tunic may be given them; and to these a mantle shall not be given without necessity and permission of the prelate; knowing that for a healthy friar to use three pieces of clothing is a manifest sign of lax spirit.

23. In order that poverty, so loved by the Son of God, and given to us as a mother by the Seraphic Father, may shine forth in everything we use, it is decreed that the mantle shall not extend beyond the tips of the fingers and shall be without a hood, except when making a journey; and it shall not be worn without necessity. The habit shall not go beyond the ankles in length and shall be ten feet wide, twelve feet for the corpulent Friars. The sleeves shall be no wider than is necessary to put in and draw out the arms, and long enough to reach the middle of the hand or a little longer. The tunics shall be very plain and coarse, eight or nine feet wide, and at least a half foot shorter than the habit. The hood shall be square, like those of St. Francis and his companions which still exist as relics, and as may be seen in ancient pictures, and as is described in the Book of Conformity: so that our habit be in the form of a cross to remind us that we are crucified to the world and the world to us. The girdle of the friars shall be a plain and coarse cord, with very simple knots, without any art or singularity; so that being despised by the world we may have occasion to mortify ourselves the more. Neither birettas, hats, nor anything ornamented or superfluous shall be worn.

…

25. In order that our beds may resemble somewhat that on which He died Who said: "The foxes have holes and the birds of the air nests, but the Son of Man hath no where to lay His head"; and also that we may be the more watchful and solicitous in prayer and be the more like our father St. Francis, whose bed was often the bare ground, and even like Christ, the Saint of Saints, especially in the desert, it is ordained that all the friars, except the sick and the very weak, shall sleep on a bare board, rush mat, or upon a little straw or hay; and they shall not sleep upon quilts.

26. In accordance with the example of Christ it is ordained that the young friars, and those who can, shall go barefooted, as a sign of humility, testimony of poverty, mortification of sensuality and as a good example to our

neighbor. And those who cannot do this may, in conformity with evangelical teaching and the example of our primitive fathers, wear sandals with the permission of the prelate; but they shall be simple, plain and poor, without any ornamentation.

27. In order that the friars reach the summit of most high poverty the queen and mother of all virtues, the spouse of Christ our Lord, and of our Seraphic Father, and of our most beloved Mother, we exhort all the friars not to have any attachment on earth, but always to fix their affection in heaven, using the things of this world sparingly as if by constraint, and in so far as their weakness will allow, deeming themselves rich with all their poverty. Let them be content with one spiritual book, or even with Christ crucified, and with two handkerchiefs and two drawers. And let them remember, as our Seraphic Father said, that a Friar Minor should be nothing but a mirror of every virtue, especially of poverty.

...

29. The tonsure shall be cut every twenty days, or once a month, with a pair of scissors. The friars shall wear the beard, after the example of Christ most holy, and of all our first saints, since it is something manly, natural, severe, despised and austere.

Chapter Seven

90. To remove every danger from subjects and superiors, no friar shall hear the confessions of seculars without the permission of the chapter, or of the Father Vicar General. Since this office demands not merely a good and sufficient understanding but a ripe experience, it shall not be exercised save by those who are qualified. The friars appointed to hear confessions shall do so only in particular cases, when charity demands. Thus they shall avoid every danger and mental distraction, and remain composed and recollected in Christ so that without any obstacle they may walk more securely on the road to their heavenly home.

91. Let the friars confess at least twice a week, and receive holy communion every fortnight, or oftener if they wish, and their superiors deem it expedient. During Advent and Lent they shall receive holy communion every Sunday. And let the friars, according to the apostolic admonition, carefully examine themselves beforehand, remembering on the one hand their own nothingness and unworthiness, and on the other hand, this sublime gift of God given to us with such great charity, so that they may not receive it to the injury of their souls but rather to their increase in light, grace and virtue. And this most august and divine sacrament, wherein our dearest Savior so lovingly condescends to abide with us always, shall be reserved in all our churches in a place of great cleanliness and shall be regarded by all with the greatest reverence. Let the friars remain before it and pray as if they were already in their heavenly country with the holy angels.

92. When the friars happen to be absent from the monastery they may confess to other priests.

...

Chapter Nine

110. Preaching the word of God, after the example of Christ, the Master of life, is one of the most honorable, useful, exalted and divine duties in the Church of God, on the fulfillment of which the salvation of mankind largely depends. We therefore ordain that no one shall be promoted to the office of preaching unless he has been examined and approved, as the Rule desires, by the general chapter or by the Father Vicar General. Nor shall the office of preacher be conferred upon anyone unless it is evident that he is of holy and exemplary life, of clear and mature judgment, of strong and ardent will, because knowledge and eloquence without charity tend in no way to edification but often to destruction. Let superiors take diligent care that in granting faculties for preaching they be not acceptors of persons, nor swayed by human friendship or favor, but have in view simply and solely God's honor, make it their aim to have a few virtuous preachers, rather than many useless ones. Thus they will follow the example of Christ, the supreme wisdom, Who from the whole Jewish nation chose only twelve apostles and seventy-two disciples, and that after long prayer.

111. In addition it is ordained that the preachers refrain from introducing into their sermons trifles, foolish stories, useless questions, curious and farfetched opinions, but after the example of the apostle St. Paul, let them preach Christ crucified, in Whom are all the treasures of wisdom and knowledge of God. This is that Divine Wisdom which St. Paul preached to the perfect [prefect]

after he had become a Christian; for as a Hebrew youth, he thought as a child, and understood as a child, and spoke as a child, of the shadows and types of the Old Testament. Let the preachers, besides quoting the holy doctors, chiefly cite Christ, Whose authority carries more weight than that of all other persons and reasons in the world.

112. The preachers shall abstain from difficult and affected phrases as unworthy of Him Who died naked and humble on the cross. Their language shall be plain, pure, simple and humble, withal holy, full of charity and aflame with zeal, after the example of St. Paul, the vessel of election, who preached, not in loftiness of speech and human eloquence, but in the power of the Holy Ghost. The preachers, therefore, are exhorted to do their utmost to imprint the Blessed Jesus on their own hearts and give Him peaceable possession of their souls, so that it may be He Who moves them to speak from the fullness of love, not merely by word but much more by their deeds, after the example of St. Paul, the doctor of the Gentiles, who did not dare to preach anything to others until Christ had enabled him first to practice it. So, also, did Jesus, our most perfect master, teach us not only by words, but by deeds. They are great in the kingdom of heaven who first do, and then teach and preach to others.

...

114. And while preaching to others, should they feel the spirit weakening, let them return to solitude, and there let them remain, till once again, full of God, the impulse of the Holy Spirit may move them to go forth to spread divine grace over the world. Thus engaged, now like Martha, now like Mary, they shall follow Christ in His mixed life, Who, after praying on the mountain, went down to the temple to preach, nay, descended from Heaven to earth to save souls.

115. We strictly forbid preachers to receive delicate food. They shall live like poor men and mendicants, as they have voluntarily promised for the love of Christ. Above all let them guard against every kind of avarice, so that preaching Jesus Christ freely and sincerely, they may gather fruit in greater abundance. When they preach, let them not beg either for themselves or for their brethren; so that, according to the teaching of the Apostle, all may know they seek not their own interests, but those of Jesus Christ,

116. Since he who does not know how to read and imitate Christ, the Book of Life, cannot have the learning necessary for preaching, preachers are forbidden to carry with them many books, so that they find all things in Christ.

117. In order that the sacred office of preaching, so precious and most pleasing to Christ, our God, Who has proved it by preaching the most salutary evangelical doctrine with so much ardor of divine charity for the welfare of our souls; in order also the better to impress on the hearts of preachers the norm and method they are to follow in the worthy exercise of preaching Christ crucified and the kingdom of heaven, in effectively procuring the conversion and the spiritual welfare of the faithful, by reproducing, as it were, and implanting Christ in their souls, we counsel and command them to use the sacred scriptures, especially the New Testament and in particular the Gospels, so that being evangelical preachers, we may fashion an evangelical people.

...

120. And in order that, while preaching to others, the preachers themselves may not become castaways, they shall sometimes leave the multitude, and, with our most sweet Savior, ascend the mountain of prayer and contemplation. There let them endeavor to become informed of the Seraphim, with divine love, so that, all aflame themselves, they may enkindle others.

121. As mentioned above it is enjoined on preachers not to carry with them many books, so that they may attentively study the most excellent book, the cross. And as it was always the intention of our beloved father that the friars have the necessary books in common and not individually, and the better to observe poverty and to remove from the hearts of the brethren all feeling of attachment, it is ordained that in each house there shall be a small room where the holy scriptures and some of the holy doctors shall be kept. But books that are really useless and make a man worldly rather than Christian (as stated above in the first chapter) shall not be kept in our houses. Let such as are found be disposed of according to the injunction of the Vicars General or Provincial.

122. And since in him who would preach worthily and in a befitting manner there is required, together with a religious and exemplary life, some knowledge of the Holy Scriptures, which cannot be acquired except by

literary study; lest so noble and useful a function as preaching should, to the greater loss of souls, decline in our congregation, we enact that there shall be devout and holy studies, abounding in charity and humility, both for the humanities and sacred letters. To these studies only such friars shall be admitted, as the Vicar Provincial and the definitors judge to be distinguished for fervent charity, praiseworthy behavior, humble and holy conversation, and at the same time, so capable of learning that they may afterwards, by their life and doctrine, be useful and productive in the house of the Lord.

28. IGNATIUS LOYOLA (1491–1556)

Born in 1491 to a noble Basque family, Ignatius Loyola early began a career as a soldier. In 1521 he was gravely wounded during a siege of Pamplona, an event that proved to be the turning point in his career. During his convalescence the only books available to him were Ludolph of Saxony's Life of Christ *and Jacopo de Voragine's* The Golden Legend, *a collection of stories about the saints. As a result of his reading, he determined to turn away from the military life and serve the will of God. Having failed to complete a pilgrimage to Jerusalem in 1522, in 1524 he began an extended program of study at the universities of Alcalá, Salamanca, and Paris.*

Ignatius's Spiritual Exercises *developed during his years at Paris, and it was there that he gathered the group who would become the foundation of the Jesuit order. In 1534 he decided to go with six followers to Jerusalem to work for the conversion of the Turks. Failing to find passage to the east from Venice, the group turned to Rome, where they formed themselves into a formal religious order that received papal approval in 1540.*

The Jesuits combined an intense spirituality with a great emphasis on the importance of education. They have often been portrayed as the shock troops of the Counter-Reformation, but this is a caricature of the order. They were deeply devoted to the Church, and to the pope as its leader, and they took a vow of obedience directly to the pope. They were driven, however, by a positive desire to reform the Church, rather than by a particularly anti-Protestant agenda, and they were one of the most important instruments of Catholic reform. By the time of Ignatius's death in 1556, there were more than a thousand members of his order working as missionaries and educators throughout the known world.

Letter on Obedience

To the province of Portugal

Ignatius of Loyola sends greetings to his brethren of the Society of Jesus in Portugal, and wishes them the grace and everlasting love of Christ our Lord.

1. It is a cause of deep consolation to me, my dear brothers in Christ, to hear of the eager efforts you are making in your striving after the highest perfection in virtue and in God's service. It is owing to His bounty that, having once called you to this way of life, He keeps you in it, as might be expected of His mercy, and guides you to that happy goal attained by those whom He has chosen.

2. Of course, I wish you to be perfect in all spiritual gifts and adornments. But it is especially in the virtue of obedience, as you have heard from me on other occasions, that I am anxious to see you signalize yourselves. I desire this, not only because of the rare and outstanding blessings connected with obedience, as may be seen from the many distinguished proofs and examples of it to be found in Holy Scripture, in both the Old and the New Testaments; but also because, as we read in St. Gregory: "Obedience is the only virtue which implants the other virtues in the heart, and preserves them after they have been so implanted." With this virtue flourishing, the others will surely flourish and bring forth the fruits which I look for in your hearts, and which He requires Who by His saving obedience redeemed the human race which had been laid low and destroyed by

the sin of disobedience, "becoming obedient unto death, even to the death on the cross" [Phil. 2:8].

3. We may the more readily allow other religious orders to surpass us in the matter of fasting, watching, and other austerities in their manner of living, which all of them devoutly practice according to their respective institutes. But in the purity and perfection of obedience and the surrender of our will and judgment, it is my warmest wish, beloved brethren, to see those who serve God in this Society signalize themselves. Indeed, the true and genuine sons of this Society should be recognized by this characteristic, that they never regard the individual himself whom they obey, but in him Christ our Lord for Whose sake they obey. For the superior is not to be obeyed because he is prudent, or kind, or divinely gifted in any other way, but for the sole reason that he holds the place of God and exercises the authority of Him Who says, "He who hears you hears me, and he who despises you despises me" [Luke 10:16]. On the other hand, there should not be the least remissness in obedience to him, at least insofar as he is superior, because he happens to be less prudent or less experienced, since he is the representative of Him Whose wisdom cannot be mistaken, and Who will make good whatever is lacking in his representative, even though it be uprightness or other good qualities. Christ our Lord expressly declared this, when He said: "The scribes and Pharisees have sat on the chair of Moses," adding immediately, "all things, therefore, that they command you observe and do, but do not act according to their works" [Matt. 23:2, 3].

4. For this reason it is my desire that you devote yourselves to an unremitting effort, and make it a practice to recognize Christ our Lord in any superior you may have, and with all devotion, reverence and obey the Divine Majesty in Him. This will seem the less surprising if you take note that St. Paul bids us obey our civil and pagan superiors as we would Christ, from Whom flows all legitimate authority. He writes to the Ephesians: "Slaves, obey your masters according to the flesh, with fear and trembling in the sincerity of your heart, as you would Christ: not serving to the eye as pleasers of men, but as slaves of Christ, doing the will of God from your heart, giving your service with good will as to the Lord and not to man ..." [Eph. 6:5–7].

From this you yourselves can gather how a religious ought to regard one whom he has chosen not only as a superior, but expressly as Christ's representative, to be his guide and adviser: I mean, whether he should look upon him as a mere man, or as Christ's vicar.

5. Now, this is a point on which you should have a thorough understanding and which I am anxious to see solidly established in your minds, that the first and lowest degree of obedience is exceedingly imperfect, since it does not go beyond the bare execution of a command. In fact, it should not be called obedience at all, unless it rises to the second degree which makes the superior's will the subject's own, and not only conforms it to the superior's will in the actual carrying out of the command, but begets also a conformity of desires. In this way what one wishes the other wishes and what one rejects the other rejects. This is what we read in Holy Scripture: "Obedience is better than sacrifice" [1 Kings 15:22], which is thus explained by St. Gregory: "In other sacrifices the flesh of another is slain, but in obedience our own will is sacrificed." Precisely because this faculty of the mind is so precious, the surrender of it to our Lord and Creator in obedience should be held to be of great value.

6. In how great and perilous an error are they involved who, not only in matters pertaining to flesh and blood, but even in those which in other respects are holy and very spiritual, such as fasts, prayers, and other works of devotion, think they are justified in withdrawing from the will and command of their superior! Let them give heed to what Cassian wisely observes in the *Conference of the Abbot Daniel*: "It is one and the same kind of disobedience to break the command of the superior, whether it be done from an interest in work or a desire of ease, and as harmful to disregard the rules of the monastery by going to sleep as by remaining awake. Finally, it would be just as bad to fail to obey the command of the Abbot, whether you did it to read or to sleep." Martha's activity was holy and holy was Magdalen's contemplation, and holy the penitence and tears with which she bathed the feet of Christ our Lord. But these things, it must be noted, were to be done in Bethania, a name which the interpreters say means "House of Obedience." According to St. Bernard, it would seem that our Lord wished to point out to us that neither the zeal of good actions, nor the repose of holy contemplation, nor the penitent's tears would have been acceptable to Him anywhere but in Bethania.

7. As far as you can, therefore, my dear brothers, make a complete surrender of your wills. Dedicate as a free gift to your Creator, through His ministers, this liberty which He has bestowed upon you. Be sure of this, that it is no slight benefit to your free will to be allowed to restore it completely to Him from Whom you received it. In doing so, you not only do not lose it, but you even add to it and perfect it, when you conform your own will to that most certain norm of all righteousness, the will

of God, which is interpreted for you by him who governs you in God's name.

8. Therefore, you must maintain a watchful guard against ever trying at any time to wrest the superior's will, which you should think of as God's, into agreement with your own. To do this would be not to conform your own will to God's, but to endeavor to rule God's by yours, and thus reverse the order of His Divine Wisdom. Great is the mistake of those whom self-love has blinded into thinking themselves obedient when they have by some stratagem bent the superior's will to their own wishes. Hear what St. Bernard, a man of exceptional experience in this matter, has to say: "Whoever either openly or covertly tries to have his spiritual father enjoin him what he himself desires, deceives himself if he flatters himself into thinking that he is a true follower of obedience. For in this he does not obey his superior, but rather his superior obeys him."

If this is true, whoever wishes to attain the virtue of obedience must rise to this second degree, in which he not only fulfills the superior's commands, but even makes the superior's will his own, or rather strips himself of his own will to clothe himself with God's will as proposed to him by his superior.

9. But he who wishes to make an absolutely complete offering of himself must in addition to his will include his understanding, which is the third and highest degree of obedience. The result will be that he not only identifies his will with that of the superior, but even his thought, and submits his own judgment to the superior's judgment, to the extent that a devout will can bend the understanding. For although this faculty is not endowed with the will's liberty and is naturally borne to assent to whatever is presented to it as true, nevertheless, in many instances, where the evidence of the known truth is not coercive, the intellect under the influence of the will may be inclined to this side rather than to that. In such circumstances everyone who makes profession of obedience must bow to the judgment of the superior.

As a matter of fact, obedience is a whole-burnt offering in which the entire man, without the slightest reserve, is offered in the fire of charity to his Creator and Lord by the hands of His ministers. It is at the same time a complete surrender in which a religious freely yields up his own rights for the purpose of being governed and possessed by Divine Providence through the agency of his superiors. It cannot be denied, therefore, that obedience includes not only the execution, which carries the superior's command into effect, and the will by doing so with a glad heart, but, in addition, it includes also the judgment, so that whatever the superior commands and thinks right ought to appear right and proper to the inferior, to the extent, as I have said, that the will has power to bend the understanding.

10. Would to God that this obedience of the understanding and judgment were as well understood by men and put into practice as it is pleasing to God and necessary for anyone leading the religious life! This necessity can be seen from a consideration of the heavenly bodies, where, if one is to have any effect upon another, or communicate its movement to it, this body must be subject and subordinate to the first. The same is true among men. If one is to be moved by another's authority, as is done in obedience, he who is in the position of the inferior must accommodate himself to the commands and views of his superior, if the influence of the latter is to reach him and have any effect on him. Now, this subjection and subordination cannot exist unless there be a conformity of will and judgment between the subject and the superior.

11. Once more then, if we look to the end and purpose of obedience, it is just as possible for the intellect as for the will to be deceived as to what is good for us. And therefore, as the will is united with the superior's will to keep it from error, so the understanding must conform to the judgment of the superior to keep from being misled. "Lean not on thine own prudence," is the warning of Holy Scripture [Prov. 3:5].

Even in the temporal affairs of life, the wise think that the truly prudent man should have little confidence in his own prudence, especially when personal interests are at stake, in which men who are not easy in mind can hardly ever be good judges. Now, if in our own personal affairs we ought to think more of the judgment and advice of another, even when he is not our superior, how much more should we think of that judgment and advice when he is our superior, a man to whom we have surrendered ourselves to be ruled as to God's representative and the interpreter of His holy will!

Certain it is that in men and matters spiritual even greater caution is necessary, seeing that there is greater danger in a spiritual course when one runs along in it without the check of counsel and direction. In the *Conference of Abbot Moses,* Cassian observes: "By no other vice does the devil so lead a monk on in order to hurl him headlong to destruction, as when he persuades him to disregard the counsel of his superiors and trust to his own judgment and decision."

12. What is more, without this obedience of the intellect, obedience of the will and execution cannot possibly be what they should. For nature has so arranged matters

that what are called the appetitive powers of the soul must follow the apprehensive; and the will cannot long obey without violence when there is disagreement in the judgment. One may obey for some time perhaps, under the common misunderstanding that obey we must even if commanded amiss. But such obedience cannot last, with the resulting failure in perseverance, or at least in the perfection of obedience—which consists in obeying cheerfully and lovingly. And there can be no love or cheerfulness as long as such a conflict exists between action and judgment. We fail in zest and punctuality, when we question whether it is good or not to obey a command. We fail in that glorious simplicity of blind obedience, when we examine a command to see whether it is right or not, and even pass sentence against the superior because he asks us to do something we do not like. We fail in humility, because if from one point of view we obey, from another we prefer ourselves to our superior. We fail in courage in difficult tasks. In a word, all the perfection and dignity of this virtue is lost.

On the other hand, we have instead pain, discontent, delays, weariness, complaints, excuses and other faults which are far from trivial and completely strip obedience of its value and merit. It is this that leads St. Bernard to say, speaking of those who become disgruntled when the commands of the superior are little to their taste: "If you begin to grieve at this, to judge your superior, to murmur in your heart, even though you outwardly fulfill what is commanded, this is not the virtue of patience [obedience], but a cloak over your malice." Peace and tranquility of soul he certainly shall not enjoy who has in his own heart the cause of his disturbance and unrest, I mean the conflict between his own judgment and the obligations of obedience.

13. This is why the Apostle, wishing to safeguard the spirit of unity, which is the binding force of every society, is so much in earnest when he urges all to be of one mind and one heart [Rom. 15:15; 1 Cor. 1:10; 2 Cor. 13:11; Phil. 2:2]. He knows that if the faithful agree in will and judgment, they will be a mutual and unfailing help to each other. Now if there must be one and the same understanding between the members and the head, it is easy to see whether it is more reasonable for the head to agree with the members, or the members with the head. From all I have thus far said, you can see quite clearly the absolute necessity of this obedience of the understanding.

14. But how perfect is this obedience, and at the same time how pleasing to God, can be seen from this, that what is most excellent in man and beyond all price is consecrated to God. Secondly, because one who thus obeys becomes a living holocaust, most pleasing to His Divine Majesty, seeing that he keeps nothing at all for himself. And finally because of the difficulty which the obedient man experiences in overcoming himself for God's love, since he resists the inclination which is natural to all men: to think for themselves and to follow their own opinion. From these considerations it follows that, although obedience seems to be a perfection of the will, since it makes it prompt and ready at the beck of the superior, yet it has to do also with the understanding itself, as we have pointed out, and should bring it to think what the superior thinks. Thus the whole power of the soul, its will and intelligence, will be brought to bear on a prompt and perfect performance of what is commanded.

15. I think I hear you say, beloved brethren, that you have no doubt about your needing this virtue, and that you would like very much to know how you can acquire it in its perfection. With St. Leo I answer, "To the humble nothing is hard, nothing difficult to the meek." If you have humility, if you have meekness, God will have the goodness to help you stand by your promise not only cheerfully but even lovingly.

16. In addition to these practices I especially recommend three others which will be a great help to you in your efforts to acquire this obedience of the understanding.

The first is that, as I said in the beginning, you do not take a personal view of your superior and think of him as a mere man, subject to error and adversity, but as Christ Himself Who is Supreme Wisdom, Boundless Goodness and Infinite Charity, Who can neither be deceived nor will deceive you. And since you are well aware that it was out of love for God that you have taken this yoke of obedience upon yourselves, in the thought that in carrying out the superior's will you would be more certain to be carrying out God's will, you should not have the slightest doubt that the most faithful love of God will continue to guide you by the hands of those whom He has placed over you. You should, therefore, listen to their words when they command you, as though they were the very words of Christ Himself. The Apostle, writing to the Colossians and encouraging subjects to be obedient to their superiors, says on this point: "Whatever you do, work at it from the heart as for the Lord and not for men, knowing that from the Lord you will receive the inheritance as your reward. Serve the Lord Christ" [Col. 3:23, 24]. And St. Bernard: "Whether it be God or man, His vicar, who commands anything, we must obey with equal diligence and show equal reverence, on the supposition, however, that man commands nothing that is contrary to God." Thus if you behold not man with the eyes of the body, but God with the eyes of the soul, you will surely not find it difficult to conform your will and judgment to that norm of conduct which you yourselves have chosen.

17. The second practice is that in your own mind you always make a serious effort to defend the superior's command, or even his thought, but never to find fault with it. To do this it will be a help if you are always favorably disposed to any order he may give. You will thus obey, not only without annoyance, but even with a glad heart, because, as St. Leo tells us, "It is not hard to serve when we love what is commanded."

18. There is a third and last way of bringing the judgment into subjection. It is easier and safer and much used by the holy Fathers. Make up your minds that whatever the superior commands is the command and will of God Himself. Just as in accepting a truth which the Catholic Church puts before you, you at once bring into play all the powers of mind and heart, so in carrying out any order whatever of the superior, you should be swept on by a kind of blind passion to obey, without making even the slightest enquiry into the command. It is thus we must believe that Abraham acted when he was told to offer his son, Isaac, in sacrifice [Gen. 22:1–13]. Thus, in the days of the New Testament, some of those holy fathers of whom Cassian speaks, as the abbot John who without a single thought as to whether it would do any good or not, with great and prolonged labor watered a dry stick for a whole year on end, when told to do so: or whether it was possible, when he strove so mightily to move a huge rock which many men with their combined strength could not have budged. We see that heaven sometimes approved this kind of obedience with miracles. Not to mention others, with whom you are well acquainted, Maurus the disciple of St. Benedict, went into a lake on the order of his superior and did not sink. Another, at the word of his superior captured a lioness and brought her home. Now this manner of subjecting one's judgment so as unhesitatingly to approve or praise in one's own mind any command of the superior is not only the practice of holy men, but must be imitated by those who desire to practice perfect obedience in everything, except where sin is clearly involved.

19. But for all that, you are not forbidden to lay before your superior something that occurs to you and that seems to be at variance with his mind, and which you think might be called to his attention. You should, however, first consult the Lord in prayer. There is, of course, some danger of being deceived by self-love in such instances, and to guard against it and your own judgment you should, both before and after submitting your difficulty, be completely indifferent, not only with regard to undertaking or dropping the proposal itself, but you should be ready even to approve and think best whatever decision the Superior makes.

20. What I have said of obedience should be the practice of individuals towards their immediate superiors, and of rectors and local superiors towards their provincials, and of provincials towards the general, and of the general, finally, towards him whom God has placed over him, I mean, His vicar on earth. In this way a perfect subordination of authority will be maintained, with the resulting harmony and love, without which neither the proper government of our Society nor of any other congregation whatever could be preserved.

It is in this way that Divine Providence "ordereth all things sweetly" [Wisd. 8:1], leading to their particular ends the lowest by means of the midmost, and the midmost by means of the highest. Among the angels there is likewise this graded subordination of one hierarchy to another, and in the heavenly bodies and all their movements an orderly and close connection and interrelation is kept, all movement coming from the one Supreme Mover in perfect order, step by step, to the lowest.

We see the same thing on earth, not only in every civilized government, but especially in the Church's hierarchy, where officials and their activities draw their authority from the one universal Vicar of Christ our Lord. The better this subordination and gradation is kept, the better and smoother will be the government. But when it is absent, anyone can see how deplorable are the results wherever men are assembled together. It is my earnest desire, therefore, to see this virtue flourish as vigorously in this Society which God has to some extent entrusted to me, as though the well-being and continued existence of our Society depended on it alone.

21. Not to go beyond the limits I set myself at the beginning of this letter, I beg of you in the name of our Lord Jesus Christ, Who gave Himself to us not only as a teacher of obedience, but also as a model of it, to bend every effort to acquire this virtue, and, all athirst for so glorious a victory, to gain complete mastery over yourselves, that is, over the sublimest and most difficult part of your souls, your will, I mean, and understanding. For

it is in this way that the true and solid knowledge of God our Lord will draw your souls to Him completely, and rule and govern you throughout the whole course of this mortal pilgrimage, until at last He leads you and many others who have been helped by your efforts and example to that last and most blissful end, which is life everlasting.

I earnestly commend myself to your prayers.
Rome, March 26, 1553.

29. TERESA OF AVILA (1515–82)

St. Teresa of Avila was the granddaughter of a converso, *a converted Jew, who moved his family to Avila after his conversion. She showed early signs of religious piety, setting off at the age of seven with her brother Rodrigo to the land of the Moors to have her head cut off for Christ, though in her early teens she became caught up in the stories of romance and chivalry so popular in Spain. In 1531 her father sent her to school with the Augustinian nuns of Our Lady of Grace in Avila, in the hopes of turning her away from her frivolous interests. While in the convent Teresa began to think of entering the religious life, and, over her father's objections, she finally joined the Carmelite monastery of the Incarnation in 1535.*

Teresa made her profession two years later, but by then her health was deteriorating. Attempts to treat her condition almost killed her, and she was paralyzed for three years. After the intercession of St. Joseph, she walked again, but her health remained a constant problem. Her spiritual life was also less than satisfactory, and it was only in the late 1550s that the conversion took place that changed the course of her life. She began to experience both a new level of prayer and new visions, which she feared came from the devil. The Inquisition was particularly active in Spain in the late sixteenth century, and Teresa was anxious to ensure that her new experiences were orthodox. In order to explain and understand these experiences, she confided in a series of confessors, whose questions led to the writing of her Life.

Spiritual Testimonies

33

(Place uncertain, 1572–73)

A prophetic vision of victory for her Carmel

I saw a great tempest of trials and that just as the children of Israel were persecuted by the Egyptians, so we would be persecuted; but that God would bring us through dry-shod, and our enemies would be swallowed up by the waves.

34

(Beas, 1575)

A spiritual token

One day when I was staying at our monastery in Beas, our Lord told me that since I was His bride I should make requests of Him, for He had promised that whatever I asked He would grant me. And as a token He gave me a beautiful ring, with a precious stone resembling an amethyst but with a brilliance very different from any here on earth, and He placed the ring on my finger. I write this with confusion at seeing the goodness of God and my wretched life, for I deserved hell. But, alas, daughters, pray for me and be devoted to St. Joseph who can do a great deal. I'm writing this foolishness…

35

(Ecija, Andalusia, May 23, 1575)

The vow of obedience to Father Gratian

1. On the second day after Pentecost, while at Ecija, a person was recalling a great favor she had received from our Lord on the vigil of this feast. Desiring to do something very special in His service, she thought it would be good to promise from that time on not to hide any fault or sin she had committed in her whole life from the one who stood in God's place. Even though she had made a vow of obedience, this promise seemed to involve something

more, because there's no obligation like this toward one's superiors. And she also promised to do all that this confessor might tell her—with regard to serious matters, of course—providing it would not go against her vow of obedience. And even though keeping this promise was hard for her in the beginning, she made it.

2. The first reason why she decided to do so was the thought that she was rendering some service to the Holy Spirit; the second was that she chose a person who was a great servant of God and a learned man, who would help her serve the Lord more.

This learned man knew nothing about the above until some days after she had made the promise. He was Friar Jerome Gratian of the Mother of God.

36

(Beas, April, 1575)

The vow of obedience to Father Gratian

Material having to do with my conscience and soul. Let no one read it even though I be dead, but give it to the Father Master Gratian.

IHS

1. In 1575, during the month of April, while I was at the foundation in Beas, it happened that the Master Friar Jerome Gratian of the Mother of God came there. I had gone to confession to him at times, but I hadn't held him in the place I had other confessors, by letting myself be completely guided by him. One day while I was eating, without any interior recollection, my soul began to be suspended and recollected in such a way that I thought some rapture was trying to come upon me; and a vision appeared with the usual quickness, like a flash of lightning.

2. It seemed to me our Lord Jesus Christ was next to me in the form in which He usually appears, and at His right side stood Master Gratian himself, and I at His left. The Lord took our right hands and joined them and told me He desired that I take this master to represent Him as long as I live, and that we both agree to everything because it was thus fitting.

3. I remained with very great assurance that the vision was from God. The remembrance of the two confessors I had gone to and followed for a long time and to whom I owed a great deal made me undecided. The remembrance of one especially made me put up strong resistance, since it seemed to me I was offending him; for I had great respect and love for him. In spite of this I felt assurance from the vision that such an action suited me, and also comfort coming from the thought that this going about consulting different minds with different opinions was now to end. For some, by not understanding me, made me suffer very much; although I never gave up any of them until either they moved away or I did, because I thought the fault was mine. Twice more the Lord returned to tell me in different words not to fear since He gave Master Gratian to me. So I resolved not to do otherwise, and I made the proposal within myself to carry out the Lord's request for the rest of my life, to follow Father Gratian's opinion in everything as long as it wasn't clearly offensive to God—and I was certain it would not be; for, according to some things I have heard, I believe he has made the same promise I have made, of doing the more perfect thing in all matters.

4. I was left with a peace and comfort so great I was amazed, and I felt certain the Lord wanted this, for it doesn't seem to me the devil could give such great peace and comfort of soul. It seems to me I remained outside myself in a way I don't know how to describe, but each time I recall this vision I again praise our Lord and remember that verse which says, *Qui posuit fines suos in pace;* and I want to be consumed in the praises of God.

It seems to me this promise must be for His glory, and so I again propose never to make a change.

5. The second day of Pentecost, after this resolution, while on our way to Seville, we heard Mass in a hermitage in Ecija and remained there for siesta. While my companions were in the hermitage and I was alone in the sacristy there, I began to think of the wonderful favor the Holy Spirit had granted me on the vigil of that feast of Pentecost. Great desires came over me to render Him a special service, but I couldn't find anything that wasn't done. I recalled that although I had made a vow of obedience, it wasn't of a kind I could obey with perfection; and the thought came to me that it would be pleasing to the Holy Spirit to promise what I had proposed in regard to the friar, Father Jerome. On the one hand it seemed to me I wouldn't be doing anything by such a promise, and on the other hand it struck me as something very arduous when I reflected that with superiors you don't reveal your interior state; and that if you don't get along well with one superior, there is finally a change, and another one comes along; and that this promise would mean remaining without any freedom either interiorly or exteriorly throughout life. And I felt pressed a little, and even very much, not to go through with it.

6. This very resistance that my thoughts caused in my will reproached me. It seemed to me there was already

something presenting itself to me that I wasn't doing for God and which I had always fled. The fact is the difficulty so bothered me I don't think I did anything in my life, not even in making profession, over which I felt within myself greater resistance, except when I left my father's house to become a nun. This resistance was the reason I didn't consider my love for this Father; but rather, I then considered the matter as though it regarded a stranger. Nor did I consider his good qualities, but only whether it would be good to make this promise for the Holy Spirit. The doubts that arose as to whether or not it would be of service to God, I believe, caused me to delay.

7. At the end of a period of battle, the Lord gave me great confidence so that it seemed to me I made that promise for the Holy Spirit, and that the Spirit was obliged to give the Father light so that he in turn might give it to me. It also seemed I was to recall that it was our Lord Jesus Christ who had given me the light. And at this point I knelt down and promised that for the rest of my life I would do everything Master Gratian might tell me, as long as there was nothing in opposition to God or my superiors to whom I was obliged. It was my intention that this would apply only in serious matters so as to avoid scruples; for example, when I insist with Father Jerome about some trifling thing in regard to his comfort or mine, and he in turn tells me not to speak of it any more. For such insistence implies no lack of obedience or intention to hide knowingly any of my faults or sins. And not hiding these also involves more than what one is obliged to with superiors. In sum, it was my intention to hold him in the place of God, interiorly and exteriorly.

8. I don't know if I merited, but it seemed to me I did something great for the Holy Spirit, at least all I knew how; and so I remained with great satisfaction and happiness, and I have remained so since then. And although I feared I might be restricted, I was left with greater freedom; and I was more confident our Lord would grant Father Gratian new favors for this service I rendered to God and that I might share in them and receive light in everything.

Blessed be He who created a person who so pleased me that I could dare do this. […]

58

(Seville, 1576)

Account of her spiritual life for the Inquisitor of Seville

1. Forty years ago this nun took the habit. And from the beginning she has turned her thoughts to the mysteries and the Passion of our Lord and to her sins without ever thinking about supernatural experiences; rather, she has thought about how quickly creatures or things come to an end. And she has spent some periods of the day reflecting on these matters without it even passing through her mind to desire anything more, for her opinion of herself has been such that she has seen that she doesn't deserve even to think about God.

2. She spent about twenty-two years in this way with great dryness, devoting time also to reading good books. It was eighteen years ago that she began to discuss—about three years before the actuality—her first monastery of discalced nuns which she founded in Avila. For, as it seemed to her, she began sometimes to receive interior locutions, and she saw some visions and experienced revelations. She never saw anything, nor has seen anything, of these visions with her bodily eyes. Rather, the representation came like a lightning flash, but it left as great an impression upon her and as many effects as it would if she had seen it with her bodily eyes, and more so.

3. She was terrified, for sometimes she didn't even dare remain alone during the day. Since she couldn't avoid the experiences no matter how much she tried, she went about terribly afflicted, fearing lest she be deceived by the devil. She began to discuss the matter with spiritual persons of the Society of Jesus, among whom were: Father Araoz who happened to go to Avila, for he was the commissary of the Society of Jesus; Father Francis, with whom she spoke twice, who had been duke of Gandia; a provincial of the Society, named Gil González, who is now in Rome and one of the four counselors; also the present provincial of Castile, although she did not speak so much with him; Baltasar Alvarez, who is now rector in Salamanca and who was her confessor for six years; the rector at Cuenca, named Salazar; and, not for long, the rector at Segovia, named Santander; the rector at Burgos, whose name is Ripalda, who was even very unfavorable to her until she talked with him; Doctor Pablo Hernández of Toledo, who was a consultant to the Inquisition; and another, Ordóñez, who was rector at Avila. In short, wherever she went she sought out those who were most esteemed.

4. She spoke frequently with Friar Peter of Alcántara, and it was he who did a great deal for her.

5. During this time (for more than six years), she was put to the test, shed many tears, and underwent much affliction; and the greater the trials the more favors she received. Often she experienced suspension of the faculties while in prayer, and even outside of it. Many prayers were said and Masses offered that God might lead her by another path, for she had the greatest fear when she was

not in prayer, although in all things touching upon the service of God she clearly understood there was improvement, and no vainglory or pride. On the contrary, she felt embarrassed before those who knew about the favors, and regretted speaking about these favors more than she did speaking about her sins; for it seemed to her that her confessors would laugh at her and attribute these favors to the foolish things of women.

6. It was about thirteen years ago, a little more or less, that the Bishop of Salamanca went there, for he was the Inquisitor, I believe, in Toledo and had been here. For the sake of greater assurance she arranged to speak with him and gave him an account of everything. He told her this whole matter was something that didn't belong to his office because all that she saw and understood strengthened her ever more in the Catholic faith. For she always was and is firm in the faith, and she experiences the strongest desires for the honor of God and the good of souls. These desires are such that for one soul she would allow herself to be killed many times. Since he saw she was so concerned, he told her she should write to Master Avila—who was alive—a long account of everything, for he was a man who understood much about prayer; and that with what he would write her, she could be at peace. She did so, and he replied giving her much assurance. Her account was of such a kind that all the learned men who saw it—for they were her confessors—said it was very helpful for information about spiritual things. They ordered her to make a copy and write another little book for her daughters in which she could give some counsels, for she was prioress.

7. In spite of all this, she was not without fears at times, and it seemed to her that spiritual people could be deceived as well as she. She wanted to speak with very learned men, even though they might not be given to prayer, for she only wanted to know whether all her experiences were in conformity with Sacred Scripture. And she was sometimes consoled, thinking that even though she may have deserved to be deceived because of her sins, God would not permit so many persons to be deceived since they desired to give her light.

8. With this thought in mind she began to discuss these favors with Dominican Fathers because previous to such experiences she often had these Fathers as confessors. The following are the ones whom she consulted. Friar Vicente Barrón was her confessor for a year and a half in Toledo, when she was there for a foundation, for he was consultant to the Inquisition and a very learned man. He gave her much assurance. (And all of them told her that since she didn't offend God and knew she was wretched, she had nothing to fear.) The Master, Friar Domingo Báñez (who is now consultant to the Holy Office in Valladolid) was her confessor for six years, and she always kept in contact with him by letter when something new presented itself. She consulted with Master Chaves. Besides Friar Domingo Báñez, she consulted Friar Pedro Ibáñez, who was then a professor in Avila and a most learned man; and another Dominican whose name was Friar Garcia de Toledo. She consulted the Father Master, Friar Bartolomé de Medina, who has a professor's chair at Salamanca, and who she knew had a very bad opinion of her because he had heard about these experiences. And she thought he better than anyone would tell her if she were being deceived. She consulted him a little more than two years ago when she came to Salamanca. She arranged to go to confession to him and gave him a long account of everything, and she provided that he see what she had written so that he might understand her life better. He assured her very much—more than all of them—and became her close friend. She also made her confession for a time to the Father Master Friar Felipe de Meneses, when she went to Valladolid for a foundation and he was the prior or rector of that College of St. Gregory. Having heard about these things, he went with great charity to speak to her in Avila, wanting to know if she was being deceived, and pointing out that if she wasn't, there was no reason for so much criticism of her; and he was very satisfied. She also took the matter up with a Dominican provincial, named Salinas, who was a very spiritual man and a great servant of God; and with another professor, now in Segovia, named Friar Diego de Yanguas, who has a truly keen mind.

9. During so many years in which she was subject to those fears, she had the opportunity to consult with others, especially since she went to so many places for foundations. They all tested her because they all wanted to be certain in giving her light; by this light they assured her and were assured themselves.

10. She ever was and ever is subject to all that the holy Catholic faith holds, and all her prayer and the prayer in the houses she has founded is for the increase in the faith. She used to say that if any of her experiences were to induce her to turn against the Catholic faith or the law of God, she would have no need to go in search of proof, for then she would see it was the devil.

11. She never did anything based on what she understood in prayer. Rather, if her confessors told her to do the contrary, she did it immediately, and always informed them about everything. She never believed so decidedly that an experience was from God that, no matter how

much they told her it was, she would swear to the fact; although by reason of the effects and great favors that were granted her in some matters, the experience may have seemed to her to be from the good spirit. But she always desired virtues, and this desire she urged upon her nuns, saying that the most humble and mortified would be the most spiritual.

12. What she has written she gave to the Father Master, Friar Domingo Báñez, who is in Valladolid. For it is with him that she more often discusses and has discussed these experiences. She thinks he has presented her written account to the Holy Office in Madrid. In all of it she submits to the correction of the Catholic faith and of the Church. No one has blamed her, for these experiences are not within anyone's power; and our Lord doesn't ask the impossible.

13. Since an account was given to so many because of the great fear she was undergoing, many of these experiences were told around, which was for her an extraordinary torment and cross. She says that this suffering was not caused by humility but by the fear that these things would be attributed to women's fancy. She went to the extreme of not submitting herself to the judgment of any person who she thought believed that everything was from God, for she feared that then the devil would deceive both him and her. She discussed her soul more willingly with anyone who she saw was more fearful, although it also caused her grief to deal with those who completely despised these experiences—they did so to try her—for some of these seemed to her to be very much from God. And she did not want them to give definite condemnation of the experiences simply because they didn't see any reason for them. Nor did she want them to act as though everything were from God, for she understood very well that there could be some deception. For this reason it never seemed to her that she could have complete assurance where there could be danger. She tried as hard as she could not to offend God in anything and always to obey. By these two means she thought she could free herself even if her experience were from the devil.

14. From the time she began to receive supernatural experiences, her spirit was always inclined to seek what was most perfect, and it almost habitually had great desires for suffering. In persecutions—for she experienced many—she found consolation and a special love for her persecutors. There was a great desire for poverty and solitude, and to leave this exile so as to see God. Because of these effects and other similar ones, she began to grow calm since it seemed to her that a spirit that left these virtues in her would not be bad. And those with whom she discussed this idea agreed. However, this thought didn't make her stop fearing; but it did help her to advance with less worry. Never did her spirit persuade her to hide anything, but always to obey.

15. She never saw anything with her bodily eyes, as has been said. But what she saw was so delicate and intellectual that sometimes at the beginning she thought she had imagined it; at other times she couldn't think such a thing. Nor did she ever hear with her bodily ears—except twice; and these times she didn't hear what was being said, nor did she know.

16. These experiences were not continual, but only came sometimes when there was a need, as once when she endured for some days certain unbearable interior torments and a disturbing inner fear about whether the devil was deceiving her, as is explained more at length in the account of her life and also of her sins, in which her sins were made public as were her other experiences. That time, her fear made her forget her worth. And while in this indescribable state of affliction, merely by hearing the words within, "It is I, do not be afraid," the soul was left so quiet and courageous and confident that it couldn't understand where such a great blessing came from. For neither her confessor nor many learned men with many words sufficed to give her that peace and quiet that were given with these words; nor did these learned men suffice at other times, until she was strengthened by some vision. Without this strength she would have been unable to suffer such great trials, contradictions, and sicknesses, which have been without number. And it happens that she is never without some kind of suffering. There is more and less of it; but ordinarily there are always pains with much other sickness, although since she has been a nun she has been afflicted with more suffering.

17. If some service she renders the Lord or the favors He grants her suddenly come to mind, even though she frequently recalls the favors, she cannot think of them for long as she can of her sins, which are always tormenting her like foul-smelling mud. That she committed so many sins and served God so little must be the reason she is not tempted to vainglory.

18. She was never persuaded concerning any spiritual experience of hers unless it was completely clean and chaste, and there was above all a great fear of offending God our Lord and the desire to do His will in everything. This latter she begs of Him always. And in her opinion she is so determined not to turn from His will that there is nothing her confessors or superiors might tell her about what they think would be of service to God that

she would fail to carry out, confident that the Lord helps those who are resolved to render Him service and glory.

19. Relative to this service, she no more thinks of herself or of her own gain than if she did not exist, insofar as she and her confessors understand concerning herself. Everything on this paper is the full truth, and your Reverence can check with her confessors if you want, and with all the persons who have dealt with her during the past twenty years. Very habitually, her spirit moves her to the praises of God; and she would want everyone to be praising Him even were this to cost her a great deal. That all be praising Him is the source of her desire for the good of souls. And upon seeing how the exterior things of this world are like dung, and how precious the interior are—for the two are incomparable—she has come to have little esteem for the things of the world.

20. The kind of vision your Reverence asked me about is a kind in which nothing is seen, neither interiorly nor exteriorly, because the vision is not an imaginative one. But without seeing anything, the soul understands who it is—and even where the representation is—more clearly than if it saw the person, except that nothing in particular is represented. It's as though we were to feel that another is beside us, and because it is dark don't see that person; yet certainly we know the other is there. However this comparison is insufficient, for one who is in darkness knows in some way, either by hearing a noise or having seen the person before, that someone is there, or knows it from previous knowledge. Here, there is nothing of this; but without any exterior or interior word, the soul understands most clearly who it is and where He is, and sometimes the meaning. Where these visions come from, or how, the soul doesn't know; but they happen in this way, and while they last they cannot be ignored. When one of these visions is taken away, no matter how much the soul wants to imagine it as it was, its efforts are to no avail because what it forms is seen to be something imagined and not a presence; for this presence is not in its power to produce. And so it is with all the supernatural experiences. This inability to produce them is why individuals to whom God grants such a favor don't consider themselves to be anything, for they see that their experience is a gift and that the soul can neither add nor subtract anything. And this leaves the soul with much more humility and much more love of always serving this Lord, so powerful that He can do what we cannot even understand. However much learning one may have, there are things that cannot be grasped.

May He who grants this vision be blessed forever and ever, amen.

5

Social Relations

30. THE TRIAL OF MARY AND JOSEPH

This play comes from the N-Town cycle of mystery plays. The cycle seems to have originated in East Anglia and was most likely transcribed between about 1468 and the early sixteenth century. It was written by four scribes on at least seven different kinds of paper. The cycle opens with the creation of heaven and progresses through the major stories of the Old Testament through the life of Christ and on to judgment day. It is an eclectic mixture of plays that seem to have been put together over a long period of time; the Proclamation that opens the cycle describes forty pageants, but they do not entirely correspond with the cycle as it now stands. Besides these problems with the origins of the material, it is not entirely clear how the pageant was staged, as scholars have argued for various combinations of processional and fixed-stage presentations.

The Trial of Mary and Joseph is unique to the N-Town cycle among extant English mysteries. It describes the reaction of the local community, aware of Mary and Joseph's vow of chastity, to the news of Mary's pregnancy. By placing the action in a medieval ecclesiastical court, the text gives us a popular view of that institution and its officials, as well as an insight into issues of religion, sexuality, and community.

Dramatis Personae:

    First Detractor (Raise Slander)
    Second Detractor (Backbiter)
    First Doctor of Law
    Second Doctor of Law
    Summoner
    Mary
    Joseph
    Bishop Abizacher

Here enters the play of the trial of Mary and Joseph. The first detractor says:

Ah, sirs, God save you all!
  Here is a fair people, in good faith.
  Good sirs, tell me what men call me.
  I think you can not, by this day.
  Yet I walk wide and many a-way,
  but yet where I come I do no good;
  to raise slander is all my law;
  Backbiter is my brother of blood.
  Did he not come hither at all this day?
  Now, would God that he were here
  and by my troth I dare well say
  that if we two together appear

more slander we two shall raise
   within an hour, throughout this town,
   than ever there was these thousand years,
   or else I curse you, both up and down!
   Now, by my troth, I have a sight
   even of my brother. Lo! Here he is!
   Welcome brother, my troth I pledge.
   Your gentle mouth let me now kiss.

2ND DETRACTOR
Gramercy, brother. So have I bliss,
   I am full glad we meet this day!

1ST DETRACTOR
Right so am I, brother, indeed.
   Much gladder than I can say.
   But yet, good brother, I pray you,
   tell all these people what is your name.
   For if they knew it, my life I wager,
   they would worship you and speak great fame.

2ND DETRACTOR
I am Backbiter, that preaches all game,
   both liked and known in many a-place.

1ST DETRACTOR
By my troth I said the same,
   and yet some said you should have evil grace.

2ND DETRACTOR
Hark, Raise Slander, can you not tell
   of any new thing that has happened of late?

1ST DETRACTOR
Within a short while a thing befell,
   I think you will laugh right well there-at.
   For, in truth, a great amount of hate,
   if it be known, will grow from it.

2ND DETRACTOR
If I may raise, therewith, debate,
   I shall not spare the seed to sow.

1ST DETRACTOR
Sir, in the temple a maid there was
   call maid Mary, the truth to tell.
   She seemed so holy within that place
   men said she was fed by a holy angel.
   She made a vow never to lie with a man,
   but to live a chaste and clean virgin.
   How ever it be, her womb does swell
   and is as great as yours or mine!

2ND DETRACTOR
Yes, that old shrew Joseph, my troth I pledge,
   was so enamored on that maid
   that when he had sight of her beauty
   he ceased not until he had her assayed.

1ST DETRACTOR
Ah, no, no! Well worse she has him paid!
   Some fresh young gallant she loves well more
   that his legs to her has laid.
   And that does grieve the old man sore!

2ND DETRACTOR
By my troth, all may well be!
   For fresh and fair she is to sight,
   and such a morsel, as it seems to me,
   would cause a young man to have delight.

1ST DETRACTOR
Such a young damsel, of beauty bright,
   and of shape so comely, also
   of her tail often-times lain by,
   and right ticklish under the toe.

2ND DETRACTOR
That old cuckold was evilly beguiled
   by that fresh wench when he was wed.
   Now must he father another man's child
   and with his labor he shall be fed.

1ST DETRACTOR
A young man may do more cheer in bed
   to a young wench than may an old:
   that is the cause that such law is read,
   that many a man is a cuckold!

Here, the Bishop Abizacher is seated between two doctors of law, and hearing this defamation, speaks to the detractors, saying:

BISHOP
Hark you fellows! Why speak such shame
   of that good virgin fair, maid Mary?
   You are cursed, to defame her so!
   She that is of life so good and holy,
   of her to speak such villainy,
   you make my heart very heavy in mood.
   I charge you to cease of your false cry
   for she is a relation of my own blood!

2ND DETRACTOR
Sibling of your kin, though she be,
   all great with child her womb does swell.
   Do call her hither and yourself shall see
   that it is truth, what I you tell.

1ST DETRACTOR
Sir, for your sake I shall keep counsel.
   I am right loath to grieve you.
   But listen, sirs, listen to what says the bell,
   our fair maid now goes great with child.

FIRST DOCTOR OF LAW
Take good heed, sirs, what you do say.
   Advise you well, what you present.
   If this be found false another day
   full sorely shall you your tale repent.

2ND DETRACTOR
Sir, the maid, in truth, is good and gentle,
   both comely and gay, and a fair wench,
   and craftily with help, she can consent
   to set a cuckold on the high bench.

2ND DOCTOR OF LAW
You are too busy in your language!
   I hope to God to prove you false!
   It would be a great shame if she should behave so
   or with such sin to cause mischief.

BISHOP
This evil tale does grieve my heart!
   Of her to hear such dalliance!
   If she is found in such behavior
   she shall sorely rue her governance.
Sym Summoner! In haste wend you your way.
   Bid Joseph and his wife by name
   to appear at the court this day;
   here to purge them of their defame.
Say that I hear of them great shame
   and that causes me great heaviness.
   If they are clean, without blame,
   bid them come hither and show witness.

SUMMONER
All right sir, I shall them call
   here at your court to appear.
   And if I may meet them at all
   I hope right soon they shall be here.
Away sirs! Let me come near!
   A man of worship comes to this place!
   It seems to me you need learn of courtesy!
   Take off your hoods, with an evil grace!
Do me some worship before my face,
   or, by my troth, I'll make you!
   If I roll you up in my course,
   for fear I shall make your arse quake!
But, yet, if you give me some reward
   I will withdraw my great rough tooth.
   Gold and silver I will not forsake,
   even as all summoners do.
Ah, Joseph, good day with your fair spouse.
   My lord, the bishop, has for you sent.
   It is told to him that in your house
   a cuckold's bow each night is bent.

He that shot the bolt is likely to be brought low.
   Fair maid, that is a tale that you can best tell.
   Now, by your troth, tell your intent.
   Did not the archer please you right well?

MARY
Of God in heaven I take witness
   that sinful work was never my thought.
   I am yet a maid, of pure cleanness,
   just as I was in to this world brought.

SUMMONER
No other witness shall be sought.
   You are with child! Every man may see!
   I charge you both. You shall not tarry,
   but to the bishop come forth with me.

JOSEPH
To the bishop with you we go.
   Of our vindication we have no doubt.

MARY
Almighty God shall be our friend
   when the truth is tried out.

SUMMONER
Yes, in this way excuse themselves all scoundrels,
   when their own sin does defame them.
   But they then begin to bow lowly
   when they are guilty and found in blame.
Therefore, come forth, cuckold by name,
   the bishop shall question your life.
   Come forth also goodly dame,
   a clean housewife, as I suppose.
I will tell you without any gloss,
   if you were mine, without fail
   I would each day tweak your nose
   if you did bring me such a pack.
My lord the bishop, here have I brought
   this goodly couple at your bidding,
   and it seems to me by her freight,
   "Fair child lallay" soon must she sing.

1ST DETRACTOR
If you bring a cradle to her
   you might save money in her purse.
   Because she is your young cousin,
   I pray you sir, let her never fare the worse.

BISHOP
Alas, Mary, what have you done?
   I am ashamed even for your sake.
   How have you changed your holy thought?
   Did old Joseph, with strength you take?
Or have you chosen another mate
   by whom you are thus brought to shame?

Tell me, who has done this injury,
   how have you lost your holy name?

MARY
My name, I hope, is safe and sound.
   God to witness, I am a maid;
   of fleshly lust and ghostly wound
   —in deed, nor in thought—I never assayed.

1ST DOCTOR OF LAW
How shall your womb thus be arrayed,
   so greatly swollen as that it is,
   but if some man had you o'er-laid
   your womb should never be so great, indeed.

2ND DOCTOR OF LAW
Hark, you, Joseph. I am afraid
   that you have worked this open sin.
   This woman you have thus betrayed
   with great flattering or some false trick.

2ND DETRACTOR
Now, by my troth, you hit the pin!
   With that purpose in faith I hold.
   Tell now how you thus her did win
   or acknowledge yourself for a cuckold.

JOSEPH
She is for me a true clean maid,
   and I for her am clean also.
   Of fleshly sin I never assayed
   since when she was wedded to me.

BISHOP
You shall not escape from us yet so.
   First you shall tell us another story.
   Straight to the altar you shall go,
   the drink of vengeance to attempt.
   Here is the bottle of God's vengeance.
   This drink shall now be your vindication.
   This has such virtue, by God's ordinance,
   that, whatever man drinks of this potion
   and goes certainly in procession
   here in this place about this altar,
   if he is guilty, some mark
   shall show it plainly in his face.
   If you are guilty, tell us the cause.
   Be not too bold over God's might.
   If you presume and are guilty,
   God will grieve you many-fold.

JOSEPH
I am not guilty as I first told.
   Almighty God, I take witness!

BISHOP
Then drink what you hold in haste
   and address yourself to the procession.

Here Joseph drinks and circles the altar seven times, saying:

JOSEPH
This drink I take with meek intent.
   As I am guiltless to God I pray,
   Lord, as you are omnipotent,
   on me you show the truth this day.
   About this altar I take the way,
   O gracious God help your servant,
   as I am guiltless against yon maid
   of your mercy grant me your hand this time.

SUMMONER
This old shrew may not well go.
   Long he tarries to go about.
   Lift up your feet, set forth your toes,
   or by my troth, you'll get a clout!

2ND DETRACTOR
Now sir, evil luck comes to your snout!
   What ails your legs, now to be lame?
   You did put them right freshly out
   when you did play with yon young dame!

1ST DETRACTOR
I pray to God, give him mischance!
   His legs here do fold for age,
   but with this damsel, when he did dance,
   the old churl had right great courage!

SUMMONER
The shrew was then set in a dotage
   and had good lust that time to play.
   Did she not give you broth for a meal,
   when you had finished, to comfort your brain?

JOSEPH
O gracious God, help me at this time,
   against these people that do me defame.
   As I never more did touch her side,
   help me this day from worldly shame.
   About this altar, to keep my fame
   vii times I have gone round about.
   If I am worthy to suffer blame,
   O rightful God, my sin show out!

BISHOP
Joseph, with heart, thank God the Lord,
   whose high mercy does excuse you.
   For your vindication we shall record
   That you did never muse on sin with her.
   But Mary, yourself may not refuse.
   All great with child we see you stand.
   What mysterious man misused you?
   Why have you sinned against your husband?

MARY
I trespassed never with earthly man.
> Thereof I hope, through God's dispensation,
> here to be purged before your sight
> from all sin clean, like as my husband.
> Take me the bottle out of your hand.
> Here shall I drink before your face.
> About this altar then shall I walk
> vii times to go by God's grace.

1ST DOCTOR OF LAW
See this bold liar would presume
> against God to test his might.
> Though God's vengeance should her consume
> she will not tell her false delight.
> You are with child! We see in sight.
> To us your womb does you accuse.
> There was never woman yet in such plight
> that from mankind her could excuse.

1ST DETRACTOR
In faith, I suppose that this woman slept
> outside, all covered while that it snowed.
> And a flake thereof into her mouth crept
> and thereof the child in her womb does grow.

2ND DETRACTOR
Then beware, dame, for this is well known:
> when it is born, if that the sun shines
> it will turn to water again, as I believe,
> for snow unto water does always return.

2ND DOCTOR OF LAW
With God's high might you should not joke!
> Advise you well of your purging.
> If you are guilty you may not escape.
> Beware ever of God, that rightful justice.
> If God with vengeance sets on you his eyes,
> not only you, but all your kin is shamed.
> Better it is to tell the truth, consider,
> than to grieve God and anger him.

MARY
I trust in his grace, I shall never grieve him.
> His servant I am in word, deed and thought,
> a maid undefiled I hope he shall me prove.
> I pray you, stop me not.

BISHOP
Now, by that good Lord that all this world has
>   wrought,
> if God on you shows any manner of token,
> vindication, I believe, was never so dearly bought,
> if I may, on you, in any way be avenged.
> Hold here the bottle and take a large drink
> and about the altar go in your procession.

MARY
To God, in this case, my cause I have handed.
> Lord, through your help I drink of this potion.

Here the blessed virgin drinks from the potion and afterwards circles the altar saying:

> God, as I never knew of man's stain,
> but ever have lived in true virginity,
> send me this day your holy consolation
> that all these fair people may see my cleanness.
> O gracious God, as thou hast chosen me
> To be thy mother, to be born of me,
> save your tabernacle that is kept clean for you
> which now is put at reproof and scorn.
> Gabriel told me with words here in my presence
> that you, of your goodness, would become my child.
> Help now, of your highness, that my worship is
>   not lost.
> O dear son, I pray you, help your mother mild.

BISHOP
Almighty God, what may this mean?
> For all the drink of God's potion,
> this woman with child is fair and clean,
> without foul spot or stain.
> I cannot, by no imagination,
> prove her guilty and sinful of life.
> It shows openly by her vindication,
> she is clean maid, both mother and wife.

1ST DETRACTOR
By my father's soul, here is a great trick!
> Because she is a relation of your kin
> the drink is changed by some false scheme
> so that she will have no shame this time.

BISHOP
Because you think that we do falsehood,
> and because you did first them defame,
> you shall right here, despite your head,
> before all these people, drink of the same!

1ST DETRACTOR
Sir, in good faith, one draught I pull,
> if these two drinkers have not spent it all.

Here he drinks and, feeling a pain in the head, falls and says

> Out, out, alas! What ails my skull?
> Ah! My head with fire I think is burnt!
> Mercy good Mary, I do me repent
> of my cursed and false language.

MARY
Now good Lord in heaven omnipotent,
   of his great mercy your sickness assuage.
BISHOP
We all on our knees fall here on the ground.
   You, God's handmaid praying for grace,
   all cursed language and shame unsound,
   good Mary, forgive us here in this place.
MARY
Now, God forgive you all your trespass
   and also forgive you all defamation
   that you have said, both more and less,
   to my hindrance and stain.
BISHOP
Now blessed virgin we thank you all
   of your good heart and great patience.
   We will go with you home to your hall
   to do you service with high reverence.
MARY
I thank you heartily of your benevolence.
   On to your own house I pray you go
   and take these people home with you hence.
   I am not disposed to pass from hence.

BISHOP
Then farewell maiden and pure virgin.
   Farewell true handmaid of God in bliss.
   We all to you lowly incline
   and take our leave of you as is worthy.
MARY
Almighty God guide your ways.
   For that high Lord is most of might.
   May he speed you so that you will not miss
   to have of him in heaven a sight.
JOSEPH
Honored in heaven by that high Lord,
   whose endless grace is so abundant
   that he does show the true record
   of each man that is his true servant.
   That Lord to worship with heart pleasant
   we both are bound right on this place,
   which our vindication did us grant
   and prove us pure by high grace.
MARY
For truth, good spouse, I thank him highly
   of his good grace for our vindication.
   Our cleanness is known full openly
   by virtue of his great consolation.

They exit with joy.

---

31. *MALLEUS MALEFICARUM*

The Malleus Maleficarum *(The Hammer of Witches) was published in 1486 by the Dominicans Jacob Sprenger (c. 1436–95) and Heinrich Kramer (also known as Institoris; c. 1430–1505). It appeared in the middle of the era of witch-hunting: witchcraft prosecutions had begun in the thirteenth century, with the development of the inquisitorial procedure. The essence of this procedure was that cases against suspected offenders were brought by the authorities, based on information provided by the public. Once the suspect had been denounced, the judge could begin the investigation, or "inquisition." The accused was rarely allowed a lawyer, and the main aim of the procedure was to convince the accused to confess and be reconciled to the Church, rather than to determine guilt or innocence. Such a confession could be obtained by torture.*

   The idea of the witch was fully developed by the early fifteenth century; familiar ideas such as the witch's sabbath and nocturnal flight, which were entirely absent from early prosecutions, were common by the 1430s. The Malleus Maleficarum *comes from this period, before the mass persecutions of the witch-craze in the sixteenth and seventeenth centuries. Although it is one of the most famous of the witch-hunting manuals of the period, it does not feature some of the more graphic elements of the witch's habits, such as the witch's sabbath. However, it is notable for its virulent misogyny. It also shares one of the central problems of the source material for witchcraft in that it gives us the perceptions of the learned persecutors of witches, rather than witches themselves or their victims.*

Malleus Maleficarum

Part 1, Question 6

CONCERNING WITCHES WHO COPULATE WITH DEVILS

WHY IT IS THAT WOMEN ARE CHIEFLY ADDICTED TO EVIL SUPERSTITIONS

There is also, concerning witches who copulate with devils, much difficulty in considering the methods by which such abominations are consummated. On the part of the devil: first, of what element the body is made that he assumes; secondly, whether the act is always accompanied by the injection of semen received from another; thirdly, as to time and place, whether he commits this act more frequently at one time than at another; fourthly, whether the act is invisible to any who may be standing by. And on the part of the women, it has to be inquired whether only they who were themselves conceived in this filthy manner are often visited by devils; or secondly, whether it is those who were offered to devils by midwives at the time of their birth; and thirdly, whether the actual venereal delectation of such is of a weaker sort. But we cannot here reply to all these questions, both because we are only engaged in a general study, and because in the second part of this work they are all singly explained by their operations, as will appear in the fourth chapter, where mention is made of each separate method. Therefore let us now chiefly consider women; and first, why this kind of perfidy is found more in so fragile a sex than in men. And our inquiry will first be general, as to the general conditions of women; secondly, particular, as to which sort of women are found to be given to superstition and witchcraft; and thirdly, specifically with regard to midwives, who surpass all others in wickedness.

WHY SUPERSTITION IS CHIEFLY FOUND IN WOMEN

As for the first question, why a greater number of witches is found in the fragile feminine sex than among men; it is indeed a fact that it were idle to contradict, since it is accredited by actual experience, apart from the verbal testimony of credible witnesses. And without in any way detracting from a sex in which God has always taken great glory that His might should be spread abroad, let us say that various men have assigned various reasons for this fact, which nevertheless agree in principle. Wherefore it is good, for the admonition of women, to speak of this matter; and it has often been proved by experience that they are eager to hear of it, so long as it is set forth with discretion.

For some learned men propound this reason; that there are three things in nature, the Tongue, an Ecclesiastic, and a Woman, which know no moderation in goodness or vice; and when they exceed the bounds of their condition they reach the greatest heights and the lowest depths of goodness and vice. When they are governed by a good spirit, they are most excellent in virtue; but when they are governed by an evil spirit, they indulge the worst possible vices.

This is clear in the case of the tongue, since by its ministry most of the kingdoms have been brought into the faith of Christ; and the Holy Ghost appeared over the Apostles of Christ in tongues of fire. Other learned preachers also have had as it were the tongues of dogs, licking the wounds and sores of the dying Lazarus. As it is said: With the tongues of dogs ye save your souls from the enemy.

For this reason St. Dominic, the leader and father of the Order of Preachers, is represented in the figure of a barking dog with a lighted torch in his mouth, that even to this day he may by his barking keep off the heretic wolves from the flock of Christ's sheep.

It is also a matter of common experience that the tongue of one prudent man can subdue the wrangling of a multitude; wherefore not unjustly Solomon sings much in their praise, in *Proverbs* x[:13]: In the lips of him that hath understanding wisdom is found. And again, The tongue of the just is as choice silver: the heart of the wicked is little worth [Prov. 10:20]. And again, The lips of the righteous feed many; but fools die for want of wisdom [Prov. 10:21]. For this cause he adds in chapter xvi, The preparations of the heart belong to man; but the answer of the tongue is from the Lord [Prov. 16:1].

But concerning an evil tongue you will find in *Ecclesiasticus* xxviii[:14]: A backbiting tongue hath disquieted many, and driven them from nation to nation: strong cities hath it pulled down, and overthrown the houses of great men. And by a backbiting tongue it means a third party who rashly or spitefully interferes between two contending parties.

Secondly, concerning Ecclesiastics, that is to say, clerics and religious of either sex, St. John Chrysostom speaks on the text, He cast out them that bought and sold from the temple. From the priesthood arises everything good, and everything evil. St. Jerome in his epistle to Nepotian says: Avoid as you would the plague a trading priest, who has risen from poverty to riches, from a low to a high estate. And Blessed Bernard in his 23rd Homily *On the Psalms* says of clerics: If one should arise as an open heretic, let him be cast out and put to silence; if he is a violent enemy, let all good men flee from him. But how are we to know which ones to cast out or to flee from? For they are confusedly friendly and hostile, peaceable and quarrelsome, neighborly and utterly selfish.

And in another place: Our bishops are become spearmen, and our pastors shearers. And by bishops here is meant those proud abbots who impose heavy labors on their inferiors, which they would not themselves touch with their little finger. And St. Gregory says concerning pastors: No one does more harm in the Church than he who, having the name or order of sanctity, lives in sin; for no one dares to accuse him of sin, and therefore the sin is widely spread, since the sinner is honored for the sanctity of his order. Blessed Augustine also speaks of monks to Vincent the Donatist: I freely confess to your charity before the Lord our God, which is the witness of my soul from the time I began to serve God, what great difficulty I have experienced in the fact that it is impossible to find either worse or better men than those who grace or disgrace the monasteries.

Now the wickedness of women is spoken of in *Ecclesiasticus* xxv[:15]: There is no head above the head of a serpent and there is no wrath above the wrath of a woman. I had rather dwell with a lion and a dragon than to keep house with a wicked woman. And among much which in that place precedes and follows about a wicked woman, he concludes: All wickedness is but little to the wickedness of a woman. Wherefore St. John Chrysostom says on the text, It is not good to marry (Matthew xix[:10]). What else is woman but a foe to friendship, an unescapable punishment, a necessary evil, a natural temptation, a desirable calamity, a domestic danger, a delectable detriment, an evil of nature, painted with fair colors! Therefore if it be a sin to divorce her when she ought to be kept, it is indeed a necessary torture; for either we commit adultery by divorcing her, or we must endure daily strife. Cicero in his second book of *The Rhetorics* says: The many lusts of men lead them into one sin, but the one lust of women leads them into all sins; for the root of all woman's vices is avarice. And Seneca says in his *Tragedies:* A woman either loves or hates; there is no third grade. And the tears of a woman are a deception, for they may spring from true grief, or they may be a snare. When a woman thinks alone, she thinks evil.

But for good women there is so much praise, that we read that they have brought beatitude to men, and have saved nations, lands, and cities; as is clear in the case of Judith, Debbora, and Esther. See also 1 Corinthians vii[:13]: If a woman hath a husband that believeth not, and he be pleased to dwell with her, let her not leave him. For the unbelieving husband is sanctified by the believing wife. And *Ecclesiasticus* xxvi[:1]: Blessed is the man who has a virtuous wife, for the number of his days shall be doubled. And throughout that chapter much high praise is spoken of the excellence of good women; as also in the last chapter of *Proverbs* [31:10–31] concerning a virtuous woman.

And all this is made clear also in the New Testament concerning women and virgins and other holy women who have by faith led nations and kingdoms away from the worship of idols to the Christian religion. Anyone who looks at Vincent of Beauvais (in *Spe. Histor.*, XXVI. 9) will find marvellous things of the conversion of Hungary by the most Christian Gilia and of the Franks by Clotilda, the wife of Clovis. Wherefore in many vituperations that we read against women, the word woman is used to mean the lust of the flesh. As it is said: I have found a woman more bitter than death, and a good woman subject to carnal lust.

Others again have propounded other reasons why there are more superstitious women found than men. And the first is, that they are more credulous; and since the chief aim of the devil is to corrupt faith, therefore he rather attacks them. See *Ecclesiasticus* xix[:4]: He that is quick to believe is light-minded, and shall be diminished. The second reason is, that women are naturally more impressionable, and more ready to receive the influence of a disembodied spirit; and that when they use this quality well they are very good, but when they use it ill they are very evil.

The third reason is that they have slippery tongues, and are unable to conceal from their fellow-women those things which by evil arts they know; and, since they are weak, they find an easy and secret manner of vindicating themselves by witchcraft. See *Ecclesiasticus* as quoted above: I had rather dwell with a lion and a dragon than to keep house with a wicked woman. All wickedness is but little to the wickedness of a woman. And to this may be added that, as they are very impressionable, they act accordingly.

There are also others who bring forward yet other reasons, of which preachers should be very careful how they make use. For it is true that in the Old Testament the Scriptures have much that is evil to say about women, and this because of the first temptress, Eve, and her imitators; yet afterwards in the New Testament we find a change of name, as from Eva to Ave (as St. Jerome says), and the whole sin of Eve taken away by the benediction of MARY, Therefore preachers should always say as much praise of them as possible.

But because in these times this perfidy is more often found in women than in men, as we learn by actual experience, if anyone is curious as to the reason, we may add to what has already been said the following: that since they are feebler both in mind and body, it is not surprising that they should come more under the spell of witchcraft.

For as regards intellect, or the understanding of spiritual things, they seem to be of a different nature from men; a fact which is vouched for by the logic of the authorities, backed by various examples from the Scriptures. Terence says: Women are intellectually like children. And Lactantius (*Institutiones*, III): No woman understood philosophy except Temeste. And *Proverbs* xi, as it were describing a woman, says: As a jewel of gold in a swine's snout, so is a fair woman which is without discretion.

But the natural reason is that she is more carnal than a man, as is clear from her many carnal abominations. And it should be noted that there was a defect in the formation of the first woman, since she was formed from a bent rib, that is, a rib of the breast, which is bent as it were in a contrary direction to a man. And since through this defect she is an imperfect animal, she always deceives. For Cato says: When a woman weeps she weaves snares. And again: When a woman weeps, she labors to deceive a man. And this is shown by Samson's wife, who coaxed him to tell her the riddle he had propounded to the Philistines, and told them the answer, and so deceived him. And it is clear in the case of the first woman that she had little faith; for when the serpent asked why they did not eat of every tree in Paradise, she answered: Of every tree, etc.—lest perchance we die. Thereby she showed that she doubted, and had little faith in the word of God. And all this is indicated by the etymology of the word; for *Femina* comes from *Fe* and *Minus*, since she is ever weaker to hold and preserve the faith. And this as regards faith is of her very nature; although both by grace and nature faith never failed in the Blessed Virgin, even at the time of Christ's Passion, when it failed in all men.

Therefore a wicked woman is by her nature quicker to waver in her faith, and consequently quicker to abjure the faith, which is the root of witchcraft.

And as to her other mental quality, that is, her natural will; when she hates someone whom she formerly loved, then she seethes with anger and impatience in her whole soul, just as the tides of the sea are always heaving and boiling. Many authorities allude to this cause. *Ecclesiasticus* xxv: There is no wrath above the wrath of a woman. And Seneca (*Tragedies*, VIII): No might of the flames or of the swollen winds, no deadly weapon, is so much to be feared as the lust and hatred of a woman who has been divorced from the marriage bed (*Medea*).

This is shown too in the woman who falsely accused Joseph, and caused him to be imprisoned because he would not consent to the crime of adultery with her (Genesis [39:7–20]). And truly the most powerful cause which contributes to the increase of witches is the woeful rivalry between married folk and unmarried women and men. This is so even among holy women, so what must it be among the others? For you see in Genesis xxi[:9–11] how impatient and envious Sarah was of Hagar when she conceived: how jealous Rachel was of Leah because she had no children (Genesis xxx[:1]): and Hannah, who was barren, of the fruitful Peninnah (1 Sam. 1[:2–6]): and how Miriam (Numbers xii[:1]) murmured and spoke ill of Moses, and was therefore stricken with leprosy: and how Martha was jealous of Mary Magdalen, because she was busy and Mary was sitting down (Luke x[:38–40]). To this point is Ecclesiasticus xxxvii[:11]: Neither consult with a woman touching her of whom she is jealous. Meaning that it is useless to consult with her, since there is always jealousy, that is, envy, in a wicked woman. And if women behave thus to each other, how much more will they do so to men.

Valerius Maximus tells how, when Phoroneus, the king of the Greeks, was dying, he said to his brother Leontius that there would have been nothing lacking to him of complete happiness if a wife had always been lacking to him. And when Leontius asked how a wife could stand in the way of happiness, he answered that all married men well knew. And when the philosopher Socrates was asked if one should marry a wife, he answered: If you do not, you are lonely, your family dies out, and a stranger inherits; if you do, you suffer perpetual anxiety, querulous complaints, reproaches concerning the marriage portion, the heavy displeasure of your relations, the garrulousness of a mother-in-law, cuckoldom, and no certain arrival of an heir. This he said as one who knew. For St. Jerome in his *Contra Jovinianum* says: This Socrates had two wives, whom he endured with much patience, but could not be rid of their contumelies and clamorous vituperations. So one day when they were complaining against him, he went out of the house to escape their plaguing, and sat down before the house; and the women then threw filthy water over him. But the philosopher was not disturbed by this, saying, "I knew that the rain would come after the thunder."

There is also a story of a man whose wife was drowned in a river, who, when he was searching for the body to take it out of the water, walked up the stream. And when he was asked why, since heavy bodies do not rise but fall, he was searching against the current of the river, he answered: "When that woman was alive she always, both in word and deed, went contrary to my commands;—therefore I am searching in the contrary direction in case even now she is dead she may preserve her contrary disposition."

And indeed, just as through the first defect in their intelligence they are more prone to abjure the faith; so through their second defect of inordinate affections and passions they search for, brood over, and inflict various vengeances, either by witchcraft, or by some other means. Wherefore it is no wonder that so great a number of witches exist in this sex.

Women also have weak memories; and it is a natural vice in them not to be disciplined, but to follow their own impulses without any sense of what is due; this is her whole study, and all that she keeps in her memory. So Theophrastus says: If you hand over the whole management of the house to her, but reserve some minute detail to your own judgment, she will think that you are displaying a great want of faith in her, and will stir up strife; and unless you quickly take counsel, she will prepare poison for you, and consult seers and soothsayers; and will become a witch.

But as to domination by women, hear what Cicero says in the *Paradoxes*. Can he be called a free man whose wife governs him, imposes laws on him, orders him, and forbids him to do what he wishes, so that he cannot and dare not deny her anything that she asks? I should call him not only a slave, but the vilest of slaves, even if he comes of the noblest family. And Seneca, in the character of the raging Medea, says: Why do you cease to follow your happy impulse; how great is that part of vengeance in which you rejoice? Where he adduces many proofs that a woman will not be governed, but will follow her own impulse even to her own destruction. In the same way we read of many women who have killed themselves either for love or sorrow because they were unable to work their vengeance.

St. Jerome, writing of Daniel, tells a story of Laodice, wife of Antiochus king of Syria; how, being jealous lest he should love his other wife, Berenice, more than her, she first caused Berenice and her daughter by Antiochus to be slain, and then poisoned herself. And why? Because she would not be governed, but would follow her own impulse. Therefore St. John Chrysostom says not without reason: O evil worse than all evil, a wicked woman, whether she be poor or rich. For if she be the wife of a rich man, she does not cease night and day to excite her husband with hot words, to use evil blandishments and violent importunations. And if she have a poor husband she does not cease to stir him also to anger and strife. And if she be a widow, she takes it upon herself everywhere to look down on everybody, and is inflamed to all boldness by the spirit of pride.

If we inquire, we find that nearly all the kingdoms of the world have been overthrown by women. Troy, which was a prosperous kingdom, was, for the rape of one woman, Helen, destroyed, and many thousands of Greeks slain. The kingdom of the Jews suffered much misfortune and destruction through the accursed Jezebel, and her daughter Athaliah, queen of Judah who caused her son's sons to be killed, that on their death she might reign herself; yet each of them was slain. The kingdom of the Romans endured much evil through Cleopatra, Queen of Egypt, that worst of women. And so with others. Therefore it is no wonder if the world now suffers through the malice of women.

And now let us examine the carnal desires of the body itself, whence has arisen unconscionable harm to human life. Justly may we say with Cato of Utica: If the world could be rid of women, we should not be without God in our intercourse. For truly, without the wickedness of women, to say nothing of witchcraft, the world would still remain proof against innumerable dangers. Hear what Valerius said to Rufinus: You do not know that woman is the Chimaera, but it is good that you should know it; for that monster was of three forms; its face was that of a radiant and noble lion, it had the filthy belly of a goat, and it was armed with the virulent tail of a viper. And he means that a woman is beautiful to look upon, contaminating to the touch, and deadly to keep.

Let us consider another property of hers, the voice. For as she is a liar by nature, so in her speech she stings while she delights us. Wherefore her voice is like the song of the Sirens, who with their sweet melody entice the passersby and kill them. For they kill them by emptying their purses, consuming their strength, and causing them to forsake God. Again Valerius says to Rufinus: When she speaks it is a delight which flavors the sin; the flower of love is a rose, because under its blossom there are hidden many thorns. See *Proverbs* v, 3–4: Her mouth is smoother than oil; that is, her speech is afterwards as bitter as absinthium. [Her throat is smoother than oil. But her end is as bitter as wormwood.]

Let us consider also her gait, posture, and habit, in which is vanity of vanities. There is no man in the world who studies so hard to please the good God as even an ordinary woman studies by her vanities to please men. An example of this is to be found in the life of Pelagia, a worldly woman who was wont to go about Antioch tired and adorned most extravagantly. A holy father, named Nonnus, saw her and began to weep, saying to his companions, that never in all his life had he used such diligence to please God; and much more he added to this effect, which is preserved in his orations.

It is this which is lamented in *Ecclesiastes* vii, and which the Church even now laments on account of the great multitude of witches. And I have found a woman more bitter than death, who is the hunter's snare, and her heart is a net, and her hands are bands. He that pleaseth God shall escape from her; but he that is a sinner shall be caught by her. More bitter than death, that is, than the devil: *Apocalypse* vi, 8, His name was Death. For though the devil tempted Eve to sin, yet Eve seduced Adam. And as the sin of Eve would not have brought death to our soul and body unless the sin had afterwards passed on to Adam, to which he was tempted by Eve, not by the devil, therefore she is more bitter than death.

More bitter than death, again, because that is natural and destroys only the body; but the sin which arose from woman destroys the soul by depriving it of grace, and delivers the body up to the punishment for sin.

More bitter than death, again, because bodily death is an open and terrible enemy, but woman is a wheedling and secret enemy.

And that she is more perilous than a snare does not speak of the snare of hunters, but of devils. For men are caught not only through their carnal desires, when they see and hear women: for St. Bernard says: Their face is a burning wind, and their voice the hissing of serpents: but they also cast wicked spells on countless men and animals. And when it is said that her heart is a net, it speaks of the inscrutable malice which reigns in their hearts. And her hands are as bands for binding; for when they place their hands on a creature to bewitch it, then with the help of the devil they perform their design.

To conclude. All witchcraft comes from carnal lust, which is in women insatiable. See *Proverbs* xxx[:15]: There are three things that are never satisfied, yea, a fourth thing which says not, It is enough; that is, the mouth of the womb. Wherefore for the sake of fulfilling their lusts they consort even with devils. More such reasons could be brought forward, but to the understanding it is sufficiently clear that it is no matter for wonder that there are more women than men found infected with the heresy of witchcraft. And in consequence of this, it is better called the heresy of witches than of wizards, since the name is taken from the more powerful party. And blessed be the Highest Who has so far preserved the male sex from so great a crime: for since He was willing to be born and to suffer for us, therefore He has granted to men this privilege.

32. SIR THOMAS MORE (1478–1535)

More (see selection 7) is remembered not only as King Henry's most principled opponent but also as the author of Utopia *(1516), one of the great books of the Northern Renaissance. Sharing with his close friends Erasmus and John Colet a strong belief in the need for church reform, he wrote of a previously unknown island where charity, reason, cooperation, and virtue operated. This mythical island of Utopia (No Place) he contrasted to the England he knew. The book is also an evocative expression of the values of northern humanism, a movement More strongly supported both privately and officially.*

Utopia

BOOK I

HENRY VIII, the unconquered King of England, a prince adorned with all the virtues that become a great monarch, having some differences of no small consequence with Charles, the most serene Prince of Castile, sent me into Flanders, as his ambassador, for treating and composing matters between them. I was colleague and companion to that incomparable man Cuthbert Tunstall, whom the King with such universal applause lately made Master of the Rolls, but of whom I will say nothing; not because

I fear that the testimony of a friend will be suspected, but rather because his learning and virtues are too great for me to do them justice, and so well known that they need not my commendations unless I would, according to the proverb, "Show the sun with a lantern." Those that were appointed by the Prince to treat with us, met us at Bruges, according to agreement; they were all worthy men. The Margrave of Bruges was their head, and the chief man among them; but he that was esteemed the wisest, and that spoke for the rest, was George Temse, the Provost of Casselsee; both art and nature had concurred to make him eloquent: he was very learned in the law; and as he had a great capacity, so by a long practice in affairs he was very dexterous at unravelling them.

After we had several times met without coming to an agreement, they went to Brussels for some days to know the Prince's pleasure. And since our business would admit it, I went to Antwerp. While I was there, among many that visited me, there was one that was more acceptable to me than any other, Peter Giles, born at Antwerp, who is a man of great honor, and of a good rank in his town, though less than he deserves; for I do not know if there be anywhere to be found a more learned and a better bred young man: for as he is both a very worthy and a very knowing person, so he is so civil to all men, so particularly kind to his friends, and so full of candor and affection, that there is not perhaps above one or two anywhere to be found that are in all respects so perfect a friend. He is extraordinarily modest, there is no artifice in him; and yet no man has more of a prudent simplicity: his conversation was so pleasant and so innocently cheerful, that his company in a great measure lessened any longings to go back to my country, and to my wife and children, which an absence of four months had quickened very much. One day as I was returning home from mass at St. Mary's, which is the chief church, and the most frequented of any in Antwerp, I saw him by accident talking with a stranger, who seemed past the flower of his age; his face was tanned, he had a long beard, and his cloak was hanging carelessly about him, so that by his looks and habit I concluded he was a seaman.

As soon as Peter saw me, he came and saluted me; and as I was returning his civility, he took me aside, and pointing to him with whom he had been discoursing, he said: "Do you see that man? I was just thinking to bring him to you."

I answered, "He should have been very welcome on your account."

"And on his own too," replied he, "if you knew the man, for there is none alive that can give so copious an account of unknown nations and countries as he can do; which I know you very much desire."

Then said I, "I did not guess amiss, for at first sight I took him for a seaman."

"But you are much mistaken," said he, "for he has not sailed as a seaman, but as a traveler, or rather a philosopher. This Raphael, who from his family carries the name of Hythloday, is not ignorant of the Latin tongue, but is eminently learned in the Greek, having applied himself more particularly to that than to the former, because he had given himself much to philosophy, in which he knew that the Romans have left us nothing that is valuable, except what is to be found in Seneca and Cicero. He is a Portuguese by birth, and was so desirous of seeing the world that he divided his estate among his brothers, ran the same hazard as Americus (Amerigo) Vespucci, and bore a share in three of his four voyages, that are now published; only he did not return with him in his last, but obtained leave of him almost by force, that he might be one of those twenty-four who were left at the farthest place at which they touched, in their last voyage to New Castile. The leaving him thus did not a little gratify one that was more fond of traveling than of returning home to be buried in his own country; for he used often to say that the way to heaven was the same from all places; and he that had no grave had the heaven still over him. Yet this disposition of mind had cost him dear, if God had not been very gracious to him; for after he, with five Castilians, had traveled over many countries, at last, by strange good fortune, he got to Ceylon, and from thence to Calicut, where he very happily found some Portuguese ships, and, beyond all men's expectations, returned to his native country."

When Peter had said this to me, I thanked him for his kindness, in intending to give me the acquaintance of a man whose conversation he knew would be so acceptable; and upon that Raphael and I embraced each other. After those civilities were passed which are usual with strangers upon their first meeting, we all went to my house, and entering into the garden, sat down on a green bank, and entertained one another in discourse. He told us that when Vespucci had sailed away, he and his companions that stayed behind in New Castile, by degrees insinuated themselves into the affections of the people of the country, meeting often with them, and treating them gently: and at last they not only lived among them without danger, but conversed familiarly with them; and got so far into the heart of a prince, whose name and country I have forgot, that he both furnished them plentifully with all things necessary, and also with the conveniences of traveling; both boats when they went by water, and wagons when they traveled over land: he sent with them a very faithful guide, who was to introduce and recommend them to such other princes as they had a mind to see: and after many days' journey, they came to towns and cities, and to commonwealths, that were both happily governed and well-peopled. Under the equator, and as far on both sides of it as the sun moves, there lay vast deserts that were parched with the perpetual heat of the sun; the soil was withered, all things looked dismally, and all places were either quite uninhabited, or abounded with wild beasts and serpents, and some few men that were neither less wild nor less cruel than the beasts themselves.

But as they went farther, a new scene opened, all things grew milder, the air less burning, the soil more verdant, and even the beasts were less wild: and at last there were nations, towns, and cities, that had not only mutual commerce among themselves, and with their neighbors, but traded both by sea and land, to very remote countries. There they found the conveniences of seeing many countries on all hands, for no ship went any voyage into which he and his companions were not very welcome. The first vessels that they saw were flat-bottomed, their sails were made of reeds and wicker woven close together, only some were of leather; but afterward they found ships made with round keels and canvas sails, and in all respects like our ships; and the seamen understood both astronomy and navigation. He got wonderfully into their favor, by showing them the use of the needle, of which till then they were utterly ignorant. They sailed before with great caution, and only in summer-time, but now they count all seasons alike, trusting wholly to the lodestone, in which they are perhaps more secure than safe; so that there is reason to fear that this discovery, which was thought would prove so much to their advantage, may by their imprudence become an occasion of much mischief to them. But it were too long to dwell on all that he told us he had observed in every place, it would be too great a digression from our present purpose: whatever is necessary to be told, concerning those wise and prudent institutions which he observed among civilized nations, may perhaps be related by us on a more proper occasion. We asked him many questions concerning all these things, to which he answered very willingly; only we made no inquiries after monsters, than which nothing is more common; for everywhere one may hear of ravenous dogs and wolves, and cruel man-eaters; but it is not so easy to find States that are well and wisely governed.

As he told us of many things that were amiss in those newly discovered countries, so he reckoned up not a few things from which patterns might be taken for correcting the errors of these nations among whom we live; of which an account may be given, as I have already promised, at some other time; for at present I intend only to relate those particulars that he told us of the manners and laws of the Utopians: but I will begin with the occasion that led us to speak of that commonwealth. After Raphael had discoursed with great judgment on the many errors that were both among us and these nations; had treated of the wise institutions both here and there, and had spoken as distinctly of the customs and government of every nation through which he had passed, as if he had spent his whole life in it, Peter, being struck with admiration, said: "I wonder, Raphael, how it comes that you enter into no king's service, for I am sure there are none to whom you would not be very acceptable: for your learning and knowledge both of men and things, are such that you would not only entertain them very pleasantly, but be of great use to them, by the examples you could set before them and the advices you could give them; and by this means you would both serve your own interest and be of great use to all your friends."

"As for my friends," answered he, "I need not be much concerned, having already done for them all that was incumbent on me; for when I was not only in good health, but fresh and young, I distributed that among my kindred and friends which other people do not part with till they are old and sick, when they then unwillingly give that which they can enjoy no longer themselves. I think my friends ought to rest contented with this, and not to expect that for their sake I should enslave myself to any king whatsoever."

"Soft and fair," said Peter, "I do not mean that you should be a slave to any king, but only that you should assist them, and be useful to them."

"The change of the word," said he, "does not alter the matter."

"But term it as you will," replied Peter, "I do not see any other way in which you can be so useful, both in private to your friends, and to the public, and by which you can make your own condition happier."

"Happier!" answered Raphael; "is that to be compassed in a way so abhorrent to my genius?

"Now I live as I will, to which I believe few courtiers can pretend. And there are so many that court the favor of great men, that there will be no great loss if they are not troubled either with me or with others of my temper."

Upon this, said I: "I perceive, Raphael, that you neither desire wealth nor greatness; and indeed I value and admire such a man much more than I do any of the great men in the world. Yet I think you would do what would well become so generous and philosophical a soul as yours is, if you would apply your time and thoughts to public affairs, even though you may happen to find it a little uneasy to yourself: and this you can never do with so much advantage, as by being taken into the counsel of some great prince, and putting him on noble and worthy actions, which I know you would do if you were in such a post; for the springs both of good and evil flow from the prince, over a whole nation, as from a lasting fountain. So much learning as you have, even without practice in affairs, or so great a practice as you have had, without any other learning, would render you a very fit counsellor to any king whatsoever."

"You are doubly mistaken," said he, "Mr. More, both in your opinion of me, and in the judgment you make of things: for as I have not that capacity that you fancy I have, so, if I had it, the public would not be one jot the better, when I had sacrificed my quiet to it. For most princes apply themselves more to affairs of war than to the useful arts of peace; and in these I neither have any knowledge, nor do I much desire it: they are generally more set on acquiring new kingdoms, right or wrong, than on governing well those they possess. And among the ministers of princes, there are none that are not so wise as to need no assistance, or at least that do not think themselves so wise that they imagine they need none; and if they court any, it is only those for whom the prince has much personal favor, whom by their fawning and flatteries they endeavor to fix to their own interests: and indeed Nature has so made us that we all love to be flattered, and to please ourselves with our own notions. The old crow loves his young, and the ape her cubs. Now if in such a court, made up of persons who envy all others, and only admire themselves, a person should but propose anything that he had either read in history or observed in his travels, the rest would think that the reputation of their wisdom would sink, and that their interest would be much depressed, if they could not run it down: and if all other things failed, then they would fly to this, that such or such things pleased our ancestors, and it were well for us if we could but match them. They would set up their rest on such an answer, as a sufficient confutation of all that could be said, as if it were a great misfortune, that any should be found wiser than his ancestors; but though they willingly let go all the good things that were among those of former ages, yet if better things are proposed they cover themselves obstinately with this excuse of reverence to past times. I have met with these proud, morose, and absurd judgments of things in many places, particularly once in England."

"Were you ever there?" said I.

"Yes, I was," answered he, "and stayed some months there not long after the rebellion in the west was suppressed with a great slaughter of the poor people that were engaged in it. I was then much obliged to that reverend prelate, John Morton, Archbishop of Canterbury, Cardinal, and Chancellor of England: a man," said he, "Peter (for Mr. More knows well what he was), that was not less venerable for his wisdom and virtues than for the high character he bore. He was of a middle stature, not broken with age; his looks begot reverence rather than fear; his conversation was easy, but serious and grave. He sometimes took pleasure to try the force of those that came as suitors to him upon business, by speaking sharply though decently to them, and by that he discovered their spirit and presence of mind, with which he was much delighted, when it did not grow up to impudence, as bearing a great resemblance to his own temper; and he looked on such persons as the fittest men for affairs. He spoke both gracefully and weightily; he was eminently skilled in the law, had a vast understanding and a prodigious memory; and those excellent talents with which nature had furnished him were improved by study and experience. When I was in England the King depended much on his counsels, and the government seemed to be chiefly supported by him; for from his youth he had been all along practiced in affairs; and having passed through many traverses of fortune, he had with great cost acquired a vast stock of wisdom, which is not soon lost when it is purchased so dear.

"One day when I was dining with him there happened to be at table one of the English lawyers, who took occasion to run out in a high commendation of the severe execution of justice upon thieves, who, as he said, were then hanged so fast that there were sometimes twenty on one gibbet; and upon that he said he could not wonder enough how it came to pass, that since so few escaped, there were yet so many thieves left who were still robbing in all places. Upon this, I who took the boldness to speak freely before the cardinal, said there was no reason to wonder at the matter, since this way of punishing thieves was neither just in itself nor good for the public; for as the severity was too great, so the remedy was not effectual; simple theft not being so great a crime that it ought to cost a man his life, no punishment however severe being able to restrain those from robbing who can find out no other way of livelihood. 'In this,' said I, 'not only you in England, but a great part of the world imitates some ill masters that are readier to chastise their scholars than to teach them. There are dreadful punishments enacted against thieves, but it were much better to make such good provisions by which every man might be put in a method how to live, and so be preserved from the fatal necessity of stealing and of dying for it.'

"'There has been care enough taken for that,' said he, 'there are many handicrafts, and there is husbandry, by which they may make a shift to live unless they have a greater mind to follow ill courses.'

"'That will not serve your turn,' said I, 'for many lose their limbs in civil or foreign wars, as lately in the Cornish rebellion, and some time ago in your wars with France, who being thus mutilated in the service of their king and country, can no more follow their old trades, and are too old to learn new ones: but since wars are only accidental things, and have intervals, let us consider those things that fall out every day. There is a great number of noblemen among you, that are themselves as idle as drones, that subsist on other men's labor, on the labor of their tenants, whom, to raise their revenues, they pare to the quick. This indeed is the only instance of their frugality, for in all other things they are prodigal, even to the beggaring of themselves: but besides this, they carry about with them a great number of idle fellows, who never learned any art by which they may gain their living; and these, as soon as either their lord dies or they themselves fall sick, are turned out of doors; for your lords are readier to feed idle people than to take care of the sick; and often the heir is not able to keep together so great a family as his predecessor did. Now when the stomachs of those that are thus turned out of doors grow keen, they rob no less keenly; and what else can they do? for when, by wandering about, they have worn out both their health and their clothes, and are tattered, and look ghastly, men of quality will not entertain them, and poor men dare not do it, knowing that one who has been bred up in idleness and pleasure, and who was used to walk about with his sword and buckler, despising all the neighborhood with an insolent scorn as far below him, is not fit for the spade and mattock: nor will he serve a poor man for so small a hire, and in so low a diet as he can afford to give him.'

"To this he answered: 'This sort of men ought to be particularly cherished, for in them consists the force of the armies for which we have occasion; since their birth inspires them with a nobler sense of honor than is to be found among tradesmen or ploughmen.'

"'You may as well say,' replied I, 'that you must cherish thieves on the account of wars, for you will never want the one as long as you have the other; and as robbers prove sometimes gallant soldiers, so soldiers often prove brave robbers; so near an alliance there is between those two sorts of life. But this bad custom, so common among you, of keeping many servants, is not peculiar to this nation. In France there is yet a more pestiferous sort of people, for the whole country is full of soldiers, still kept up in time of peace, if such a state of a nation can be called a peace: and these are kept in pay upon the same account that you plead for those idle retainers about noblemen; this being a maxim of those pretended statesmen that it is necessary for the public safety to have a good body of veteran soldiers ever in readiness. They think raw men are not to be depended on, and they sometimes seek occasions for making war, that they may train up their soldiers in the art of cutting throats; or as Sallust observed, for keeping their hands in use, that they may not grow dull by too long an intermission. But France has learned to its cost how dangerous it is to feed such beasts.

"'The fate of the Romans, Carthaginians, and Syrians, and many other nations and cities, which were both overturned and quite ruined by those standing armies, should make others wiser: and the folly of this maxim of the French appears plainly even from this, that their trained soldiers often find your raw men prove too hard for them; of which I will not say much, lest you may think I flatter the English. Every day's experience shows that the laborers in the towns, or the rustics in the country, are not afraid of fighting with those idle gentlemen, if they are not disabled by some misfortune in their body, or dispirited by extreme want, so that you need not fear that those well-shaped and strong men (for it is only such that noblemen love to keep about them, till they spoil them) who now grow feeble with ease, and are softened with their effeminate manner of life, would be less fit for action if they were well bred and well employed. And it seems very unreasonable that for the prospect of a war, which you need never have but when you please, you should maintain so many idle men, as will always disturb you in time of peace, which is ever to be more considered than war. But I do not think that this necessity of stealing arises only from hence; there is another cause of it more peculiar to England.'

"'What is that?' said the cardinal.

"'The increase of pasture,' said I, 'by which your sheep, which are naturally mild, and easily kept in order, may be said now to devour men, and depopulate, not only villages, but towns; for wherever it is found that the sheep of any soil yield a softer and richer wool than ordinary, there the nobility and gentry, and even those holy men the abbots, not contented with the old rents which their farms yielded, nor thinking it enough that they, living at their ease, do no good to the public, resolve to do it hurt instead of good. They stop the course of agriculture, destroying houses and towns, reserving only the churches, and enclose grounds that they may lodge their sheep in them. As if forests and parks had swallowed up too little of the land, those worthy countrymen turn the best inhabited places into solitudes, for when an insatiable wretch, who is a plague to his country, resolves to enclose many thousand acres of ground, the owners as well as tenants are turned out of their possessions, by tricks, or by main force, or being wearied out with ill-usage, they are forced to sell them. By which means those miserable people, both men and women, married and unmarried, old and young, with their poor but numerous families (since country business requires many hands), are all forced to change their seats, not knowing whither to go; and they must sell almost for nothing their household stuff, which could not bring them much money, even though they might stay for a buyer. When that little money is at an end, for it will be soon spent, what is left for them to do, but either to steal and so to be hanged (God knows how justly), or to go about and beg? And if they do this, they are put in prison as idle vagabonds; while they would willingly work, but can find none that will hire them; for there is no more occasion for country labor, to which they have been bred, when there is no arable ground left. One shepherd can look after a flock which will stock an extent of ground that would require many hands if it were to be ploughed and reaped. This likewise in many places raises the price of corn.

"'The price of wool is also so risen that the poor people who were wont to make cloth are no more able to buy it; and this likewise makes many of them idle. For since the increase of pasture, God has punished the avarice of the owners by a rot among the sheep, which has destroyed vast numbers of them; to us it might have seemed more just had it fell on the owners themselves. But suppose the sheep should increase ever so much, their price is not like to fall; since though they cannot be called a monopoly, because they are not engrossed by one person, yet they are in so few hands, and these are so rich, that as they are not pressed to sell them sooner than they have a mind to it, so they never do it till they have raised the price as high as possible. And on the same account it is, that the other kinds of cattle are so dear, because many villages being pulled down, and all country labor being much neglected, there are none who make it their business to breed them. The rich do not breed cattle as they do sheep, but buy them lean, and at low prices; and after they have fattened them on their grounds sell them again at high rates. And I do not think that all the inconveniences this will produce are yet observed, for as they sell the cattle dear, so if they are consumed faster than the breeding countries from which they are brought can afford them, then the stock must decrease, and this must needs end in great scarcity; and by these means this your island, which seemed as to this particular the happiest in the world, will suffer much by the cursed avarice of a few persons; besides this, the rising of corn makes all people lessen their families as much as they can; and what can those who are dismissed by them do, but either beg or rob? And to this last, a man of a great mind is much sooner drawn than to the former.

"'Luxury likewise breaks in apace upon you, to set forward your poverty and misery; there is an excessive vanity in apparel, and great cost in diet; and that not only in noblemen's families, but even among tradesmen, among the farmers themselves, and among all ranks of persons. You have also many infamous houses, and, besides those that are known, the taverns and alehouses are no better; add to these, dice, cards, tables, foot-ball, tennis, and quoits, in which money runs fast away; and those that are initiated into them, must in the conclusion betake themselves to robbing for a supply. Banish these plagues, and give orders that those who have depopulated so much soil, may either rebuild the villages they have pulled down, or let out their grounds to such as will do it: restrain those engrossings of the rich, that are as bad almost as monopolies; leave fewer occasions to idleness; let agriculture be set up again, and the manufacture of the wool be regulated, that so there may be work found for those companies of idle people whom want forces to be thieves, or who, now being idle vagabonds or useless servants, will certainly grow thieves at last. If you do not find a remedy to these evils, it is a vain thing to boast of your severity in punishing theft, which though it may have the appearance of justice, yet in itself is neither just nor convenient. For if you suffer your people to be ill-educated, and their manners to be corrupted from their infancy, and then punish them for those crimes to which their first education disposed them, what else is to be concluded from this, but that you first make thieves and then punish them?'

"While I was talking thus, the counsellor who was present had prepared an answer, and had resolved to resume all I had said, according to the formality of a debate, in which things are generally repeated more faithfully than they are answered; as if the chief trial to be made were of men's memories.

"'You have talked prettily for a stranger,' said he, 'having heard of many things among us which you have not been able to consider well; but I will make the whole matter plain to you, and will first repeat in order all that you have said, then I will show how much your ignorance of our affairs has misled you, and will in the last place answer all your arguments. And that I may begin where I promised, there were four things—'

"'Hold your peace,' said the cardinal; 'this will take up too much time; therefore we will at present ease you of the trouble of answering, and reserve it to our next meeting, which shall be to-morrow, if Raphael's affairs and yours can admit of it. But, Raphael,' said he to me, 'I would gladly know upon what reason it is that you think theft ought not to be punished by death? Would you give way to it? Or do you propose any other punishment that will be more useful to the public? For since death does not restrain theft, if men thought their lives would be safe, what fear or force could restrain ill men? On the contrary, they would look on the mitigation of the punishment as an invitation to commit more crimes.'

"I answered: 'It seems to me a very unjust thing to take away a man's life for a little money; for nothing in the world can be of equal value with a man's life: and if it is said that it is not for the money that one suffers, but for his breaking the law, I must say extreme justice is an extreme injury; for we ought not to approve of these terrible laws that make the smallest offences capital, nor of that opinion of the Stoics that makes all crimes equal, as if there were no difference to be made between the killing a man and the taking his purse, between which, if we examine things impartially, there is no likeness nor proportion. God has commanded us not to kill, and shall we kill so easily for a little money? But if one shall say, that by that law we are only forbidden to kill any, except when the laws of the land allow of it; upon the same grounds, laws may be made in some cases to allow of adultery and perjury: for God having taken from us the right of disposing, either of our own or of other people's lives, if it is pretended that the mutual consent of man in making laws can authorize manslaughter in cases in which God has given us no example, that it frees people from the obligation of the divine law, and so makes murder a lawful action; what is this, but to give a preference to human laws before the divine?

"'And if this is once admitted, by the same rule men may in all other things put what restrictions they please upon the laws of God. If by the Mosaical law, though it was rough and severe, as being a yoke laid on an obstinate and servile nation, men were only fined and not put to death for theft, we cannot imagine that in this new law of mercy, in which God treats us with the tenderness of a father, he has given us a greater license to cruelty than he did to the Jews. Upon these reasons it is that I think putting thieves to death is not lawful; and it is plain and obvious that it is absurd, and of ill-consequence to the commonwealth, that a thief and a murderer should be equally punished; for if a robber sees that his danger is the same if he is convicted of theft as if he were guilty of murder, this will naturally incite him to kill the person whom otherwise he would only have robbed, since if the punishment is the same, there is more security, and less danger of discovery, when he that can best make it is put out of the way; so that terrifying thieves too much, provokes them to cruelty.

"'But as to the question, What more convenient way of punishment can be found? I think it is much easier to answer what is better than to invent something worse; why should we doubt but the way that was so long in use among the old Romans, who understood so well the arts of government, was very proper for their punishment? They condemned such as they found guilty of great crimes, to work their whole lives in quarries, or to dig in mines with chains about them. But the method that I liked best, was that which I observed in my travels in Persia, among the Polylerits, who are a considerable and well-governed people. They pay a yearly tribute to the King of Persia; but in all other respects they are a free nation, and governed by their own laws. They lie far from the sea, and are environed with hills; and being contented with the productions of their own country, which is very fruitful, they have little commerce with any other nation; and as they, according to the genius of their country, have no inclination to enlarge their borders; so their mountains, and the pension they pay to the Persians, secure them from all invasions.

"'Thus they have no wars among them; they live rather conveniently than with splendor, and may be rather called a happy nation, than either eminent or famous; for I do not think that they are known so much as by name to any but their next neighbors. Those that are found guilty of theft among them are bound to make restitution to the owner, and not as it is in other places, to the prince, for they reckon that the prince has no more right to the stolen goods than the thief; but if that which was stolen is no more in being, then the goods of the thieves are estimated, and restitution being made out of them, the remainder is given to their wives and children: and they themselves are condemned to serve in the public works, but are neither imprisoned, nor chained, unless there happened to be some extraordinary circumstances in their crimes. They go about loose and free, working for the public. If they are idle or backward to work, they are whipped; but if they work hard, they are well used and treated without any mark of reproach, only the lists of them are called always at night, and then they are shut up. They suffer no other uneasiness, but this of constant labor; for as they work for the public, so they are well entertained out of the public stock, which is done differently in different places. In some places, whatever is bestowed on them, is raised by a charitable contribution; and though this way may seem uncertain, yet so merciful are the inclinations of that people, that they are plentifully supplied by it; but in other places, public revenues are set aside for them; or there is a constant tax of a poll-money raised for their maintenance. In some places they are set to no public work, but every private man that has occasion to hire workmen goes to the market-places and hires them of the public, a little lower than he would do a freeman: if they go lazily about their task, he may quicken them with the whip.

"'By this means there is always some piece of work or other to be done by them; and beside their livelihood, they earn somewhat still to the public. They all wear a peculiar habit, of one certain color, and their hair is cropped a little above their ears, and a piece of one of their ears is cut off. Their friends are allowed to give them either meat, drink, or clothes so they are of their proper color, but it is death, both to the giver and taker, if they give them money; nor is it less penal for any freeman to take money from them, upon any account whatsoever: and it is also death for any of these slaves (so they are called) to handle arms. Those of every division of the country are distinguished by a peculiar mark; which it is capital for them to lay aside, to go out of their bounds, or to talk with a slave of another jurisdiction; and the very attempt of an escape is no less penal than an escape itself; it is death for any other slave to be accessory to it; and if a freeman engages in it he is condemned to slavery. Those that discover it are rewarded—if freemen, in money; and if slaves, with liberty, together with a pardon for being accessory to it; that so they might find their account, rather in repenting of their engaging in such a design, than in persisting in it.

"'These are their laws and rules in relation to robbery, and it is obvious that they are as advantageous as they are mild and gentle; since vice is not only destroyed, and men preserved, but they are treated in such a manner as to make them see the necessity of being honest, and of employing the rest of their lives in repairing the injuries they have formerly done to society. Nor is there any hazard of their falling back to their old customs: and so little do travelers apprehend mischief from them, that they generally make use of them for guides, from one jurisdiction to another; for there is nothing left them by which they can rob, or be the better for it, since, as they are disarmed, the very having of money is a sufficient conviction: and as they are certainly punished if discovered, so they cannot hope to escape; for their habit being in all the parts of it different from what is commonly worn, they cannot fly away, unless they would go naked, and even then their cropped ear would betray them. The only danger to be feared from them is their conspiring against the government: but those of one division and neighborhood can do nothing to any purpose, unless a general conspiracy were laid among all the slaves of the several jurisdictions, which cannot be done, since they cannot meet or talk together; nor will any venture on a design where the concealment would be so dangerous and the discovery so profitable. None are quite hopeless of recovering their freedom, since by their obedience and patience, and by giving good grounds to believe that they will change their manner of life for the future, they may expect at last to obtain their liberty: and some are every year restored to it, upon the good character that is given of them.'

"When I had related all this, I added that I did not see why such a method might not be followed with more advantage than could ever be expected from that severe justice which the counsellor magnified so much. To this he answered that it could never take place in England without endangering the whole nation. As he said this he shook his head, made some grimaces, and held his peace, while all the company seemed of his opinion, except the cardinal, who said that it was not easy to form a judgment of its success, since it was a method that never yet had been tried.

"'But if,' said he, 'when the sentence of death was passed upon a thief, the prince would reprieve him for a while, and make the experiment upon him, denying him the privilege of a sanctuary; and then if it had a good effect upon him, it might take place; and if it did not succeed, the worst would be, to execute the sentence on the condemned persons at last. And I do not see,' added he, 'why it would be either unjust, inconvenient, or at all dangerous, to admit of such a delay: in my opinion, the vagabonds ought to be treated in the same manner; against whom, though we have made many laws, yet we have not been able to gain our end.' When the cardinal had done, they all commended the motion, though they had despised it when it came from me; but more particularly commended what related to the vagabonds, because it was his own observation."

33. MARTIN LUTHER (1483–1546)

The house of the Augustinian friars to which Luther (see selection 13) belonged closed as a result of the Reformation, but Luther continued to live in the monastic building with his large family (wife, six children, nieces, and nephews), students, and guests. The evening meal was often attended by even more guests and visitors, and some of the men who visited got into the habit of taking notes at table, much as they would at lectures or sermons. This Table Talk circulated from the sixteenth century onwards, and shows a more relaxed, informal side of Luther, though the reformer was aware that his conversation was being recorded. The excerpts here focus on Luther's comments on family, a new concern for the Protestant clergy.

On the Family

Youth, Not Age, Is Venturesome

December, 1532

"No good work is undertaken or done with wise reflection. It must all happen in a half-sleep. This is how I was forced to take up the office of teaching. If I had known what I know now, ten horses wouldn't have driven me to it. Moses [Num. 11:11–15] and Jeremiah [Jer. 20:7–12] also complained that they were deceived. Nor would any man take a wife if he first gave real thought to what might happen in marriage and the household."

Here Philip [Melanchthon] said that he had diligently observed that in history great deeds had never been done by old men. "This was so," said Luther, "when Alexander and Augustus were young; afterward men become too wise. They didn't do great things by deliberate choice but by a sort of impulse. If you young fellows were wise, the devil couldn't do anything to you; but since you aren't wise, you need us who are old. Our Lord God doesn't do great things except by violence, as they say. If old men were strong and young men were wise it would be worth something. The sect leaders are all young men like Icarus and Phaeton. Such are [Ulrich] Zwingli and [Andreas] Karlstadt. They are novices in the sacred Scriptures."

To Be Glad to Die Is Unnatural

December, 1532

"I don't like to see examples of joyful death. On the other hand, I like to see those who tremble and shake and grow pale when they face death and yet get through. It was so with the great saints; they were not glad to die. Fear is something natural because death is a punishment, and therefore something sad. According to the spirit one dies willingly, but according to the flesh the saying applies, 'Another will carry you where you do not wish to go' [John 21:18]. In the Psalms and other histories, as in Jeremiah, one sees how eager men were to escape death. 'Beware' Jeremiah said, 'or you will bring innocent blood upon yourselves' [Jer. 26:15]. But when Christ said, 'Let this cup pass from me' [Matt. 26:39], the meaning was different, for this was the Same who said, 'I have life and death in my hand' [John 5:21, 24]. We are the ones who drew the bloody sweat from him."

Cases of Conscience Pertaining to Marriage

December, 1532

"Cases for the consolation of consciences belong in confession and not in books. A certain man took a wife, and after bearing several children she contracted syphilis and was unable to fulfill her marital obligation. Thereupon the husband, troubled by the flesh, denied himself beyond his ability to sustain the burden of chastity. It is asked, Ought he to be allowed a second wife? I reply that one or the other of two things must happen: either he commits adultery or he takes another wife. It is my advice that he take a second wife; however, he should not abandon his first wife but should provide for her sufficiently to enable her to support her life.

"In short, there are many cases of this kind, from which it ought to be clearly seen and recognized that this is the law and that that is the gospel. The pope, who has heaped up laws, doesn't do this. He decrees thus: If a man has married two women, he should pay his nuptial obligation to the first, although she is not properly his wife, and sleep with the second. This is very bad advice to consciences. So the pope has revoked the imperial law concerning divorce without making another law, except only for a prohibition.

"I feel that judgments about marriages belong to the jurists. Since they make judgments concerning fathers, mothers, children, and servants, why shouldn't they also make decisions about the life of married people? When the papists oppose the imperial law concerning divorce, I reply that this doesn't follow from what is written, 'What God has joined together let no man put asunder' [Matt. 19:6] for the emperor puts asunder with his laws; it's not man who puts asunder, but God, for here 'man' signifies a private person. It is similar when it is written, 'You shall not kill' [Exod. 20:13], which is a command addressed to a private person and not to a magistrate.

"In such cases in which the conscience was troubled I have often offered counsel not according to the pope but according to my office, according to the gospel. Nevertheless, I warned the persons involved not to make this judgment of mine public. I said to them, 'Keep this to yourselves. If you can't keep it secret, take the consequences.' I won't make such judgments public because I don't have the authority to carry them out. It would therefore be useless. Moreover, others who are not troubled in conscience would take the judgments to be excuses for lust. But this judgment of mine is valid according to that saying of Christ, '"Whatever two or three say in my name," etc. [Matt. 18:16–20]. Accordingly the statement, 'What God has joined together,' has this meaning: Here God doesn't mean God in heaven, but God's Word, and specifically that we obey our parents and magistrates [Exod. 20:12]. God doesn't join together what happens without the consent of the father, and what I command and order my daughter is God's command to her. If there are no parents, then the closest blood relatives speak in God's stead. Consequently 'God' means God's Word, as in John [1:1], 'And the Word was God.' On the other hand, God puts asunder when my daughter marries against my will. If she knows my will she knows God's will, for God has said that what you do to anybody God does to him, as appears in many passages in Genesis, where the father is consulted and it is said that God is consulted. So Christ declares in Luke [Matt. 19:5], 'God said, The two shall become one flesh' although it was Adam who had said it. For next to God the authority of parents is divine. But the world calls God 'luck' as it does when it is said, 'what man has joined together' that is, the foolish frenzy of love has joined together."

Each Age Has Its Own Peculiar Temptations

Between May 27 and 31, 1532

"Young fellows are tempted by girls, men who are thirty years old are tempted by gold, when they are forty years old they are tempted by honor and glory, and those who are sixty years old say to themselves, 'What a pious man I have become!'"

Pope Deprived of the Blessing of Offspring

Between May 27 and 31, 1532

"That God has hated the pope appears from this, that God has deprived him of the fruit of his body. We wouldn't have received the blessing [of children] if the Lord hadn't planted the desire in us. The ardor is in both [men and women], and children are engendered as a consequence. Even if a child is unattractive when it is born, we nevertheless love it."

We Must Often Try God's Patience

Between May 27 and 31, 1532

The doctor took his son on his lap, and the child befouled him. Thereupon he [Martin Luther] said, "How our Lord God has to put up with many a murmur and stink from us, worse than a mother must endure from her child!"

Fornication and Adultery Are Both Sinful

Between June 12 and July 12, 1532

Then Ignatius inquired, "Dear Doctor, is fornication also a sin if I don't take another man's wife but an unattached wench, as long as I am myself free too?" The doctor

[Martin Luther] replied by citing Paul, "Neither the immoral . . . nor adulterers . . . will inherit the kingdom of God" [1 Cor. 6:9]. "Paul," he added, "made no distinction between fornication and adultery. I can't make a law for you. I simply point to the Scriptures. There it is written. Read it for yourself. I don't know what more I can do."

Men Cannot Get Along Without Women
Between June 12 and July 12, 1532

"Many good things may be perceived in a wife. First, there is the Lord's blessing, namely, offspring. Then there is community of property. These are some of the preeminently good things that can overwhelm a man.

"Imagine what it would be like without this sex. The home, cities, economic life, and government would virtually disappear. Men can't do without women. Even if it were possible for men to beget and bear children, they still couldn't do without women."

Marriage and Cohabitation Are God's Creation
Between June 12 and July 12, 1532

"When one looks back upon it, marriage isn't so bad as when one looks forward to it. We see that our mothers and our fathers were saints and that we have the divine commandment, 'Honor your father and your mother' [Exod. 20:12]. When I look beside myself, I see my brothers and sisters and friends, and I find that there's nothing but godliness in marriage. To be sure, when I consider marriage, only the flesh seems to be there. Yet my father must have slept with my mother and made love to her, and they were nevertheless godly people. All the patriarchs and prophets did likewise. The longing of a man for a woman is God's creation—that is to say, when nature's sound, not when it's corrupted as it is among Italians and Turks."

Children Must Be Disciplined with Understanding
Between March 28 and May 27, 1537

"Stealing is no art. It's deception, manual dexterity. Presto, and the stuff is gone! That's how the gypsies were."

Then he [Martin Luther] spoke about children and said that they should not be allowed to commit thefts. "However, one ought to observe reasonableness. If only cherries, apples, and the like are involved, such childish pranks ought not to be punished so severely; but if money, clothing, or coffers have been seized it is time to punish. My parents kept me under very strict discipline, even to the point of making me timid. For the sake of a mere nut my mother beat me until the blood flowed. By such strict discipline they finally forced me into the monastery; though they meant it heartily well, I was only made timid by it. They weren't able to keep a right balance between temperament and punishment. One must punish in such a way that the rod is accompanied by the apple. It's a bad thing if children and pupils lose their spirit on account of their parents and teachers. There have been bungling schoolmasters who spoiled many excellent talents by their rudeness. Ah, what a time we had on Fridays with the lupus [student monitor] and on Thursdays with the parts of Donatus! Then they asked each pupil to parse precisely, according to Donatus, *legeris, legere, legitur,* and even *lecti mei ars*. These tests were nothing short of torture. Whatever the method that's used, it ought to pay attention to the difference in aptitudes and teach in such a way that all children are treated with equal love."

Children Are Ingenuous at Their Play
February 26, 1539

On February 26 Master [George] Spalatin and the pastor of Zwickau, Master Leonard [Beyer], came to supper [in Luther's house]. He [Luther] had some pleasant banter with his little son Martin, who wished to defend his doll with zeal and honor and to dress her and love her. Then he said, "Such was our disposition in paradise—simple, upright, without malice. There must have been real earnestness there, just as this boy speaks about God piously and with supreme trust and just as he is sure of God. Such natural playing is best in children, who are the dearest jesters. The affected play of old fools lacks such grace. Therefore little children are the finest mockingbirds and talk naturally and honestly. Such a man was the jester Claus, who, when he befouled his boots, excused himself to the chamberlain Pfeffinger by saying that a little bird had done it."

The Simplicity of Faith in Children
February 26, 1539

Afterward, watching his son, he [Martin Luther] praised the boy's ingenuousness and innocence: "Children are better informed in the faith [than adults], for they believe very simply and without any question in a gracious God and eternal life. Oh, how good it is for children to die while they're young. To be sure, it would cause me great grief because part of my body and part of their mother's flesh and blood would die. Such natural feelings don't cease in godly parents, no matter how hardened and calloused they think they are, for feelings like these are a work of divine creation.

"Children live altogether in faith, without reason. It's as Ambrose said, 'There is lack of reason but not of faith.'"

The Consequences of Enforced Celibacy
February 26, 1539

Thereupon the conversation turned to the very harmful superstition of celibacy, which has hindered many good things, like the bringing to life of children, the activity of the state, and economic life. On the other hand, horrible crimes have proceeded from it, like fornication, adultery, incest, fluxes, dreams, fantasies, pollutions. "Ambrose therefore declares in his hymn, 'Let dreams and fantasies of the night withdraw into the distance, lest our bodies should be polluted.' If St. Ambrose, who was burdened with many cares, experienced such temptations, why shouldn't fat and lazy monks feel them? Dear God, this is no way to remedy what God has created."

Illness of Luther's Daughter Becomes Graver
September, 1542

When the illness of his daughter became graver he [Luther] said, "I love her very much. But if it is thy will to take her, dear God, I shall be glad to know that she is with thee."

Afterward he said to his daughter, who was lying in bed, "Dear Magdalene, my little daughter, you would be glad to stay here with me, your father. Are you also glad to go to your Father in heaven?"

The sick girl replied, "Yes, dear Father, as God wills."

The father said, "You dear little girl!" Then he turned away from her and said, "The spirit is willing, but the flesh is weak [Matt. 26:41]. I love her very much. If this flesh is so strong, what must the spirit be?" Among other things he then said, "In the last thousand years God has given to no bishop such great gifts as he has given to me (for one should boast of God's gifts). I'm angry with myself that I'm unable to rejoice from my heart and be thankful to God, though I do at times sing a little song and thank God. Whether we live or die, we are the Lord's [Rom. 14:8]—in the genitive singular and not in the nominative plural."

Desire to Talk with Christ Before the End
September, 1542

Turning to [George] Rorer he [Luther] said, "Be of good cheer, Master!"

He responded, "I have at some time heard a word from Your Reverence that has often comforted me, namely, 'I have prayed our Lord God that he may grant me a blessed end in order that I may depart from this life, and I'm sure he'll do it. Just before I die I'll speak with Christ, my Lord, even if it should be but a brief word.'"

The doctor said, "I'm afraid I'll go suddenly and silently, without being able to utter a single word."

Philip Melanchthon said, "Whether we live or die we are the Lord's [Rom. 14:8]. Even if you should fall down the stairs or should suddenly expire while you are writing, it wouldn't matter. Let it be! The devil hates us but God protects and keeps us."

Description of the Death of Magdalene Luther
September 20, 1542

When his daughter was in the agony of death, he [Luther] fell on his knees before the bed and, weeping bitterly, prayed that God might will to save her. Thus she gave up the ghost in the arms of her father. Her mother was in the same room, but farther from the bed on account of her grief. It was after the ninth hour on the Wednesday after the Fifteenth Sunday after Trinity in the year 1542.

The Love of Parents for Their Children
September, 1542

Often he [Martin Luther] repeated the words given above: "I'd like to keep my dear daughter because I love her very much, if only our Lord God would let me. However, his will be done! Truly nothing better can happen to her, nothing better."

While she was still living he often said to her, "Dear daughter, you have another Father in heaven. You are going to go to him."

Philip Melanchthon said, "The feelings of parents are a likeness of divinity impressed upon the human character. If the love of God for the human race is as great as the love of parents for their children, then it is truly great and ardent."

Luther's Daughter Magdalene Placed in Coffin

September, 1542

When his dead daughter was placed in a coffin, he [Martin Luther] said, "You dear little Lena! How well it has turned out for you!"

He looked at her and said, "Ah, dear child, to think that you must be raised up and will shine like the stars, yes, like the sun!"

The coffin would not hold her, and he said, "The little bed is too small for her."

[Before this,] when she died, he said, "I am joyful in spirit but I am sad according to the flesh. The flesh doesn't take kindly to this. The separation [caused by death] troubles me above measure. It's strange to know that she is surely at peace and that she is well off there, very well off, and yet to grieve so much!"

The Coffin Is Escorted from the Home

September, 1542

When people came to escort the funeral and friends spoke to him according to custom and expressed to him their sympathy, he [Luther] said, "You should be pleased! I've sent a saint to heaven—yes, a living saint. Would that our death might be like this! Such a death I'd take this very hour."

The people said, "Yes, this is quite true. Yet everybody would like to hold on to what is his."

Martin Luther replied, "Flesh is flesh, and blood is blood. I'm happy that she's safely out of it. There is no sorrow except that of the flesh."

Again, turning to others, he said, "Do not be sorrowful. I have sent a saint to heaven. In fact, I have now sent two of them" [his eight-month-old daughter Elizabeth had died August 3, 1528].

Among other things, he said to those who had come to escort the funeral as they were singing the verse in the psalm, "Lord, remember not against us former iniquities" [Ps. 79:8], "O Lord, Lord, Lord, not only former iniquities but also present ones! We are usurers, gougers, etc., and for fifteen years I read mass and conducted the abominations of the mass."

A Girl Is Harder to Raise Than a Boy

September, 1542

When she was buried he [Luther] said, "There is a resurrection of the flesh."

When he returned home from the funeral he said, "My daughter is now fitted out in body and soul. We Christians now have nothing to complain about. We know that it should and must be so, for we are altogether certain about eternal life."

Thereupon he consoled himself by saying, "After all, one must make provision for the children, especially for the poor girls. We have no right to expect that somebody else will care for them. I don't worry about the boys because a boy supports himself, no matter what country he's in, as long as he's willing to work. But the poor girls must have a staff to lean on. A boy who is in school can gather alms, and afterward he can become a fine man if he has a will to. A girl can't do this and can easily bring shame on herself. I'm very glad to give my daughter to our Lord God. According to the flesh I would gladly have had her, but since God has taken her away I am thankful to him."

A Choice Between a Wife and the Ministry

Spring, 1543

This case was put to the doctor [Luther]: There is a certain schoolmaster in Frankfurt on the Oder, a learned and godly man. He set his heart on theology and preached several times to the great admiration of his auditors. At length he was called to the office of deacon. But his wife, since she had a haughty spirit, was altogether unwilling to consent to that kind of life. She simply did not want to have a parson for a husband. The question was asked, "What should the good man do? Should he abandon his wife or the ministry of the Word?"

The doctor replied at first with a jest, "If he married a widow, as you say, he must do what she wishes." A little later he said, "If there were a real government, it could compel the old hag. For a wife is bound to follow her husband, not a husband his wife. She must be a wicked woman—indeed, a devil—to be ashamed of the ministry in which the Lord Christ himself and the dear angels were. The devil tries to slander and defame the ministry. If she were my wife I'd say to her, 'Will you go with me? Say quickly, No or Yes.' If she said No, I would at once take another wife and leave her. The trouble is that the government isn't there with its performance and doesn't watch over the ministry."

34. MARGUERITE DE NAVARRE (1492–1549)

Marguerite de Navarre was the sister of Francis I of France. She was married in 1509 to Charles, duc d'Alençon. Charles died in 1525, and two years later, Marguerite married Henri d'Albret, king of Navarre. Marguerite was a well-educated woman, and deeply involved in the contemporary literary scene, patron, most famously, of Rabelais. She was also interested in religious reform; not only was she a protector of reforming churchmen, she was also a writer of religious verse. Apart from her intellectual interests, Marguerite also played a role in the ongoing conflict between France and the emperor, negotiating her brother's release from captivity in Madrid in 1525 and participating in peace negotiations in 1529 and 1536–38.

Marguerite was not originally identified as the author of the Heptameron, *which was published first in 1558, some years after her death. It was only with the revised edition of 1559 that her name was associated with the collection, and there is still some discussion as to whether the stories were actually composed by the queen, or, as their format suggests, told by a group and gathered by her.*

The Heptameron *displays a notable concern with the question of truth. The prologue tells how the French royal family admired Boccaccio's* Decameron *(a series of 100 stories ostensibly told by seven young women and three young men sheltering in a villa outside Florence to escape the Black Death, written in the mid-fourteenth century), and how they wished to produce a French version, with one important difference: the stories were to be true. Although this project was never carried out, the* Heptameron *was a close replacement and thus carries the implication of veracity, though it is fictionalized. The stories in the collection provide insight into the courtly conventions of the period, gender relations, and the author's concerns with corruption in the Church, among other issues.*

The Heptameron

Tale 4

...

There lived in the land of Flanders a lady of such high lineage, that none more illustrious could be found. She was a widow, both her first and second husbands being dead, and she had no children living. During her widowhood she lived in retirement with her brother, by whom she was greatly loved, and who was a very great lord and married to the daughter of a King. This young Prince was a man much given to pleasure, fond of hunting, pastimes, and women, as his youth inclined him. He had a wife, however, who was of a very difficult disposition, and found no pleasure in her husband's pursuits; wherefore this Lord always took his sister along with his wife, for she was a most joyous and pleasant companion, and withal a discreet and honorable woman.

In this Lord's household there was a gentleman who, for stature, comeliness, and grace, surpassed all his fellows. This gentleman, perceiving that his master's sister was of merry mood and always ready for a laugh, was minded to try whether the offer of an honorable love would be displeasing to her.

He made this offer, but the answer that he received from her was contrary to his desires. However, although her reply was such as beseemed a Princess and a woman of true virtue, she readily pardoned his hardihood for the sake of his comeliness and breeding, and let him know that she bore him no ill-will for what he had said. But she charged him never to speak to her after that fashion again; and this he promised, that he might not lose the pleasure and honor of her conversation. Nevertheless, as time went on, his love so increased that he forgot the promise he had made. He did not, however, risk further trial of words, for he had learned by experience, and much against his will, what virtuous replies she was able to make. But he reflected that if he could take her somewhere at a disadvantage, she, being a widow, young, lusty, and of a lively humor, would perchance take pity on him and on herself.

To compass his ends, he told his master that excellent hunting was to be had in the neighborhood of his house, and that if it pleased him to repair thither and hunt three or four stags in the month of May, he could have no finer sport. The Lord granted the gentleman's request, as much for the affection he bore him as for the pleasure of the chase, and repaired to his house, which was as handsome and as fairly ordered as that of the richest gentleman in the land.

The Lord and his Lady were lodged on one side of the house, and she whom the gentleman loved more than himself on the other. Her apartment was so well arranged, tapestried above and matted below, that it was impossible to perceive a trap-door which was by the side of her bed, and which opened into a room beneath, that was occupied by the gentleman's mother.

She being an old lady, somewhat troubled by rheum, and fearful lest the cough she had should disturb the Princess, made exchange of chambers with her son. In the evening this old lady was wont to bring sweetmeats to the Princess for her collation, at which the gentleman was present; and being greatly beloved by her brother and intimate with him, he was also suffered to be present when she rose in the morning and when she retired to bed, on which occasions he always found reasons for an increase of his affection.

Thus it came to pass that one evening he made the Princess stay up very late, until at last, being desirous of sleep, she bade him leave her. He then went to his own room, and there put on the handsomest and best-scented shirt he had, and a nightcap so well adorned that nothing was lacking in it. It seemed, to him, as he looked at himself in his mirror, that no lady in the world could deny herself to one of his comeliness and grace. He therefore promised himself a happy issue to his enterprise, and so lay down on his bed, where in his desire and sure hope of exchanging it for one more honorable and pleasant, he looked to make no very long stay.

As soon as he had dismissed all his attendants he rose to fasten the door after them; and for a long time he listened to hear whether there were any sound in the room of the Princess, which was above his own. When he had made sure that all was quiet, he wished to begin his pleasant task, and little by little let down the trap-door, which was so excellently wrought, and so well covered with cloth, that it made not the least noise. Then he ascended into the room and came to the bedside of his lady, who was just falling asleep.

Forthwith, having no regard for the duty that he owed his mistress or for the house to which she belonged, he got into bed with her, without entreating her permission or making any kind of ceremony. She felt him in her arms before she knew that he had entered the room; but being strong, she freed herself from his grasp, and fell to striking, biting, and scratching him, demanding the while to know who he was, so that for fear lest she should call out he sought to stop her mouth with the bedclothes. But this he found it impossible to do, for when she saw that he was using all his strength to work her shame she did as much to baffle him. She further called as loudly as she could to her lady of honor, who slept in her room; and this old and virtuous woman ran to her mistress in her nightdress.

When the gentleman saw that he was discovered, he was so fearful of being recognized by the lady, that he descended in all haste through his trap-door; his despair at returning in such an evil plight being no less than his desire and assurance of a gracious reception had previously been. He found his mirror and candle on his table, and looking at his face, all bleeding from the lady's scratches and bites, whence the blood was trickling over his fine shirt, which had now more blood than gold about it, he said

"Beauty! now hast thou been rewarded according to thy deserts. By reason of thy vain promises I attempted an impossible undertaking, and one that, instead of increasing my happiness, will perchance double my misfortune. I feel sure that if she knows I made this foolish attempt contrary to the promise I gave her, I shall lose the honorable and accustomed companionship which more than any other I have had with her. And my folly has well deserved this, for if I was to turn my good looks and grace to any account, I ought not to have hidden them in the darkness. I should not have sought to take that chaste body by force, but should have waited in long service and humble patience till love had conquered her. Without love, all man's merits and might are of no avail."

Thus he passed the night in tears, regrets, and sorrows such as I cannot describe; and in the morning, finding his face greatly torn, he feigned grievous sickness and to be unable to endure the light, until the company had left his house.

The lady, who had come off victorious, knew that there was no man at her brother's Court that durst attempt such an enterprise save him who had had the boldness to declare his love to her. She therefore concluded that it was indeed her host, and made search through the room with her lady of honor to discover how he could have entered it. But in this she failed, whereupon she said to her companion in great anger—

"You may be sure that it can have been none other than the lord of this house, and I will make such report of him to my brother in the morning that his head shall bear witness to my chastity."

Seeing her in such wrath, the lady of honor said to her—

"Right glad am I, madam, to find you esteem your honor so highly that, to exalt it, you would not spare the life of a man who, for the love he bears you, has put it to this risk. But it often happens that one lessens what one thinks to increase; wherefore, I pray you, madam, tell me the truth of the whole matter."

When the lady had fully related the business, the lady of honor said to her—

"You assure me that he had nothing from you save only scratches and blows?"

"I do assure you that it was so," said the lady; "and, unless he find a rare surgeon, I am certain his face will bear the marks tomorrow."

"Well, since it is thus, madam," said the lady of honor, "it seems to me that you have more reason to thank God than to think of vengeance; for you may well believe that, since the gentleman had spirit enough to make such an attempt, his grief at having failed will be harder of endurance than any death you could award him. If you desire to be revenged on him, let love and shame do their work; they will torment him more grievously than could you. And if you would speak out for your honor's sake, beware, madam, lest you fall into a mishap like to his own. He, instead of obtaining the greatest delight he could imagine, has encountered the gravest vexation any gentleman could endure. So you, madam, thinking to exalt your honor, may perchance diminish it. If you make complaint, you will bring to light what is known to none, for you may rest assured that the gentleman on his side will never reveal aught of the matter. And even if my lord, your brother, should do justice to him at your asking, and the poor gentleman should die, yet would it everywhere be noised abroad that he had had his will of you, and most people would say it was unlikely a gentleman would make such an attempt unless the lady had given him great encouragement. You are young and fair; you live gaily with all; and there is no one at Court but has seen the kind treatment you have shown to the gentleman whom you suspect. Hence every one will believe that if he did this deed it was not without some fault on your side; and your honor, for which you have never had to blush, will be freely questioned wherever the story is related."

On hearing the excellent reasoning of her lady of honor, the Princess perceived that she spoke the truth, and that she herself would, with just cause, be blamed on account of the close friendship which she had always shown towards the gentleman. Accordingly she inquired of her lady of honor what she ought to do.

"Madam," replied the other, "since you are pleased to receive my counsels, having regard for the affection whence they spring, it seems to me you should be glad at heart to think that the most comely and gallant gentleman I have ever seen was not able, whether by love or by force, to turn you from the path of true virtue. For this, madam, you should humble yourself before God, and confess that it was not through your own merit, for many women who have led straighter lives than you have been humiliated by men less worthy of love than he. And you should henceforth be more than ever on your guard against proposals of love; for many have the second time yielded to dangers which on the first occasion they were able to avoid. Be mindful, madam, that love is blind, and that it makes people blind in such wise that the way appears safest just when it is most slippery. Further, madam, it seems to me that you should give no sign of what has befallen you, whether to him or to any one else, and that if he seeks to say anything on the matter, you should feign not to understand him. In this way you will avoid two dangers, the one of vainglory in the victory you have won, and the other of recalling things so pleasant to the flesh that at mention of them the chastest can only with difficulty avoid feeling some sparks of the flame, though they strive their utmost to escape them. Besides this, madam, in order that he may not think he has done anything pleasing in your sight, I am of opinion you should little by little withdraw the friendship you have been in the habit of showing him. In this way he will know how much you scorn his rashness, and how great is your goodness, since, content with the victory that God has given you, you seek no further vengeance upon him. And may God give you grace, madam, to continue in the virtue He has placed in your heart; and, knowing that all good things come from Him, may you love and serve Him better than before."

The Princess determined to abide by the advice of her lady of honor, and then fell asleep with joy as great as was the sadness of her waking lover.

On the morrow, the lord, her brother, wishing to depart, inquired for his host, and was told that he was too ill to bear the light or to hear any one speak. The Prince was greatly astonished at this, and wished to go and see the gentleman; however, learning that he was asleep, he would not awake him, but left the house without bidding him farewell. He took with him his wife and sister, and the latter, hearing the excuses sent by the gentleman, who would not see the Prince or any of the company before their departure, felt convinced that it was indeed he who had so tormented her, and that he durst not let the marks which she had left upon his face be seen. And although his master frequently sent for him, he did not return to Court until he was quite healed of all his wounds, save only one—namely, that which love and vexation had dealt to his heart.

When he did return, and found himself in presence of his victorious foe, he could not but blush; and such was his confusion, that he who had formerly been the boldest of all the company, was often wholly abashed before her. Accordingly, being now quite certain that her suspicion was true, she estranged herself from him little by little, though not so adroitly that he did not perceive it; but he durst not give any sign for fear of meeting with something still worse, and so he kept his love concealed, patiently enduring the disgrace he had so well deserved.

"This, ladies, is a story which should be a warning to those who would grasp at what does not belong to them, and which, further, should strengthen the hearts of ladies, since it shows the virtue of this young Princess, and the good sense of her lady of honor. If the like fortune should befall any among you, the remedy has now been pointed out."

"It seems to me," said Hircan, "that the tall gentleman of whom you have told us was so lacking in spirit as to be unworthy of being remembered. With such an opportunity as that, he ought not to have suffered any one, old or young, to baffle him in his enterprise. It must be said, also, that his heart was not entirely filled with love, seeing that fear of death and shame found place within it."

"And what," replied Nomerfide, "could the poor gentleman have done with two women against him?"

"He ought to have killed the old one," said Hircan, "and when the young one found herself without assistance she would have been already half subdued."

"To have killed her!" said Nomerfide. "Then you would turn a lover into a murderer? Since such is your opinion, it would indeed be a fearful thing to fall into your hands."

"If I had gone so far," said Hircan, "I should have held it dishonorable not to achieve my purpose."

Then said Geburon—

"You think it strange that a Princess, bred in all honor, should prove difficult of capture to one man. You should then be much more astonished at a poor woman who escaped out of the hands of two."

"Geburon," said Ennasuite, "I give my vote to you to tell the fifth tale, for I think you know something concerning this poor woman that will not be displeasing to us."

"Since you have chosen me," said Geburon, "I will tell you a story which I know to be true from having made inquiries concerning it on the spot. By this story you will see that womanly sense and virtue are not in the hearts and heads of Princesses alone, nor love and cunning in such as are most often deemed to possess them."

Tale 20

...

The Lord of Riant, being greatly in love with a widow lady and finding her the contrary of what he had desired and of what she had often declared herself to be, was so affected thereby that in a moment resentment had power to extinguish the flame which neither length of time nor lack of opportunity had been able to quench.

In the land of Dauphiné there lived a gentleman named the Lord of Riant; he belonged to the household of King Francis the First, and was as handsome and worshipful a gentleman as it was possible to see. He had long been the lover of a widow lady, whom he loved and revered so exceedingly that, for fear of losing her favor, he dare not solicit of her that which he most desired. Now, since he knew himself to be a handsome man and one worthy to be loved, he fully believed what she often swore to him—namely, that she loved him more than any living man, and that if she were led to do anything for any gentleman, it would be for him alone, who was the most perfect she had ever known. She at the same time begged him to rest satisfied with this virtuous love and to seek nothing further, and assured him that if she found him unreasonably aiming at more, he would lose her altogether. The poor gentleman was not only satisfied, but he deemed himself very fortunate in having gained the heart of a lady who appeared to him so full of virtue.

It would take too long to tell you his love-speeches, his lengthy visits to her, and the journeys he took in order to see her; it is enough to say that this poor martyr, consumed by so pleasing a fire that the more one burns the more one wishes to burn, continually sought for the means of increasing his martyrdom.

One day the fancy took him to go post-haste to see the lady whom he loved better than himself, and whom he prized beyond every other woman in the world. On reaching her house, he inquired where she was, and was told that she had just come from vespers, and was gone into the warren to finish her devotions there. He dismounted from his horse and went straight to the warren where she was to be found, and here he met with some of her women, who told him that she had gone to walk alone in a large avenue.

He was more than ever beginning to hope that some good fortune awaited him, and continued searching for her as carefully and as quietly as he could, desiring above all things to find her alone. He came in this way to a summer-house formed of bended boughs, the fairest and pleasantest place imaginable, and impatient to see the object of his love, he went in; and there beheld the lady lying on the grass in the arms of a groom in her service, who was as ill-favored, foul and disreputable as the Lord of Riant was handsome, virtuous and gentle.

I will not try to depict to you his resentment, but it was so great that in a moment it had power to extinguish the flame which neither length of time nor lack of opportunity had been able to impair.

"Madam," he said to her, being now as full of indignation as once he had been of love, "much good may this do you! The revelation of your wickedness has to-day cured me, and freed me from the continual anguish that was caused by the virtue I believed to be in you."

And with this farewell he went back again more quickly than he had come.

The unhappy woman made him no other reply than to put her hand to her face; for being unable to hide her shame, she covered her eyes that she might not see him who in spite of her deceit now perceived it only too clearly.

"And so, ladies, if you are not minded to love perfectly, do not, I pray you, seek to deceive and annoy an honest man for vanity's sake; for hypocrites are rewarded as they deserve, and God favors those who love with frankness."

"Truly," said Oisille, "you have kept us a proper tale for the end of the day. But that we have all sworn to speak the truth, I could not believe that a woman of that lady's condition could be so wicked both in soul and in body, and leave so gallant a gentleman for so vile a muleteer."

"Ah, madam," said Hircan, "if you knew what a difference there is between a gentleman who has worn armor and been at the wars all his life, and a well-fed knave that has never stirred from home, you would excuse the poor widow."

"I do not believe," said Oisille, "whatever you may say, that you could admit any possible excuse for her."

"I have heard," said Simontault, "that there are women who like to have apostles to preach of their virtue and chastity, and treat them as kindly and familiarly as possible, saying that but for the restraints of honor and conscience they would grant them their desire. And so these poor fools, when speaking in company of their mistresses, swear that they would thrust their fingers into the fire without fear of burning in proof that these ladies are virtuous women, since they have themselves thoroughly tested their love. Thus praised by honorable men, those women show their true nature to such as are like themselves; and they choose such as would not have courage to speak, or, if they did, would not be believed by reason of their low and degraded position."

"That," said Longarine, "is an opinion which I have before now heard expressed by jealous and suspicious men, but it may indeed be called painting a chimera. And even although it be true of one wretched woman, the same suspicion cannot attach to all."

"Well," said Parlamente, "the longer we talk in this way, the longer will these good gentlemen play the critics over Simontault's tale, and all at our own expense. So in my opinion we had better go to vespers, and not cause so much delay as we did yesterday."

The company agreed to this proposal, and as they were going Oisille said:—

"If any one gives God thanks for having told the truth to-day, Saffredent ought to implore His forgiveness for having raked up so vile a story against the ladies."

"By my word," replied Saffredent, "what I told you was true, albeit I only had it upon hearsay. But were I to tell you all that I have myself seen of women, you would have need to make even more signs of the cross than the priests do in consecrating a church."

"Repentance is a long way off," said Geburon, "when confession only increases the sin."

"Since you have so bad an opinion of women," said Parlamente, "they ought to deprive you of their honorable society and friendship."

"There are some women," he returned, "who have acted towards me so much in accordance with your advice, in keeping me far away from things that are honorable and just, that could I do and say worse to them, I should not neglect doing so, in order that I might stir them up to revenge me on her who does me so much wrong."

Whilst he spoke these words, Parlamente put on her mask and went with the others into the church, where they found that although the bell had rung for vespers, there was not a single monk present to say them.

The monks, indeed, had heard that the company assembled in the meadow to tell the pleasantest tales imaginable, and being fonder of pleasure than of their prayers, they had gone and hidden themselves in a ditch, where they lay flat on their bellies behind a very thick hedge; and they had there listened so eagerly to the stories that they had not heard the ringing of the monastery bell, as was soon clearly shown, for they returned in such great haste that they almost lacked breath to begin the saying of vespers.

After the service, when they were asked why they had been so late and had chanted so badly, they confessed that they had been to listen to the tales; whereupon, since they were so desirous of hearing them, it was granted that they might sit and listen at their ease every day behind the hedge.

Supper-time was spent joyously in discoursing of such matters as they had not brought to an end in the meadow. And this lasted through the evening, until Oisille begged them to retire so that their minds might be the more alert on the morrow, after a long, sound sleep, one hour of which before midnight was, said she, better than three after it. Accordingly the company parted one from another, betaking themselves to their respective rooms; and in this wise ended the Second Day.

35. HANS SACHS (1494–1576)

Hans Sachs was born in Nuremberg, the son of a tailor; he followed the craft of shoemaking, however, as well as becoming a celebrated poet and playwright. About 1511 he began a journey through Germany and Austria that would last five years. In Munich he began his apprenticeship as a master-singer, and in 1516 he returned to Nuremberg, where he would spend the rest of his life. It is there and in that occupation that he appears in Wagner's opera Die Meistersinger von Nürnberg *(1867). Sachs welcomed the Reformation and wrote a famous poem in 1523 in praise of Martin Luther, even though Nuremberg had not yet committed to the Reformation.*

Sachs wrote more than 4,000 master-songs. He also wrote many farces and at least eighty Fastnachtspiele *or Shrovetide plays for performance during the popular festivities associated with that season. Each lasted for about a quarter of an hour, and they were enacted in halls, taverns, courtyards, and private houses by bands of amateur players. Some of Sachs's religious plays, written in octosyllabic couplets, were presented in the churches of Nuremberg. The play that is reprinted here,* The Old Game, *was written in 1554. It has been modified for use by English theater companies and is at best a free translation from the German original. In the original, Master Hans Sachs and his neighbors did not appear: the modern version has attributed the moralizing of the last speech directly to Sachs. Nevertheless, it does offer a good example of the type of play that remained current and popular in Reformation Germany, of the subject matter, the views expressed, and the values upheld.*

The Old Game

CHARACTERS

>Hans, a Farm Laborer
>His Wife
>A Village Woman
>The Farmer
>Master Hans Sachs, a Cobbler
>Neighbors

Interior of Hans's kitchen. Entrances right and left. A large kitchen table and two chairs are the only furniture in the room. An empty washing-basket stands near the door right, and an old pig-skin and some sacks lie rolled up in one corner. A long red cloak hangs on a nail on the door right. Hans is sitting on the table swinging his legs. His Wife is sweeping the floor. A lively discussion is going on.

HANS: You did, I seen you!
WIFE: I didn't.
HANS: You did.
WIFE: I didn't.
HANS: But I says as you did! [*He thumps the table.*]
WIFE: And I say as I didn't—leastways if I did, it was all for the best. [*She flourishes with her broom round the table, and Hans draws up his legs in alarm.*] And if I say it once, Hans, I say it a hundred times, that whatsoever I may do that puts you in a rage, 'tis all that good may come out of it! Trust me, dear husband and be sure I love you well.
HANS [*gloomily*]: No woman's to be trusted till she's in her grave!
WIFE [*pausing and leaning on her broom*]: Why husband, don't you love me?
HANS: Times I do. More often I don't.
WIFE: In truth I would fain know how much you do love me. Answer me, husband.

HANS: But I can't answer, not in sober truth. You're that round-a-bout in your goings on.
WIFE: Then, when is it you love me best?
HANS [*readily*]: Why to be sure, when you do as I bids you, like a humble, willing and obedient wife. Then I'm ready enough to share my last crust of sour bread with you, and to see you lack no clothing nor finery. Then it's a pleasure to look after you, and give you good counsel. If I'm a bit cold and stern at times, why 'tis your own fault entirely.
WIFE: And how is it my own fault pray? When is it I act as you don't like?
HANS: I can give a short answer to that. When you go against my wishes, either behind of my back, or in front of my eyes.
WIFE: But tell me just what it is I do.
HANS: Oh, no end of things. Every day I suffer torments from what you say and do.
WIFE [*very persistently*]: And what is it I says and does?
HANS [*peevishly*]: Aren't I telling you? You don't manage the house as it ought to be managed, and when I points it out, you are angry and answer me back. You are always crossing me. I can't never do nothing right. Why anyone would think I was the wife and you the husband! That's not right! It puts a man against you!
WIFE: Now husband, if you let such petty things upset you, your love is worth no more than that! [*She snaps her fingers.*] If you was as fond of me as I am of you, 'twouldn't flicker in and out, but get stronger and brighter every day.
HANS [*moodily*]: Times I sit and wonder if you ever cared at all about me.
WIFE: My dear husband, whatever makes you say a silly thing like that?
HANS: Well, I can't say as I've seen many signs.
WIFE [*hurt*]: Why, I'm always calling you 'dear Hans.'

HANS [*scornfully*]: 'Dear Hans'! That sort of love is naught but talk. If you showed it in your actions now! But it's contradictions, contradictions, morning, noon and night!

WIFE: Dear Hans! [*He snorts in contempt.*] I have loved you for many a year, but I don't always show it. Let me tell you this, if you was sick unto death, I would die in your place right willingly. And if you was to die before me, mark my words I wouldn't live a moment longer, nor take a second husband, but I'd bury you with all honor in my red cloak, so as all the world should vow there was never a more loving wife. I pledge you my solemn word!

HANS [*impressed in spite of himself*]: If you'd do all that, your love must be as strong as mine. Why didn't you tell me afore?

WIFE: If I'd spoken out sooner you'd have grown slack in caring for me. But believe me, it's the truth. [*She picks up the basket.*] Well, well, after that I'm off down to the river to wring out the washing. You can stay and mind the house,

HANS: You go and get the washing, wife, and I'll stay and kill time by the fireside. [*The Wife goes out stage right with the basket, leaving the door open.*]

HANS: She's mighty proud of her love for me, and I believe that if I did die, she'd show her grief right enough. But what's the good of that? How will her tears and groans help a man when he's gone? I'd sooner have 'em when I'm alive, I might get a better time of it! There's one way I could get to the root of this, and find out if she's speaking truth. Supposing I was to stretch myself out on this very spot [*He doubles up a bit of old sacking on the table as a pillow, and lies down on the table*] and breathe all trembly and gaspy like as though it hurted! [*He gasps.*] Then when she comes back and finds me gone, what about the tears and sorrowing, and a costly burial in the red cloak she's always promised me? We shall see! Meantime, I'll put her to the test, and prove her words. She loves me? She loves me not? She loves me? She—[*Re-enter the Wife stage right with her basket filled with washing. Hans begins to draw his breath in short, sharp gasps. The Wife puts down the basket with a bang.*]

WIFE [*irritably*]: Now fool, what are you lying on the table for, like a stable-boy? Get up, and give me a hand with the washing. [*Anxiously seeing he does not move*] Oh, Hans, what is it? Are you ill? [*She shakes him vigorously. The gasps cease, and he lies quite still*] Come now, get up, dear Hans! [*She leans over him and feels his pulse. Hans opens one eye, and moves one foot slightly. The Wife smiles, as she realizes what has happened.*] I fear in truth you must be dead! Alas, I see clearly that you are dead! [*She goes to the door, closes it with a bang, and comes back wringing her hands.*] Alack-the-day! What shall I do to begin with? Weep, or have a bit of supper? Supper will be best, for if I start crying and making a to-do, the neighbors will come running, and here I shall be mourning all night long without bite or sup! Moreover I am wet through with the washing. First I'll put on dry things, then break five eggs in the frying-pan to help me cry the better. Maybe, too, I'll fetch out a cask of wine to comfort me in my great sorrow, for as the old saying goes:

Neither dance nor mourn the dead, Till you feasted be and fed.

[*She goes, singing, exits stage left. Hans sits up very indignant.*]

HANS: She's no more concerned over my death than the loss of a spoon! A cold love forsooth! [*Knock on door stage right*] Come—[*He claps his hand over his mouth, and lies down again hurriedly. The knocking continues at intervals till the Wife re-enters L. with a tankard in her hand*].

WIFE: Now I am somewhat refreshed and ready for the mourning when company comes. [*Knocking grows more insistent. She puts down the tankard on the table by Hans's feet, and begins to lament loudly.*] Woe is me! Who's that a-knocking? Woe is me! Woe is me!

[*She goes to the door, right, and opens it. As soon as her back is turned, Hans lifts his head and watches her. Enter the first neighbor, a woman from the village, who peers round inquisitively.*]

VILLAGE WOMAN: Why, neighbour, what's the matter? Why have you shut your door? [*She sees Hans and gives a scream*] Mercy me! What's that on the table? It's never your husband? [*The Wife winks, and makes violent signs. Then she draws the Neighbor nearer the table.*]

WIFE: Look, dear neighbor, while I was away down at the washing, my husband passed away. Misery me! I am stricken to the heart.

Woman [*looking at Hans, then turning away smiling*]: Ah, my dear neighbor, to think he's really dead! Him that did no ill to no one, a good neighbor, and a pious man withal. Alas and alack, I am sore grieved to hear of this. How did it come about? [*The two women sit down for a chat.*]

Wife: Well, only yesterday he cut his finger. But then he was a poor weak creature at the best of times. [*Hans wriggles.*] It's a pretty penny he's cost me of late, what with drugs and herbs and roots for hot baths. I've grudged him naught.

Woman [*bracingly*]: Well, neighbor, 'tis an everlasting pity he's dead, but since it can't be otherwise, you must resign yourself. What's done by Providence is well done.

Wife: That's true enough. But now that I have no husband, who will look after me?

Woman [*briskly*]: Why, take a second to be sure, who'll do as well for you as this good neighbor.

Wife: That cannot be yet awhile, for tomorrow Lent begins, and parson has decreed there's to be no marriages in Lent. What shall I do? I never thought to keep house without a husband, so hard as 'twill be!

Woman [*soothingly*]: There, there, let sorrow take its course. Go, fetch down your red cloak from behind the door, and wrap up the corpse, so that it'll be out of our sight.

Wife: No, no, neighbor. I must keep the old red cloak against the time I get married again. I have nothing else. [*She picks up the pig-skin.*] Here, let us sew up my husband in this pig-skin. 'Tis useless for the tannery, seeing the pig died of something catching. [*Hans wriggles again.*]

Woman: But the pig-skin is far too little. 'Twouldn't near cover the body. Come, let him have your red cloak. You always promised it him for a shroud.

Wife [*covering Hans with the skin, but leaving his feet uncovered*]: If his feet do stick out, what matter? My husband'll never heed. I have but one shroud, and that my mother gave me for a dowry. 'Tis worth at least five florins.

Woman: Oh lay him in the ground with honor! The cloak will be your last gift to him in this world. Count it not too dear. The good man is worth it! [*Loud knocking at door right. The Wife begins to moan and cry.*]

Wife: Woe, woe is me! There's someone at the door. Woe, woe is me! Go see who 'tis.

[*The Neighbor opens the door right, and the second neighbor enters. He is a middle-aged Farmer of prosperous appearance, evidently a man of standing in the village, and a churchwarden. He is followed by four or five other Neighbors, both men and women from the village, and by Hans Sachs, an old man with a white beard, wearing the leather apron of a cobbler, and a half-finished shoe sticking out of his pocket.*]

Farmer: Good dame, as we come down the street, we heard a weeping and a wailing within, so we are come straight to find out the cause.

Wife: Come right in, good neighbors, you're welcome. Come over here and see where my husband lies dead! [*The Neighbors recoil in horror, but the Wife reassures them smiling and nodding and winking*] I am undone! I'd sooner all my livestock sickened and died!

Farmer: On my oath you must have held him dear if you'd give all that to have him back again. [*He stifles a laugh, and the Neighbors make sympathetic noises.*] What livestock have you got, neighbor?

Wife [*counting on her fingers*]: In the house alone, there's a dog, two cats, a bird, two dozen mice, one dozen rats, not to speak of the black-beetles! I'd give 'em all if only he was alive!

Farmer [*solemnly*]: The love betwixt you two must have been powerful strong. Now how would it be, if you was to give a promise of three pounds of wax candles and an offering in silver in memory of him in the green grave? That might bring him to life again. I did hear t'other day of a man being fetched back by something of that sort!

Wife: Good neighbor, be silent! My husband has gone to heaven. It would be wicked and shameful to bring him down to earth again.

Farmer [*going to door*]: Then I'd best get a barrow right away, and we'll carry him down to the church.

Woman: See that the candles be not forgotten, nor the tolling of the bell.

Chorus of Neighbors: And we'll follow the corpse in procession!

Wife: Oh, neighbors, neighbors, I pray you leave me in peace! My Hans was never a man for show. Bear him to the church on the barrow, but go secretly and after dark. Let the parson and the clerks stay at home! What need has he of candles, when he'll not see them, nor of the tolling of bells when he'll never hear more? 'Twould be sinful waste of money!

FARMER [*coming back*]: But, good dame, if we bury him tonight, we must have a silver collection on the morrow among both young and old in the village, so that his soul may fare the better. [*The Neighbors shake their heads in disapproval.*]

WIFE: When my man was alive, he never gave willing to the collection, so why start now he's dead driving other folks to the alms-giving, and all for the sake of a few pence? [*She appeals to Hans*] Oh, my dear husband, what will happen to me? Shall I never see you alive no more? Oh Hans, husband of my heart, whatever shall I do next? [*Hans sits up suddenly, kicking over the tankard, and throwing aside the pig-skin.*]

HANS: I'll tell you what to do next. You listen, wife. First you go and break five eggs in the frying-pan; then you pour a cask of my wine down your throat; next you try to sew me up in a pig-skin, though you swore I should be buried in your red cloak. You better lie down quiet till you've got your wits about you again!

WIFE [*showing surprise*]: Why, husband, you're talking in your old way!

HANS [*bitterly*]: And what way would I be talking? Is this the love you boasted of so brazen? It's little I've heard nor seen of loving words and deeds this day!

WIFE: Dear Hans -

HANS: You wicked woman! You'll do for me in death same as you've done for me in life. You prize me only for what I can give you, the clothes to your back, and the roof over your head. Without them you wouldn't so much as look at me over a hedge! Bah!

WIFE: Good gracious, husband mine! Now you must despise me into the bargain. [*She laughs.*] Why I knew all the time you wasn't dead!

HANS [*amazed*]: You knew?

WIFE: Now Hans, didn't you make believe to die just to see how I should act? That was why I played the trick on you.

HANS: You knew all the time I laid on this here table I wern't dead? Oh, the artfulness of it!

WIFE [*putting her arm around him*]: If you was really to die, you know well I should behave very different.

HANS [*still hurt*]: How'd I know what you'd do? Didn't I do my best to find out?

WIFE: You ask the neighbors, they'll tell you.

NEIGHBORS: Ay, ay, she's fond of you right enough!

WOMAN: Truth is, Hans, you've mauled your hand in your own trap.

FARMER [*taking him by the arm*]: Come, come, friend, your wife's so full of cunning there's no curing her. Soon as ever she opened her eyes on this world, she was at her tricks. But bless you, my wife's as bad! Let 'em be, and come along down to the ale-house.

WOMAN: 'Twas for the best she done it. Isn't that so, Master Cobbler? [*Hans Sachs comes forward and stands in the center of the crowd,*]

HANS SACHS: I say, a joke's a joke, my friend, Like all good things, must have an end. Wives will be wives, they're all the same! So let them play the ancient game in their own way; nor seek to test a woman's love by questions, lest grey hairs and bitter sorrows wax 'twixt man and wife; so says Hans Sachs!

ALL [*repeating*]: So says Hans Sachs!

CURTAIN

---

36. MICHEL DE MONTAIGNE (1533–92)

Michel d'Eyquem de Montaigne was born in the Aquitaine region of southern France in 1533 to a family originally of bourgeois origin that had been raised into the ranks of the nobility through his father's contributions to the Italian campaign of Francis I. Impressed by the classical humanism he saw in Italy, Montaigne's father had young Michel tutored privately in Latin so that it was as familiar to him as his native French. Later he was sent to a celebrated humanist school in Bordeaux, the College de Guyenne, where he polished his education. As a result, he had an exceptionally deep knowledge of Latin literature that was always dear to him.

After some training in the law at Toulouse, Montaigne's father secured a position for him in the legal administration of the south of France, and he soon caught the eye of the royal court and the king. He was a gentleman of the chamber to Charles IX from 1561–63 and later a courtier of Henry de Bourbon, king of Navarre, the Protestant leader. On his father's death in 1568, Montaigne inherited the family estates, and in 1570 he moved to the chateau. The next year, although only 37, he abandoned public life to devote himself to reading, writing, and thought. He had established his large library in a tower on his estate, and it was there that he began to compose over the rest of his life his Essays *(or* Trials*), a genre he largely invented.*

His health began to decline in 1578 as a result of very painful kidney stones, so he set out for medicinal baths throughout Europe, keeping a travel journal that was not, however, printed until the eighteenth century. It was in 1581, while on this journey in Italy, that Montaigne learned he had been elected mayor of Bordeaux. Despite misgivings but fortified by a personal encouraging letter from the king, Montaigne returned to Bordeaux, where he served as mayor until 1585. The Wars of Religion between Protestants and Catholics raged around him and he was a moderating influence on both sides, counseling tolerance. Montaigne himself, though, remained a Roman Catholic.

Montaigne published the first edition of his Essays *in 1580, although he continued to work on them, almost until his death in 1592. He saw the world through skeptical eyes, privileging experience over abstraction and an open mind over dogmatism. He wrote that the subject of the essays was himself, as each essay offers another subjective assessment of his life, experience, reading, observation, and thought, as revealed in the passage below. He himself offered the best insight into his life and work in his motto, "Que sais-je?": "What do I know?"*

On Experience

(From Book Three: Chapter 13)

There is no desire more natural than that of knowledge. We try all ways that can lead us to it; where reason is wanting, we therein employ experience,

> "Per varios usus artem experientia fecit,
> Exemplo monstrante viam,"
>
> ["By various trials experience created art, example showing the way." —Manilius, i. 59.]

which is a means much more weak and cheap; but truth is so great a thing that we ought not to disdain any mediation that will guide us to it. Reason has so many forms that we know not which to take; experience has no fewer; the consequence we would draw from the comparison of events is unsure, by reason they are always unlike. There is no quality so universal in this image of things as diversity and variety. Both the Greeks and the Latins and we, for the most express example of similitude, employ that of eggs; and yet there have been men, particularly one at Delphos, who could distinguish marks of difference amongst eggs so well that he never mistook one for another, and having many hens, could tell which had laid it.

Dissimilitude intrudes itself of itself in our works; no art can arrive at perfect similitude: neither Perrozet nor any other can so carefully polish and blanch the backs of his cards that some gamesters will not distinguish them by seeing them only shuffled by another. Resemblance does not so much make one as difference makes another. Nature has obliged herself to make nothing other that was not unlike.

And yet I am not much pleased with his opinion, who thought by the multitude of laws to curb the authority of judges in cutting out for them their several parcels; he was not aware that there is as much liberty and latitude in the interpretation of laws as in their form; and they but fool themselves, who think to lessen and stop our disputes by recalling us to the express words of the Bible: forasmuch as our mind does not find the field less spacious wherein to controvert the sense of another than to deliver his own; and as if there were less animosity and tartness in commentary than in invention. We see how much he was mistaken, for we have more laws in France than all the rest of the world put together, and more than would be necessary for the government of all the worlds of Epicurus:

> *"Ut olim flagitiis, sic nunc legibus, laboramus."*
>
> *["As we were formerly by crimes, so we are now overburdened by laws." —Tacitus, Annal., iii. 25.]*

and yet we have left so much to the opinions and decisions of our judges that there never was so full a liberty or so full a license. What have our legislators gained by culling out a hundred thousand particular cases, and by applying to these a hundred thousand laws? This number holds no manner of proportion with the infinite diversity of human actions; the multiplication of our inventions will never arrive at the variety of examples; add to these a hundred times as many more, it will still not happen that, of events to come, there shall one be found that, in this vast number of millions of events so chosen and recorded, shall so tally with any other one, and be so exactly coupled and matched with it that there will not remain some circumstance and diversity which will require a diverse judgment. There is little relation betwixt our actions, which are in perpetual mutation, and fixed and immutable laws; the most to be desired are those that are the most rare, the most simple and general; and I am even of opinion that we had better have none at all than to have them in so prodigious a number as we have.

Nature always gives them better and happier than those we make ourselves; witness the picture of the Golden Age of the Poets and the state wherein we see nations live who have no other. Some there are, who for their only judge take the first passer-by that travels along their mountains, to determine their cause; and others who, on their market day, choose out some one amongst them upon the spot to decide their controversies. What danger would there be that the wisest amongst us should so determine ours, according to occurrences and at sight, without obligation of example and consequence? For every foot its own shoe. King Ferdinand, sending colonies to the Indies, wisely provided that they should not carry along with them any students of jurisprudence, for fear lest suits should get footing in that new world, as being a science in its own nature, breeder of altercation and division; judging with Plato, "that lawyers and physicians are bad institutions of a country."

. . .

I hate that we should be enjoined to have our minds in the clouds, when our bodies are at table; I would not have the mind nailed there, nor wallow there; I would have it take place there and sit, but not lie down. Aristippus maintained nothing but the body, as if we had no soul; Zeno comprehended only the soul, as if we had no body: both of them faultily. Pythagoras, they say, followed a philosophy that was all contemplation, Socrates one that was all conduct and action; Plato found a mean betwixt the two; but they only say this for the sake of talking. The true temperament is found in Socrates; and, Plato is much more Socratic than Pythagoric, and it becomes him better. When I dance, I dance; when I sleep, I sleep. Nay, when I walk alone in a beautiful orchard, if my thoughts are some part of the time taken up with external occurrences, I some part of the time call them back again to my walk, to the orchard, to the sweetness of that solitude, and to myself.

Nature has mother-like observed this, that the actions she has enjoined us for our necessity should be also pleasurable to us; and she invites us to them, not only by reason, but also by appetite, and 'tis injustice to infringe her laws. When I see alike Caesar and Alexander, in the midst of his greatest business, so fully enjoy human and corporal pleasures, I do not say that he relaxed his mind: I say that he strengthened it, by vigor of courage subjecting those violent employments and laborious thoughts to the ordinary usage of life: wise, had he believed the last was his ordinary, the first his extraordinary, vocation. We are great fools. "He has passed his life in idleness," say we: "I have done nothing to-day." What? have you not lived? that is not only the fundamental, but the most illustrious, of your occupations. "Had I been put to the management of great affairs, I should have made it seen what I could do." "Have you known how to meditate and manage your life? you have performed the greatest work of all." In order to shew and develop herself, nature needs only fortune; she equally manifests herself in all stages, and behind a curtain as well as without one. Have you known how to regulate your conduct, you have done a great deal more than he who has composed books.

Have you known how to take repose, you have done more than he who has taken empires and cities.

The glorious masterpiece of man is to live to purpose; all other things: to reign, to lay up treasure, to build, are but little appendices and props. I take pleasure in seeing a general of an army, at the foot of a breach he is presently to assault, give himself up entire and free at dinner, to talk and be merry with his friends. And Brutus, when heaven and earth were conspired against him and the Roman liberty, stealing some hour of the night from his rounds to read and scan Polybius in all security. 'Tis for little souls, buried under the weight of affairs, not from them to know how clearly to disengage themselves, not to know how to lay them aside and take them up again:

> "O fortes, pejoraque passi
> Mecum saepe viri! nunc vino pellite curas
> Cras ingens iterabimus aequor."

> ["O brave spirits, who have often suffered sorrow with me, drink cares away; tomorrow we will embark once more on the vast sea." —Horace, Od., i. 7, 30.]

Whether it be in jest or earnest, that the theological and Sorbonnical wine, and their feasts, are turned into a proverb, I find it reasonable they should dine so much more commodiously and pleasantly, as they have profitably and seriously employed the morning in the exercise of their schools. The conscience of having well spent the other hours, is the just and savory sauce of the dinner-table. The sages lived after that manner; and that inimitable emulation to virtue, which astonishes us both in the one and the other Cato, that humor of theirs, so severe as even to be importunate, gently submits itself and yields to the laws of the human condition, of Venus and Bacchus; according to the precepts of their sect, that require the perfect sage to be as expert and intelligent in the use of natural pleasures as in all other duties of life:

> "Cui cor sapiat, ei et sapiat palatus."

> ["He that has a learned soul also has a learned palate."]

Relaxation and facility, methinks, wonderfully honor and best become a strong and generous soul. Epaminondas did not think that to take part, and that heartily, in songs and sports and dances with the young men of his city, were things that in any way derogated from the honor of his glorious victories and the perfect purity of manners that was in him. And amongst so many admirable actions of Scipio the grandfather, a person worthy to be reputed of a heavenly extraction, there is nothing that gives him a greater grace than to see him carelessly and childishly trifling at gathering and selecting cockle shells, and playing at quoits,

> [This game, as the Dictionnaire de Trevoux describes it, is one wherein two persons contend which of them shall soonest pick up some object.]

amusing and tickling himself in representing by writing in comedies the meanest and most popular actions of men. And his head full of that wonderful enterprise of Hannibal and Africa, visiting the schools in Sicily, and attending philosophical lectures, to the extent of arming the blind envy of his enemies at Rome. Nor is there anything more remarkable in Socrates than that, old as he was, he found time to make himself taught dancing and playing upon instruments, and thought it time well spent. This same man was seen in an ecstasy, standing upon his feet a whole day and a night together, in the presence of all the Grecian army, surprised and absorbed by some profound thought. He was the first, amongst so many valiant men of the army, to run to the relief of Alcibiades, oppressed with the enemy, to shield him with his own body, and disengage him from the crowd by absolute force of arms. It was he who, in the Delian battle, raised and saved Xenophon when fallen from his horse; and who, amongst all the people of Athens, enraged as he was at so unworthy a spectacle, first presented himself to rescue Theramenes, whom the thirty tyrants were leading to execution by their satellites, and desisted not from his bold enterprise but at the remonstrance of Theramenes himself, though he was only followed by two more in all. He was seen, when courted by a beauty with whom he was in love, to maintain at need a severe abstinence. He was seen ever to go to the wars, and walk upon ice, with bare feet; to wear the same robe, winter and summer; to surpass all his companions in patience of bearing hardships, and to eat no more at a feast than at his own private dinner. He was seen, for seven-and-twenty years together, to endure hunger, poverty, the indocility of his children, and the nails of his wife, with the same countenance. And, in the end, calumny, tyranny, imprisonment, fetters, and poison. But was this man obliged to drink full bumpers by any rule of civility? he was also the man of the whole army with whom the advantage in drinking, remained. And he never refused to play at noisettes, nor to ride the hobby-horse with children, and it became him well; for all actions, says philosophy, equally become and equally honor a wise man. We have enough wherewithal to do it, and we ought never to be weary of presenting the image of this great man in all the patterns and forms of perfection. There are very few examples of life, full and pure; and we wrong our teaching every day, to propose to ourselves those that are weak and imperfect, scarce good for any one service, and rather pull us back; corrupters rather than correctors of manners. The people deceive themselves; a man goes much more easily indeed by the ends, where the extremity serves for a bound, a stop, and guide, than by the middle way, large and open; and according to art, more than according to nature: but withal much less nobly and commendably.

Greatness of soul consists not so much in mounting and in pressing forward, as in knowing how to govern and circumscribe itself; it takes everything for great, that is enough, and demonstrates itself in preferring moderate to eminent things. There is nothing so fine and legitimate as well and duly to play the man; nor science so arduous as well and naturally to know how to live this life; and of all the infirmities we have, 'tis the most barbarous to despise our being.

Whoever has a mind to isolate his spirit, when the body is ill at ease, to preserve it from the contagion, let him by all means do it if he can: but otherwise let him on the contrary favor and assist it, and not refuse to participate of its natural pleasures with a conjugal complacency, bringing to it, if it be the wiser, moderation, lest by indiscretion they should get confounded with displeasure. Intemperance is the pest of pleasure; and temperance is not its scourge, but rather its seasoning. Euxodus, who therein established the sovereign good, and his companions, who set so high a value upon it, tasted it in its most charming sweetness, by the means of temperance, which in them was singular and exemplary.

I enjoin my soul to look upon pain and pleasure with an eye equally regulated:

"*Eodem enim vitio est effusio animi in laetitia quo in dolore contractio,*"

["For from the same imperfection arises the expansion of the mind in pleasure and its contraction in sorrow." —*Cicero, Tusc. Quaes., iv. 31.*]

and equally firm; but the one gaily and the other severely, and so far as it is able, to be careful to extinguish the one as to extend the other. The judging rightly of good brings along with it the judging soundly of evil: pain has something of the inevitable in its tender beginnings, and pleasure something of the evitable in its excessive end. Plato couples them together, and wills that it should be equally the office of fortitude to fight against pain, and against the immoderate and charming blandishments of pleasure: they are two fountains, from which whoever draws, when and as much as he needs, whether city, man, or beast, is very fortunate. The first is to be taken medicinally and upon necessity, and more scantily; the other for thirst, but not to drunkenness. Pain, pleasure, love and hatred are the first things that a child is sensible of: if, when reason comes, they apply it to themselves, that is virtue.

I have a special vocabulary of my own; I "pass away time," when it is ill and uneasy, but when 'tis good I do not pass it away: "I taste it over again and adhere to it"; one must run over the ill and settle upon the good. This ordinary phrase of pastime, and passing away the time, represents the usage of those wise sort of people who think they cannot do better with their lives than to let them run out and slide away, pass them over, and baulk them, and, as much as they can, ignore them and shun them as a thing of troublesome and contemptible quality: but I know it to be another kind of thing, and find it both valuable and commodious, even in its latest decay, wherein I now enjoy it; and nature has delivered it into our hands in such and so favorable circumstances that we have only ourselves to blame if it be troublesome to us, or escapes us unprofitably:

"*Stulti vita ingrata est, trepida est, tota in futurum fertur.*"

["The life of a fool is thankless, timorous, and wholly bent upon the future." —*Seneca, Ep:, 15.*]

Nevertheless I compose myself to lose mine without regret; but withal as a thing that is perishable by its condition, not that it molests or annoys me. Nor does it properly well become any not to be displeased when they die, excepting such as are pleased to live. There is good husbandry in enjoying it: I enjoy it double to what others do; for the measure of its fruition depends upon our more or less application to it. Chiefly that I perceive mine to be so short in time, I desire to extend it in weight; I will stop the promptitude of its flight by the promptitude of my grasp; and by the vigor of using it compensate the speed of its running away. In proportion as the possession of life is more short, I must make it so much deeper and fuller.

Others feel the pleasure of content and prosperity; I feel it too, as well as they, but not as it passes and slips by; one should study, taste, and ruminate upon it to render condign thanks to Him who grants it to us.

37. THOMAS DELONEY

Neither the birth nor the death date of Thomas Deloney is certain, and most of what we know about him centers on his published work. A silk-weaver by profession, with enough education to translate Latin, he began publishing in the early 1580s. Famous first as a ballad-writer, Deloney got involved in political protest in the 1590s, when London weavers complained about the encroachments of French and Dutch weavers in their business. Jack of Newbury *was his first of four works of fiction, and one of the first of this new genre in England. Its hero is a cloth-worker who both demonstrates the rising economic power of the merchant class and suggests its value as a force for social and moral stability. Deloney's work was tremendously popular:* Jack of Newbury, *for example, went through seventeen editions by 1700. Deloney died, most likely in London, before 1600.*

The most pleasant and delectable history of John Winchcomb, otherwise called Jack of Newbury: and first of his love and pleasant life

Chapter 1

In the days of King Henry the eighth, that most noble and victorious prince, in the beginning of his reign, John Winchcomb, a broadcloth weaver, dwelt in Newberry, a town in Berkshire, who because he was a man of a merry disposition and honest conversation, was wonderfully well-beloved of rich and poor, specially because in every place where he came, he would spend his money with the best, and was not at any time found a churl of his purse. Wherefore being so good a companion, he was called by old and young Jack of Newberry: a man so generally well known in all his country for his good fellowship, that he could go in no place but he found acquaintance; by means whereof, Jack could no sooner get a crown, but immediately he found means to spend it; yet had he ever this care, that he would always keep himself in comely and decent apparel: neither at any time would he be overcome in drink, but so discreetly behave himself with honest mirth, and pleasant conceits, that he was every gentleman's companion.

After Jack had long led this pleasant life, being (though he were but poor) in good estimation, it was his Master's chance to die, and his Dame to be a widow, who was a very comely ancient woman, and of reasonable wealth. Wherefore she, having a good opinion of her man John, committed unto his government the guiding of all her work-folks for the space of three years together, in which time she found him so careful and diligent that all things came forward and prospered wonderfully well. No man could entice him from his business all the week, by whatever entreaty they could use, so much that in the end some of the wild youths of the town began to deride and scoff at him....

Nevertheless, every Sunday in the afternoon, and every holy-day, Jack would keep them company, and be as merry as a pie, and having still good store of money in his purse, one or other would ever be borrowing of him, but never could he get penny of it again: which when Jack perceived, he would never after carry above twelve pence at once in his purse: and that being spent, he would straight return home merrily, taking his leave of the company in this sort.

My masters, I thank you, it's time to pack home.
For he that wants money is counted a mome [a fool]:

And twelve pence a Sunday being spent in good cheer,
To fifty two shillings amounts in the year;
Enough for a craftsman that hews by his hands:
And he that exceeds it shall purchase no lands.
For that I spend this day, I'll work hard tomorrow.
For woe is that party that seeketh to borrow.
My money doth make me full merry to be;
And without my money none careth for me:
Therefore wanting money, what should I do here?
But hast home, and thank you for all my good cheer?

Thus Jack's good government and discretion was noted by the best and most substantial men of the town, so that it wrought his great commendations, and his Dame thought herself not a little blessed to have such a servant, that was so obedient unto her, and so careful for her profit. For she had never had an apprentice that yielded her more obedience than he did, or was more dutiful, so that by his good example he did as much good as by his diligent labor and careful travail. His singular virtue being noted by the widow, she began to cast a very good countenance to her man John, and to use very much talk with him in private; and first by way of communication, she would tell him what suitors she had, and also the great offers they made her, what gifts they sent her, and the great affection they bore her, seeking his opinion in the matter.

When Jack found the favor to be his Dame's secretary, he thought it an extraordinary kindness: and guessing by the yarn it would prove a good web, began to question with his Dame this way: "although it does not become me, your servant, to pry into your secrets, nor to be busy about matters of your love: yet since it has pleased you to conference with me in those causes, I ask you, let me entreat you to know their names that are your suitors, and their profession."

"Marry John" said she, "that you shall, and I ask you, take a cushion and sit down by me."

"Dame" quoth he, "I thank you: but there is no reason I should sit on a cushion till I have deserved it." "If you have not you might have done" said she, "but some soldiers never find favor."

John replied, "that makes me indeed to want favor: for I never dare try maidens because they seem coy, nor wives for fear of their husbands, nor widows fearing their disdainfulness."

"Tush John" quoth she, "he that fears and doubts womankind cannot be counted mankind, and take this for a principle 'all things are not as they seem.' But let us leave this, and proceed to our former matter. My first suitor dwells at Wallingford, by trade a tanner, a man of good wealth, and his name is Crafts, of nice appearance and very good behavior, a widower, well thought of among his neighbors. He has appropriate land, a fair house well furnished, never a child in the world, and he loves me well enough."

"Why then Dame" quoth John, "you were best to have him."

"Is that your opinion?" quoth she. "Now trust me, it is not mine, for I find two special reasons to the contrary: the one is, that he being over-worn in years, makes me over-loth to love him: and the other, that I know one nearer hand."

"Believe me, Dame" quoth Jack, "I perceive store is no sore, and proffered ware is worse by ten in the hundred than that which is sought: but I pray who is your second suitor?"

"John" quoth she, "it may seem immodesty in me to expose my lovers' secrets: yet seeing your discretion and being persuaded of your secrecy, I will show you. The other is a man of middle years, but yet a bachelor, by occupation a tailor, and dwelling at Hungerford: by report a very good husband, such a one as has crown's good store, and he professes much good will to me. As for his person, he may please any woman."

"Aye, Dame" quoth John, "because he pleases you."

"Not so" said she, "for my eyes are impartial judges in that case, and although my opinion may be contrary to others, if his art does not deceive my eye-sight, he is worthy of a good wife, both for his person and conditions."

"Then trust me Dame" quoth John, "for so much as you are without doubt of yourself that you will prove a good wife, and so well persuaded of him, I should think you could make no better a choice."

"Truly John" quoth she, "there are also two reasons that move me not to like him: the one, that being so large a ranger, he would at home be a stranger: and the other, that I like better one nearer hand."

"Who is that?" quoth Jack.

She says "the third suitor is the parson of Spinhomland, who has a proper living, who is of holy conversation and good estimation, [and] whose affection to me is great."

"No doubt Dame" quoth John, "you may do wonderfully well with him, where you shall have no care but to serve God, and to make ready his meat."

"John" quoth she, "the flesh and the spirit agrees not: for he will be so bent to his book that he will have little mind of his bed, for one month's studying for a sermon will make him forget his wife a whole year."

"Truly Dame" quoth John, "I must needs speak in his behalf and the rather for that he is a man of the Church, and your so near neighbor, to whom (as I guess) you bear the best affection: I do not think that he will be so much bound to his book or subject to the spirit, but that he will remember a woman at home or abroad."

"Well John" quoth she, "I know my mind is not that way: for I like better one nearer hand."

"No marvel" quoth Jack "you are so peremptory, seeing you have so much choice: but I pray you Dame" quoth he, "let me know this fortunate man that is so highly placed in your favor?"

"John" quoth she, "they are worthy to know nothing, that cannot keep something: that man (I tell thee) must go nameless: for he is lord of my love, and king of my desires: there is neither tanner, tailor, nor parson may compare with him, his presence is a preservative to my health, his sweet smiles my heart's solace, and his words heavenly music to my ears."

"Why then Dame" quoth John, "for your body's health, your heart's joy, and your ears' delight, delay not the time, but entertain him with a kiss, make his bed next yours, and chop up the match in the morning."

"Well" quoth she, "I perceive your consent is quickly given for any, having no care how I am matched as long as I am matched: I know, I know, I could not let you go so lightly, being loth that any one should have you, unless I could love her as well as myself."

"I thank you for your kindness and good will, good Dame" quoth he, "but it is not wisdom for a young man that can scarcely keep himself to take a wife, therefore I hold it best to lead a single life. For I have heard say that many sorrows follow marriage, especially where want remains, and besides it is a hard matter to find a constant woman: for as young maids are fickle, so are old women jealous: the one a grief too common, the other a torment intolerable."

"What John?" quoth she, "consider that maidens' fickleness proceeds of vain fancies, but old women's jealousy of super-abounding love and therefore the more to be borne besides."

"But Dame" quoth he, "many are jealous without cause: for is it sufficient for their mistrusting natures to take exceptions at a shadow, at a word, at a look, at a smile, nay at the twinkle of an eye, which neither man nor woman is able to expel? I knew a woman that was ready to hang herself, just for seeing her husband's shirt hang on a hedge with her maid's smock."

"I grant that this fury may haunt some" quoth she, "yet there be many other that complain not without great cause."

"Why, is there any cause that should move jealousy?" quoth John.

"Aye, by S. Mary there is" quoth she, "for would it not grieve a woman (being one every way able to delight her husband) to see him forsake her, despise and contemn her, being never so merry as when he is in other company, sporting abroad from morning till noon, from noon till night, and when he comes to bed, if he turns to his wife, it is in such solemnness and wearisome drowsy lameness, that it brings rather loathsomeness than any delight? Can you then blame a woman in this case to be angry and displeased? I'll tell you what, among brute beasts it is a grief intolerable: for I heard my grand-dame tell, that the bellwether of her flock fancying one of the ewes above the rest, and seeing Gratis the Shepherd abusing her in abominable sort (subverting the law of nature) could by no means bear that abuse, but watching opportunity for revenge, on a time found the said shepherd sleeping in the field, and suddenly ran against him in such violent sort, that by the force of his intertwined horns, he beat the brains out of the shepherd's head and slew him. If then a sheep could not endure that injury, think not that women are so sheepish to suffer it."

"Believe me" quoth John, "if every horn maker should be so plagued by a horned beast, there should be less horns made in Newbery by many in a year. But Dame" quoth he, "to make an end of this prattle, because it is an argument too deep to be discussed between you and I, you shall hear me sing an old song, and so we will depart to supper." . . .

Then calling the rest of her servants, they fell to their meat merrily, and after supper, the Goodwife went abroad for her recreation, to walk a while with one of her neighbors. And in the mean space John went up into his chamber, and there began to meditate on this matter, thinking about what were best to do: for he perceived that his Dame's affection was great towards him. Knowing therefore the woman's disposition, and further, that her estate was reasonably good, and considering besides, that he should find a house ready furnished, servants ready taught, and all other things necessary for his trade, he thought it best not to let slip that good occasion, lest he should never come to the like. But again, when he considered her years to be unfitting to his youth, and that having once been his Dame she would (perhaps) so disdain to be governed by him that had been her poor servant that it would prove a bad bargain [and] doubting many inconveniences that might grow from that, he therefore resolved to be silent rather than to proceed further. So he went straight to bed, and the next morning settled himself close to his business.

...

Thus the matter rested for two or three days, in which space she daily devised which way she might obtain her desire, which was to marry her man.

Thus it passed on from Bartholomew-tide till it was near Christmas, at which time the weather was so wonderfully cold that all the running rivers round about the town were frozen very thick. The widow, being very loth to lie without company any longer, on a cold winter's night made a great fire and sent for her man John. Having also prepared a chair and a cushion, she made him sit down therein, and sending for a pint of good sack, they both went to supper.

In the end, bedtime coming on, she caused her maid in a merriment to pluck off his hose and shoes, and caused him to be laid in his master's best bed, standing in the best chamber, hung round about with very fair curtains. John being thus preferred, thought himself a gentleman, and lying soft, after his hard labor and a good supper, quickly fell asleep.

About midnight, the widow being cold on her feet crept into her man's bed to warm them. John, feeling one lift up the clothes, asked who was there. "O good John it is I" quoth the widow. "The night is so extreme cold, and my chamber walls so thin, that I am likely to be frozen in my bed, so rather than in any way hazard my health, I thought it much better to come here and try your courtesy, to have a little room beside you."

John, being a kind young man, would not say her nay, and so they spent the rest of the night both together in one bed. Early in the morning she arose and made herself ready, and willed her man John to run and fetch her a torch with all speed, "for" quoth she, "I have earnest business to do this morning." Her man did so. Which done, she made him carry the torch before her until she came to Saint Bartholomew's chapel, where Sir John the priest, with the clerk and sexton, stood waiting for her.

"John" quoth she, "turn into the chapel, for before I go further I will make my prayers to St. Bartholomew so shall I speed the better in my business."

When they had gone in the priest, according to his order, came to her and asked where the bridegroom was.

Quoth she, "I thought he would have been here before me." "Sir" quoth she, "I will sit down and say over my [rosary]-beads, and by that time he will come."

John mused at this matter, to see that his Dame should so suddenly be married, and he hearing nothing of it before. The widow rising from her prayers, the priest told her that the bridegroom had not yet come.

"Is it true?" quoth the widow. "I promise you I will wait no longer for him, even if he were as good as George a Green, and therefore hurry up" quoth she, "and marry me to my man John."

"Why Dame" quoth he, "you do but jest."

"I believe, John" quoth she, "I do not jest, for so I mean it shall be, and do not stand strangely, but remember that you promised me on your faith not to hinder me when I came to the church to be married, but rather to set it forward. Therefore set your torch aside and give me your hand, for none but you shall be my husband."

John, seeing no remedy, consented, because he saw the matter could not otherwise be amended and they were married without delay.

When they came home, John entertained his Dame with a kiss, which the other servants seeing, thought him somewhat saucy. The widow caused the best cheer in the house to be set on the table, and to breakfast they went, causing her new husband to be set in a chair at the table's end, with a fair napkin laid on his trencher, then she called out the rest of her servants, willing them to sit down and take part of their good cheer. They, wondering to see their fellow John sit at the table's end in their old master's chair, began heartily to smile, and openly to laugh at the matter, especially because their Dame so naturally sat by his side. When she perceived this, she asked if that were all the manners they could show before their master. "I tell you" quoth she, "he is my husband, for this morning we were married, and therefore henceforward look you acknowledge your duty towards him."

...

The next day the report was all over town that Jack of Newberry had married his Dame, so that when the woman walked abroad, every one bade God give her joy: some said that she was matched to her sorrow, saying that so lusty a young man as he would never love her, being so ancient. Whereupon the woman made answer that she would take him down in his wedding shoes, and would try his patience in the prime of his lustiness: to which many of her gossips encouraged her. Every day therefore for the space of a month after she was married, it was her ordinary custom to go forth in the morning among her gossips and acquaintance to make merry and not to return home till night, without any regard of her household. At her coming home her husband did very often admonish her very gently, showing what great inconvenience would grow from this, which sometimes she would take gently and sometimes disdainfully, saying,

"I am now in very good case, that he that was my servant just the other day will now be my master; this is what happens when a woman makes her foot her head. The day has been, when I might have gone forth when I wished, and come in again when it pleased me without any control, and now I must be subject to every Jack's check." "I am sure" quoth she, "that by my gadding abroad and careless spending, I waste no goods of yours. I, pitying your poverty, made you a man and master of the house, but not so that I would become your slave. I scorn, I tell you truly, that such a youngling as yourself should so correct my conceit and give me instructions as if I were not able to guide myself: but truly, truly, you shall not use me like a baby nor bridle me like an ass, and seeing my going abroad grieves you, where I have gone out one day, I will go abroad three; and for one hour, I will stay five."

"Well" quoth her husband, "I trust you will be better advised." And with that he went from her about his business, leaving her sweating in her fustian furies.

Thus the time passed on, till on a certain day she had been abroad in her wonted manner and staying out very late, he shut the doors and went to bed. About midnight she came to the door and knocked to come in: to whom he, looking out of the window, answered this way:

"What? Is it you that keeps such a knocking? I pray you go away and request the constable to provide you a bed, for this night you shall have no lodging here."

"I hope" quoth she, "you will not shut me out of doors like a dog, or let me lie in the streets like a strumpet."

"Whether like a dog or drab" quoth he, "all is one to me, knowing no reason but that as you have stayed out all day for your delight so you may lie forth all night for my pleasure. Both birds and beasts at the night's approach repair to their rest and observe a convenient time to return to their habitation. Look but upon the poor spider, the frog, the fly, and every other silly worm, and you shall see all these observe time to return to their home: and if you, being a woman, will not do the like, content yourself to bear the brunt of your own folly and so farewell."

The woman, hearing this, made piteous moan, and very humbly entreated him to let her in and to pardon this offence, and while she lived vowed never to do the like. Her husband at length being moved with pity towards her, slipped on his shoes, and came down in his shirt. The door being opened, in she went quaking, and as he was about to lock it again, in very sorrowful manner she said, "Alacke husband, what hap have I? My wedding ring was even now in my hand, and I have let it fall about the door: good sweet John come forth with the candle and help me seek it."

The man immediately did so, and while he sought for that which was not there to be found, she whipped into the house, and quickly clapping to the door, she locked her husband out. He stood calling with the candle in his hand to come in, but she made as if she heard not. Right away she went up into her chamber, and carried the key with her, but when he saw she would not answer he presently began to knock as loud as he could at the door. At last she thrust her head out at the window, saying "Who is there?" "'Tis I" quoth John, "what do you mean by this? I pray you come down and open the door that I may come in."

"What sir" quoth she, "is it you? Have you nothing to do but dance about the streets at this time of night, and like a sprite of the buttery hunt after crickets, are you so hot that the house cannot hold you?"

"Nay, I pray you sweetheart" quoth he, "do not gibe any longer, but let me in."

"O sir, remember" quoth she, "how you stood just now at the window, like a judge on the bench, and taunting, kept me out of my own house. How now Jack, am I even with you? What, John my man, were you so lusty to lock your Dame out of doors? Sirra, remember you bade me go to the constable to get lodging, now you have leisure to try if his wife will prefer you to a bed. You, sir sauce, that made me stand in the cold till my feet froze and my teeth chattered, while you stood preaching of birds and beasts, telling me a tale of spiders, flies, and frogs: go try now if any of them will be so friendly to let you have lodging. Why do you not go man? Fear not to speak with them; for I am sure you shall find them at home. I do not think they are such ill husbands as you, to be abroad at this time of night."

With this John's patience was greatly moved, insomuch that he deeply swore that if she would not let him in, he would break down the door.

"Why John" quoth she, "you need not be so hot, your clothing is not so warm, and because I think this will be a warning for you against another time, how you shut me out of my house, catch, there is the key, come in at your pleasure, and go to bed to your fellows, for you shall not lie with me tonight."

With that she closed the casement, and went to bed, locking the chamber door fast. Her husband knew it was in vain to seek to come into her chamber, and being no longer able to endure the cold, found a place among his apprentices, and there slept soundly. In the morning his wife rose early, and merrily made him a caudle, and bringing it up to his bedside, asked him how he did.

Quoth John, "troubled with a shrew, who the longer she lives, the worse she is, and as the people of Illyria kill men with their looks, so she kills her husband's heart with untoward conditions." "But trust me wife" quoth he, "seeing I find you of such crooked qualities, that (like the spider) you turn the sweet flowers of good counsel into venomous poison, from henceforth I will leave you to your own willfulness, and neither vex my mind, nor trouble myself to restrain you: which if I had wisely done last night, I had kept the house in quiet, and myself from cold."

"Husband" quoth she, "think that women are like starlings, which will burst their gall before they will yield to the fowler: or like the fish Scolopendra, that cannot be touched without danger. Notwithstanding, as the hard steel yields to the hammer's stroke, being used to his kind, so will women to their husbands, where they are not too much crossed. And seeing you have sworn to give me my will, I vow likewise that my willfulness shall not offend you. I tell you husband, the noble nature of a woman is such that for their loving friends they will not stick (like the pelican) to pierce their own hearts to do them good. And therefore forgiving each other all injuries past, having also tried one another's patience, let us quench these burning coals of contention with the sweet juice of a faithful kiss and shaking hands, bequeath all our anger to the eating up of this caudle."

Her husband courteously consented and after this time they lived long together in most godly, loving and kind sort, until in the end she died, leaving her husband wonderfully wealthy.

38. JUAN LUIS VIVES (1492–1540)

Vives was born in Valencia in 1492, of converso *parents (converts to Christianity from Judaism), and studied Latin and Greek in Spain and scholastic philosophy at the University of Paris (1509–12). Unhappy with the rigid scholasticism of Paris, he moved to Bruges, where he became tutor to the young Cardinal de Croy, Archbishop of Toledo. Moving in 1517 to Louvain with his pupil, Vives began teaching at the university until the death of his patron, de Croy, led to his requiring a more secure income.*

In 1522 Vives was offered a chair at the Spanish University of Alcala but stopped en route in England, where he was invited to teach Greek at Oxford. He also received the patronage of King Henry VIII and Queen Catherine of Aragon, serving as tutor to Princess Mary in 1527–28 and enjoying the company of leading English humanists. His support of Queen Catherine during the divorce proceedings resulted in his leaving England permanently. Vives is best known as an educator whose treatises stressed not only Christian virtue and classical studies but also vernacular languages as the foundations of knowledge, as well as specifically addressing the education of women; but, like his friend Thomas More, he was much concerned with the plight of the poor. His 1526 On Assistance to the Poor *recommends a system of poor relief in Bruges (then a city of about 50,000) and criticizes the Church for not attending sufficiently to the problem. In the early sixteenth century the problem of poverty seemed unusually pressing; changing patterns of landholding were forcing people off the land, bad harvests were leading to starvation, and changing economic patterns meant an unprecedented and incomprehensible level of inflation. These problems were most clearly manifested in quickly growing cities, where both religious and economic change meant that old patterns of poor relief were either unacceptable or ineffective, or both. Vives died in Bruges in 1540.*

On Assistance to the Poor

The obligations of administrators in a city toward the poor

My references here are to the state and the administrator, who is to the former as a soul is to the body. The soul quickens and animates not merely this or that part, but the entire body; thus, the magistrate may never disregard a portion of his governance.

Those who fancy only the wealthy and despise the poor are like doctors who are not concerned about healing the hands or the feet because they are at some distance from the heart. Just as this treatment would bring injury to the whole man, so in the state the weak may not be neglected without danger to the strong. The poor will rob when they are pressed through necessity; yet the judge does not think it important to pay attention to the cause, a small matter to him. These poor envy the rich, and are angered and resentful that the wealthy have so much money to lavish on jesters, dogs, harlots, asses, packhorses, and elephants. In the meantime, the poor themselves do not have the means to feed their starving children. The former proudfully and insolently flaunt their wealth, which has been wrung from these destitute and others like them.

. . .

A mutual danger imperils the commonwealth from the contagion of disease. It happens too often that one man has brought into the community some serious and dreadful disease, such as the plague, or syphilis, or the like, causing others to perish. What sort of situation is this, when in every church—especially at the solemn and most heavily attended feasts—one is obliged to enter into the church proper between two rows or squadrons of the sick, the vomiting, the ulcerous, the diseased with ills whose very names cannot be mentioned. And more, this is the only entrance for boys and girls, the aged and the pregnant! Do you think these are made of such iron that, fasting as they are, they are not revolted by this spectacle—especially since ulcers of this sort are not only forced upon the eyes but upon the nose as well, the mouth, and almost on the hands and body as they pass through? How shameless such begging! I will not even discuss the fact that some who have just left the side of one dead of the plague mingle with the crowd.

These two matters—how diseases may be cured and how their contagion to others can be suppressed—must not be neglected by administrators of the state. Further, a wise government, solicitous for the common good, will not leave so large a part of the citizenry in a condition of uselessness, harmful to themselves and to others. When the general funds have been expended, those without means of subsistence are driven to robbery in the city and on the highways; others commit theft stealthily; women of eligible years put modesty aside and, no longer holding to chastity, put it on sale for a bagatelle (and then, can never be persuaded to abandon this detestable practice); old women take up regular pandering and then sorcery, which promotes procuring. Children of the needy receive a deplorable upbringing. Together with their brood, the poor are cast out of the churches and wander over the land; they do not receive the sacraments and they hear no sermons. We do not know by what law they live, nor what their practices or beliefs. Actually, the discipline of the church has collapsed so completely that no ministrations are offered without an attendant charge. Clerics scorn the reference to selling, yet they force the people into recompense. Even the bishop of a diocese does not consider such shorn sheep as belonging to his fold and pasture.

So, there is no one to see that these beggars go to confession or receive communion with others at the Lord's Supper. Since they never hear instructions, they inevitably judge things by false standards and lead most disorderly lives. If it happens in some way that they come into money, they are intolerable because of their base and discreditable upbringing. So it follows that those vices (which I cited earlier) are not so much the fault of the poor as of the administrators who do not provide adequate regulations for the good government of the people. Rather, they consider themselves chosen to preside exclusively over legal suits concerning money or to pass sentences on crimes.

On the contrary, it is much more important for magistrates to work on ways of producing good citizens than on punishing or restraining evil-doers. How much less need there would be of punishment if these matters were attended to in the first place! The Romans of ancient times provided in such manner for their citizens that no one needed to beg; hence begging was forbidden in the Twelve Tables. The Athenians took the same preventive measures for their populace. Again, the Lord gave to the Jewish people a peculiar law, hard and intractable, such as became a people of similar temperament; yet in Deuteronomy He commands them to such precautions that, so far as it was within their power, there was to be no indigent or beggar among them, especially in that year of rest so acceptable to the Lord. In such manner are all people to live; for them the Lord Jesus was buried—with the Old Law and ceremonials and the "old man"—and rose again in a regeneration of life and spirit. Unquestionably, it is a scandal and disgrace that we Christians confront everywhere in our cities so many poor and indigent, we to whom no injunction has been more explicitly commanded than charity (I might say, the only one).

Wherever you turn, you encounter poverty and want, always along with those who are obliged to hold out their hands for a dole. In a state, anything ravaged or ruined by time or fortune is renewed, such as walls, ditches, ramparts, streams, institutions, customs, laws themselves; so it would be equally reasonable to reform that method of poor relief which in various ways in the passage of time has become outmoded. The most eminent men, and others interested in the welfare of the city, have devised some salutary measures: taxes have been eased; public lands have been turned over to the poor for cultivation; certain surplus funds have been distributed by the state—things which we have seen even in our own day. However, measures of this sort require specific conditions which appear only too rarely in our times. Recourse must be made, therefore, to other more appropriate and more enduring solutions.

Identification and registration of the poor

Someone may ask me: "How do you propose to relieve such numbers?" If true charity dwelt in us, if it were truly a law (though compulsion is not necessary for one who loves), it would hold all things in common. One man would regard another's distress as though it were his own. As it is, however, no one extends his concern beyond his own home, and sometimes not even beyond his own room or himself personally. Too many are not sufficiently concerned about their own parents or children or brothers or wife. Therefore, since human countermeasures must be employed—especially among those for whom divine commands are ineffective—I suggest the following plan.

Some of the poor live in places usually called "hospitals"—the Greek word is Ptochotrophia, but I will use the more familiar word—and others beg in public; still others endure their afflictions as best they can in their own places. I define a hospital as any place where the sick are fed and nursed, where a given number of indigent persons are supported, boys and girls educated, abandoned infants nourished, the insane confined, and the blind allowed to spend their days. Rulers of states must understand that these institutions are part of their responsibilities.

No one may circumvent the founders' stipulations in setting up these institutions; these must remain inviolable. With these one should interpret not merely the words but attend primarily to their jurisdiction (as in deeds of trust) and intent (as in wills). On this point, no doubt it was the donors' desire that the funds left by them should be distributed to the best possible purposes and used in the worthiest places; they were not so much concerned by whom this should be done, or how, as that it should be done.

In the next place, there is nothing so free in the state that it could not be subject to inquiry by those who administer the government. Liberty is found in yielding obedience to the magistrates of the community rather than in that encouragement to violence or in the opportunity for widespread license in whatever direction caprice may lead. No one can remove his property from the custody and control of the state unless he gives up his citizenship. Even more, he may not even give up his life, which is of more importance and value than property. Indeed, everyone has acquired his property with the help of the state, as if it were a gift, and can keep and hold his wealth only through the state.

Therefore, going in twos and with a secretary, the Senators should visit each of these institutions and inspect it. They should write a full account of its condition, of the number of inmates, their names, who supports them there, and the reason for each person's being there. These results should be reported to the Councilors and the Senate in assembly.

Those who suffer poverty at home should be registered also, along with their family, by two Senators for each parish, their needs ascertained, their manner of living up until then, and the reason for their decline into poverty. It will be easy to discover from their neighbors what kind of individuals they are, how they live, and what their habits are. However, the testimony of one pauper should not be taken too seriously concerning another pauper, for the one would not be free from jealousy of the other. The Councilors and Senate should be informed of all these things. If someone suddenly becomes destitute, he should notify them through one of the Senators; then his situation can be judged adequately, on the basis of his condition and circumstances.

Beggars in good health who wander about with no fixed dwelling-place should submit their names, and state the reason for their mendicancy to the Senate—however, in some open place or vacant lot, so that their filth may not pollute the Senate chamber. Beggars who are ill should do likewise in the presence of two or four Senators apart, along with a doctor, so that the eyes of the entire Senate may be spared. Witnesses should be sought out by both classes of paupers to testify in regard to their manner of life.

The Senators appointed to make these examinations and perform these duties should be given authority to coerce and compel obedience, even to the point of imprisonment, so that the Senate will be aware of the recalcitrant.

Means of providing necessities for these disadvantaged

From the outset this principle must be accepted which the Lord imposed on the human race as a punishment for its many sins—that each man should eat the bread which is the fruit of his labor. When I use the word "eat" or "nourish" or "support," I do not intend to suggest food alone, but clothes, shelter, fuel, and light; in a word, everything that is related to the sustenance of the body.

None among the poor should be idle, provided, of course, that he is fit for work by his age and health. As the Apostle writes to the Thessalonians [2 Thes. 3:10–12]–

> For even when we were with you, we commanded that if anyone will not work, then let him not eat. For we hear that some who walk among you in disorderly manner do not work at all, but are mere busybodies. Now, those who are like that we denounce, and exhort in the Lord Jesus Christ that they work in silence and eat their own bread.

And the Psalmist promises a double joy, both in this life and in the next, to him who has eaten out of the labor of his own hands. Therefore, no one must be permitted to live indolently in the state; rather, as in a well-ordered home, everyone has his own role and its related tasks to perform. As the saying goes, "By doing nothing, men learn to do evil."

Breakdowns in health and age must be taken into consideration. However, in order that a pretense of sickness or infirmity may not be foisted on you—which happens quite frequently—the opinion of physicians must be consulted. Impostors are to be penalized. Of the able-bodied vagrants, those who are aliens should be returned to their own country—as is provided for, according to Imperial law—but they should be supplied with money for the journey. It would be inhuman to send a destitute man on a journey with no provision for the trip; otherwise such a person might question, What is this measure other than commanding him to pillage on the way? If they are from areas ravaged by war, then the teaching of Paul must be borne in mind: that among those who have been baptized in the blood of Christ, there is neither Greek nor pagan, neither Frenchman nor Lowlander, but a new and elevated creature. Hence, these should be treated as though they were native-born.

Should the native-born poor be asked whether they have learned a trade? Yes, and those who have not—if they are of suitable age—should be taught the one to which they are most strongly attracted, provided that it is practical, or else a similar or related occupation. For example, if it is not possible for him to sew clothing, he could sew what they call *caligas* (soldiers' boots). If a craft is too difficult, or if he is too slow in learning, another and easier task should be assigned to him, all the way down to one in which he could be sufficiently instructed in a very short time, such as digging, drawing water, carrying loads, pushing a wheelbarrow, serving magistrates, running errands, carrying letters or mail packets, or driving the scheduled horses.

Even those who have dissipated their fortunes in dissolute living—through gaming, harlots, excessive luxury, gluttony, and gambling—should be given food, for no one should die of hunger. However, smaller rations and more irksome tasks should be assigned to them so that they may be an example to others. Perhaps they would come to repent of their prior life and not relapse as easily into the same vices, restrained as they are by the lack of food and the duress of their tasks. They must not die of hunger, but they must feel its pangs.

. . .

Since funds for such measures of support were originally given for the poor, they should be spent on the poor. I would like to remind bishops, theologians, and abbots of this, but will write for them elsewhere. I would hope that they would do these things spontaneously, without being urged on by me.

...

The able-bodied who remain in the hospitals like drones, living by the sweat of others, should leave and be put to work. However, some must be allowed to remain because of a given estate—such as the law of gentility—or the prerogative willed by a generous benefactor or because of having made over their property to the institution. Even in these cases, they should be obliged to work in the hospital so that the result of their labors may be shared by all. If anyone healthy and robust ask to be allowed to remain because of his love for the home and for his companions, he could be granted this favor, but on the same condition.

No one should be attracted by the money that was contributed earlier for pious works. This warning is not without foundation. For there are those who, from servants, have become masters. Ladies living delicately in splendor and luxury were originally admitted to perform works of piety; but now, having thrust out the poor or else keeping them grudgingly, they have become haughty mistresses. This office of ministration must be taken from them so that they will not grow fat from the pennies of the starving poor; so let them perform the duty which they came there to do. They should be intent upon ministering to the sick, like those widows of the early church who were so highly praised by the Apostles. In the balance of their time, they could pray, read, spin, weave, or occupy themselves in some good and honest labor—all of which Jerome advises for even the richest and most aristocratic matrons.

The blind should not be allowed to sit idle or wander about aimlessly. There are many occupations in which they might be employed. Some are suited for academic training; these should be allowed to study since their aptitude for letters is no small thing. Others are suited to the art of music; they could sing, pluck the lute, or play the flute. Others might turn weavers' wheels, work treadmills, tread winepresses, or blow bellows in the smithies. Still other blind are particularly skilled in making little boxes and chests, fruit-baskets and cages. Women who are blind could spin and wind yarn. Since it is easy enough to find employment for them, none of the blind should be willing to sit idle or avoid work. Laziness and a love of ease are the reasons for pretending they cannot do things, not physical defect.

The infirm and the aged, too, should have lighter tasks assigned them suited to their age and strength. No one is so feeble or lacking in strength that he can do nothing. It follows that the evil thoughts and affections likely in the minds of the idle will be controlled by those who are employed and intent upon work.

Then, when all the leeches have been eliminated from the hospitals, the resources of each institution should be examined, taking into account its regular expenses, annual revenues, and the money on hand. Treasure rooms and superfluous trappings should be eliminated, since they are only toys for children or misers, useless in a life of piety. Then, assign to each of the hospitals as many of the sick poor as it will seem proper, taking care that the food is not so scanty that their hunger will not be easily satisfied. This is one of the essentials in the care of those who are sick in body or mind, for invalids often grow worse from an inadequate diet. On the other hand, there should be no luxury by which they might easily fall into bad practices.

Now let us refer to the insane. Since there is nothing in the world more excellent than man, and nothing more excellent in man than his mind, particular care should be given to its welfare. It should be considered the highest of ministries to restore the mind of others to sanity, or to keep them sane and rational. Therefore, when a man of disturbed mental faculties is brought to the hospital, first of all, it must be determined whether his insanity is congenital or has resulted from some environmental cause, and whether there is hope for health or whether the case is completely hopeless. One ought to feel a compassion before such a great disaster to this noblest of human faculties. He who has suffered so should be treated with such care and delicacy that the cure will not enlarge or increase the condition, such as would result from mocking, exciting, or irritating him, approving and applauding the foolish things which he says or does, and inciting him to act more ridiculously, applying a stimulus, as it were, to his absurdity and stupidity. What could be more inhuman than to drive a man to insanity just for the sake of laughing at him and entertaining oneself with such a misfortune!

Remedies suited to the individual patient should be prescribed. Some need care and attention to their mode of living. Others need mild and gentle treatment so that, like wild animals, they may gradually grow less violent. Some require education. Some may need force and chains, but these should be used in such a way that the patients will not become the more violent because of them. Above all, as far as it is possible, tranquility must be introduced into their minds, for it is through this that reason and mental health return.

If the hospitals cannot accommodate all the diseased beggars, one or more homes should be built, as many as are necessary, where they can be treated separately. A doctor, a pharmacist, and male and female nurses should be hired. Doing this is what nature (as well as a builder of ships) does, locating the repugnant in one place so that it may not offend the rest of the body. Likewise, those afflicted with a loathsome or contagious disease should sleep and eat their food in a place apart so that their repulsive condition, or the infection itself, may not creep over the rest of the population—or else there will never be an end to disease.

When a patient recovers, he should be treated in the same manner as the rest who are healthy. He should be sent out to work unless, out of compassion, he would prefer to remain serving in the hospital with his particular skills.

For the poor who live at home, work should be furnished by the public officials, by the hospitals, or by private citizens. If their work is not enough to supply their needs, whatever seems adequate should be added to their earnings.

Investigators into the needs of the poor should perform their task humanely and kindly. While nothing should be given if the judgment on their needs is unfavorable, still intimidation should never be applied unless deemed necessary in dealing with the refractory or the rebels against public authority.

This one law should be inviolable: "If anyone request money or exert influence in favor of a person supposedly in need, he should not receive it; instead, there should be a penalty according as the Senate sees fit." It should always be permissible to inform the Senate of the needs of others. The administrators of charities—or whoever may be appointed by the Senate—should find the balance, and give alms in proportion to the need. This is to guard against the situation in the future when wealthy men, preserving their own moneys, might demand that money which belongs to the destitute should be expended on their own servants, domestics, relatives, and friends. Such favoritism steals from those who need it so much more, as we have already seen happen in the hospitals.

Provisions for children

A hospital must be established for abandoned children where they may be reared. If mothers are known, they should nurture the infants until the sixth year. After this age, all such children would enter a publicly supported school where they would be educated in letters and morals, and be maintained.

As far as possible, this school should be in charge of men who are trustworthy and who have a solid and broad education themselves, so that they may pour out their culture into this basic school with their own example. No greater danger for the sons of the poor exists than a cheap, inferior, and demoralizing education. In order to secure teachers of this upright character, magistrates should spare no expense. At relatively small cost, the latter will thus perform great service to the state over which they preside.

The students should learn to live frugally, but neatly and clean, and to be content with little. They should be protected from all forms of dissipation. They must not develop habits of intemperance and gluttony, becoming slaves of the belly. Otherwise, when they are deprived of something that their appetite calls for, they will shamelessly take up begging, as we have seen some do the moment they do not get, not just the food, but even their condiments such as mustard, sauce, or some such trifle.

They should be taught not only reading and writing but, above all, the duty of a Christian and right attitudes toward things.

I suggest a similar school for girls, in which they can be taught the fundamentals of literacy. If one girl is particularly qualified for studies and inclined to them, she should be permitted to progress farther, provided that the courses coincide with the development of her character. In addition to spinning, sewing, weaving, embroidery, cooking, and home management, all girls should be taught a virtuous perspective and morality as well as modesty, frugality, gentleness, good manners, and, primarily, chastity (convinced, as they ought to be, of the excellence of this virtue in women).

Any of the boys who are particularly skilled at letters should be retained by the school to become teachers themselves; later on, they might become candidates for the priesthood. The others should learn the trades in which they are most interested.

Supervisors and their duties

Two supervisors should be appointed every year from among the members of the Senate, eminent individuals of obvious integrity, to become acquainted with the way of life of the poor, of boys, youths, and old men alike.

With regard to boys, inquiry should be made concerning their occupations, the progress they are making, the sort of lives they lead, the talents they possess, the promise they show, and, if any one of them is in trouble, who is to blame. From these corrections can be made.

In regard to young adults and old men, the supervisors should inquire if they are living according to the laws governing them. Such investigators should also inquire most carefully concerning old women, who are master-hands at pandering and sorcery. Further, they should study whether all of these persons lead a frugal and sober life. Those who frequent gaming places and wine and beer taverns should be penalized. If reprimands have no effect, such persons should be punished severely.

A system of penalties should be devised in each state, as judged applicable by its wisest and most prestigious citizens. The same measures do not apply equally to all places and times; some men are influenced by some things, and others, by other things. In any case, the fraud of idle, lazy men must be guarded against so that deception has no profit.

I would also suggest that the supervisors investigate as well the youth who are the sons of the wealthy. It could be very valuable to the well-being of the state if they were to oblige such young men to render an account to the magistrates (as though to fathers) concerning their use of time, and what activities and occupations they follow. This could prove a greater alms than that which is distributed to the poor.

In ancient times, this service was provided by the office of Questor, or Censor, among the Romans, and among the Athenians in the court of Areopagus. When the old practices had deteriorated, they were revived by the Emperor Justinian in codifying the duties of the Questor. These included the injunction to survey all persons—both ecclesiastical and secular, of whatever rank and fortune—asking who they were, from whence they came, and for what reason they were there. That same law allowed no one to live in idleness.

39. WILLIAM SHAKESPEARE (1564–1616)

Shakespeare was born in Stratford-upon-Avon, the son of a prosperous glover. He married young (to Anne Hathaway, 1555/6–1623) but went to London to pursue a career as an actor and playwright. He was a prodigious author, producing all or much of at least 38 plays, sonnets, and other poetical works. He became a successful theatrical entrepreneur, forming companies of players with several patrons and partners, resulting in great fame and some considerable wealth. He is considered perhaps the greatest writer in the English language, and his work provides a deep insight into the human condition, both in his own time and for all times. He retired to his native Stratford where he died in 1616. The famous speech that follows, which Shakespeare puts into the mouth of the Greek hero Ulysses (Odysseus), reflects the Renaissance concept of the social hierarchy as part of the natural order.

Ulysses on Degree

From Troilus and Cressida, I.iii.75–137

ULYSSES Troy, yet upon his basis, had been down,
   And the great Hector's sword had lack'd a master,
   But for these instances.
   The specialty of rule hath been neglected:
   And, look, how many Grecian tents do stand
   Hollow upon this plain, so many hollow factions.   80
When that the general is not like the hive
To whom the foragers shall all repair,
   What honey is expected? Degree being vizarded,
The unworthiest shows as fairly in the mask.
The heavens themselves, the planets and this center
   Observe degree, priority and place,
Insisture, course, proportion, season, form,
Office and custom, in all line of order;
   And therefore is the glorious planet Sol
In noble eminence enthroned and sphere   90
   Amidst the other; whose medicinable eye
Corrects the ill aspects of planets evil,
And posts, like the commandment of a king,

Sans cheque to good and bad: but when
    the planets
In evil mixture to disorder wander,
What plagues and what portents! what mutiny!
What raging of the sea! shaking of earth!
Commotion in the winds! frights, changes, horrors,
Divert and crack, rend and deracinate
The unity and married calm of states   100
Quite from their fixure! O, when degree is shaked,
Which is the ladder to all high designs,
Then enterprise is sick! How could communities,
Degrees in schools and brotherhoods in cities,
Peaceful commerce from dividable shores,
The primogenitive and due of birth,
Prerogative of age, crowns, scepters, laurels,
But by degree, stand in authentic place?
Take but degree away, untune that string,
And, hark, what discord follows! each
    thing meets   110
In mere oppugnancy: the bounded waters
Should lift their bosoms higher than the shores
And make a sop of all this solid globe:
Strength should be lord of imbecility,
And the rude son should strike his father dead:
Force should be right; or rather, right and wrong,
Between whose endless jar justice resides,
Should lose their names, and so should
    justice too.
Then every thing includes itself in power,
Power into will, will into appetite;   120
And appetite, an universal wolf,
So doubly seconded with will and power,
Must make perforce an universal prey,
And last eat up himself. Great Agamemnon,
This chaos, when degree is suffocate,
Follows the choking.
And this neglection of degree it is
That by a pace goes backward, with a purpose
It hath to climb. The general's disdain'd
By him one step below, he by the next,   130
That next by him beneath; so every step,
Exampled by the first pace that is sick
Of his superior, grows to an envious fever
Of pale and bloodless emulation:
And 'tis this fever that keeps Troy on foot,
Not her own sinews. To end a tale of length,
Troy in our weakness stands, not in her
    strength.

6

Discovering New Worlds Abroad

GOING WEST

40. CHRISTOPHER COLUMBUS (1451–1506)

Colombus was born in Genoa into a family of artisans. He had little formal education but was a voracious reader who acquired considerable knowledge of geography, history, navigation, and cartography, as well as mastering later in life several languages, including Portuguese, Spanish, and Latin. His first experiences at sea were on Genoese trading vessels traveling to the eastern Mediterranean and into northern Europe. A brother had moved to Portugal where he worked as a cartographer, and Columbus spent time with him in Lisbon after 1479, even marrying there and having a son, Diego.

Some of his experience at sea also took him down the coast of Africa, where he acquired some knowledge of the currents and wind patterns on the Atlantic. The Ottoman conquest of Constantinople in 1453 and the new dangers and expense involved in dealing with Muslim-controlled regions drove him to believe that a safer, faster, and cheaper way for Europeans to access the very lucrative luxury and spice trade with the East was to sail west across the Atlantic. Columbus reached this conclusion based on a very inaccurate estimate of the distances between Europe and Japan, and a miscalculation of the circumference of the earth, despite the fact that the ancients had correctly determined its measurement of about 25,000 miles. Columbus estimated that Japan lay just 3,000 miles from the Canary Islands, when the actual distance is 12,178 miles.

To test his theory, he twice asked the king of Portugal—in 1485 and 1487—for ships and support for a voyage of discovery. He was rejected, as he was by his native Genoa, Venice, and England. In 1486 he sought an audience with the king and queen of Castile and Aragon, Ferdinand the Catholic and Isabella. They listened to his plans, but a learned advisory council rejected his plan as well, because it, too, realized that his distances were incorrectly determined. But the monarchs of the only recently dynastically united kingdoms were in need of money and new ventures. Consequently, they refused to reject Columbus altogether; rather, they placed him on a kind of retainer and asked for more evidence.

The successful defeat of the Muslims of Granada in 1492 and the uniting of the Iberian peninsula into the kingdom of Spain left Ferdinand and Isabella very short of money; and Columbus was relentless in his supplications to the Most Catholic monarchs. Eventually, the king and queen yielded to his entreaties and, with help from Italian investors as well as the Spanish treasury, Columbus was granted three ships and crews to discover and claim new territory for Spain and establish new commercial links with the East. Columbus was richly rewarded in titles and a share of any wealth he found, and the right to serve as viceroy of any newly discovered territory, as reflected in this excerpt.

Columbus made four voyages to the New World between 1492 and 1503, visiting islands in the Caribbean and assuming the vice-regal authority he had been promised. Charges of incompetence and brutality were, however, levelled against him and his brothers. So in 1500 he was arrested and sent back to Spain as a prisoner. There can be no doubt that Columbus was cruel and harsh in his role as governor. Nevertheless, the king of Spain ordered him freed, restored his wealth, and even financed his final voyage; however, his position as viceroy was not restored to him and another administrator was put in charge of the newly discovered territory. Columbus returned to Spain, where he died in 1506, believing until the end of his life that he had discovered islands off the coast of Asia rather than an entirely new continent.

The Privileges Accorded to Columbus by Ferdinand and Isabella

Granada Capitulations promising to confer on Columbus the offices of admiral, viceroy, and governor of the islands and mainland he might discover and the title of Sir.

Granada, 30 April 1492

[1] Sir Fernando and Lady Isabel, by the grace of God king and queen of Castile, Leon, Aragon, Sicily, Granada, Toledo, Valencia, Galicia, the Balearics, Seville, Sardinia, Cordoba, Corsica, Murcia, Jaen, the Algarve, Algeciras, Gibraltar and the Canary Islands, count and countess of Barcelona, lords of Vizcaya and Molina, dukes of Athens and Neopatria, counts of Roussillon and Cerdagne, marquises of Oristano and Goceano.

Because you, Christopher Columbus, are going at our command with some of our ships and personnel to discover and acquire certain islands and mainland in the Ocean Sea, and it is hoped that, with the help of God, some of the islands and mainland in the Ocean Sea will be discovered and acquired by your command and expertise, it is just and reasonable that you should be remunerated for placing yourself in danger for our service.

Wanting to honor and bestow favor for these reasons, it is our grace and wish that you, Christopher Columbus, after having discovered and acquired these islands and mainland in the Ocean Sea, will be our admiral of the islands and mainland that you discover and acquire and will be our admiral, viceroy, and governor of them. You will be empowered from that time forward to call yourself Sir Christopher Columbus, and thus your sons and successors in this office and post may entitle themselves sir, admiral, viceroy, and governor of them.

You and your proxies will have the authority to exercise the office of admiral together with the offices of viceroy and governor of the islands and mainland that you discover and acquire. You will have the power to hear and dispose of all the lawsuits and cases, civil and criminal, related to the offices of admiral, viceroy, and governor, as you determine according to the law, and as the admirals of our kingdoms are accustomed to administer it. You and your proxies will have the power to punish and penalize delinquents as well as exercising the offices of admiral, viceroy, and governor in all matters pertaining to these offices. You will enjoy and benefit from the fees and salaries attached, belonging, and corresponding to these offices, just as our high admiral enjoys and is accustomed to them in the admiralty of our kingdoms.

[2] With this our writ or its transcript certified by a public clerk, we order Prince Sir Juan, our most dear and very beloved son, and the princes, dukes, prelates, marquises, counts, masters, priors, and commanders of the orders; royal councillors, judges of our appellate court, and judges and any other justices of our household, court, and chancery; subcommanders and commanders of our

castles, forts, and buildings; all municipal councils, royal judges, *corregidores*, municipal judges, sheriffs, appeals judges, councilmen, parish delegates, commissioned and noncommissioned officers, municipal officials, and voting citizens of all the cities, towns, and villages of these our kingdoms and domains and of those that you may conquer and acquire; captains, masters, mates, warrant officers, sailors and ship's crews; and each and every one of our subjects and citizens now and in the future, that, having discovered and acquired any islands and mainland in the Ocean Sea, once you or your designated representative have performed the oath and formalities required in such cases, from then on you shall be accepted and regarded for the rest of your life, and your sons and successors after you forevermore, as our admiral of the Ocean Sea and viceroy and governor of the islands and mainland that you, Sir Christopher Columbus, discover and acquire.

[All these officials and people] shall put into effect everything pertaining to these offices, together with you and the proxies you appoint to the offices of admiral, viceroy, and governor. They shall pay and cause to be paid to you the salary, fees, and other perquisites of these offices. They shall observe and cause to be observed for you all the honors, gifts, favors, liberties, privileges, prerogatives, exemptions, immunities, and each and all of the other things that, by virtue of the offices of admiral, viceroy, and governor, you should receive and that should be paid to you fully and completely, in such a way that nothing will be withheld from you. They shall not place or consent to place hindrance, or obstacle against you in any way.

[3] For with this writ we grant to you from now on the offices of admiral, viceroy, and governor as a hereditary right forevermore, and we grant you actual and prospective possession of them, as well as the authority to administer them and collect the dues and salaries attached and pertaining to each of them.

[4] If it should be necessary for you, and you should request it of them, we command our chancellor, notaries, and other officials who preside over the table with our seals to give, issue, forward, and seal our letter of privilege with the circle of signatures, in the strongest, firmest, and most sufficient manner that you may request and find necessary. None of you or them shall do otherwise in any way concerning this, under penalty of our displeasure and a fine of 10,000 *maravedis* for our treasury on each person who does the contrary.

[5] Furthermore, we command the man who shows you this writ to summon you to appear before us in our court, wherever we may be, within fifteen days of having been cited, under the same penalty. Under this same penalty, we command every public clerk who may be summoned for this purpose to give the person showing this writ to him a certificate to that effect, inscribed with his rubric, so that we may know how well our command is obeyed.

[6] Given in our city of Granada on the thirtieth day of the month of April in the year of the birth of our Lord Jesus Christ one thousand four hundred and ninety-two.

I, the King

I, the Queen

[7] I, Juan de Coloma, secretary of the king and queen our lords, had this written at their command.

[8] Approved in form: Rodericus, doctor.

[9] Registered: Sebastian de Olano. Francisco de Madrid, chancellor.

Instructions to Columbus for colonization of the Indies, Burgos, 23 April 1497

[1] Sir Christopher Columbus, our admiral, viceroy and governor of the Ocean Sea.

In our opinion, the things that must be done and implemented, with the help of God our lord, above and beyond that which, by another of our writs, you and the bishop of Badajoz must provide for the settlement of the Indies and continent discovered and placed under our sovereignty, of those islands and mainland still to be discovered in the region of the Indies in the Ocean Sea, and of the people who, by our command, are already there and will go to live there in the future, are the following:

[2] First. When, God willing, you are in the Indies you shall endeavor with all diligence to encourage and lead the natives of the Indies to serve us and remain benignly under our sovereignty and subjection in peace and order, and especially to convert them to our holy Catholic faith. They and those who are going to live in the Indies shall be administered the holy sacraments by the monks and priests who are already there and those going now, so that God our lord may be served and their consciences may be satisfied.

[3] Item. From now until we order further, 330 persons may go with you, whom you shall choose with such qualifications and professions as stipulated in the instructions. If it seems to you that some of the instructions should be adjusted, however, by adding to some occupations and professions while reducing others, you or your proxy can do so, as you think will contribute to our service as well as the welfare and advantageous governance of the Indies.

[4] Item. When, God willing, you are in the Indies, you shall establish another settlement or fortress on the island of La Espanola, on the other side of the island from the one already in existence, near the gold mine in the place and form that seems best to you.

[5] Item. Near this new settlement or the one that is already established or in some other location that seems well situated to you, establish and introduce plowing and animal husbandry, so that the persons who are or will be residing on the island can sustain themselves better and more economically.

In order best to accomplish this, give to the farmers now going to the Indies up to fifty *cahices* of the wheat and barley being sent there, on loan for sowing, and up to twenty yokes of oxen, mares, or other plow stock. Farmers who receive the grain shall plow, sow, and obligate themselves to return [an equivalent amount of] grain to you at harvest time in addition to paying the tithe on what is harvested.

The farmers may sell the remaining grain to the Christians for as much as they can, provided that the prices do not cause undue hardship for those purchasing it. If the latter should occur, you, our admiral, or your representative must set and enforce a maximum price.

[6] Item. The 330 persons going to the Indies must be paid their wages at the rate that has been paid up to now. Instead of the maintenance that they are usually given, they must be provided with some of the grain that we are ordering sent there: to each person one *fanega* of wheat every month and 12 *maravedis* per day to buy other necessary food. This is to be issued to them by you, our admiral, or your proxy, and the agents of our chief accountants in the Indies. Our treasurer in the Indies shall pay them according to your roster, vouchers, and writs in the stipulated manner.

[7] Item. If you the admiral believe that it would be advantageous to our service if the total number of persons were increased from 330, you may do so up to a total of 500 persons, on the condition that the wages and food of these extra persons are paid from any merchandise and valuables acquired in the Indies, without our ordering provisions for them from elsewhere.

[8] Item. The persons who remain in the Indies shall be paid the wages owed them according to the roster, in the manner stipulated. Those who are not on the payroll are to be compensated for their service as appears best to you, and those who have worked for others likewise.

[9] Item. The posts, salaries, and wages of commanders and other principal persons and officials who live and serve there ought to be remunerated according to what seems proper to you, our admiral, taking into consideration the qualifications of each person and what work each has done and will do. In addition to this, when, God willing, the means to bestow favors in the Indies exists, we shall issue further instructions on how to do so. These shall be awarded by our officials, who will be notified to issue and pay them in the prescribed manner.

[10] Item. When the heirs of the abbot Gallego and Andres de Salamanca who died in the Indies appear, they should be paid the value of the casks and barrels that were used and confiscated from them for having gone to the Indies contrary to our prohibition.

[11] Item. Concerning the settlement of estates for those who die in the Indies, it seems to us the procedure should be observed that you described in a section of your report to us, which is as follows:

[12] "Many foreigners and citizens have died in the Indies, and I ordered, by virtue of the powers that I have from Your Highnesses, that they should draw up wills and that these should be executed. I gave responsibility to Escobar, citizen of Seville, and Juan de Leon, citizen of La Isabela, faithfully to discharge all this by paying what the deceased owed, if their executors had not paid it, as well as recovering all their property and wages. All this must be recorded by magistrates and public clerks. Everything accumulated should be placed in a chest with three locks: the executors will have one key, a monk another, and I the third. The money of the deceased shall be placed in this chest and remain there for up to three years, so that the heirs will have time to come for it or send to claim it. If they do not claim it in this time, it should be distributed in good works for their souls."

[13] Likewise, it seems to us that the gold obtained in the Indies should be minted and made into coins of Granada *excelentes* as we have ordered in these our kingdoms, in order to avoid the making of counterfeits from this gold in the Indies.

[14] In order to coin the money, we order that you take the persons, dies, and tools necessary, for which purpose we give you complete power, with the condition that the money coined in the Indies conforms to the ordinances that we now order to be made about the coining of money. The craftsmen who do the coining must observe these ordinances, under the stipulated penalties.

[15] Item. It seems to us that the Indians who have agreed to pay the ordered tax should wear a token of brass or lead that they can hang from the neck. The design or mark on this token should be changed each time one pays, so that it will be known if someone has not paid. Every time persons are found on the island without this

token hanging from the neck, have them arrested and given some light penalty.

[16] Because it will be necessary to appoint a diligent and trustworthy person to collect and receive the tribute, it is our wish and command that ... should have this office. From the tribute and merchandise that he receives, collects, and causes to be paid, he shall take and keep for himself five pesos, *medidas*, or *libras* per hundred, which is one-twentieth of what he is to receive and cause to be collected and received.

I, the King I, the Queen

[17] By order of the king and queen. Fernan Alvarez de Toledo.

[18] Agreed.

41. GONZALO FERNANDEZ DE OVIEDO (1478–1557)

Gonzalo Fernandez de Oviedo was born in Madrid and educated at the royal court. He was present at the return of Columbus from his first voyage to the New World and he knew the admiral's sons. In 1514 he took his first trip to the New World, in the same expedition as Bernal Díaz, acting as inspector of gold smelting. He spent many years there in various administrative and military positions, crossing the Atlantic twelve times. He died in Valladolid in 1557.

Most of Oviedo's output was historical. In 1526 he wrote a short natural history of the Indies, describing the flora and fauna, customs and mineral wealth of the new discovery. His work was well received at the Spanish court, and he was appointed General Chronicler of the Indies. In 1535 he published the first part of the General and Natural History of the Indies, *and he continued to work on the project until 1548, though the complete text was not published in his lifetime. Much of the history is an eyewitness account, but as chronicler of the Indies, Oviedo was given the authority to require accounts from all royal officials in the conquest. Oviedo uses this information, but he makes it clear to his reader when he is not speaking from personal knowledge, and indeed indicates any reservations he has as to the accuracy of his source. Oviedo was acutely aware of the intellectual problems posed by the discovery of the New World, and of the growing tension between the knowledge acquired by experience and the venerated learning of the ancients. He emphatically chooses experience, reminding the reader of his intimate familiarity with his subject material, though his broad education in the classics is also clear from his writing.*

General and Natural History of the Indies

BOOK II

CHAPTER 2

The origin and character of Christopher Columbus, first Admiral of the Indies, and common opinions of his motives in embarking on his discoveries

Some say that these lands were first known many centuries ago, and that their situation was written down and the exact latitudes noted in which they lay, but their geography and the sea routes by which they were to be reached were forgotten, and that Christopher Columbus, a learned man well read in the science of cosmography, set out to make a fresh discovery of these islands. I am inclined to believe this theory for reasons that I will explain in later chapters. But it is right to accept this man, to whom we owe so much, as the prime mover of this great enterprise, which he initiated for the benefit of all now living and those who shall live after us.

I will say that Christopher Columbus, as I've heard from men of his nation, was a native of the province of Liguria, in which lies the city and lordship of Genoa. Some give his birthplace as Savona, or a small town or village called Nervi, on the Levant coast two leagues from Genoa, but the most reliable story is that he came from Cugureo, which is also near Genoa. He was a man of decent life and parentage, handsome and well-built, and of more than average height and strength. His eyes were lively and his features well proportioned. His hair was chestnut brown and his complexion rather ruddy and blotchy; he was well spoken, cautious and extremely intelligent. He had good Latin and great cosmographical knowledge; he was charming when he wished to be and very testy when annoyed. His ancestors came from the city of Piacenza in Lombardy, which lies on the banks of the Po, and were members of the ancient family of Pelestrel. In the lifetime of his father Dominico, Christopher Columbus, now a well-educated young man who had attained his majority, left Italy for the Levant and traveled over the greater part of the Mediterranean, where he learnt navigation and put it to practical use. After several voyages in these restricted waters, having a mind for greater enterprises and wider prospects, he decided to see the great ocean and left for Portugal. Here he lived for some time in the city of Lisbon. From there, or wherever else he was, as a grateful son he sent some part of all he earned to his old father, whom he helped to support and who lived in some poverty with hardly enough money for his bare needs.

There is a story that a caravel sailing from Spain to England with a cargo of merchandise and provisions, wines and other goods, not to be found in England and generally sent there from Spain, was overwhelmed by such violent contrary winds that it was forced to run west for many days, in the course of which it sighted one or more of the Indies. A landing was made on one of these islands and naked people were seen like those found here today. When the winds, which had brought them here against their will, died down, they took aboard water and wood and sailed back on to their previous course. The story goes on to say that as the greater part of the ship's cargo consisted of food and wine the crew had sufficient to keep them alive on this long and arduous voyage and to make the return passage, meeting with favorable weather. They reached Europe safely and made for Portugal. The voyage had been extremely long and dangerous and they had all the time been greatly afraid. Moreover, though the winds had driven them swiftly on their course, the journey there and back had lasted four or five months, or possibly even more. In the course of that time almost all the ship's crew died. The only men to land in Portugal were the pilot and three or four of the sailors, and all these were so ill that they also died a short time after their arrival.

The story goes that this pilot was a close friend of Christopher Columbus and had some knowledge of the quadrant, and that he marked the position of this land he had discovered. He is said to have given this information very privately to Columbus, asking him to make a map and place upon it this land which he had seen. Columbus is said to have welcomed him into his house as a friend and got him medical treatment, for by now he was very sick. Nevertheless he died like the others; thus Columbus remained with sole knowledge of these islands, and this he kept to himself. According to some accounts, this pilot was an Andalusian, others make him Portuguese, others a Basque. Some accounts say that Columbus was at that time in the island of Madeira, others in the Cape Verde Islands and that it was at this or that place the caravel arrived and there that Columbus heard of these lands. Whether these events took place or not cannot be decided with certainty, but this romantic story is in common circulation in the form that I have set down. In my opinion it is a fiction. As St. Augustine says: "When the facts are obscure, it is better to exercise doubt than to argue an uncertain case." It is better to doubt what we do not know than to insist on facts that are not proven.

CHAPTER 3

The author's opinions concerning the alleged discovery and description of the islands by the Ancients

In the last chapter I gave a common story concerning the previous discovery of the Indies. Now I will set down my beliefs concerning Christopher Columbus's motives and the knowledge which emboldened him, as a man of some learning, to undertake this great enterprise, so memorable to the men of his and future times. He rightly recognized that these lands had been forgotten, for he had found them described—and of this I am in no doubt at all—as one-time possessions of kings of Spain. I should like to quote Aristotle on this matter. On leaving the Straits of Gibraltar for the Atlantic ocean, he said, some Carthaginian merchants discovered a large island which had never been discovered before and was inhabited only by wild animals. It was therefore entirely wild and covered with large trees. It had great rivers on which ships could sail and was very fertile; everything that was planted there germinated and produced an abundant crop. This island was very remote, lying far off the coast of Africa at a distance of several days' sailing. On reaching it, these Carthaginian merchants, inspired by the fertility of the soil and the mildness of the climate, began to settle and build farms and villages. On learning this the Carthaginians in their senate proclaimed under pain of death that thenceforth none should sail for this land and that all those who had been there should be put to death.

For the fame of this island was so high that if any other nation or empire were to hear of it it would conquer it and thus become a very formidable enemy to Carthage and its liberties.

This story is included in the repertory of Brother Theophilus de Ferrariis of Cremona, in his *Vitae regularis sacri ordinis predicatorum* which cites Aristotle's *De admirandis in natura auditis*.

[Oviedo now tells the story of the legendary Hesperus, twelfth king of Spain in descent from Tubal Cain, who was present at the fall of the Tower of Babel. He bases a long and fanciful argument on the fabulous histories of Beroso and Isidore of Seville, and on the evidence of various early geographers proves that the Fortunate Islands, known as the Hesperides after King Hesperus, were not the Canaries, as was generally assumed, but the Indies themselves. From this he develops an argument that, while admitting Columbus's courage, minimizes his achievement and suggests that he was not discovering but rediscovering the New World.]

The islands known as the Hesperides mentioned by Sebosus and Solinus, Pliny and Isidore must undoubtedly be the Indies and must have belonged to the Kingdom of Spain ever since Hesperus's time, who, according to Beroso, reigned 1,650 years before the birth of Our Lord. Therefore, if we add the 1,535 years since Our Savior came into the world, the kings of Spain have been lords of the Hesperides for 3,193 years in all. So by the most ancient rights on this account and for other reasons that will be stated during the description of Christopher Columbus's voyages, God has restored this realm to the kings of Spain after many centuries. It appears therefore that divine justice restored to the fortunate and Catholic Kings Ferdinand and Isabel[la], conquerors of Granada and Naples, what had always been theirs and belongs to their heirs in perpetuity. In their time and by their commands, the admiral Christopher Columbus discovered this New World (or a very large part of it), which had been completely forgotten: during the reign of his Imperial Majesty, our Lord Charles V, these regions have been more widely explored and his empire thus largely extended.

All the authors whom I have mentioned indicate that these Hesperides were in fact the Indies, and I believe that Columbus followed their authority (or perhaps that of others that were known to him) when he set out on his long voyage, boldly risking so many dangers in search of the lands that he found. Whether or not he was guided by this knowledge, he undertook a journey into these seas which none had undertaken before him and which neither he nor any other sailor would have risked without the authority of these early geographers.

CHAPTER 4

That Christopher Columbus was the first to teach the Spaniards to navigate by taking the altitudes of the sun and the North Star. He goes to Portugal and other lands, seeking help and support for his project of discovering the Indies. The Catholic sovereigns, Ferdinand and Isabella, receive information about him, and at their command he makes his discovery.

Many are of the opinion (which is well supported by convincing arguments) that Christopher Columbus was the first in Spain to teach the art of navigating the wide ocean seas by measuring the height in degrees of the sun and the North Star. He was the first to practice the art, for, before his time, though it was taught in the schools, few (in fact none) had dared to try it out at sea. For this is a science which cannot be translated into actual knowledge unless it is practiced in very large stretches of sea far from the coasts. Till then steersmen, pilots and seamen had exercised their craft by trial and error, relying on the knowledge of the captain or pilot, but not scientifically as is done today with our present knowledge of the seas. They steered as in the Mediterranean, along the shores of Spain and Flanders, the rest of Europe and Africa, and everywhere else, by hugging the coast. But in order to sail in search of provinces as distant as the Indies are from Spain, the pilot must make use of the science of the quadrant, which is practicable only in such vast expanses of sea as those lying between here [Santo Domingo, where Oviedo was writing] and Europe or our possessions in the Spicelands at the western end of the mainland of these Indies.

Impelled by his desire for discovery and having achieved practical mastery of the secret of navigation (touching the plotting of the course), Columbus set about seeking support. Perhaps he relied on this scientific mastery, perhaps on information received from the pilot, who is said to have given him an account of these unknown lands, either in Portugal, or in the Azores (supposing this story to be true), perhaps on the authorities mentioned in my last chapter or perhaps he was impelled in some other way. In any case, Columbus worked through his brother Bartholomew on King Henry VII of England (father of the present King Henry VIII) to support him and equip him with ships in which to discover these western seas, offering to give him great wealth and to increase his realm and estates with new kingdoms and lordships.

After consulting his counsellors and certain men whom he had asked to examine Columbus's proposals, the King laughed at the idea, considering all that Columbus said to be nonsense.

In no way disconcerted when Columbus saw that his services would not be accepted in England, he began to open negotiations of the same kind with King John II of Portugal. King John was no more convinced by Columbus, although he was living and had married in that kingdom and by his marriage had become a subject of Portugal. Uninfluenced by this, King John refused either to support or aid Columbus in his project and put no trust in him.

He decided therefore to go to Castile, and on arriving at Seville made the acquaintance of the illustrious and brave Don Enrique Guzman, Duke of Medina-Sidonia. Not finding in him the support that he was seeking, he moved on to open new negotiations with the illustrious Don Luis de la Cerda, first Duke of Medina Celi, who also found his proposals fantastic, though some say that this duke agreed to equip Columbus in his city of Puerto de Sancta Maria, but was refused a license to do so by the Catholic sovereigns. Therefore, since theirs was the highest authority, Columbus went to their most serene Catholic Majesties—King Ferdinand and Queen Isabella, and spent some time at their court in great poverty, meeting with no response from those to whom he spoke.

Remaining there in great straits he endeavored to persuade those fortunate sovereigns to support him and equip some caravels, in which he might discover this new world (or regions unknown to him at this time) in their royal name. But this project was alien to the ideas of those to whom he proposed it. It did not please them, nor did they share the hopes of its great success in which Columbus alone believed. Not only did they attach little credit to his ideas; they actually considered that he was talking nonsense. He persisted in his suit for almost seven years, repeatedly holding out great prospects of wealth and riches for the crown of Castile. But as his cloak was poor and ragged, he was considered a dreamer and everything he said was taken to be fantastic. Being an unknown foreigner he found none to back him. What is more, the projects which he laid before them were great and unheard of. But see God's care in giving the Indies to their rightful owners! The offer had been made to the mighty kings of England and of Portugal and to those two rich dukes I have mentioned. He did not permit any of them to risk the small sum that Columbus asked. Disappointed by all these princes, Columbus went in search of the Catholic sovereigns, whom he found occupied at that time in their holy war against the Moors of the Kingdom of Granada.

It is no marvel that such Catholic princes should be more concerned with winning souls for salvation than with treasure and new estates which would only increase their royal cares and responsibilities, nor that they decided to back this project of discovery. But let no one believe that this alone could account for their good fortune, for eye had never seen, nor ear heard, nor human heart dreamed of the rewards prepared by God for those who love Him. These and many other blessings fell to our good sovereigns for their faithful service to Jesus Christ and their fervent desire for the spread of His holy faith. It was for this purpose that the Lord brought Christopher Columbus to their notice, for He sees the ends of the earth and all that happens beneath the sky. And when in due season this great business was concluded, it was God's purpose that was to be fulfilled.

During the time when Columbus was at court he lodged at the house of Alonso de Quintanilla, chief accountant to the Catholic sovereigns, a man of importance greatly devoted to their service and anxious for the extension of their power. Pitying Columbus's poverty he gave him food and money for his needs. In him Columbus found more support and understanding than in anyone else in Spain. On this gentleman's introduction, Columbus was received by the most reverend and illustrious Pedro Gonzalez de Mendoza, Cardinal of Spain and Archbishop of Toledo, who, on giving Columbus a first hearing, recognized him as a man of fair speech and learning who argued his case well. Realizing that he had a good intelligence and great knowledge he formed a favorable impression of Columbus and took pain to back him.

Thanks to the support of the cardinal and of Quintanilla, Columbus was received by the King and Queen and they immediately attached some credit to his written proposals and petitions. The business was finally concluded while the sovereigns were besieging the great and famous city of Granada [the last Moorish city in Spain], in the year 1492. From their royal camp which they had built in the midst of their army and had named Santa Fé the blessed sovereigns concluded their agreement with Columbus; there, in the camp-city of the Holy Faith and in the holy faith that lay in their Highnesses' hearts, this discovery had its beginnings.

Not content with the holy and victorious enterprise which they had in hand, and by which they finally subdued all the Moors in Spain, who had insulted and maltreated Christians since the year 720 (as many chroniclers agree), these blessed princes, in addition to bringing the whole of Spain to our Catholic religion, decided to send an expedition in search of this new world and propagate the Christian faith there, for they devoted every hour to the service of God. For this holy purpose they ordered Columbus to be dispatched, giving him authority under the royal seal to hire three caravels of the type he required in Andalusia, with all necessary crews and provisions, for this long voyage whose only hope of success lay in the pious zeal and holy purpose of these Christian princes, under whose auspices and by whose commands this great adventure began. And since he needed money for his expedition, sufficient to prepare his ships and set out on the first discovery of the Indies, on account of the costly war this was lent him by Luis de Santangel, the financial secretary. A first grant and agreement was made by the sovereigns to Columbus in the city of Santa Fé, in the Kingdom of Granada, on 18 April 1492, before secretary Juan de Coloma. And the agreement was confirmed by a royal appointment given to him thirteen days later in the city of Granada on 30 April of the same year 1492, and with this authority Columbus departed, as has been said, and went to the city of Palos de Moguer, where he prepared for his voyage.

42. BERNAL DÍAZ (1492–1581)

Bernal Díaz was born in Medina del Campo in Spain, and he died at the age of 89 on his estates in Guatemala. He was over 70 when he began writing his story of the Conquest, and at one point almost gave up on it, before finishing it at about the age of 84. Díaz was the last survivor of the Conquest of Mexico, and his narrative has the value of an eyewitness account. Díaz himself recognized that he was no great stylist, and this embarrassment at his lack of polish was largely responsible for his almost abandoning the project. However, his concern at his own shortcomings was outweighed by his annoyance at the inaccuracy of other accounts of the Conquest, and his desire to present the true version of events eventually drove him to finish his narrative.

Díaz's account not only has the vivid detail of the personal account, but is also imbued with his own awareness of the magnitude of the conquerors' accomplishment. He was no idealist, and he recognized the greed of the soldiers and their cruelty to the Aztecs. However, he was also aware of their sense of mission, and was convinced that the success of such a small and isolated group could be attributed only to the intervention of God, who, in Díaz's eyes, clearly wished New Spain and its inhabitants to be ruled by Charles V and the Catholic Church.

The Expedition of Francisco Hernández de Córdoba

I, Bernal Díaz del Castillo, governor of the town of Santiago, in Guatemala, author of this very true and faithful history, have now finished it, in order that it may be published to the world. It treats of the discovery and total conquest of New Spain; and how the great city of Mexico and several other towns were taken, up to the time when peace was concluded with the whole country; also of the founding of many Spanish cities and towns, by which we, as we were in duty bound, extended the dominion of our sovereign.

In this history will be found many curious facts worthy of notice.... What I have written in this book I declare and affirm to be strictly true. I myself was present at every battle and hostile encounter. Indeed, these are not old tales or romances of the seventh century; for, if I may so say, it happened but yesterday what is contained in my history. I relate how, where, and in what manner these things took place; as an accredited eyewitness of this I may mention our very spirited and valorous captain Don Hernando Cortes, marquis del Valle Oaxaca, who wrote an account of these occurrences from Mexico to his imperial majesty Don Charles the Fifth, of glorious memory; and likewise the corresponding account of the viceroy Don Antonio de Mendoza. But, besides this, you have only to read my history and you see it is true.

I have now completed it this 26th day of February, 1568, from my day-book and memory, in this very loyal city of Guatemala, the seat of the royal court of audience. I also think of mentioning some other circumstances which are for the most part unknown to the public.

Chapter I

THE TIME OF MY DEPARTURE FROM CASTILE, AND WHAT FURTHER HAPPENED TO ME

In the year 1514 I departed from Castile in the suite of Pedro Arias de Avila, who had just then been appointed governor of Terra Firma. At sea we had sometimes bad and sometimes good weather, until we arrived at Nombre Dios, where the plague was raging: of this we lost many of our men, and most of us got terrible sores on our legs, and were otherwise ill. Soon after our arrival, dissensions arose between the governor and a certain wealthy cavalier, named Vasco Nuñez de Balboa, who had brought this province to subjection, and was married to one of the daughters of Avila. As, however, suspicion had been excited against him, owing to a plan he had formed of making a voyage to the South Sea at his own expense, for which he required a considerable body of troops, his own father-in-law deposed him and afterwards sentenced him to decapitation.

While we were spectators of all this, and saw, moreover, how other soldiers rebelled against their superior officers, we learnt that the island of Cuba had just been conquered, and that a nobleman of Quellar, named Diego Velasquez, was appointed governor there. Upon this news some of us met together, cavaliers and soldiers, all persons of quality who had come with Pedro Arias de Avila, and asked his permission to proceed to the island of Cuba: this he readily granted, not having sufficient employment for so great a number of men as he had brought with him from Spain. Neither was there any further conquest to be made in these parts; all was in profound peace, so thoroughly had his son-in-law Balboa subdued the country, besides which it was but small in extent and thinly populated. As soon, therefore, as we had obtained leave, we embarked in a good vessel and took our departure. Our voyage was most prosperous, so that we speedily arrived at Cuba. The first thing we did was to pay our respects to the governor, who received us with great kindness, and made us a promise of the first Indians that might be discharged. Three years, however, passed away since our first arrival in Terra Firma and stay at Cuba, still living in the expectation of the Indians which had been promised us, but in vain. During the whole of this time we had accomplished nothing worthy of notice: we therefore, the 110 who had come from Terra Firma, with some others of Cuba, who were also without any Indians, met together to concert measures with a rich cavalier named Francisco Hernández de Córdoba, who, besides being a person of wealth, possessed great numbers of Indians on the island. This gentleman we chose for our captain; he was to lead us out on voyages for the discovery of new countries, where we might find sufficient employment.

We purchased three vessels, two of which were of considerable burden; the third was given us by the governor, Diego Velasquez, on condition namely, that we should first invade the Guanajas islands, which lie between Cuba and the Honduras, and bring him thence three cargoes of Indians, whom he wanted for slaves; this he would consider as payment for the vessel. We were, however, fully aware that it was an act of injustice which Diego Velasquez thus required at our hands, and gave him for answer: that neither God nor the king had commanded us to turn a free people into slaves. When he learnt our determination, he confessed that our project for the discovery of new countries was more praiseworthy, and he furnished us with provisions for our voyage.

We had now three vessels and a sufficient supply of cassava bread, as it is there made from the juca root. We also purchased some pigs, which cost us three pesos apiece; for at that time there were neither cows nor sheep on the island of Cuba: to this I must also add a scanty supply of other provisions; while every soldier took with him some glass beads for barter. We had three pilots; of whom the principal one, who had the chief command of our vessels, was called Anton de Alaminos, a native of Palos; the two others were Camacho de Triana, and Juan Alvarez el Manquillo of Huelva. In the same way we hired sailors, and furnished ourselves with ropes, anchors, water-casks, and other necessaries for our voyage, all at our own expense and personal risk.

After we had met together, in all 110, we departed for a harbor on the north coast of Cuba, called by the natives Ajaruco. The distance from this place to the town of San Cristobal, then recently built, was twenty-four miles; for the Havana had then only been two years in our possession. In order that our squadron might not want for anything really useful, we engaged a priest at the town of San Cristobal. His name was Alonso Gonzalez, and by fair words and promises we persuaded him to join us. We also appointed, in the name of his majesty, a treasurer, called Beruardino Miguez, a native of Saint Domingo de la Calzada. This was done in order that if it pleased God we should discover any new countries, where either gold, silver, or pearls were to be found, there might be amongst us a qualified person to take charge of the fifths for the Emperor. After everything had been thus properly ordered and we had heard mass said, we commended ourselves to God, our Lord Jesus Christ, and the Virgin Mary his blessed mother, and set out on our voyage, as I shall further relate.

Chapter II

OF THE DISCOVERY OF YUCATAN, AND THE BATTLE WE FOUGHT THERE WITH THE NATIVES

We sailed in the year 1517 from the harbor of Jaruco and left the Havana. This harbor lies on the north coast of Cuba, and is so called by the natives. After twelve days' sail we had passed the coast of Saint Antonius, which in Cuba is called the country of the Guanatavies, a wild tribe of Indians. We now made for the wide ocean, steering continually towards the west, totally ignorant of the shoals and currents or of the winds which predominate in this latitude. Certainly most hazardous on our part, and indeed we were very soon visited by a terrible storm, which continued two days and two nights, in which the whole of us had nigh perished.

After the storm had abated and we had changed our course, we came in sight of land on the twenty-first day after our departure from Cuba, which filled every heart with joy and thanks towards God. This country had never been discovered before, nor had any one ever heard of it. From our ships we could perceive a considerable sized town, which lay about six miles from the sea shore. On account of its magnitude, and because it was larger than any town in Cuba, we gave it the name of *Grand Cairo*.

We resolved that our smallest vessel should near the shore as much as possible, to learn the nature of the spot and look out for a good anchorage. One morning, the 5th of March, we perceived five large canoes full of men coming towards us as swift as their paddles and sails could bring them from the town just mentioned. These canoes were hollowed out of the trunks of large trees, after the manner of our kneading troughs. Many of them were big enough to hold from forty to fifty Indians.

As these Indians approached us in their canoes, we made signs of peace and friendship, beckoning at the same time to them with our hands and cloaks to come up to us that we might speak with them; for at that time there was nobody amongst us who understood the language of Yucatan or Mexico. They now came along side of us without evincing the least fear, and more than thirty of them climbed on board of our principal ship. We gave them bacon and cassava bread to eat, and presented each with a necklace of green glass beads. After they had for some time minutely examined the ship, the chief, who was a *cazique* [military leader], gave us to understand by signs that he wished to get down again into his canoe and return home, but that he would come the next day with many more canoes in order to take us on shore. These Indians wore a kind of cloak made of cotton, and a small sort of apron which hung from their hips half-way down to the knee, which they termed a *maltates*. We found them more intelligent than the Indians of Cuba, where only the women wear a similar species of apron made of cotton, which hangs down over their thighs, and is called by them a *nagua*.

But to continue my narrative. Very early the morning following, our *cazique* again called upon us: this time he brought with him twelve large canoes and a number of rowers. He made known to our captain, by signs, that we were good friends and might come to his town: he would give us plenty to eat with everything we wanted, and could go on shore in his twelve canoes. I shall never forget how he said, in his language, *con escotoch, con escotoch*, which means, come with me to my houses yonder. We therefore called the spot Punta de Cotoche, under which name it stands on the sea charts.

In consideration of all these friendly invitations from the *cazique* to accompany him to his village, our captain held a short consultation with us, when we came to the resolution to lower our boats, take the smallest of our vessels with us, and so proceed together with the twelve canoes all at once on shore, as the coast was crowded with Indians from the above-mentioned village. This was accordingly done, and we all arrived there at the same time. The *cazique* seeing us now landed, but that we made no signs of going to his village, again gave our captain to understand, by signs, that we should follow him to his habitation, making at the same time so many demonstrations of friendship, that a second consultation was held as to whether we should accompany him or not. This was carried in the affirmative, but we took every precaution to be upon our guard, marching in close order with our arms ready for action. We took fifteen crossbows with a like number of matchlocks, and followed the *cazique*, who was accompanied by a great number of Indians.

As we were thus marching along, and had arrived in the vicinity of several rocky mountains, the *cazique* all at once raised his voice, calling aloud to his warriors, who it seemed were lying wait in ambush, to fall upon us and destroy us all. The *cazique* had no sooner given the signal, than out rushed with terrible fury great numbers of armed warriors, greeting us with such a shower of arrows, that fifteen of our men were immediately wounded. These Indians were clad in a kind of cuirass made of cotton, and armed with lances, shields, bows, and slings; with each a tuft of feathers stuck on his head. As soon as they had let fly their arrows, they rushed forward and attacked us man to man, setting furiously to with their lances, which they held in both hands. When, however, they began to feel the sharp edge of our swords, and saw what destruction our crossbows and matchlocks made among them, they speedily began to give way. Fifteen of their number lay dead on the field.

At some distance from the spot where they had so furiously attacked us was a small place in which stood three houses built of stone and lime. These were temples in which were found many idols made of clay which were of a pretty good size; some had the countenances of devils, others those of females: some again had even more horrible shapes, and appeared to represent Indians committing horrible offences. In these temples we also found small wooden boxes containing other of their gods with hellish faces, several small shells, some ornaments, three crowns, and other trinkets, some in the shape of fish, others in the shape of ducks, all worked out of an inferior kind of gold. Seeing all this, the gold, and the good architectural style of the temples, we felt overjoyed at the discovery of this country; for Peru was not discovered till sixteen years after. While we were fighting with the Indians, the priest Gonzalez ordered the gold and small idols to be removed to our ships by two Indians whom we had brought with us from Cuba. During the skirmish we took two of the natives prisoners, who subsequently allowed themselves to be baptised and became Christians. One was named Melchior and the other Julian; both were tattooed about the eyes. The combat with the natives now being at an end, we resolved to re-embark, and prosecute our voyage of discovery further along the coast towards the west. Having dressed the wounds of our men we again set sail.

Chapter III

DISCOVERY OF THE COAST OF CAMPEACHY
Continuing the course we had previously determined upon, more westward along the coast, we discovered many promontories, bays, reefs, and shallows. We all considered this country to be an island, because our pilot, Anton de Alaminos, persisted in it. During daytime we proceeded with all caution, but lay to at nights. After sailing in this way for fourteen days, we perceived another village which appeared to us of considerable magnitude. Here was a bay with an inner harbor, and it appeared to us that there might also be some river or small stream where we could take in fresh water, which latter had become very scarce, as our supply in the casks, which were none of the best, was fast diminishing; for, as the expedition was fitted out solely by persons in poor circumstances, we had not been able to purchase good ones. It happened to be Sunday Lazari when we landed, and we therefore named this place in honor of this day, although we were well aware that the Indians called it the land of *Campeachy*.

In order that the whole of us might land at the same time, we determined to go on shore in our smallest vessel and three boats, all of us well armed, to be ready in case we should meet with a similar encounter as at the cape of Cotoche. The sea in these bays and roads is very shallow, so that our vessels were forced to anchor at more than three miles distance from the shore. Thus, having taken precautions, we landed near the village, but were still a good way from the place where we intended to fill our casks. From this spot the natives also had their water; for we now found that there was no rivulet in the neighborhood.

When we had brought our casks on shore, filled them with water, and were about to embark again, about fifty Indians from the village came up to us. They all wore stately mantles made of cotton, appeared friendly disposed, and to be *caziques*. They asked us, by signs, what our business was there? We told them to take in water, and that we were about to re-embark. They further pointed with their hands to the rising of the sun, and asked us whether we came from that quarter, at the same time pronouncing the word *Castilan, Castilan*; but at that moment we did not pay any particular attention to the word Castilan. In the course of this interview, however, they gave us to understand that we might go with them to their village.

We held a consultation amongst ourselves as to whether we should accept the invitation, and at length unanimously agreed to follow them, but to use the utmost circumspection. They took us to some large edifices, which were strongly put together, of stone and lime, and had otherwise a good appearance. These were temples, the walls of which were covered with figures representing snakes and all manner of gods. Round about a species of altar we perceived several fresh spots of blood. On some of the idols there were figures like crosses, with other paintings representing groups of Indians. All this astonished us greatly as we had neither seen nor heard, of such things before. It appeared to us that the inhabitants had just been sacrificing some Indians to their gods, to obtain from them the power to overcome us.

There were great numbers of Indians with their wives who received us with pleasing smiles, and otherwise made every show of friendship; but their numbers gradually increasing we began to entertain fears that it would end in the same hostile manner as at Cape Cotoche. While we were thus looking on, a number of Indians approached us clad in tattered cloaks, each carrying a bundle of dried reeds, which they arranged in order on the ground. Among them we also perceived two troops of men armed with bows, lances, shields, slings, and stones, having their cotton cuirasses on. At the head of these, and at some distance from us stood the chiefs. At this moment ten Indians came running out of another temple, all dressed in long white robes, while the thick hair of their heads was so entangled and clotted with blood that it would have been an impossibility to have combed or put it in order without cutting it off. These personages were priests, and in New Spain are commonly termed *Papas*. I repeat it, that in New Spain they are termed papas, and I will therefore in future call them by that name. These papas brought with them a kind of incense, which looked like resin, and is termed by them copal. They had pans made of clay filled with glowing embers, and with these they perfumed us. They also gave us to understand by signs that we should leave their country before the bundles of reeds, which had been brought and were going to be set fire to, should be consumed, otherwise they would attack and kill us every man.

Upon this they ordered the bundles to be lighted, and as soon as they began to burn, all were silent, nor did they utter another syllable. Those, on the contrary, who had ranged themselves in order of battle, began to play on their pipes, blow their twisted shells, and beat their drums. When we saw what their real intentions were, and how confident they appeared, it of course reminded us that our wounds which we had received at Cape Cotoche were not yet healed; that two of our men had died of the consequences, whom we had been obliged to throw overboard. As the number of Indians continued to increase, we became alarmed, and resolved to retreat to the shore in the best order we could. In this way we marched along the coast until we arrived at that spot where our boats and the small vessels lay with the water-casks. Not far distant from this place stood a rock in the midst of the sea; for, on account of the vast numbers of Indians, we durst not venture to re-embark where we had at first landed, as they would no doubt have fallen upon us while we were getting into our boats.

After we had thus managed to get our water safe on board and re-embark at the small harbor which the bay here forms, we continued our course for six days and six nights without interruption, the weather being very fine. But now the wind suddenly veered round to the north and brought stormy weather, as is always the case with a north wind on this coast. The storm lasted twenty-four hours, and indeed we had nearly all of us met with a watery grave, so boisterous was the sea. In order to save ourselves from total destruction we cast anchor near the shore. The safety of our ship now depended upon two ropes, and had they given way we should have been cast on shore. Oh, in what a perilous situation we were then placed! Had we been torn away from our anchors we must have been wrecked off the coast! But it was the will of Providence that our old ropes and cables should preserve us. When the storm had abated we continued our course along the coast and kept in as much as possible, that we might take in water when required. For, as I have before stated, our casks were old and leaky; nor was the best economy used with the water, for we thought by going on shore we should be certain either to meet with some spring or obtain it by digging wells. Thus coasting along we espied a village from our ships, and about three miles further on there was a kind of inner harbor, at the head of which it appeared to us there might be some river or brook; we therefore resolved to land here.

The water, as I have above mentioned, being uncommonly shallow along this coast, we were compelled to anchor our two larger vessels at about three miles distance from the shore, fearing they might otherwise run aground. We then proceeded with our smallest vessel and all our boats in order to land at the above-mentioned inner harbor. We were, however, quite upon our guard, and carried along with us, besides the water-casks, our arms, crossbows, and muskets.

It was about midday when we landed. The distance from here to the village, which was called Potonchan, might be three miles. Here we found some wells, corn plantations, and stone buildings. Our water-casks were soon filled, but we could not succeed to get them into our boats on account of an attack made upon us by great numbers of the inhabitants. I will, however, break off here and relate the battle we fought, in the next chapter.

Chapter IV

HOW WE LANDED IN A BAY CLOSE TO SOME CORN PLANTATIONS, NEAR THE HARBOR OF POTONCHAN, AND OF THE ATTACK THAT WAS MADE UPON US THERE

While we were busy taking in water, near the above-mentioned houses and corn plantations, great numbers of Indians were making towards us from the village of Potonchan, as it is termed by the natives. They had all their cotton cuirasses on, which reached to their knees, and were armed with bows, lances, shields, and swords. The latter were shaped like our broadswords, and are wielded with both hands. They also had slings and stones, their bunches of feathers on, and their whole bodies painted with white, brown, and black colors. They approached us in profound silence, as if they came with the most peaceable intentions, and inquired of us by signs if we came from the rising of the sun, thereby pronouncing the very same words which the inhabitants of St. Lazaro had used: namely, *Castilan, Castilan*. We told them, likewise by signs that we indeed came from the rising of the sun. We certainly did not understand what they meant; nevertheless it was something for us to reflect on, while it at the same time gave rise to a variety of conjectures, since the natives of St. Lazaro had used the identical words.

It was about the hour of Ave Maria, when the Indians approached us in this manner. A few rural houses were scattered round about the neighborhood. We took the precaution to post watches in different quarters, and upon the whole kept a sharp look out, as the manner in which the natives were assembling seemed to forebode very little good. When we had closed our ranks and taken every necessary precaution, our ears were assailed by the cries and yells of large bodies of Indians who were advancing from different quarters. As they were all armed for battle we could no longer doubt that some evil design was lurking behind; we therefore held a consultation with our captain as to the course we should adopt. Many were of opinion that the best we could do would be to re-embark ourselves in all haste; but, as is always the case in critical moments, one advised this and another that, and so this proposal was overruled as unadvisable, for the vast numbers of Indians would certainly fall upon us while we were getting into our boats and we should all stand in danger of being killed. Others again, among which number I also was, were of opinion that the enemy should be attacked that very night; for, according to the old saying, he who strikes the first blow remains master of the field; but we might make up our minds that each of us singly would have to encounter thirty Indians at least.

Day now began to dawn, and we emboldened each other to meet the coming severe conflict by putting our trust in God and commending our cause to him, while everyone was determined to defend himself to the utmost. As soon as daylight had fully broken forth, we perceived more troops of armed natives moving towards the coast with flying colors. They had on their feather-knots, and were provided with drums, bows, lances, shields, and joined themselves to the others who had arrived in the night. They divided themselves into different bodies, surrounded us on all sides, and commenced pouring forth such showers of arrows, lances, and stones, that more than eighty of our men were wounded at the first onset. They next rushed furiously forward and attacked us man to man: some with their lances, others with their swords and arrows, and all this with such terrible fury that we were compelled also to show them earnest. We dealt many a good thrust and blow amongst them, keeping up at the same time an incessant fire with our muskets and crossbows; for while some loaded others fired. At last, by dint of heavy blows and thrusts we forced them to give way; but they did not retreat further than was necessary, in order that they might still continue to hem us in in all safety; constantly crying out in their language, *Al calachoni, al calachoni*; which signifies, kill the chief! And sure enough our captain was wounded in no less than twelve different places by their arrows. I myself had three; one of which was in my left side and very dangerous, the arrow having pierced to the very bone. Others of our men were wounded by the enemy's lances, and two were carried off alive; of whom, one was called Alonzo Bote, the other was an old Portuguese.

Perceiving how closely we were hemmed in on all sides by the enemy, who not only kept constantly pouring in fresh troops but were copiously supplied on the field of battle with meat, drink, and quantities of arrows, we soon concluded that all our courageous fighting would not advance us a step. The whole of us were wounded, many shot through the neck, and more than fifty of our men were killed. In this critical situation we determined to cut our way manfully through the enemy's ranks and make for the boats, which fortunately lay on the coast near at hand. We therefore firmly closed our ranks and broke through the enemy. At that moment you should have heard the whizzing of their arrows, the horrible yell they set up, and how the Indians provoked each other to the combat, at the same time making desperate thrusts with their lances. But a still more serious misfortune awaited us; for as we made a simultaneous rush to our boats, they soon sunk or capsized, so that we were forced to cling to them as well as we could; and in this manner by swimming we strove to make the best of our way to the small vessel, which was now in all haste coming up to our assistance. Many of our men were even wounded while climbing into the vessel, but more particularly those who clung to its side; for the Indians pursued us in their canoes and attacked us without intermission. With the greatest exertions and help of God we thus got out of the hands of this people.

After we had gained our vessels we found that fifty-seven of our men were missing, besides the two whom the Indians had carried off alive, and five whom we had thrown overboard, who had died in consequence of their wounds and extreme thirst. The battle lasted a little longer than half an hour. The spot where it took place was certainly called Potonchan. Our seamen, however, gave it the name of Bahia de Mala Pelea (the bay of the disastrous engagement), as it stands on the maps. As soon as we found ourselves in safety we returned thanks to Almighty God for the preservation of our lives. Our wounded, however, had still great sufferings to undergo, as we had nothing but salt water to wash their wounds with, which caused them to swell very much. Some of our men swore most bitterly against our chief pilot Alaminos, and the conduct he had pursued; he having steadfastly maintained that this was an island and not a continent. I must, however, break off here, and relate what further happened to us, in the next chapter.

Chapter V

WE RESOLVE TO RETURN TO CUBA. THE EXTREME THIRST WE SUFFERED, AND ALL THE FATIGUES WE UNDERWENT UNTIL OUR ARRIVAL IN THE PORT OF HAVANA

After we had got into our vessels, as above related, and returned thanks to God for our preservation, we commenced dressing our wounds. None of us had escaped without two, three, or four wounds. Our captain had as many as twelve, and there was only one single soldier who came off whole. We therefore determined to return to Cuba; but as most of the sailors who had accompanied us on shore were also wounded, we had not sufficient hands to work the sails, we were therefore forced to set fire to our smallest vessel and leave it to the mercy of the waves, after taking out all the ropes, sails, and anchors, and distributing the sailors who were not wounded equally among the two other vessels. We had, however, to struggle with another far greater evil. This was our great want of fresh water; for although we had filled our barrels and casks near Potonchan, we did not succeed to bring them off, owing to the furious attack of the natives and the hurry we were in to get on board: thus we had been compelled to leave them behind and return without a single drop of water. We suffered most intensely from thirst, and the only way we could in some measure refresh our parched tongues was to hold the edges of our axes between our lips. Oh, what a fearful undertaking it is to venture out on the discovery of new countries, and place one's life in danger, as we were obliged to do! Those alone can form any idea of it who have gone through the hard school of experience.

We now kept as close into the shore as possible, to look out for some stream or creek where we might meet with fresh water. After thus continuing our course for three days we espied an inlet or mouth of some river as we thought, and sent a few hands on shore in the hopes of meeting with water. These were fifteen sailors who had remained on board during the battle at Potonchan, and three soldiers who had been only slightly wounded. They carried along with them pickaxes and three small casks. But the water in the inlet was salt, and wherever they dug wells it was equally bad. They nevertheless filled the casks with it, but it was so bitter and salty as to be unfit for use. Two soldiers who drank of it became ill of the consequences. The water here swarmed with lizards; we therefore gave this place the name of Lizard Bay, under which name it stands on the sea charts.

But, to continue my history, I must not forget to mention that while our boats were on shore in search of water, there suddenly arose such a violent tempest from the north-east that our ships were nigh being cast on shore. For, as we were forced to lay to, the wind blowing hard from the north and north-east, our position was extremely dangerous, from a scarcity of ropes.

When the men who had gone on shore with our boats perceived the danger we were in, they hastened to our assistance, and cast out additional anchors and cables. In this way we lay for two days and two nights. After the expiration of that time we again heaved our anchors and steered in the direction of Cuba. Our pilot Alaminos here held a consultation with the two others, when they concluded that the best plan would be to get, if possible, into the latitude of Florida, which, according to their charts and furthest measurement, could not be more than 210 miles distant; for they assured us if we could get into the latitude of Florida, we should have a better and speedier sail to the Havana. It turned out exactly as they had said; for Alaminos had been in these parts before, having accompanied Juan de Leon when he discovered Florida, about ten or twelve years previously. After four days' sail we crossed this gulf and came in sight of Florida.

43. STEPHEN PARMENIUS OF BUDA (C. 1541–83)

Stephen Parmenius was born in Buda, Hungary, sometime after 1541. He was a Calvinist, and was educated by the leading scholars of his own nation but was then sent abroad in 1579 to polish his learning at leading western European universities. Reaching England in 1581, he was patronized by Sir Henry Unton and sent up to Oxford, residing at Christ Church, where he began a friendship with Richard Hakluyt, to whom this letter is addressed. Parmenius then went down to London, where he entered the circle of Sir Humphrey Gilbert, as a consequence of a learned Latin poem in his honor. Now very much part of the group of gentlemen interested in exploration, Parmenius decided to join Gilbert's next voyage to record in Latin verse this great adventure of his age. He landed at St. John's, Newfoundland, in 1583 and was anxious to explore the island, but the dense forests made the interior impenetrable. He continued down the coast but the ship on which he was sailing foundered and he was lost, either on Cape Breton or Sable Island. The poem, then, was never completed.

Letter to ... Richard Hakluyt ... From St. John's Harbor, Newfoundland, 1583

To his distinguished friend and brother, Richard Hakluyt, Master of Arts and Philosophy, Christ Church College, Oxford

GREETINGS. I was not intending to write to you at the time when your promise of a letter came to mind. Last June you thought that you would be following us, and I had therefore left word that you should be told about my situation by Dr Humfrey [master of Magdalen College, Oxford]: but this would not satisfy you. So I shall write to you in almost the same words, because I have no leisure at the moment for new ideas and different *façons de parler*.

In the end we actually set sail from England, belatedly, on June 11, leaving port and dry land at Plymouth. The fleet consisted of five ships, the biggest of which had been provided by the admiral's brother and separated herself from us, for some unknown reason, on the third day. The rest of us carried on sailing together until July 23, when visibility was obscured by thick mist and we all took different courses.

We sighted the first land on our own on August 1, at about latitude 50°, after we had gone down, a few days previously, beyond 41 degrees in the hope of finding southerly winds, which however never blew for us at their usual time. It was what your people call Penguin Island, owing to the number of that sort of bird there. But we neither saw the birds nor reached the island, because the winds were calling us elsewhere. And yet we all met in the same place, a little way out of the harbor which had been planned as our common destination (and that within two hours of each other), by the great goodness of God and to our own delight. The spot is a place in Newfoundland, between latitudes 47 and 48°, which they call St John's.

The admiral himself has had somewhat the harder hit company, because of their large numbers and the cramped quarters of his ship, and he has already lost two of them from dysentery: there is good hope for the rest. Of our own men (for I attached myself to Maurice Browne, a young man of high character), two were drowned in some accident: but the rest are safe and a good deal more robust. I myself was never more healthy.

We put in to this place on August 3, and on the 5th the admiral took these regions into the possession and authority of himself and of the realm of England, having passed certain laws about religion and obedience to the Queen of England. At the moment we are regaling ourselves rather more cheerfully and sumptuously. For you will surely have gathered, from considering the length of time we took, what sort of winds we have used and how exhausted we were able to become. From now on we shall not go short of anything, because apart from the English we have come across some twenty Portuguese and Spanish ships in this place, and they, being no match for us, will not allow us to go hungry. The English group, although strong enough themselves and unthreatened by us, attend us with all deference and kindness, respecting the authority of our letters patent from the Queen.

Now I ought to tell you about the customs, territories and inhabitants: and yet what am I to say, my dear Hakluyt, when I see nothing but desolation? There are inexhaustible supplies of fish, so that those who travel here do good business. Scarcely has the hook touched the bottom before it is loaded with some magnificent catch. The whole terrain is hilly and forested: the trees are for the most part pine. Some of these are growing old and others are just coming to maturity, but the majority have fallen with age, thus obstructing a good view of the land and the passage of travelers, so that no advance can be made anywhere. All the grass is tall, but scarcely any different from ours. Nature seems even to want to struggle towards producing corn; for I found some blades and ears that resembled rye and they seem capable of being adapted easily to cultivation and sowing in the service of man. There are blackberries in the woods, or rather very sweet strawberries growing on bushes. Bears sometimes appear round the shelters and are killed: but they are white, so far as I have been able to make out from their skins, and smaller than ours. I am not clear whether there are any inhabitants in this area, nor have I met anyone who was in a position to say (and who could be, I ask you, since it is impossible to travel any distance). Nor do we know any better whether there is any metal in the mountains; and for the same reason, even though their appearance may indicate underlying minerals.

We made representations to the admiral to burn the forests down, so as to clear an open space for surveying the area; nor was he averse to the idea, if it had not seemed likely to bring a considerable disadvantage. For some reliable people asserted that, when this had occurred by accident at some other settlement post, no fish had been seen for seven whole years, because the seawater had been turned bitter by the turpentine that flowed down from the trees burning along the rivers.

At this time of the year the weather is so hot that if the fish which are put to dry in the sun were not regularly turned over they could not be prevented from scorching. But the huge masses of ice out to sea have taught us how cold it is in winter. Some of our company have reported that in the month of May they were stuck for sixteen whole days on end in so much ice that some of the icebergs were sixty fathoms thick; and when their sides facing the sun melted, the entire mass was turned over, as it were on a sort of pivot, in such a way that what had previously been facing upwards was then facing down, to the great danger of any people at hand, as you can well imagine. The atmosphere on land is moderately clear, but there is continuous fog over the sea toward the east. And on the sea itself around the Bank (which is what they call the place about forty miles off shore where the bottom can be reached and they start catching fish) there is scarcely a day without rain.

When we have provided for all our requirements in this place we shall advance southwards, with God's help; and the more that is reported about the regions we are making for, the greater will our expectations be from day to day.

So much for us; now I want to hear about you. But I fear my wish may be in vain. But, above all, I would especially like to know how my patron Unton is taking my absence. He will have my ready respect and service as long as I live. I sincerely hope that this expedition of ours will be of some service to his own project. Now it remains that you should think me yours, and so much yours that no-one else is more so. May the Son of God prosper our efforts to such an extent that you also can take part. Goodbye, Hakluyt, my most delightful and distinguished friend: keep me in your affection.

Yours, Stephen Parmenius of Buda

GOING EAST

44. RICHARD HAKLUYT (C. 1552–1616)

Hakluyt was the son of a prosperous skinner and was educated at Westminster School and Christ Church, Oxford, where he took his degree in 1574. He remained a scholar, earning an M.A. in 1577 and was ordained as a priest. Hakluyt began teaching at the university, and devoted his energy to the comprehensive study of geography, supported after 1583 by a pension arranged by Elizabeth's chief minister, Sir William Cecil, in order to further English knowledge of exploration. His first book, concerning the discovery of America, appeared in 1582. The next year he was appointed the secretary to the English ambassador in Paris, where he continued his research and in 1584 produced a book, commissioned by Sir Walter Raleigh and dedicated to Queen Elizabeth, recommending English colonial settlements in America. Hakluyt returned to England, where in 1589 he published his Principal Navigations, Voyages and Discoveries of the English Nation, *a collection of travel narratives, both ancient and contemporary, which he continued to expand and enlarge throughout the 1590s and early 1600s. He was an adviser to the East India Company and the Virginia Company, though he never traveled farther than Paris. Hakluyt is buried in Westminster Abbey.*

ROBERT THORNE (1492–1532)

Robert Thorne the younger was a merchant of Bristol who inherited both his father's trade with Seville and his passion for exploration. In 1532 he became M.P. for Bristol, implying that he was a man of some standing in the city. He invested in Sebastian Cabot's voyage to South America in 1526–30, and around the same time began arguing for a northern route to the fabled Spice Islands, the source of a remarkably lucrative trade that had been largely monopolized by the Portuguese in the early years of the century. The circumnavigation of the globe by Ferdinand Magellan and Sebastian Del Cano under Spanish auspices between 1519 and 1522 had also given the Spanish access to trade with the East, and Thorne was anxious that English merchants should find their own route to riches. He believed that the territory discovered by John Cabot (Newfoundland) and claimed for England was really an extension of the Indies. Thorne also underestimated the distance, the dangers, and the complications of ice and cold, even producing a map indicating how that route might be sailed. With his brother Nicholas he supported the creation of a grammar school in Bristol with particular focus on navigational instruction and foreign languages.

The book made by the right worshipful Mr. Robert Thorne in the year 1527 in Seville, to Dr. Ley, lord ambassador for King Henry the eighth, to Charles the Emperor, being an information of the parts of the world, discovered by him and the king of Portugal: and also of the way to the Moluccas by the North

… to write unto your lordship of the new trade of spicery of the emperor, there is no doubt but that the islands are fertile with cloves, nutmegs, mace, and cinnamon, and that the said islands, with others thereabout, abound with gold, rubies, diamonds, balass-rubies, garnets, jacincts [sapphires], and other stones and pearls, as all other lands that are under and near the Equinoctial.… And I see that the preciousness of these things is measured after the distance that is between us and the things that we have appetite for. For in this navigation of the spicery it was discovered that these islands set nothing by gold, but set more by a knife and a nail of iron, than by their quantity of gold: and with reason, as the thing more necessary for man's service. And I doubt not but that our corn and seeds should be as precious to them, if they might have them, as their spices are to us: and likewise the pieces of glass that here we have counterfeited are as precious to them, as their stones are to us: which is seen daily by the experience of those that have trade thither.

….

In the year 1484 the king of Portugal thought about arming certain caravels to discover this spicery. Then, as he feared that once the islands were discovered, every other prince would send and trade thither, so that the cost and peril of discovering should be his, and the profit common: first he gave knowledge of his plan to all Christian princes, saying that he would seek amongst the infidels new possessions of regions, and therefore would make a certain army: and that if any of them would help in the cost of the said army, he should enjoy his part of the profit or honor that should come of it. And then this discovering was thought to be a strange and uncertain thing. Now they say, that all the princes of Christendom answered, that they would be no part of such an army, nor yet of the profit that might come of it. After which he gave knowledge to the pope of his purpose and of the answer of all the princes, desiring him that seeing that none would help in the costs, that he would judge all that should be found and discovered to be of his jurisdiction, and command that no other princes should intermeddle therewith. The pope said not as Christ says, *Quis me constituit judicem inter vos* [Who has made me a judge between you]? He did not refuse, but making himself as lord and judge of all, not only granted that all that should be discovered from Orient to Occident, should be the king of Portugal's, but also, that upon great censures no other prince should discover but he....

After this in the year 1492 the king of Spain, intending to discover lands toward the west without making any such diligence or taking license of the king of Portugal, armed certain caravels and then discovered this West India, especially two islands of the said India, that in this map I set forth, naming the one la Dominica, and the other Cuba, and brought certain gold from thence. Of which, when the king of Portugal had knowledge, he sent to the king of Spain, requiring him to give him the said islands, for by the sentence of the pope all that should be discovered was his, and that he should not proceed further in the discovery without his license.... So that it seems that the king of Spain answered, that what the king of Portugal asked was reasonable, and that to be obedient to that which the pope had decreed, he would give him the ... islands of the Indies.... [The king of Portugal] consented to the king of Spain, that touching this discovering they should divide the world between them two, and that all that should be discovered from Cape Verde, where this map begins to be counted in the degrees of longitude, to 180 of the said scale of longitude, which is half the world toward the Orient and finishes in this map right over against a little cross made at the said 180 degrees, to be the king of Portugal's.

....

But now touching what your lordship wrote, whether that which we discovered touches the aforesaid coasts: once it appears plainly, that the Newfound land that we discovered is all a mainland with the West Indies ... and so continues of coast more than 5000 leagues of length, as by this map appears. For from the said New lands it proceeds toward the west to the Indies, and from the Indies returns toward the Orient, and after turns southward up till it comes to the straits of Todos Santos, which I reckon to be more than 5000 leagues.

So that to the Indies it should seem that we have some title, at least that for our discovering we might trade thither as others do. But all this is nothing near the spicery.

Now then if from the said Newfound lands the sea is navigable, there is no doubt that by sailing northward and passing the Pole, descending to the Equinoctial line, we shall hit these islands, and it should be a much shorter way than either the Spaniards or the Portuguese have.

....

And even if we did not go to the said islands, for that they are the emperor's or the king of Portugal's, we should by the way and coming once to the line Equinoctial, find lands no less rich of gold and spicery, as all other lands are under the said line Equinoctial: and also should, if we may pass under the north, enjoy the navigation of all Tartary, which should be no less profitable to our commodities of cloth than these spiceries to the emperor and the king of Portugal.

But it is a general opinion of all cosmographers that passing the seventh clime, the sea is all ice and the cold so much that none can suffer it. And hitherto they had all the same opinion, that under the line Equinoctial the land was uninhabitable for too much heat.

Yet since (by experience it is proved) that no land is so much habitable nor more temperate. And to conclude, I think the same should be found under the north, if it were experimented. For as all judge, *Nihil fit vacuum in rerum natura* [nothing in nature is made to be empty]: So I judge, there is no land uninhabitable, nor sea innavigable.

45. SIR MARTIN FROBISHER (C. 1535–94)

Frobisher began his career as a teenager sailing on voyages to the African coast as part of a variety of attempts by English merchants to gain some part of the profitable Portuguese trade in the area. He was captured by the Portuguese in 1554 and held until 1556 or 1557. After his release he seems to have developed an active career as a privateer, seizing enemy ships under license, but a stubborn unwillingness to differentiate between friendly and enemy vessels meant that he was frequently in trouble. After an obscure period where he appears to have acted as a double agent for the Privy Council, Frobisher set out on his first attempt to find the north-west passage to China in 1576. He passed Baffin Island and encountered a group of Inuit, but worsening weather forced him to return home. He made another attempt in 1577, though this time the primary focus was on finding valuable minerals, with China as a secondary goal. On the third trip, in the summer of 1578, Frobisher once again mined ore, which turned out to be worthless, and traveled as far as Hudson Strait. With the collapse of the financial promise of the voyage, the search for a north-west passage was suspended, and Frobisher returned to his career as a privateer until distinguishing himself during the defeat of the Spanish Armada.

Dionise Settle's identity is unclear. He was not listed as a member of Frobisher's crew and his account seems to be personal rather than official.

The second voyage of Captain Frobisher, made to the West and Northwest regions, in the yere 1577 ... Written by Master Dionise Settle

On Whit Sunday, being the sixth-and-twentieth day of May, in the year of our Lord God 1577, Captain Frobisher departed from Blackwall with one of the Queen's Majesty's ships called the Aid, of nine score ton or thereabout, and two other little barques, one called the Gabriel ... and the other the Michael ... accompanied with seven score gentlemen, soldiers, and sailors, well furnished with victuals and other provisions necessary for one half year on this, his second year, for the further discovering of the passage to Cathay and other countries thereunto adjacent, by west and north-west navigations: which passage or way is supposed to be on the north and north-west parts of America, and the said America to be an island surrounded with the sea, through which our merchants might have course and recourse with their merchandise from our northernmost parts of Europe to those Oriental coasts of Asia in much shorter time and with greater benefit than any others, to their no little commodity and profit....

Upon which considerations the day and year before expressed, he departed from Blackwall to Harwich, where making an accomplishment of things necessary, the last of May we hoisted up sails, and with a merry wind the 7th of June we arrived at the islands called Orchades, or vulgarly Orkney ... We departed here hence the 8th of June, and followed our course between west and north-west until the 4th of July, all which time we had no night, but that easily and without any impediment, we had, when we were so disposed, the fruition of our books, and other pleasures to pass away the time, a thing of no small moment to such as wander in unknown seas and long navigations, especially when both the winds and raging surges pass their common and wonted course. This benefit lasts in those parts not six weeks, while the sun is near the tropic of Cancer, but where the pole is raised to 70 or 80 degrees it continues longer....

The 4th of July we came within the making of Friesland. From this shore, ten or twelve leagues, we met great islands of ice of half a mile, some more, some less in compass, showing above the sea thirty or forty fathoms, and as we supposed fast on ground, where, with our lead, we could scarce sound the bottom for depth.

Here, in place of odoriferous and fragrant smells of sweet gums and pleasant notes of musical birds, which other countries in more temperate zones do yield, we tasted the most boisterous Boreal blasts, mixed with snow and hail, in the months of June and July, nothing inferior to our intemperate winter.... All along this coast ice lies as a continual bulwark, and so defends the country, that those who would land there incur great danger. Our general attempted to go on shore three days together with the ship boat, which, because he could not accomplish it without great danger, he deferred until a more convenient time....

From hence we departed the 8th of July, and the 16th of the same we came with the making of land, which land our general the year before had named the Queen's Forehand, being an island, as we judge, lying near the supposed continent with America, and on the other side, opposite to the same, one other island, called Halles Isle, after the name of the master of the ship, near adjacent to the firm land, supposed continent with Asia. Between the which two islands there is a large entrance or strait, called Frobisher's Strait, after the name of our general, the first finder thereof....

At our first coming, the straits seemed to be shut up with a long wall of ice, which gave no little cause of discomfort unto us all; but our general (to whose diligence, imminent dangers and difficult attempts seemed nothing in respect of his willing mind for the commodity of his prince and country), with two little pinnaces prepared of purpose, passed twice through them to the east shore, and the islands thereunto adjacent; and the ship, with the two barques, lay off and on something farther into the sea from the danger of the ice.

Whilst he was searching the country near the shore, some of the people of the country showed themselves, leaping and dancing, with strange shrieks and cries, which gave no little admiration to our men. Our general, desiring to allure them unto him by fair means, caused knives and other things to be proffered unto them, which they would not take at our hands; but being laid on the ground, and the party going away, they came and took up, leaving something of theirs to countervail the same. At the length, two of them, leaving their weapons, came down to our general and master, who did the like to them, commanding the company to stay, and went unto them, who, after certain dumb signs and mute congratulations, began to lay hands upon them, but they cleverly escaped, and ran to their bows and arrows and came fiercely upon them, not respecting the rest of our company, which were ready for their defence, but with their arrows hurt divers of them. We took the one, and the other escaped....

The day following, being the 19th of July, our captain returned to the ship with good news of great riches, which showed itself in the bowels of those barren mountains, wherewith we were all satisfied.

Within four days after we had been at the entrance of the straits, the north-west and west winds dispersed the ice into the sea, and made us a large entrance into the Straits, that without impediment, on the 19th July, we entered them; and the 20th thereof our general and master, with great diligence, sought out and sounded the west shore, and found out a fair harbor for the ship and barques to ride in, and named it after our master's mate, Jackman's Sound, and brought the ship, barques, and all their company to safe anchor, except one man which died by God's visitation.

At our first arrival, after the ship rode at anchor, our general, with such company as could well be spared from the ships, in marching order entered the land, having special care by exhortations that at our entrance thereinto we should all with one voice, kneeling upon our knees, chiefly thank God for our safe arrival; secondly, beseech Him that it would please His Divine Majesty long to continue our Queen, for whom he, and all the rest of our company, in this order took possession of the country; and thirdly, that by our Christian study and endeavor, those barbarous people, trained up in paganry and infidelity, might be reduced to the knowledge of true religion, and to the hope of salvation in Christ our Redeemer, with other words very apt to signify his willing mind and affection towards his prince and country, whereby all suspicion of an undutiful subject may credibly be judged to be utterly exempted from his mind. All the rest of the gentlemen, and others, deserve worthily herein their due praise and commendation....

After this order we marched through the country, with ensign displayed, so far as was thought needful, and now and then heaped up stones on high mountains and other places, in token of possession, as likewise to signify unto such as hereafter may chance to arrive there that possession is taken in the behalf of some other prince by those which first found out the country....

Our general certain days searched this supposed continent with America, and not finding the commodity to answer his expectations, after he had made trial thereof, he departed thence, with two little barques, and men sufficient, to the east shore, being he supposed continent of Asia, and left the ship, with most of the gentlemen soldiers and sailors, until such time as he either thought good to send or come for them.

The stones on this supposed continent with America be altogether sparkled and glister in the sun like gold; so likewise doth the sand in the bright water, yet they verify the old proverb, "All is not gold that glistereth."

On this west shore we found a dead fish floating, which had in his nose a horn, straight and torquet, of length two yards lacking two inches, being broken in the top, where we might perceive it hollow, into which some of our sailors putting spiders they presently died. I saw not the trial hereof, but it was reported unto me of a truth, by the virtue whereof we supposed it to be the sea unicorn.

After our general had found out good harbor for the ship and barques to anchor in, and also such store of gold ore as he thought himself satisfied withal, he returned to the Michael, whereof Master Yorke aforesaid was captain, accompanied with our master and his mate, who coasting along the west shore, not far from whence the ship rode, they perceived a fair harbor, and willing to sound the same, at the entrance thereof they espied two tents of seal skins, unto which the captain, our said master, and other company resorted. At the sight of our men the people fled into the mountains; nevertheless, they went to their tents, where, leaving certain trifles of ours as glasses, bells, knives, and such like things, they departed, not taking anything of theirs except one dog. They did in like manner leave behind them a letter, pen, ink, and paper, whereby our men whom the captain lost the year before, and in that people's custody, might (if any of them were alive) be advertised of our presence and being there.

On the same day, after consultation, all the gentlemen, and others likewise that could be spared from the ship, under the conduct and leading of Master Philpot (unto whom, in our general's absence, and his lieutenant, Master Beast, all the rest were obedient), went ashore, determining to see if by fair means we could either allure them to familiarity, or otherwise take some of them, and so attain to some knowledge of those men whom our general lost the year before.

At our coming back again to the place where their tents were before, they had removed their tents farther into the said bay or sound, where they might, if they were driven from the land, flee with their boats into the sea. We, parting ourselves into two companies, and compassing a mountain, came suddenly upon them by land, who, espying us, without any tarrying fled to their boats, leaving the most part of their oars behind them for haste, and rowed down the bay, where our two pinnaces met them and drove them to shore. But if they had had all their oars, so swift are they in rowing, it had been lost time to have chased them.

When they were landed they fiercely assaulted our men with their bows and arrows, who wounded three of them with our arrows, and perceiving themselves thus hurt they desperately leaped off the rocks into the sea and drowned themselves; which if they had not done but had submitted themselves, or if by any means we could have taken alive (being their enemies as they judged), we would both have saved them, and also have sought remedy to cure their wounds received at our hands. But they, altogether void of humanity, and ignorant what mercy means, in extremities look for no other than death, and perceiving that they should fall into our hands, thus miserably by drowning rather desired death than otherwise to be saved by us. The rest, perceiving their fellows in this distress, fled into the high mountains. Two women, not being so apt to escape as the men were, the one for her age, and the other being encumbered with a young child, we took. The old wretch, whom divers of our sailors supposed to be either a devil or a witch, had her buskins plucked off to see if she were cloven-footed, and for her ugly hue and deformity we let her go; the young woman and the child we brought away. We named the place where they were slain Bloody Point, and the bay or harbor Yorke's Sound, after the name of one of the captains of the two barques.

Having this knowledge both of their fierceness and cruelty, and perceiving that fair means as yet is not able to allure them to familiarity, we disposed ourselves, contrary to our inclination, something to be cruel, returned to their tents, and made a spoil of the same, where we found an old shirt, a doublet, a girdle, and also shoes of our men, whom we lost the year before; on nothing else unto them belonging could we set our eyes.

Their riches are not gold, silver, or precious drapery, but their said tents and boats made of the skins of red deer and seal skins, also dogs like unto wolves, but for the most part black, with other trifles, more to be wondered at for their strangeness than for any other commodity needful for our use.

Thus returning to our ship the 3rd of August, we departed from the west shore, supposed firm with America, after we had anchored there thirteen days, and so the 4th thereof we came to our general on the east shore, and anchored in a fair harbor named Anne Warwick's Sound, and to which is annexed an island, both named after the Countess of Warwick—Anne Warwick's Sound and Isle.

In this isle our general thought good for this voyage to freight both the ships and barques with such stone or gold mineral as he judged to countervail the charges of his first and this his second navigation to these countries, with sufficient interest to the venturers whereby they might both be satisfied for this time and also in time to come (if it please God and our prince) to expect a much more benefit out of the bowels of those septentrional parallels, which long time hath concealed itself....

In the meantime of our abode here some of the country people came to show themselves unto us sundry times from the main shore, near adjacent to the said isle. Our general, desirous to have some news of his men whom he lost the year before, with some company with him repaired with the ship boat to commune or sign with them for familiarity, whereunto he is persuaded to bring them. They at the first show made tokens that three of his five men were alive, and desired pen, ink, and paper, and that within three or four days they would return, and, as we judged, bring those of our men which were living with them....

Another time, as our said general was coasting the country with two little pinnaces, whereby at our return he might make the better relation thereof, three of the crafty villains with a white skin allured us to them. Once again our general, for that he hoped to hear of his men, went towards them; at our coming near the shore whereon they were we might perceive a number of them lie hidden behind great stones, and those three in sight laboring by all means possible that some would come on land; and perceiving we made no haste, by words nor friendly signs, which they used by clapping their hands, and being without weapon, and but three in sight, they sought further means to provoke us thereunto. One alone laid flesh on the shore, which we took up with the boat-hook as necessary victuals for the relieving of the man, woman, and child whom we had taken, for that as yet they could not digest our meat; whereby they perceived themselves deceived of their expectation for all their crafty allurements. Yet once again to make, as it were, a full show of their crafty natures and subtle sleights, to the intent thereby to have entrapped and taken some of our men, one of them counterfeited himself impotent and lame of his legs, who seemed to descend to the water's side with great difficulty, and to cover his craft the more one of his fellows came down with him, and in such places where he seemed unable to pass, he took him on his shoulders, set him by the water's side, and departed from him, leaving him, as it should seem, all alone; who, playing his counterfeit pageant very well, thought thereby to provoke some of us to come on shore, not fearing but that one of us might make our party good with a lame man.

Our general, having compassion of his impotency, thought good, if it were possible, to cure him thereof; wherefore he caused a soldier to shoot at him with his calever, which grazed before his face. The counterfeit villain cleverly fled without any impediment at all, and got him to his bow and arrows, and the rest from their lurking holes with their weapons, bows, arrows, slings, and darts. Our general caused some calevers to be shot off at them, whereby, some being hurt, they might hereafter stand in more fear of us.

This was all the answer for this time we could have of our men, or of our general's letter. Their crafty dealing at these three several times being thus manifest unto us, may plainly show their disposition in other things to be correspondent. We judged that they used these stratagems thereby to have caught some of us for the delivering of the man, woman, and child, whom we had taken.

They are men of a large corporature, and good proportion; their color is not much unlike the sunburnt countryman, who laboreth daily in sun for his living.

They wear their hair something long, and cut before either with stone or knife, very disorderly. Their women wear their hair long, knit up with two loops, showing forth on either side of their faces, and the rest faltered upon a knot. Also, some of their women tint their faces proportionally, as chin, cheeks, and forehead and the wrists of their hands, whereupon they lay a color which is dark azurine.

They eat their meat all raw, both flesh, fish, and fowl, or something parboiled with blood, and a little water, which they drink. For lack of water, they will eat ice that is hard frozen as pleasantly as we will do sugar-candy, or other sugar.

If they, for necessity's sake, stand in need of the premises, such grass as the country yieldeth they pluck up and eat, not daintily, or saladwise, to allure their stomachs to appetite, but for necessity's sake, without either salt, oils, or washing, like brute beasts devouring the same. They neither use table, stool, or table-cloth for comeliness: but when they are imbrued with blood, knuckle deep, and their knives in like sort, they use their tongues as apt instruments to lick them clean; in doing whereof they are assured to lose none of their victuals.

They keep certain dogs, not much unlike wolves, which they yoke together, as we do oxen and horses, to a sled or trail, and so carry their necessaries over the ice and snow, from place to place, as the captain, whom we have, made perfect signs. And when those dogs are not apt for the same use, or when with hunger they are constrained for lack of other victuals, they eat them, so that they are as needful for them, in respect of their bigness, as our oxen are for us.

They apparel themselves in the skins of such beasts as they kill, sewed together with the sinews of them. All the fowl which they kill they skin, and make thereof one kind of garment or other to defend them from the cold....

Those beasts, fishes, and fowls which they kill are their meat, drink, apparel, houses, bedding, hose, shoes, thread, and sails for their boats, with many other necessaries, whereof they stand in need, and almost all their riches.

The houses are tents made of seal skins, pitched up with four fir quarters, four-square, meeting at the top, and the skins sewed together with sinews, and laid thereupon; they are so pitched up, that the entrance into them is always south, or against the sun.

They have other sort of houses, which we found not to be inhabited, which are raised with stones and whalebones, and a skin laid over them to withstand the rain, or other weather; the entrance of them being not much unlike an oven's mouth, whereunto, I think, they resort for a time to fish, hunt, and fowl, and so leave them until the next time they come thither again.

Their weapons are bows, arrows, darts, and slings. Their bows are of wood, of a yard long, sinewed on the back with firm sinews, not glued to, but fast girded and tied on. Their bow strings are likewise sinews. Their arrows are three pieces, nocked with bone and ended with bone; with those two ends, and the wood in the midst, they pass not in length half a yard, or little more. They are feathered with two feathers, the pen end being cut away, and the feathers laid upon the arrow with the broad side to the wood, insomuch, that they seem, when they are tied on, to have four feathers. They have likewise three sorts of heads to those arrows; one sort of stone or iron, proportioned like to a heart; the second sort of bone much like unto a stopt head, with a hook on the same, the third sort of bone likewise, made sharp at both sides, and sharp pointed. They are not made very fast, but lightly tied to, or else set in a nocke, that, upon small occasion, the arrow leaveth these heads behind them; they are of small force except they be very near when they shoot.

Their darts are made of two sorts: the one with many forks of bones in the fore end, and likewise in the midst; their proportions are not much unlike our toasting-irons, but longer; these they cast out of an instrument of wood very readily. The other sort is greater than the first aforesaid, with a long bone made sharp on both sides, not much unlike a rapier, which I take to be their most hurtful weapon....

I can suppose their abode or habitation not to be here, for that neither their houses nor apparel are of such force to withstand the extremity of cold that the country seemeth to be infected withal; neither do I see any sign likely to perform the same.

Those houses, or rather dens, which stand there, have no sign of footway, or anything else trodden, which is one of the chiefest tokens of habitation. And those tents, which they bring with them, when they have sufficiently hunted and fished, they remove to other places; and when they have sufficiently stored them of such victuals as the country yieldeth, or bringeth forth, they return to their winter stations or habitations. This conjecture do I make for the infertility which I perceive to be in that country.

They have some iron, whereof they make arrow-heads, knives, and other little instruments, to work their boats, bows, arrows, and darts withal, which are very unapt to do anything withal, but with great labor.

It seemeth that they have conversation with some other people, of whom for exchange they should receive the same. They are greatly delighted with anything that is bright or makes a sound....

As the country is barren and unfertile, so are they rude, and of no capacity to culture the same to any perfection; but are contented by their hunting, fishing, and fowling, with raw flesh and warm blood, to satisfy their greedy paunches, which is their only glory....

The 23rd August, after we had satisfied our minds with freight sufficient for our vessels, though not our covetous desires, with such knowledge of the country, people, and other commodities as are before rehearsed, the 24th thereof we departed there hence: the 17th of September we fell with the Land's End of England, and so to Milford Haven, from whence our general rowed to the court for order to what port or haven to conduct the ship.

46. RICHARD HAKLUYT (C. 1552–1616)
Notes given in 1580 to Mr. Arthur Pet, and to Mr. Charles Jackman, sent by the merchants of the Muscovy Company for the discovery of the Northeast strait

The Muscovy Company was founded by Richard Chancellor (1521–56), Sebastian Cabot (1477–1557), and Sir Hugh Willoughby (d. 1554) to develop trade with Muscovy and to search for a north-east passage to China, which would allow the English to gain the riches of the East while avoiding the Portuguese-dominated route around Africa and across the Indian

Ocean. The Company was chartered by Queen Mary in 1555 and was successful in establishing English trading rights in Muscovy, which at that time was politically and diplomatically isolated. Although neither the founders nor later Muscovy traders were successful in finding a feasible overland route to China via Russia, they were loath to give up on the idea, given the wealth the Portuguese had garnered in Asian trade. The instructions given to Arthur Pet and Charles Jackman demonstrate both the growing experience of the Company in long-distance trade and their hopes for the route.

Notes in writing, besides more privy by mouth, that were given by Mr. Richard Hakluyt of Eton in the County of Hereford, Esquire, Anno 1580 to Mr. Arthur Pet and to Mr. Charles Jackman, sent by the merchants of the Muscovy Company for the discovery of the Northeast strait, not altogether unfit for some other enterprises of discovery, hereafter to be taken in hand.

What respect of islands is to be had, and why

Whereas the Portuguese have certain ports and fortifications to thrust into by the way in their course to their Indies in the Southeast, to divers great purposes: so you are to see what islands and what ports you need to have by the way in your course to the Northeast. For which cause I wish you to enter into consideration of the matter, and to note all the islands, and to set them down in plat [i.e., on the map], to two ends: that is to say, that we may devise to take the benefit by them, and also foresee how by them the savages or civil princes may in any sort annoy us in our purposed trade that way.

And since the people to whom we intend to go in this voyage are not Christians, it would be better if the mass of our commodities were always in our own disposition, and not at the will of others. Therefore it would be better if we sought out some small island in the Scythian sea, where we might plant, fortify, and staple safely, from whence (as time should serve) we might feed those heathen nations with our commodities without overloading them, or without venturing our whole mass in the bowels of their country.

....

RESPECT OF HAVENS AND HARBORS

And if no such islands may be found in the Scythian sea toward the firm of Asia, then you are to search out the ports that are about Nova Zembla, all along the tract of that land, to the end that you may winter there the first year if you are hindered by contrary winds, and to the end that if we may in a short time come to Cambalu and unlade and set sail again for return without venturing there at Cambalu, that you may on your way come as far in return as a port about Nova Zembla: so that the summer following, you may the sooner be in England for the more speedy sale of your East commodities, and for the speedier discharge of your mariners if you cannot go forward and back in the same summer.

And touching the tract of the land of Nova Zembla, toward the east out of the arctic circle in the more temperate zone, you are to have regard: for if you find the soil planted with people, it is likely that in time an ample sale of our warm woolen clothes may be found. And if there are no people at all there to be found, then you shall specially note what plenty of whales, and of other fish is to be found there, to the end we may turn our new found land fishing or island fishing or our whalefishing that way, for the aid and comfort of our new trades to the northeast to the coasts of Asia.

RESPECT OF FISH AND CERTAIN OTHER THINGS

And if the air upon that tract may be found temperate, and the soil yielding wood, water, land and grass, and the seas fish, then we may plant on that mainland the offals of our people, as the Portuguese do in Brazil, and so they may in our fishing in our passage, and in divers ways yield commodity to England by harboring and victualling us.

And it may be that the inland there may yield masts, pitch, tar, hemp, and all things for the navy, as plentifully as Eastland doth.

....

IF A STRAIT IS FOUND, WHAT IS TO BE DONE, AND WHAT GREAT IMPORTANCE IT MAY HAVE

And if there is a strait in the passage into the Scythian seas, the same is specially and with great regard to be noted, especially if the same strait is narrow and to be kept. I say it is to be noted as a thing that has much importance, for what prince soever shall be lord of the same, and shall possess the same, as the king of Denmark possesses the strait of Denmark, only he shall have the trade out of these regions into the northeast parts of the world for himself and for his private profit or for his subjects only, or to enjoy the wonderful benefit of the toll of the same as the king of Denmark enjoys in his straits, by allowing the merchants of other princes to pass that way. If any such strait is found, the elevation, the high or low land, the havens near, the length of the straits, and all other such circumstances are to be set down for many purposes: and all the mariners in the voyage are to be sworn to keep close all such things, so that other princes do not prevent us of the same after our return upon the disclosing of the mariners, if any such thing should happen.

WHICH WAY THE SAVAGE MAY BE MADE ABLE TO PURCHASE OUR CLOTH AND THEIR OTHER WANTS

If you find any island or mainland populous, and that the same people have need of cloth, then are you to devise what commodities they have to purchase the same.

If they are poor, then are you to consider of the soil, and how by any possibility the same may be made to enrich them, so that hereafter they may have something to purchase the cloth.

If you enter into any main by portable river and find any great woods, you are to note what kind of timber they are of, that we may know whether they are for pitch, tar, masts, dealboard, clapboard, or for building of ships or houses, for so, if the people have no use of them, they may perhaps be brought to use.

NOT TO VENTURE THE LOSS OF ANY ONE MAN

You must have great care to preserve your people, since your number is so small, and not to venture any one man in any way.

TO BRING HOME BESIDES MERCHANDIZE CERTAIN TRIFLES

Bring home with you (if you may) from Cambalu or other civil place, one or other young man, even if you leave one for him.

Also if the fruits of the countries will not of themselves last, dry them and so preserve them.

And bring with you the kernels of pears and apples, and the stones of such stonefruits as you shall find there.

Also the seeds of all strange herbs and flowers, for such seeds of fruits and herbs coming from another part of the world, and so far off, will delight the fancy of many for their strangeness, and because the same may grow and continue the delight for a long time.

If you arrive at Cambalu or Quinsay, to bring thence the map of that country, for so shall you have the perfect description, which is to great purpose.

To bring thence some old printed book, to see whether they have had print there before it was devised in Europe as some write.

....

THINGS TO BE MARKED TO MAKE CONJECTURES BY

To take special note of their buildings and of the ornaments of their houses within.

Take a special note of their apparel and furniture, and of the substance that the same is made of, from which a merchant may make an estimate as well of their commodity, as also of their wants.

To note their shops and warehouses, and with what commodities they abound, the price also.

....

THINGS TO BE CARRIED WITH YOU, WHEREOF MORE OR LESS IS TO BE CARRIED FOR A SHOW OF OUR COMMODITIES TO BE MADE

Kerseys of all orient colors, specially of stamell, broadcloth of orient colors also.

...

Felts of various colors.
Taffeta hats.
Deep caps for mariners colored in stamel[l], whereof if ample sale may be found, it would turn to an infinite commodity of the common poor people by knitting.
Quilted caps of Levant taffeta of various colors, for the night.
Knit stocks of silk of orient colors.
Knit stocks of jersey yarn of orient colors, whereof if ample sale might follow the poor multitude should be set in work.
Stocks of kersey of various colors for men and for women.
Garters of silk of several kinds, and of various colors.
Girdles of buff and all other leather, with gilt and ungilt buckles, specially waist girdles, waist girdles of velvet.
Gloves of all sorts, knit and of leather.
Gloves perfumed.
Points of all sorts of silk, thread, and leather, of all manner of colors.

Shoes of Spanish leather of various colors, of various length, cut and uncut.
Shoes of other leather.
Velvet shoes and pantophles [slippers].
These shoes and pantophles to be sent this time, rather for a show than for any other cause.
Purses, knit and of leather.
Nightcaps, knit and other.
A garnish of pewter for a show of a sale of that English commodity, bottles, flagons, spoons, etc. of that metal.
Glasses of English making.
Venice glasses.
Looking glasses for women, great and fair.

....

Spectacles of the common sort.
Others of crystal, trimmed with silver and otherwise.

Hourglasses. } {Combs of boxwood.
Combs of ivory. } {Combs of horn.

Linen of various sorts.
Handkerchiefs with silk of several colors wrought.
Glazen eyes to ride with against dust.
Knives in sheaths both single and double, of good edge.
Needles great and small of every kind.
Buttons greater and smaller, with molds of leather and not of wood, and such as are durable of double silk, and that of sundry colors.
Boxes with weights for gold, and of every kind of the coin of gold, good and bad, to show that the people here use weight and measure, which is a certain show of wisdom and of certain government settled here.

All the several silver coins of our English monies to be carried with you to be showed to the governors at Cambalu, which is a thing that shall in silence speak to wise men more than you imagine.

....

SAFFRON
To try what sale you may have of saffron, because this realm yields the best of the world, and for the tillage and other labors may set the poor greatly in work to their relief.

AQUAVITÆ
By new devises wonderful quantities may be made here, and therefore to seek the sale.

BLACK CONEYS' SKINS
To try the sale at Cambalu, because it lies towards the north, and because we abound with the commodity and may spare it.

THREAD OF ALL COLORS
The sale thereof may set our people in work.

COPPER SPURS AND HAWKS' BELLS
To see the sale for it may set our people in work.

A NOTE AND CAVEAT FOR THE MERCHANT
That before you offer your commodities for sale, you endeavor to learn what commodities the country there has. For if you bring thither velvet, taffeta, spice, or any such commodity that you yourself desire to lade yourself home with, you must not sell yours dear, least hereafter you purchase theirs not so cheap as you wish.

7

Imagining New Worlds at Home

47. WILLIAM CAXTON (B. 1415–24, D. 1492)

William Caxton was born in Kent. His parents apprenticed him to a mercer, Robert Large, who later became mayor of London, suggesting that the Caxtons were a family of some substance. The mercers were heavily involved in overseas trade, and Caxton seems to have traveled regularly to Bruges. By 1462 he had settled in that city and was the governor of the English nation of the Merchant Adventurers Company, a prominent position. While in Bruges Caxton probably dealt in the manuscript trade from the Low Countries, and this may have led to his interest in printing. He decided to produce English translations of fashionable Burgundian texts, and in 1469 he began a translation of Le Recueil des Histoires de Troye. In late 1473 or early 1474 he published his translation of the Recueil, *the* Recuyell of the Histories of Troy, *the first book printed in English. However, Caxton discovered that he could not sell books in English from the continent and in 1476 he moved to England and set up a press near Westminster Abbey. From his shop he sold imported books as well as his own material. Throughout his career he remained a merchant who focused on the book trade, rather than a printer as such. Between 1476 and his death in 1492 he published almost one hundred books, many of which he had translated himself from French. They included romances, saints' lives, medieval versions of the classics, and religious treatises. He was careful to ensure that the books he printed would sell, and thus he focused on well-known material, or famous translators. Caxton was both a skilled marketer of books and an insightful critic; many of his prefaces to his translations explain why people should read these particular books, allowing us an unusual insight into the reading taste of the period.*

Prologue to the Translation of the Eneydos [*Caxton's translation of the* Aeneid]

After diverse works made, translated and achieved, having no work in hand, I was sitting in my study where many pamphlets and books lay. It happened that a little book in French came to my hand, recently translated out of Latin by some noble clerk of France, which book is called *Eneydos,* written in Latin by that noble poet and great clerk Virgil. In this book I saw and read how, after the general destruction of the great Troy, Aeneas departed bearing his old father Anchises upon his shoulders, his little son Ilus on his hand, his wife with many other people following, and how he took ship and departed, with all the story of his adventures that he had before he came to the achievement of his conquest of Italy, as all along shall be shown in this present book. I had great pleasure in this book because of the fair and honest terms and words in French. I never saw its like before, nor any so pleasant or so well ordered and it seemed to me that this book should be required for noble men to see, as much for the eloquence as the histories, for many hundreds of years ago the said book of *Eneydos*, with many other works, was made and learned daily in schools, especially in Italy and other places, which history the said Virgil made in metre.

And when I had advised me in the said book, I deliberated and concluded to translate it into English. Forthwith I took a pen and ink and wrote a leaf or two, which I looked over again to correct it. And when I saw the fair and strange terms therein, I thought that it should not please some gentlemen who lately blamed me, saying that in my translations I had overcurious terms which could not be understood by the common people, and desired me to use old and homely terms in my translations. I would be glad to satisfy every man, and to do so I took an old book and read it, and certainly the English was so rough and broad that I could not understand it well. And also my lord abbot of Westminster recently showed me certain documents written in old English to reduce it into our English now used. And certainly it was written in such a way that it was more like German than English and I could not reduce or bring it to be understood.

And certainly our language now used varies far from that which was used and spoken when I was born. For we Englishmen are born under the rule of the moon, which is never steadfast but ever wavering, waxing one season and waning and decreasing another season. And the common English that is spoken in one shire varies from another in so much that in my day it happened that certain merchants were in a ship on the Thames to sail over the sea to Zeeland and for lack of wind they waited and went to land to refresh themselves. And one of them called Sheffield, a mercer, came into a house and asked for food and especially he asked for *eggys*. And the good wife answered that she could speak no French. And the merchant was angry, for he also could speak no French, but he would have eggs and she did not understand him. And then at last another said that he would have *eyren* and then the good wife said that she understood him well. Lo, what should a man in these days now write, *egges* or *eyren*, certainly it is hard to please every man because of diversity and change of language. For in these days every man that has any reputation in his country will utter his communication and matters in such manners and terms that few men will understand him. And some honest and great clerks have been with me and desired me to write the most curious terms that I could find. And thus between plain rude and curious I stand abashed, but in my judgment the common terms that are used daily are more easily understood than the old and ancient English.

And for as much as this present book is not for a rude uplandish man to labor therein nor to read it, but only for a clerk and a noble gentleman that experiences and understands feats of arms, love and noble chivalry, therefore in a middle way between both I have reduced and translated this said book into our English, not over rough or curious but in such terms as shall be understood by God's grace according to my copy. And if any man will busy himself in reading it and find terms that he cannot understand, let him go read and learn Virgil or the epistles of Ovid and there he shall easily see and understand all, if he has a good reader and informer. For this book is not for every rude and ignorant man to see, but for clerks and true gentlemen that understand gentleness and science.

Then I pray all those that will read this little treatise to hold me excused for the translating of it. For I acknowledge myself ignorant of cunning to attempt such a high and noble work, but I pray Master John Skelton, late created poet laureate in the university of Oxford, to oversee and correct this said book and to address and expound where fault is found to those that shall require it. For I know that he is able to expound and english every difficulty that is therin, for he has recently translated the epistles of Tully [Cicero] and the book of Diodorus Siculus and divers other works out of Latin into English, not in rough and old language, but in polished and ornate terms with craft, as he that has read Virgil, Ovid, Tully and all the other noble poets and orators unknown to me. And he has also read the nine muses and understands their musical sciences and to which of them each science is appropriate. I suppose he has drunk of Helicon's well. Then I pray him and such other to correct, add or take away where he or they will find fault, for I have only followed my copy in French as nearly as I could. And if any word is said therin well, I am glad, and if otherwise I submit my said book to their correction.

Which book I present unto the highborn, my future natural and sovereign lord Arthur, by the grace of God prince of Wales, duke of Cornwall and earl of Chester, first begotten son and heir unto our most dread natural and sovereign lord and most Christian King Henry the VII, by the grace of God king of England and of France and lord of Ireland, beseeching his noble grace to receive it in thank of me his most humble subject and servant. And I shall pray unto almighty God for his prosperous increasing in virtue, wisdom and humanity that he may be equal with the most renowned of all his noble progenitors.

And so to live in this present life that after this transitory life he and we all may come to everlasting life in heaven. Amen.

48. MIGUEL DE CERVANTES (1547–1616)

Born in Alcala de Henares, Cervantes enjoyed a brief humanist education in Madrid under Juan Lopez de Hoyos, but he augmented this study with wide reading and travel, visiting Italy, for example, and acquiring a deep appreciation for Italian Renaissance culture. He was also a soldier and fought—and was wounded—at the great naval battle of Lepanto in 1571, in which the Christian Holy League defeated the Turkish fleet. Later, however, Cervantes was captured and sold into slavery in Algiers, and not ransomed until 1580.

Returning to Spain, he was appointed a collector of taxes to be used to assemble the Armada of Philip II against England, but he was imprisoned because of problems with his accounts. In prison on several other occasions for debt, he began to write Don Quixote *while in jail. It is a satire on the tales of chivalry so popular in Spain at the time, following the adventures of its hero, Don Quixote, and his servant, Sancho Panza, and like the Caxton prologue above, it also gives us a glimpse into the ways in which the invention of print changed reading culture. This early novel became the most popular work of Spanish literature when printed (part one in 1605, part two in 1615), and it made its author's fortune. Cervantes died in Madrid in 1616.*

Don Quixote: *Dedication to the Duke of Béjar and the Prologue*

Dedication To the Duke of Béjar Marquis of Gibraleón, Count of Benalcázar and Bañares, Viscount of La Puebla de Alcocer, Lord of the Towns of Capilla, Curiel, and Burguillos

Confident of the courteous reception and honors that Your Excellency bestows on all sorts of books, as a prince so inclined to favor the fine arts, chiefly those which by their nobility do not submit to the service and bribery of the vulgar, I have decided to publish *The Ingenious Gentleman Don Quixote of La Mancha* in the shelter of Your Excellency's most illustrious name. And with the obeisance I owe to such grandeur, I beg you to receive it graciously under your protection, so that in this shadow, though deprived of those precious ornaments of elegance and erudition that clothe works composed in the houses of those who know, it may dare appear with assurance before the judgment of some who, trespassing the bounds of their own ignorance, condemn with more rigor and less justice the writings of others. It is my earnest hope that Your Excellency's wisdom will consider my honorable purpose and will not disdain the littleness of so humble a service.

Prologue

Idle reader: you may believe me, without my having to swear, that I would have liked this book, as it is the child of my brain, to be the fairest, gayest, and cleverest that could be imagined. But I could not counteract Nature's law that everything shall beget its like; and what, then, could this sterile, uncultivated wit of mine beget but the story of a dry, shriveled, eccentric offspring, full of thoughts of all sorts and such as never came into any other imagination—just what might be begotten in a prison, where every misery is lodged and every doleful sound makes its dwelling? Tranquility, a cheerful retreat, pleasant fields, bright skies, murmuring brooks, peace of mind, these are the things that go far to make even the most barren muses fertile and cause them to bring into the world offspring that fill it with wonder and delight.

Sometimes when a father has an ugly, unattractive child, the love he bears him so blindfolds his eyes that he does not see its defects; on the contrary, he considers them marks of intelligence and charm and talks of them to his friends as wit and grace. I, however—for though I pass for the father, I am the stepfather of Don Quixote—I have no desire to go with the current of custom or to implore you, dearest reader, almost with tears in my eyes, as others do, to pardon or excuse the defects you may perceive in this child of mine. You are neither its relative nor its friend, your soul is your own and your will as free as any man's, you are in your own house and master of it as much as the king of his taxes, and you know the common saying, "A man's home is his castle"—all of which exempts and frees you from every consideration and obligation. And you can say what you will about the story without fear of being abused for any ill or rewarded for any good you may say of it.

My wish would be simply to present it to you plain and unadorned, without the embellishment of a prologue or the lengthy catalogue of the usual sonnets, epigrams, and eulogies, such as are commonly put at the beginning of books. For I can tell you, though composing it cost me considerable effort, I found nothing harder than the making of this prologue you are now reading. Many times I took up my pen to write it, and many I laid it down again, not knowing what to write. One of these times, as I was pondering with the paper before me, a pen behind my ear, my elbow on the desk, and my cheek in my hand, thinking of what I should say, there came in unexpectedly a certain lively, clever friend of mine, who, seeing me so deep in thought, asked the reason; to which I, making no mystery of it, answered that I was thinking of the prologue I had to write for the story of Don Quixote, which so troubled me that I had a mind not to write any at all—nor even publish the achievements of so noble a knight.

"For, how could you expect me not to feel uneasy about what that ancient lawgiver they call the Public will say when it sees me, after slumbering so many years in the silence of oblivion, coming out now with all my years upon my back, and with a book as dry as a bone, devoid of invention, meager in style, poor in conceits, wholly wanting in learning and doctrine, without quotations in the margin or annotations at the end, after the fashion of other books I see, which, though on fictitious and profane subjects, are so full of maxims from Aristotle and Plato and the whole herd of philosophers that they fill the readers with amazement and convince them that the authors are men of learning, erudition, and eloquence. And then, when they quote the Holy Scriptures, anyone would say they are St. Thomases or other doctors of the Church, observing as they do a decorum so ingenious that in one sentence they describe a distracted lover and in the next deliver a devout little sermon that it is a pleasure and a treat to hear and read. Of all this there will be nothing in my book, for I have nothing to quote in the margin or to note at the end, and still less do I know what authors I follow in it, to place them at the beginning, as all do, under the letters A, B, C, beginning with Aristotle and ending with Xenophon or Zoilus or Zeuxis, though one was a slanderer and the other a painter. Also my book must do without sonnets at the beginning, at least sonnets whose authors are dukes, marquises, counts, bishops, ladies, or famous poets. Though if I were to ask two or three friendly tradesmen, I know they would give me some, and such that the productions of those that have the highest reputation in our Spain could not equal.

"In short, my friend," I continued, "I am determined that Señor Don Quixote shall remain buried in the archives of his own La Mancha until Heaven provides someone to garnish him with all those things he stands in need of; because I find myself, through my incapacity and want of learning, unequal to supplying them, and because I am by nature indolent and lazy about hunting for authors to say what I myself can say without them. Hence, my friend, the cogitation and abstraction you found me in, and what you have heard from me is sufficient cause for it."

Hearing this, my friend, giving himself a slap on the forehead and breaking into a hearty laugh, exclaimed, "Before God, brother, now am I disabused of an error in which I have been living all this long time I have known you, all through which I have taken you to be shrewd and sensible in all you do; but now I see you are as far from that as the heaven is from the earth. Is it possible that things of so little moment and so easy to set right can occupy and perplex a ripe wit like yours, accustomed to break through and crush far greater obstacles? By my faith, this comes, not of any want of ability, but of too much indolence and too little thinking. Do you want to know if I am telling the truth? Well, then, pay attention to me, and you will see how, in the opening and shutting of an eye, I sweep away all your difficulties and supply all those deficiencies which you say check and discourage you from bringing before the world the story of your famous Don Quixote, the light and mirror of all knight-errantry."

"Say on," said I, listening to his talk. "How do you propose to make up for my diffidence and reduce to order this chaos of perplexity I am in?"

To which he answered, "Your first difficulty, about the sonnets, epigrams, or complimentary verses which you lack for the beginning and which ought to be by persons of importance and rank, can be removed if you yourself take a little trouble to write them. You can afterwards baptize them and give them any name you like, fathering them on Prester John of the Indies or the Emperor of Trebizond, who I know were said to have been famous poets. And even if they were not, and any pedants or bachelors should attack you and question the fact, don't let it bother you two *maravedis*' worth, for even if they prove a lie against you, they cannot cut off the hand you wrote it with.

"As to references in the margin to the books and authors from whom you take the maxims and sayings you put into your story, all you have to do is work in any sentence or scraps of Latin you may happen to know by heart, or at any rate that will not give you much trouble to look up. Thus when you speak of freedom and captivity, you can insert *Non bene pro toto libertas venditur auro* [one should not sell his liberty for any price: medieval fable] and then refer in the margin to Horace, or whoever said it. Or, if you allude to the power of death, you can bring in *Pallida mors æquo pulsat pede pauperum tabernas,/ Regumque turres* [pale death strikes without distinction the hovels of the poor and the towers of kings: Horace].

"If it is the friendship and the love God commands us to feel towards our enemy, go at once to the Holy Scriptures, which you can do with a very small amount of research, and quote no less than the words of God himself: *Ego autem dico vobis: diligite inimicos vestros* [but I say unto you, love your enemies: Matt. 5:44]. If you speak of evil thoughts, turn to the Gospel: *De corde exeunt cogitationes malæ* [from out of the heart proceed evil thoughts: Matt. 15:19]. If of the fickleness of friends, there is Cato, who will give you his couplet: *Donec eris felix muttos numerabis amicos,/ Tempora si fuerint nubila, solus eris* [while you are prosperous you will have many friends; but when times are troubled you will be alone: Ovid]. With these and such like bits of Latin they will take you for a grammarian at all events, and that nowadays is no small honor and profit.

"With regard to adding annotations at the end of the book, you may safely do it in this way. If you mention any giant in your book, arrange for it to be the giant Goliath, and with this alone, which will cost you almost nothing, you have a grand note, for you can put *The giant Golias or Goliath was a Philistine whom the shepherd David slew by a mighty stone—cast in the Terebinth valley, as is related in the Book of Kings,* in the chapter where you find it written.

"Next, to prove yourself a man of erudition in polite literature and a cosmographer, manage to mention the river Tagus in your story, and there you are at once with another fine annotation, setting forth *The river Tagus was so called after a King of Spain: it has its source in such and such a place and falls into the ocean, kissing the walls of the famous city of Lisbon, and it is a common belief that it has golden sands,* etc.

"If you should have anything to do with robbers, I will give you the story of Cacus, for I know it by heart; if with loose women, there is the Bishop of Mondoñedo, who will lend you Lamia, Laida, and Flora, any reference to whom will bring you great credit; if with hardhearted ones, Ovid will furnish you with Medea; if with witches or enchantresses, Homer has Calypso, and Virgil Circe; if with valiant captains, Julius Cæsar himself will lend you himself in his own *Commentaries;* and Plutarch will give you a thousand Alexanders. If you should deal with love, and if you have a smattering of Italian, you can go to Leon the Hebrew, who will supply you to your heart's content; or if you should not care to go to foreign countries, you have at home Fonseca's *Of the Love of God,* in which is condensed all that you or the most imaginative mind can want on the subject.

"In short, all you have to do is to manage to quote these names or refer to these stories I have mentioned, and leave it to me to insert the annotations and quotations, and I swear by all that's good to fill your margins and use up four sheets at the end of the book.

"Now let us come to those references to authors which other books have and you need for yours. The remedy for this is very simple: you have only to look up some book that quotes them all, from A to Z as you say yourself, and then insert the very same list in your book, and though the deception may be obvious, because you had so little need to make use of them, that is no matter; there will probably be some stupid enough to believe that you have made use of them all in this simple, straightforward story of yours. At any rate, if it answers no other purpose, this long catalogue of authors will serve to give instant authority to your book.

"Besides, no one will trouble himself to verify whether you have followed them or whether you have not, since it cannot possibly matter to him; especially as, if I understand it correctly, this book of yours has no need of any of those things you say it lacks, for it is, from beginning to end, an attack upon the books of chivalry, of which Aristotle never dreamed or St. Basil said a word or Cicero had any knowledge. Nor do the niceties of truth nor the observations of astrology come within the range of its fanciful nonsense; nor have geometrical measurements or refutations of the arguments used in rhetoric anything to do with it; nor does it have any reason to preach to anybody, mixing up things human and divine, a sort of motley in which no Christian understanding should dress itself. It has only to avail itself of imitation in its writing, and the more perfect the imitation the better the work will be. And as this piece of yours aims at nothing more than to destroy the authority and influence which books of chivalry have in the world and with the public, there is no need for you to go begging for aphorisms from philosophers, precepts from Holy Scripture, fables from poets, speeches from orators, or miracles from saints, but merely to take care that your sentences flow musically, pleasantly, and plainly, with clear, proper, and well-placed words, setting forth your purpose to the best of your power, and putting your ideas intelligibly, without confusion or obscurity.

"Strive, too, that in reading your story the melancholy may be moved to laughter, and the merry made merrier still; that the simple shall not be wearied, that the judicious shall admire the invention, that the grave shall not despise it, or the wise fail to praise it. Finally, keep your aim fixed on the destruction of that ill-founded edifice of the books of chivalry, hated by so many yet praised by many more; for if you succeed in this you will have achieved no small success."

In profound silence I listened to what my friend said, and his observations made such an impression on me that, without attempting to question them, I admitted their soundness, and out of them I determined to make this prologue, in which gentle reader, you will perceive my friend's good sense, my good fortune in finding such an adviser in such a time of need, and why you find—to your relief—the story of Don Quixote of La Mancha so straightforward and free of extraneous matter. This famous knight is held by all the inhabitants of the district of the Campo de Montiel to have been the chastest lover and the bravest knight that has for many years been seen in that region. I have no desire to magnify the service I am rendering to you in making you acquainted with so renowned and honored a knight, but I do desire your thanks for the acquaintance you will make with the famous Sancho Panza, his squire, in whom, to my thinking, I have given you condensed all the squirely virtues that are scattered throughout the swarm of the vain books of chivalry. And so may God give you health and not forget me. *Vale.*

49. MIGUEL DE CERVANTES (1547–1616)

Don Quixote

The station in life and the pursuits of the famous gentleman, Don Quixote de la Mancha

In a village of La Mancha the name of which I have no desire to recall, there lived not so long ago one of those gentlemen who always have a lance in the rack, an ancient buckler, a skinny nag, and a greyhound for the chase. A stew with more beef than mutton in it, chopped meat for his evening meal, scraps for a Saturday, lentils on Friday, and a young pigeon as a special delicacy for Sunday, went to account for three-quarters of his income. The rest of it he laid out on a broadcloth greatcoat and velvet stockings for feast days, with slippers to match, while the other days of the week he cut a figure in a suit of the finest homespun. Living with him were a housekeeper in her forties, a niece who was not yet twenty, and a lad of the field and market place who saddled his horse for him and wielded the pruning knife.

This gentleman of ours was close on to fifty, of robust constitution but with little flesh on his bones and a face that was lean and gaunt. He was noted for his early rising, being very fond of the hunt. They will try to tell you that his surname was Quijada or Quesada—there is some difference of opinion among those who have written on the subject—but according to the most likely conjectures we are to understand that it was really Quejana. But all this means very little so far as our story is concerned, providing that in the telling of it we do not depart one iota from the truth.

You may know, then, that the aforesaid gentleman, on those occasions when he was at leisure, which was most of the year around, was in the habit of reading books of chivalry with such pleasure and devotion as to lead him almost wholly to forget the life of a hunter and even the administration of his estate. So great was his curiosity and infatuation in this regard that he even sold many acres of tillable land in order to be able to buy and read the books that he loved, and he would carry home with him as many of them as he could obtain.

Of all those that he thus devoured none pleased him so well as the ones that had been composed by the famous Feliciano de Silva, whose lucid prose style and involved conceits were as precious to him as pearls; especially when he came to read those tales of love and amorous challenges that are to be met with in many places, such a passage as the following, for example: "The reason of the unreason that afflicts my reason, in such a manner weakens my reason that I with reason lament me of your comeliness." And he was similarly affected when his eyes fell upon such lines at these: " … the high Heaven of your divinity divinely fortifies you with the stars and renders you deserving of that desert your greatness doth deserve."

The poor fellow used to lie awake nights in an effort to disentangle the meaning and make sense out of passages such as these, although Aristotle himself would not have been able to understand them, even if he had been resurrected for that sole purpose. He was not at ease in his mind over those wounds that Don Beliants gave and received; for no matter how great the surgeons who treated him, the poor fellow must have been left with his face and his entire body covered with marks and scars. Nevertheless, he was grateful to the author for closing the book with the promise of an interminable adventure to come; many a time he was tempted to take up his pen and literally finish the tale as had been promised, and he undoubtedly would have done so, and would have succeeded at it very well, if his thoughts had not been constantly occupied with other things of greater moment.

He often talked it over with the village curate, who was a learned man, a graduate of Sigüenza, and they would hold long discussions as to who had been the better knight, Palmerin of England or Amadis of Gaul; but Master Nicholas, the barber of the same village, was in the habit of saying that no one could come up to the Knight of Phoebus, and that if anyone *could* compare with him it was Don Galaor, brother of Amadis of Gaul, for Galaor was ready for anything—he was none of your finical knights, who went around whimpering as his brother did, and in point of valor he did not lag behind him.

In short, our gentleman became so immersed in his reading that he spent whole nights from sundown to sunup and his days from dawn to dusk in poring over his books, until, finally, from so little sleeping and so much reading, his brain dried up and he went completely out of his mind. He had filled his imagination with everything that he had read, with enchantments, knightly encounters, battles, challenges, wounds, with tales of love and its torments, and all sorts of impossible things, and as a result had come to believe that all these fictitious happenings were true; they were more real to him than anything else in the world. He would remark that the Cid Ruy Díaz had been a very good knight, but there was no comparison between him and the Knight of the Flaming Sword, who with a single backward stroke had cut in half two fierce and monstrous giants. He preferred Bernardo del Carpio, who at Roncesvalles had slain Roland despite the charm the latter bore, availing himself of the stratagem which Hercules employed when he strangled Antaeus, the son of Earth, in his arms.

He had much good to say for Morgante who, though he belonged to the haughty, overbearing race of giants, was of an affable disposition and well brought up. But, above all, he cherished an admiration for Rinaldo of Montalbán, especially as he beheld him sallying forth from his castle to rob all those that crossed his path, or when he thought of him overseas stealing the image of Mohammed which, so the story has it, was all of gold. And he would have liked very well to have had his fill of kicking that traitor Galalón, a privilege for which he would have given his housekeeper with his niece thrown into the bargain.

At last, when his wits were gone beyond repair, he came to conceive the strangest idea that ever occurred to any madman in this world. It now appeared to him fitting and necessary, in order to win a greater amount of honor for himself and serve his country at the same time, to become a knight-errant and roam the world on horseback, in a suit of armor; he would go in quest of adventures, by way of putting into practice all that he had read in his books; he would right every manner of wrong, placing himself in situations of the greatest peril such as would redound to the eternal glory of his name. As a reward for his valor and the might of his arm, the poor fellow could already see himself crowned Emperor of Trebizond at the very least; and so, carried away by the strange pleasure that he found in such thoughts as these, he at once set about putting his plan into effect.

The first thing he did was to burnish up some old pieces of armor, left him by his great-grandfather, which for ages had lain in a corner, moldering and forgotten. He polished and adjusted them as best he could, and then he noticed that one very important thing was lacking: there was no closed helmet, but only a morion, or visorless headpiece, with turned-up brim of the kind foot soldiers wore. His ingenuity, however, enabled him to remedy this, and he proceeded to fashion out of cardboard a kind of half-helmet, which, when attached to the morion, gave the appearance of a whole one. True, when he went to see if it was strong enough to withstand a good slashing blow, he was somewhat disappointed; for when he drew his sword and gave it a couple of thrusts, he succeeded only in undoing a whole week's labor. The ease with which he had hewed it to bits disturbed him no little, and he decided to make it over. This time he placed a few strips of iron on the inside, and then, convinced that it was strong enough, refrained from putting it to any further test; instead, he adopted it then and there as the finest helmet ever made.

After this, he went out to have a look at his nag; and although the animal had more cuartos, or cracks, in its hoof than there are quarters in a real, and more blemishes than Gonela's steed which *tantum pellis et ossa fuit,* it nonetheless looked to its master like a far better horse than Alexander's Bucephalus or the Babicca of the Cid. He spent all of four days in trying to think up a name for his mount; for—so he told himself—seeing that it belonged to so famous and worthy a knight, there was no reason why it should not have a name of equal renown. The kind of name he wanted was one that would at once indicate what the nag had been before it came to belong to a knight-errant and what its present status was; for it stood to reason that, when the master's worldly condition changed, his horse also ought to have a famous, high-sounding appellation, one suited to the new order of things and the new profession that it was to follow.

After he in his memory and imagination had made up, struck out, and discarded many names, now adding to and now subtracting from the list, he finally hit upon "Rocinante," a name that impressed him as being sonorous and at the same time indicative of what the steed had been when it was but a hack, whereas now it was nothing other than the first and foremost of all the hacks in the world.

Having found a name for his horse that pleased his fancy, he then desired to do as much for himself, and this required another week, and by the end of that period he had made up his mind that he was henceforth to be known as Don Quixote, which, as has been stated, has led the authors of this veracious history to assume that his real name must undoubtedly have been Quijada, and not Quesada as others would have it. But remembering that the valiant Amadis was not content to call himself that and nothing more, but added the name of his kingdom and fatherland that he might make it famous also, and thus came to take the name of Amadis of Gaul, so our good knight chose to add his place of origin and become "Don Quixote de la Mancha"; for by this means, as he saw it, he was making very plain his lineage and was conferring honor upon his country by taking its name as his own.

And so, having polished up his armor and made the morion over into a closed helmet, and having given himself and his horse a name, he naturally found but one thing lacking still: he must seek out a lady of whom he could become enamored; for a knight-errant without a lady-love was like a tree without leaves or fruit, a body without a soul.

"If," he said to himself, "as a punishment for my sins or by a stroke of fortune I should come upon some giant hereabouts, a thing that very commonly happens to knights-errant, and if I should slay him in a hand-to-hand encounter or perhaps cut him in two, or, finally, if I should vanquish and subdue him, would it not be well to have someone to whom I may send him as a present, in order that he, if he is living, may come in, fall upon his knees in front of my sweet lady, and say in a humble and submissive tone of voice, 'I, lady, am the giant Caraculiambro, lord of the island Malindrania, who has been overcome in single combat by that knight who never can be praised enough, Don Quixote de la Mancha, the same who sent me to present myself before your Grace that your Highness may dispose of me as you see fit'?"

Oh, how our good knight reveled in this speech, and more than ever when he came to think of the name that he should give his lady! As the story goes, there was a very good-looking farm girl who lived nearby, with whom he had once been smitten, although it is generally believed that she never knew or suspected it. Her name was Aldonza Lorenzo, and it seemed to him that she was the one upon whom he should bestow the title of mistress of his thoughts. For her he wished a name that should not be incongruous with his own and that would convey the suggestion of a princess or a great lady; and, accordingly, he resolved to call her "Dulcinea del Toboso," she being a native of that place. A musical name to his ears, out of the ordinary and significant, like the others he had chosen for himself and his appurtenances.

The first sally that the ingenious Don Quixote made from his native heath

Having, then, made all these preparations, he did not wish to lose any time in putting his plan into effect, for he could not but blame himself for what the world was losing by his delay, so many were the wrongs that were to be righted, the grievances to be redressed, the abuses to be done away with, and the duties to be performed. Accordingly, without informing anyone of his intention and without letting anyone see him, he set out one morning before daybreak on one of those very hot days in July. Donning all his armor, mounting Rocinante, adjusting his ill-contrived helmet, bracing his shield on his arm, and taking up his lance, he sallied forth by the back gate of his stable yard into the open countryside. It was with great contentment and joy that he saw how easily he had made a beginning toward the fulfillment of his desire.

No sooner was he out on the plain, however, than a terrible thought assailed him, one that all but caused him to abandon the enterprise he had undertaken. This occurred when he suddenly remembered that he had never formally been dubbed a knight, and so, in accordance with the law of knighthood, was not permitted to bear arms against one who had a right to that title. And even if he had been, as a novice knight he would have had to wear white armor, without any device on his shield, until he should have earned one by his exploits. These thoughts led him to waver in his purpose, but, madness prevailing over reason, he resolved to have himself knighted by the first person he met, as many others had done if what he had read in those books that he had at home was true. And so far as white armor was concerned, he would scour his own the first chance that offered until it shone whiter than any ermine. With this he became more tranquil and continued on his way, letting his horse take whatever path it chose, for he believed that therein lay the very essence of adventures.

And so we find our newly fledged adventurer jogging along and talking to himself. "Undoubtedly," he is saying, "in the days to come, when the true history of my famous deeds is published, the learned chronicler who records them, when he comes to describe my first sally so early in the morning, will put down something like this: 'No sooner had the rubicund Apollo spread over the face of the broad and spacious earth the gilded filaments of his beauteous locks, and no sooner had the little singing birds of painted plumage greeted with their sweet and mellifluous harmony the coming of the Dawn, who, leaving the soft couch of her jealous spouse, now showed herself to mortals at all the doors and balconies of the horizon that bounds La Mancha—no sooner had this happened than the famous knight, Don Quixote de la Mancha, forsaking his own downy bed and mounting his famous steed, Rocinante, fared forth and began riding over the ancient and famous Campo de Montiel.'"

And this was the truth, for he was indeed riding over that stretch of plain.

"O happy age and happy century," he went on, "in which my famous exploits shall be published, exploits worthy of being engraved in bronze, sculptured in marble, and depicted in paintings for the benefit of posterity. O wise magician, whoever you be, to whom shall fall the task of chronicling this extraordinary history of mine! I beg of you not to forget my good Rocinante, eternal companion of my wayfarings and my wanderings."

Then, as though he really had been in love: "O Princess Dulcinea, lady of this captive heart! Much wrong have you done me in thus sending me forth with your reproaches and sternly commanding me not to appear in your beauteous presence. O lady, deign to be mindful of this your subject who endures so many woes for the love of you."

And so he went on, stringing together absurdities, all of a kind that his books had taught him, imitating insofar as he was able the language of their authors. He rode slowly, and the sun came up so swiftly and with so much heat that it would have been sufficient to melt his brains if he had had any. He had been on the road almost the entire day without anything happening that is worthy of being set down here; and he was on the verge of despair, for he wished to meet someone at once with whom he might try the valor of his good right arm. Certain authors say that his first adventure was that of Puerto Lápice, while others state that it was that of the windmills; but in this particular instance I am in a position to affirm what I have read in the annals of La Mancha; and that is to the effect that he went all that day until nightfall, when he and his hack found themselves tired to death and famished. Gazing all around him to see if he could discover some castle or shepherd's hut where he might take shelter and attend to his pressing needs, he caught sight of an inn not far off the road along which they were traveling, and this to him was like a star guiding him not merely to the gates, but rather, let us say, to the palace of redemption. Quickening his pace, he came up to it just as night was falling.

By chance there stood in the doorway two lasses of the sort known as "of the district"; they were on their way to

Seville in the company of some mule drivers who were spending the night in the inn. Now, everything that this adventurer of ours thought, saw, or imagined seemed to him to be directly out of one of the storybooks he had read, and so, when he caught sight of the inn, it at once became a castle with its four turrets and its pinnacles of gleaming silver, not to speak of the drawbridge and moat and all the other things that are commonly supposed to go with a castle. As he rode up to it, he accordingly reined in Rocinante and sat there waiting for a dwarf to appear upon the battlements and blow his trumpet by way of announcing the arrival of a knight. The dwarf, however, was slow in coming, and as Rocinante was anxious to reach the stable, Don Quixote drew up to the door of the hostelry and surveyed the two merry maidens, who to him were a pair of beauteous damsels or gracious ladies taking their ease at the castle gate.

And then a swineherd came along, engaged in rounding up his drove of hogs—for, without any apology, that is what they were. He gave a blast on his horn to bring them together, and this at once became for Don Quixote just what he wished it to be: some dwarf who was heralding his coming; and so it was with a vast deal of satisfaction that he presented himself before the ladies in question, who, upon beholding a man in full armor like this, with lance and buckler, were filled with fright and made as if to flee indoors. Realizing that they were afraid, Don Quixote raised his pasteboard visor and revealed his withered, dust-covered face.

"Do not flee, your Ladyships," he said to them in a courteous manner and gentle voice. "You need not fear that any wrong will be done you, for it is not in accordance with the order of knighthood which I profess to wrong anyone, much less such highborn damsels as your appearance shows you to be."

The girls looked at him, endeavoring to scan his face, which was half-hidden by his ill-made visor. Never having heard women of their profession called damsels before, they were unable to restrain their laughter, at which Don Quixote took offense.

"Modesty," he observed, "well becomes those with the dower of beauty, and, moreover, laughter that has not good cause is a very foolish thing. But I do not say this to be discourteous or to hurt your feelings; my only desire is to serve you."

The ladies did not understand what he was talking about, but felt more than ever like laughing at our knight's unprepossessing figure. This increased his annoyance, and there is no telling what would have happened if at that moment the innkeeper had not come out. He was very fat and very peaceably inclined; but upon sighting this grotesque personage clad in bits of armor that were quite as oddly matched as were his bridle, lance, buckler, and corselet, mine host was not at all indisposed to join the lasses in their merriment. He was suspicious, however, of all this paraphernalia and decided that it would be better to keep a civil tongue in his head.

"If, Sir Knight," he said, "your Grace desires a lodging, aside from a bed—for there is none to be had in this inn—you will find all else that you may want in great abundance."

When Don Quixote saw how humble the governor of the castle was—for he took the innkeeper and his inn to be no less than that—he replied, "For me, Sir Castellan, anything will do, since

Arms are my only ornament,
My only rest the fight, etc."

The landlord thought that the knight had called him a castellan because he took him for one of those worthies of Castile, whereas the truth was, he was an Andalusian from the beach of Sanlúcar, no less a thief than Cacus himself, and as full of tricks as a student or a page boy.

"In that case," he said,

"Your bed will be the solid rock,
Your sleep: to watch all night.

This being so, you may be assured of finding beneath this roof enough to keep you awake for a whole year, to say nothing of a single night."

….

Of the good fortune which the valorous Don Quixote had in the terrifying and never-before-imagined adventure of the windmills, along with other events that deserve to be suitably recorded

At this point they caught sight of thirty or forty windmills which were standing on the plain there, and no sooner had Don Quixote laid eyes upon them than he turned to his squire and said, "Fortune is guiding our affairs better than we could have wished; for you see there before you, friend Sancho Panza, some thirty or more lawless giants with whom I mean to do battle. I shall deprive them of their lives, and with the spoils from this encounter we shall begin to enrich ourselves; for this is righteous warfare, and it is a great service to

God to remove so accursed a breed from the face of the earth."

"What giants?" said Sancho Panza.

"Those that you see there," replied his master, "those with the long arms some of which are as much as two leagues in length."

"But look, your Grace, those are not giants but windmills, and what appear to be arms are their wings which, when whirled in the breeze, cause the millstone to go."

"It is plain to be seen," said Don Quixote, "that you have had little experience in this matter of adventures. If you are afraid, go off to one side and say your prayers while I am engaging them in fierce, unequal combat."

Saying this, he gave spurs to his steed Rocinante, without paying any heed to Sancho's warning that these were truly windmills and not giants that he was riding forth to attack. Nor even when he was close upon them did he perceive what they really were, but shouted at the top of his lungs, "Do not seek to flee, cowards and vile creatures that you are, for it is but a single knight with whom you have to deal!"

At that moment a little wind came up and the big wings began turning.

"Though you flourish as many arms as did the giant Briareus," said Don Quixote when he perceived this, "you still shall have to answer to me."

He thereupon commended himself with all his heart to his lady Dulcinea, beseeching her to succor him in this peril; and, being well covered with his shield and with his lance at rest, he bore down upon them at a full gallop and fell upon the first mill that stood in his way, giving a thrust at the wing, which was whirling at such a speed that his lance was broken into bits and both horse and horseman went rolling over the plain, very much battered indeed. Sancho upon his donkey came hurrying to his master's assistance as fast as he could, but when he reached the spot, the knight was unable to move, so great was the shock with which he and Rocinante had hit the ground.

"God help us!" exclaimed Sancho, "did I not tell your Grace to look well, that those were nothing but windmills, a fact which no one could fail to see unless he had other mills of the same sort in his head?"

"Be quiet, friend Sancho," said Don Quixote. "Such are the fortunes of war, which more than any other are subject to constant change. What is more, when I come to think of it, I am sure that this must be the work of that magician Frestón, the one who robbed me of my study and my books, and who has thus changed the giants into windmills in order to deprive me of the glory of overcoming them, so great is the enmity that he bears me; but in the end his evil arts shall not prevail against this trusty sword of mine."

"May God's will be done," was Sancho Panza's response. And with the aid of his squire the knight was once more mounted on Rocinante, who stood there with one shoulder half out of joint. And so, speaking of the adventure that had just befallen them, they continued along the Puerto Lápice highway; for there, Don Quixote said, they could not fail to find many and varied adventures, this being a much traveled thoroughfare. The only thing was, the knight was exceedingly downcast over the loss of his lance.

"I remember," he said to his squire, "having read of a Spanish knight by the name of Diego Pérez de Vargas, who, having broken his sword in battle, tore from an oak a heavy bough or branch and with it did such feats of valor that day, and pounded so many Moors, that he came to be known as Machuca, and he and his descendants from that day forth have been called Vargas y Machuca. I tell you this because I too intend to provide myself with just such a bough as the one he wielded, and with it I propose to do such exploits that you shall deem yourself fortunate to have been found worthy to come with me and behold and witness things that are almost beyond belief."

"God's will be done," said Sancho. "I believe everything that your Grace says; but straighten yourself up in the saddle a little, for you seem to be slipping down on one side, owing, no doubt, to the shaking-up that you received in your fall."

"Ah, that is the truth," replied Don Quixote, "and if I do not speak of my sufferings, it is for the reason that it is not permitted knights-errant to complain of any wound whatsoever, even though their bowels may be dropping out."

"If that is the way it is," said Sancho, "I have nothing more to say; but, God knows, it would suit me better if your Grace did complain when something hurts him. I can assure you that I mean to do so, over the least little thing that ails me—that is, unless the same rule applies to squires as well."

Don Quixote laughed long and heartily over Sancho's simplicity, telling him that he might complain as much as he liked and where and when he liked, whether he had good cause or not; for he had read nothing to the contrary in the ordinances of chivalry. Sancho then called his master's attention to the fact that it was time to eat. The knight replied that he himself had no need of food at the moment, but his squire might eat whenever he chose. Having been granted this permission, Sancho seated himself as best he could upon his beast, and, taking out from his saddlebags the provisions that he had stored there, he rode along leisurely behind his master, munching his victuals and taking a good, hearty swig now and then at the leather flask in a manner that might well have caused the biggest-bellied tavernkeeper of Málaga to envy him. Between draughts he gave not so much as a thought to any promise that his master might have made him, nor did he look upon it as any hardship, but rather as good sport, to go in quest of adventures however hazardous they might be.

The short of the matter is, they spent the night under some trees, from one of which Don Quixote tore off a withered bough to serve him as a lance, placing it in the lance head from which he had removed the broken one. He did not sleep all night long for thinking of his lady Dulcinea; for this was in accordance with what he had read in his books, of men of arms in the forest or desert places who kept a wakeful vigil, sustained by the memory of their ladies fair. Not so with Sancho, whose stomach was full, and not with chicory water. He fell into a dreamless slumber, and had not his master called him, he would not have been awakened either by the rays of the sun in his face or by the many birds who greeted the coming of the new day with their merry song.

Upon arising, he had another go at the flask, finding it somewhat more flaccid than it had been the night before, a circumstance which grieved his heart, for he could not see that they were on the way to remedying the deficiency within any very short space of time. Don Quixote did not wish any breakfast; for, as has been said, he was in the habit of nourishing himself on savorous memories. They then set out once more along the road to Puerto Lápice, and around three in the afternoon they came in sight of the pass that bears that name.

"There," said Don Quixote as his eyes fell upon it, "we may plunge our arms up to the elbow in what are known as adventures. But I must warn you that even though you see me in the greatest peril in the world, you are not to lay hand upon your sword to defend me, unless it be that those who attack me are rabble and men of low degree, in which case you may very well come to my aid; but if they be gentlemen, it is in no wise permitted by the laws of chivalry that you should assist me until you yourself shall have been dubbed a knight."

"Most certainly, sir," replied Sancho, "Your Grace shall be very well obeyed in this; all the more so for the reason that I myself am of a peaceful disposition and not fond of meddling in the quarrels and feuds of others. However, when it comes to protecting my own person, I shall not take account of those laws of which you speak, seeing that all laws, human and divine, permit each one to defend himself whenever he is attacked."

"I am willing to grant you that," assented Don Quixote, "but in this matter of defending me against gentlemen you must restrain your natural impulses."

"I promise you I shall do so," said Sancho. "I will observe this precept as I would the Sabbath day."

As they were conversing in this manner, there appeared in the road in front of them two friars of the Order of St. Benedict, mounted upon dromedaries—for the she-mules they rode were certainly no smaller than that. The friars wore travelers' spectacles and carried sunshades, and behind them came a coach accompanied by four or five men on horseback and a couple of muleteers on foot. In the coach, as was afterwards learned, was a lady of Biscay, on her way to Seville to bid farewell to her husband, who had been appointed to some high post in the Indies. The religious were not of her company although they were going by the same road.

The instant Don Quixote laid eyes upon them he turned to his squire. "Either I am mistaken or this is going to be the most famous adventure that ever was seen; for those black-clad figures that you behold must be, and without any doubt are, certain enchanters who are bearing with them a captive princess in that coach, and I must do all I can to right this wrong."

"It will be worse than the windmills," declared Sancho. "Look you, sir, those are Benedictine friars and the coach must be that of some travelers. Mark well what I say and what you do, lest the devil lead you astray."

"I have already told you, Sancho," replied Don Quixote, "that you know little where the subject of adventures is concerned. What I am saying to you is the truth, as you shall now see."

With this, he rode forward and took up a position in the middle of the road along which the friars were coming, and as soon as they appeared to be within earshot he cried out to them in a loud voice, "O devilish and monstrous beings, set free at once the highborn princesses whom you bear captive in that coach, or else prepare at once to meet your death as the just punishment of your evil deeds."

The friars drew rein and sat there in astonishment, marveling as much at Don Quixote's appearance as at the words he spoke. "Sir Knight," they answered him, "we are neither devilish nor monstrous but religious of the Order of St. Benedict who are merely going our way. We know nothing of those who are in that coach, nor of any captive princesses either."

"Soft words," said Don Quixote, "have no effect on me. I know you for what you are, lying rabble!" And without waiting for any further parley he gave spur to Rocinante and, with lowered lance, bore down upon the first friar with such fury and intrepidity that, had not the fellow tumbled from his mule of his own accord, he would have been hurled to the ground and either killed or badly wounded. The second religious, seeing how his companion had been treated, dug his legs into his she-mule's flanks and scurried away over the countryside faster than the wind.

Seeing the friar upon the ground, Sancho Panza slipped lightly from his mount and, falling upon him, began stripping him of his habit. The two mule drivers accompanying the religious thereupon came running up and asked Sancho why he was doing this. The latter replied that the friar's garments belonged to him as legitimate spoils of the battle that his master Don Quixote had just won. The muleteers, however, were lads with no sense of humor, nor did they know what all this talk of spoils and battles was about; but, perceiving that Don Quixote had ridden off to one side to converse with those inside the coach, they pounced upon Sancho, threw him to the ground, and proceeded to pull out the hair of his beard and kick him to a pulp, after which they went off and left him stretched out there, bereft at once of breath and sense.

Without losing any time, they then assisted the friar to remount. The good brother was trembling all over from fright, and there was not a speck of color in his face, but when he found himself in the saddle once more, he quickly spurred his beast to where his companion, at some little distance, sat watching and waiting to see what the result of the encounter would be. Having no curiosity as to the final outcome of the fray, the two of them now resumed their journey, making more signs of the cross than the devil would be able to carry upon his back.

Meanwhile Don Quixote, as we have said, was speaking to the lady in the coach.

"Your beauty, my lady, may now dispose of your person as best may please you, for the arrogance of your abductors lies upon the ground, overthrown by this good arm of mine; and in order that you may not pine to know the name of your liberator, I may inform you that I am Don Quixote de la Mancha, knight-errant and adventurer and captive of the peerless and beauteous Doña Dulcinea del Toboso. In payment of the favor which you have received from me, I ask nothing other than that you return to El Toboso and on my behalf pay your respects to this lady, telling her that it was I who set you free."

One of the squires accompanying those in the coach, a Biscayan, was listening to Don Quixote's words, and when he saw that the knight did not propose to let the coach proceed upon its way but was bent upon having it turn back to El Toboso, he promptly went up to him, seized his lance, and said to him in bad Castilian and worse Biscayan, "Go, *caballero,* and bad luck go with you; for by the God that created me, if you do not let this coach pass, me kill you or me no Biscayan."

Don Quixote heard him attentively enough and answered him very mildly, "If you were a *caballero,* which you are not, I should already have chastised you, wretched creature, for your foolhardiness and your impudence."

"Me no *caballero?*" cried the Biscayan. "Me swear to God, you lie like a Christian. If you will but lay aside your lance and unsheath your sword, you will soon see that you are carrying water to the cat! Biscayan on land, gentleman at sea, but a gentleman in spite of the devil, and you lie if you say otherwise."

"'You shall see as to that presently,' said Agrajes," Don Quixote quoted. He cast his lance to the earth, drew his sword, and, taking his buckler on his arm, attacked the Biscayan with intent to slay him. The latter, when he saw his adversary approaching, would have liked to dismount from his mule, for she was one of the worthless sort that are let for hire and he had no confidence in her; but there was no time for this, and so he had no choice but to draw his own sword in turn and make the best of it. However, he was near enough to the coach to be able to snatch a cushion from it to serve him as a shield; and then they fell upon each other as though they were mortal enemies. The rest of those present sought to make peace between them but did not succeed, for the Biscayan with his disjointed phrases kept muttering that if they did not let him finish the battle then he himself would have to kill his mistress and anyone else who tried to stop him.

The lady inside the carriage, amazed by it all and trembling at what she saw, directed her coachman to drive on a little way; and there from a distance she watched the deadly combat, in the course of which the Biscayan came down with a great blow on Don Quixote's shoulder, over the top of the latter's shield, and had not the knight been clad in armor, it would have split him to the waist.

Feeling the weight of this blow, Don Quixote cried out, "O lady of my soul, Dulcinea, flower of beauty, succor this your champion who out of gratitude for your many favors finds himself in so perilous a plight!" To utter these words, lay hold of his sword, cover himself with his buckler, and attack the Biscayan was but the work of a moment; for he was now resolved to risk everything upon a single stroke.

As he saw Don Quixote approaching with so dauntless a bearing, the Biscayan was well aware of his adversary's courage and forthwith determined to imitate the example thus set him. He kept himself protected with his cushion, but he was unable to get his she-mule to budge to one side or the other, for the beast, out of sheer exhaustion and being, moreover, unused to such childish play, was incapable of taking a single step. And so, then, as has been stated, Don Quixote was approaching the wary Biscayan, his sword raised on high and with the firm resolve of cleaving his enemy in two; and the Biscayan was awaiting the knight in the same posture, cushion in front of him and with uplifted sword. All the bystanders were trembling with suspense at what would happen as a result of the terrible blows that were threatened, and the lady in the coach and her maids were making a thousand vows and offerings to all the images and shrines in Spain, praying that God would save them all and the lady's squire from this great peril that confronted them.

But the unfortunate part of the matter is that at this very point the author of the history breaks off and leaves the battle pending, excusing himself upon the ground that he has been unable to find anything else in writing concerning the exploits of Don Quixote beyond those already set forth. It is true, on the other hand, that the second author of this work could not bring himself to believe that so unusual a chronicle would have been consigned to oblivion, nor that the learned ones of La Mancha were possessed of so little curiosity as not to be able to discover in their archives or registry offices certain papers that have to do with this famous knight. Being convinced of this, he did not despair of coming upon the end of this pleasing story, and Heaven favoring him, he did find it, as shall be related in the second part.

50. NOSTRADAMUS (MICHEL DE NOSTRADAME, 1503–66)

Michel de Nostradame was born in 1503. Both of his grandfathers were medical doctors and philosophers, and they saw to his early education. He enrolled in the University of Avignon, where he developed his early interest in astronomy and astrology, but he eventually decided to pursue the family tradition in medicine. In 1522 he went to Montpellier, one of the best medical schools of the period. In 1525 the university was closed as a wave of plague rolled through southern France. Nostradamus decided to fight the plague, and he met with a remarkable degree of success. His fame led to the offer of a teaching position when the university reopened. Nostradamus felt restricted by the academic routine, however, and he took up an offer from Joseph Scaliger, one of the best-known scholars in Europe, to come to Agen and study with him. He settled there, but after another wave of plague killed his wife and two small children, his reputation suffered, he fought with Scaliger, and he had a brush with heresy charges.

In 1538 he left Agen and began to travel through France and Italy. It was at this time that his interest in astrology seems to have broadened into an interest in prophecy. Through this period he continued to practice medicine with some success, but he was regarded with suspicion both by fellow doctors and by the Inquisition. In 1547 he finally settled in Salon, where he married again. In 1550 he began to publish his almanacs, and in 1554 his Presages *appeared. Following their success he began to rely more heavily on his prophetic powers, and between 1554 and 1565 he produced his* Centuries—*collections of 100 quatrains of prophetic verse. He died a famous man in 1566.*

Letter to King Henri II of France

Salon, 27 June, 1558

To the most invincible, very puissant, and most Christian Henry King of France the Second: Michael Nostradamus, his most humble, most obedient servant and subject, wishes victory and happiness.

For that sovereign observation that I had, O most Christian and very victorious King, since that my face, long obscured with cloud, presented itself before the deity of your measureless Majesty, since that in that I have been perpetually dazzled, never failing to honor and worthily revere that day, when first before it, as before a singularly humane majesty, I presented myself. I searched for some occasion by which to manifest good heart and frank courage, by the means of which I might grow into greater knowledge of your serene Majesty. I soon found in effect it was impossible for me to declare it, considering the contrast of the solitariness of my long obnubilation and obscurity, and my being suddenly thrust into brilliancy, and transported into the presence of the sovereign eye of the first monarch of the universe. Likewise I have long hung in doubt as to whom I ought to dedicate these three *Centuries*, the remainder of my Prophecies amounting now to a thousand. I have long meditated on an act of such audacity. I have at last ventured to address your Majesty, and was not daunted from it as Plutarch, that grave author, relates in the life of Lycurgus, that, seeing the gifts and presents that were made in the way of sacrifice at the temples of the immortal gods in that age, many were staggered at the expense, and dared not approach the temple to present anything.

Notwithstanding this, I saw your royal splendor to be accompanied with an incomparable humanity, and paid my addresses to it, not as to those Kings of Persia whom it was not permissible to approach. But to a very prudent and very wise Prince I have dedicated my nocturnal and prophetic calculations, composed out of a natural instinct, and accompanied by a poetic fervor, rather than according to the strict rules of poetry. Most part, indeed, has been composed and adjusted by astronomical calculation corresponding to the years, months, and weeks, of the regions, countries, and for the most part towns and cities, throughout Europe, Africa, and a part of Asia, which nearest approach [or resemble] each other in all these climates, and this is composed in a natural manner. Possibly some may answer—who, if so, had better blow his nose [that he may see the clearer by it]—that the rhythm is as easy to be understood, as the sense is hard to get at. Therefore, O most gracious King, the bulk of the prophetic quatrains are so rude, that there is no making way through them, nor is there any interpreter of them. Nevertheless, being always anxious to set down the years, towns, and regions cited, where the events are to occur, even from the year 1585, and the year 1606, dating from the present time, which is the 14th of March, 1557.

Then passing far beyond to things which shall happen at the commencement of the seventh millenary, deeply calculated, so far as my astronomic calculus, and other knowledge, has been able to reach, to the time when the adversaries of Jesus Christ and of His Church shall begin to multiply in great force. The whole has been composed and calculated on days and hours of best election and disposition, and with all the accuracy I could attain to at a moment [blessed] *Minerva libera et non invita,* [when Minerva was free and favorable] my calculations looking forward to events through a space of time to come that nearly equals that of the past even up to the present, and by this they will know in the lapse of time and in all regions what is to happen, all written down thus particularly, immingled with nothing superfluous.

Notwithstanding that some say, *Quod de futuris non est determinata omnino veritas,* [There can be no truth entirely determined for certain which concerns the future] I will confess, Sire, that I believed myself capable of presage from the natural instinct I inherit of my ancestors, adjusted and regulated by elaborate calculation, and the endeavor to free the soul, mind, and heart from all care, solicitude, and anxiety, by resting and tranquilizing the spirit, which finally has all to be completed and perfected in one respect *tripode oeneo* [by the brazen tripod]. With all this there will be many to attribute to me as mine, things no more mine than nothing. The Almighty alone, who strictly searches the human heart, pious, just, and pitiful, is the true Judge; to Him I pray to defend me from the calumny of wicked men. Such persons, with equal calumny, will bring into question how all your ancient progenitors the Kings of France have cured the evil; how those of other nations have cured the bite of serpents; others have had a certain instinct in the art of divination, and other faculties that would be too long to recount here. Notwithstanding such as cannot be restrained from the exercise of the malignancy of the evil spirit, [there is hope that] by the lapse of time, and after my extinction here on earth, my writings will be more valued than during my lifetime.

However, if I err in calculation of ages, or find myself unable to please all the world, may it please your Imperial Majesty to forgive me, for I protest before God and His saints, that I purpose to insert nothing whatever in writing this present Epistle that shall militate against the true Catholic Faith, whilst consulting the astronomical calculations to the very best of my knowledge. For the stretch of time of our forefathers [i.e., the age of the world] which has gone before is such, submitting myself to the direction of the soundest chronologists, that the first man, Adam, was about one thousand two hundred and forty years before Noah, not computing time by Gentile records, such as Varro has committed to writing, but taking simply the Sacred Scriptures for the guide in my astronomic reckonings, to the best of my feeble understanding. After Noah, from him and the universal deluge, about one thousand and fourscore years, came Abraham, who was a sovereign astrologer according to some; he first invented the Chaldaean alphabet. Then came Moses, about five hundred and fifteen or sixteen years later. Between the time of David and Moses five hundred and seventy years elapsed. Then after the time of David and the time of our Savior and Redeemer, Jesus Christ, born of a pure Virgin, there elapsed (according to some chronographers) one thousand three hundred and fifty years....

I fully confess that all proceeds from God, and for that I return Him thanks, honor, and immortal praise, and have mingled nothing with it of the divination which proceeds *a fato,* but *a Deo, a natura,* [which proceeds from fate, but from God, and nature] and for the most part accompanied with the movement of the celestial courses. Much as, if looking into a burning mirror [we see], as with darkened vision, the great events, sad or portentous, and calamitous occurrences that are about to fall upon the principal worshippers. First upon the temples of God, secondly upon such as have their support from the earth [i.e., by the kings], this decadence draweth nigh, with a thousand other calamitous incidents that in the course of time will be known to happen.

For God will take notice of the long barrenness of the great Dame, who afterwards will conceive two principal children. But, she being in great danger, the girl she will give birth to with risk at her age of death in the eighteenth year, and not possible to outlive the thirty-sixth, will leave three males and one female, and he will have two who never had any of the same father. The three brothers will be so different, though united and agreed, that the three and four parts of Europe will tremble. By the youngest in years will the Christian monarchy be sustained and augmented; heresies spring up and suddenly cast down, the Arabs driven back, kingdoms united, and new laws promulgated. Of the other children the first shall possess the furious crowned Lions, holding their paws upon the bold escutcheon. The second, accompanied by the Latins, shall penetrate so far that a second trembling and furious descent shall be made, descending Mons Jovis [at Barcelona] to mount the Pyrenees, shall not be translated to the antique monarchy, and a third inundation of human blood shall arise, and March for a long while will not be found in Lent. The daughter shall be given for the preservation of the Christian Church, the dominator falling into the Pagan sect of new infidels, and she will have two children, the one fidelity, the other infidelity, by the confirmation of the Catholic Church. The other, who to his great confusion and tardy repentance wished to ruin her, will have three regions over a wide extent of leagues, that is to say, Rumania, Germany, and Spain, which will entail great intricacy of military handling, stretching from the 50th to the 52nd degree of latitude. And they will have to respect the more distant religions of Europe and the north above the 48th degree of latitude, which at first in a vain timidity will tremble, and then the more western, southern, and eastern will tremble. Their power will become such, that what is brought about by union and concord will prove insuperable by warlike conquest. By nature they will be equal, but exceedingly different in faith.

After this the sterile Dame, of greater power than the second, shall be received by two nations, by the first made obstinate by him who had power over all, by the second, and third, that shall extend his forces towards the circuit of the east of Europe; [arrived] there his standards will stop and succumb, but by sea he will run on to Trinacria and the Adriatic with his mirmidons. The Germans will succumb wholly and the Barbaric sect will be disquieted and driven back by the whole of the Latin race. Then shall begin the grand Empire of Antichrist in the Atila and Xerxes, [who is] to descend with innumerable multitudes, so that the coming of the Holy Spirit, issuing from the 48th degree, shall make a transmigration, chasing away the abomination of Antichrist, that made war upon the royal person of the great vicar of Jesus Christ, and against His Church, and reign *per tempus, et in occasione temporis* [for a time, and to the end of time]. This will be preceded by an eclipse of the sun, more obscure and tenebrose than has ever been since the creation of the world, up to the death and passion of Jesus Christ, and from thence till now. There will be in the month of October a grand revolution [translation] made, such that one would think that the librating body of the earth had lost its natural movement in the abyss of perpetual darkness. There will be seen precursive signs in the springtime, and after extreme changes ensuing, reversal of kingdoms, and great earthquakes [i.e., wars]. All this accompanied with the procreations of the New Babylon [Paris], a miserable prostitute big with the abomination of the first holocaust [death of Louis XVI]. It will only continue for seventy-three years seven months.

Then there will issue from the stock so long time barren, proceeding from the 50th degree, [one] who will renovate the whole Christian Church. A great peace, union, and concord will then spring up between some of the children of races [long] opposed to each other and separated by diverse kingdoms. Such a peace shall be set up, that the instigator and promoter of military faction by means of the diversity of religions, shall dwell attached to the bottom of the abyss, and united to the kingdom of the furious, who shall counterfeit the wise. The countries, towns, cities, and provinces that had forsaken their old customs to free themselves, enthralling themselves more deeply, shall become secretly weary of their liberty, and, true religion lost, shall commence by striking off to the left, to return more than ever to the right.

Then replacing holiness, so long desecrated by their former writings [circulating slanders], afterwards the result will be that the great dog will issue as an irresistible mastiff [Napoleon?] who will destroy everything, even to all that may have been prepared in time past, till the churches will be restored as at first, and the clergy reinstated in their pristine condition; till it lapses again into whoredom and luxury, to commit and perpetrate a thousand crimes. And drawing near to another desolation, then, when she shall be at her highest and sublimest point of dignity, the kings and generals [*mains militaires*] will come up [against her], and her two swords will be taken from her, and nothing will be left her but the semblance of them. "From which by the means of the crookedness that draweth them, the people causing it to go straight, and not willing to submit unto them by the end opposite to the sharp hand that toucheth the ground they shall provoke." Until there shall be born unto the branch a long time sterile, one who shall deliver the French people from the benign slavery that they voluntarily submitted to, putting himself under the protection of Mars, and stripping Jupiter [Napoleon I] of all his honors and dignities, for the city constituted free and seated in another narrow Mesopotamia. The chief and governor shall be cast from the midst, and set in a place of the air, ignorant of the conspiracy of the conspirators [Fouché, Duc d'Otranto, etc.] with the second Thrasibulus, who for a long time had prepared all this. Then shall the impurities and abominations be with great shame set forth and manifested to the darkness of the veiled light, shall cease towards the end of his reign, and the chiefs of the Church shall evince but little of the love of God, whilst many of them shall apostatize from the true faith.

Of the three sects [Lutheran, Catholic, and Mahometan], that which is in the middle, by the action of its own worshippers, will be thrown a little into decadence. The first totally throughout Europe, and the chief part of Africa exterminated by the third, by means of the poor in spirit, who by the madness engendered of libidinous luxury, will commit adultery [i.e., apostatize]. The people will pull down the pillar, and chase away the adherents of the legislators, and it shall seem, from the kingdoms weakened by the Orientals, that God the Creator has loosed Satan from the infernal prisons, to make room for the great Dog and Dohan [Gog and Magog], which will make so great and injurious a breach in the Churches, that neither the reds nor the whites, who are without eyes and without hands [meaning the latter Bourbons, "who learn nothing and forget nothing"], cannot judge of the situation, and their power will be taken from them. Then shall commence a persecution of the Church such as never was before. Whilst this is enacting, such a pestilence shall spring up that out of three parts of mankind two shall be removed. To such a length will this proceed that one will neither know nor recognize the fields or houses, and grass will grow in the streets of the cities as high as a man's knees. To the clergy there shall be a total desolation, and the martial men shall usurp what shall come back from the City of the Sun [Rome], and from Malta and the Islands of Hières [off Marseilles], and the great chain of the port shall be opened that takes its name from the marine ox [Bosphorus]....

Had I wished to give to every quatrain its detailed date, it could easily have been done, but it would not have been agreeable to all, and still less to interpret them, Sire, until your Majesty should have fully sanctioned me to do this, in order not to furnish calumniators with an opportunity to injure me. Always reckoning the years since the creation of the world to the birth of Noah as being 1506 years, and from that to the completion of the building of the ark at the period of the universal deluge 600 years elapsed (let them be solar years, or lunar, or mixed), I hold that the Scripture takes them to be solar. At the conclusion of this 600 years, Noah entered the ark to escape the deluge. The deluge was universal over the earth, and lasted one year and two months. From the conclusion of the deluge to the birth of Abraham there elapsed 295 years, and 100 years from that to the birth of Isaac. From Isaac to Jacob 60 years. From the time he went into Egypt until his coming out of it was 130 years, and from the entry of Jacob into Egypt to his exit was 436 years; and from that to the building of the Temple by Solomon in the fortieth year of his reign, makes 480 years. From the building of the Temple to Jesus Christ, according to the supputation of the Hierographs, there passed 490 years. Thus by this calculation that I have made, collecting it out of the sacred writings, there are about 4173 years and eight months less or more. Now, from Jesus Christ, in that there is such a diversity of opinion, I pass it by, and having calculated the present prophecies in accordance with the order of the chain which contains the revolution, and the whole by astronomical rule, together with my own hereditary instinct. After some time, and including in it the period Saturn takes to turn between the 7th of April up to the 25th of August; Jupiter from the 14th of June to the 7th of October; Mars from the 17th of April to the 22nd of June; Venus from the 9th of April to the 22nd of May; Mercury from the 3rd of February to the 24th of the same; afterwards from the 1st of June to the 24th of the same; and from the 25th of September to the 16th of October, Saturn in Capricorn, Jupiter in Aquarius, Mars in Scorpio, Venus in Pisces, Mercury within a month in Capricorn, Aquarius, and Pisces; the moon in Aquarius, the Dragon's head in Libra, the tail in her sign opposite. Following the conjunction of Jupiter to Mercury, with a quadrin aspect of Mars to Mercury, and the head of the Dragon shall be with a conjunction of Sol with Jupiter, the year shall be peaceful without eclipse.

Then will be the commencement [of a period] that will comprehend in itself what will long endure [i.e., the vulgar advent of the French Revolution], and in its first year there shall be a great persecution of the Christian Church, fiercer than that in Africa [by the Vandals from 1439 to 1534], and this will burst out [*durera*] the year one thousand seven hundred and ninety-two; they will think it to be a renovation of time. After this the people of Rome will begin to reconstitute themselves [in 1804, when Napoleon is emperor], and to chase away the obscurity of darkness, recovering some share of their ancient brightness, but not without much division and continual changes. Venice after that, in great force and power, shall raise her wings very high, not much short of the force of ancient Rome. At that time great Byzantine sails, associated with the Piedmontese by the help and power of the North, will so restrain them that the two Cretans will not be able to maintain their faith. The arks built by the ancient warriors will accompany them to the waves of Neptune. In the Adriatic there will be such permutations, that what was united will be separated, and that will be reduced to a house which before was a great city, including the Pampotan and Mesopotamia of Europe, to 45, and others to 41, 43, and 47. And in that time and those countries the infernal power will set the power of the adversaries of its law against the Church of Jesus Christ. This will constitute the second Antichrist, which will persecute that Church and its true vicar, by means of the power of the temporal kings, who in their ignorance will be reduced by tongues that will cut more than any sword in the hands of a madman....

After that Antichrist will be the infernal prince. Then at this last epoch, all the kingdoms of Christianity, as well as of the infidel world, will be shaken during the space of twenty-five years, and the wars and battles will be more grievous, and the towns, cities, castles, and all other edifices will be burnt, desolated, and destroyed with much effusion of vestal blood, married women and widows violated, sucking children dashed and broken against the walls of town; and so many evils will be committed by means of Satan, the prince infernal, that nearly all the world will become undone and desolated. Before the events occur certain strange birds [imperial eagles] will cry in the air, "To-day! to-day!" and after a given time will disappear [June, 1815]. After this has endured for a certain length of time [twenty-five years he has said before, 1790 to 1815], there will be almost renewed another reign of Saturn, the age of gold [this might be the discovery of California, but for what follows]. God the Creator shall say, hearing the affliction of His people, Satan shall be precipitated and bound in the bottomless abyss, and then shall commence between God and men a universal peace. There he shall abide for the space of a thousand years, and shall turn his greatest force against the power of the Church, and shall then be bound again.

How justly are all these figures adapted by the divine letters to visible celestial things, that is to say, by Saturn, Jupiter, and Mars, and others in conjunction with them, as may be seen more at large by some of the quatrains! I would have calculated it more deeply, and adapted the one to the other; but, seeing, O most serene King, that some who are given to censure will raise a difficulty, I shall take the opportunity to retire my pen and seek my nocturnal repose. "*Multa etiam, O Rex potentissime proeclara, et sane to brevi ventura, sed omnia in hac tua Epistola, innectere non possumus, nec volumus, sed ad intellegenda quondam facta, horrida fata pauca libanda sunt, quamvis tanta sit in omnes tua amplitudo et humanitas homines, deosque pietas, ut solos amplissimo et Christianissimo Regis nomine, et ad quem summa totius religionis auctoritas deferatur dignus esse videare.*" But I shall only beseech you, O most clement King, by this your singular and most prudent goodness, to understand rather the desire of my heart, and the sovereign wish I have to obey your most excellent Majesty, ever since my eyes approached so nearly to your solar splendor, than the grandeur of my work can attain to or acquire.

Faciebat Michael Nostradamus.

SEVEN: IMAGINING NEW WORLDS AT HOME

51. THE FUGGER NEWSLETTERS (1568–1604)

The Fugger family began to build their banking fortune in the late fifteenth century. Through the sixteenth century they loaned money to various European rulers, most importantly the house of Habsburg which ruled central Europe, the Netherlands, Spain, Italy, and much of the New World. As security for the money, the Habsburgs gave the Fuggers interests in their mines, their lands, and their administration. By the middle of the sixteenth century the bankers had business interests that covered the Empire and stretched beyond to the New World and the Far East.

In 1655 the Emperor Ferdinand III bought the Fugger family library, of which the newsletters were a part. The newsletters originated with Count Philip Edward Fugger (1546–1618), who had a voracious appetite for news. Aware of his interests, the employees of the branch offices added news of current events in their various parts of the world to routine dispatches sent to the head office. The count seems to have added to this collection from news sources available in his home city of Augsburg. As the collection grew, the count had the unwieldy mass of material copied, and it was this collection that entered the imperial library. It is difficult to tell which of the items are actually from Fugger correspondents and which from the news sheets of the time, though the item on the witch Walpurga Hausmann is probably of the latter variety.

105. *The Famous Alchemist Bragadini*

From Venice, the 1st day of November 1589.

Your Grace will no doubt have learnt from the weekly reports of one Marco Antonio Bragadini, called Mamugnano. He is the bastard son of a nobleman here and was born in Cyprus. He is reported to be able to turn base metal into gold. Our government has had him conveyed hither under safe escort because the Inquisition has put him under ban. He is forty years old and was formerly possessed of no mean fortune, but spent it in riotous living. Then for a time he was mint-master to the Grand Duke Francis. From thence he came to the late Pope Gregory, who held him in great esteem. He thus obtained several thousand ducats. But when these too had been spent, he became a Capuchin and had taken his second vows. But since he could not subject himself to the strict rule of the order, he absconded without dispensation (hence the excommunication bar by the Holy Office) and betook himself to France. There he served several princes incognito. Latterly he has returned again to Bergamo in Italy and has exhibited his art in Valcamonica and in a short time increased his fortune to over and above two hundred thousand crowns. He has expounded his craft to several persons and it had got so far that he was prevailed upon to come here of his free will. Such a host of princes and lords beleaguered him that he was scarcely safe, although he had a bodyguard of fifty archers. This man is now here in this city, holds banquets daily for five hundred people and lives in princely style in the Palazzo Dandolo on the Giudecca. He literally throws gold about in shovelfuls. This is his recipe: he takes ten ounces of quicksilver, puts it into the fire and mixes it with a drop of liquid, which he carries in an ampulla. Thus it promptly turns into good gold. He has no other wish but to be of good use to his country, the Republic. The day before yesterday he presented to the Secret Council of Ten two ampullas with this liquid, which have been tested in his absence. The first test was found to be successful and it is said to have resulted in six million ducats. I doubt not but that this will appear mighty strange to Your Grace. It verily sounds like a fairy tale, but Your Grace will surely believe us, for everything is so obvious that it cannot be doubted. The confectioning of this liquid is, however, his secret, for in his letter of safe conduct he made express demand that he be not forced to divulge this. He also craves nothing more from this our Government but that it may exercise good watch over his life and his person. In return he will provide them with gold in sufficiency according to their demands. He has already made known that he is greatly amazed at the ignorance of the world, in not discovering this art before, considering that little is requisite for this achievement. This is truly marvellous and quite novel to all of us. The alchemists have taken heart of grace again and are working night and day. One hears of nothing but of this excellent man who, as already stated, has no other wish but to serve his country.

From Venice, the 8th day of December 1589.

You have learnt latterly that the craft of the alchemist Marco Bragadini after being tested has been approved of. The tests have shown this sufficiently. The most noble personages here address him by the title "Illustrissimo" and feast with him daily. The Duke speaks to him in the second person. By day noblemen attend upon him, by night he is guarded by armed barges. Whereas so many strange people have arrived here, the Government holds in readiness three fully equipped galleys.

From Venice, the 16th day of December 1589.

The alchemist is said to be at work now in making five thousand sequins per month at the request of our rulers. Thereafter he will make fifteen or sixteen millions more which he has promised to hand over to it. Day by day he shows himself in great pomp. He makes his friends presents of twenty thousand and more ducats at a time. Monday last he gave a banquet in honor of the Duc de Luxembourg, the French Catholic Ambassador in Rome, which, without counting all kinds of special confectionery, cost near upon six hundred crowns.

From Rome, the 16th day of December 1589.

The Venetian Ambassador has solemnly besought the Pope that Mamugnano, the alchemist, who now resides in Venice, may remain there without molestation by the Holy Office, on account of his being a former Capuchin. Thereupon the Pope made answer that he was not a little surprised at the afore-mentioned Rulers putting so much faith in that man. Though his art might be found to be successful, yet it only could accrue unto him by the help of Satan.

From Venice, the 4th day of January 1590.

It is said of our Mamugnano that his craft for transforming quicksilver into gold does suffice for small quantities, but fails to produce larger ones. It is reported that the night before last he made two ingots in the presence of some of our patrician aldermen, each one of the weight of one pound. There no longer exists any doubt in the matter. Discussion, however, is rife amongst some of this city's philosophers as to whether Mamugnano can renew the material wherewith he has made his gold, once it is used up. Some say yes, and others say no, so that it is doubtful what they really think about it.

106. Gold from New Spain

From Venice, the 12th day of January 1590.

News reaches us from Lyons that letters from Lisbon of the 18th day of December of the past year report the arrival in Seville from New Spain of the fleet with eight millions in gold. More ships are expected to arrive shortly, which had to remain behind on account of storms. They are bringing a further four millions. This cause for the delay in the arrival of the first ships is the fact that they took their course several degrees higher than is their wont in order to escape the English cruisers who were waiting for them on the usual degree. The other ships have probably taken their course along other degrees for the same reason.

107. Bragadini works on

From Venice, the 19th day of January 1590.

Mamugnano changed a pound of quicksilver into gold some days ago. But he is not satisfied with this weight, because he has been asked by several persons to produce a larger sum.

109. Further Successes by Bragadini

From Venice, the 26th day of January 1590.

Concerning the alchemist, Mamugnano, no one harbors doubts any longer about his daily experiments in changing quicksilver into gold. It was realized that his craft did not go beyond one pound of quicksilver, however much various persons begged him to produce more. Thus the belief is now held that his allegations to produce a number of millions have been a great fraud, in which he caused people to believe. For he who can make a small amount of gold should also be able to produce a large quantity. This is the question upon which learned professors hold dispute. Meanwhile he has cut down his expenses, also reduced his banqueting, and is seen about with a smaller suite than formerly. It is reported from Spain that the King has concluded an agreement with the Genoese for a loan of five millions towards the end of the months of March and April, one million during the middle of July and the last during the middle of September.

From Venice, the 26th day of January 1590.

The alchemist Mamugnano is making gold here for his needs. He is intending this Shrovetide to hold a joyous masque in the Square of St. Stephen, for which purpose he is having sent hither six fine stallions from Mantua.

110. Printing of the Bible for the Heathen

From Rome, the 26th day of January 1590.

The Pope has learned with particular satisfaction that the Grand Duke of Florence is willing to have the books of the Bible printed here at his expense in the Chaldean, Arabic, Syrian and Ethiopian languages, and to have them expedited to these countries. These people have complained that hitherto they had to live in blindness for the lack of biblical writings and they demand to be instructed in the Christian Faith.

111. Adultery at the Court of Saxe-Coburg

From Strasburg, the 7th day of February of the year 1590 of the old calendar.

John Casimir is said to be in sore trouble concerning his consort, for she has committed adultery with a Pole. The latter has had intercourse with her seven or eight times, and upon each occasion she presented him with a hundred crowns. When these things became bruited abroad, he was taken into strict custody to the Palace of Mannheim, about two miles distant from the city of Worms. Not long ago he escaped, but was caught again in the Palatinate. By order of the said Duke, several hundredweight of iron were fastened to his person, so that he may not be able to flee again. May God console him and all such as are afflicted!

The Princess has been divested of all her princely apparel and raiment. She is reported to be wearing the clothing of one of her former tiring women and to be in durance no less hard than her lover. Only an old woman is let in to her.

Otherwise information has been received that the alchemist of Venice has been instigated by the Grand Vizier to pass himself off as an alchemist and an artist in order thus to gain admittance to the city of Venice. This scheme has been, however, discovered, and the alchemist will not escape punishment.

112. Genoese Money for the League

From Venice, the 9th day of February 1590.

Tidings come from France that the Spinolas, wealthy Genoese merchants who did a large business in Paris, have collected a goodly part of the moneys owing to them from such countries as France, England and the Netherlands. Finding themselves possessed in Paris of so large a sum in cash as near on four hundred thousand crowns, they dared not remove it, because they were afeared that it might be taken from them. Still less did they wish to take it to Italy or Spain because trade there is at a standstill. They are now offering this sum to the League, and His Royal Majesty of Spain has promised its repayment in Spain. In Rouen there are other Spanish merchants, who possess a still larger fortune, which they also wish to offer to the League.

It is said that Mamugnano has won near on ten thousand ducats gambling with several noblemen, so that rumor hath it that he is as clever at gambling as at making gold. He is reported to have produced in these latter days ten thousand gold crowns at one sitting, which fact is confirmed by a credible witness, who was present on that occasion.

113. Attempt to Poison Philip II

From Venice, the 6th day of April 1590.

A terrifying miracle, so they say, has occurred in Spain. One morning, as the King after praying in his oratory before a crucifix, which he held in great devotion, as was his daily custom, wished to kiss the image of Christ, the latter turned away from him. This greatly horrified and frightened the King and he once more began to pray that God might forgive him his sins. He thereupon once more tried to kiss the image of Christ, which again withdrew from him. When the King had perceived this with great concern and affliction, he sent for his Father Confessor, to whom he related this miracle. The latter then began praying to God that He might reveal this secret unto him. When he had concluded his prayers, he told the King to send for two of his most eminent councillors and bid them kiss the crucifix. They did so and soon thereafter fell sick and died. Some aver that the crucifix was poisoned so that the King might lose his life thereby.

114. Execution of Two Children

From Vienna, the 24th day of April 1590.

Yesterday two boys, the one thirteen and the other seventeen years of age, were put to death by fire and sword. For some time they had caused much damage through setting fire to property. May God guard henceforth all the children of pious parents!

115. Another Burning of Witches

From Schwab-München, the 4th day of May 1590.

Last Wednesday the innkeeper's wife of Möringen and the baker's wife of Bobingen were tried here for their misdeeds in witchcraft. Mine hostess is a short, stout, seventy-year-old doxy, who had taken to her accursed witchery when eighteen years of age. This she has practiced fifty-two years, and it is easy to imagine what havoc she has wrought in such a long time. As the result of fervent petitioning, her sentence has been lightened inasmuch as she was first strangled and then only burned.

The other was only seduced to this work of the Devil by Ursula Krämer, who was the first to be executed here. So far, she has not perpetrated any sore misdeeds, but so much has she owned to, that her life is forfeit. Even on her day of judgment she still thought she could vindicate herself, and even at the place of execution I myself heard her say that she was dying innocent. Most unwillingly did she submit to her fate. But in the end she was reconciled to it and prayed long to God that He might pardon her misdeeds.

This morn another woman was brought hither from Möringen. Only half a year ago she married off one of her sons to a widow, who is said to be of the same craft. Thus it is hoped that it may incriminate others here. To-morrow or next week some more are to be brought here, but no one knows from whence. There is much discussion here about the hostess of Göggingen. May the Lord grant that this be but idle talk.

116. Fresh Deeds of the Alchemist of Venice

From Venice, the 11th day of May 1590.

Whereas Mamugnano, the alchemist, passed some time in a village a certain distance from here, and several persons suspected him of making gold for other people, his rooms were sealed at the request of his creditors. By order of the Signori Capitani, however, one room was unsealed again.

During the last days a large fish was caught by the fishers near Malamocco. It weighs more than a thousand pounds, according to our weights, and measures twenty spans. It has two wide wings, eyes as large as those of an ox, and a round, small mouth with two teeth, one in the upper and one in the lower jaw. They are almost as thick as a finger and the fish has a strange color. What kind of a fish it is the fishermen are as yet unable to say.

We have just learned that Mamugnano, the alchemist, has returned here. The Pope is said to have granted him absolution, but he had to make a donation of five thousand crowns and enter the Order of the Knights of Malta.

52. GALILEO GALILEI (1564–1642)

Galileo was born in Pisa, the son of a celebrated musician. He entered the University of Pisa in 1583 to study medicine but left two years later without a degree, despite his remarkable abilities in science and mathematics. He continued to study privately and conduct experiments, which gave him sufficient fame to permit him to return to Pisa as a professor in 1589; however, his later experiments resulted in conclusions that contradicted the received scientific curriculum based on Aristotle. Consequently, he left Pisa in 1592 to teach at the celebrated University of Padua, where he taught mathematics and physics for over 18 years and where he built a strong reputation as an experimental scientist. His particular interest was in motion, so he adapted the invention of a Dutch lens maker to build the most powerful telescope in Europe. His observations could now include planetary motion—why and how the heavens seem to move. He published his conclusion in 1610 in his Starry Messenger, *a book that proved that the surface of the moon was not perfect but cratered and mountainous and that Jupiter had moons of its own. His conclusions implied that the traditional geocentric universe (the earth is the center around which all other celestial bodies move) was incorrect; rather the sun was the center. In so doing he was supporting the results of a Polish priest, Nicholas Copernicus (1473–1543), who in 1543 published similar conclusions. Galileo's adoption of this Copernican theory caused the Church in 1616 to demand he no longer teach or hold these opinions, as they were contrary to Aristotle, Scripture, and Church dogma, although in 1624 Pope Urban VIII, a former friend of the astronomer, moderated this position, allowing Galileo to continue his work as long as he treated the Copernican argument as a mathematical abstraction. Despite this warning, Galileo continued to observe and write, publishing his greatest work,* A Dialogue on the Two Great World Systems, *in 1632. He was consequently summoned to Rome, where he was tried by the Inquisition. Now an old man and almost blind, he was threatened with being burned as a contumacious heretic, so he recanted, even though he knew his position was correct. Galileo was sentenced to perpetual house arrest in Florence. He died in 1642 and is buried in a great tomb in the church of Santa Croce in Florence.*

Letter to Madame Christina of Lorraine, grand duchess of Tuscany, Concerning the Use of Biblical Quotations in Matters of Science [1615]

Galileo Galilei to the most serene grand duchess mother:

Some years ago, as Your Serene Highness well knows, I discovered in the heavens many things that had not been seen before our own age. The novelty of these things, as well as some consequences which followed from them in contradiction to the physical notions commonly held among academic philosophers, stirred up against me no small number of professors—as if I had placed these things in the sky with my own hands in order to upset nature and overturn the sciences. They seemed to forget that the increase of known truths stimulates the investigation, establishment, and growth of the arts; not their diminution or destruction.

Showing a greater fondness for their own opinions than for truth, they sought to deny and disprove the new things which, if they had cared to look for themselves, their own senses would have demonstrated to them. To this end they hurled various charges and published numerous writings filled with vain arguments, and they made the grave mistake of sprinkling these with passages taken from places in the Bible which they had failed to understand properly, and which were ill suited to their purposes.

These men would perhaps not have fallen into such error had they but paid attention to a most useful doctrine of St. Augustine's, relative to our making positive statements about things which are obscure and hard to understand by means of reason alone. Speaking of a certain physical conclusion about the heavenly bodies, he wrote: "Now keeping always our respect for moderation in grave piety, we ought not to believe anything inadvisably on a dubious point, lest in favor to our error we conceive a prejudice against something that truth hereafter may reveal to be not contrary in any way to the sacred books of either the Old or the New Testament."

Well, the passage of time has revealed to everyone the truths that previously set forth; and, together with the truth of the facts, there has come to light the great difference in attitude between those who simply and dispassionately refused to admit the discoveries to be true, and those who combined with their incredulity some reckless passion of their own. Men who were well grounded in astronomical and physical science were persuaded as soon as they received my first message. There were others who denied them or remained in doubt only because of their novel and unexpected character and because they had not yet had the opportunity to see for themselves. These men have by degrees come to be satisfied. But some, besides allegiance to their original error, possess I know not what fanciful interest in remaining hostile not so much toward the things in question as toward their discoverer. No longer being able to deny them, these men now take refuge in obstinate silence, but being more than ever exasperated by that which has pacified and quieted other men, they divert their thoughts to other fancies and seek new ways to damage me.

I should pay no more attention to them than to those who previously contradicted me—at whom I always laugh, being assured of the eventual outcome—were it not that in their new calumnies and persecutions I perceive that they do not stop at proving themselves more learned than I am (a claim which I scarcely contest), but go so far as to cast against me imputations of crimes which must be, and are, more abhorrent to me than death itself. I cannot remain satisfied merely to know that the injustice of this is recognized by those who are acquainted with these men and with me, as perhaps it is not known to others.

Persisting in their original resolve to destroy me and everything mine by any means they can think of, these men are aware of my views in astronomy and philosophy. They know that as to the arrangement of the parts of the universe, I hold the sun to be situated motionless in the center of the revolution of the celestial orbs while the earth rotates on its axis and revolves about the sun. They know also that I support this position not only by refuting the arguments of Ptolemy and Aristotle, but by producing many counterarguments; in particular, some which relate to physical effects whose causes can perhaps be assigned in no other way. In addition there are astronomical arguments derived from many things in my new celestial discoveries that plainly confute the Ptolemaic system while admirably agreeing with and confirming the contrary hypothesis. Possibly because they are disturbed by the known truth of other propositions of mine which differ from those commonly held, and therefore mistrusting their defense so long as they confine themselves to the field of philosophy, these men have resolved to fabricate a shield for their fallacies out of the mantle of pretended religion and the authority of the Bible. These they apply, with little judgment, to the refutation of arguments that they do not understand and have not even listened to.

First they have endeavored to spread the opinion that such propositions in general are contrary to the Bible and are consequently damnable and heretical. They know that it is human nature to take up causes whereby a man may oppress his neighbor, no matter how unjustly, rather than those from which a man may receive some just encouragement. Hence they have had no trouble in finding men who would preach the damnability and heresy of the new doctrine from their very pulpits with unwonted confidence, thus doing impious and inconsiderate injury not only to that doctrine and its followers but to all mathematics and mathematicians in general. Next, becoming bolder, and hoping (though vainly) that this seed which first took root in their hypocritical minds would send out branches and ascend to heaven, they began scattering rumors among the people that before long this doctrine would be condemned by the supreme authority. They know, too, that official condemnation would not only suppress the two propositions which I have mentioned, but would render damnable all other astronomical and physical statements and observations that have any necessary relation or connection with these.

In order to facilitate their designs, they seek so far as possible (at least among the common people) to make this opinion seem new and to belong to me alone. They pretend not to know that its author, or rather its restorer and confirmer, was Nicholas Copernicus; and that he was not only a Catholic, but a priest and a canon. He was in fact so esteemed by the church that when the Lateran Council under Leo X took up the correction of the church calendar, Copernicus was called to Rome from the most remote parts of Germany to undertake its reform. At that time the calendar was defective because the true measures of the year and the lunar month were not exactly known. The Bishop of Fossombrone, then in charge of this matter, assigned Copernicus to seek more light and greater certainty concerning the celestial motions by means of constant study and labor. With Herculean toil he set his admirable mind to this task, and he made such great progress in this science and brought our knowledge of the heavenly motions to such precision that he became celebrated as an astronomer. Since that time not only has the calendar been regulated by his teachings, but tables of all the motions of the planets have been calculated as well.

Having reduced his system into six books, he published these at the instance of the Cardinal of Capua and the Bishop of Culm. And since he had assumed his laborious enterprise by order of the supreme pontiff, he dedicated this book *On the Celestial Revolutions* to Pope Paul III. When printed, the book was accepted by the holy Church, and it has been read and studied by everyone without the faintest hint of any objection ever being conceived against its doctrines. Yet now that manifest experiences and necessary proofs have shown them to be well grounded, persons exist who would strip the author of his reward without so much as looking at his book, and add the shame of having him pronounced a heretic.

All this they would do merely to satisfy their personal displeasure conceived without any cause against another man, who has no interest in Copernicus beyond approving his teachings.

Now as to the false aspersions which they so unjustly seek to cast upon me, I have thought it necessary to justify myself in the eyes of all men, whose judgment in matters of religion and of reputation I must hold in great esteem. I shall therefore discourse of the particulars which these men produce to make this opinion detested and to have it condemned not merely as false but as heretical. To this end they make a shield of their hypocritical zeal for religion. They go about invoking the Bible, which they would have minister to their deceitful purposes. Contrary to the sense of the Bible and the intention of the holy Fathers, if I am not mistaken, they would extend such authorities until even in purely physical matters—where faith is not involved—they would have us altogether abandon reason and the evidence of our senses in favor of some biblical passage, though under the surface meaning of its words this passage may contain a different sense.

I hope to show that I proceed with much greater piety than they do, when I argue not against condemning this book, but against condemning it in the way they suggest—that is, without understanding it, weighing it, or so much as reading it. For Copernicus never discusses matters of religion or faith, nor does he use arguments that depend in any way upon the authority of sacred writings which he might have interpreted erroneously. He stands always upon physical conclusions pertaining to the celestial motions, and deals with them by astronomical and geometrical demonstrations, founded primarily upon sense experiences and very exact observations. He did not ignore the Bible, but he knew very well that if his doctrine were proved, then it could not contradict the Scriptures when they were rightly understood. And thus at the end of his letter of dedication, addressing the pope, he said:

> If there should chance to be any exegetes ignorant of mathematics who pretend to skill in that discipline, and dare to condemn and censure this hypothesis of mine upon the authority of some scriptural passage twisted to their purpose, I value them not, but disdain their unconsidered judgment. For it is known that Lactantius—a poor mathematician though in other respects a worthy author—writes very childishly about the shape of the earth when he scoffs at those who affirm it to be a globe. Hence it should not seem strange to the ingenious if people of that sort should in turn deride me. But mathematics is written for mathematicians, by whom, if I am not deceived, these labors of mine will be recognized as contributing something to their domain, as also to that of the Church over which Your Holiness now reigns.

Such are the people who labor to persuade us that an author like Copernicus may be condemned without being read, and who produce various authorities from the Bible, from theologians, and from Church Councils to make us believe that this is not only lawful but commendable. Since I hold these to be of supreme authority, I consider it rank temerity for anyone to contradict them—when employed according to the usage of the holy Church. Yet I do not believe it is wrong to speak out when there is reason to suspect that other men wish, for some personal motive, to produce and employ such authorities for purposes quite different from the sacred intention of the holy Church.

Therefore I declare (and my sincerity will make itself manifest) not only that I mean to submit myself freely and renounce any errors into which I may fall in this discourse through ignorance of matters pertaining to religion, but that I do not desire in these matters to engage in disputes with anyone, even on points that are disputable. My goal is this alone; that if, among errors that may abound in these considerations of a subject remote from my profession, there is anything that may be serviceable to the holy Church in making a decision concerning the Copernican system, it may be taken and utilized as seems best to the superiors. And if not, let my book be torn and burnt, as I neither intend nor pretend to gain from it any fruit that is not pious and Catholic. And though many of the things I shall reprove have been heard by my own ears, I shall freely grant to those who have spoken them that they never said them, if that is what they wish, and I shall confess myself to have been mistaken. Hence let whatever I reply be addressed not to them, but to whoever may have held such opinions.

The reason produced for condemning the opinion that the earth moves and the sun stands still is that in many places in the Bible one may read that the sun moves and the earth stands still. Since the Bible cannot err, it follows as a necessary consequence that anyone takes an erroneous and heretical position who maintains that the sun is inherently motionless and the earth movable.

With regard to this argument, I think in the first place that it is very pious to say and prudent to affirm that the holy Bible can never speak untruth—whenever its true meaning is understood. But I believe nobody will deny that it is often very abstruse, and may say things which are quite different from what its bare words signify. Hence in expounding the Bible if one were always to confine oneself to the unadorned grammatical meaning, one might fall into error. Not only contradictions and propositions far from true might thus be made to appear in the Bible, but even grave heresies and follies. Thus it would be necessary to assign to God feet, hands, and eyes, as well as corporeal and human affections, such as anger, repentance, hatred, and sometimes even the forgetting of things past and ignorance of those to come. These propositions uttered by the Holy Ghost were set down in that manner by the sacred scribes in order to accommodate them to the capacities of the common people, who are rude and unlearned. For the sake of those who deserve to be separated from the herd, it is necessary that wise expositors should produce the true senses of such passages, together with the special reasons for which they were set down in these words. This doctrine is so widespread and so definite with all theologians that it would be superfluous to adduce evidence for it.

Hence I think that I may reasonably conclude that whenever the Bible has occasion to speak of any physical conclusion (especially those which are very abstruse and hard to understand), the rule has been observed of avoiding confusion in the minds of the common people which would render them contumacious toward the higher mysteries. Now the Bible, merely to condescend to popular capacity, has not hesitated to obscure some very important pronouncements, attributing to God himself some qualities extremely remote from (and even contrary to) His essence. Who, then, would positively declare that this principle has been set aside, and the Bible has confined itself rigorously to the bare and restricted sense of its words, when speaking but casually of the earth, of water, of the sun, or of any other created thing? Especially in view of the fact that these things in no way concern the primary purpose of the sacred writings, which is the service of God and the salvation of souls—matters infinitely beyond the comprehension of the common people.

This being granted, I think that in discussions of physical problems we ought to begin not from the authority of scriptural passages, but from sense-experiences and necessary demonstrations; for the holy Bible and the phenomena of nature proceed alike from the divine Word, the former as the dictate of the Holy Ghost and the latter as the observant executrix of God's commands. It is necessary for the Bible, in order to be accommodated to the understanding of every man, to speak many things which appear to differ from the absolute truth so far as the bare meaning of the words is concerned. But Nature, on the other hand, is inexorable and immutable; she never transgresses the laws imposed upon her, or cares a whit whether her abstruse reasons and methods of operation are understandable to men. For that reason it appears that nothing physical which sense-experience sets before our eyes, or which necessary demonstrations prove to us, ought to be called in question (much less condemned) upon the testimony of biblical passages which may have some different meaning beneath their words. For the Bible is not chained in every expression to conditions as strict as those which govern all physical effects; nor is God any less excellently revealed in Nature's actions than in the sacred statements of the Bible. Perhaps this is what Tertullian meant by these words:

> We conclude that God is known first through Nature, and then again, more particularly, by doctrine; by Nature in His works, and by doctrine in His revealed word.

From this I do not mean to infer that we need not have an extraordinary esteem for the passages of holy Scripture. On the contrary, having arrived at any certainties in physics, we ought to utilize these as the most appropriate aids in the true exposition of the Bible and in the investigation of those meanings which are necessarily contained therein, for these must be concordant with demonstrated truths. I should judge that the authority of the Bible was designed to persuade men of those articles and propositions which, surpassing all human reasoning, could not be made credible by science, or by any other means than through the very mouth of the Holy Spirit.

Yet even in those propositions which are not matters of faith, this authority ought to be preferred over that of all human writings which are supported only by bare assertions or probable arguments, and not set forth in a demonstrative way. This I hold to be necessary and proper to the same extent that divine wisdom surpasses all human judgment and conjecture.

But I do not feel obliged to believe that that same God who has endowed us with senses, reason, and intellect has intended to forego their use and by some other means to give us knowledge which we can attain by them. He would not require us to deny sense and reason in physical matters which are set before our eyes and minds by direct experience or necessary demonstrations. This must be especially true in those sciences of which but the faintest trace (and that consisting of conclusions) is to be found in the Bible. Of astronomy, for instance, so little is found that none of the planets except Venus are so much as mentioned, and this only once or twice under the name of "Lucifer." If the sacred scribes had had any intention of teaching people certain arrangements and motions of the heavenly bodies, or had they wished us to derive such knowledge from the Bible, then in my opinion they would not have spoken of these matters so sparingly in comparison with the infinite number of admirable conclusions which are demonstrated in that science. Far from pretending to teach us the constitution and motions of the heavens and the stars, with their shapes, magnitudes, and distances, the authors of the Bible intentionally forbore to speak of these things, though all were quite well known to them. Such is the opinion of the holiest and most learned Fathers, and in St. Augustine we find the following words:

> It is likewise commonly asked what we may believe about the form and shape of the heavens according to the Scriptures, for many contend much about these matters. But with superior prudence our authors have forborne to speak of this, as in no way furthering the student with respect to a blessed life—and, more important still, as taking up much of that time which should be spent in holy exercises. What is it to me whether heaven, like a sphere, surrounds the earth on all sides as a mass balanced in the center of the universe, or whether like a dish it merely covers and overcasts the earth? Belief in Scripture is urged rather for the reason we have often mentioned; that is, in order that no one, through ignorance of divine passages, finding anything in our Bibles or hearing anything cited from them of such a nature as may seem to oppose manifest conclusions, should be induced to suspect their truth when they teach, relate, and deliver more profitable matters. Hence let it be said briefly, touching the form of heaven, that our authors knew the truth but the Holy Spirit did not desire that men should learn things that are useful to no one for salvation.

The same disregard of these sacred authors toward beliefs about the phenomena of the celestial bodies is repeated to us by St. Augustine in his next chapter. On the question whether we are to believe that the heaven moves or stands still, he writes thus:

> Some of the brethren raise a question concerning the motion of heaven, whether it is fixed or moved. If it is moved, they say, how is it a firmament? If it stands still, how do these stars which are held fixed in it go round from east to west, the more northerly performing shorter circuits near the pole, so that heaven (if there is another pole unknown to us) may seem to revolve upon some axis, or (if there is no other pole) may be thought to move as a discus? To these men I reply that it would require many subtle and profound reasoning to find out which of these things is actually so; but to undertake this and discuss it is consistent neither with my leisure nor with the duty of those whom I desire to instruct in essential matters more directly conducing to their salvation and to the benefit of the holy Church.

From these things it follows as a necessary consequence that, since the Holy Ghost did not intend to teach us whether heaven moves or stands still, whether its shape is spherical or like a discus or extended in a plane, nor whether the earth is located at its center or off to one side, then so much the less was it intended to settle for us any other conclusion of the same kind. And the motion or rest of the earth and the sun is so closely linked with the things just named, that without a determination of the one, neither side can be taken in the other matters. Now if the Holy Spirit has purposely neglected to teach us propositions of this sort as irrelevant to the highest goal (that is, to our salvation), how can anyone affirm that it is obligatory to take sides on them, and that one belief is required by faith, while the other side is erroneous? Can an opinion be heretical and yet have no concern with the salvation of souls? Can the Holy Ghost be asserted not to have intended teaching us something that does concern our salvation? I would say here something that was heard from an ecclesiastic of the most eminent degree: "That the intention of the Holy Ghost is to teach us how one goes to heaven, not how heaven goes."

53. JOHN SHUTE (D. 1563)

John Shute was likely born in Devon, although the date of his birth is unknown. He appears to have been a member of the painter and stainers' guild in London and had achieved some small reputation as a painter of miniatures. At some point in the 1540s he seems to have entered the service of Edward Seymour (1500–52), duke of Somerset, and Lord Protector of England during the minority of his young nephew, Edward VI (r. 1547–53). Shute may have been involved with Sir William Thynne in the building of Somerset House in London and perhaps Thynne's own country house, Longleat. But, after Somerset's fall in 1549, Shute appears to have migrated to the household of his successor, John Dudley, duke of Northumberland, for whom he might have designed part of Dudley castle. It was Northumberland who at his own expense sent Shute to Italy to study architecture. Shute was in Italy by 1550, but we have no documentation of his time or activities while there. The result of this journey is The First and Chief Grounds of Architecture, *printed in 1563, the year of Shute's death. This is the first English treatise on architecture and is heavily illustrated with engravings, almost certainly by Shute himself. The book is, however, mostly a digest of Sebastiano Serlio's (d. 1554) work in Italian. Shute is also indebted to Vitruvius's Ten Books on Architecture and its commentators. The great majority of Shute's treatise is concerned with the classical orders of building, as is much of Serlio's. Shute is one of the first Englishmen to refer to himself as an architect, and he introduced not only the new styles of Italian Renaissance building into England but its vocabulary as well, using for the first time words such as* symmetry.

The First and Chief Groundes of Architecture used in all the auncient and famous monymentes: with a farther & more ample discourse uppon the same, than hitherto hath been set out by any other

The Dedicatory Letter to Queen Elizabeth and to the Reader

To the Most High and Excellent Princess Elizabeth by the grace of God Queen of England, France, and Ireland, defender of the faith, etc.

It is both rightly and excellently affirmed of Marcus Tullius Cicero, in his first book *de officiis* (right Excellent Princess and my most gracious sovereign Lady) that no man is borne into this world for his prime and singular weale, because our Country chiefly, partly our parents, and partly our kinsfolk do require as it were a duty of us, and recompense for that the which we have received and like as the members of man's body be diverse in number, and have according to their diversity diverse and peculiar properties so is it a good and well settled commonwealth: in which there is no office so base, or handy work so simple which is not necessary and profitable for the same. And as the members of the body doing without impediments their natural duties the whole body is in an healthful harmony and able to perform all that belongeth to the same; so is it in a public weale when all men in their calling, do labor not only for their own gain, but also for the profit and commodity of our Country, which things when I according to my small capacity did way with myself, I was as it were stirred forward to do my duty unto this my Country wherein I live and am a member. And so much the rather, for that being servant unto the Right honorable Duke of Northumberland in 1550. It pleased his grace for my further knowledge to maintain me in Italy there to confer with theologies of the skillful masters of architecture, and also to view such ancient Monuments hereof as are yet extant, whereupon at my return, presenting his grace with the fruits of my travails, it pleased the same to show them unto that noble king Edward the VI, your majesty's most dear brother of famous memory, whose delection and pleasure was to see it, and such like. And having the said tricks and devises as well of sculpture and painting as also of Architecture, yet in my keeping, I thought it good at this time to let forth some part of the same for the profit of others, especially touching Architecture wherein I do follow not only the writings of learned men, but also do ground myself in my own experience and practice, gathered by the sight of the monuments in Italy. And because all the members of the body have chiefly and principally a duty to the head, as governor of the whole, and without which, all the other can not live; so my duty enforceth me most sovereign lady (the perfect and natural head next unto God of this our commonwealth) to show a token of the same unto your highness, in presenting these my poor and simple labours whereunto I am the rather boldened considering your highness delight in all kind of good learning, and perfect skill in the tongues and sciences, most humbly beseeching your royal majesty to vouchsafe to let this my small travail and work pass under your noble perfection and defense: and I according to my bound and duty shall pray to God for your long life and prosperous reign, with peace and tranquility to his honor and glory. Amen.

Your majesty's most humble and obedient subject,
John Shute

John Shute, Painter and Architect: Unto the Loving and Friendly Readers

Amongst all other things (gentle and loving reader) wherewith the divine providence of almighty God hath most liberally, and plentifully, endowed mankind: there is nothing either for the dignity and worthiness of the thing itself, or for the wonderful estimation and price which in all times it hath been in, more excellent, precious, and commendable then learning, knowledge and science, the which alone causeth mortal men to be most like immortal Gods: and as it taketh out of their minds that rude and uncomely admiration wherewith through ignorance the simple in most vain trifles are wonderfully occupied. So to the wise be monuments and works skillfully practiced and carefully left both commendable and marvelous: yea and such as neither the injuries of any storms and tempest can clean waste and consume, no nor (as it seemeth) the envy of man or spoil of enemies deface and overthrow, either that which is greatest of all, time itself can deface or cast out of mind. And amongst all other studies there is none in my simple judgment of this sort that deserveth greater praise, than that which is of the Greeks named Architectonica, and of the Latins, Architecture (I think not altogether unfit or unaptly called by me termed in English, the art and trade to raise up and make excellent edifices and buildings) the which like as in all other ages before hath been in marvelous account and estimation, as full well appeareth by diverse learned Philosophers and famous princes that embraced the same as Plato, Aristotle, Pliny, who were excellent therein as their works will witness. Alexander Magnus, Julius Caesar, Vespasian, Adrian with many other ancient Greeks and Romans which labored to advance their name thereby who left many arguments of their virtue, high intents and doings by the same with many other famous [men], of which Pliny maketh mention. Vitruvius and Frontyne [Frontinus], of later days men praiseworthy very studious and painful therein so in us seemeth it not only to crave the wonted commendation, but also to be most necessary and profitable as well by the condition of the time as necessity of the thing itself. And surely such is the amplitude and largeness (I may well say perfection) of this faculty, that without some acquaintance with many other arts ye shall not enter into the deep secrets: for it hath a natural society and as it were by a certain kindred and affinity is knit unto all the Mathematicals, which sciences and knowledges are friends and a maintainer of diverse rational arts: so that without a mean acquaintance or understanding in them neither painters, masons, goldsmiths, embroiderers, carvers, joiners, glassers, gravers, in all manner of metals and diverse others more can obtain any worthy praise at all. Now all these being branches of that foresaid foundation, stock, or science shall bring forth the fruits of it to their great profits, and commodity of the realm, which continuing and thoroughly practiced in the same by time shall increase riches, worship, and fame. Considering with myself the manifold commodities and profits that should redownde to a great many lovers of the same and contrary wise what a loss and hindrance it hath been to them that lack the languages and learning who of necessity hath remained in ignorance to their great loss and discommodity of the Realme, notwithstanding I know well there hath been a multitude and at this time be very many learned men who hath (through travail received) the full perfection of the prudent lady *Scientia*, of whom so deeply learned I crave pardon for my rude rashness that I having but tasted a certain sweetness of her excellency and liberality, wherefore natural love hath drawn me to advance her reputation and honor, according to my poor ability and good will, the thing nothing garnished as it ought to be, but most briefly and plainly with such demonstrations that it might edify them which of a long time have desired and reached at it to attain also for the encouraging of those which earnestly studied and favored it, I thought it therefore good to let out and commit to writing in our native language, part of those things which (both by great labor and travail, at the first for my private commodity I searched out and for my own pleasure out of diverse as well Latin and Italian, as French and Dutch writers), I have diligently gathered, as also passed many countries and regions to see, both in Rome amongst the antiquities and in the most notable places of Italy, where are most excellent buildings, and intending to write of Architecture or buildings, I thought it best neither with the lightest or least profitable part thereof to begin, nor altogether after the most slender sort to handle that which I purposed to entreat upon. I have therefore taken my first entrance into the writings of this art, at the five antique pillars or columns, commonly named of the places and persons partly where and of they were invented, and partly of their virtues and properties of those that were likened unto, which pillars' names are these as followeth: Tuscana, Dorica, Ionica, Corinthia, and Conposita. The treatise of these pillars, as it hath in it most delection and pleasure in the beauty and comeliness of the workmanship appertaining unto them so though at the beginning, it be mingled with a little asperity and as it were bitterness (for the difficulty and hardness wherewith as both principals and also other things of any excellency at the first are customed to be, it is somewhat cumbrous) yet it is both so necessary and profitable, that neither without it any man may attain to any estimable part of the rest of this science, and with it as by a clue of thread or plain pathway a man may most easily pierce and lightly pass over the most dark and unknown corners of the whole process thereof. But to speak of the worthiness of this part of Architecture it seemeth almost altogether superfluous, wherefore taking these to suffice in the part to be said, I will now show what trade and order I do follow in the declaration of the measures, proportions, and garnishments of these before-mentioned pillars. For so much therefore as in teaching of all arts three things are chiefly considered that is to say diligence in giving the precepts, aptness in choosing plain and evident examples, and last of all practice and experience of the teacher, I have for the first part taken for my author chiefly to be followed the noble and excellent writer Vitruvius, one of the most perfect of all the antiques, and for that neither any one man in what art so ever it be is absolute, and that other singular men of the antiques and he in many points do disagree and differ, which Sebastianus Serlius, a marvelous cunning artificer in our time in many places of his works learnedly doth declare, I have added unto him upon whatsoever in anything seemed needful the opinion and meaning of the said expert writer Sebastianus, here and there also where I thought meet I have joined the mind and judgment of one Gulielmus Philander, a notable man which about the year of our lord 1546 wrote unto the French king annotations upon Vitruvius, concerning this matter or such like. Now for examples which are necessarily required to the opening of such dark matters, I have everywhere through the whole process of this present treatise after the precepts of lightening of them set both demonstration and figure, and as for practice and experience of these things which I teach, I assure the most gentle reader and all other that shall be readers of this my little work that I have put no title in any part thereof concerning the proportion and symmetry to use the accustomed term of the art of the forenamed columns, which I have not as well seen and measured in Italy, from whence they can first unto us amongst the antique works as read and studied in England in the Antique writers, that I might with so much more perfection write of them as both the reading of the thing and seeing it in deed is more than only bear reading of it. This small and simple treatise of mine I can not tell whither with like felicity brought to his perfection as with no small labor and study for this time ended, I thought meet as the first fruits of my poor attempts and endeavors to leave as a duty and debt of me to be paid, and that well received of all men, I shall think of myself most happy, and if not of all persons, yet at the least wise of such as be honest esteemers and accepters of other men's diligence and studies. The which if it come to pass, both I shall be glad of my labors in these things bestowed and for the love of my natural countrymen be furthermore encouraged hereafter to attempt greater things. Thus almighty God preserve thee in godly exercises to his pleasure forever. Amen.

54. JEAN BODIN (1530–96)

Jean Bodin was a French social and political philosopher, economist, occultist, historian, and lawyer. He was first educated in a Carmelite monastery and even took initial vows as a monk; however, he was freed from these and went in 1549 to Paris to study at the humanist institution of the Collège des trois langues (Collège de France) and the Sorbonne. Later he pursued his legal education in Toulouse. He was attached to the Parlement of Paris and was later elected a representative to the Estates General. Although he remained a Roman Catholic, he was hardly a zealot. Consequently, he fell into the circle called Les Politiques, a group of like-minded theorists who sought an end to the Wars of Religion through pragmatism and enlightened policy enforced by a strong central monarchy. After the assassination of Henry III in 1589, Bodin briefly supported the Catholic League to keep the Huguenot Henry of Navarre from becoming king of France, despite his adherence to the interconfessional pragmatism of Les Politiques.

In 1576 he wrote his most influential book, Six Books on the Commonwealth (Six Livres de la République), *in which he argues in favor of an absolute monarchy, responsible only to God. In his argument he uses the principles of geography and climate developed earlier, in his* Method for the Easy Comprehension of History, *that France is best suited by nature to a powerful hereditary monarchy. His* Method *presents a systematic method of studying history with the purpose of establishing universal law. The following extract contains parts of his theory that climate and geographical features determined the character and, therefore, the political dispositions of men. Those who were born in temperate zones, such as the French, were predisposed to moderation and good sense in the conduct of affairs.*

Method for the Easy Comprehension of History

Let us therefore adopt this theory, that all who inhabit the area from the forty-fifth parallel to the seventy-fifth toward the north grow increasingly warmer within, while the southerners, since they have more warmth from the sun, have less from themselves. In winter the heat is collected within, but in summer it flows out. Whereby it happens that in winter we are more animated and robust, in summer more languid. The same reason usually makes us hungrier in winter so that we eat more than in summer, especially when the north wind blows. The south wind has the opposite effect, that is to say, living things are less hungry, as Aristotle wrote. So it comes to pass that when the Germans visit Italy, or the French, Spain, we observe that they eat more frugally or suffocate. This accident happened to Philip, duke of Austria, when he dined according to his usual custom in Spain. But the Spanish, who live frugally in their fatherland, in France are more voracious than the French. Let it serve as evidence that the shepherds commonly say that when the herds and the flocks go down to the south they are wasted with fasting; they are more active in the north. Nor is it remarkable that Leo the African wrote he had seen almost no herds of oxen or horses and only a few flocks of sheep in Africa; the ewes gave only a little milk. In contrast, the; flocks of the Germans and the Scythians are praised by almost all writers. This ought not to be attributed to the fact that they have better pastures than the southerners, as Pliny thought, but to the climate. For the strength of inward heat brings it about that those who live in northerly lands are more active and robust than the southerners. Even in the opposite area, beyond Capricorn's circle, the same thing happens: the further men move from the equator the larger they grow, as in the land of the Patagonians, who are called giants, in the very same latitude as the Germans. This, then, is the reason why Scythians have always made violent attacks southward; and what seems incredible, but is nevertheless true, the greatest empires always have spread southward—rarely from the south toward the north. The Assyrians defeated the Chaldeans; the Medes, the Assyrians; the Greeks, the Persians; the Parthians, the Greeks; the Romans, the Carthaginians; the Goths, the Romans; the Turks, the Arabs; and the Tartars, the Turks. The Romans, on the contrary, were unwilling to advance beyond the Danube. After Trajan had built a stone bridge of remarkable size across the Danube (for it is said that it had twenty pylons, of which the fragments even now remain), he did indeed conquer the Dacians completely. But when Hadrian understood that these tribes were not easily kept in subjection and did not submit to defeat, he ordered the bridge to be destroyed. Let us, however, cite more recent examples.

The French often suffered serious defeat at the hands of the English in France itself and almost lost their territory;

they could never have penetrated into England, had they not been invited by the inhabitants. The English, on the other hand, were frequently overwhelmed by the Scots, and although they fought for control for more than 1,200 years, yet they could not drive the Scots from a small part of the island, even when in resources and numbers they were as much superior to the Scots as they were inferior to the French. It is not a fact, as the English complain, that the contest was unequal because of French hostility, for when the Roman Empire was tottering the South Britons were forced to call the Anglo-Saxons for protection, lest they should fall into servitude under the Scots. Yet the men who withstood the onslaughts of the Scots were not willing to attack at home. I omit the serious incursions into Europe and Asia of the Scythians, Parthians, Turks, Tartars, Muscovites, Goths, Huns, and Suessiones, since the list is endless. Unless I err, this is what Ezekiel, Jeremiah, Isaiah, and the remaining Prophets threaten so many times: wars from the north, soldiers, horsemen, and the coming downfall of empires …

The Africans, with dry, cold, and very hard bodies, bear work and heat patiently … Yet they cannot bear the cold, since they have no internal heat, unlike the Scythians, who endure external heat with difficulty, since they are abundantly supplied within. In the same way horses, by their very nature warm and wet, live with difficulty in Ethiopia, but more easily in Scythia. On the other hand, asses, dry and cold, are lively in Africa, tired in Europe, nonexistent in Scythia …

The chief discussion is about the peoples who dwell from the thirtieth parallel to the sixtieth, because we know their history, about which we must form an opinion. We have almost no material for other peoples, but by this illustration we shall learn what must be believed about all. The Mediterranean peoples, then, as far as concerns the form of the body, are cold, dry, hard, bald, weak, swarthy, small in body, crisp of hair, black-eyed, and clear-voiced. The Baltic peoples, on the other hand, are warm, wet, hairy, robust, white, large-bodied, soft-fleshed, with scanty beards, bluish grey eyes, and deep voices. Those who live between the two show moderation in all respects. But this one thing is open to question: that the southerners, weak by the consent of all, are yet hard; the northerners, indeed, are robust, and yet soft. In opposition to this, Hippocrates and almost all the other writers said that Scythians and mountaineers who resemble the type of the Scythians were hard, wild, and born to endure labor. Among these conflicting opinions of historians and philosophers, however, we shall judge correctly about history, as well as reconcile with Hippocrates and Alexander, Livy, Tacitus, Polybius, Plutarch, and Caesar, who reported that the French and the Germans were impatient of work, if we grant that the northerners in a cold region patiently bear labor, but in a warm region dissolve in sweat and languish. With this the account of Agathias about the Germans and of Krantz about the Scandinavians agree—that they wage war willingly in the winter, but rarely in the summer.

In contrast, the southerners easily endure heat suited to their nature, although they become more energetic in a cold region, languid in a warm one. And so, as I hear, in their language the Spanish women usually call the Germans "soft fish." But the Celts and the Belgae, when they come into Italy or Provence, are tortured by the mosquitoes and vermin to an unusual extent because of the softness of their skin. The natives, due to their toughness, are not annoyed so much …

The southerners are not so avaricious as they are parsimonious and stingy; the Scythians, on the other hand, are extravagant and rapacious. Since they know that they are at a disadvantage, they are usually suspicious. This trait our men formerly knew well enough. Holster related to me the additional fact that spies and listeners in Gothland hide in public inns, for suspicion arises from want of knowledge. They do not have intercourse with southerners unless they are sober, and when they feel themselves deceived, they draw back, or often anticipate by deceiving the strangers, or as a last resort use force. Whereby it happens that by universal consent they are supposed to be as perfidious as the southerners. (Of this fact the old historians were entirely ignorant, because they had no intercourse with the Scythians.) Later, when they left their homes, they revealed their character. Since the Franks came from Germany into France (for the Germans boast that the French are of Teutonic origin), it is in keeping that Procopius, in speaking of the Franks, commented: "This race is the most likely of all to betray their faith." And Vopiscus said: "It is customary for the Franks to break their faith laughingly." Hence, Alciati wrote that a scorpion's tail was tossed at the Germans. This proverb we retain in France in the vulgar tongue—with due apologies, may it be said, lest our discourse should seem to harm the name of any race. I am not discussing this particular characteristic, but the inborn nature of each race. In this trait, however, the Germans are exceeded to a considerable degree by the Danes and the Norwegians, from whom they differ widely. Certainly greater perfidy or cruelty of people toward princes or of princes among themselves was never engendered than between Christian and Gustavus, between Danes and Swedes. From these races originate also the Normans, who, the common people believe, are unreliable.

But if from want of reasoning and wisdom the northerners cannot control their appetites and furthermore are regarded as intemperate, suspicious, perfidious, and cruel why are the southerners much more cruel and perfidious even than these? Here again I seek the decision in history. It is evident that by nature the southerners have the greatest gifts of ability; thus Columella, in Book I, chapter iii, declared: "It is well known that the Carthaginians, a very acute race, said 'the field must be weaker than the ploughman.'" Concerning the Egyptians who fought against Caesar, Hirtius said: "These very clever men shrewdly constructed the things they saw made by us, so that our men seemed to imitate their work." A little later the same author added, "The race of Egyptians is much given to treachery." Moreover, who does not know how artfully and how long the Carthaginians eluded the power of the Romans? Nevertheless, they always practiced incredible cruelty against the enemy, as may be seen in the Punic War and also in that combat which the Spendii and the Carthaginians, both Phoenicians, waged against each other. As Polybius said, "It far exceeded all wars of which we have heard in cruelty and all kinds of crimes." Yet the things related by Polybius about the cruelty of the Carthaginians would seem ludicrous if anyone compared them with the history of Leo the African, or even with the unheard-of cruelty of Muley-Hasan and his sons, which not so long ago they practiced against the citizens and then against each other. For Muley-Hasan, driven from the kingdom whence he had driven his father, came as a suppliant to Emperor Charles, suffering from the loss of his eyes, which had been burnt out through the brutal violence of his brother.

... Then the powers which are attributed to the senate or to magistrates have a significance distinct from sovereignty. Otherwise, it must be confessed, the sovereignty would be vested in those who had received it from others. If this seems absurd, what Polybius affirmed ought also to seem absurd—that the sovereignty of the state was partly in the people, partly in the senate, partly in the consuls. Furthermore, he thought that the form of government seemed to be mixed—aristocracy, monarchy, and democracy. This opinion Dionysius and Cicero adopted; then Machiavelli, Contarini, Thomas More, Garimberto, and Manutius vehemently approved it. We must refute them in debate, because this subject is of great importance for the thorough comprehension of the history of states. When the restoration of liberty to the people was mooted with bitter contention among the Florentines and it did not seem sage, and indeed was dangerous, to spread the secrets of empire among the throng, it was decided that after they had segregated the dregs of the plebs, who could not legally hold office, the laws must be ordained and the magistrates must be elected by the people. Other matters were to be regulated through the senate and the popular magistrates. For thus Guicciardini wrote.

From this, also, it is made plain that the right of sovereignty is chiefly displayed in these specified attributes. Therefore, in every state one ought to investigate who can give authority to magistrates, who can take it away, who can make or repeal laws—whether one citizen or a small part of the citizens or a greater part. When this has been ascertained, the type of government is easily understood. There can be no fourth, and indeed none can be conceived, for virtue and viciousness do not create a type of rule. Whether the prince is unjust or worthy, nevertheless the state is still a monarchy. The same thing must be said about oligarchy and the rule of the people, who, while they have no powers but the creation of magistrates, still have the sovereignty, and on them the form of government necessarily depends. We shall then call the form one of optimates, or else popular (let us use these words in order that we may not rather often be forced to use the names aristocracy, oligarchy, democracy, ochlocracy, according to the type of virtue or vice); much more so if in addition to the creation of magistrates there is also power over war and peace, life and death. Moreover, it is evident that these things have always been so, not only in a monarchy but also in a government of optimates or in a popular state … But not to take endless examples from history, we shall use as examples Athenians, Romans, and Venetians, in order to show that what they taught about the mixed type of the Roman state is false.

55. FRANÇOIS RABELAIS (C. 1483–1553)

Rabelais was born sometime between 1483 and 1490 near Chinon, the son of a lawyer and landowner. Sent to a Franciscan monastery, Rabelais took priest's orders by 1521 but spent much time and energy studying Greek. His superiors objected, so Rabelais left the Franciscans and entered a Benedictine monastery, where he became secretary to the abbot, who shared his interest in humanism.

Leaving the monastery at some time before 1530, Rabelais traveled to Paris, perhaps to study medicine. He matriculated in medicine at Montpellier in 1530 and accepted the position of physician in a hospital in Lyon in 1532. His doctorate in medicine was granted by Montpellier in 1537.

Rabelais traveled to Rome on two occasions (1533, 1535) in the suite of Cardinal Jean du Bellay. He subsequently entered another Benedictine monastery in France, St Maur, but accepted in 1537 an appointment as a physician in Metz. Although he remained in the Roman Church, Rabelais had several illegitimate children, knew a number of French Protestants, and satirized the theologians of the Sorbonne. The faculty of theology retaliated in 1543 by condemning his work. Rabelais died in 1553.

The publication of Pantagruel *in 1532 was followed soon after by* Gargantua. *These works tell the story of the two eponymous giants, following their adventures and celebrating their love of eating, drinking, and the other pleasures of the flesh. Informed by a brilliant satiric wit and deep sympathy with the human condition, this large, rollicking collection of stories has remained among the most popular of all Renaissance books.*

Gargantua *and* Pantagruel

How Gargantua Had the Abbey of Thélème Built for the Monk

There remained the monk to provide for. Gargantua wanted to make him Abbot of Seuilly, but the friar refused. He wanted to give him the Abbey of Bourguêil or that of Saint-Florent, whichever might suit him best, or both, if he had fancy for them. But the monk gave a peremptory reply to the effect that he would not take upon himself any office involving the government of others.

"For how," he demanded, "could I govern others, who cannot even govern myself? If you are of the opinion that I have done you, or may be able to do you in the future, any worthy service, give me leave to found an abbey according to my own plan."

This request pleased Gargantua, and the latter offered his whole province of Thélème, lying along the River Loire, at a distance of two leagues from the great Forest of Port-Huault. The monk then asked that he be permitted to found a convent that should be exactly the opposite of all other institutions of the sort.

"In the first place, then," said Gargantua, "you don't want to build any walls around it; for all the other abbeys have plenty of those."

"Right you are," said the monk, "for where there is a wall (*mur*) in front and behind there is bound to be a lot of *murmur*-ing, jealousy and plotting on the inside."

Moreover, in view of the fact that in certain convents in this world there is a custom, if any woman (by which, I mean any modest or respectable one) enters the place, to clean up thoroughly after her wherever she has been—in view of this fact, a regulation was drawn up to the effect that if any monk or nun should happen to enter this new convent, all the places they had set foot in were to be thoroughly scoured and scrubbed. And since, in other convents, everything is run, ruled, and fixed by hours, it was decreed that in this one there should not be any clock or dial of any sort, but that whatever work there was should be done whenever occasion offered. For, as Gargantua remarked, the greatest loss of time he knew was to watch the hands of the clock. What good came of it? It was the greatest foolishness in the world to regulate one's conduct by the tinkling of a time-piece, instead of by intelligence and good common sense.

Another feature: Since in those days women were not put into convents unless they were blind in one eye, lame, hunchbacked, ugly, misshapen, crazy, silly, deformed, and generally of no account, and since men did not enter a monastery unless they were snotty-nosed, underbred, dunces, and troublemakers at home—

"Speaking of that," said the monk, "of what use is a woman who is neither good nor good to look at?"

"Put her in a convent," said Gargantua.

"Yes," said the monk, "and set her to making shirts."

And so, it was decided that in this convent they would receive only the pretty ones, the ones with good figures and sunny dispositions, and only the handsome, well-set-up, good-natured men.

Item: Since in the convents of women, men never entered, except underhandedly and by stealth, it was provided that, in this one, there should be no women unless there were men also, and no men unless there were also women.

Item: Inasmuch as many men, as well as women, once received into a convent were forced and compelled, after a year of probation, to remain there all the rest of their natural lives—in view of this, it was provided that, here, both men and women should be absolutely free to pick up and leave whenever they happened to feel like it.

Item: Whereas, ordinarily, the religious take three vows, namely, those of chastity, poverty and obedience, it was provided that, in this abbey, one might honorably marry, that each one should be rich, and that all should live in utter freedom.

With regard to the lawful age for entering, the women should be received from the age of ten to fifteen years, the men from the age of twelve to eighteen.

How the Abbey of the Thelemites Was Built and Endowed

For the building and furnishing of the abbey, Gargantua made a ready-money levy of two-million-seven-hundred-thousand-eight-hundred-thirty-one of the coins known as "big woolly sheep"; and for each year, until everything should be in perfect shape, he turned over, out of the toll-receipts of the Dive River, one-million-six-hundred-sixty-nine-thousand "sunny crowns" and the same number of "seven-chick pieces." For the foundation and support of the abbey, he made a perpetual grant of two-million-three-hundred-sixty-nine-thousand-five-hundred-fourteen "rose nobles," in the form of ground-rent, free and exempt of all encumbrances, and payable every year at the abbey gate, all of this being duly witnessed in the form of letters of conveyance.

As for the building itself, it was in the form of a hexagon, so constructed that at every corner there was a great round tower sixty paces in diameter, all these being of the same size and appearance. The River Loire flowed along the north elevation. Upon the bank of this river stood one of the towers, named Arctic, while, proceeding toward the east, there was another, named Calaer, following it another, named Anatole, then another, named Mesembrine, another after it, named Hesperia, and finally, one named Cryere. Between every two towers, there was a distance of three-hundred-twelve paces. To the building proper, there were six stories in all, counting the underground cellars as one. The second story was vaulted, in the form of a basket handle. The rest were stuccoed with plaster of Paris, in the manner of lamp bottoms, the roof being covered over with a fine slate, while the ridge-coping was lead, adorned with little mannikins and animal figures, well grouped and gilded. The eaves-troughs, which jutted out from the walls, between the mullioned windows, were painted with diagonal gold and blue figures, all the way down to the ground, where they ended in huge rainspouts, all of which led under the house to the river.

This building was a hundred times more magnificent than the one at Bonivet, at Chambord, or at Chantilly; for in it there were nine-thousand-three-hundred-thirty-two rooms, each equipped with a dressing room, a study, a wardrobe, and a chapel, and each opening into a large hall. Between the towers, in the center of the main building, was a winding stair, the steps of which were partly of porphyry, partly of Numidian stone, and partly of serpentine marble, each step being twenty-two feet long and three fingers thick, with an even dozen between each pair of landings. On each landing were two fine antique arches, admitting the daylight, while through these arches, one entered a loggia of the width of the stair, the chair itself running all the way to the roof and ending in a pavilion. From this stair one could enter, from either side, a large hall, and from this hall the rooms.

From the tower known as Arctic to the one called Cryere, there were fine large libraries, in Greek, Latin, Hebrew, French, Tuscan, and Spanish, separated from each other according to the different languages. In the middle of the building was another and marvelous stairway, the entrance to which was from outside the house, by way of an arch thirty-six feet wide. This stair was so symmetrical and capacious that six men-at-arms, their lances at rest, could ride up abreast, all the way to the roof. From the tower Anatole to Mesembrine, there were large and splendid galleries, all containing paintings representative of deeds of ancient prowess, along with historical and geographical scenes …

What Kind of Dwelling the Thelemites Had

In the middle of the lower court was a magnificent fountain of beautiful alabaster, above which were the three Graces with cornucopias, casting out water through their breasts, mouths, ears, eyes, and the other openings of their bodies.

The interior of the portion of the dwelling that opened upon this court rested upon great pillars of chalcedony and of porphyry, fashioned with the finest of antique workmanship. Above were splendid galleries, long and wide, adorned with paintings, with the horns of deer, unicorns, rhinoceroses, and hippopotamuses, as well as with elephants' teeth and other objects interesting to look upon.

The ladies' quarters extended from the tower Arctic to the Mesembrine gate. The men occupied the rest of the house. In front of the ladies' quarters, in order that the occupants might have something to amuse them, there had been set up, between the first two outside towers, the lists, the hippodrome, the theater, and the swimming-pools, with wonderful triple-stage baths, well provided with all necessary equipment and plentifully supplied with water of myrrh.

Next the river was a fine pleasure-garden, in the center of which was a handsome labyrinth. Between the towers were the tennis courts and the ball-grounds. On the side by the tower Cryere was the orchard, full of all sorts of fruit trees, all of them set out in the form of quincunxes. Beyond was the large park, filled with every sort of savage beast. Between the third pair of towers were the targets for arquebus, archery, and crossbow practice. The servants' quarters were outside the tower Hesperia and consisted of one floor only, and beyond these quarters were the stables. In front of the latter stood the falcon-house, looked after by falconers most expert in their art. It was furnished annually by the Candians, the Venetians, and the Sarmatians, with all kinds of out-of-the-ordinary birds: eagles, gerfalcons, goshawks, sakers, lanners, falcons, sparrow-hawks, merlins, and others, all so well trained and domesticated that, when these birds set out from the castle for a little sport in the fields, they would take everything that came in their way. The hunting kennels were a little farther off, down toward the park.

All the halls, rooms and closets were tapestried in various manners, according to the season of the year. The whole floor was covered with green cloth. The bedding was of embroidered work. In each dressingroom was a crystal mirror, with chasings of fine gold, the edges being trimmed with pearls; and this mirror was of such a size that—it is the truth I am telling you—it was possible to see the whole figure in it at once. As one came out of the halls into the ladies' quarters, he at once encountered the perfumers and the hair-dressers, through whose hands the gentlemen passed when they came to visit the ladies.

These functionaries each morning supplied the women's chambers with rose, orange, and "angel" water; and in each room a precious incense-dish was vaporous with all sorts of aromatic drugs.

...

How the Thelemites Were Governed in Their Mode of Living

Their whole life was spent, not in accordance with laws, statutes, or rules, but according to their own will and free judgment. They rose from bed when they felt like it and drank, ate, worked, and slept when the desire came to them. No one woke them, no one forced them to drink or to eat or do any other thing. For this was the system that Gargantua had established. In the rule of their order there was but this one clause:

DO WHAT THOU WOULDST

for the reason that those who are free born and well born, well brought up, and used to decent society possess, by nature, a certain instinct and spur, which always impels them to virtuous deeds and restrains them from vice, an instinct which is the thing called honor. These same ones, when, through vile subjection and constraint, they are repressed and held down, proceed to employ that same noble inclination to virtue in throwing off and breaking the yoke of servitude, for we always want to come to forbidden things; and we always desire that which is denied us.

In the enjoyment of their liberty, the Thelemites entered into a laudable emulation in doing, all of them, anything which they thought would be pleasing to one of their number. If anyone, male or female, remarked: "Let us drink," they all drank. If anyone said: "Let us play," they all played. If anyone suggested: "Let us go find some sport in the fields," they all went there. If it was hawking or hunting, the ladies went mounted upon pretty and easy-paced nags or proud-stepping palfreys, each of them bearing upon her daintily gloved wrist a sparrowhawk, a lanneret, or a merlin. The men carried the other birds.

They were all so nobly educated that there was not, in their whole number, a single one, man or woman, who was not able to read, write, sing, play musical instruments, and speak five or six languages, composing in these languages both poetry and prose.

In short, there never were seen knights so bold, so gallant, so clever on horse and on foot, more vigorous, or more adept at handling all kinds of weapons than were they. There never were seen ladies so well groomed, so pretty, less boring, or more skilled at hand and needlework and in every respectable feminine activity. For this reason, when the time came that any member of this abbey, either at the request of his relatives or from some other cause, wished to leave, he always took with him one of the ladies, the one who had taken him for her devoted follower, and the two of them were then married. And if they had lived at Thélème in devotion and friendship, they found even more of both after their marriage, and remained as ardent lovers at the end of their days, as they had been on the first day of their honeymoon.

The Letter Which Pantagruel at Paris Received from His Father Gargantua

Pantagruel studied very hard, you may be sure of that, and profited greatly from it; for he had a two-fold understanding, while his memory was as capacious as a dozen casks and flagons of olive oil. And while he was residing there, he received one day a letter from his father, which read as follows:

My very dear Son:

Among all the gifts, graces, and prerogatives with which that sovereign plastician, Almighty God, has endowed and adorned human nature in its beginnings, it seems to me the peculiarly excellent one is that by means of which, in the mortal state, one may acquire a species of immortality, and in the course of a transitory life be able to perpetuate his name and his seed. This is done through that line that issues from us in legitimate marriage. By this means, there is restored to us in a manner that which was taken away through the sin of our first parents, of whom it was said that, inasmuch as they had not been obedient to the commandment of God the Creator, they should die, and that, through their death, the magnificent plastic creation which man had been should be reduced to nothingness. By this means of seminal propagation, there remains for the children that which was lost to the parents, and for the grandchildren that which, otherwise, would have perished with the children; and so, successively down to the hour of the last judgment when Jesus Christ shall have rendered to God the Father His specific realm, beyond all danger and contamination of sin; for then shall cease all begettings and corruptions, and the elements shall forgo their incessant transmutations, in view of the fact that the peace that is so desired shall then have been consummated and perfected, and all things shall have been brought to their period and their close.

It is not, therefore, without just and equitable cause that I render thanks to God, my Savior, for having given me the power to behold my hoary old age flowering again in your youth: for when, by the pleasure of Him who rules and moderates all things, my soul shall leave this human habitation, I shall not feel that I am wholly dying in thus passing from one place to another, so long as, in you and through you, my visible image remains in this world, living, seeing, and moving among men of honor and my own good friends, as I was wont to do. My own conduct has been, thanks to the aid of divine grace—not, I confess, without sin, for we are all sinners, and must be continually beseeching God to efface our sins—but at least, without reproach.

For this reason, since my bodily image remains in you, if the manners of my soul should not likewise shine there, then you would not be held to have been the guardian and the treasury of that immortality which should adhere to our name; and the pleasure I should take in beholding you would accordingly be small, when I perceive that the lesser part of me, which is the body, remained, while the better part, which is the soul, through which our name is still blessed among men, had become degenerate and bastardized. I say this, not out of any doubt of your virtue, of which you have already given me proof, but to encourage you, rather, to profit still further, and to go on from good to better. And I am now writing you, not so much to exhort you to live in this virtuous manner, as to urge you to rejoice at the fact that you are so living and have so lived, that you may take fresh courage for the future. In order to perfect and consummate that future, it would be well for you to recall frequently the fact that I have spared no expense on you, but have aided you as though I had no other treasure in this world than the joy once in my life, of seeing you absolutely perfect in virtue, decency, and wisdom, as well as in all generous and worthy accomplishments, with the assurance of leaving you after my death as a mirror depicting the person of me, your father—if not altogether as excellent and as well formed an image as I might wish you to be, still all that I might wish, certainly, in your desires.

But while my late father of blessed memory, Grandgousier, devoted all his attention to seeing that I should profit from and be perfected in political wisdom, and while my studious labors were equal to his desires and perhaps even surpassed them, nevertheless, as you can readily understand, the times were not so propitious to letters as they are at present and I never had an abundance of such tutors as you have. The times then were dark, reflecting the unfortunate calamities brought about by the Goths who had destroyed all fine literature; but through divine goodness, in my own lifetime light and dignity have been restored to the art of letters, and I now see such an improvement that at the present time I should find great difficulty in being received into the first class of little rowdies—I who, in the prime of my manhood, and not wrongly so, was looked upon as the most learned man of the century. I do not say this in any spirit of vain boasting, even though I might permissibly do so—you have authority for it in Marcus Tullius, in his book on Old Age, as well as in that maxim of Plutarch's that is to be found in his book entitled How One May Praise One's Self Without Reproach—but I make the statement, rather, to give you the desire of climbing higher still.

Now all the branches of science have been reestablished and languages have been restored: Greek, without which it is a crime for any one to call himself a scholar, Hebrew, Chaldaic, and Latin; while printed books in current use are very elegant and correct. The latter were invented during my lifetime, through divine inspiration, just as, on the other hand, artillery was invented through the suggestion of the devil. The world is now full of scholarly men, learned teachers, and most ample libraries; indeed, I do not think that in the time of Plato, of Cicero, or of Papinian, there ever were so many advantages for study as one may find today. No one, longer, has any business going out in public or being seen in company, unless he has been well polished in the workshop of Minerva. I see brigands, hangmen, freebooters, and grooms nowadays who are more learned than were the doctors and preachers of my time. What's this I'm saying? Why, even the women and the girls have aspired to the credit of sharing this heavenly manna of fine learning. Things have come to such a pass that, old as I am, I have felt it necessary to take up the study of Greek, which I had not contemned, like Cato, but which I never had had the time to learn in my youth. And I take a great deal of pleasure now in reading the *Morals* of Plutarch, the beautiful *Dialogues* of Plato, the *Monuments* of Pausanias, and the *Antiquities* of Athenaeus, as I wait for the hour when it shall please God, my Creator, to send for me and to command me to depart this earth.

For this reason, my son, I would admonish you to employ your youth in getting all the profit you can from your studies and from virtue. You are at Paris and you have your tutor, Epistemon; the latter by word-of-mouth instruction, the former by praiseworthy examples, should be able to provide you with an education.

It is my intention and desire that you should learn all languages perfectly: first, the Greek as Quintilian advises; secondly the Latin; and finally the Hebrew, for the sake of the Holy Scriptures, along with the Chaldaic and the Arabic, for the same purpose. And I would have you form your style after the Greek, in imitation of Plato, as well as on the Latin, after Cicero. Let there be no bit of history with which you are not perfectly familiar. In this you will find the various works which have been written on cosmography to be of great help.

As for the liberal arts, geometry, arithmetic, and music, I gave you some taste for these while you were still a little shaver of five or six; keep them up; and as for astronomy endeavor to master all its laws; do not bother about divinatory astrology and the art of Lully, for they are mere abuses and vanities.

As for civil law, I would have you know by heart the best texts and compare them with philosophy.

As for a knowledge of the facts of nature, I would have you apply yourself to this study with such curiosity that there should be no sea, river, or stream of which you do not know the fish; you should likewise be familiar with all the birds of the air, all the trees, shrubs, and thickets of the forest, all the grasses of the earth, all the metals hidden in the bellies of the abysses, and the precious stones of all the East and South: let nothing be unknown to you.

Then, very carefully go back to the books of the Greek, Arabic, and Latin physicians, not disdaining the Talmudists and the Cabalists, and by means of frequent dissections, see to it that you acquire a perfect knowledge of that other world which is man. And at certain hours of the day form the habit of spending some time with the Holy Scriptures. First in Greek, the New Testament and the Epistles of the Apostles; and then, in Hebrew, the Old Testament.

In short, let me see you an abysm of science, for when you shall have become a full-grown man, you will have to forsake your quiet life and leisurely studies, to master the art of knighthood and of arms, in order to be able to defend my household and to succor my friends in all their undertakings against the assaults of evildoers.

In conclusion, I would have you make a test, to see how much profit you have drawn from your studies; and I do not believe you can do this in any better fashion than by sustaining theses in all branches of science, in public and against each and every comer, and by keeping the company of the learned, of whom there are as many at Paris as there are anywhere else.

But since, according to the wise Solomon, wisdom does not enter the malevolent soul, and since science without conscience is but the ruin of the soul, it behooves you to serve, love, and fear God and to let all your thoughts and hopes rest in Him, being joined to Him through a faith formed of charity, in such a manner that you can never be sundered from Him by means of sin. Look upon the scandals of the world with suspicion. Do not set your heart upon vain things, for this life is transient but the word of God endures eternally. Be of service to all your neighbors and love them as yourself. Respect your teachers, shun the company of those whom you would not want to be like, and do not receive in vain the graces which God has bestowed upon you. And when you feel that you have acquired all the knowledge that is to be had where you now are, come back to me, so that I may see you and give you my blessing before I die.

My son, may the peace and grace of Our Lord be with you! Amen.

From Utopia, this seventeenth day of the month of March.

Your Father,
Gargantua

When he had received and read this letter, Pantagruel took fresh courage, and was inflamed to profit more than ever from his studies; to such a degree that, seeing him so study and profit, you would have said that his mind among his books was like a fire among brushwood, so violent was he and so indefatigable.

---

56. WILLIAM SHAKESPEARE (1564–1616)

This scene from The Merchant of Venice *illustrates the complexities of Shakespeare's mind, with multiple interwoven plots, essential classical allusions, philosophical references, and an unerring sense of character and human nature. The neoplatonic ideal of love as redemptive is present in the play, and the role of music and beauty affirmed.*

The Merchant of Venice

SCENE I. Belmont. Avenue to PORTIA'S house. Enter LORENZO and JESSICA

LORENZO
The moon shines bright: in such a night as this,
    When the sweet wind did gently kiss the trees
    And they did make no noise, in such a night
    Troilus methinks mounted the Troyan walls
    And sigh'd his soul toward the Grecian tents,
    Where Cressid lay that night.

JESSICA
In such a night
    Did Thisbe fearfully o'ertrip the dew
    And saw the lion's shadow ere himself
    And ran dismay'd away.

LORENZO
In such a night
    Stood Dido with a willow in her hand
    Upon the wild sea banks and waft her love
    To come again to Carthage.

JESSICA
In such a night
    Medea gather'd the enchanted herbs
    That did renew old Aeson.

LORENZO
In such a night
    Did Jessica steal from the wealthy Jew
    And with an unthrift love did run from Venice
    As far as Belmont.

JESSICA
In such a night
    Did young Lorenzo swear he loved her well,
    Stealing her soul with many vows of faith
    And ne'er a true one.

LORENZO
In such a night
    Did pretty Jessica, like a little shrew,
    Slander her love, and he forgave it her.

JESSICA
I would out-night you, did no body come;
  But, hark, I hear the footing of a man.

Enter STEPHANO

LORENZO
Who comes so fast in silence of the night?
STEPHANO
A friend.
LORENZO
A friend! what friend? your name, I pray you, friend?
STEPHANO
Stephano is my name; and I bring word
  My mistress will before the break of day
  Be here at Belmont; she doth stray about
  By holy crosses, where she kneels and prays
  For happy wedlock hours.
LORENZO
Who comes with her?
STEPHANO
None but a holy hermit and her maid.
  I pray you, is my master yet return'd?
LORENZO
He is not, nor we have not heard from him.
  But go we in, I pray thee, Jessica,
  And ceremoniously let us prepare
  Some welcome for the mistress of the house.
…
LORENZO
Sweet soul, let's in, and there expect their coming.
  And yet no matter: why should we go in?
  My friend Stephano, signify, I pray you,
  Within the house, your mistress is at hand;
  And bring your music forth into the air.

Exit STEPHANO

  How sweet the moonlight sleeps upon this bank!
  Here will we sit and let the sounds of music
  Creep in our ears: soft stillness and the night
  Become the touches of sweet harmony.
  Sit, Jessica. Look how the floor of heaven
  Is thick inlaid with patines of bright gold:
  There's not the smallest orb which thou behold'st
  But in his motion like an angel sings,
  Still quiring to the young-eyed cherubins;
  Such harmony is in immortal souls;
  But whilst this muddy vesture of decay
  Doth grossly close it in, we cannot hear it.

Enter Musicians

  Come, ho! and wake Diana with a hymn!
  With sweetest touches pierce your mistress' ear,
  And draw her home with music.

Music

JESSICA
I am never merry when I hear sweet music.
LORENZO
The reason is, your spirits are attentive:
  For do but note a wild and wanton herd,
  Or race of youthful and unhandled colts,
  Fetching mad bounds, bellowing and neighing loud,
  Which is the hot condition of their blood;
  If they but hear perchance a trumpet sound,
  Or any air of music touch their ears,
  You shall perceive them make a mutual stand,
  Their savage eyes turn'd to a modest gaze
  By the sweet power of music: therefore the poet
  Did feign that Orpheus drew trees, stones and floods;
  Since nought so stockish, hard and full of rage,
  But music for the time doth change his nature.
  The man that hath no music in himself,
  Nor is not moved with concord of sweet sounds,
  Is fit for treasons, stratagems and spoils;
  The motions of his spirit are dull as night
  And his affections dark as Erebus:
  Let no such man be trusted. Mark the music.

Enter PORTIA and NERISSA

PORTIA
That light we see is burning in my hall.
  How far that little candle throws his beams!
  So shines a good deed in a naughty world.
NERISSA
When the moon shone, we did not see the candle.
PORTIA
So doth the greater glory dim the less:
  A substitute shines brightly as a king
  Unto the king be by, and then his state
  Empties itself, as doth an inland brook
  Into the main of waters. Music! hark!
NERISSA
It is your music, madam, of the house.
PORTIA
Nothing is good, I see, without respect:
  Methinks it sounds much sweeter than by day.

NERISSA
Silence bestows that virtue on it, madam.
PORTIA
The crow doth sing as sweetly as the lark,
    When neither is attended, and I think
    The nightingale, if she should sing by day,
    When every goose is cackling, would be thought
No better a musician than the wren.
How many things by season season'd are
    To their right praise and true perfection!
Peace, ho! the moon sleeps with Endymion
And would not be awaked.

Music ceases

LORENZO
That is the voice,
    Or I am much deceived, of Portia.
PORTIA
    He knows me as the blind man knows
        the cuckoo,
By the bad voice.

LORENZO
Dear lady, welcome home.

8

Renaissance and Reformation Politics

57. SIR THOMAS ELYOT (C. 1490–1546)

Sir Thomas Elyot was the son of a Wiltshire judge and landowner. He was educated privately and enjoyed a very diverse education in many disciplines. His training in the law seems to have come by serving under his father as clerk of assizes for the western circuit after 1511, a position he held even after his father's death and his inheriting the family estates. A dispute over another inheritance brought him to Wolsey's attention, and Elyot was appointed Clerk of the Privy Council, for which he received a knighthood. In 1531 Elyot was sent as ambassador to the emperor Charles V in order to argue King Henry VIII's case for a divorce from Catherine of Aragon.

Elyot cannot have been a strong advocate for Henry, because he was a close friend of Thomas More and his wife had been associated with More's household. This ambiguity was reflected in Elyot's failure to receive any advantage from his appointments as a commissioner to review Wolsey's estates and, more significantly, the suppression of monastic houses. Indeed, he wrote letters to Thomas Cromwell pleading to be relieved of some offices, such as High Sheriff in two counties, because he had been reduced to poverty as a consequence of his embassies and other expenses in the service of the Crown.

Nevertheless, despite his sympathy for Queen Catherine and the Catholic position, he was again named ambassador to the emperor in 1535–36 and was returned as M.P. for Cambridge from 1539–42. It was on his Cambridgeshire estate that he died in 1546.

Elyot was an early and influential proponent of humanism in England. He was very well read in classical as well as continental authors, including Erasmus. In a long list of important works, including translations from Greek and Latin writers, a book on health, a collection of moral tags, and a dictionary, his fame rested mostly on The Book Named the Governor. *This was intended as a treatise for the education of those whose rank and expectations would lead them to positions of authority and power in the state. It is rich in classical allusions and owes much to similar books, such as Erasmus's* Education of a Christian Prince. *But Elyot stands out in the breadth of the education he recommends for privileged youths, as the following excerpt on training in dancing illustrates.*

The Boke Named the Governour

Chapter 20: Of the first beginning of dancing and the old estimation thereof

There are several opinions of the original beginning of dancing. The poets claim that when Saturn, who had devoured various of his children, wished to do the same with Jupiter, Rhea, Jupiter's mother, directed that Curetes (who were men of arms in that country) should dance in armor, playing with their swords and shields, in such a way that by that new and pleasant scheme, they should assuage the melancholy of Saturn. In the meantime Jupiter was conveyed into Phrygia and when Saturn pursued him there Rhea similarly taught the people there, called Coribantes, to dance in another form, by which Saturn was likewise soothed and appeased. This fable resembles the history of the Bible, in the first book of Kings, where it is remembered that Saul, whom God chose from a keeper of asses to be king of Jews, (who in stature excelled and was above all other men by a head) declining from the laws and precepts of God was possessed of an evil spirit which often tormented and vexed him and he found no other remedy but that David, who was king after him, but at that time a decorous child, by playing sweetly on a harp reduced his mind into its pristine estate. During the time that David played, whom God also had predestined to be a great king and a great prophet; for the sovereign gifts of grace and of nature that he was endowed with Almighty God said of him that he had found a man after his heart and pleasure. But now let us return to speak of dancing.

Some interpreters of poets imagine that Proteus, who is supposed to have turned himself into several figures—sometimes like a serpent, sometimes like a lion, other times like water, another time like the flame of fire—signifies only that he was an agile and crafty dancer, who in his dance could conjure the inflexions of the serpent, the soft and delectable flowing of the water, the swiftness and mounting of the fire, the fierce rage of the lion, the violence and fury of the leopard. This explanation is not to be disparaged, since it is not unreasonable. But there is another opinion which I will relate, more for the merry fantasy that is contained in it than for any faith or credit that is to be given to it. Over Syracuse (a great and ancient city in Sicily) there reigned a cruel tyrant called Gelo, who by horrible tyrannies and oppressions brought himself to be hated by all his people. Perceiving this, lest by communication together they should conspire any rebellion against him, he prohibited under terrible threats that no man or woman should speak to another, but instead of words they should use in their necessary affairs behaviors, tokens, and movements with their feet, hands, and eyes, which used for necessity at first, eventually grew to a perfect and delectable dancing. And Gelo, notwithstanding his foolish nicety, eventually was slain most miserably by his people.

But even if this history were true, dancing did not first begin at this time, for Orpheus and Museus, the most ancient of poets, and also Homer, who were long before Gelo, make mention of dancing. And in Delus, which was the most ancient temple of Apollo, no solemnity was done without dancing. Also in India, where the people honor the sun, they assemble together and when the sun first appears they greet him together in a dance, supposing that since he moves without perceptible noise, it pleases him best to be greeted the same way, that is to say with a pleasant motion and silence. The interpreters of Plato think that the wonderful and incomprehensible order of the celestial bodies, I mean stars and planets, and their harmonious motions gave to them that intensity, and by the deep search of reason behold their courses, in the several diversities of number and time, a form of imitation of a similar motion which they called dancing. For this reason the nearer they approached to that temperance and subtle modulation of the said superior bodies, the more perfect and commendable is their dancing: this is closest to the truth of any opinion that I have hitherto found.

There are other fables which I omit for this present time. And now I will express in what estimation dancing was had in the ancient time; and also several forms of dancing from ancient times; and also several forms of dancing: not all, but those which had in them the appearance of virtue or cunning.

When the ark of God (in which was put the tables of the commandments, the staff with which Moses divided the Red Sea and did the miracles in the presence of Pharaoh king of Egypt, and a portion of manna with which the children of Israel were fed forty years in the desert) was recovered from the Philistines and brought to the city of Gaba, the holy king David, wearing a linen surplice, danced before the said ark with a great number of instruments of music following him, at which his wife Michal, the daughter of king Saul, disdained and scorned him, with which (as holy scripture says) almighty God was much displeased. And David, not ceasing, danced joyously through the city, in that manner honoring that solemn feast, which was one of the chief and principal [feasts] among the Jews: with which God was more pleased, than with all the other observances that then were done to him at that time.

I will not trouble the readers with the innumerable ceremonies of the gentiles, which were included in dancing, since they ought to be numbered among superstitions. But I will declare how wise men and valiant captains embraced dancing as a sovereign and profitable exercise.

Licurgus, who first gave laws to the Lacedaemons, (a people in Greece) ordained that the children there should be taught as diligently to dance in armor as to fight, and that in time of war they should move in battle against their enemies in the form and manner of dancing.

Similarly the old inhabitants of Ethiopia dance at the joining of their battles, and when the trumpets and other instruments sound, and in place of a quiver they have their darts set about their heads like rays or beams of the sun, with which they believe that they put their enemies in fear. Also it was not permissible for any of them to cast any dart at his enemy except while dancing. And not only this rough people esteemed dancing so much but also the most noble of the Greeks, who for their excellence in prowess and wisdom, were called half gods, such as Achilles and his son Pirrhus, and various others. For this reason Homer recites dancing among the high benefits that God gives to man, for he says in the first book of the *Iliad*:

God grants to some man prowess martial
To another dancing, with song harmonical.

Suppose that the Romans, who in gravity of manners passed the Greeks, did not have great pleasure in dancing? Did not Romulus, the first king of the Romans, ordain certain priests and ministers to the god Mars, (whom he boasted was his father?) which priests, forasmuch as certain times they danced about the city with targets that they imagined to fall from heaven, were called in Latin *Salli* which may be translated into English as dancers. They continued for such a long time in reverence among the Romans that until they were Christianized, the noble men and princes there, using much diligence and suit, coveted to be of the college of the said dancers.

Moreover the most noble emperors delighted in dancing, perceiving there to be a perfect measure which may be called modulation in it: in which some dancers of old time so wonderfully excelled that they would plainly express in dancing, without any words or ditty, histories with the whole circumstance of affairs contained in them; of which I shall relate two marvelous experiences. At Rome in the time of Nero, there was a noble philosopher called Demetrius who was of that sect called *Cinici* (in English doggish), because they abandoned all modesty in their words and acts. This Demetrius, often reproving dancing, would say that it was nothing but a counterfeiting with the feet and hands of the harmony that was shown before in the rebecke [an early violin], shalme [an early oboe], or other instrument, and that the motions were but vain and separate from all understanding and of no purpose or efficacy. Hearing this, a famous dancer, one that was not without good learning, as it seemed, and remembered many histories, came to Demetrius and said to him "Sire, I humbly desire you refuse not to do me that honesty with your presence, in beholding me dance, which ye shall see me do without the sound of any instrument, and then if it shall seem to you worthy of dispraise, utterly banish and confound my science," which Demetrius granted. The young man danced the adultery of Mars and Venus, and expressed in [his dance] how Vulcan, husband of Venus, being informed of it by the sun, laid snares for his wife and Mars, also how they were wounded and tied in Vulcan's net, how all the gods came to the spectacle, and finally how Venus, all ashamed and blushing, fearfully desired her lover Mars to deliver her from that peril, and the rest contained in the fable. He did this with so subtle and crafty gesture, with such a plain declaration of every act in the matter (which of all things is most difficult) with such a grace and beauty, with a wit so wonderful and pleasant, that Demetrius, as it seemed, rejoicing and delighting at this, cried with a loud voice "O man, I do not only see, but also hear what you do, and it seems also to me, that you speak with your hands." This saying was confirmed by all those that were present at that time.

The same young man sang and danced one time before the emperor Nero, when a strange king was also present who understood no other language but of his own country, yet notwithstanding the man danced so aptly and plainly, as his custom was, that the strange king, although he did not perceive what he said, understood every deal of the matter, and when he had taken his leave of the emperor to depart, the emperor offered to give to him anything that he thought might be to his benefit. "You may" said the king "bounteously reward me if you lend me the young man that danced before your majesty." Nero wondered and asked him why he so pressingly desired the dancer, or what benefit the dancer might be unto him. "Sir" said the king, "I have various cousins and neighbors who are of several languages and manners, for which reason I often need many interpreters. Wherefore if I had this man with me and should have anything to do with my neighbors, he would so with his face and gesture express everything to me and teach them to do the same, that from henceforth I should not have need of any interpreter."

Also the ancient philosophers commended dancing, insomuch as Socrates, the wisest of all the Greeks in his time, and from whom all the sects of philosophers, as from a fountain, were derived, was not ashamed to account dancing among the serious disciplines, for the commendable beauty, for the apt and proportionate moving, and for the crafty disposition and fashioning of the body. It is to be considered, that in the said ancient time there were various manners of dancing which varied in the names, as they did in tunes of the instrument, similarly, we have at this day. But those names, some were general, some were special: the general names were given of the universal form of dancing, whereby was represented the qualities or conditions of several estates: for example, the majesty of princes was shown in that dance, which was named and belonged to tragedies; dissolute motions and wanton countenances, in that which was called *Cordax* and pertained to comedies, wherein only men of base behavior danced. Also the form of battle and fighting in armor was expressed in those dances which were called *Enopliae*. Also there was a kind of dancing called *hormus*, of all the others most like that which is used at this time, in which young men and maidens danced: the man expressing in his motion and countenance, strength and courage, fit for the wars; the maiden moderation and modesty, which represent a pleasant conjunction of fortitude or temperance. Instead of these we have now base dances: bargnets, pavions, turgions, and rounds. And as for the special names, they were taken as they are now either from the names of the first inventors, or from the measure and number that they contain, or from the first words of the ditty which the song contains, from which the dance was made. In all of the said dances, there was a concinnity of moving the foot and body, expressing some pleasant or profitable affects or motions of the mind. Here a man may behold what craft there was in the ancient time in dancing which at this day no man can imagine or contrive. But if men would now apply the first part of their youth, that is to say from seven years to twenty, effectually in the liberal sciences and knowledge of histories, they should revive the ancient form as well of dancing as of other exercises, in which they might take not only pleasure but also profit and commodity.

Chapter 21: *Wherefore in the good order of dancing a man and a woman dance together*

It is diligently to be noted that the company of man and woman in dancing, both of them observing one number and time in their moving, was not begun without special consideration as well for the necessary conjunction of those two persons, as for the intimation of sundry virtues which are represented by them. And forasmuch as by the joining of a man and a woman in dancing may be signified matrimony, I could in declaring the dignity and commodity of that sacrament make entire volumes if it were not so commonly known to all men, that almost every friar limiter [a friar licensed to beg within limits] carries it written in his bosom. For this reason, lest in repeating a thing so frequent and common my book should be as distasteful or cloying to the readers as such merchant preachers are now to their customers, I will reverently take my leave of divines. And for my parte I will endeavor myself to assemble out of the books of ancient poets and philosophers matter as well fitted to my purpose and as new or at least infrequent or seldom heard of by those who have not read very many authors in Greek [or] in Latin.

But now to my purpose. In every dance of a most ancient custom, there dance together a man and a woman, holding each other by the hand or the arm, which betokens concord. Now it behooves the dancer, and also the beholders of them, to know all qualities incident to a man and also all qualities likewise pertaining to a woman.

A man in his natural perfection is fierce, hardy, strong in opinion, covetous of glory, desirous of knowledge, desiring by generation to bring forth his like. The good nature of a woman is to be mild, timorous, tractable, benign, of sure remembrance and modest. Various other qualities of each of them might be found out, but these are most apparent, and for this time sufficient.

For this reason when we behold a man and a woman dancing together, let us suppose there to be a concord of all the said qualities being joined together as I have set them in order. And the moving of the man would be more vehement, [that] of the woman more delicate, and with less advancing of the body, signifying the courage and strength that ought to be in a man, and the pleasant soberness that should be in a woman. And in this way fierceness joined with mildness makes severity. Hardiness with timorousness makes magnanimity, that is to say valiant courage. Willful opinion and tractability (which is to be easily persuaded and moved) and constancy a virtue.

Covetousness of glory adorned with benignity causes honor. Desire of knowledge with sure remembrance procures sapience [wisdom]. Modesty joined to appetite of generation makes continence, which is a mean between chastity and inordinate lust. These qualities, in this way being knit together and signified in the personages of man and woman dancing, express or set out the figure of true nobility, which in the higher estate [it] is contained, the more excellent is the venue.

Chapter 22: How dancing may be an introduction to the first moral virtue called prudence

As I have already affirmed, the principal cause of this my little enterprise is to declare an induction or mean, how children of gentle nature or disposition may be trained in to the way of virtue with a pleasant facility. And forasmuch as it is very expedient that there be mixed with study some honest and moderate amusement, or at the least way recreation, to re-comfort and quicken the vital spirits, lest they long travailing or being much occupied in contemplation or remembrance of things grave and serious, might happen to be fatigued or perchance oppressed. And therefore Tully, who scarcely ever found any time vacant from study, permitted in his first book of offices, that men may use play and amusement: yet still in such a way as they use sleep and other manner of quiet [times]—when they have sufficiently disposed earnest matters and weighty importance.

Now because there is no pastime to be compared to that in which may be found both recreation and meditation of virtue, I have among all honest pastimes where there is exercise of the body, noted dancing to be of excellent utility, including in it wonderful figures, which the Greeks call *Ideae*, of virtues and noble qualities, and specially of the commodious virtue called prudence, which Tully defines to be the knowledge of things which ought to be desired and followed and also of those which ought to be fled from or eschewed. And it is named by Aristotle the mother of virtues, by other philosophers it is called the captain or mistress of virtues, by some the housewife, forasmuch as by her diligence she investigates and prepares places fit and convenient, where other virtues shall execute their powers or offices. For this reason, as Salomon says, as water shows the faces of those that behold it, so to men that are prudent the secrets of men's hearts are openly discovered. This virtue is so commodious to man, and as it were the porch of the noble palace of man's reason by which other virtues shall enter, it seems to me expedient, that as soon as opportunity may be found, a child or young man may be led to it. And because the study of virtue is tedious for the most part for those that flourish in young years, I have devised how in the form of dancing now late used in this realm among gentlemen, the whole description of this virtue, prudence, may be found out and well perceived, as well by the dancers as by those who, standing by, will be diligent beholders and markers, having first my instruction surely graven in the table of their remembrance. For which reason all those who have their courage steered toward true honor or perfect nobility, let them approach to this pastime, and either themselves prepare to dance, or else at least behold with watching eyes other that can dance truly, keeping just measure and time. But to the understanding of this instruction, they must mark well the several motions and measures which in true form of dancing is to be specially observed.

The first moving in every dance is called honor, which is a reverent inclination or curtsey with a long deliberation or pause, and is only one motion including the time of three other motions or setting forth of the foot: by that may be signified that at the beginning of all our acts we should do due honor to God, which is the root of prudence: which honor is made up of these three things, fear, love and reverence; and that in the beginning of all things we should advisedly, with some tract of time, behold and foresee the success of our enterprise.

By the second motion, which is two in number, may be signified celerity and slowness: which two, although they seem to discord in their effects and natural properties therefore they may be well resembled to the brawl in dancing (for in our English tongue we say men brawl, when between them is altercation in words) yet of them two springs an excellent virtue whereunto we lack a name in English. Wherefore I am constrained to usurp a Latin word calling it Maturity; which word though it be strange and dark, yet by declaring the virtue in a few words, the name once brought in custom, shall be as easy to understand as other words late come out of Italy and France, and made denizens among us.

Maturity is a mean between two extremities, wherein nothing lacketh or excedeth: and is in such estate, that it may neither increase nor diminish without losing the denomination of Maturity. The Greeks in a proverb do express it properly in two words, which I cannot otherwise interpret in English, but "spede slowly."

Also of this word Maturity, sprang a noble and precious sentence, recited by Sallust in the battle against Cataline which is in this manner or like: Consult before thou enterprise anything: and after thou has taken counsel, it is expedient to do it maturely.

Maturum in Latin may be interpreted ripe or ready: as fruit, when it is ripe, it is at the very point to be gathered and eaten and every other thing, when it is ready, it is at the instant after to be occupied. Therefore that word maturity is translated to the acts of man, that when they be done with such moderation, that nothing in the doing may be seen superfluous or indigent, we may say, that they be maturely done: reserving the words, ripe and ready to fruit and other things separate from affairs, as we have now in usage. And this do I now remember for the necessary augmentation of our language.

In the excellent and most noble emperor Octavius Augustus, in whom reigned all nobility, nothing is more commended, than that he had frequently in his mouth this word *Matura*, do maturely. As he should have said, do neither too much nor too little: too soon nor too late: too swiftly nor slowly: but in due time and measure.

Now I trust I have sufficiently expounded the virtue called Maturity, which is the mean or mediocrity between sloth and celerity commonly called speediness: and so have I declared what utility may be taken of a brawl in dancing.

---

58. DESIDERIUS ERASMUS OF ROTTERDAM (C. 1466–1536)

Erasmus (see Chapter Two) published this treatise in 1516, at the height of his career. He may have aspired to the position of tutor to Prince Charles in 1504, but that position subsequently went to the future Pope Adrian VI, a man who was presumably well-positioned to raise Charles as a Christian prince. Here Erasmus is marking a new appointment as councillor to Charles, a position which carried no duties but which should have brought him a comfortable income. The treatise is dedicated to Charles as he became king of Aragon and thus moved from the years of formal humanistic education to the actual exercise of power. The proper maintenance and exercise of power was a topic of some concern at the time, as the publication of Thomas More's Utopia *in the same year and Machiavelli's* Prince *just three years earlier demonstrates. Erasmus assumes the value of political stability in this treatise and considers how a prince should rule in the best interests of his subjects to maintain that stability and justify his power. Charles's advice to his son Philip (Selection 60) as he handed over power at the end of his career provides a remarkable comparison with Erasmus's advice.*

The Education of a Christian Prince

TO THE MOST ILLUSTRIOUS PRINCE CHARLES, GRANDSON OF THE INVINCIBLE CAESAR MAXIMILIAN, DESIDERIUS ERASMUS OF ROTTERDAM SENDS GREETINGS

Wisdom is not only an extraordinary attribute in itself, Charles, most bountiful of princes, but according to Aristotle no form of wisdom is greater than that which teaches a prince how to rule beneficently. Accordingly, Xenophon was quite correct in saying in his *Oeconomicus* that he thought it something beyond the human sphere and clearly divine, to rule over free and willing subjects. That kind of wisdom is indeed to be sought by princes, which Solomon as a youth of good parts, spurning all else, alone desired, and which he wished to be his constant companion on the throne. This is that purest and most beautiful wisdom of Sunamite, by whose embraces alone was David pleased, he that wisest son of an all-wise father. This is the wisdom which is referred to in *Proverbs*: "Through me princes rule, and the powerful pass judgment." Whenever kings call this wisdom into council and exclude those basest of advisers—ambition, wrath, cupidity, and flattery—the state flourishes in every way and, realizing that its prosperity comes from the wisdom of the prince, rejoices rightly in itself with these words: "All good things together come to me with her [i.e., wisdom]." Plato is nowhere more painstaking than in the training of his guardians of the state. He does not wish them to excel all others in wealth, in gems, in dress, in statues and attendants, but in wisdom alone. He says that no state will ever be blessed unless the philosophers are at the helm, or those to whom the task of government falls embrace philosophy. By "philosophy" I do not mean that which disputes concerning the first beginnings of primordial matter, of motion and infinity, but that which frees the mind from the false opinions and the vicious predilections of the masses and points out a theory of government according to the example of the Eternal Power. It was something such as this that Homer had in mind when [he had] Mercury protect Ulysses against the potions of Circe with the molu flower. And not without reason did Plutarch say that no one serves the state better than he who imbues the mind of the prince, who provides and cares for everyone and everything, with the best of ideas and those most becoming a prince. On the other hand, no one brings so serious a blight upon the affairs of men as he who has corrupted the heart of the prince with depraved ideas and desires. He is no different from one who has poisoned the public fountain whence all men drink. Likewise Plutarch judges not inapposite that celebrated remark of Alexander the Great: Departing from the talk he had had with Diogenes the Cynic, and still marveling at his philosophic spirit, so proud, unbroken, unconquered, and superior to all things human, he said, "If I were not Alexander, I should like to be Diogenes." Nay, as great authority is exposed to so many storms, the more was that spirit of Diogenes to be sought after, since he could rise to the measure of such towering tumults.

But as much as you surpass Alexander in good fortune, mighty prince Charles, so much do we hope you will surpass him in wisdom. For he had gained a mighty empire, albeit one not destined to endure, solely through bloodshed. You have been born to a splendid kingdom and are destined to a still greater one. As Alexander had to toil to carry out his invasions, so will you have to labor to yield, rather than to gain, part of your power. You owe it to the powers of heaven that you came into a kingdom untainted with blood, bought through no evil connection. It will be the lot of your wisdom to keep it bloodless and peaceful. You have the inborn nature, the soundness of mind, the force of character, and you have received training under the most reliable preceptors. So many examples from your ancestors surround you on every side that we all have the highest hopes that Charles will some day do what the world long hoped his father Philip would do. And he [Philip] would not have disappointed the popular expectation if death had not cut him off before his time. And so, although I am not unaware that your highness does not need the advice of anyone, and least of all my advice, yet it has seemed best to set forth the likeness of the perfect prince for general information, but addressed to you. In this way those who are being brought up to rule great kingdoms will receive their theory of government through you and take their example from you. At the same time the good from this treatise will spread out to all under your auspices, and we of your entourage may manifest somewhat by these first fruits, as it were, the zeal of our spirit toward you.

We have done into Latin Isocrates's precepts on ruling a kingdom. We have fashioned ours, set off with subject headings so as to be less inconvenient to the reader, after the fashion of his, but differing not a little from his suggestions. That sophist was instructing a young king, or rather a tyrant: one pagan instructing another. I, a theologian, am acting the part of teacher to a distinguished and pure-hearted prince—one Christian to another. If I were writing these things for a prince of more advanced age, I should perhaps come under the suspicions of some for flattery or impertinence. But since this little book is dedicated to one who, although he evidences the highest hopes for himself, is still so youthful and so recently installed in his power that he could not as yet do many things which people are wont to praise or censure in princes, I am free from suspicion on both charges and cannot appear to have sought any object beyond the public welfare. That, to the friends of kings (as to kings themselves), ought to be the only aim. Among the countless distinctions and praises which virtue, by the will of God, will prepare for you, this will be no small part: Charles was such a one that anyone could without the mark of flattery present [to him] the likeness of a pure and true Christian prince, which the excellent prince would happily recognize, or wisely imitate as a young man always eager to better himself. With best wishes.

. . . .

The teacher should enter at once upon his duties, so as to implant the seeds of good moral conduct while the senses of the prince are still in the tenderness of youth, while his mind is furthest removed from all vices and tractably yields to the hand of guidance in whatever it directs. He is immature both in body and mind, as in his sense of duty. The teacher's task is always the same, but he must employ one method in one case, and another in another. While his pupil is still a little child, he can bring in his teachings through pretty stories, pleasing fables, clever parables. When he is bigger, he can teach the same things directly.

When the little fellow has listened with pleasure to Aesop's fable of the lion and the mouse or of the dove and the ant, and when he has finished his laugh, then the teacher should point out the new moral: the first fable teaches the prince to despise no one, but to seek zealously to win to himself by kindnesses the heart of even the lowest peasant (plebs), for no one is so weak but that on occasion he may be a friend to help you, or an enemy to harm you, even though you be the most powerful. When he has had his fun out of the eagle, queen of the birds, that was almost completely done for by the beetle, the teacher should again point out the meaning: not even the most powerful prince can afford to provoke or overlook even the humblest enemy. Often those who can inflict no harm by physical strength can do much by the machinations of their minds. When he has learned with pleasure the story of Phaeton, the teacher should show that he represents a prince who, while still headstrong with the ardor of youth, but with no supporting wisdom, seized the reins of government and turned everything into ruin for himself and the whole world. When he has finished the story of the Cyclops who was blinded by Ulysses, the teacher should say in conclusion that the prince who has great strength of body, but not of mind, is like Polyphemus. Who has not heard with interest of the government of the bees and ants? When temptations begin to descend into the youthful heart of the prince, then his tutor should point out such of these stories as belong in his education. He should tell him that the king never flies far away, has wings smaller in proportion to the size of its body than the others, and that he alone has no sting. From this the tutor should point out that it is the part of a good prince always to remain within the limits of his realm; his reputation for clemency should be his special form of praise. The same idea should be carried on throughout. It is not the province of this treatise to supply a long list of examples, but merely to point out the theory and the way. If there are any stories that seem too coarse, the teacher should polish and smooth them over with a winning manner of speech. The teacher should give his praise in the presence of others, but only within the limits of truth and proportion. His scoldings should be administered in private and given in such a way that a pleasing manner somewhat breaks the severity of his admonition. This is especially to be done when the prince is a little older. Before all else the story of Christ must be firmly rooted in the mind of the prince. He should drink deeply of His teachings, gathered in handy texts, and then later from those very fountains themselves, whence he may drink more purely and more effectively. He should be taught that the teachings of Christ apply to no one more than to the prince.

The great mass of people are swayed by false opinions and are no different from those in Plato's cave who took the empty shadows as the real things. It is the part of a good prince to admire none of the things that the common people consider of great consequence, but to judge all things on their own merits as "good" or "bad." But nothing is truly "bad" unless joined with base infamy. Nothing is really "good" unless associated with moral integrity.

. . . .

But here some one of those frumps at the court, more stupid and worthless than any woman you could name, will interrupt with this: "You are making us a philosopher, not a prince." "I am making a prince," I answer, "although you prefer a worthless sot like yourself instead of a real prince!" You cannot be a prince, if you are not a philosopher; you will be a tyrant. There is nothing better than a good prince. A tyrant is such a monstrous beast that his like does not exist. Nothing is equally baneful, nothing more hateful to all. Do not think that Plato rashly advanced the idea, which was lauded by the most praiseworthy men, that the blessed state will be that in which the princes are philosophers, or in which the philosophers seize the principate. I do not mean by philosopher, one who is learned in the ways of dialectic or physics, but one who casts aside the false pseudo-realities and with open mind seeks and follows the truth. To be a philosopher and to be a Christian is synonymous in fact. The only difference is in the nomenclature.

What is more stupid than to judge a prince on the following accomplishments: his ability to dance gracefully, dice expertly, drink with a gusto, swell with pride, plunder the people with kingly grandeur, and do all the other things which I am ashamed even to mention, although there are plenty who are not ashamed to do them? The common run of princes zealously avoids the dress and manner of living of the lower classes. Just so should the true prince be removed from the sullied opinions and desires of the common folk. The one thing which he should consider base, vile, and unbecoming to him is to share the opinions of the common people who never are interested in anything worthwhile. How ridiculous it is for one adorned with gems, gold, the royal purple, attended by courtiers, possessing all the other marks of honor, wax images and statues, wealth that clearly is not his, to be so far superior to all because of them, and yet in the light of real goodness of spirit to be found inferior to many born from the very dregs of society.

What else does the prince, who flaunts gems, gold, the royal purple, and all the other trappings of fortune's pomp in the eyes of his subjects, do but teach them to crave and admire the very sources from which spring the foulest essence of nearly all crimes that are punishable by the law of the prince? In others, frugality and simple neatness may be ascribed to want, or parsimony, if you are less kind in your judgment. These same qualities in a prince are clearly an evidence of temperance, since he uses sparingly the unlimited means which he possesses.

What man is there whom it becomes to stir up crimes and then inflict punishment for them? What could be more disgusting than for him to permit himself things he will not let others do? If you want to show yourself an excellent prince, see that no one outshines you in the qualities befitting your position—I mean wisdom, magnanimity, temperance, integrity. If you want to make trial of yourself with other princes, do not consider yourself superior to them if you take away part of their power or scatter their forces; but only if you have been less corrupt than they, less greedy, less arrogant, less wrathful, and less headstrong.

No one will gainsay that nobility in its purest form becomes a prince. There are three kinds of nobility: the first is derived from virtue and good actions; the second comes from acquaintance with the best of training; and the third from an array of family portraits and the genealogy or wealth. It by no means becomes a prince to swell with pride over this lowest degree of nobility, for it is so low that it is nothing at all, unless it has itself sprung from virtue. Neither must he neglect the first, which is so far the first that it alone can be considered in the strictest judgment. If you want to be famous do not make a display of statues or paintings; if there is anything praiseworthy in them, it is due to the artist whose genius and work they represent. Far better it is to make your character the monument to your good parts. If all else is lacking, the very appurtenances of your majesty can remind you of your duty. What does the anointing mean if not greatness, leniency, and clemency on the part of the prince, since cruelty is almost always the companion of great power? What does the gold mean, except outstanding wisdom? What significance has the sparkle of the gems, except extraordinary virtues as different as possible from the common run? What does the warm rich purple mean, if not the essence of love for the state? And why the scepter, unless as a mark of a spirit clinging strongly to justice, turned aside by none of life's diversions? But if the prince has none of these qualities, these symbols are not ornaments to him, but stand as accusations against him. If a necklace, a scepter, royal purple robes, a train of attendants are all that make a king, what is to prevent the actors who come on the stage decked with all the pomp of state from being called king? What is it that distinguishes a real king from the actor? It is the spirit befitting a prince. I mean he must be like a father to the state. It is on this basis that the people swore allegiance to him. The crown, the scepter, the royal robes, the collar, the sword belt are all marks or symbols of good qualities in the good prince; in a bad one, they are accusations of vice.

Watchfulness must increase in proportion to his meanness, or else we will have a prince like many we read about of old. (May we never see the like again!) If you strip them of their royal ornaments and inherited goods, and reduce them to themselves alone, you will find nothing left except the essence of an expert at dice, the victor of many a drinking bout, the fierce conqueror of modesty, the craftiest of deceivers, an insatiable pillager; a creature steeped in perjury, sacrilege, perfidy, and every other kind of crime. Whenever you think of yourself as a prince, remember you are a Christian prince! You should be as different from even the noble pagan.

. . .

They are also wrong who win the hearts of the masses by largesse, feasts, and gross indulgence. It is true that some popular favor, instead of affection, is gained by these means, but it is neither genuine nor permanent. In the meanwhile the greed of the populace is developed, which, as happens, after it has reached large proportions thinks nothing is enough. Then there is an uprising, unless complete satisfaction is made to their demands. By this means your people are not won, but corrupted. And so by this means the [average] prince is accustomed to win his way into the hearts of the people after the fashion of those foolish husbands who beguile their wives with blandishments, gifts, and complaisance, instead of winning their love by their character and good actions. So at length it comes about that they are not loved; instead of a thrifty and well-mannered wife they have a haughty and intractable one; instead of an obedient spouse they find one who is quarrelsome and rebellious. Or take the case of those unhappy women who desperately try to arouse love in their husbands' hearts by giving them drugs, with the result that they have madmen instead of sane lovers.

The wife should first learn the ways and means of loving her husband and then let him show himself worthy of her love. And so with the people—let them become accustomed to the best, and let the prince be the source of the best things. Those who begin to love through reason, love long. In the first place, then, he who would be loved by his people should show himself a prince worthy of love; after that it will do some good to consider how best he may win his way into their hearts. The prince should do this first so that the best men may have the highest regard for him and that he may be accepted by those who are lauded by all. They are the men he should have for his close friends; they are the ones for his counselors; they are the ones on whom he should bestow his honors and whom he should allow to have the greatest influence with him. By this means everyone will come to have an excellent opinion of the prince, who is the source of all good will. I have known some princes who were not really evil themselves who incurred the hatred of the people for no other reason than that they granted too much liberty to those whom universal public sentiment condemned. The people judged the character of the prince by these other men.

For my part, I should like to see the prince born and raised among those people whom he is destined to rule, because friendship is created and confirmed most when the source of good will is in nature itself. The common people shun and hate even good qualities when they are unknown to them, while evils which are familiar are sometimes loved. This matter at hand has a twofold advantage to offer, for the prince will be more kindly disposed toward his subjects and certainly more ready to regard them as his own. The people on their part will feel more kindness in their hearts and be more willing to recognize his position as prince. For this reason I am especially opposed to the accepted [idea of] alliances of the princes with foreign, particularly with distant, nations.

The ties of birth and country and a mutual spirit of understanding, as it were, have a great deal to do with establishing a feeling of good will. A goodly part of this feeling must of necessity be lost if mixed marriages confuse that native and inborn spirit. But when nature has laid a foundation of mutual affection, then it should be developed and strengthened by every other means. When the opposite situation is presented, then even greater energy must be employed to secure this feeling of good will by mutual obligations and a character worthy of commendation. In marriage, the wife at first yields entirely to the husband, and he makes a few concessions to her and indulges her whims until, as they come really to know one another, a firm bond unites them; so it should be in the case of a prince selected from a foreign country. Mithridates learned the languages of all the peoples over whom he ruled, and they were said to be twenty in number. Alexander the Great, however barbarous the peoples with whom he was dealing, at once used to imitate their ways and customs and by this method subtly worked himself into their good graces.

Alcibiades has been praised for the same thing. Nothing so alienates the affections of his people from a prince as for him to take great pleasure in living abroad, because then they seem to be neglected by him to whom they wish to be most important. The result of this is that the people feel that they are not paying taxes to a prince (since the moneys are spent elsewhere and totally lost as far as they are concerned) but that they are casting spoils to foreigners. Lastly, there is nothing more harmful and disastrous to a country, nor more dangerous for a prince, than visits to faraway places, especially if these visits are prolonged; for it was this, according to the opinion of everyone, that took Philip from us and injured his kingdom no less than the war with the Gelrii, which was dragged out for so many years. The king bee is hedged about in the midst of the swarm and does not fly out and away. The heart is situated in the very middle of the body. Just so should a prince always be found among his own people.

There are two factors, as Aristotle tells us in his *Politics*, which have played the greatest roles in the overthrow of empires. They are hatred and contempt. Good will is the opposite of hatred; respected authority, of contempt. Therefore it will be the duty of the prince to study the best way to win the former and avoid the latter. Hatred is kindled by an ugly temper, by violence, insulting language, sourness of character, meanness, and greediness; it is more easily aroused than allayed. A good prince must therefore use every caution to prevent any possibility of losing the affections of his subjects. You may take my word that whoever loses the favor of his people is thereby stripped of a great safeguard. On the other hand, the affections of the populace are won by those characteristics which, in general, are farthest removed from tyranny. They are clemency, affability, fairness, courtesy, and kindliness. This last is a spur to duty, especially if they who have been of good service to the state see that they will be rewarded at the hands of the prince. Clemency inspires to better efforts those who are aware of their faults, while forgiveness extends hope to those who are now eager to make recompense by virtuous conduct for the shortcomings of their earlier life and provides the steadfast with a happy reflection on human nature. Courtesy everywhere engenders love—or at least assuages hatred. This quality in a great prince is by far the most pleasing to the masses.

Contempt is most likely to spring from a penchant for the worldly pleasures of lust, for excessive drinking and eating, and for fools and clowns—in other words, for folly and idleness. Authority is gained by the following varied characteristics: in the first place wisdom, then integrity, self-restraint, seriousness, and alertness. These are the things by which a prince should commend himself, if he would be respected in his authority over his subjects. Some have the absurd idea that if they make the greatest confusion possible by their appearance, and dress with pompous display, they must be held in high esteem among their subjects. Who thinks a prince great just because he is adorned with gold and precious stones? Everyone knows he has as many as he wants. But in the meanwhile what else does the prince expose except the misfortunes of his people, who are supporting his extravagance to their great cost? And now lastly, what else does such a prince sow among his people, if not the seeds of all crime? Let the good prince be reared in such a manner and [continue to] live in such a manner that from the example of his life all the others (nobles and commoners alike) may take the model of frugality and temperance. Let him so conduct himself in the privacy of his home as not to be caught unawares by the sudden entrance of anyone. And in public it is unseemly for a prince to be seen anywhere, unless always in connection with something that will benefit the people as a whole. The real character of the prince is revealed by his speech rather than by his dress. Every word that is dropped from the lips of the prince is scattered wide among the masses. He should exercise the greatest care to see that whatever he says bears the stamp of [genuine] worth and evidences a mind becoming a good prince.

Aristotle's advice on this subject should not be overlooked. He says that a prince who would escape incurring the hatred of his people and would foster their affection for him should delegate to others the odious duties and keep for himself the tasks which will be sure to win favor. Thereby a great portion of any unpopularity will be diverted upon those who carry out the administration, and especially will it be so if these men are unpopular with the people on other grounds as well. In the matter of benefits, however, the genuine thanks redound to be prince alone. I should like to add also that gratitude for a favor will be returned twofold if it is given quickly, with no hesitation, spontaneously, and with a few words of friendly commendation. If anything must be refused, refusal should be affable and without offense. If it is necessary to impose a punishment, some slight diminution of the penalty prescribed by law should be made, and the sentence should be carried out as if the prince were being forced [to act] against his own desires. It is not enough for the prince to keep his own character pure and uncorrupted for his state. He must give no less serious attention, in so far as he can, to see that every member of his household—his nobles, his friends, his ministers, and his magistrates—follows his example. They are one with the prince, and any hatred that is aroused by their vicious acts rebounds upon the prince himself. But, someone will say, this supervision is extremely difficult to accomplish. It will be easy enough if the prince is careful to admit only the best men into his household, and if he makes them understand that the prince is most pleased by that which is best for the people. Otherwise it too often turns out that, due to the disregard of the prince in these matters or even his connivance in them, the most criminal men (hiding under cover of the prince) force a tyranny upon the people, and while they appear to be carrying out the affairs of the prince, they are doing the greatest harm to his good name. What is more, the condition of the state is more bearable when the prince himself is wicked than when he has evil friends; we manage to bear up under a single tyrant. Somehow or other the people can sate the greed of one man without difficulty: it is not a matter of great effort to satisfy the wild desires of just one man or to appease the vicious fierceness of a single individual, but to content so many tyrants is a heavy burden. The prince should avoid every novel idea in so far as he is capable of doing so; for even if conditions are bettered thereby, the very innovation is a stumbling block. The establishment of a state, the unwritten laws of a city, or the old legal code are never changed without great confusion. Therefore, if there is anything of this sort that can be endured, it should not be changed but should either be tolerated or happily diverted to a better function. As a last resort, if there is some absolutely unbearable condition, the change should be made, but [only] gradually and by a practiced hand.

The end which the prince sets for himself is of the greatest consequence, for if he shows little wisdom in its selection he must of necessity be wrong in all his plans. The cardinal principle of a good prince should be not only to preserve the present prosperity of the state but to pass it on more prosperous than when he received it. To use the jargon of the Peripatetics, there are three kinds of "good"—that of the mind, that of the body, and the external good. The prince must be careful not to evaluate them in reverse order and judge the good fortune of his state mainly by the external good, for these latter conditions should only be judged good in so far as they relate to the good of the mind and of the body; that is, in a word, the prince should consider his subjects to be most fortunate not if they are very wealthy or in excellent bodily health but if they are most honorable and self-controlled, if they have as little taste for greed and quarreling as could be hoped for, and if they are not at all factious but live in complete accord with one another. He must also beware of being deceived by the false names of the fairest things, for in this deception lies the fountainhead from which spring practically all the evils that abound in the world. It is no true state of happiness in which the people are given over to idleness and wasteful extravagance, any more than it is true liberty for everyone to be allowed to do as he pleases. Neither is it a state of servitude to live according to the letter of just laws. Nor is that a peaceful state in which the populace bows to every whim of the prince; but rather [is it peaceful] when it obeys good laws and a prince who has a keen regard for the authority of the laws. Equity does not lie in giving everyone the same reward, the same rights, the same honor; as a matter of fact, that is sometimes a mark of the greatest unfairness.

A prince who is about to assume control of the state must be advised at once that the main hope of a state lies in the proper education of its youth. This Xenophon wisely taught in his *Cyropaedia*. Pliable youth is amenable to any system of training. Therefore the greatest care should be exercised over public and private schools and over the education of the girls, so that the children may be placed under the best and most trustworthy instructors and may learn the teachings of Christ and that good literature which is beneficial to the state. As a result of this scheme of things, there will be no need for many laws or punishments, for the people will of their own free will follow the course of right.

Education exerts such a powerful influence, as Plato says, that a man who has been trained in the right develops into a sort of divine creature, while on the other hand, a person who has received perverted training degenerates into a monstrous sort of savage beast. Nothing is of more importance to a prince than to have the best possible subjects.

The first effort, then, is to get them accustomed to the best influences, because any music has a soothing effect to the accustomed ear, and there is nothing harder than to rid people of those traits which have become second nature to them through habit. None of those tasks will be too difficult if the prince himself adheres to the best manners. It is the essence of tyranny, or rather trickery, to treat the common citizen as animal trainers are accustomed to treat a savage beast: first they carefully study the way in which these creatures are quieted or aroused, and then they anger them or quiet them at their pleasure. This Plato has painstakingly pointed out. Such a course is an abuse of the emotions of the masses and is no help to them. However, if the people prove intractable and rebel against what is good for them, then you must bide your time and gradually lead them over to your end, either by some subterfuge or by some helpful pretense. This works just as wine does, for when that is first taken it has no effect, but when it has gradually flowed through every vein it captivates the whole man and holds him in its power.

If sometimes the whirling course of events and public opinion beat the prince from his course, and he is forced to obey the [exigencies of the] time, yet he must not cease his efforts as long as he is able to renew his fight, and what he has not accomplished by one method he should try to effect by another.

59. JUAN LUIS VIVES (1492–1540)

In Renaissance Europe, the letter was not just a means of private communication, but an important humanist genre. Letters addressed to a single individual could be intended to circulate widely, as with Erasmus's letter to Jodocus Jonus (selection 8) or Gallileo's letter to the Grand Duchess Christina (selection 52), or be addressed to a larger group, such as Katharina Zell's letter to Strasbourg (selection 18) or Ignatius Loyola's letter to the province of Portugal (selection 28). Even private letters served a wide variety of functions—requesting favors, building and maintaining relationships, sharing information, offering advice, reproof or complaint—between people of widely varying status, personality and interests. In a status- and style-conscious age, letter-writing could be fraught with difficulties, and a number of humanists provided guides to aid the confused or unwary. Vives's was first published in 1534, and appeared in 43 editions in the sixteenth century, usually in collections with other letter-writing manuals such as those by Erasmus and Celtis, or together with Vives's Colloquia.

For biographical information on Vives, see selection 38.

On the Writing of Letters

To Senor Idiáquez, Secretary of Charles V

1. When I was setting about, my dear Idiáquez, to publish a brief work on the composition of letters, which are of great utility in every walk of life, it seemed proper to me to inscribe it with a dedication to your name. It is not that you have need of these prescriptions of mine, since in the acquisition of this skill, you have Cicero and Pliny as mentors and guides, in whose footsteps you tread with singular success, winning the admiration of all those who know how quickly you have realized your goals in the study of Latin. But it is rather that this treatise seems ideally suited to one who must daily write a great number of Latin epistles (both in your own name and in that of the Emperor Charles) on matters of great importance. Finally, in view of our close friendship and mutual goodwill, whatever comes from one of us cannot fail to bring great pleasure to the other.

2. A letter is a conversation by means of the written word between persons separated from each other. It was invented to convey the mental concepts and thoughts of one person to another as a faithful intermediary and bearer of a commission. "The purpose of the letter," said Saint Ambrose to Sabinus, "is that though physically separated we may be united in spirit. In a letter the image of the living presence emits its glow between persons distant from each other, and conversation committed to writing unites those who are separated. In it we also share our feelings with a friend and communicate our thoughts to him." The Greeks called it an epistle from the verb "to send," as if one were to say in Latin *missoria*, a word not found in established usage. Among those present to each other there is no need of a letter unless perhaps you intend to deal with something in definite and explicit language, as Suetonius recounts of Caesar Augustus, who in private conversation of some importance, even with his wife Livia, would speak from written notes, for fear of saying too much or too little if he were to speak *ex tempore*, and we read in Tacitus of that arrogant master of Rome who never had any dealings with his slaves except by gesture or in writing.

3. Likewise, writing tablets were invented for the use of those who lived in the same city and neighborhood, but either had little desire or opportunity to see each other, or in any case could more conveniently commit the matter to writing. There is frequent mention of these writing tablets in Cicero, Tacitus and others. Letters in early antiquity were employed for the sole purpose of conveying news of public or private affairs to an absent party, reporting what had been done, what was likely to happen, what was going on, what they wished would be done or not done. We see that Cicero's letters, especially those to Titus Atticus, are of this type. Later, everything that could be said or written fell into the confines of the letter. Cicero wrote to Curio: "You are well aware that there are many kinds of letters, but one thing is beyond doubt: the reason why letter-writing was invented was to inform those not present of anything that it would be to our interest or theirs for them to know. For the rest there are two kinds of letters that I particularly enjoy: one is the familiar, humorous letter, the other austere and serious." Thus the true genuine letter is that by which we signify to someone what it is important for him or for us to know in the conduct of one's affairs, such as, in general, letters of information, petition, recommendation, advice, admonishment and any others of this kind which make up for the absence of the writer.

4. Afterwards there were added letters of consolation, reconciliation, instruction, and letters of discussion that treated of every argument of philosophy, law, ancient history, in short, of all branches of learning and of all those topics which would be committed to writing even among those who often frequent each other's company. Thus Plato writes to Dionysius and others on philosophy; Seneca writes to Lucilius; Jerome, Ambrose, Augustine and Cyprian write to various persons on sacred subjects. The books of Cato the Censor and of many jurisconsults on queries and responses in the form of a letter may be cited. I do not wish for the present to discuss how widely the name letter should be applied, but certainly if we agree that whatever bears a salutation is to be called a letter, what is to prevent us from calling the *Tusculan Disputations* or the *De finibus* letters to Brutus, the essays *De senectute* and *De amicitia* letters to Atticus, the *De officiis* a letter to his son Marcus, or if you were to preface the salutation "To the jury" to the *Pro Milone* or the *In Verrem*, would they then qualify as letters? But as a woman who puts on cuisses or girds herself with a sword does not by that token become a man, so not every book to which a salutation is prefixed becomes a letter, unless it takes on the nature and qualities of a letter, as we shall demonstrate immediately. Pliny put it well when he said "It is one thing to write history, but another to write a letter," signifying that they are distinct in nature.

On Invention

5. We shall combine invention in letters with a part of the disposition of the subject matter, especially in the exordium of the letter, because often these cannot readily be

separated. Indeed the rules concerning both of them are the same in several respects. Many people who are about to write a letter struggle over the introduction as if they were navigating among reefs, and they would easily complete the rest of the journey if they had only escaped the treachery of the harbor. At the outset it must be said that all invention, not only in the letter but in any other kind of speech or discourse, as also in what we are saying now, is not at all a matter of skill, but of proficiency. It is the product of ability, memory, judgment and experience. In the transmission of skills we can be of help but we do not make perfect: recommendations are given, but not a complete training. Consequently, no one should expect to acquire a full comprehension of the art of letter-writing or of any other type of literary skill either in this section or in others, or from myself or any other writer or teacher. There are some who condemn as useless rules that do not immediately make a stupid man brilliant or one with no training an expert. Therefore, let this stand as the first rule, that we facilitate and further invention by these formulas, but that they will have no effect of themselves unless they are joined with experience and practice. With this premise I come now to the main subject.

6. One who sets about to write a letter should consider who the writer is and to whom he is writing and on what subject; who we are to him, and who he is in his own right. As to ourselves, we may be either strangers or acquaintances, friends or enemies, casual or dubious friends, or open and close friends, equals or unequals, from various points of view: family, social station, learning, age. Then, concerning the addressee, we must consider his family background: plebeian or patrician, well-born or of lowly origins: his personal resources—opulent, conspicuous, moderate, humble, non-existent; his legal status, free or slave. We must determine whether he is outspoken or secretive, of good or bad reputation, leisurely or occupied, cobbler or tailor; we must consider his learning: great, poor, average; whether he is a theologian, doctor, philosopher, lawyer, experienced or otherwise; his character and morals—stern or good-natured, lax or severe, mild-mannered or irascible, affable or haughty, easy or difficult, sharp-witted or dull. All these things may easily be surveyed in a single mental reflection, in a moment's time. Frequently you must plead in excuse that you write as a complete stranger or as a mere casual acquaintance, or that you are writing to a person of great importance, or to one who may think you are of unfriendly disposition. This must be made clear from the beginning, for it is a natural tendency that once the letter is opened and the writer's name is read, the recipient of the letter will wonder whether it is sent by a stranger or by someone not especially endeared to him, or by an enemy. And so in his mind he condemns the writer right from the start for impudence, temerity, arrogance or insanity, with the result that he does not so much repudiate the letter as conceive a dislike for its author, all the more intensely if he is haughty or ill-tempered and inclined to feelings of antipathy. Therefore one must make allowance for this eventuality, for, even in the forum new orators were compelled before proceeding to plead their case to give some personal background explaining why they were speaking: as Cicero did in the *Pro Roscio Amerino*, the first speech he delivered before a jury, and in the *Pro Lege Manilia*, his first speech before the people.

7. The opening therefore must be drawn either from yourself or from things pertaining to you, or from the recipient or things pertaining to him, or from the subject itself on which you are writing, in the form of a short introduction. Concerning yourself, somewhat in the following manner: that you have always loved and cherished him; that you have on every occasion held him in the highest esteem and spoken well of him; that you regret that you have remained unknown to him for so long or were only slightly acquainted with a man whom you have always so admired for his talent and virtue; or that you regret that this suspicion presented itself to his mind concerning your good will towards him, since you continue to count that friendship as one of your principal blessings. You will adduce, if you can, some proof of your friendly sentiments towards him; you will cast blame on those who were envious of your friendship, or even on the addressee himself, but in a restrained manner and without any harshness, or on your own imprudence and inexperience; or you will openly confess your guilt, if the circumstances require it, indicating your repentance and your resolution to give some concrete demonstration of how well-disposed you now are towards him. If you begin with things pertaining to yourself, you will point out some friendship that you have in common with him, or was shared by your fathers. If you open the letter with references to him, you will say, as in letters of reconciliation, that you were induced to write to him by the talent, literary accomplishments, humane character, and moral excellence that you admired in him; that although you were a stranger to him, in his extraordinary kindness and zeal for doing good he welcomes all into his friendship. Moreover, owing to his literary reputation and wisdom, it was impossible either that he could be unknown to anyone or think that anyone was unknown to him or not his concern. The same could be said of power, for a prince or a king, to whom one must resort as if for sanctuary, can-

not make any distinction between those who are known or unknown; all those who have entrusted themselves to his care have sufficient recognition.

8. We must take particular care to make it appear that we have been more influenced by his virtues than attracted by his good fortune, but in the enumeration of his virtues there should be no semblance of flattery. Rather we shall show that we have either discovered it for ourselves, if we have benefitted from some good action of his, or have heard it from others, who have experienced it, or have learned of it or witnessed it of ourselves. Accordingly we shall adduce some concrete evidence of his accomplishments, as in the case of men of learning, from books published by him, speeches delivered, lectures or disputations. And we shall mention especially those good qualities of his that are most appropriate to the substance of our letter, as his clemency, if we are seeking pardon; his friendly nature, if we seek his friendship; his generosity, if we solicit a favor; his wisdom and uprightness, if it is counsel that we desire.

9. If the letter begins with things pertaining to him, allusion may be made to some common friendship or friendship between your fathers. From the subject matter of the letter, that it is a noble, learned and subtle argument, and therefore worthy of our writing to him about it; or an urgent matter, and therefore we were compelled to take refuge in him, as to a sacred altar, just as in connection with wealth one has recourse to a rich man, or in matters of justice to a judge, a king, or a magistrate. It may be stated that we preferred to undergo suspicion of any vice whatever, even if it would have grave consequences for us, at least in the mind of the person whom we esteem so highly, rather than not write. You may recall to him that necessity is a very powerful weapon, which none can resist, that it is more honorable when something is done for another; or that the matter is of such a nature that when he becomes thoroughly acquainted with it, he will not consider you rash or presumptuous in writing about it, but a man completely without guile and vigorous in the pursuit of good. On the contrary he would have considered you remiss had you neglected it. One must also apologize to a friend for writing about something which you could have dealt with personally. Cicero wrote to Lucceius: "Often, when I attempted to discuss this subject with you privately, I was inhibited by a kind of almost backward bashfulness, but now that I am not in your presence I shall set forth my thoughts more confidently, for a letter does not blush."

10. This is the first encounter, which, as the character in the comedy says, is the hardest; after this the rest is more effortless and easier to manage. Therefore in the first letter we must take great pains that in the eyes of this new acquaintance we do not come under suspicion of some vice, like impudence or arrogance or loquacity or ostentation or cunning or pedantic affectation or excessive and parasitical flattery or scurrility or ignorance or imprudence. For there is much at stake in the first contact, as in cases that are still fragile and delicate before they fuse. Nor do I think that I need remind anyone that not everything is suitable for all persons. You must determine to whom you can express your admiration, to whom you can mention parental ties of hospitality, or the care of subordinates. But if you have no need of giving any reason for your writing to him, then you will take into consideration who it is to whom you are writing, for this will set the tone for the whole letter.

11. To a prosperous, haughty person the letter must be more respectful, but without flattery: to one who is stern and disagreeable, use a more mild and reserved style: to one who is unsophisticated or dull-witted, a more lucid style is called for: to a clever person, the style must be more studied and ornate, if he takes pleasure in that and regards it as an expression of respect: to a learned man, use a style more consonant with that of the ancient writers: to a busy man, be brief: to a man of leisure, be more expansive, if you think he will appreciate it: to a jovial person, write in a sprightly manner: to a kindly person, be less anxious about detail: to a severe person, be somewhat solemn: to one who is easy-going, be light-hearted: to a gloomy person, gloomy: to a faithful friend, express yourself openly and with great confidence: to an uncertain friend, be more cautious, but in such a manner that he thinks he is loved and that you truly love him. This is the law of nature, this is what Christ commands, more valid than the law of nature, with the result that one who does not love in return will be deservedly condemned for ingratitude. You should write to an enemy in such a way that you expect that he may become your friend and that a return to your favor remains always possible and feasible. All harshness should be absent and you should demonstrate a certain gentleness even towards an enemy. And it will be best to remember our profession of faith, whereby we are forbidden to hate anyone. Thus you will show him that you wish that he be corrected, not damned, and that you hate the vice, but love the person. To one of equal rank and one who is dear to you you will write in a simple and familiar manner: to one less intimate, more cautiously, but courteously and without condescension: to one beneath your rank, in a kindly manner, so that you do not appear to speak down to him, but on an equal footing, even to

people of very humble circumstances. Good morals recommend this, and religious piety commands it. Examples will be readily at hand from experience.

12. To be banned altogether from all human experience is that deceitful, insipid, inept type of letter, in which all indications of intentions are blurred. So insincere and flattering are such letters that there is no way of discerning the writer's intent, e.g., those letters that go by the name of courtly and polite. For human thought, enveloped by the ponderous mass of the body, is impenetrable; it is made manifest to a certain extent in speech. But if this too is completely feigned and disguised, what do we have left to understand our fellow man? What kind of communication and fellowship will exist among mankind when no one will be able to distinguish a well-wisher from an ill-wisher, will give welcome to the wolf instead of the sheep, or will flee from the sheep in fear of the wolf's ferocity? But this is the object of another program of learning. Now to the subject matter of letters.

60. EMPEROR CHARLES V (1500–58)

Son of the duke of Burgundy and the heir to Ferdinand and Isabella of Spain, Charles of Habsburg was born and educated in the Netherlands. In 1506 he became duke of Burgundy and in 1516 king of Spain; three years later he was elected Holy Roman Emperor. His reign was characterized by his struggle with France, which lasted over 30 years, and by the Protestant Reformation, which began in the German-speaking lands of his empire. It was also during his reign that Spain consolidated its New World empire and tried to contain the Turkish advance into Europe and the Mediterranean. In 1557 Charles abdicated and divided his immense dynastic inheritance between his brother, Ferdinand, who became Holy Roman Emperor, and his son, Philip, who became King of Spain and ruler of the Habsburg territories in Italy, the Low Countries, and the New World. Charles retired to a monastery, where he died in 1558.

Philip II of Spain (1527–98)

Charles V's son Philip II assumed rule of Spain, the Low Countries, Naples, Sicily, Milan, and the Spanish Empire in the New World. He married Queen Mary I of England in 1554 and was given the title but not the authority of king. Philip extended his dominions through the conquest of Portugal and weakened Turkish power in the Mediterranean by defeating the Ottomans at Lepanto in 1571. However, during his reign the Low Countries revolted against Spanish rule, and the Armada sent to conquer England in 1588 was destroyed. Ruling his vast empire from his office in the enormous palace and monastery of the Escorial that he had constructed near Madrid, Philip presided over the height of Spanish power and the beginnings of Spain's cultural Golden Age.

The Emperor Charles V: Advice to His Son

I have resolved, my dear son, to remit to your hands the sovereignty of my dominions, having told you several times that I had formed this design.... Since the number of princes who have divested themselves of their supreme power in order to invest their successors with it is very small, you shall understand from this how great the love is that I bear to you, how thoroughly I am persuaded of your goodness, and how much I desire your increasing greatness, seeing that rather than remain in possession of the sovereignty over my realms to the end of my life (as do nearly all other princes) I prefer to follow such rare examples and reduce myself from sovereign to the status of a subject....

I will not further stress this point, and I think I need not endeavor to exhort you to imitate the conduct which I have adhered to during the course of my life, nearly all of which I have passed in difficult enterprises and laborious employment, in the defence of the empire, in propagating the holy faith of Jesus Christ, and in preserving my peoples in peace and security. I will only say that at the beginning of your reign the two advantages you have—of being my son and of looking like me—will, if I am not mistaken, win for you the love of your subjects; in addition, you on your side must treat them so well that in due course you will have no need of memories of me to assist you in preserving their affection.

Do not imagine, my very dear son, that the pleasure of ruling so many peoples, and the freedom which flatters the feelings of sovereign princes, are not mixed with some bitterness and linked with some trouble. If one knew what goes on in the hearts of princes one would see that the suspicions and uncertainties which agitate those whose conduct is irregular torment them day and night, while those who govern their realms wisely and sensibly are overwhelmed by various worries which give them no rest. And truly, if you weigh in a fair balance, on the one hand, the prerogatives and preeminences of sovereignty, and on the other the work in which it involves you, you will find it a source of grief rather than of joy and delight. But this truth looks so much like a lie that only experience can make it believable.

You must know that the charge of ruling the realms which today I place upon your shoulders is more trying than the government of Spain which is a kingdom of ancient inheritance, firm and assured; whereas the acquisition of the states of Flanders, Italy, and the other provinces into whose possession you are to enter, is more recent, and they are exposed to more difficulties and upheavals, especially because they have for neighbors powerful and belligerent princes. Furthermore, the great number and vast extent of these states and kingdoms increases the cares and troubles of him who rules them; as the addition of a small piece to a reasonable burden will overwhelm him who carries it, or as superfluous food cannot but cause indigestion in a stomach which has taken sufficient nourishment....

Remember, the prince is like a mirror exposed to the eyes of all his subjects who continually look to him as a pattern on which to model themselves, and who in consequence without much trouble discover his vices and virtues. No prince, however clever and skillful he may be, can hope to hide his actions and proceedings from them. If during his life he can shut their mouths and prevent them from making his irregularities and excesses public, they will after his death convey the memory of them to posterity. Therefore adhere to so just and orderly a conduct towards your peoples that, seeing the trouble you take to govern them well, they will come to rely entirely on your prudence and take comfort from your valor; and in this way there will grow between you and them a reciprocal love and affection....

It is certain that people submit to the rule of their princes more readily of their own free will than when they are kept in strict bondage, and that one can retain their services better by love than by violence. I admit that the power which rests on a sovereign's gentle kindness is less absolute than that which rests only on fear; but one must also agree that it is more solid and enduring....

A prince must preserve his credit with the merchants, which he will easily achieve if he takes precise care to pay them both their capital and the interest arising on it. You should especially act thus with the Genoese because, being involved in your kingdoms through the money they lend, they will be attached to you; without which you would have to garrison their city which they would not suffer without great difficulty. In this way you will make yourself master of Genoa, which is a most important place in Italy, just as the king of France has attached the Florentines to his interests through their trade with Lyons.

And since it is impossible for princes (especially those possessing several realms) to govern all alone, they must be assisted by ministers who will help them to carry so heavy a burden. From which it follows that it is extremely important to have honest and intelligent ones. I will therefore say a little more on this subject.

The three principal qualities called for in a minister are sound sense, love of his prince, and uprightness. Sound sense makes them capable of administration; love ensures that they have their master's interests at heart; and uprightness helps them to discharge their business efficiently.... But while it is difficult to find such men, you must do all you can, and spare no trouble, to acquire them when you meet them; for experience shows that all princes who have had this advantage have ruled their peoples with glory and success, although they themselves might be full of faults.... Certainly it is high wisdom in a prince, when by nature he is not sufficiently competent to govern his realms himself, to know how to choose those who are and to put trust in them. In this way he enjoys the abilities of several persons joined together, and he will gain much advantage, more than those who have only their own knowledge to fall back on. But that prince may be called very unfortunate who has neither the ability to rule by himself nor the good sense to follow wise counsels. . . . Do not think that any prince, however wise and able he may be, can do without good ministers. . . .

In criminal matters, where it is a question of life and other corporal pains, see to it that the judges modify severity with some mildness, and mildness with severity, and that they pay regard to the case, the persons, the circumstances of place and time, the manner in which the deed was done, and other like considerations. For those who govern states ought to accommodate themselves to the occasion and to the condition of affairs; otherwise they have reason to fear that they may be accused of having respect of persons. In effect, in order to follow the rules of sense and justice, one should consider the nature of cases, and when these are entirely alike one must proceed in the same manner; for injustice does not consist in judging now severely and now mildly, but in imposing different sentences in similar circumstances.

True, this would seem in part to contradict what I said before about laws being inflexible and immutable; but that referred to the dead law which should always be enforced according to its meaning and tenor. This is not so in the living law, which is the prince; his ministers, in executing the dead law, must keep in mind the point of which we have just spoken, provided that in expounding the law they do not violate it. For the prince and the judges have a right to interpret law, and they should thoroughly examine all the circumstances of a case in order to arrive at an equitable decision. . . . Take care that your courts lean rather to mildness than to severity and cruelty, except that in particular cases, for the sake of example and to deter criminals, they should not fail to exact rigorous execution.

Lavish display on special occasions will give you great authority; ordinary dress, following common usage, will gain you popularity. Use the same with respect to your table and in other things, taking care that excess of show do not lead your subjects to dislike you, nor conformity with their habits and too much familiarity cause them to despise you. In peace time, you should engage in occupations worthy of a prince, such as doing things useful to your peoples, repairing bridges, improving roads, building houses, beautifying churches, palaces and squares, rebuilding town walls, reforming the religious orders, establishing schools, colleges, universities, law courts, and similar things. . . . But I ought to warn you that all this must be done without exacting new taxes from them, for their burdens are already grievous, no matter what purpose you have in mind when imposing them. . . .

61. JOHN KNOX (C. 1514–72)

John Knox was educated at St. Andrews University and was ordained a priest in the late 1530s. At some point in the mid-1540s he converted to Protestantism, and from the beginning he was associated with the leaders of the fledgling movement. In 1547 he was captured when St. Andrews castle was taken by French Catholic forces, and he spent 19 months serving on the galleys and ministering to his fellow captives. After his release he spent several years as a royal chaplain in England, but eventually he rejected the Edwardian church as insufficiently reformed. On Mary's accession in 1553 he moved to the continent, where he spent time with English exile communities in Frankfurt and Geneva. In 1558 he published his most famous work, The First Blast of the Trumpet. *The resounding argument in the opening, that women should not bear rule, was not an unusual position to hold, and while Knox is often perceived as a misogynist, he had many warm and mutually supportive relationships with female parishioners. Knox's* Blast *resonates for the clarity with which he argued that it was against the law of God for a woman to rule, and for the unfortunate timing that saw it written the reign of Catholic Mary but published in the reign of Protestant Elizabeth. Though Knox argued that Elizabeth's rule was based upon divine providence and thus outside the usual prohibition, the queen remained unimpressed. Knox returned to Scotland in 1559 and took an active role in the development of the Scottish church.*

The First Blast of the Trumpet against the Monstrous Regiment of Women

My purpose is thrice to blow the trumpet in the same matter, if God so permit. Twice I intend to do it without name, but at the last blast to take the blame upon myself, that all others may be purged.

The First Blast To Awake Women Degenerate

To promote a woman to bear rule, superiority, dominion, or empire above any realm, nation, or city is repugnant to nature, contumely to God, a thing most contrarious to his revealed will and approved ordinance, and, finally, it is the subversion of good order, of all equity and justice.

In the probation of this proposition I will not be so curious as to gather whatsoever may amplify, set forth, or decor the same; but I am purposed, even as I have spoken my conscience in most plain and few words, so to stand content with a simple proof of every member, bringing in for my witness God's ordinance in nature, his plain will revealed in his word, and the minds of such as be most ancient amongst godly writers.

And first, where that I affirm the empire of a woman to be a thing repugnant to nature, I mean not only that God by the order of his creation hath spoiled woman of authority and dominion, but also that man hath seen, proved, and pronounced just causes why that it so should be. Man, I say, in many other cases blind, doth in this behalf see very clearly, for the causes be so manifest that they cannot be hid. For who can deny but it repugns to nature that the blind shall be appointed to lead and conduct such as do see, that the weak, the sick and impotent persons shall nourish and keep the whole and strong, and, finally, that the foolish, mad, and frenetic shall govern the discreet and give counsel to such as be sober of mind? And such be all women compared unto man in bearing of authority. For their sight in civil regiment is but blindness, their counsel foolishness, and judgment frenzy, if it be rightly considered. I except such as God, by singular privilege and for certain causes known only to himself, hath exempted from the common rank of women, and do speak of women as nature and experience do this day declare them.

Nature, I say, doth paint them forth to be weak, frail, impatient, feeble, and foolish, and experience hath declared them to be unconstant, variable, cruel, and lacking the spirit of counsel and regiment. And these notable faults have men in all ages espied in that kind, for the which not only they have removed women from rule and authority, but also some have thought that men subject to the counsel or empire of their wives were unworthy of all public office. For thus writes Aristotle in the second of his *Politics*: "What difference shall we put," says he, "whether that women bear authority or the husbands that obey the empire of their wives be appointed to be magistrates? For what ensues the one must needs follow the other, to wit, injustice, confusion, and disorder." The same author further reasons that the policy or regiment of the Lacedemonians (who other ways amongst the Grecians were most excellent) was not worthy to be reputed nor accounted amongst the number of commonwealths that were well governed, because the magistrates and rulers of the same were too much given to please and obey their wives.

What would this writer, I pray you, have said to that realm or nation where a woman sits crowned in parliament amongst the midst of men? Oh fearful and terrible are thy judgments, O Lord, which thus hast abased man for his iniquity! I am assuredly persuaded that if any of those men, which illuminated only by the light of nature did see and pronounce causes sufficient why women ought not to bear rule nor authority, should this day live and see a woman sitting in judgment or riding from parliament in the midst of men, having the royal crown upon her head, the sword and scepter borne before her in sign that the administration of justice was in her power; I am assuredly persuaded, I say, that such a sight should so astonish them that they should judge the whole world to be transformed into Amazons, and that such a metamorphosis and change was made of all the men of that country (as poets do feign was made of the companions of Ulysses), or at least that albeit the outward form of men remained; yet should they judge that their hearts were changed from the wisdom, understanding, and courage of men to the foolish fondness and cowardice of women. Yea, they further should pronounce that where women reign or be in authority that there must needs vanity be preferred to virtue, ambition and pride to temperance and modesty, and, finally, that avarice, the mother of all mischief, must needs devour equity and justice.

But lest that we shall seem to be of this opinion alone, let us hear what others have seen and decreed in this matter. In the rules of the law thus it is written: "Women are removed from all civil and public office, so that they neither may be judged, neither may they occupy the place of the magistrate, neither yet may they be speakers for others." The same is repeated in the third and in the sixteenth books of the *Digests* where certain persons are forbidden, *Ne pro aliis postulent*, that is, that they be no speakers nor advocates for others. And among the rest are women forbidden, and this cause is added, that they do not against modesty intermeddle themselves with the causes of others, neither yet that women presume to use the offices due to men. The law in the same place doth further declare that a natural modesty ought to be in womankind which most certainly she loses whenever she takes upon her the office and estate of man. As in Calpurnia was evidently declared, who, having license to speak before the Senate, at length became so impudent and importune that by her babbling she troubled the whole assembly and so gave occasion that this law was established.

In the first book of the *Digests* it is pronounced that the condition of the woman in many cases is worse than of the man. As in jurisdiction, says the law, in receiving of cure and tuition, in adoption, in public accusation, in declaration, in all popular action, and in motherly power, which she hath not upon her own sons. The law further will not permit that the woman give anything to her husband, because it is against the nature of her kind, being the inferior member, to presume to give anything to her head. The law doth moreover pronounce womankind to be most avaricious, which is a vice intolerable in those that should rule or minister justice. And Aristotle, as before is touched, doth plainly affirm that wheresoever women bear dominion there must needs the people be disordered, living and abounding in all intemperance, given to pride, excess, and vanity. And finally, in the end, that they must needs come to confusion and ruin.

Would to God the examples were not so manifest. To the further declaration of the imperfections of women, of their natural weakness and inordinate appetites, I might adduce histories proving some women to have died for sudden joy; some for unpatience to have murdered themselves; some to have burned with such inordinate lust that, for the quenching of the same, they have betrayed to strangers their country and city; and some to have been so desirous of dominion that, for the obtaining of the same, they have murdered the children of their own sons. Yea, and some have killed with cruelty their own husbands and children. But to me it is sufficient (because this part of nature is not my most sure foundation) to have proved that men, illuminated only by the light of nature, have seen and have determined that it is a thing most repugnant to nature that women rule and govern over men. For those that will not permit a woman to have power over her own sons will not permit her, I am assured, to have rule over a realm; and those that will not suffer her to speak in defense of those that be accused, neither that will admit her accusation intended against man, will not approve her that she shall sit in judgment, crowned with the royal crown, usurping authority in the midst of men.

But now to the second part of nature, in the which I include the revealed will and perfect ordinance of God; and against this part of nature, I say that it doth manifestly repugn that any woman shall reign or bear dominion over man. For God, first by the order of his creation and after by the curse and malediction pronounced against the woman by the reason of her rebellion, hath pronounced the contrary.

First, I say that woman in her greatest perfection was made to serve and obey man, not to rule and command him. As St. Paul doth reason in these words: "Man is not of the woman but the woman of the man. And man was not created for the cause of the woman, but the woman for the cause of man, and therefore ought the woman to have a power upon her head" (that is, a coverture in sign of subjection). Of which words it is plain that the Apostle meaneth that woman in her greatest perfection should have known that man was lord above her, and therefore, that she should never have pretended any kind of superiority above him no more than do the angels above God the creator or above Christ Jesus their head. So, I say that in her greatest perfection woman was created to be subject to man.

But after her fall and rebellion committed against God there was put upon her a new necessity, and she was made subject to man by the irrevocable sentence of God pronounced in these words: "I will greatly multiply thy sorrow and thy conception. With sorrow shalt thou bear thy children, and thy will shall be subject to thy man, and he shall bear dominion over thee." Hereby may such as altogether be not blinded plainly see that God by his sentence hath dejected all woman from empire and dominion above man. For two punishments are laid upon her, to wit, a dolor, anguish, and pain as oft as ever she shall be mother, and a subjection of herself, her appetites and will, to her husband and to his will. From the former part of the malediction can neither art, nobility, policy, nor law made by man deliver womankind; but whosoever attaineth to that honor to be mother proveth in experience the effect and strength of God's word.

But, alas, ignorance of God, ambition, and tyranny have studied to abolish and destroy the second part of God's punishment, for women are lifted up to be heads over realms and to rule above men at their pleasure and appetites. But horrible is the vengeance which is prepared for the one and for the other: for the promoters and for the persons promoted, except they speedily repent. For they shall be dejected from the glory of the sons of God to the slavery of the devil and to the torment that is prepared for all such as do exalt themselves against God. Against God nothing be more manifest than that a woman shall be exalted to reign above man. For the contrary sentence hath he pronounced in these words: "Thy will shall be subject to thy husband, and he shall bear dominion over thee." As God should say: "Forasmuch as thou hast abused thy former condition, and because thy free will hath brought thyself and mankind into the bondage of Satan, I therefore will bring thee in bondage to man. For where before thy obedience should have been voluntary, now it shall be by constraint and by necessity; and that because thou hast deceived thy man, thou shalt therefore be no longer mistress over thine own appetites, over thine own will nor desires. For in thee there is neither reason nor discretion which be able to moderate thy affections, and therefore they shall be subject to the desire of thy man. He shall be lord and governor, not only over thy body, but even over thy appetites and will." This sentence, I say, did God pronounce against Eve and her daughters, as the rest of the Scriptures doth evidently witness. So that no woman can ever presume to reign over man, but the same she must needs do in despite of God and in contempt of his punishment and malediction.

I am not ignorant that the most part of men do understand this malediction of the subjection of the wife to her husband and of the dominion which he beareth above her; but the Holy Ghost giveth to us another interpretation of this place, taking from all women all kind of superiority, authority, and power over man, speaking as followeth by the mouth of St. Paul: "I suffer not a woman to teach, neither yet to usurp authority above man." Here he nameth women in general, excepting none, affirming that she may usurp authority above no man. And that he speaketh more plainly in another place in these words: "Let women keep silence in the congregation, for it is not permitted to them to speak, but to be subject as the law saith." These two testimonies of the Holy Ghost be sufficient to prove whatsoever we have affirmed before and to repress the inordinate pride of women, as also to correct the foolishness of those that have studied to exalt women in authority above man, against God, and against his sentence pronounced.

But that the same two places of the Apostle may the better be understand, it is to be noted that in the latter, which is written in the First Epistle to the Corinthians, the fourteenth chapter, before the Apostle had permitted that all persons should prophesy one after another, adding this reason: "that all may learn and all may receive consolation." And lest that any might have judged that amongst a rude multitude and the plurality of speakers many things, little to purpose, might have been affirmed, or else that some confusion might have risen, he addeth: "the spirits of the prophets are subject to the prophets." As he should say, God shall always raise up some to whom the verity shall be revealed, and unto such ye shall give place, albeit they sit in the lowest seats. And thus the Apostle would have prophesying an exercise to be free to the whole church, that everyone should communicate with the congregation what God have revealed to them, providing that it were orderly done.

But from this general privilege he secludeth all woman, saying, "Let women keep silence in the congregation." And why, I pray you, was it because that the Apostle thought no woman to have any knowledge? No, he giveth another reason, saying, "Let her be subject as the law saith." In which words is first to be noted that the Apostle calleth this former sentence pronounced against woman a law, that is, the immutable decree of God, who by his own voice hath subjected her to one member of the congregation, that is, to her husband. Whereupon the Holy Ghost concludeth that she may never rule nor bear empire above man. For she that is made subject to one may never be preferred to many, and that the Holy Ghost doth manifestly express, saying, "I suffer not that woman usurp authority above man." He saith not, "I will not that woman usurp authority above her husband"; but he nameth man in general, taking from her all power and authority to speak, to reason, to interpret, or to teach, but principally, to rule or to judge in the assembly of men. So that woman, by the law of God and by the interpretation of the Holy Ghost, is utterly forbidden to occupy the place of God in the offices aforesaid, which he hath assigned to man, whom he hath appointed and ordained his lieutenant in earth, secluding from that honor and dignity all woman, as this short argument shall evidently declare.

The Apostle taketh power from all women to speak in the assembly. Ergo, he permitteth no woman to rule above man. The former part is evident, whereupon doth the conclusion of necessity follow. For he that taketh from woman the least part of authority, dominion, or rule will not permit unto her that which is greatest. But greater it is to reign above realms and nations, to publish and to make laws, and to command men of all estates, and, finally, to appoint judges and ministers, than to speak in the congregation. For her judgment, sentence, or opinion, proposed in the congregation, may be judged by all, may be corrected by the learned and reformed by the godly. But woman, being promoted in sovereign authority, her laws must be obeyed, her opinion followed, and her tyranny maintained, supposing that it be expressly against God and the profit of the commonwealth, as to manifest experience doth this day witness. And therefore, yet again, I repeat that which before I have affirmed, to wit, that a woman promoted to sit in the seat of God, that is, to teach, to judge, or to reign above man, is a monster in nature, contumely to God, and a thing most repugnant to his will and ordinance. For he hath deprived them, as before is proved, of speaking in the congregation and hath expressly forbidden them to usurp any kind of authority above man.

How then will he suffer them to reign and have empire above realms and nations? He will neither, I say, approve it, because it is a thing most repugnant to his perfect ordinance, as after shall be declared and as the former Scriptures have plainly given testimony. To the which to add anything were superfluous were it not that the world is almost now come to that blindness that whatsoever pleaseth not the princes and the multitude, the same is rejected as doctrine newly forged and is condemned for heresy. I have therefore thought good to recite the minds of some ancient writers in the same matter, to the end that such as altogether be not blinded by the devil may consider and understand this my judgment to be no new interpretation of God's Scripture but to be the uniform consent of the most part of godly writers since the time of the Apostles.

Tertullian, in his book of women's apparel, after that he hath shewed many causes why gorgeous apparel is abominable and odious in a woman, addeth these words, speaking, as it were, to every woman by name: "Dost thou not know," saith he, "that thou art Eve? The sentence of God liveth and is effectual against this kind, and in this world of necessity it is that the punishment also live. Thou art the port and gate of the devil. Thou art the first transgressor of God's law; thou didst persuade and easily deceive him whom the devil durst not assault. For thy merit (that is for thy death) it behooved the son of God to suffer the death, and doth it yet abide in thy mind to deck thee above thy skin coats?" By these and many other grave sentences and quick interrogations did this godly writer labor to bring every woman in contemplation of herself, to the end that every one, deeply weighing what sentence God had pronounced against the whole race and daughters of Eve, might not only learn daily to humble and subject themselves in the presence of God, but also that they should avoid and abhor whatsoever thing might exalt them or puff them up in pride, or that might be occasion that should forget the curse and malediction of God.

And what, I pray you, is more able to cause woman to forget her own condition than if she be lifted up in authority above man? It is a thing very difficile to a man (be he never so constant) promoted to honors not to be tickled somewhat with pride (for the wind of vainglory doth easily carry up the dry dust of the earth). But as for woman, it is no more possible that she, being set aloft in authority above man, shall resist the motions of pride than it is able to the weak reed or to the turning weathercock not to bow or turn at the vehemency of the unconstant wind. And therefore the same writer expressly forbiddeth all women to intermeddle with the office of man. For thus he writeth in his book *De Virginibus Velandis*: "It is not permitted to a woman to speak in the congregation, neither to teach, neither to baptize, neither to vindicate to herself any office of man." The same he speaketh yet more plainly in the preface of his sixth book written against Marcion, where he recounting certain monstrous things which were to be seen at the sea called Euxinum. Amongst the rest he reciteth this as a great monster in nature, that "woman in those parts were not tamed nor embased by consideration of their own sex and kind; but that all shame laid apart, they made expenses upon weapons and learned the feats of war, having more pleasure to fight than to marry and be subject to man." Thus far of Tertullian, whose words be so plain that they need no explanation. For he that taketh from her all office appertaining to man will not suffer her to reign above man; and he that judgeth it a monster in nature that a woman shall exercise weapons must judge it to be a monster that a woman shall be exalted above a whole realm and nation. Of the same mind is Origen and divers others. Yea, even till the days of Augustine, whose sentences I omit to avoid prolixity.

Augustine in his twenty-second book written against Faustus proveth that a woman ought serve her husband as unto God, affirming that in no thing hath woman equal power with man, saving that neither of both have power over their own bodies. By which he would plainly conclude that woman ought never to pretend nor thirst for that power and authority which is due to man. For so he doth explain himself in another place: affirming that woman ought to be repressed and bridled betimes, if she aspire to any dominion; alleging that dangerous and perilous it is to suffer her to proceed, although it be in temporal and corporal things. And thereto he addeth these words: "God seeth not for a time, neither is there any new thing in his sight and knowledge" meaning thereby that what God hath seen in one woman, as concerning dominion and bearing of authority, the same he seeth in all. And what he hath forbidden to one, the same he also forbiddeth to all. And this most evidently yet in another place he writeth, moving this question: "How can woman be the image of God, seeing," saith he, "she is subject to man and hath none authority, neither to teach, neither to be witness, neither to judge, much less to rule or bear empire?" These be the very words of Augustine, of which it is evident that this godly writer doth not only agree with Tertullian, before recited, but also with the former sentence of the law which taketh from woman not only all authority amongst men but also every office appertaining to man.

To the question how she can be the image of God, he answereth as followeth. "Woman," saith he, "compared to other creatures is the image of God, for she beareth dominion over them; but compared unto man, she may not be called the image of God, for she beareth not rule and lordship over man, but to obey him," etc. And how that woman ought to obey man, he speaketh yet more clearly in these words: "The woman shall be subject to man as unto Christ." "For woman," saith he, "hath not her example from the body and from the flesh, that so she shall be subject to man as the flesh is unto the spirit. Because that the flesh in the weakness and mortality of this life striveth and striveth against the spirit, and therefore would not the Holy Ghost give example of subjection to the woman of any such thing," etc. This sentence of Augustine ought to be noted of all women, for in it he plainly affirmeth that woman ought to be subject to man, that she never ought more to desire pre-eminence above him than that she ought to desire above Christ Jesus.

With Augustine agreeth in every point St. Ambrose, who thus writeth in his Hexameron: "Adam was deceived by Eve, and not Eve by Adam, and therefore just it is that woman receive and acknowledge him for governor whom she called to sin, lest that again she slide and fall by womanly facility." And writing upon the Epistle to the Ephesians, he saith, "Let women be subject to their own husbands as unto the Lord; for the man is head to the woman, and Christ is head to the congregation, and he is the savior of the body; but the congregation is subject to Christ; even so ought women to be to their husbands in all things." He proceedeth further, saying, "Women are commanded to be subject to men by the law of nature, because that man is the author or beginner of the woman; for as Christ is head of the church, so is man of the woman. From Christ the church took beginning, and therefore it is subject unto him; even so did woman take beginning from man that she should be subject."

Thus we hear the agreeing of these two writers to be such that a man might judge the one to have stolen the words and sentences from the other, and yet, plain it is that, during the time of their writing, the one was far distant from the other. But the Holy Ghost, who is the spirit of concord and unity, did so illuminate their hearts and direct their tongues and pens that, as they did conceive and understand one truth, so they did pronounce and utter the same, leaving a testimony of their knowledge and posterity.

If any think that all these former sentences be spoken only of the subjection of the married woman to her husband, as before I have proved the contrary by the plain words and reasoning of St. Paul, so shall I shortly do the same by other testimony of the foresaid writers. The same Ambrose, writing upon the second chapter of the First Epistle to Timothy, after he hath spoken much of the simple arrayment of women, he addeth these words: "Woman ought not only to have simple arrayment, but all authority is to be denied unto her, for she must be in subjection to man..."

---

62. QUEEN ELIZABETH I OF ENGLAND (1533–1603)

Elizabeth I was the daughter of Henry VIII and Anne Boleyn and followed her younger brother Edward VI and older sister Mary to the throne of England in 1558. Born three years before her mother was executed for adultery, Elizabeth's youth combined political insecurity with the best contemporary education available. The young queen expressed herself with force and facility in Latin, Greek, French, and Italian, as well as English. While many of the surviving speeches attributed to her were written down after the event by servants or onlookers, the clarity and style of the queen's rhetoric remains fairly consistent. Elizabeth died without marrying in 1603 and was succeeded by James I of England (r. 1603–25) and VI of Scotland (r. 1567–1625).

Sir William Cecil (1520–98) was born at Stamford in Lincolnshire and entered St. John's College, Cambridge in 1535, where he enjoyed a full humanist curriculum. In the 1540s he advanced in government circles, building relationships with Protestant humanists at home and abroad. Cecil largely withdrew from politics during the reign of Queen Mary, though he was willing to serve when called upon, but in these years he spent much time in the service of Princess Elizabeth, who named him her secretary of state on the first day of her reign. Cecil and Elizabeth did not always agree, but his lifelong service to her married the humanist ideal of objective and truthful council with a deep and abiding personal and political loyalty.

Queen Elizabeth's First Speech, Hatfield, November 20, 1558

Queen Elizabeth's speech to her secretary and other her lords before her Coronation

WORDS SPOKEN BY HER MAJESTY TO MR: CECIL:
I give you this charge that you shall be of my Privy Council and content yourself to take pains for me and my realm. This judgment I have of you: that you will not be corrupted with any manner of gift, and that you will be faithful to the state, and that without respect of my private will, you will give me that counsel that you think best, and if you shall know anything necessary to be declared to me of secrecy, you shall show it to myself only. And assure yourself I will not fail to keep taciturnity therein, and therefore herewith I charge you.

WORDS SPOKEN BY THE QUEEN TO THE LORDS:
My lords, the law of nature moves me to sorrow for my sister; the burden that has fallen upon me makes me amazed; and yet, considering I am God's creature, ordained to obey His appointment, I will thereto yield, desiring from the bottom of my heart that I may have assistance of His grace to be the minister of His heavenly will in this office now committed to me. And as I am but one body naturally considered, though by His permission a body politic to govern, so I shall desire you all, my lords (chiefly you of the nobility, everyone in his degree and power), to be assistant to me, that I with my ruling and you with your service may make a good account to almighty God and leave some comfort to our posterity in earth. I mean to direct all my actions by good advice and counsel. And therefore, considering that various of you are of the ancient nobility, having your beginnings and estates from my progenitors, kings of this realm, and thereby ought in honor to have the more natural care for maintaining of my estate and this commonwealth; some others have been of long experience in governance and enabled by my father of noble memory, my brother, and my late sister to bear office; the rest of you being upon special trust lately called to her service only and trust, for your service considered and rewarded; my meaning is to require of you all nothing more but faithful hearts in such service as from time to time shall be in your powers towards the preservation of me and this commonwealth. And for counsel and advice I shall accept you of my nobility, and such others of you the rest as in consultation I shall think meet and shortly appoint, to the which also, with their advice, I will join to their aid, and for ease of their burden, others meet for my service. And they which I shall not appoint, let them not think the same for any disability in them, but for that I do consider a multitude doth make rather discord and confusion than good counsel. And of my goodwill you shall not doubt, using yourselves as appertaineth to good and loving subjects.

Richard Mulcaster's Account of Queen Elizabeth's Speech and Prayer during Her Passage through London to Westminster the Day before Her Coronation, January 14, 1559

Richard Mulcaster (1531/2–1611) was a schoolmaster and author. Educated at Cambridge and Oxford, he settled in London in 1559 as a Member of Parliament and participated in the pageant welcoming the new queen into London. Around the same time he began to work as a teacher and became the headmaster of the Merchant Taylors' School in London in 1561, serving in that role until 1586. He later became the headmaster of St. Paul's school. From these institutions Mulcaster both influenced a number of boys who would play an important role in the public life of England and mingled with many of the most prominent figures of his day. He wrote two books on education, of which the Elementarie *is best known, not only for its thoughtful and advanced ideas on education, but also for its spirited defense of the value of English as a literary and intellectual language.*

And on the other side, her grace, by holding up her hands and merry countenance to such as stood far off, and most tender and gentle language to those that stood nigh to her grace, did declare herself no less thankfully to receive her people's goodwill than they lovingly offered it unto her. To all that wished her grace well she gave hearty thanks, and to such as bade God save her grace she said again, God save them all, and thanked them with all her heart. So that on either side there was nothing but gladness, nothing but prayer, nothing but comfort. The queen's majesty rejoiced marvelously to see it so exceedingly showed toward her grace which all good princes have ever desired: I mean, so earnest love of subjects, so evidently declared even to her grace's own person being carried in the midst of them. The people, again, were wonderfully ravished with welcoming answers and gestures of their princess, like to the which they had before tried at her first coming to the Tower from Hatfield. This her grace's loving behavior, preconceived in the people's heads, upon these considerations was thoroughly confirmed and indeed implanted a wonderful hope in them touching her worthy government in the rest of her reign. For in all her passage she did not only show her most gracious love toward the people in general, but also privately. If the baser personages had either offered her grace any flowers or such like as a signification of their goodwill, or moved to her any suit, she most gently, to the common rejoicing of all the lookers-on and private comfort of the party, stayed her chariot and heard their requests.

So that if a man should say well, he could not better term the City of London that time than a stage wherein was showed the wonderful spectacle of a noble-hearted princess toward her most loving people and the people's exceeding comfort in beholding so worthy a sovereign and hearing so princelike a voice. . . .

Out at the windows and penthouses of every house did hang a number of rich and costly banners and streamers, till her grace came to the upper end of Cheap. And there, by appointment, the right worshipful Master Ranulph Cholmley, recorder of the City, presented to the queen's majesty a purse of crimson satin richly wrought with gold, wherein the City gave unto the queen's majesty a thousand marks in gold, as Master Recorder did declare briefly unto the queen's majesty, whose words tended to this end: that the lord mayor, his brethren and commonality of the City, to declare their gladness and goodwill towards the queen's majesty, did present her grace with that gold, desiring her grace to continue their good and gracious queen and not to esteem the value of the gift, but the mind of the givers. The queen's majesty with both her hands took the purse and answered to him again marvelous pithily, and so pithily that the standers-by, as they embraced entirely her gracious answer, so they marveled at the couching thereof, which was in words truly reported these:

I thank my lord mayor, his brethren, and you all. And whereas your request is that I should continue your good lady and queen, be ye ensured that I will be as good unto you as ever queen was to her people. No will in me can lack, neither do I trust shall there lack any power. And persuade yourselves that for the safety and quietness of you all I will not spare, if need be, to spend my blood. God thank you all.

Which answer of so noble an hearted princess, if it moved a marvelous shout and rejoicing, it is nothing to be marveled at, since both the heartiness thereof was so wonderful, and the words so jointly knit.

But because princes be set in their seat by God's appointing and therefore they must first and chiefly tender the glory of Him from whom their glory issueth, it is to be noted in her grace that forsomuch as God hath so wonderfully placed her in the seat of government over this realm, she in all doings doth show herself most mindful of His goodness and mercy showed unto her. And amongst all other, two principal signs thereof were noted in this passage. First in the Tower, where her grace, before she entered her chariot, lifted up her eyes to heaven and said:

O Lord, almighty and everlasting God, I give Thee most hearty thanks that Thou hast been so merciful unto me as to spare me to behold this joyful day. And I acknowledge that Thou hast dealt as wonderfully and as mercifully with me as Thou didst with Thy true and faithful servant Daniel, Thy prophet, whom Thou deliveredst out of the den from the cruelty of the greedy and raging lions. Even so was I overwhelmed and only by Thee delivered. To Thee (therefore) only be thanks, honor, and praise forever, amen.

The second was the receiving of the Bible at the Little Conduit in Cheap. For when her grace had learned that the Bible in English should there be offered, she thanked the City therefore, promised the reading thereof most diligently, and incontinent commanded that it should be brought. At the receipt whereof, how reverently did she with both her hands take it, kiss it, and lay it upon her breast, to the great comfort of the lookers-on! God will undoubtedly preserve so worthy a prince, which at His honor so reverently taketh her beginning. For this saying is true and written in the book of truth: he that first seeketh the kingdom of God shall have all other things cast unto him.

Now, therefore, all English hearts and her natural people must needs praise God's mercy, which hath sent them so worthy a prince, and pray for her grace's long continuance amongst us.

63. THEODORE BEZA (1519–1605)

Beza was born in Vezelay, France, into a distinguished family of royal administrators, lawyers, and clerics (his uncle was abbot of Froimont). He began his education in Paris but transferred to Orleans, and later Bourges, before returning to Orleans to study law. In addition to his legal studies, Beza became interested in classical literature and was influenced by humanist scholarship. After he qualified as a lawyer in 1539, he left for Paris to establish a reputation. His family managed to secure ecclesiastical benefices to support him; and his uncle proposed that Beza eventually take orders so that he might succeed him as abbot of Froimont. Initially, his fame derived from his Latin poetry, as he had printed in 1548 a book of poems that revealed him as one of his generation's most accomplished humanist poets. That same year, however, he fully embraced the teachings of John Calvin to which he had been introduced in Orleans and Bourges. Consequently, in the fall of 1548 he fled to Geneva, where he was warmly received by Calvin himself. The now married Beza left Geneva to assume a position as professor of Greek in Lausanne and continued to write not only poetry but also Calvinist tracts, including in 1554 a treatise justifying Calvin's burning of Michael Servetus (1509/11–53). After serving on several missions to other Protestant congregations, Beza returned to Geneva, where he was appointed professor of Greek and later theology. Despite this, Beza traveled widely, attempting to secure the Calvinist cause in France and elsewhere in Europe. In so doing he established a great reputation as a speaker, theologian, and thinker. As a result, on Calvin's death in 1564 Beza succeeded him as the center of the Calvinist structure of Geneva. He continued to teach, however, and also reinforced Geneva as the center for Calvinist theology after the reformer's death. His own theological works were very influential, including his Greek edition of the New Testament (1565). The St. Bartholomew's massacre in France (1572), the events of the French Wars of Religion, and his experience guiding the city state of Geneva inspired Beza to write in 1574 his Right of Magistrates. *Originally written in Latin and published anonymously in Germany out of fear of French royal reprisals, this central work of political resistance theory argued that it was the right of legitimate magistrates to depose a tyrannical monarch. It is a complex argument described with a lawyer's precision and a theologian's recognition of the ultimate authority of God. The foundation is a kind of contract theory among God, the king, and his subjects. In it a ruler's duty to both God and his people is affirmed, with the obligation of lesser authorities in the state to remedy either royal impiety (not obeying divine law) and royal tyranny (breaking the positive and natural laws that govern the community). The* Right of Magistrates *made Beza a leading member of the so-called* monarchomachs, *those Huguenot theorists who argued for the limitation of royal power. Beza died in Geneva in 1605.*

On the Right of Magistrates

I. Should magistrates as well as God be unconditionally obeyed?

The only will that is a perpetual and immutable criterion of justice is the will of the one God and none other. Hence Him alone we are obliged to obey without exception. Princes too would have to be obeyed implicitly if they were always the voice of God's commandments. But since the opposite too often happens, an exception is imposed upon obedience, when their commands are irreligious or iniquitous. Irreligious commands are those which order us to do what the First Table of God's Law forbids, or forbid us to do what it commands. Iniquitous commands are those that cannot be obeyed without violating or neglecting the charity we owe our fellow men according to our station public or private. And I can prove this assertion by evident reasons and examples.... [Various passages and examples from Scripture are cited, the general tenor of which is that one must obey God rather than man.]

II. To what extent should a subject assume the justice of commands?

Having established this foundation, I shall be glad to examine in detail some related points that have troubled many consciences. First, it is often asked whether a magistrate is bound to justify all of his commands to everyone. I say no and hold rather that loyal subjects should presume well of their rulers and not inquire too closely into complicated matters that are beyond their grasp and station. But if their consciences are troubled nonetheless, they may and should inquire, by modest and pacific means, as to the reason and equity of what they are commanded to do or to refrain from doing. For the clear injunction of the Apostle still abides, that "anything done without faith (which is done, that is with a doubting conscience) is sin." (Romans 14:23) And, of course, if a command is clearly irreligious or iniquitous, what we have said above applies.

III. How far should disobedience extend?

It is also asked how far disobedience to irreligious or iniquitous commands of rulers should extend. My answer is that each man must have regard to his vocation, and whether it is general and public or is private. If your magistrate commands you to do what God forbids, as did Pharaoh the midwives of Egypt and Herod when he ordered his followers to slay the innocents, it is your duty to refuse to act.... But if the tyrant forbids you to do what God has commanded, then you will not have done your duty merely by refusing to obey the tyrant, but you must render obedience to God. Thus, Obadiah not only refused to kill the prophets, but gave them refuge and nourishment against the will of Ahab and Jezebel....

[The point is illustrated by further biblical examples and is extended to all obligations under natural law.]

IV. What are the remedies of a subject injured by a lesser magistrate?

The further question now arises as to what a man of good conscience should do, not where he is asked to do a wrong, but where the wrong is done to him. This I hold to be a complicated question for which distinctions must be drawn.

If the magistrate who wrongs a subject is beneath another who is sovereign, the aggrieved subject may appeal to the sovereign according to the law, as St. Paul appealed to Caesar to prevent the wrong being done him by Festus, the governor of Judea. But here private subjects must keep two considerations in mind. They should proceed exclusively by legal means, and then only insofar as it is expedient. For when that same St. Paul was outraged and whipped at Philippi by an ill-advised magistrate acting contrary to his rights as a Roman citizen, and without even hearing his case, he decided that patience would better serve God's glory and pursued his rights no further, merely admonishing the magistrates for their violation of the law. But if it should happen, as it does all too often in our time, that one of two lower magistrates does violence to the other, against the express will of their sovereign, then, I say, it is always licit for the aggrieved magistrate, after he has tried all milder means, to take his stand upon the law and to repel illegal violence by resort to arms, as Nehemiah did against Sanballat and his adherents.

V. Is resistance to a superior magistrate always illicit and seditious?

But what if the source of outrage should be the sovereign magistrate himself? Jesus Christ and all the martyrs afterwards surely teach us that injustice should be suffered patiently, and that it is the glory of Christians to suffer injustice at the hands of others while doing none themselves. Is there then no remedy at all, it will be asked, against a sovereign who abuses his dominion against all law divine and human? A remedy does exist, and it is to be found in human institutions, although in saying this I hope that no one will infer that I support those fanatic Anabaptists and other seditious and mutinous people who, I believe, deserve rather to be hated by all and to be punished severely for their crimes. For to put the matter properly, those who teach that notorious tyranny may be resisted in good conscience are not denying good and legitimate rulers the authority that God has given them, nor are they encouraging rebellion. On the contrary, the authority of magistrates cannot be stabilized, nor that public peace, which is the end of a true governance, preserved unless tyranny is prevented from arising or else abolished when it does. The question, then, is to see if there is some means, in accord with justice and the will of God, by which subjects may curb manifest tyranny on the part of a sovereign magistrate, by force of arms if need be.

To resolve this question I would begin by pointing out that peoples do not come from rulers; that peoples, whether they have chosen to be governed by a single prince or by a number of elected notables, are older than these rulers; and that peoples, accordingly, are not created for their rulers, but rulers rather for their peoples, just as a guardian is created for the ward, not the ward for the guardian, and the shepherd for the flock, not the flock for the shepherd. And although this is all self-evident, it can be confirmed by the history of every nation, for even God, having chosen Saul to rule in place of Samuel at the people's request, willed that the people, in addition, should establish and receive Saul as their king. David, too, though God's own choice, did not exercise royal power until he received the votes and free consent of the tribes of Israel. And although the right to the throne became hereditary in the line of David by divine decree (unless there was some exceptional obstacle, as when the Egyptians and then the kings of Assyria tyrannized God's people), it was arranged that of the race of David only he whom the people had approved should reign, so that although the kingdom was hereditary as to family because God had so ordained, it was nonetheless elective as to individuals. . . . [There follow additional examples from the Old Testament, opinions of ancient philosophers, and citations to St. Paul.] Yet some people so recommend patience and prayers to God that they condemn all who do not yield their necks [to violence] as rebels and false Christians. So slippery is this terrain that I beg the reader to remember all that I have said above so as to draw no evil consequence from what I am about to say upon this point. I praise Christian patience as a virtue to be especially commended, and I avow that it is to be assiduously cultivated in men as the pathway to eternal bliss. I detest seditions and disorders of all kinds as horrible monstrosities, and I agree that in affliction most of all we should depend on God alone. I admit that prayers united with repentance are proper and necessary remedies to tyranny since it is most often an evil or scourge sent by God for the chastisement of nations. But for all of this, I deny that it is illicit for peoples oppressed by notorious tyranny to make use of lawful remedies in addition to repentance and prayers, and I now present the reasons for my view.

VI. Do subjects have any remedy against a legitimate sovereign who has become a notorious tyrant?

We must now take up a question which, not without reason is hotly debated in our day. What in good conscience may be done by subjects if their sovereign magistrate, who is otherwise legitimate, becomes a notorious tyrant? Is the authority of a sovereign who has changed into a notorious tyrant so sacred and inviolable that subjects must endure him unresisting? And if they may resist, may they go so far as to resort to arms?

I reply that there are three kinds of subjects. Some are purely private persons who have no public office. Others, like the sovereign, are magistrates but are underneath him and so subaltern or inferior. The third class includes those who in ordinary matters do not exercise sovereign power but are established to check and bridle the sovereign magistrate. And as these classes differ, so must my answer vary.

Private Persons

As for private persons: if they have expressly and voluntarily consented to the dominion of a usurper, as the Roman people accepted Augustus and his successors, or if their legitimate ruler has become a notorious tyrant, as did Abimelech among the Israelites, the Thirty at Athens, the Decemvirs at Rome, and others elsewhere, then, I say, unless a private person has a special calling from God, which I do not deal with here, they may not, on his own initiative, answer force with force but must either go into exile or bear the yoke with trust in God (although, as we said at the beginning, he must never make himself the instrument of tyranny against another or fail to do his duty to God and to his fellow men).

Here our previous responses may perhaps be cited in objection. In discussing the two other kinds of tyranny, we said that even private persons were obliged to resist with all their strength. And at first glance it might seem that attempted usurpation by a private person and tyrannical use of legitimate dominion are the same, and that the same solution should apply in either case. But on closer inspection we discover a very considerable difference between these two cases, which appear to be so similar. A man who invades against others who are in no way subject to him (even if he wishes to rule equitably, as we read of Peisistratus and Demetrios of Phaleros at Athens) may rightfully be stopped by force of arms, and by anyone, no matter what his station, since there is no obligation whatsoever towards him. But a ruler who has been avowed by his people may abuse his dominion and still retain his authority over private subjects because the obligation to obey him was publicly contracted by common consent and cannot be withdrawn and nullified at the pleasure of a private individual. Were it otherwise, infinite troubles would ensue even worse than the tyranny itself, and a thousand tyrants would arise on the pretext of suppressing one.

And yet another argument, weightier than all the others that might be brought forward to the contrary, is the authority of God's word, which is unfailingly clear. St. Paul, speaking of the duty of a private citizen, not only forbids resistance to any magistrate, inferior as well as sovereign, but commands obedience for conscience's sake. St. Peter also orders us to honor kings, presumably remembering the reproof he received from his Master when, as a private person, he drew his sword against the public power, even though it was being misused against his Master. And yet there is none who does not know what kind of men the emperors of those days were, i.e., Tiberius and Nero; or what most of the provincial governors were like. The same attitude was later adopted by the faithful martyrs who were cruelly persecuted by inhuman tyrants, and not only when emperors persecuted Christians according to imperial law, but even when they faithlessly transgressed standing edicts passed in favor of the Christians, as did the Emperor Julian the Apostate.

My conclusion, then, is that it is illicit for any private subject to use force against a tyrant whose dominion was freely ratified beforehand by the people. And if in private contracts a promise is so sacred that we must keep it even when it leads to loss there is an even greater duty on the part of private persons not to disavow an obligation that was entered into by public agreement.

Lesser Magistrates

I come now to the lesser magistrates who hold a lower rank between the sovereign and the people. I do not mean officers of the king's household, who are devoted rather to the king than the kingdom, but those who have public or state responsibilities either in the administration of justice or in war. In a monarchy, therefore, the latter are called "officers of the crown," and thus of the kingdom rather than the king, which are two quite different things. Such, in [imperial] Rome, were the consuls, the praetors, the prefect of the city, the governors that were still appointed by the people and the Senate under the Empire, and similar officers of the Republic or of the Empire, who, for that reason, were called "magistrates of the Roman people" even in the period of the last emperors. In Israel they were the leaders of the twelve tribes; the captains of thousands, of hundreds, and of fifties; and the elders of the people. This arrangement, established under Moses, was not abolished with the change from aristocracy to monarchy, but was retained, and organized with more precision under Solomon. And in our day they are the officers of the various Christian kingdoms among whom may be numbered dukes, marquises, counts, viscounts, barons, chatelains, whose estates and offices were at one time public and conferred in the ordinary legal way and have since become hereditary, without, however, any change in the nature of their right and their authority. And we must also include the elected officers of towns such as maires, viguiers, consuls, capitouls, syndics, echevins, and so on.

Now, although all these officers are beneath their sovereign in that they take commands from him and are installed in office and approved by him, they hold, properly speaking, not of the sovereign but of the sovereignty. That is why, when the sovereign magistrate dies, they nonetheless remain in office, just as the sovereignty itself remains intact. It is true that the newly succeeding administrator of the sovereignty confirms their dignities as also the privileges of towns (which is a custom first introduced into the Roman empire by the Emperor Tiberius according to Suetonius in his life of Vespasian, but which was unknown in ancient France, except in cases where the crown did not descend from father to son). But this does not imply that the sovereign is the author and source of their rights, since the sovereign himself does not enter into true possession of his sovereign administration until he has sworn fealty to the sovereignty and accepted the conditions attached to his oath, in the same way that he subsequently administers the oath to the above-mentioned officers. Hence confirmation of this sort resembles a feudal investiture where there is a new vassal or a new lord. It does not confer any new right but is simply the renewed recognition of an old one on the occasion of a change of persons.

It is thus apparent that there is a mutual obligation between the king and the officers of a kingdom; that the government of the kingdom is not in the hands of the king in its entirety, but only the sovereign degree; that each of the officers has a share in accord with his degree; and that there are definite conditions on either side. If these conditions are not observed by the inferior officers, it is the part of the sovereign to dismiss and punish them, but only for definite cause and according to the procedures prescribed by the law of the realm, and not otherwise, unless he is himself to violate the oath he took to exercise his office in conformity with law. If the king, hereditary or elective, clearly goes back on the conditions without which he would not have been recognized and acknowledged, can there be any doubt that the lesser magistrates of the kingdom, of the cities, and of the provinces, the administration of which they have received from the sovereignty itself, are free of their oath, at least to the extent they are entitled to resist flagrant oppression of the realm which they swore to defend and protect according to their office and their particular jurisdiction? What, it will be asked? Is a ruler, previously regarded as sovereign and inviolable, suddenly to be considered a private person at the whim of some subordinate, and then pursued and attacked as if a public enemy? Not at all, I say, for this would open the door to all kinds of miserable seditions and conspiracies. I am speaking, in the first place, of a clearly flagrant tyranny and of a tyrant who endures no remonstrations. Furthermore, I do not speak of removing a tyrant from his throne, but only of resistance against open violence according to one's rank, for I have already shown that an obligation entered into by common agreement cannot be nullified at the discretion of any individual, no matter who he is and no matter how just his complaint.

On the other hand, it is by the sovereignty itself that lesser officers are charged with enforcing and maintaining law among those committed to their charge, to which duty they are further bound by oath. (And they are not absolved from this oath by the delinquency of a king who has turned tyrant and flagrantly violated the conditions to which he swore and under which he was received as king.) Is it not then reasonable, by all law divine and human, that more should be permitted to these lesser magistrates, in view of their sworn duty to preserve the law, than to purely private persons without office? I say, therefore, that they are obliged, if reduced to that necessity, and by force of arms where that is possible, to offer resistance to flagrant tyranny, and to safeguard those within their care, until such time as the Estates, or whoever holds the legislative power of the kingdom or the empire, may by common deliberation make further and appropriate provision for the public welfare. This, moreover, is not to be seditious or disloyal towards one's sovereign, but to be loyal fully and to keep one's faith toward those from whom one's office was received against him who has broken his oath and oppressed the kingdom he ought to have protected. This was the right on which Brutus and Lucretius acted against Tarquin the Proud at Rome (even though their private interests were involved to some extent as well). To resist flagrant tyranny, Brutus as tribune of the knights and Lucretius as prefect of the city assembled the Roman people, by whose authority the tyrant was driven from his kingdom and his possessions confiscated. And had they been able to lay hands on him, they would doubtless have condemned his person according to the law, which he had violated and not upheld as was his duty. For to say that the sovereign is not subject to the law is surely the false maxim of detestable flatterers, not of a subject loyal to his prince. On the contrary, there is not a single law to which the ruler is not bound in the conduct of his government, since he has sworn to be the protector and preserver of them all. . . . [After quotations from Marcus Aurelius and Trajan, there follow two examples from Scripture: David's armed resistance against Saul for purposes of self-defense and the rebellion of the priestly city of Libnah against Jehoram.]

These two examples, quite apart from the arguments above, are, in my opinion, so clear and authentic as to give sufficient assurance to the consciences of lesser magistrates who, after trying every other remedy, find it necessary to resort to arms to protect those within their charge from flagrant tyranny, and thus seek not to stir up rebellion but to stop it. And it is well known that in the days of our forefathers the tyranny of those who ruled the Swiss was the occasion for the municipal magistrates of the Swiss to assert the liberty that people now enjoy.

Sources

Anonymous.
"Consilium de Emendanda Ecclesia," from *The Catholic Reformation: Savonarola to Ignatius Loyola*. Edited by John C. Olin. New York: Harper & Row, 1969; "The Capuchin Constitutions of 1536," from *The Catholic Reformation: Savonarola to Ignatius Loyola*. Edited by John C. Olin. New York: Harper & Row, 1969.

Beza, Theodore.
"On the Right of Magistrates," from *Constitutionalism and Resistance in the Sixteenth Century*. Edited by Julian H. Franklin. New York: Pegasus, 1969.

Bodin, Jean.
"Method for the Easy Comprehension of History," from *Culture & Belief in Modern Europe 1450–1600*. Edited by David Englander. Oxford: Basil Blackwell, 1990. Copyright © 1990 Oxford Basil Blackwell. Reproduced with permission of Blackwell Publishing Ltd.

Calvin, John.
"Reply to Sadoleto," from *A Reformation Debate: John Calvin and Jacopo Sadoleto*. Edited by John C. Olin. 1969.

Celtis, Conrad.
"Oration Delivered Publicly in the University of Ingolstadt," from *The Northern Renaissance*. Edited by Lewis W. Spitz. New Jersey: Prentice-Hall, 1972.

Cervantes, Miguel de.
"Don Quixote: Dedication to the Duke of Bejar and the Prologue," from *Don Quixote: A Norton Critical Edition: The Ormsby Translation, Revised*. Edited by Joseph Jones and Kenneth Douglas. New York: W.W. Norton, 1981. Copyright © 1981 by W. W. Norton & Company, Inc. Used by permission of W.W. Norton & Company, Inc.; Excerpts from *Don Quixote*, from *The Northern Renaissance*. Edited by Lewis W. Spitz. New Jersey: Prentice-Hall, 1972.

Charles V (Emperor).
"Advice to His Son," from *Renaissance and Reformation: 1300 to 1648*, 3rd ed. Edited by Geoffrey R. Elton. Upper Saddle River, NJ: Pearson Education, 1976. © 1976. Reprinted by permission of Pearson Education, Inc., Upper Saddle River, NJ.

Columbus, Christopher.
"Granada Capitulations, promising . . . Columbus the Offices of Admiral, Viceroy and Governor of the Islands and Mainland He Might Discover . . . April 1492," from "Instructions to Columbus for Colonization of the Indies, Burgos, 23 April 1497," in *The Book of Privileges*. Edited by Helen Nader. Eugene, OR: Wipf and Stock, 2004. Used by permission of Wipf and Stock Publishers. www.wipfandstock.com.

Erasmus, Desiderius.
Excerpts from "Letter to Jodocus Jonas on Vitrier and Colet" and "The Paraclesis," from *Christian Humanism and the Reformation: Selected Writings of Desiderius Erasmus*. Translated by John C. Olin. New York: Harper & Row, 1965. Copyright © 1965 by John C. Olin. Reprinted by permission of HarperCollins Publishers.

Fernandez de Oviedo, Gonzalo.
"General and Natural History of the Indies," from *The Four Voyages of Christopher Columbus*. Edited by J.M Cohen. Harmondsworth: Penguin, 1969. Reprinted by permission of Penguin Books Ltd.

Filastre, Cardinal Guillaume.
"Diary of the Council of Constance," from *The Council of Constance: The Unification of the Church*. Translated by Louise Ropes Loomis. New York: Columbia University Press, 1961. Copyright © 1961 Columbia University Press. Reprinted with permission from the publisher.

Fish, Simon.
"A Supplication of Beggars," from *The Protestant Reformation*. Edited by Lewis W. Spitz. Englewood Cliffs, NJ: Prentice-Hall, 1966.

Galilee, Galileo.
"Letter to the Grand Duchess Christina," from *Discoveries and Opinions of Galileo*. Edited by Stillman Drake. New York: Knopf, 1957. Copyright © 1957 by Stillman Drake. Used by permission of Doubleday, an imprint of the Knopf Doubleday Publishing Group, a division of Random House LLC. All rights reserved.

Knox, John.
"The First Blast of the Trumpet against the Monstrous Regiment of Women," from *The Political Writings of John Knox*. Edited by Marvin Breslow. Washington: Folger Books, 1985. Reprinted by permission of the author.

Loyola, Ignatius.
"Letter on Obedience," from *St. Ignatius' Own Story as Told to Luis Gonzalez de Camara with a Sampling of His Letters*. Translated by William J. Young. Chicago: Henery Regnery Co., 1956.

Luther, Martin.
Excerpt from "To the Christian Nobility," from *Luther's Works*, Vol. 44. Edited by Helmut T. Lehmann. Minneapolis, MN: Concordia Publishing/Fortress Press. Reprinted by permission of Augsburg Fortress Publishers; "Admonition to Peace" and "Against the Robbing and Murdering Hordes," from *Luther's Works*, Vol. 46. Edited by Helmut T. Lehmann. Minneapolis, MN: Concordia Publishing/Fortress Press. Reprinted by permission of Augsburg Fortress Publishers; "Luther on Family etc.," from *Luther's Works*, Vol. 54. Edited by Helmut T. Lehmann. Minneapolis, MN: Concordia Publishing/Fortress Press. Reprinted by permission of Augsburg Fortress Publishers.

Melancthon, Philip.
"Funeral Oration over Luther (1546)," from *The Protestant Reformation*. Edited by Lewis W. Spitz. Englewood Cliffs, NJ: Prentice-Hall, 1966.

More, Thomas.
"Letter to the Professors and Masters of the University of Oxford," from *Renaissance Letters*. Edited by R.J. Clements and L. Levant. New York: New York University Press, 1976. Reprinted by permission of New York University Press.

Muntzer, Thomas.
"A Highly Provoked Defense," from *The Collected Works of Thomas Muntzer*. Translated and edited by Peter Matheson. Edinburgh: T&T Clark, 1988. © Peter Matheson, editor and translator, 1988, T&T Clark, an imprint of Bloomsbury Publishing Plc.

Nostradamus, Michel de.
"Letter to King Henri II of France," from *Renaissance Letters*. Edited by R.J. Clements and L. Levant. New York: New York University Press, 1976. Reprinted by permission of New York University Press.

Parmenius, Stephen.
"Letter to . . . Richard Hakluyt . . . from St John's Harbour Newfoundland, 1583," from *The New Found Land of Stephen Parmenius*. Edited by D.B. Quinn and N.M. Cheshire. Toronto: University of Toronto Press, 1972. Copyright © 1972 University of Toronto Press. Reprinted with the permission of the publisher.

Peter of Mladonovice.
"The End of the Saintly and Reverend Master John Hus," from *John Hus at the Council of Constance*. Translated by Matthew Spinka. New York: Columbia University Press, 1965. Copyright © 1965 Columbia University Press. Reprinted with permission from the publisher.

Piccolomini, Aeneas Silvius.
Excerpt from the First Book of the *Commentaries*, from *De Gestis Concilii Basiliensis Commentarium: Libri II*. Translated by May and Smith. Oxford: Oxford University Press, 1967. By permission of Oxford University Press.

Rabelais, François.
Excerpts from *Gargantua* and *Pantagruel*, from *The Northern Renaissance*. Edited by Lewis W. Spitz. New Jersey: Prentice-Hall, 1972.

Sach, Hans.
"The Old Game," from *Culture & Belief in Modern Europe 1450–1600*. Edited by David Englander. Oxford: Basil Blackwell, 1990. Copyright © 1990 Oxford Basil Blackwell. Reproduced with permission of Blackwell Publishing Ltd.

SOURCES

Servetus, Michael.
"On the Errors of the Trinity," from *The Two Treatises of Servetus on the Trinity*. Harvard Theological Studies, XVI. Cambridge, MA: Harvard University Press, 1932.

Teresa of Avila.
"Spiritual Testimonies," from *The Collected Works of St. Teresa of Avila*, Vol. 1. Translated by Kieran Kavanaugh and Otilio Rodriguez. Washington, DC: ICS Publications, 1976. Copyright © 1976 by Washington Province of Discalced Carmelites, ICS Publications, 2131 Lincoln Road, N.E., Washington, DC, 20002–1199, U.S.A. www.icspublications.org.

Vives, Juan Luis.
Excerpt from *On Assistance to the Poor*. Translated by Alice Tobriner. Toronto: University of Toronto Press. (Renaissance Society of America reprint series). Reprinted by permission of the Renaissance Society of America; "On the Writing of Letters," from *J.L. Vives: De Conscribendis Epistolis*. Edited by C. Fantazzi. Amsterdam: E.J. Brill, 1989. Reprinted by permission of Koninklijke BRILL NV.

von Grumbach, Argula.
"To Adam Von Thering," from *Argula von Grumbach, A Woman's Voice in the Reformation*. Edited by Peter Matheson. Edinburgh: T&T Clark, 1995. © Peter Matheson, T&T Clark, an imprint of Bloomsbury Publishing Plc.

Ximenes, Cardinal Francisco.
"Prologue to the Polyglot from Catholic Reform," from *Cardinal Ximenes to the Council of Trent 1495–1563*. Edited by John C. Olin. New York: Fordham University Press, 1990. Reprinted by permission of Fordham University Press.

Zell, Katharina Schütz.
"Letter to . . . Strasbourg," from *The Writings of a Protestant Reformer in Sixteenth-Century Germany*. Translated and edited by Church Mother Elsie McKee. Chicago: University of Chicago Press, 2006. Copyright © 2006 University of Chicago Press. Reprinted by permission of the publisher.